TELLING NEW MEXICO

TELLING NEW MEXICO
A New History

edited by Marta Weigle

with Frances Levine *and* Louise Stiver

Museum of New Mexico Press
Santa Fe

Dedicated in gratitude to
Michael and Marianne O'Shaughnessy

Contents

Territory of New Mexico (1896). 1:760320, 1 inch = 12 miles. Oil-on-canvas painting based on a rendering by Miera y Pacheco, about 1760. Photograph by Blair Clark. Courtesy History Collection (NMHM/DCA) 9599/45.

PREFACE

Telling New Mexico: A New History anticipates two centennials: that of the Museum of New Mexico in 2009 and that of statehood for New Mexico in 2012. The first is marked in May 2009 when the New Mexico History Museum opens behind the venerable Palace of the Governors on the Santa Fe plaza. The second becomes official at 1:35 P.M. on January 6, 2012, a hundred years after President William Howard Taft signed the proclamation admitting New Mexico as the forty-seventh state, following by some four years the forty-sixth (Oklahoma, November 16, 1907) and preceding by some five weeks the forty-eighth (Arizona, February 14, 1912).

The new history museum houses a core exhibition that displays New Mexico history from its prehistoric sequences to the present in broad thematic and temporally based sections. In the spring of 2006, during the planning for the exhibit, nearly twenty authors were solicited to write pieces for an associated collection of essays that would "craft the overall scope of a New Mexico that will be published during our opening year." As the initial group of writers and subjects changed, the editors complemented the newly written essays with reprinted selections from publications dating as early as 1941 (by Haniel Long) and as recently as the summer of 2007 (by Jennifer Nez Denetdale). These reprinted articles appear here with their original dates of publication. There are now fifty-two contributions from forty-seven contributors.

By November 2007 the volume's working title, "Telling New Mexico: History, Memory, Museum," had been replaced with the present one: *Telling New Mexico: A New History.* The first part, "Light, Land, Water, Wind," situates this history in the landscape. It is followed by six parts that roughly correspond to sections in the new museum's core exhibition. The essays in "Beyond History's Records" tell of the region's precontact indigenous peoples, and "The Northern Province" covers the colonial period, from Coronado's 1540 expedition to Mexican independence from Spain in 1821. "Linking Nations" is set during the Mexican period, 1821–46. "Becoming the Southwest" treats the years from the 1848 Treaty of Guadalupe Hidalgo, which ended the Mexican-American War of 1846–48, and the 1850 "Organic Act Establishing the Territory of New Mexico" through statehood and well into the twentieth century. "The 'New' New Mexico" tells of the decades from statehood in 1912 through the 2005 dedication of the Bosque Redondo Memorial in Fort Sumner. Finally, "My New Mexico" offers personal (hi) stories from 1939 through the 2005 dedication of sculptor Cliff Fragua's statue of Po'pay, leader of the Pueblo Revolt of 1680, in the U.S. Capitol's National Statuary Hall collection. Director Frances Levine provides the epilogue, "Telling New Mexico into the Twenty-First Century: The New Mexico History Museum."

Volume editor Marta Weigle briefly introduces each part of the book. She also compiled the notes on sources, the bibliography of published references cited, and the contributor notes on sources at the end of the book. Under the direction of senior curator Louise Stiver, most of the illustrations were selected from maps, photographs, and artifacts in the collections of the New Mexico History Museum. Infrastructure editor Kay Hagan researched rights and permissions for text and illustrations and wrote caption text. Acknowledgments for the entire book project conclude this new history.

PART ONE

LIGHT, LAND, WATER, WIND

Telling natural New Mexico speaks of cosmogonic light (Page), geologic epic (Crumpler, Long), and a litany of mountains (deBuys). The essential work of water in this semiarid country resounds in an ethnography of the Taos Valley *acequia* (ditch) irrigation system (Rodríguez) and in memoirs of windmills around Clovis (Dickey) and the deep wells and "copper water" of the Santa Rita mine that eventually swallowed the town it surrounded (Jones). The flow of *Po-wa-ha* (water-wind-breath) through earth, sky, and living beings is the creative life force of Pueblo cosmology (Swentzell). The Pueblos' sacred narrative of emergence from the underworlds into this one echoes in the personal experience narrative of a 1940s tour into Carlsbad Cavern (Long); both recount pilgrimage.

Mesa near Acoma. Photograph by Mark Nohl.

Natural New Mexico:
Light

Jake Page (1995)

The most important natural area in New Mexico exists wherever one goes in the state. It is the sky overhead. For overhead is the great light show, the special quality people find in New Mexico that they cannot quite describe (the English language, perhaps the richest in the world in numbers of words, lacks fine distinctions about matters that are both meteorological and aesthetic). The sky and its sun are, in New Mexico, the soulcatchers. In one place in fifteen minutes, the sky may change from an overall gray that produces a few snowflakes, to a blue deeper than any ocean with breathlessly light clouds almost hurtling across it, to an opaque yellow as the spring winds hit, shifting enormous quantities of Arizona "topsoil" eastward.

In New Mexico, on a proper day, every leaf of every creosote bush, every lavender wild-aster petal, every sunstruck rock face on a mountain miles off, stands out with a clarity that is existential. In such a light, the importance of a single rock, an individual flower, the existence of life itself, can strike one suddenly — fresh and poignant. What is distant seems near; what is near seems searingly real, insistent, poised. And with each change in the arc of the sun, especially at the beginning and end of its daily career, and with each passing cloud when they are present, the entire stage setting for the Creation is new, something never seen before.

The Sandia Mountains, for example, which lie like a blessed guard dog in silent enormity to the east of New Mexico's largest city, Albuquerque, are named for the color of the inside of a watermelon. Given the right configuration of things in the evening sky, the mountains glow as if from within, and the name makes sense. But the Sandias change color, mood, and even shape many times in every hour of daylight. They are the playmates of the sun, which, even as it clips behind the western horizon with nothing but high clouds to turn gold and copper and apricot and vermilion, doesn't want to relinquish its place — doesn't want to go to bed. The glow remains, an amber cloud presides over a gunmetal-gray veil of distant rain, and distant canyons emit countershafts of pale light.

At such moments, a visible hymn is in the air, sung with an elegaic purity.

Every vista in the state, every landform and ecosystem, whether it is unimaginable miles away or within the confines of an adobe wall, is a creature of New Mexico's elusive, even angelic light.

The English novelist of the twenties D. H. Lawrence saw it somewhat differently. In fact, he grew quite terrified of the New Mexico landscape. He wrote: "The first moment I saw the brilliant, proud morning shine high up over the deserts of Santa Fe, something stood still in my soul, and I started to attend.... Never is the light more pure and overweening than there, arching with a royalty almost cruel over the hollow, uptilted world."

Few have looked for the first time upon the many landscapes of New Mexico without feeling an upwelling of emotion, a sense of their own size. "Rising out of long forgotten seas like a massive shrug of shoulders," wrote John Dewitt McKee, a professor of English, in the 1950s, "the mountains stand firm and hold us. Volcanic cones against the sky, monuments to the grandeur of past violence, hold us too, in something that approaches awe." And then come the aftereffects. McKee said: "The land itself by slow degrees takes those who come to it and shapes them till they fit, till they take the color of the desert, till they can look almost unwaveringly at the sky. This is the land then."

And so it remains today, under its uptilted world of sky and light.

Land of Volcanoes

Larry S. Crumpler (2001)

What makes New Mexico exceptional? There are many points of view, some more frequently mentioned than others. New Mexicans are poor at boasting, so one would be excused if unable to answer immediately the question, "What is geologically exceptional about New Mexico?"

When you think about it, each of the other Four Corners states seems to have a geologic specialty. Arizona is the Grand Canyon State. Utah is the Dinosaur State, and Colorado is the Rocky Mountain State. In New Mexico the landscape is geologically young and dynamic. It so happens that its volcanoes are a profound reason why the landscape here is so unique.

In the same way that uniqueness and diversity is New Mexico's specialty in culture and art, diversity of volcanic landforms is its geologic specialty. Like a bird sanctuary where birdwatchers may see many different species in one small area, New Mexico is a "volcano sanctuary" to volcanologists. The fact is, this is one of the best places on the continent to see the landforms associated with volcanoes. New Mexico is "the Volcano State."

Many Western states certainly have volcanoes, and some really spectacular and grandiose ones, too. But in keeping with the theme of diversity and subtle characteristics of art and culture in New Mexico, grandiose is not the point. The volcanoes here are refined, world-class examples of many different volcanic landforms, many of which are either not as well-preserved or not as abundant elsewhere. The volcanoes of New Mexico are also the framework on which much of our

The Valle Grande caldera, a volcanic basin filled with rich grassland that has supported livestock for centuries, about 1960.

most scenic ecology is based. It is a grand outdoor gallery of young volcanoes with exotic and artistic Southwestern mesas and desert vistas thrown in for visual relief. It is a giant museum of volcanoes.

Given this diversity and scenic appeal of volcanic landscapes, it should be no surprise that 20 percent of the U.S. national parks and monuments based on volcanic landscapes are in New Mexico. That is more than in Arizona, Idaho, Oregon and Washington combined.

Volcanoes are exotic. Only a relative handful of the world's population actually lives near volcanoes because most of Earth's surface consists of sedimentary rocks or old, eroded granitic rocks. But volcanoes are everywhere in New Mexico. Most of the state's cities (Santa Fe, Ratón, Taos, Grants, Quemado, Truth or Consequences and Las Cruces) have volcanoes nearby. New Mexico's largest city, Albuquerque, might well be called "the City of Volcanoes." There are more types of volcanoes within an hour's drive of Albuquerque than any other comparable city on the continent. The Valles Caldera, San Felipe volcano, and Cerros del Río volcanoes lie to the north; Mount Taylor and the Albuquerque volcanoes to the west; and Isleta, Los Lunas and Cat Hills volcanoes lie to the south, to name a few. In fact, all of the major centers of art and commerce along the Río Grande are near young volcanoes.

New Mexico's geologic specialty could also be subtitled "the Rift Valley State." The Río Grande rift, running the length of New Mexico, is one of only a handful of big, young continental rifts in the world, East Africa being one of the other ones. The Río Grande rift is one reason why there are many young scoria (cinder) cones and lava flows dotting the Río Grande Valley and adjacent llanos. Rift valleys are exotic on dry land — New Mexico is one of those exotic places.

Like Kilimanjaro and other big volcanoes in East Africa, Mount Taylor, a large cascade-type volcano, now broods just outside the margin of the Río Grande rift. The summit of Mount Taylor is in the shape of a large amphitheater that faces Albuquerque. Most of the peaks of Mount Taylor, as seen from Albuquerque, are really the rim of this amphitheater. The amphitheater does not owe its shape entirely to erosion; it may have started out as a Mount St. Helens-like summit crater that was gradually widened and deepened by erosion over the 2 million years since its eruption.

The Valles Caldera near Los Alamos is a monument to the large scales attainable by volcanoes in New Mexico. It is a resurgent caldera, a type in which the central floor has bulged upward to form a central peak, in this case, Cerro Redondo. The bulging occurred over a period of hundreds of thousands of years following the actual catastrophic eruption of great flowing clouds of ash that today forms the cliffs of Bandelier Tuff. The underlying magma chamber was nearly emptied by the eruption, causing the surface to collapse and form the Valles Caldera.

Valles Caldera in fact is the prototype used to identify other calderas of this type throughout the world. Yellowstone is a later-identified and less visually obvious example of this type of volcano. Similar and older, but awesome because they rank among some of the biggest volcanoes on Earth, are the now-eroded calderas of the Datil-Mogollón region of New Mexico. The biggest is estimated to have been larger than 25 miles across.

Even the youngest lava flows here have significance beyond New Mexico. The Carrizozo lava flow (Valley of Fires State Park) and McCartys lava flow (El Malpais National Monument) erupted about 5,000 and 3,000 years ago respectively. But they are also two of the largest young lava flows in the world. The eruptions were nonviolent by volcanic standards. In each case several cubic kilometers of lava oozed out over the space of several years to fill their respective valleys. Many of the geological terms for surface features and technical details of lava flows were first defined here in New Mexico from the McCartys lava flow, not Hawaii.

Besides big volcanoes, New Mexico abounds in small scoria cone volcanoes. Who has not seen Capulín Volcano, which is a type example. Scoria cones tend to come in clusters that volcanologists call "volcanic fields." Classic volcanic fields include the Ratón-Clayton; Zuni-Bandera; Potrillo, near Las Cruces; Cerros del Río, west of Santa Fe; Red Hill, west of Quemado; Ocaté, near Fort Union and Wagon Mound; Taos Plateau; and Mesa Chivato, north of Mount Taylor. Young volcanic steam-explosion craters, resembling meteor craters, are fairly rare in most volcanic regions but abundant in New Mexico. Examples are Zuni Salt Lake crater and Kilbourne Hole crater, near Las Cruces as well as in the Potrillo area, White Rock Canyon, Mesa Chivato and around Elephant Butte.

New Mexico has some truly unique volcanic landforms not seen elsewhere. Exposed in the side of the East Grants Ridge, just north of Grants, is the best example in the world of a small scoria cone in cross section. Due to extensive back-wasting of the mesa edges surrounding Mount Taylor, particularly along the Río Puerco, the "heads" of many small volcanoes have been completely removed by erosion, leaving behind their "necks," or interior plugs of hardened lava and cinder. Cabezón Peak is one of the larger of many examples in the Río Puerco Valley, which is home to the largest collection and best-exposed examples of the insides of small volcanoes in the world.

What about volcanic eruptions in the future? There are no active volcanoes in New Mexico right now, but the conditions exist to make a new one. Molten rock, or magma, is even now spreading out like pancake batter between deep rock layers about 12 miles below the surface in an area between Belén and Socorro. Referred to as the Socorro magma body, it is actually the source of many of New Mexico's earthquakes. Less perfect examples of this phenomenon occur at Yellowstone, Mammoth Lake and Death Valley. The Socorro magma body may erupt someday — or maybe not. It is too early to tell. But volcanism in New Mexico has continued off and on for tens of millions of years. So it is unlikely that it stopped magically 3,000 years ago with the eruption of the McCartys lava flow at El Malpais.

3

The Sangre de Cristo Mountains

William deBuys

The Rocky Mountains, spine of the continent, give birth to the Rio Grande in southern Colorado and fork to either side. In the west they become the San Juan range, which diminishes from its Colorado heights to a long tangle of ridges in New Mexico. East of the river the mountains form a rugged sierra walling the grassy sea of the Great Plains from the increasingly arid country of the intermountain West. The exotic name of these mountains, Sangre de Cristo — Blood of Christ — derives, according to one legend, from a distant time when Pueblo Indians slaughtered Spanish missionaries who had come to save them from the presumed perdition of their paganism. One of these missionaries, at the moment of his martyrdom, prayed to God for a sign that his death would not be in vain, and as though in response, the snowcapped peaks of the sierra were suddenly bathed in a vivid crimson — they glowed with the Blood of Christ! (Julyan 1998, 323). The legend gives no hint about how word of this miracle got out (and the question is an interesting one, because the sole believing witness to the event was instantly hacked to bits), but the commonplace of sunsets reddening the Sangres helps keep the tale alive.

The actual history of the name is more mundane. Long known to Spanish colonists simply as the Sierra Madre, the mountains are broken by a relatively accessible pass near present-day Walsenburg, Colorado. As early as 1779 the river flowing west from the pass was identified on maps by the name Sangre de Cristo. The name was subsequently applied to the pass itself, and ultimately, courtesy of railroad publicists eager

Threshing grain near Tres Ritos, north-central New Mexico, about 1940. Photograph by Wyatt Davis.

to enhance the region's tourist appeal, to the entire mountain range (Wroth 1983). This last extension of the name was additionally cemented in the public mind by the nineteenth-century florescence of the passionately religious Penitente Brotherhood, which became famous for penitential practices such as self-flagellation and Holy Week reenactments of the original shedding of the Sangre de Cristo. It is poetic that the mountains where the Penitentes were and are still strongest should bear the name of the object of their devotion.

The Sangres stretch farther south than any other spur of the Rockies and yield to a landscape of mesas and plains not far from Santa Fe, at the small, tough town of Pecos, New Mexico. You could hardly say that the Rockies whittle down to a mild end. The mountains above Pecos and Santa Fe soar to altitudes over thirteen thousand feet, and their canyons and ridges are home to elk, deer, bighorn sheep, black bear, and cougar. Almost all the mountain country is now included in the Carson and Santa Fe National Forests, and although numerous small farming and ranching communities lie scattered through the lower elevations, higher up, where the two national forests jointly manage the Pecos Wilderness, the land appears to be as free from sustained human effect as any in the Southwest. (But *appears* is the operative word here, for suppression of fire, alteration of wildlife populations, and other human-caused phenomena, no doubt including climate change, have loosed a cascade of consequences that leave the high mountains, notwithstanding their beauty and ecological resilience, far from pristine. In this, they have much company, for virtually every ecosystem on earth bears the imprint of humankind's touch.)

At the foot of the high peaks that rise treeless and windswept from the dark forests of the Sangres also rise the headwaters of the nine-hundred-mile Rio Pecos as well as tributary sources of the nearby Rio Grande and the distant Mississippi. Like any other mountain range, particularly one that divides the waters of major river systems, these mountains are collectively a kind of pivot in the natural history of the region. The land below them is made from their eroded wastes; they change and channel the weather and divide one environmental region, one flora and fauna, from another. Equally as barriers to communication and conquest and as sources of valuable water, timber, game, and grazing, they have played a fundamental role in human affairs.

And what remarkable affairs they have been. The history of New Mexico is as rich as it is long. Anyone who studies it is at pains to remember that New Mexico has been part of the United States for little more than a century and a half, and for a century more than that it belonged to Spain and Mexico. And before the coming of the Spaniards, for much longer, it indisputably belonged to Native, village-dwelling agriculturalists and to a diverse array of semisedentary and nomadic tribes.

Mountains offer a fine vantage from which to view the history of a region, and New Mexico is a land of mountains. Much of my work over the years has focused on the mountain country that fills the triangle formed by Santa Fe, Las Vegas, and Taos. Within this triangle most of the decisive events in New Mexico's early history took place. The mountains were a valued goal to some of the people who came to them, and an obstacle to others. In every case, they were always an actor as well as a stage, for their influence reached to the heart of every enterprise.

In different ways, at different scales, and at different times, something similar might be said for the other mountain ranges of New Mexico: the Chuskas, which birthed so much of the history and lore of the Navajos; the Jemez, with the spectacular Valles Caldera at its core; the Sandia and Manzano Mountains, which rise like fins of rock and forest from the sun-baked center of the state; the Mogollon, Pinos Altos, and Black Mountains and other, smaller ranges that embrace the lonesome headwaters of the Gila River; the limestone Guadalupes, whose hollow innards conceal vast systems of caves and caverns; and the majestic Sacramento Mountains, where winter snowcaps gleam teasingly above the unbounded deserts of the south.

These names, however, are only a beginning. The roll call of New Mexico mountains is long; it becomes a kind of chant, a song of place, a litany evocative of the

wildness of the American West, the panoramas of its land, and the heritage of both
Native and Spanish and Mexican North America. The names feel good on the tongue
as they are said, and they feel even better in the mind as each one evokes a different
history and relationship, a different distillation of hope, survival, devotion, and experience. There are the Nacimientos and the Turkeys, the Zuni, the Ortiz, and the San
Pedros. There are two San Mateo ranges, one that enfolds sacred Mount Taylor and
another that guards part of the rim of the stunning Plains of San Augustine. There are
the Sawtooth, Datil, and Magdalena Mountains, plus the Gallinas and the Capitans.
Brooding above the daunting Jornada del Muerto stand the San Andreas, Oscura,
Caballo, and Fra Cristóbal Mountains. There are isolated peaks and ranges that rise
like islands out of desert seas: the Organs, the Franklins, the Pyramids, the Alamo
Huecos, the Tres Hermanas, the two ranges called the Hatchets, big and little, the Burros, also big and little, and the Floridas, whose name, pronounced correctly, does *not*
sound like the citrus-growing state (you put the accent on the *i*) — it sounds instead
like something native to New Mexico. There are the Cookes Range, the Cedar Mountain Range, the Good Sight Mountains, the Cornudas, the Brokeoffs, and the Sierra
de las Uvas, the last of which suggests (falsely) the sweetness and moisture of grapes
amid the arid monotony of rock and sand. And down in the boot heel of the state,
there are the Animas and the Peloncillo Mountains, where the pull of ecological kinship from the Sierra Madre Occidental of Mexico is like a breeze that never calms.

The Rockies may end at the southern extremity of the Sangre de Cristo range,
but it is an ending only in the sense that the continuous chain of high mountains
abruptly becomes discontinuous. The mountains break like a string of pearls and yield
their parts, the pearls scattering across the land, each one related to the next, but each
one standing separate and apart, and each one a jewel.

In the late seventies and early eighties I wrote a book about the Sangre de
Cristo Range — *Enchantment and Exploitation: The Life and Hard Times of a New
Mexico Mountain Range* — in a not-altogether conscious attempt to understand the
place where, as a young man, I had come to live. I was not native to the mountains
but had come there from elsewhere. At some level, writing about the place was my
way of laying claim to belonging to it. The mountains — or at least the isolated valley
where I lived — had begun to feel like home, and by writing about the land and its
people I wanted to answer the fundamental question *Where am I?* and I wanted to
understand my *place.*

Luckily for me the place I wanted to understand was — and still is — one of the
most remarkable points of convergence, in terms of both natural history and cultural history, to be found on the continent. No other region in North America so richly combines
ecological and human diversity, and in this regard the Sangres are a microcosm of New
Mexico, which among the fifty states is similarly conspicuous as a redoubt of diversity.

The Sangre de Cristo range stands with its feet in the near-desert of the arid
Rio Grande Valley and its head in the alpine tundra of thirteen-thousand-foot peaks.

Between those extremes lie as many as nine or ten discrete ecological zones, depending on how you classify them. Even more impressive is the mix of cultures one finds in the Sangres. The Pueblo Indians and their ancestors have made their homes there for at least two thousand years, and for the last four hundred they have shared their land with the sons and daughters of Spanish-speaking pioneers from Mexico. The Hispanic *pobladores* of northern New Mexico built their adobe villages in scores of irrigable valleys nestled in the mountains' lower slopes, and there these remarkable communities remain today, in many cases still isolated, weather-beaten, and, to most Anglo Americans, foreign.

I received my introduction to the Sangres in 1972 as a research assistant to a social scientist who was writing a book on aspects of the region's cultures. I was given license to pursue my research however I desired — whether in saloons or elementary schools did not matter, so long as I conveyed such findings as I made to my employer. Unfortunately, this ideal arrangement ended in failure. I found it impossible to write intelligently about the people of the region when I knew so little about the demanding physical environment in which they dwelled. I realized that until I understood something of the influence of the land, I could not begin to understand the people whose lives and history bound them to it.

A few years later I had the opportunity to pursue that intuition, and I set out to become a student of the land and to express what I learned in a manuscript that eventually became *Enchantment and Exploitation*. I was not trying to compose a "regional study" in an academic sense. Rather, I wanted to capture a sense of the land's being — a sense, that is, of place.

The most important thing I learned was that a society's relationship to land is reciprocal: society both changes the physical world and is changed by it. I also learned that the study of those changes offered an excellent means to illuminate the main themes of the cultural history of New Mexico.

In adapting to environment, a society alters the land both purposefully (clearing fields for agriculture, building dams on rivers) and by accident (overgrazing, climate change). In turn its people tend to find themselves obliged to adapt to the changes they have wrought — sometimes by changing the environment still further, which is the Anglo way, the way of dams for irrigation and more dams for desalination. At every step in the process of adaptation and change there are opportunities for choosing between alternatives, and people's choice of one alternative over another depends in large measure upon their outlook and priorities — in a word, upon their culture.

Culture provides a filter through which people perceive the environment around them and their relation to it. It screens out certain influences or possibilities while allowing others to pass on to awareness, sometimes greatly intensified. For the Pueblos the landscape was (and, casinos notwithstanding, still is) manifestly spiritual, especially in certain locations and at certain times. The mountain peaks were sources of spiritual energy; the lakes were doors to an underworld. The land and sky were living things that the Pueblo people supplicated through elaborate rituals to ensure the orderly progression of the seasons and the stability of their communities.

To the Hispanos of New Mexico the land was not sacred in the same sense it was for the Pueblos. As Catholics and Christians they assented that holiness of place abided mainly in the church and other sanctified locations, but the land was still not altogether inanimate. It was the mother and protector of their traditional subsistence pastoralism. It had a spirit with which they identified and allied themselves and which they felt to be almost palpable. In many cases the land was also a communal thing, belonging not to individuals but to whole villages and groups of villages as a collective possession.

Initially in the Anglo view, the land of New Mexico and other western territories possessed little by way of spiritual or communal qualities. Land was mainly a commodity, which, like wheat or iron ore, might be advantageously bought and still more advantageously sold. Toward the end of the nineteenth century, however, new ideas based on a kind of scientifically oriented communalism gained increasing currency, along with the argument that certain land, particularly the high mountain forests, should be held in trust for all members of society in order to protect water quality, timber supplies, and other resources. The forest reserves, later renamed national forests, were the result.

Never entirely separate from this communalism was the notion, expressed in the creation of many national parks, that certain wild lands possessed a spiritual quality of vital importance to our national way of life. At the urging of Aldo Leopold and others, this idea was eventually elaborated into a system of wilderness areas that first existed within the national forests and later grew to include land managed by other agencies. The system got its start in New Mexico. In 1924 the 559,324-acre Gila Wilderness, in southwest New Mexico, became the nation's first wilderness area, and forty years later the concept of wilderness was formalized by federal legislation creating the National Wilderness Preservation System. Both the Pecos Wilderness, in the southern Sangres, and the Gila Wilderness are leading examples of this system, which in early 2007, according to Steve Capra of the New Mexico Wilderness Association, comprised thirty units totaling 1,638,722 acres in New Mexico.

Plenty of irony abides in the concept of wilderness, especially in New Mexico. As applied to public land in the United States, it is intended to commemorate the frontier conditions that helped shape American national identity. But wilderness preservation became popular only after the Native people, who made the frontier a frontier, had been safely driven from the wild lands that had long been their homes. In New Mexico, moreover, it is hard to look at the concept of frontier from just one point of view, and the longer you look at it, the more complex and culturally nuanced it becomes.

The ancient Pueblos recognized that their world was bounded by a kind of frontier, although the word is a poor translation for the depth of their thought. Their circle of sacred mountains might be said to have marked a frontier. Within the mountains' perimeter, the work of creation was considered to be complete, and the Pueblo gods ruled with unchallenged authority. But outside the ring of mountains, the world was less finished, less ripe, less orderly. The contrast of distant worlds did not particularly inhibit travel — Puebloans traveled far and wide across the region — but to journey outside the embrace of the sacred mountains required special preparation, for in a sense the traveler was stepping off the spiritual map of the world. It was equivalent to being, in the oldest, most meaningful sense of the word, in wilderness.

The first of the region's two greatest revolutions commenced when strangers marched up out of wilderness to the south in 1540. With the Spanish *entrada* and the subsequent colonization of New Mexico, the prehistoric world of the Pueblos and their tribal neighbors suddenly became historical. Initially the Spanish-speaking *pobladores*, the settlers and populators of a frontier empire, were merely the acolytes of a frantic search for mineral treasure, but as the colonists' dreams of wealth and glory faded, they became the principals in one of Spain's most audacious and problematic efforts to spread Iberian civilization throughout the New World. Up the long trail from Mexico they came, carrying in their veins not just the blood of Old World Spain, along with portions of Moorish North Africa, but the blood of Indian Mexico as well. They settled into the valleys and edges of the mountains of northern New Mexico and fashioned a new cultural identity from their struggles there; they became *New Mexicans*. These Hispanic Southwesterners (who from their point of view were *norteños*, or northerners) are seldom mentioned in the books that present American history to schoolchildren, but their story is as much a part of the North American colonial experience as that of the Pilgrims or the Virginia planters.

They had to be uncommonly resilient to survive. Because they consumed most of what they produced and exported little that was particularly valuable or irreplaceable to the centers of colonial power from which they were governed, the empire they represented spent little of its treasure on their protection. Hemmed in by forbidding mountains, inhospitable deserts, and hostile tribes, the colony of New Mexico did not prosper so much as it persisted. Erased by the Pueblo Revolt of 1680 and then reestablished, for a long time it held to life like a beleaguered desert plant, with one long thin taproot that reached to Mexico and a scant few leaves in Albuquerque, Santa Fe, Santa Cruz, and Taos.

Under pressure from warring Comanches, the frontiers of the colony actually shrank inward for a time in the middle eighteenth century. After don Juan Bautista de Anza defeated the massed Comanche tribes under Cuerno Verde in 1779, the frontiers of New Mexico began to move outward again, ushering in a period of sustained discovery and cultural growth. But those frontiers soon met the limits imposed by towering mountains in the north and deserts and the indomitable Navajos to the west. On the grassy plains to the east, after a half-century of slow expansion, the Hispanic frontier of New Mexico collided with the still more vigorous west-moving frontier of Anglo American expansion. This was the second of New Mexico's great revolutions.

The trappers and merchants who trekked across the Great Plains were men still look-ing for their country and still finding and stealing it. They were followed by ranchers and farmers, miners, lawyers, thieves, soldiers, and tourists who came piling into New Mexico in wave after wave. Each wave broke against the territory's chromatic moun-tains and mesas, leaving an indelible imprint.

The second half of the nineteenth century brought a subtle shift in the tide of Anglo conquest. The presence of army survey teams mapping the land in close detail and making an inventory of its resources presaged the rise of scientific and entrepre-neurial approaches to land use, strongly aided and subsidized by the federal govern-ment. This period also saw a radical disjuncture in the natural history of the region, catalyzed by the arrival of the railroad and the consequent linking of New Mexico to distant markets and sources of capital. Exploitation of the land soon reached a new and unsustainable intensity. Grasslands were grazed to exhaustion, then forests burned to create more grasslands, which in short order were also overgrazed. Plant ecologies were ruptured by overuse and then re-formed, often with newly introduced species replacing beleaguered native ones.

The human population also grew, and in a relatively short span of time, grizzly bear, wolves, elk, bighorn sheep, and other species were exterminated from long-held habitats. In many areas erosion sapped the strength of the soil, and arroyos lowered the water table, preparing the way for the alternate miseries of drought and flood. As the land grew weaker and poorer, the vitality of the human economy in many parts of New Mexico also began to decline, reaching a nadir in the shared hardships of the Great Depression. In response, New Mexicans attempted, at first slowly and falter-ingly, to seek new balances in their use of the land, balances that are still evolving.

The story of the land continues to develop, as does the story of New Mexico's intertwined yet distinct cultures. In great cities like New York and San Francisco one can find as much or more cultural diversity, and in isolated enclaves on some Indian reservations and in Appalachia or southern Louisiana one finds historical continuities as long or longer. But nowhere can one find diversity and continuity combined as richly as in New Mexico, and particularly in the Hispanic and Pueblo homeland in the "deep north" of the state.

The survival of the region's indigenous cultures is, in part, an accident of geography. Because New Mexico possessed scant mineral resources and few attrac-tions of other kinds, and because hundreds of miles of bleak and dangerous territory separated it from the economic centers of both New Spain and nineteenth-century Anglo America, neither imperial nation undertook to colonize New Mexico with much energy or enterprise. Both Spain and the United States found that New Mexico, unlike coastal California or the eastern half of Texas, was mostly unsettleable, at least with preindustrial technologies. The arable land of the territory consisted almost exclusively of narrow river and stream valleys that were too few and too widely scat-tered to allow the growth of large agricultural populations. Instead the landscape produced a dispersed pattern of settlement consisting of many small enclaves of population and culture. These mostly Pueblo and Hispano villages became bastions of cultural preservation, for they were at once so self-sufficient that they had little need for the outside world and yet so poor that the outside world had little need of them. In isolation they persisted for many generations, changing little.

And so they persist today, changing much more now, facing threats unimaginable a century or even a generation ago, yet still distinct, still quintessentially and inimitably *New Mexican*, like the land they have shaped and been shaped by. May they and their land so continue.

Blessing the water at the ditch that serves La Joya and Contreras, central New Mexico, 1987. Photograph by Nancy Hunter Warren.

4

Waterways: Acequias

Sylvia Rodríguez (2006)

In New Mexico, the Arabic derivation *acequia* refers to both a canal structure and a social institution whereby river water is diverted and distributed via gravity flow among a community of irrigators or water right user-owners called *parciantes*. Historically, acequias made possible the Spanish colonial settlement of the semiarid Upper Rio Grande Valley of New Mexico, starting in the late 16th century. Acequias appropriated and transformed whatever irrigation structures and practices were operating among Pueblos in the Upper Rio Grande Valley at the time of European contact.

During the colonial and Mexican periods and into the American era, acequias proliferated. For roughly 350 years, they formed a core component of the technological infrastructure of New Mexico's agropastoral economy. Their local, interlocking networks of canals transformed and shaped the entire riparian ecology of the region. The body of irrigation law brought from Spain and adapted through customary practice to frontier conditions became incorporated into territorial and finally New Mexico state water law.

Today's acequia associations are political subdivisions of the state. Local associations of parciantes elect a *mayordomo* and commissioners to oversee the annual operations of the acequias and to maintain, use, improve, and defend them. At the start of the 21st century, approximately one thousand acequia associations still existed in New Mexico. The humble earthen ditches crisscrossing the fields and arable valleys along the Rio Grande and its tributaries are arguably the oldest living, non-indigenous public works system in North America.

Acequias occupy a paradoxical position along the hypothetical water-control continuum between extremes of centralized control at one pole and autonomy or consensus at the other. Historically, acequias partake of both extremes. At the outset, they were a colonial or colonizing institution. In concert with roads, architecture, mines, and the agriculture they supported, acequias transformed the indigenous landscape radically and forever. Subordinated workers dug the first colonial ditches. Yet despite invasive beginnings, acequias became integral to the New Mexican environment.

In our own era, acequia associations continue to promote a fluctuating balance between cooperation and competition, as well as seasonal, face-to-face interaction among parciantes on a ditch. They are a democratic institution in that parciantes elect their mayordomo and commissioners, with usually one vote per parciante. Ownership of water rights is normally inherited but can transfer with the land. Nowadays, a water right is also a prime commodity bought and sold separately from the land to which it was once implicitly attached, and it can be transferred to urban uses. The market in detachable water rights escalates with each passing year. Use rights to a ditch depend on exercise through irrigation, compliance with rules, and proportional contribution to maintenance of the system. Each ditch operates according to its own variant of a common set of principles. Some are written as law; some are observed, spoken, but not written; and others are simply unspoken practice....

Acequia Practice

Acequia practice encompasses the annual spring cleaning of the ditch and other work of repair, maintenance, and improvement; changing the headgate and dividing the water; and attending meetings of the parciantes. Irrigating the fields, orchards, and gardens is the basic secular activity, and far from the simplest. Stanley Crawford's (1988) memoir, *Mayordomo*, about his year of service as mayordomo on a ditch in Dixon, in southern Taos County, offers the most detailed account of everyday acequia activities. His narrative begins and ends with cleaning the ditch but also covers the daily tasks — repair, crisis management, planning, improvement, dues collection, record keeping, meeting, and negotiation — that make up the seasonal operation of an acequia.

Curiously, Crawford never describes the actual process of irrigation. Perhaps, like riding a horse or driving a car, it is taken for granted and laborious to explain. Irrigation involves bodily skill learned through observation in the context of practice. Practitioners do not describe it in the abstract or narrate it outside its execution. Irrigation is kinesthetic, visual, spatial, technical, and interactive, but not especially verbal.

Anyone who has watched the minimalist gestures of a parciante irrigating a field will allow that at first glance it does not look like much. Yet anyone who has tried to control the gravity-driven flow of water over an irregular gradient of variably porous, plowed ground so that it will soak in slowly, deeply, and evenly will tell you how difficult this job is. Success requires experience, patience, knowledge, and control. One must be familiar with the terrain and responsive to the contingencies of weather and water flow. One must not lose the water or let it get away. Given the undeniable power of flowing water, little apparent exertion can become a mark of skill rather than lassitude. Each act of irrigation is particular to a piece of land. My own first attempt years ago at what looked like a simple project ended in ruined, washed-out rows and tears of frustration and shock. I failed to anticipate the force of the water as it rushed off the mountain and over my neatly planted rows of seeds. Seventy-eight-year-old Corina Santistevan of Cordillera put it this way:

> But there was, there is, a real craft about how to irrigate a field. It isn't done, it can't be done, by just anybody. I have been paying for people to do it for me, and they don't know how to irrigate. They either flood one spot, or they never get the water to another, and they don't have the sense of how the water runs. (April 1996)

La saca, or *la limpia de la acequia* (the annual spring cleaning of the ditch), requires each parciante to contribute labor toward physical maintenance of the system. Each parciante goes, sends a *peón* (surrogate), or pays for hired labor, according to how much acreage he or she irrigates. Contribution to ditch maintenance is proportional. On the morning of the designated day, each worker arrives with a shovel and spends the day clearing away underbrush and digging dirt and debris out of the ditch. The mayordomo marks and calls out the sections and supervises the labor. This is the *tarea* (task) to which generations of parciantes have committed their sons from the age of puberty. Today, most parciantes hire or pay for peones rather than go, or they send their sons. Each spring, a few young boys can still be found performing this rite of passage on their acequia madre. Some ditches take more than one day to clean. Along with irrigation, la limpia enables parciantes to become familiar with their ditches and keep their use rights. It is a day of common labor by the members — or their peones — of an acequia community. It affirms and socializes members into a cooperative, subsistence institution. "Ditch cleanings are all very much the same," Crawford (1988, 224) writes, "and in this they often feel more like ritual than work." The warm glow of mutualism notwithstanding, Crawford still perceived an underlying tension in acequia work:

> The collective power of a ditch crew of twenty or thirty men can often be felt as threatening or dangerous, but what holds it in restraint are the conventions and traditions that have evolved out of hundreds of years of maintaining acequias — a complex social fabric binds a ditch crew together far more than the character of a mayordomo or the commissioners, recalling it to a sense of common purpose and preventing the inevitable disputes from flaring into political divisiveness or even physical violence. (Crawford 1988, 23-24)

Meetings are the major venue for the cooperative, organization, and managerial aspects of acequia practice. Each acequia must hold an annual meeting to elect the mayordomo and commissioners and to deal with other routine ditch business. Parciantes also hold meetings to deal with crisis situations and the rationing of water during drought. New Mexico state statute requires mayordomos and commissioners to meet each spring to decide how the water will be divided on their common stream under pending conditions. A parciante meets with the mayordomo at a given time and headgate to transfer the water from one ditch to another. Crawford evokes the everyday seesaw of structure and agency played out among individuals and families through time along a ditch. The medium of meetings is public language, employed as an instrument of organization, control, and power.

The mayordomo plays a key role in the New Mexican community acequia complex. The mayordomo and commissioners manage all ditch business. They supervise la saca, preside over meetings, resolve minor disputes between parciantes, and organize repair jobs. The mayordomo assigns the water and manages the reparto de agua according to custom. Each tributary and acequia madre has its own, distilled out of generations of struggle and negotiation or conciliation among parciantes or between parciantes and pueblo irrigators over their respective shares of river water. Each reparto synthesizes principles of law with the pragmatics of compromise. Some customs, such as the ones governing the division of water on the Río Pueblo and the Río Lucero, enjoy the force and formality of a legal decree or agreement. Others persist in memory and practice but go unwritten and jurally unrecognized.

Today's parciantes describe mayordomos of a generation or two ago as powerful, authoritarian figures regarded with a mixture of respect, trust, and fear. Gus García put it succinctly: "They were like dictators, and what the mayordomo said was the law and you did it" (personal communication with the author, July 1995). A good mayordomo must know and uphold the customary repartos on his ditches, as well as on the river as a whole. He must be fair and evenhanded, possess intimate knowledge of local topography and hydraulics, and be able to deliver the water despite adversity or conflict. He must command respect. The authoritarian nature of the position is counterbalanced by the fact that parciantes in good standing on a ditch elect the mayordomo and the commissioners. The mayordomo is both a leader and an equal among peers.

Mayordomos are still respected, and the position carries status along with responsibility. They exert less power, however, and are less feared than in the old days when nearly everyone farmed for a living. State statute has spread the mayordomo's former power among the commissioners. A person's boss can potentially impact household economy the way the mayordomo of the acequia once did. Today people rarely seek the role of mayordomo and often accept it reluctantly, under subtle, irresistible pressure. The acequia association pays the mayordomo a modest stipend that hardly covers the hours, miles, worry, and labor involved. The variety of mayordomos is as diverse as the ditches themselves. Some are adept and fair; others are inept or self-serving. Acequias and their mayordomos have always had to adapt to local conditions shaped by larger forces. These days, officers are as preoccupied with defending their acequia rights in court as with dividing the water or maintaining their ditch.

Peñasco, New Mexico, 1943, modern gelatin silver photograph, 11 x 14 inches.
Photograph by John C. Collier Jr.

5.

Windscapes:
Chronicles of Neglected Time

Roland F. Dickey (1983)

When I was a boy, barbershops had big mirrors on facing walls and each reflection was caught by its opposite and sent back and forth at the speed of light, smaller and smaller, forever and ever. Prosperous men of the town came in for daily shaves, working stiffs and youngsters got payday haircuts, and the barbers, between stropping razors and brushing soap into foam, primed all of them to recite intimate news and Santa Fe Railway rumors and dirty jokes. From these small-town dramas I believed I was learning what growing up was all about, and ever since then my mind has repeated scenes, each more distant and less detailed than the last, as fleeting as the images in that long-ago looking-glass land.

Like the puffing Boreas that livens old maps, the Wind personified seems always to be lurking somewhere in my memories of eastern New Mexico. Channeled in the mountainless corridor that divides the continent from Canada to Mexico, the wind certainly was "the Force" in our lives, and we learned to stay tuned to its presence or absence. I never got used to the wind, and whenever it rose above a "cool summer breeze" it seemed the most hated and feared element that Nature concocts. "There's nothing between us and the North Pole but a barbed-wire fence," the saying goes, and wind on the high plains carries salvation and disaster, "chill factor" and moisture, desiccation and dust.

The auditorium in Clovis High School, where we passed notes in study hall and carved our initials in the varnished seats, had an all-purpose stage set in front of which graduation and other formal events took place. Painted by some nostalgic woodland artist, it showed a deciduous forest in the full foliage of summer, cool and green and dappled with shadows. Very few of us had ever seen such a landscape — it was a hundred miles to any forest, a thousand to one like that. The reminiscences of my childhood are not set against a wooded glade, but on a tarmac-flat grassland turned to dry farming by homesteaders.

For starters: November 11, 1918. The little town of Clovis is two miles away, its black water tower rising like a wrong-font exclamation point above rows of houses level as lines of type. The Santa Fe Shops' whistle, normally heard four times a day, is bellowing like a wounded bull. The locomotives are releasing steam in hoots and howls. It is the long-hoped-for Armistice of World War I. My mother, her hair and her apron flying in the wind, is standing by the barbed-wire fence, shading her eyes, staring toward the town. I am four years old, and my collie dog and I are running to join her. Mrs. Mitchell, the nearest neighbor, is hurrying down the lane in our direction. End of tableau.

Not every year is a 1066, and certain scenes, especially seasonal ones, take place so often that they blend into an undated medley. Every year along that same wire fence the prickly pear comes into saffron-yellow bloom, glistening brown beetles wallow in its pollen, red ants police their circular territories as cleanswept as an adobe yard in Rio Arriba. Beyond the fence are acres of wheat, blue-green and ripening to straw-gold. A horse-drawn mechanical reaper bends the ripe heads in the path of little cutting daggers. Men in gangs of twos and threes fork the cut wheat into wagons, jump up and down to pack the load. They drive teams to a clattering dragon of a threshing machine and force-feed it forkfuls of hay. A red-brown stream of grain spews from a small pipe; straw and dust billow from a big blower.

It might be a clean, sharp-edged mural by Grant Wood, except that the threshing machine balks and jams and the International Harvester tractor belches and sputters. "IHC" it says on the tractor radiator. "It means In Hell Constantly," says the tractor mechanic. The hundred-foot rubberized belt that keeps the tractor's sparks away from the hay, twisted in a figure 8 to turn the thresher belt wheel opposite from the tractor flywheel, slips and tears. The men shovel and fork and sweat and curse. All are itchy and coughing from chaff and dust. So much for romantic rural life.

At noon "the thrashers," as we call friendly neighbors who exchange labor at harvest time, wash their hands and the front part of their faces, sit jammed together at the table, shovel in the food, slop coffee, are boisterous with each other, bashful with my mother. Most of them are hard-muscled and sunburned. "Why is Uncle Ralph so *white*?" I ask my mother. "Because he works in an office," she tells me.

Same field, another year. A cyclone, a sky-high spinning top, is swinging toward our house. I am lingering, fascinated. My mother is screaming for me to get into the storm cellar — until now a cool underground storehouse for milk and meat. The tornado veers off, taking its revenge elsewhere.

Much more companionable are "dust devils," slim columns of wind-whipped soil swaggering across the land like Navajo gods. Adelaide Lubbock describes an Australian version, "a 'willy-willy' or whirlwind, twirled a pillar of red dust in a dervish dance across the paddocks."

The annual spring dust storms in the Southwest are as abrasive as emery cloth, but the "Dust Bowl" days of the 1930s were frightening because they spelled immediate and long-term tragedy. Like any natural calamity, the experience was unwanted but memorable. A writhing, orange curtain of dust, wide as the horizon and half-a-mile high, rolled out of the north like an army of tanks gone mad. It really appeared to *roll* — like a tornado on its side.

We urged the animals and the poultry into shelter, battened down whatever we could, and waited indoors, hoping the roof would hang on. First came a rattling scurry of tumbleweeds, and then the world went brown and cold.

Next morning the sky was tinted but cloudless, the air still and ominous like the eye of a hurricane. The windmill still stood. Fences were drifted with dunes of sand and soil. In the house — sills, furniture, floors — a quarter-inch of silt. The horses and cattle emerged from the barn rheumy-eyed and snorting. Our own nerves were raw from a night of creaking timbers, gravel-brushed windowpanes, gritty blankets. My mother sighed as she rinsed sand from the dishes to set the breakfast table and steeled herself to face another broom-and-dustpan day.

"It was not uncommon for a sandstorm to last all day and all night, without letting up," said Mrs. Bert McCullough, an early settler in Clovis. "The tubs and washboilers and buckets, clothing and quilts and blankets that happened to be hanging out would all go blowing past with the sand. If the wind happened to be from the north, they all landed against the Santa Fe right-of-way fence and you could go there after the sand had subsided and find most anything you had lost; but if the wind was from the west, the things went on through town and probably to Texico…you never saw them again."

Memory is triggered by any of our senses, and the wind tapping rigging on a metal flagpole reminds me of flagpoles I have known…at schools, hospitals, public squares, military installations. A pair of schoolboy brothers, Boy Scouts both, whose duty it was to lower the flag, would quarrel and almost come to blows each afternoon as to which would fold the flag, and how it *should* be done. And decades later — a confrontation between college men over whether the flag should be lowered to half-mast in the wake of the Kent State tragedy.

The clicking flag-rope sound carries me on to *windmills* — those Martian flowers that once sucked subsurface water from the plains. What was called "the cut-off wire" on our windmill collected static electricity (but not lightning) during storms, and sparks jumped across to the well pipe as on a busy telegraph key.

In those days, long before the deep primordial water table was being drained by electric pumps and circular irrigation systems, our lives centered around the windmill, a veritable polestar. We kept one ear on the wind, and although the big wheel and tail of the mill machinery would yaw automatically — that is, turn sideways in rising wind and reduce speed — it could be ripped apart like a loose sail.

At the first sound of pump rods plunging up and down at a suicidal rate, we would rush to draw down the cable that furled the long fletched tail against the wheel, narrow-edge to the wind. During a gale this called for the weight and strength of two people on the 2-by-4 cut-off brake. The steel wheel would squawk and groan as it fought the wind, turning this way and that like an animal cornered.

Our water, 300 feet below, was pulled to the surface by the mill-wheel that raised and lowered a series of 20-foot hickory rods screwed together with brass couplings, at the bottom of which a primitive piston pump sat in the water table. Periodically, leather gaskets in its valve had to be renewed, an all-day job of disassembling the entire system.

A 10-foot multibladed propeller translated wind energy to raise hundreds of pounds of water and pump-rods. This circular propeller fan was made up of 20 galvanized steel blades (some models had vanes of wood) to give it high initial torque to overcome the inertia of the pump. A simple gear system converted rotary motion into up-and-down strokes. The mechanism was mounted at the top of a 35-foot wooden tower intended to catch the smallest breeze, but it took an eight-mile-an-hour wind to drive the propeller.

Ironically, winds were lightest during the driest season, and our neighbors were as likely as we to run out of water for themselves and their livestock. In the worst of times, to obtain a few gallons of water, my father would climb the tower and turn by hand the mill wheel with its sharp steel blades. My mother would stand and watch him and wring her hands. Windmill accidents were not uncommon, and a sudden shift of wind could sweep a man off the upper platform.

Perhaps it was a blessing that few trees grew on the plains, for trees, fence posts, and barbed wire drew lightning. We heard stories of cattle crowding into fence corners during a storm and being electrocuted.

Shortly before I was born, my mother was knocked unconscious by a lightning bolt that struck nearby. Fortunately Mrs. Mitchell saw the flash and ran to the rescue. I have the impression that pioneer women were always running, skirts held high, across miles of prairie to save each other. My family had a late-blooming Victorian reticence that was a great handicap to my social education. Early in my mother's marriage, a well-meaning neighbor lady told her that a woman would have only one sharp pain before childbirth. When her first, my older brother, was imminent, she had a sharp pain and sent my father pell-mell on horseback for the doctor. Old Dr. Westerfield, this time not offering his usual "Got the same thing m'self, ma'am," just laughed at my father and sent him home. By the time he got back, Mrs. Mitchell had delivered the baby.

At age 18, during a sandstorm, I swore right in front of the Fox Drug Store never to spend another spring in Clovis. I never did, but sometimes I dream about it. Not everything the wind brought was unpleasant. Like a rich relative, the rains didn't come often enough, but they were very welcome. Temporary lakes collected in eroded hollows and toads chorused deliriously. "Buffalo beans" came into bloom and produced hard little fruits that country kids gathered and threw at each other in school — an annual ritual reserved for piñon shells in other parts of New Mexico.

"The first rain in a dry land!" writes Jessamyn West. "It smells better than lilies in July, or the ocean, or the wind in sun-washed pines, or the irrigated patch of alfalfa you reach after a long haul through dry hills. It is hard to smell that sweetness and believe in death."

Ulysses, carrying an oar, walked away from the sea until he found a people who asked him what it was. Fifty years ago, what could an inlander, a plainsman, have carried toward the sea to arouse a sailor's curiosity? A lariat might have been mistaken for boat gear, but a sharp, curved blade from a windmill....

Explosion in front of number 3 steam shovel at Santa Rita mine, December 16, 1916.

6

Minescapes: Memories of Santa Rita

Paul M. Jones (1985)

The town of Santa Rita was a small copper mining town located in southwestern New Mexico. The town has a colorful history, having been mined by the Spanish as far back as 1800 and for an undetermined period before that was known by the Indians of the Southwest. It is probable that the first European to come in contact with copper from the Santa Rita deposits was in 1535 when one of Cabeza de Baca's companions, Andres Dorantes, was given a large copper rattle or bell which is thought to have come from there. Kit Carson and other famous frontiersmen visited and/or worked there. The Spanish abandoned the mine in about 1873, largely due to constant raids by the Apaches, the most fierce fighters of the Indian tribes, and an American named James Pattie assumed operation. From that period on, the huge copper deposits were under almost continuous development.

In 1909 a young mining engineer named John Sully became instrumental in starting the mine on its way to becoming one of the largest copper producers in the United States, and remained actively involved in its operation until his death in 1933. In the late fifties and early sixties the town was demolished in order to utilize the rich ore body on which it perched. A way of life was gone forever, and a deep sentimental attachment has developed among the ex-residents who remember the good and bad times of their lives there during the Great Depression, pestilence and other such earth shaking events, with a feeling of great loss and emptiness....

My First Memory of Santa Rita

We arrived in Santa Rita in 1923 when I was at the ripe old age of four years. We moved into one of the "yellow bungalows" perched north of the road above the Hill School on Santa Rita Hill. My father, a farm boy from central Texas with a knack for machinery learned while operating a steam threshing machine, graduated into drilling oil wells, (mostly wildcats), in such places as Plainview, Ranger, Crossplains, and many of the early boomtowns. He had now accepted a job with the then Nevada Consolidated Copper Company as a driller and was to build what was known as a Standard Rig and drill a deep well to obtain a supply of water for the mine and town. The derrick was a four-legged wooden tower with a long wooden belt house leading back to a steam engine, identical to those used during the early oil explorations.

The site of the well is about one mile out of town on the old Georgetown road and it is still known as the 700 well. It turned out to be about twenty-two hundred feet deep and was somewhat of an accomplishment in that day and time....

What a Beautiful Sight

During the twenties and early thirties, nearly all the mining machinery operated in the "pit" was steam powered. What a sight that mine was at night! From our house perched high on Santa Rita Hill, and I mean that "perched" literally, for it truly was, we had an excellent view of both "pits." I can only liken it to a seat high in the grandstand and on the third base line at a baseball game. There was an almost constant stream of bright red sparks being shot high into the air from the smokestacks of the "dinkey" engines pulling ore trains from the mine, and from the steam shovels used to load the trains. Also the bright headlights on the "dinkeys" played along the sides of the "pit" as they laboriously hauled the ore trains in giant circles out of the "pit" and to the level of the rest of the world. The earth in the mine consisted of many colors, among them red, white, brown, green, and blue. Imagine the constantly changing view as the train highlighted each color in turn! Mixed in among all this were many pinpoints of light both singly and in groups scurrying all around as busy as ants on a hot summer day. These were lanterns used by labor gangs, laying track for the trains and steamshovels, ore samplers and others, attending to a multitude of tasks. In addition to all this, there were numerous fires, built, I believe, from used railroad ties around which the men gathered to eat their lunch, and to warm themselves at intervals. I strongly suspect that on a cold winter's night a good many new ties were burned.

Now you take all the displays of color described above and add to it a cacophony set up by the steam whistles of the "dinkeys" and steamshovels, the sound of ore falling into the ore cars as the steamshovels loaded them, giant gears grinding, steam engines puffing, and a multitude of other sounds from many sources, add it all together, and you have a copper mine showing off with sound and brilliant color, and pulsating with a rhythm almost as if it had a life of its own!

The Town of Santa Rita

The downtown portion of Santa Rita was situated on an "island" between the two pits which formed a huge ellipse, and was accessible only by a road passing through a portion of the pits where they joined on the east and west ends of the ellipse. On this "island" was situated the Company Store, the Post Office, Judge Green's confectionery, Kiner's Baker (Remember Ralph Kiner of baseball fame?), the Chino Club, the General Office, a community church, the Time Office, a mortuary, various mine repair shops, a corral, a dormitory for single men, a teacherage where single female teachers lived, the Chino Mess, homes for all the mine officials, and many homes for employees. At one time it was generally considered that only the elite lived "downtown" and all us common folk lived on the surrounding hills. This idea was probably more in the minds of us youngsters than the adults since children will favor those with whom they are most in contact, and there was probably some childish jealously [sic] involved.

The majority of the employees' homes were located on the hills generally north of the mine. From west to east there was the Ballpark, Booth Hill, Iron Hill, and Santa Rita Hill. Immediately east of Santa Rita Hill was a rather deep canyon which divided the town. Rising out of this canyon to the east was what I have always known as Blair Hill. It must have been due to the fact that Jim Blair, the chief of the Santa Rita law force, lived at the top of the steepest part of the hill near the Catholic Church....

Random Recollections of Santa Rita

Have you ever seen a copper railroad spike or copper CrackerJack prizes? They were pretty common when I lived in Santa Rita. We called the water that accumulated in the pit and other places "copper water" but in reality it was copper sulfate of varying strengths. We would often place the metal toys we got out of CrackerJacks in the copper water and when we retrieved them the next day they would have a nice, shiny copper coating. In some places, usually in the bottom of the pit where we weren't supposed to be, the concentration was great enough to coat a pocket knife blade with copper after only swishing it through the water, shaking it off and returning it to one's pocket.

One time, when we lived on the edge of the north pit there was a flood and the pit was deep in water. I believe that this flood resulted in the construction of the huge cement flume that extended from the east and all the way around the north pit at about the third level from the top, to the west end where the water was returned to Santa Rita Canyon. I remember that it was called the million dollar flume. I can still visualize the tops of smoke stacks and the tips of the booms on the steam shovels peeking out above the water. Some of the machinery was no doubt totally submerged and I have often wondered, based on my experience with CrackerJack toys, if it turned out to be the first all copper mining machinery in the world.

The pools of copper water in the bottom of the pits were a beautiful blue-green and occasionally migrating ducks would understandably mistake the water for a normal lake and would alight there. It was tragic indeed, to see many dead ducks floating on the surface poisoned by copper water!

It should be noted, however, that this water had its uses. The water was pumped out of the pits and to a location west of town in Santa Rita Canyon where it was allowed to run over scrap metal. The copper was precipitated out and I am told that ninety-nine percent pure copper was recovered. The method used in those days was rather crude compared to that used today. A much more sophisticated method is now in use that is highly efficient and cost effective....

Were You Born Here?

If your birth occurred at the old Santa Rita Hospital, you are eligible for membership in the "Society of Persons Born in Space." Officers of the Society are Jack Schmitt, Chief Astronaut; and Gilbert Moore, Program Director. Write to Moore,...Ogden, Utah,...for more information.

The "Society of Persons BORN IN SPACE" is alive and will thrive...with your help.

Membership in this society is restricted to people born in the old Santa Rita Hospital when it was located on a piece of ground which is no longer there. Those born in that hospital in the good old days came into the world at a spot which is now a few hundred feet in the air in the North Pit of Kennecott's Chino Mine. Therefore, the originators of the Society claim "that we were born in space."

The Society came into being in 1976 at a banquet in Salt Lake City honoring the Apollo 17 lunar mission. Jack Schmitt, Apollo 17 Lunar Module Pilot, and Gilbert Moore, General Manager of Thiokol's Astro-Met Plant, Wasatch Division, were reminiscing about the good old days in New Mexico and discovered that both were born a few years apart in the Santa Rita Hospital. One thing lead to another, and the Society was formed with Schmitt as Chief Astronaut and Moore as Program Director.

If you, or someone you know, was born in the Old Santa Rita Hospital, and is therefore, eligible for membership in the Society, write to R. Gilbert Moore,...Ogden, Utah....Mr. Moore will confirm your membership in the Society by sending you a proclamation acknowledging your birth in the "Santa Rita Spaceport."

7

Pueblo Space:
An Understated Sacredness

Rina Swentzell (1985)

Last summer as I stood on Tsikumu, one of Santa Clara Pueblo's sacred mountains, I was most impressed by the wind, the beauty of the clouds, and the flow of the hills below. There is a shrine on Tsikumu with a few well-placed stones which define an area scattered with cornmeal and a deeply-worn path in the bedrock. No special structure celebrates the sacredness of this place. Architecturally, it is understated, almost inconspicuous.

Tsikumu is typical of Pueblo shrines in that it is visually disappointing. It is, nevertheless, a special place because it is a place of access to the underworld from which the Pueblo People emerged. It is the doorway of communication between the many simultaneous levels of Pueblo existence. Tsikumu allows for a flow of energy between this plane of reality and other concurrent realities. Understanding the visual understatement of the Tsikumu shrine, and other Pueblo shrines, is important to understanding Pueblo sacred space.

Visually and physically understating shrines, or for that matter, Pueblo community and house forms, stems from the very nature of Pueblo cosmology. At the center of the Pueblo belief system is the conviction that people are not separate from nature and natural forces. This insoluble connection with nature has existed from the beginning of time. The goal of human existence is to maintain wholeness or oneness with the natural universe. Pueblo people emerged from the underworld — from the inside of the earth.

Puye Cliffs ruins at Santa Clara Pueblo, 1946. Photograph by Harold Kellogg.

The Tewa were living in Sipohene beneath Sandy Place Lake far to the north. The world under the lake was like this one, but it was dark. Supernaturals, men and animals lived together and death was unknown. (Ortiz 1969, 13)

After emerging from the darkness of the earth, the people founded their worlds (Pueblos) by first finding the centers.

The water spider spread his legs to the north and to the south, to the west and to the east, and then he said to the priests and the chiefs, "Now indeed I have measured it. Here is the center of the earth and here you must build your city!" But they said, "We have been hunting for the center of the earth for a long time, and wish to be sure." So they asked Rainbow to measure it also. So the Rainbow stretched his bright arch to the north and to the south, to the west and to the east, measuring the distance. Then he too gave his decision: "Here at this place is the heart of the earth." (Carr 1979, 17)

The "heart of the earth" or "*bu-ping-geh*" (heart of the Pueblo) for the Tewa people is the open community space within the village where ritual dances and other community activities happen. The "*bu-ping-geh*" contains the literal center of the earth or the "*nan-sipu*," which translates as the belly-root of the earth. Each Pueblo's cosmos encircles the *nan-sipu* and the surrounding mountains, where the sky and earth touch, are the boundaries of the well-organized spaces for people, animals, and spirits to live.

As at Tsikumu, all the boundary points, secondary level shrines and *nan-sipu* (center) of this well-organized cosmos are marked by a very inconspicuous stone or grouping of stones. This physical understating of sacred places is typical of Pueblo thinking because it is believed that it is better to understate than to overstate — to be one with everything rather than to be separate or conspicuous. There is, then, little need to create or cause distinctions — among people, or objects or, even, places. Since every thing, every body and every place is sacred and has essential worth, there is no need to individuate. The Christian myth of "fallen man," who is contaminated, has no counterpart in Pueblo mythology. Nowhere in Pueblo myths do humans experience a fall from "God's" grace. The people and their world are sacred and indivisible.

The shrines, boundary markers and centers, then, serve as constant reminders of the religious, symbolic nature of life. Because this realm of existence and other realms exist simultaneously, there is a continuous flow between levels of existence. Because the *nan-sipu* (center) is the symbolic point from which the people emerged, the shrines (as Tsikumu) are points where the possibility for contact with different levels of existence happen. Thus the cosmos becomes a continuous flowing whole, with visible connections between the seen and the unseen, the tangible and the intangible.

Being religiously ego-centric, Pueblo people do live at the center of the universe. Their world is sacramental. It is a world thoroughly impregnated with the energy, purpose and sense of the creative natural forces. It is all one. Sacredness, then, is recognizable in everyday life. The purpose of life for Pueblo people is to be intimately united with nature, intimately connected with everything in the natural world. Everything is included in that connectedness. Houses, for instance, are "fed" cornmeal after construction so that they may have a good life. The physical community (*O-wing-geh*), or place where people live, is periodically healed by the Bear or medicine society. Sacralization of the entire world is easy to achieve because humans are not separate from other life forms, not created to have dominion over other life forms, not on a higher rung of living, not closer to God. Directional forces of the world are cyclical and move in and out of the earth rather than upward towards the heavens. Clay (dirt) is talked to because it is of the earth and shares in the flow of life. That flow described as *Po-wa-ha* (water-wind-breath), is the essence of life. Existence is not determined by a physical body or other physical manifestation but by the breath, which is symbolized by the movement of the water and wind. It is the breath which flows without distinction through the entirety of animate and inanimate existences. The *Po-wa-ha*, then, is the creative force causing life, much as the Christian God is the originator and creator of Christian existence.

The *Po-wa-ha* is non-discriminatory; the profane and secular overlap with the sacred and solemn. On a recent trip to Chaco Canyon a non-Indian friend expressed anger at his girlfriend for unknowingly stepping on a part of the reconstructed walls of Pueblo Bonito. The act, to him, was sacrilegious. I was puzzled. I felt nothing sacrilegious had occurred, for as a child I climbed the Puye Cliff ruins in full view of my parents and great grandmother, who expressed no particular concern. I was not admonished, as a child, for enjoying sitting or standing on the *nan-sipu* in the *bu-ping-geh* of Santa Clara Pueblo. I now figure it was because I was not considered spiritually distinct from the stone or the walls of Puye cliff. I could not cause desacralization. No one can cause desacralization because the concept of original sin is lacking in Pueblo thought. We are not a fallen people, and, therefore, are still blessed with being one with our natural context. We flow in the *Po-wa-ha* along with all other manifestations of life.

Further, the belief that the *Po-wa-ha* flows through inanimate, as well as animate, beings allows buildings, ruins, places, to have life spans and to come and go as do other forms of life. Buildings and defined spaces are allowed to have birth and death. There is general acceptance that houses, human bodies, plant forms are temporary abodes through which the *Po-wa-ha* flows. They share in the essence of life which gives them cycles of life — birth and death. Traditional Santa Clara Pueblo with its soluble mud structures is an organic unit expanding, contracting and changing with other life forms and forces.

For the Pueblos, then, the entire world is a special, sacred place. Tsikumu, with its few gathered and well-placed stones, is a soft spoken reminder that all life is sacred.

8

The Carlsbad Cavern

Haniel Long (1941)

Tourist travel through the Carlsbad Caverns
fell a little short last month, but it was the third
successive April in which more than 11,000
persons saw the underground wonders.

– Las Cruces, New Mexico,
Sun-News, May 2, 1940

The Carlsbad Caverns are an event of inward and outward living in a different way from the Grand Canyon. Other visitors to the Canyon at the time you are there can hardly matter much to you. You do not brush elbows with them; most of them you do not even see, and those you do see you are not likely to see twice. They come by train, and stay a day or so, or they come by car, and are off again in an hour or so, or when they please. The Canyon is something you have to face by yourself. Only a tiny proportion of visitors descend the trail through the heaped-up temples and towers of colored earth. The rest of the tourists take the Canyon through their eyes and generally through colored glasses. The Canyon is a somewhat formal affair, too. The scenic views are along forest boulevards or stone walks that seem to have been there a long time, and all the buildings melt into the timelessness of the fir groves that envelop them. There is a great hush, and a great air of decorum, as though an important personage had just died. As a young man said, you see the Canyon in a top hat.

This loneliness and formality and sense of being cut off from the comforts of your kind help make the Canyon a

From the 1941 New Mexico State Tourist Bureau booklet, New Mexico "Land of Enchantment." *Note tourists' semiformal cave-going attire.*

deep experience. The Cavern can be as deep an experience, but you do not continue on your way thinking only of the fantasia of substance under the surface of the earth. You have in mind also the people you went underground with, for they give you as much cause for thought as the stalactites and stalagmites. Going through the Cavern is a folk festival. You must be at the Cavern at a set time, and become part of a group of hundreds of people; and with this party, under the eye of the rangers, take a walk of six subterranean miles. In the course of descending, ascending, hurrying, pausing, sauntering, sidling, you stop for a forty-five-minute luncheon at a cafeteria in an enormous and well-lighted chamber. If you aren't acquainted with a dozen or so people by now, it will happen here, or else what a pity.

The approach to the entrance of the Cavern is all that it should be. You reach the summits of the wide hills by a valley from the plains, full of bare boulders of limestone and bushes with metallic green leaves that whisper gently of hell. The small yucca gives way to the joshua tree, which is a success in the way of psychic disturbance, and then bands of ocotillas appear, insanely beckoning you this way and that with long green arms on which grow tiny leaves like the leaves of trees. The heat is so intense on a July morning that you know if you were stripped of your clothes on those slopes you would be singing your swan song in five minutes.

You can go to the Grand Canyon by train, but not to the Cavern. I remember that the Brothers in charge of a boys' school in Santa Fe once wrote back to the headquarters of their order in France for permission to hire a 'bus, to take the boys to

Carlsbad. Their superiors replied that it would be better for the boys to go on bicycles. The brothers had forgotten to tell the French priests that from Santa Fe the distance is 350 miles, with stretches of thirty and forty miles without house or water. I doubt whether anybody ever bicycles to Carlsbad or to the Grand Canyon, or walks to them, either. These spots are not on the knapsack routes. Even the nearest towns are too far away. It is a pity. Properly there should be a lack of ease about a pilgrimage; shrines should offer a certain difficulty, it is only right. But most of the meccas in the Southwest are so many miles away from anywhere that it seems funny; only the motorist can go, and if it is a dirt road, he may well go in fear and trembling.

This condition which seems suitable to a pilgrimage, that it should not be a bed of roses, is met at the Cavern from the time you get out of your car. To begin with you do a great deal of waiting. You wait while standing in line at the information and ticket windows, in the scorching sun of that hill-top. Then you wait with your kind on the curving stone terraces of the path, until the appointed hour. You have time to get acquainted with a few near-by souls. If you came up at sunset the evening before to witness the night flight of the bats, and to hear the ranger lecturing about them, you probably have already struck up acquaintances. The ranger poised himself on a rock at some distance from his audience, but the air was clear and I am sure I heard him say there were between three and five million bats, and that they ate each night between eight and eleven tons of insects, within a circle of 150 miles. These facts seem to me as fantastic as what I later saw in the Cavern.

Every day the year round people come, hundreds of them, in every kind of dress, of every age, in every sort of car, from every state, from foreign lands, and they all can produce $1.50 to get in.

We were discussing why we had come, a group of Americans who had just met.

"I always wanted to see the Cavern," said a young man from the Texas oil fields. He had been paid the Saturday before, and was on a two weeks' vacation. He was with two other boys from the oil country, and one of them owned the car, and had enough money on his person to get all three safely home. They were in their shirtsleeves.

There were four girls from Grand Rapids, schoolteachers, who had been on the road a month and were now returning home from the West coast. So far the trip had cost them thirty-five dollars apiece, because they did their own cooking.

"We wanted to see the West, and this is one of the high points of it," explained the talkative member. "I think this is going to be a thrill. We are going to the Mammoth Cave too, but that will be an anticlimax. It's been a wonderful trip. I hate to go home again."

"I wouldn't dare go home to Houston without seeing the Cavern," said a young man making up to the talkative girl. "What would they think? Everyone in Houston has been to the Cavern, and that's the first question they ask you."

A man who was with his wife and two young children said, "I'd give a penny to know why I am here."

A thirteen-year-old schoolgirl with black pigtails said, "People like to see things and see them together." Her eyes reminded me of dark shining birds.

The young man with her, in his bare arms but carrying a prudent wool jacket, said, "Isn't it the old wish to make a pilgrimage? We can't kill off those old wishes. We are full of them. They stick. But now it's the twentieth century and we're Americans, so when we go on a pilgrimage we go in our cars."

He was a hotel clerk on his vacation.

"You've got to go somewhere," said the oil-field boy.

"Won't you be cold?" I asked him.

"I'm so hot I'd just as soon be cold. I didn't even bother to take my coat out of the car."

When we first entered the Cavern the air at 56 degrees seemed quite chilly, but I suppose you adjust to it soon, if you are a young furnace. For a while people looked attentively at nature's marvels. But it is impossible to be overcome by anything very long, and talking recommenced, low talking. There were a dozen rangers along, ready to answer questions. One ranger gave a talk about what happens when water seeps through limestone, and everybody was interested and listened. The ranger also asked us to obey orders and not touch anything or stray from the path. The crowd seemed well enough behaved, and I doubt whether anyone would have strayed from the path under any circumstances.

He said too that Governor Miles had just brought a cavalcade of 'buses full of school-children to the Cavern, and the government let them through free. He told the schoolteachers to come back with their children and it wouldn't cost them a thing. That offer was a move in the right direction, but if you lived a long way from the Cavern it would cost a lot of money to bring even one 'busload of children. That is the real problem. All school-children in the country ought to see Carlsbad. It belongs to them, and is part of their education.

Detective William Martin went into the Cavern once for a fugitive from justice. The man, who was a murderer, went down with the crowd and stayed down. His idea was to hide overnight and come up to the surface with the tourists the next day. Martin and two officers followed him with gasoline lamps. They called him, and kept calling, and whether it was the disturbing echoes or his terror from being alone in the utter dark, he soon came running to give himself up. He cried, "Put me in jail — then I'll know where I am!"

It would be cold and clammy, but perhaps you could stick it out down there overnight with a good light and a good novel. This poor fellow had neither, and maybe a bad conscience.

The place is so well illuminated for the tourists' visit that the usual fear people have of being underground is absent. The vistas are extraordinary. I liked particularly watching the hundreds of human beings coming down the circling paths. The Cavern is well ventilated in an unknown way, but the smoke from cigarettes and pipes takes a while to clear out, and hangs in a gray pall at a distance. You see the people through it. It's like a dream out of Dante or Doré.

As we came up out of the earth, a woman of middle age told me she had visited the Cavern once before, with a man of eighty and his wife, who was very nearly that age.

"He had been in this neighborhood as a boy," she said, "and had gone about a lot on horseback. He often rode by the entrance of the Cavern and wished he could go in. He went back East and grew up, and time passed, and at last came the news that the government had made it possible for people to enter the Cavern and walk six of the thirty-five underground miles. This man kept talking to his wife about it, and at last they decided to go when they had a chance. Several years later the chance came. We spent the night at Carlsbad, and the old lady was so tired from the motor trip that she fainted on the hotel stairway. We didn't see how she could stand the Cavern if she couldn't stand the trip. But she had her mind made up. We got a doctor, and then we got in touch with a park official. He was an understanding man, and he saw it was important that those two old people should be given their heart's desire. So, when we got to the cave entrance, we found that he had assigned special guides to take care of them. These guides practically carried the old lady through the part of the Cavern we saw. We didn't make the complete descent, but we went down far enough. I never saw such reverence and such delight, both at once, as those two old people had on their faces."

I was thinking about that story when I first caught sight of the daylight again. As I approached it, it seemed a sickly green, but when I came close to it and stepped into it, it changed to a most beautiful light, unbelievably rich and pure. I was glad the old couple, too, could have had that experience. It seemed to me the most vivid of the whole journey. As we have nothing to compare the sun with, we have no way of knowing the wonder of it.

Die newen Inseln, so hinder Hispaniam gegen Orient: Bey dem Landt Indie gelegen (1570). No scale. Courtesy Fray Angélico Chávez History Library (NMHM/DCA).

PART TWO

BEYOND HISTORY'S RECORDS

"Beyond history's records," the Southwestern land, its water-courses, and archaeological evidence tell of "four distinctive prehistoric civilizations," among them the ancestors of "the Pueblo peoples [who] are the only one of the cultural groups identifiable as long ago as two millennia that have survived with clearly unbroken cultural continuity into the last quarter of the twentieth century." These horticulturalists were joined by "the late-coming Southern Athapaskans, who arrived in the Southwest as hunters and gatherers not more than a century before the first Europeans" and then branched into the Navajo and Apache peoples (Ortiz). Pueblo (Kennedy and Simplicio), Navajo (Iverson), and Apache (Tiller) oral traditions recount a time of emergence into this world, movement within it, and the deeds of culture heroes and heroines who made it habitable. European and later Euroamerican contact "stopped" this world and forced it into the chronology of history's written records and the purview of a different heroism.

Aerial view of Chaco Canyon, 1929. Photograph by Charles A. Lindbergh.

9

Indian People of
Southwestern North America

Alfonso Ortiz (1979)

"We have lived upon this land from days beyond history's records, far past any living memory, deep into the time of legend. The story of my people and the story of this place are one single story. No man can think of us without thinking of this place. We are always joined together" (Henry et al. 1970, 35). This is the statement of a Taos Pueblo man.

So it is with much of Southwestern North America. Here Indian people remain in their traditional homelands, and much that is vital in life remains as it was, timeless. Here is the oldest continuous record of human habitation on the continent outside of Mesoamerica, a habitation that has fashioned this region into a humanized landscape suffused with ancient meanings, myths, and mysteries. Here, as well, is a land of diversity, both of landscape and of ways of life upon that landscape....

When the Southwest was first seen with European eyes, those of Francisco Vásquez de Coronado and the men of his expedition of 1540, both the land and the people of the Southwest were already very diverse and very old. One has only to think of the great multi-hued gaps in the earth, such as Bryce and the Grand Canyon, Zion and Canyon de Chelly, or of the gigantic and majestic spires of red sandstone comprising nature's own sculpture in Monument Valley, to slip into a geological time perspective. One's spatial sense as well as one's temporal sense grows immense in the Southwest before the vast distances and topographical diversity that open out before one's eyes when looking down from any high vantage point. Here, truly, the imagination soars and the very spirit is set free. The spirit is further moved, and the temporal sense further broadened, by contemplation of the various native groups upon this land, many of whom were encountered in 1540 near where they are, and living very much as they do in the last quarter of the twentieth century.

These various peoples have their own rhythms to complement the diverse rhythms of the variegated Southwestern landscape. Within this region one can move, for example, from the Seri fishermen on Mexico's far northwest coast to Yuman, Piman, and Pueblo farmers who live along each of the great watercourses, from a few hundred feet above sea level to more than 7,000 feet above. Over all of this and beyond, up close to timberline, roamed the hunters, gatherers, and raiders, most of whom mixed the three pursuits with bravado. There are the Yavapai and Walapai, known as the Upland Yumans to distinguish them from the agricultural Riverine Yumans, and the Athapaskan-speaking Apache and Navajo. These groups have been able to retain a somewhat nomadic existence even in contemporary life, through sheep and cattle raising and social events such as dances and rodeos.

Interspersed among these contemporary groups, the evidence of the most ancient inhabitants is everywhere. Some artifacts, like petroglyphs and chipped stone, may date back untold millennia; others, like potsherds and pit houses, may go back only to the time of Christ. Although the knowledge of human events in this area beyond a few millennia removed is as yet far from complete, it is known that cultigens and the knowledge of pottery making had come up from Mexico centuries before the dawn of Christianity. These and other Mesoamerican imports were embraced by the hunting and gathering peoples of the Southwest in diverse ways, which coalesced into four distinctive prehistoric civlizations. These four — Anasazi, Mogollon, Hohokam, and Hakataya — were in the process of formation by the beginning of the European Christian era. It is, indeed, the presence of Mesoamerican influence, in belief systems as well as more tangible realms, that most clearly gives the Southwest an underlying continuity beneath its diversities and distinguishes the Southwest from the areas surrounding it.

This is not to imply that the Southwest can be understood as a frontier or periphery of Mesoamerica. While it is important to trace continuities between Mesoamerica and the Southwest, it is essential to stress that the various peoples of the Southwest fashioned unique cultural syntheses from elements of diverse provenance. This synthesizing activity continues today, in contemporary efforts to combine the eternal verities of native life with the benefits and unavoidable impositions of the encompassing American and Hispanic societies.

The boundaries and characteristics of the Southwest and its status as a culture area have long been debated (Kirchhoff 1954; Woodbury 1979). It is important to recognize that, because of the very diversity of the Southwest, various subareas within it, as well as the inhabitants of these subareas, may have more in common with the land and people of regions adjoining them than they do with other tribes within the Southwest.

Boundaries should be treated with caution, as they tend to limit and rigidify thought, as is shown by the earlier acceptance of the United States-Mexico boundary as the southern border of the Southwest, despite broad continuities in geography and culture that extend across the border and well into Mexico. The west, which is defined principally by the Colorado River, forms the closest geological and cultural break that there is in the Southwest, but it is only a relative one because there is such a vast expanse of desert west of the river itself. To the northwest, well away from the western slope of the Rockies, the land is very much like the Great Basin, and the people who adjoin it, such as the Hopi, have linguistic and other cultural affinities with tribes of the Great Basin. To the northeast and east, where the Southwest gradually merges with the Plains, the peoples who adjoin also have much in common. Hence the people of the northern Rio Grande Pueblos and the Jicarilla Apache manifest many Plains-derived customs, from arts and adornment to songs and ceremonies. There is, and has always been, free and frequent movement among the peoples of these adjoining areas, whether it be for trading, courting, religious and healing ceremonies, or some other purpose.

An appropriate gateway to the Southwest, and to a closer look at the various peoples and landscapes of the area, is from the northeast through Raton Pass. This pass lies high on the east side of the great continental divide, which runs like a backbone down the middle of the Southwest. Here one may break free of the Colorado Rockies and look down upon the vast expanse of small mountain ranges, mesas, and valleys that make up the northern region of the Southwest. The immense and diverse landscape that opens out before the eye here is truly one of the most breathtaking views in North America. Upon descending Raton Pass one enters the northern region of the Southwest, a landscape of multi-hued bluffs, spires, and canyons. At dawn and dusk, especially, these present a dazzling array of colors and shadows. This northern country is one face of the Southwest, which the Pueblo peoples and, later, the Navajo and Apache have made their own.

Another face of the Southwest is that of the watercourses of the arboreal desert on the west side of the continental divide, principally the Gila and the Salt rivers, where the prehistoric Hohokam culture flourished. The Hohokam adapted very well to the challenges of life on this searing landscape that, apart from the few watercourses that thread their way through, can be most inhospitable. The land is so hot in the summer that the air just above it quivers before the naked eye, as if there were ghostly presences about in broad daylight. At the hottest time of day the vibrations of the earth can cause objects in the distance, or even the horizon itself, to waver so much that one cannot trust one's own eyes. Sometimes the pressures of air, heat, and sand unite in an explosive combination that may send as many as six whirlwinds at a time dancing off across the landscape.

The Hohokam peoples contemplated these whirlwinds and recorded their impressions on petroglyphs and pottery. Before their civilization began to fade early in this millennium they constructed an extensive and efficient system of irrigation canals along both the Gila and Salt rivers. This waterworks system remains their most impressive monument and legacy. The agricultural Pimas and river Yumans, who succeeded the Hohokam on their land and are probably direct descendants of them, also contemplate the whirlwind in song and myth, and they record their own impressions on basketry as well as on pottery. They further respond and give meaning to this otherwise forbidding landscape in dreams and dream journeys, their distinctive form of spiritual expression.

A third face of the Southwest is provided by the rugged Gila Mountains of southwestern New Mexico, where arose the Mimbres culture, a branch of the more far-flung Mogollon prehistoric culture. From here, high up on the Gila River's watershed, one can look over what is the most concentrated topographical diversity in the Southwest. Early in the morning at first light, and at night, one may be treated to sights on these mountain slopes that stir the imagination. In the morning the evergreens appear as if they have wrapped themselves in splendid white garments, for the silver-hued frost shimmers like satin before the gathering light of day. And, during clear nights, one can watch ethereal white fingers of mist creep down the mountain slopes or between canyon walls silently, ever so silently.

If one follows out the many narrow, sparkling, serpentine streams that gather themselves together as the Gila River on the eastern flank of the continental divide, one can, in a relatively short time, traverse through several life-zones, from the snow pack of the Canadian life-zone to the desert of the Lower Sonoran. The floral and faunal life also change, of course, and abruptly. The ancient Mimbres people were quite aware of these topographical, floral, and faunal differences, for they moved regularly through all of them, and their imaginations dwelled upon them. And in this imaginative dwelling lies one key to understanding their greatest cultural legacy, their pottery. They had not much that was impressive in the way of habitation or other cultural artifacts, but they more than made up for it with their pottery, which in design was the finest produced by Indians north of Mexico. The many delicate, graceful, conventionalized designs of beetles, rabbits, turtles, bears, and other animals and insects attest to much imaginative musing on the varied fauna of their ever-changing land. They were equally skilled in executing abstract designs, but, centuries and centuries removed, no one can really be sure what brought these forms into being.

By the beginning of the second millennium A.D., even before the passing of the Hohokam, the Mimbres people were absorbed by the expanding and closely related Pueblo peoples to the north. Some may have also migrated to the south, into modern-day Mexico. The Mimbres people, of unquestionable artistic genius, would remain much more of an enigma to scholars if their continuing influence were not so readily apparent in the pottery made by Pueblo people in every generation since their own passing.

The Pueblo peoples are the only one of the cultural groups identifiable as long ago as two millennia that have survived with clearly unbroken cultural continuity into the last quarter of the twentieth century. In their greatest time, from the tenth through the thirteenth centuries, they built and occupied the great architectural wonders at Chaco Canyon, Mesa Verde, Casa Grande, and numerous other places spread out over what are now five large states. During this time they ranged from mountain to canyon and even to the higher desert elevations. During the persistent drought that haunted the Southwest in the last quarter of the thirteenth century, the Pueblo people began contracting into the great valley of the Rio Grande and its tributaries. Only the Hopi, then as now, enigmatically hung on and persisted in farming successfully in a region with no permanent or semipermanent watercourses.

The other Pueblo groups maintained their way of life — characterized in essence by intensive horticulture, an elaborate ceremonial cycle, and a cohesive social organization — in the villages of adobe and stone that, for the most part, are strung along the Rio Grande and its tributaries like beads upon a crooked string. These villages all blend in with their surroundings so that one never knows one is approaching a Pueblo until one is right upon it. The architecture of the Pueblos is gentle and unobtrusive, as, indeed, are the Pueblo peoples' very character, customs, institutions, and art forms. The Pueblo peoples have shown a genius for maintaining that which is most essential to their lives while also receiving, absorbing, and reinvigorating the decaying "vines" — to use the appropriate and evocative Tewa metaphor — of other ways of life. Hence, the Pueblo legacy has been to endure.

In addition to these four identifiable prehistoric cultural traditions of the northern Southwest, there were others in northern Mexico, but these, with the exception of the Casas Grandes region, are not at all well known. These prehistoric hunter-gatherers and small-scale farmers remain opaque to scholars for the most part because they have been little studied. A major additional group in the Southwest are the late-coming Southern Athapaskans, who arrived in the Southwest as hunters and gatherers not more than a century before the first Europeans.

These Athapaskans came into the Southwest from the north, "threading the labyrinthine canyons with their eyes on the stars" (Waters 1950). Once in the Southwest they divided, with most of the Navajos staying in the northwest country of sandy washes and red bluffs and box canyons. In this dry country, after even a mild rainfall, such fragrances emanate from the land that the earth itself seems to smell grateful for the moisture. The small mountain ranges are widely scattered, and red or pale green limestone bluffs may run for miles. These cliffs gleam at eveningtide, as the shadows skirt their folds. Appropriately enough, one of these long high bluffs is named by the Navajo, Woman's Skirt Mountain.

Yet, the land of the Navajo does not differ from that of the Pueblos along any absolute dimension; the two peoples differ, rather, in how they live upon the land. Unlike the Pueblos, the Navajo remain thinly spread out within the box canyons, or at the base of the cliffs, of their far-flung land. While they have proved themselves to be extremely adaptable, with many becoming quite successful cultivators, sheep herding and raiding were more amenable to them, and they moved about a great deal. In addition to agriculture, the Navajo absorbed many other Pueblo ideas and institutions, along with quite a few Pueblo people themselves, mainly refugees from the Spaniards. What the Navajo have learned from the Pueblos and, later, from the Spaniards and Americans, has been blended with their still seminomadic life-style to form a unique, flexible, and vital synthesis.

What is most distinctive and striking about the Navajo people and their culture is their aesthetic tradition. The woven rugs and silver jewelry, impressive as they are by themselves, ultimately have their roots in the traditional dry paintings of Navajo religion. And the dry paintings, in their turn, are but concrete pictorial representations of the great sings or chants that comprise the living vitality of Navajo religion. Hence, the entire Navajo aesthetic tradition is inspired by what are at once prayers, myths, poetry, and sacred scripture rendered into song.

Their Athapaskan siblings, those who were to be called Apaches, moved onto the higher mountain vastnesses after centuries of raiding with impunity all over the Southwest. There they, in their turn, have stayed, as guardians of the watersheds of some of the major feeder streams of the great rivers.

The diversity of the Southwest was both increased and threatened by the arrival of the Spaniards in 1540 and, further, by the American onslaught beginning in the early nineteenth century. The Coronado expedition into the Southwest was inspired by Fray Marcos de Niza's exaggerated 1539 report of the riches of the region. De Niza had spotted the Zuni Pueblos from afar, presumably at dawn or in the late afternoon sun, when the Pueblos may glow with a golden hue, and assumed he was near the famed cities of gold.

Coronado explored the Pueblo country for two years without finding the hoped-for riches, and his report dispelled Spanish enthusiasm for the region for a half-century. It was not until 1598 that Juan de Oñate set up a colony in Pueblo country, after several exploring expeditions headed by others. The Spanish government demanded labor and tribute from the Pueblos and vigorously attempted to suppress native religion. These practices eventually led the Pueblos to unite in revolt in 1680, and they managed to expel the Spaniards until 1692. In that year Diego de Vargas re-entered Pueblo country, though it was not until 1696 that he gained control over the entire Rio Grande Pueblo area. The Spaniards had learned from the Pueblo Revolt and were gentler in their demands in the next century and a half. However, the Pueblos had learned as well and maintained their ceremonial life out of the view of the Spaniards, while adopting the veneer of Roman Catholicism.

10

First Contact at Hawikku (Zuni): The Day the World Stopped

Tom R. Kennedy and Dan Simplicio

The fallout from that cultural cataclysm known as first contact ripples across time. For many descendants of the first Native peoples to encounter Europeans, the challenge continues to be to balance a world set off its mark with the realities of today's world. Ground zero for the beginning of this social cataclysm was at the A:shiwi (Zuni) ancestral village of Hawikku on July 7, 1540 — the day the world stopped.

According to the creation epic of the A:shiwi people, recent time began when they emerged onto this, the Fourth World, at a place in the Grand Canyon. After an arduous migration across much of what is now the Southwest, the A:shiwi people were led by the A:hayuda, the Twin War Gods, to their destined home, Halona:wa Idiwana, the Middle Place — present-day Zuni Pueblo. Eventually, six A:shiwi villages became established and known as centers of trade, connecting purveyors of goods from northern areas with providers of shells, copper beads, and parrot feathers from regions to the south. Stories about these active trade communities also journeyed with the goods.

Lure of the fabled "Seven Cities of Cíbola" brought Spanish conquering explorers northward. Fact becomes convoluted, however, by bestowing on an African and a Frenchman the actual honors of being the first "Spanish" outsiders to reach the Southwest, one year before Coronado. Although this unlikely pair often appears more like a footnote to history, their story is worth remembering for its wonderfully human perspective and color.

Haloná Pueblo at Zuni, west-central New Mexico, from the south, about 1880. Photograph by Ben Wittick.

According to Spanish accounts, a fabulous place of wealth existed somewhere to the north of New Spain, more or less at the boundary of present-day Mexico. Stories told by Native traders from these regions and repeated by the conquistador Nuño de Guzmán described a place of great wealth where a large population lived in many cities and people dressed in cotton, worked with copper, possessed precious stones, and grew corn. At various times during the 1530s, small, ill-equipped Spanish expeditions attempted without success to discover what became known as the "seven cities of wealth" — a place imagined to be the next fabulous Eldorado of gold and riches.

In 1539, after the marooned explorer Álvar Núñez Cabeza de Vaca found his way to Mexico City bringing further accounts of mysterious wealthy places to the north, yet another attempt was made to discover this fabled land. Viceroy Antonio de Mendoza dispatched an exploratory party led by a priest, Fray Marcos de Niza (of Nice, France), and guided by the African Estevan, a slave who had recently arrived in New Spain with Cabeza de Vaca. A small contingent of Indian porters and curious followers completed the assemblage. The sketchy details of this expedition challenge the imagination and, like a good tale, raise more questions than answers.

Estevan's own back-story seems equally incredible. Originally from the small mountain village of Azamor in what is now Morocco, North Africa, he found himself a personal slave to Andrés Dorantes de Carranza, a Spanish captain on the ill-fated Narváez expedition sailing for the New World. The expedition eventually foundered on the Gulf Coast, leaving four surviving crew members, including Estevan and Cabeza de Vaca, to set off on foot in an attempt to return to New Spain, somewhere to the west.

The trek, which Cabeza de Vaca later detailed in his writings, took ten arduous years as the men slowly traveled through mostly hostile Indian territories. In addition to gaining new knowledge about the people and customs they encountered, they began to hear stories about the "lands of wealth." Estevan in particular adopted the colorful attire of a shaman, adorned with feathers and bells, and carried a gourd rattle in an effort to impress the Indians he met. Once back in New Spain, Estevan was sold to Viceroy Mendoza, who eventually commissioned the explorations north.

Estevan proved to be an able guide, translating information learned from the Indian communities met along the way. He reported to Fray Marcos that Indians along the route called the place they sought "Cíbola," a name in the A:shiwi language loosely translated as "buffalo." Ironically, this name is similar to *tsibolo:wa,* which is what the Zunis called the Spaniards, in reference to their abundant facial hair. Indian traders described Cíbola as having a vigorous trade in buffalo hides and products as well as in turquoise and other materials.

As the land of Cíbola drew close, Fray Marcos dispatched Estevan, with a smaller contingent of Indians, to explore ahead more rapidly. Each day's findings were to be reported back to Marcos by a messenger carrying a white wooden cross fashioned in a size to indicate the importance of that day's discoveries.

Estevan arrived at Hawikku some time in advance of Fray Marcos, thus taking the honor as both an outsider and as an African of experiencing first contact with a Native people in the Southwest. Unfortunately, bravura met with skepticism undermined this momentous occasion. Estevan's pretentious attire, gourd rattle, and bold demeanor failed to impress the Hawikku leaders, who demanded that he remain outside the walled village. His claim that he came from a land of white men, although he himself was dark, as well as his demands for women and valuables apparently created great suspicion. Estevan was reported to have been killed as he boldly attempted to enter the village.

The killing of Estevan marked the first volley in this clash of cultures and secured his significance in the larger story. He is forever immortalized in Zuni ceremonialism through references and portrayals. As the first African to set foot in a place that would later be known as North America, he holds a critical place in African American history. Unfortunately, Estevan's behavior also represented a collision between the patriarchal order of the Old World and a matrilineal order in the New World. This social calamity resulted from Estevan's demand for Zuni women, which violated the strict norms of a matrilineal society and resulted in his death. These monumental collisions ultimately had even greater effect on the A:shiwi.

Upon learning about Estevan's encounters with the A:shiwi from the few badly beaten survivors who returned, Marcos hastened his return to New Spain, very possibly without ever having seen Hawikku. Nonetheless, he enhanced his report with an embellished description of Cíbola as being bigger than Mexico City.

A year later, on July 7, 1540, Francisco Vázquez de Coronado arrived on the plain of Hawikku with a well-armed expedition of Spanish horsemen and foot soldiers and a large entourage of Indian porters and followers. Zuni oral history describes how a small group of Zuni men on the annual pilgrimage encountered the Spanish expedition. The group's leader silently laid a line of corn meal on the sand in front of them, indicating their solemn task and cautioning the newcomers not to cross. In the first blatant disregard of A:shiwi cultural sovereignty, the Spaniards crossed the line and attacked Hawikku.

Spanish accounts describe a fierce battle involving several hundred Cíbola warriors who eventually fell back to the walled village. The intensive battle and siege led to the deaths of at least twenty Hawikku warriors as well as a near fatal attack on Coronado himself, who was knocked from his horse. Coronado later noted that his bright armor and plumed helmet undoubtedly presented him as an obvious target. The next morning the Spaniards reported finding that the inhabitants of Hawikku had withdrawn, leaving the village undefended. Coronado entered Hawikku and claimed the region and its inhabitants for the Spanish Crown. Day one of the "new world order" had begun.

The half-starved Spanish force was pleased to find Hawikku's ample stocks of stored corn and beans and flocks of turkeys. Though he described the village in disparaging terms, Coronado was impressed enough that he gave it the name New Granada, because he said it resembled that important Spanish city. Hawikku's inhabitants soon returned on the promise of no further retribution and agreed to cooperate henceforth. They informed the Spaniards that prophecies had foretold their coming fifty years before.

The Spaniards reported that there were six to seven settled villages in "Cevola," but no gold. After stern rebukes from the Spanish commanders, Fray Marcos was sent back to Mexico City in disgrace, though a detailed reading of his explorations show them to be fairly accurate. Coronado left behind at Hawikku three mestizos — Indians of mixed blood — who probably shared knowledge and insights about the Spaniards. The next ninety years, however, saw very few visits from Spaniards.

By 1629, Spanish Franciscan missionaries had begun directing the building of missions at Hawikku and at nearby Halona:wa, present-day Zuni. This period of more or less permanent Spanish presence among the A:shiwi people introduced many new ways. In addition to the new religion and Spanish language, the Franciscans introduced new construction technologies such as hooded fireplaces, along with the massive architecture of mission buildings. They also introduced new foods such as wheat and leavened breads, peaches, domestic animals such as sheep, pigs, cattle, and horses, new cooking methods using beehive-shaped ovens, and new forms of bureaucratic government. Although the A:shiwi undoubtedly recognized the value of many of these new ways, such innovations challenged former ways of living, speaking, and thinking.

Advantageous as they may have been, domesticated animals presented a dichotomy that affected both time and space and altered the physical landscape. The large grazing animals soon competed with the natural wildlife for sustenance. Grasslands were quickly decimated even as domesticated animals both provided benefits and created dependence within a new concept of economy. The horse proved the greatest influence in altering space and time. Before the Spaniards arrived, the Zunis and other Natives of the continent understood only one mode of traversing the landscape: on foot. Equally significant for social and economic change was the use of animals for transport, along with wheeled vehicles. Today the only exceptions are for ceremonial practices or pilgrimages, which are conducted on foot or occasionally on horseback.

After almost five centuries of contact with the outside world, the A:shiwi people can still proudly assert their presence, identity, and continuity of culture. Yet the trauma of those first centuries of Spanish domination can be noted in the absence of many oral history accounts, as well as the explanation that "Zunis don't choose to remember the difficult times." But as the list of cultural fallout attests, the legacy and challenges of first contact remain deep and continuing. Yesterday's cultural collisions have spawned the agendas for today's tribal leaders and their communities.

Two recent examples clearly illustrate the aftermath of the cultural cataclysms of first contact at Zuni: the restoration of Our Lady of Guadalupe (the Old Zuni) Mission and the development of the exhibit *Hawikku: Echoes from Our Past* at the A:shiwi A:wan Museum and Heritage Center, Zuni's community museum.

In the heart of Halona Idiwana, Zuni's historic Middle Village, stands the Old Zuni Mission, the ubiquitous symbol of outside influence and domination. For almost four centuries, generations of Zunis have fulfilled life-long cultural obligations in the shadow of this mighty adobe structure. Once a flagship of Franciscan faith, the Old Mission today struggles from benign neglect and community controversy.

Spanish Franciscan missionaries strategically placed their missions as implements of social control, to limit if not eliminate indigenous religious practices. With the placement of Our Lady of Guadalupe Mission over the pueblo's existing burial grounds, Zuni's ceremonial and sacred space became compromised. Desecration of such sacred spaces was what led to the destruction of Catholic missions throughout the Southwest and to legacies of lingering controversies in Pueblo communities.

From its founding in 1629 to its final heyday in the 1820s, Our Lady of Guadalupe Mission was nurtured by a cadre of dedicated Spanish missionaries. It received special attention from Spanish religious authorities, if not always from the local A:shiwi community. The noted Spanish cartographer and artist Bernardo Miera y Pacheco created the church's elaborate baroque altar around 1776. It was clearly described in Spanish accounts and photographed as early as 1873. But for almost 150 years, from the end of the Spanish era in 1821 until its restoration in the late 1960s, the Old Mission experienced continuous decline. A collaboration between the National Park Service, the Gallup Catholic Diocese, and the Zuni Tribe sought to restore the Old Mission to some semblance of its former glory, both for use by the local parish and to serve as a historic landmark to support tourism.

Soon after the restoration of the Old Mission, artist Alex Seowtewa, at the invitation of the parish priest, began what has become his monumental life's work, painting murals on the church walls. These life-size renderings of Zuni Ko'ko, or Kachina dancers, on the north and south walls represent the annual cycle of Zuni ceremonial observances in full color and detail. Although the artist easily explains this juxtaposition of cultures and beliefs, traditionalists in the Zuni community and even many of the Catholic faith view the images with alarm.

As the images grew in size and dominance on the Old Mission walls, so did their notoriety. Now nearing forty years of presence, the murals have taken on a life of their own, first as a compelling venue for visitors and second as a source of concern for the community. With growing visitation of the Old Mission by people from around the world, and with the dominating presence of scaffolding, equipment, and paints, the Zuni Catholic parish found continued use of the building increasingly difficult to justify and in 2004 returned the building to the tribe. As an art historian involved in researching the Old Mission's history remarked, "The Ko'ko won!" Yet the story reveals even more complexity.

Equally problematic has been the continued deterioration of the Old Mission adobe structure because of moisture retention in the walls — an inherent defect caused by the misguided restoration technique of cement-plastering adobe walls. Now both structural walls and the interior plaster on which the murals lie are seriously threatened. And here collide past and present cultural realities.

For Zuni traditionalists skeptical about the presence of the Old Mission murals, the deteriorating condition of the structure represents nothing more than nature taking its course. The Ko'ko are calling their images home. Therefore nothing should be done to conserve the paintings or interfere with the natural process. More moderate voices in the Zuni community side with conventional historic preservation notions of conserving significant structures for their educational value as well as the economic potential from tourism. The dilemma thrusts itself before tribal leadership for a solution — continued fallout from that first cultural cataclysm.

A second example deeply intertwined in the circumstance of first contact is the story of Hawikku itself and involves the emergence of anthropology and the museum profession. The telling of the Hawikku story through a major exhibition was an obvious priority of the A:shiwi A:wan Museum and Heritage Center. Of critical importance was the existence of twenty thousand artifacts excavated from Hawikku and now in the collection of the newly established National Museum of the American Indian. The artifacts had been removed from Zuni early in the twentieth century, researched and well documented but never featured in a major exhibition. It was right that Zuni should take the lead in telling this story.

From the earliest accounts about the Seven Cities of Cíbola, the Zuni region and people have captured the imagination of the outside world. Not coincidentally, the disciplines of cultural research and anthropology have included Zuni in their own myths of origin. From the young Frank H. Cushing in the 1880s, whose "participant observation" became a cornerstone of anthropological methodology, through an honor roll of founding anthropologists in the first half of the twentieth century, research at Zuni became a rite of passage of sorts. A wealth of writings, documentation, and reports attempted to capture the essence of Zuni culture. This almost relentless attention caused one recent tribal official to exclaim, "We don't need this — we have been studied to death — *we* know who we are!"

Central to this focus on Zuni was the excavation of Hawikku by archaeologist Frederick W. Hodge from 1917 to 1923. Interestingly, Hodge had served as Cushing's field assistant at Zuni some thirty years before. Because Hawikku was a well-preserved site with great historic significance, Hodge's goal was to uncover what life was like at the time of first contact. His multiyear excavations at Hawikku remain one of the largest archaeological endeavors in the Southwest, involving at least thirty-eight Zuni workmen and a virtual who's who of early archaeologists. The excavation site did not disappoint, producing a steady stream of artifact crates that flowed from Zuni to Gallup by wagon and on to New York City by train.

Eventually a total of twenty thousand artifacts arrived for caretaking at the Heye Foundation's Museum of the American Indian. For the next eighty years these Zuni treasures lived an isolated and cramped life on shelves in the heart of the Bronx. With the creation of the National Museum of the American Indian as part of the Smithsonian Institution in the late 1980s, some of Zuni's patrimony was one step closer to home.

For the Zuni community of the time, the excavation at Hawikku was highly divisive. It split the community between Progressives, who supported the endeavor, and Traditionalists, who opposed it. Fortunately for the archaeologists, the Progressives in tribal leadership positions at the time enabled the excavation to proceed. Until the loan to the A:shiwi Museum in 2001 of two hundred or so Hawikku artifacts for exhibition, very few in the Zuni community even knew that this treasure of their cultural patrimony existed.

The opening of *Hawikku: Echoes from Our Past* in 2002 represented a significant completion of a cycle of history by the Zuni community. Not only were some of Zuni's "children" finally home, as one community member expressed it, but the story itself was of and by the A:shiwi people. Zuni was at last telling its story from its perspective. Even the adobe building housing the exhibit — Zuni's first trading post, located adjacent to the original Cushing house — had a direct connection to the early work of Cushing and Hodge.

The exhibit presents, from the perspective of Hawikku and its artifacts, the story of the A:shiwi people from the earliest migration epic through historic eras to present realities. Positive contributions as well as negative effects of Spanish and American influence are portrayed. The literal and figurative turning point in the exhibit is the presentation of Hodge's excavations at Hawikku. Although the Zuni community's debate over the excavation failed to halt the endeavor, it nonetheless served as an important step toward critically scrutinizing all subsequent excavations of ancestral sites. The exhibit closes with an examination of future opportunities for Zuni community members to take increasing control over their affairs.

But it is the list of issues on the Hawikku exhibit title wall that serves to ground the visitor's experience in the realities of the present. These statements, in both Zuni and English, remind local and outside visitors that these echoes from the past are the latest links in a chain of events that began with first contact and continue to be the major concerns of the Zuni community and its leaders today. In this way, *Hawikku: Echoes from Our Past* can serve as a powerful tool for community empowerment, progress, and resolution.

Sovereignty, *hon yamande yanillaba.* How much do we control our own affairs?

Land, *dehwa:we.* What is "our land"?

Water, *k'ya:we.* Who controls our river?

Language, *bena:we.* What will ensure that the Zuni language continues to be spoken?

Religion, *dewsu' haydoshna:we.* How can we be both "traditional" and modern?

Culture, *ko' le'hoī hon a:dey'one.* How much change can our culture take?

Cultural copyrights, *haydoshna: a:dehyakk'yanak'yanna.* How can we protect our cultural knowledge?

Arts, *anikwa:we.* How can we protect our arts economy?

Population, *ko:wi'hoī a:ho'i a:dey'ona.* Can we continue to support our population growth?

Education, *I:yanikk'yanakya.* How can we educate our youth in both modern and our cultural ways?

Health, *dikwahna' yan'illi:we.* What will end our community's epidemics of chronic diseases and social concerns?

Environment, *ulohnanne*. How can we better care for our land to
    honor Mother Earth?

Like the echo from a distant cultural tidal wave, first contact continues to resonate
and affect present generations of Zunis and other Native peoples. Hawikku, ground
zero for this cultural cataclysm, remains a significant symbol of a momentous event
that forever altered all subsequent realities for the people of the Southwest. The final
chapters of this story continue to be told.

Navajo sandpainter at work, about 1925–35. Photograph by T. Harmon Parkhurst.

II

Diné (Navajo) History: "Black Clouds Will Rise"

Peter Iverson (2002)

> After we get back to our country it will brighten up again and the Navajos will be as happy as the land, black clouds will rise and there will be plenty of rain.
>
> — *Barboncito, 1868*

Beginnings

It begins with the land. It begins with the first light of morning. It begins with the white shell mountain. It begins with spring. Luci Tapahonso (1997) writes:

> Hayoolkaalgo Sisnajini nihi neel'iih leh.
> Blanca Peak is adorned with white shell.
> Blanca Peak is adorned with morning
>   light....
> She is the brightness of spring.
> She is Changing Woman returned....
> Because of her we think and create
> Because of her we make songs.
> Because of her, the designs appear as we
>   weave.
> Because of her, we tell stories and laugh.

Before this land, this light, this mountain, this season, there could be no Diné. So rooted in this particular place, this extraordinary environment, are the Navajos that one cannot imagine them else-where. The mountains are placed there for the Diné; they are to live within these mountains.

But one can imagine a certain scene, a vital moment in their history. It is the summer of 1868. Most of the Diné are in exile — incarcerated on a decidedly differ-ent earth hundreds of miles from their homeland. Their leaders are negotiating with federal representatives about their future residence. Barboncito declares: "Our grand-fathers had no idea of living in any country except our own.... When the Navajos were first created four mountains and four rivers were pointed out to us, inside of which we should live, that was to be our country and was given to us by the first woman of the Navajo tribe."

General William Tecumseh Sherman raises the possibility of sending the people to Indian Territory. Barboncito responds: "I hope to God you will not ask me to go to any other country except my own." When the Navajos eventually persuade the government negotiators to allow them to go home, they are overjoyed. Barboncito says: "After we get back to our country it will brighten up again and the Navajos will be as happy as the land, black clouds will rise and there will be plenty of rain" (*Treaty* 1968, 5-6). As the people made their way back toward their home country, the old men and the old women began to weep with gladness when they first saw Tsoodził (Mount Taylor), the sacred mountain that marks the southern Navajo boundary. They had returned to Diné Bikéyah — the Navajo country — where the Holy People wished them to live. The agreement forged at Fort Sumner — the Treaty of 1868 — clearly marked a major turning point in Navajo history. Had the Navajos been coerced into permanent exile in Oklahoma, their history would have been decidedly different.

That is, in fact, what their traditional oral histories proclaim. Through con-sideration of these stories one can begin to gain an essential appreciation for the nature of Diné identity and understand why the Navajos have been so tenacious in the defense of their land....

The Emergence

The stories say that the Navajos emerged into this world after a long and difficult journey that took them from the First World (the Black World) to the Second World (the Blue World) to the Third World (the Yellow World) to the Fourth World (the Glittering World). First Man (Áłtsé Hastiin) and First Woman (Áłtsé Asdzą́ą́) are formed in the Black World, which also contained various Insect Beings.

Quarreling in the Black World among the Insect Beings forces them to climb to the Blue World, where Blue Birds (Dólii), Blue Hawks (Ginitsoh Dootł'izhí), Blue Jays (Jigí), and Blue Herons (Táłtl'ááh Ha'alééh) resided, together with other Insect Beings. First Man and First Woman soon discovered different animals, including Wolves (Ma'iitsoh), Wildcats (Nashdoiłbáhí), Badgers (Nahashcd'id), Kit Foxes

(Ma'iiłtsooí), and Mountain Lions (Nashdoitsoh) (primarily based on Yazzie 1971; also see Zolbrod 1984, Levy 1998).

Once again, quarreling forced another migration, this time to the Yellow World. Here the mischievous Coyote causes problems for one and all that eventually lead to a flood that carries everyone to the Glittering World, the site of the six mountains: in the east (Blanca Peak or Sis Naajiní), the south (Mount Taylor or Tsoodził), the west (San Francisco Peaks or Dook'o'osłííd), the north (Mount Hesperus or Dibe Nitsaa), the center (Huerfano Mountain or Dził Na'oodłíí), and the east of center (Gobernador Knob or Ch'ool'į́'į). The first four mountains also were associated with a particular color and a particular season. They were the four sacred mountains that mark the traditional boundaries of Diné Bikéyah.

Now the world as the Navajos would know it continued to be shaped. The stories tell of the first hogan being constructed, the first sweat bath being taken, the four seasons being established, day and night being created, the stars being placed in the sky, and the sun and the moon coming into existence. The Glittering World encompasses both beauty and difficulty. In one episode after another, listeners hear the consequences of improper behavior, and learn about the difficulties that may ensue through carelessness or thoughtlessness. The people had to learn as well about planning and resourcefulness in order for them to survive (Yazzie 1971; Zolbrod 1984; Levy 1998).

During this time Changing Woman (Asdzáá Nádleehí) is born. Discovered on top of Gobernador Knob, she grew in twelve days to womanhood. The first puberty ceremony (Kinaaldá) was conducted for her, with many of the Holy People (Diyin Diné'é) participating. Talking God (Haashch'éłti'í) conducted the final night ceremony, when he presented the twelve Hogan songs (Hooghan Biyiin) still employed today. According to Navajo elder Mike Mitchell this ceremony represents the original Blessingway.

Changing Woman becomes pregnant and gives birth to twin boys, who become known as Born for Water (Tóbájíshchíní) and Monster (or Enemy) Slayer (Nayee' Neizghání). The twins embark upon a long and dangerous journey, filled with challenges that call upon them to employ all the good qualities emphasized in Navajo life. They visit their father, the Sun Bearer, who gives them weapons to employ against the monsters then plaguing the people. The twins return to kill One Walking Giant (Ye'iitsoh Ła'í Naagháíí), whose dried blood may be seen in the form of the lava flow near Tsoodził. They also slay Tsé Nináhálééh, the Monster Bird who lived on top of Shiprock (Tsé bit'aí, or "Winged Rock") (Yazzie 1971; Zolbrod 1984; Levy 1998; Yazzie 1984).

Although these exploits relieved the Diné of much suffering, the people needed additional help to improve their lives. Some Navajo accounts credit Changing Woman with the creation of livestock, while other stories have the twin boys returning to see the Sun Bearer, who gave them livestock as well as special prayers and medicine songs to be used for proper care of these animals. Regardless of how they were obtained, the horses are of four colors, each linked with one of the seasons and one of the sacred mountains: white, blue (or turquoise), yellow (or red), and black. Changing Woman is also important for her role in creating the first Navajo clans. She rubbed the skin from her breast, her back, and from under her arms to create Kiiyaa´áanii (Towering House), Honágháhnii (One Walks Around You), Tódích´ii´nii (Bitter Water), and Hashtł´ishnii (Mud) clans. Eventually there would be sixty clans, with perhaps a third of them tied to peoples of Puebloan descent. The clan system is matrilineal, with the individual inheriting his or her clan from his or her mother (Yazzie 1971; Zolbrod 1984; Levy 1998; Yazzie 1984).

Changing Woman, Born for Water, and Monster Slayer are central figures in Navajo history and culture. Diné traditional scholar Harry Walters concludes: "Their exploits and heroic deeds set order, balance and harmony in the world. Changing Woman's gift of mother's instinct and affection are the basis for the matrilineal clan system. The exploits of Monster Slayer and Born for Water are the basis for Navajo healing and protection ceremonials. The accomplishments of all three, mothers and sons, defined new terms and set standards of behavior on how the people should live and what to expect of life."

A proper life embodies *hózhǫ́*, defined by anthropologist Charlotte Frisbie (1987) as "continual good health, harmony, peace, beauty, good fortune, balance, and positive events in the lives of self and relatives." If chaos had prevailed prior to the fourth world, the Blessingway ceremony opens the way to an era Walters terms the Hózhǫ́ǫ́jí period. The onset of this era is tied to increased contact between and among peoples of Athabaskan and Pueblo heritage. This is the foundation for the way of life that will become known as the Navajo. Blessingway is the fundamental informing and organizational force in Navajo ceremonialism. The standard anthropological analysis posits its formulation well after European contact, with significant evolution in the 1700s, when in the wake of the Spanish return in 1692 Puebloan peoples fled their home country and often joined Navajo communities. Walters disagrees, contending that the absence of extended references to livestock in the core ceremonial tales and the emphasis on corn and corn pollen speak to an aboriginal origin.

Thus, the Blessingway ceremonial's adaptation and development are tied to a time of extended contact with Puebloan peoples, whereas the roots of the Enemy Way ceremonial may be linked to contact with people who have ties to the southern Plains, especially the Plains Apaches and the Comanches. Walters sees Plains elements in the Enemy Way, citing "the use of scalps, give-aways, name-calling songs, and the round dance." Not all Diné share this perspective, but this observation is indicative of the new questions being raised about the evolution of Navajo culture.

The Navajo traditional accounts do not contradict all of the archaeological or linguistic research that has been carried out over the past century. Navajos do not necessarily deny a connection with other Native peoples who speak a version of a language that has been classified as belonging to the Athabaskan (or Athapaskan) language category. The journey delineated in the traditional stories is not unlike the journey that non-Navajo archaeologists and linguists insist the Diné took from northwestern Canada and Alaska. There are, however, significant differences in some elements of Navajo traditional stories and the stories told by academic archaeologists and anthropologists.

Historian AnCita Benally's work helps to clarify commonalities and differences. Benally is completing her Ph.D. in history at Arizona State University. Highly regarded for her skill in the Navajo language, she is well versed in traditional Diné knowledge. She acknowledges Navajo and Apache linguistic ties, not only with Native communities in Alaska and Canada, but also with people such as the Hupas, who reside today in northern California. However, she contends that Diné tradition adds a component essential in understanding the full picture. Archaeologists and anthropologists, for example, still cannot reach a consensus on the route or routes that Athabaskans took in their migration or how these affiliated peoples became separated.

A traditional story tells of a terrible fire that lasted for a long time and permanently divided people into the two groups who are today labeled Northern Athabaskan and Southern Athabaskan. Another story relates how people traveled from south to north to find their relatives from whom they had been separated during a time of confusion and disagreement. These stories, Benally notes, assume "a time when all people considered Diné and who are called Athapaskan today were united as one people." The splintering that took place was followed by a time when different clan groups found one another and made an effort to reunify. As they also met with other groups, there often occurred exchanges of "gifts, ideas, and friendship. A number of them became a part of the traveling Diné and eventually became fully integrated into Diné society." On occasion, some of "the original Diné adopted small groups of other peoples and proclaimed them their relatives, either to share the same clan name or to become, as a group, related clans of a different name." "Diné clans adopting new people," she adds, "pledged to maintain kinship and social alliances with them."

"Today," Benally observes, "almost every single group that the Diné came in contact with through trading, marriage, war or social events is represented by a clan group." Thus, people from Jemez Pueblo, San Felipe Pueblo, the Utes, the Chiricahua Apaches, the Zunis, other Puebloans, Paiutes, and even Spanish/Mexican groups were integrated in time into the Diné. In time they all became one people. They were all Diné.

Recent archaeological research is calling into question routes of migration, length of residence, and other fundamental dimensions of aboriginal occupation of North America. Perhaps a major volcanic fire that took place roughly 1,600 years ago did have the effect reported by the traditional stories. Perhaps climate change occurred in a pattern allowing for south to north as well as north to south migration. Perhaps future archaeologists will find evidence to support the connection with the Pacific Coast that the Hupa presence connotes and of which traditional Diné stories speak but for which there is not presently "scientific" evidence. As Klara Kelley and Harris

Francis (1998) remark in an important essay, absence of evidence is not necessarily evidence of absence....

The Navajos and the Anasazi

Part of the conventional wisdom about the aboriginal Southwest has been to place the Navajos in opposition to the Anasazi. "Ana" does mean enemy in the Navajo language and Navajos are said to avoid the Anasazi sites because of their antagonism toward these communities as well as their reluctance to be in contact with places where people have died. At the same time, Puebloan communities within the region have assumed a proprietary air about the Anasazi. They have determined that when the great Anasazi population centers at Chaco Canyon, Mesa Verde, and elsewhere were abandoned during the thirteenth century, those who departed eventually joined or established new Puebloan entities. The similarity between Anasazi and Pueblo housing in and of itself has given that association a kind of obvious inevitability (*Gallup Independent*, April 29, 2000).

Particularly within the past generation, Navajos have begun to reconsider their association with the Anasazi. Some of the Diné now claim a connection between their history and Anasazi history. Given the pattern through the centuries of incorporation of other peoples or fusion of others' cultural elements with those of the Navajos, they contend, is it not possible that some of the Anasazi chose to join with other people to form the group that we now call Navajo? If one accepts Walters's notion that some of the Diné ancestors lived near Anasazi for generations, then the claim for a Navajo link to the Anasazi becomes not only possible, but probable. Alan Downer, now head of the Navajo Nation's Historic Preservation Office, has come to believe in an earlier arrival period for the Athabaskan speakers. Otherwise, he believes one must accept the notion that the Navajos had a curious proclivity for using old wood in their buildings. To the critics who say that the Diné simply employed old wood from other buildings, Downer replies, "I can't understand what would motivate these people to consistently use wood that's 200 years old" (*Gallup Independent*, April 29, 2000).

As one might well anticipate, such contentions are greeted derisively and dismissed by members of contemporary Pueblo communities, especially at Hopi, as well as by many anthropologists and archaeologists. Nevertheless, the Navajos have been sufficiently persuasive in regard to their claim for an association with the Anasazi that Chaco Canyon National Historic Park and Mesa Verde National Park have both agreed to consult the Diné as well as Pueblo communities in regard to dealing with Anasazi human remains and artifacts (e.g. Reed 2000; *New York Times*, August 20, 1996)....

Before the Spaniards came, the people who were becoming the Navajos were centered in an area to the east of the present reservation. The Dinétah ("among the Diné") in northwestern New Mexico formed an important part of the early Navajo country for more than two centuries, from the 1500s or earlier through the late 1700s, when pressures from the Spaniards as well as conflicts with the Comanches and the Utes encouraged the Diné to move out of the area.

The cradle of Navajo civilization, the place of Changing Woman's birth, the Dinétah is a rugged stretch of land to the east of present-day Farmington, New Mexico. Today the Bureau of Land Management manages most of this area. Here, in a challenging environment, the basic form of Navajo culture took shape. Although few Diné live in the area today, Dinétah remains a mecca to Navajos interested in their history and heritage....

The Navajos and the Spaniards

In the fields, in the hunt, and in battle, Navajos fully appreciated that their success hinged on more than hard work. They needed to pray, to hold the appropriate ceremonies, and to reconsider the promise of the Diné Bikéyah. They recognized that life was fragile, that harmony within oneself and within one's family could prove elusive, and that contact with others might provide new benefits or pose unanticipated dilemmas. Nevertheless, the promise of finding something better usually outweighed the danger of discovering something worse. Already it was becoming a society noteworthy for its members' willingness to look around the corner and over the next hill, for their curiosity about what might be gained by exploration and inquiry, and for their determination to do something well. Is it any wonder that others might consider joining such a people — less enamored of routine and more tolerant of innovation?

Such a society inherently embraced expansion. Once the people acquired a few horses, they wanted or needed more horses — and more land for them. Once they obtained a few sheep, they understood the benefits of having more — and the necessity of finding a place for them. Such an approach guaranteed that the Navajos would gain a reputation. They challenged other Indians' claims to particular territory. The Navajos did not think much of the notion of prior appropriation, or first in time, first in right. They opted for a pragmatic doctrine that emphasized beneficial use. This perspective guaranteed a continuing chance for prosperity, but it also ensured continuing opportunities for trouble.

Well before the Americans came, the Navajos began to develop a reputation. The Pueblo communities often welcomed them as trading partners, but resented the unwillingness of the Navajos to grant them primacy, that is, to acknowledge dutifully the Pueblo claim to prior appropriation. Pueblo villages offered bases for forays well beyond the mesas or valleys where they made their homes. Through their journeys for salt or eagle feathers or other items, their people believed that they had made such territory their own. The Navajos could not accept and did not accept this presumption. How could you call land your own when you did not live on it or near it, and if you made significant use of it only on rare occasions?

The Comanches and Utes, daring raiders in their own right, did not welcome the Navajo emergence as a force to be reckoned with in the region. These peoples delighted in their own courage, celebrated their ability to steal horses, or for that matter, people. The Navajo oral tradition brims over with accounts of Comanche and Ute attempts, sometimes successful, to steal their horses, their children, or their sisters or mothers.

The arrival of the Spaniards did not create instantaneous conflict for the Navajos, because the initial Spanish presence in the Rio Grande Valley lay well to the east of Navajo country. But the Spanish were committed to expansion, too, and even the Navajo appreciation for Spanish generosity for bringing such wonderful beings as horses, sheep, cattle, and goats could not forestall eventual conflict. The Diné would wrap such animals in the strands of their own stories, give credit to their own deities, and never even nod in the direction of New Spain for improving their lives. After all, the Spaniards did not possess turquoise horses. They did not have a chant that proclaimed:

> I am the Sun's son.
> I sat on the turquoise horse.
> He went to the opening in the sky.
> He went with me to the opening.
> The turquoise horse prances with me.
> From where we start the turquoise horse is seen.
> The lightning flashes from the turquoise horse.
> The turquoise horse is terrifying.
> He stands on the upper circle of the rainbow.
> The sunbeam is in his mouth for his bridle.
> He circles around all the people of the earth
> With their goods.
> Today he is on my side
> And I shall win with him. (O'Bryan 1956, 157-63)

New Spain changed the lives, altered the cultures, and influenced the destinies of all Native peoples in the region. However, as the pioneering student of the Southwest Edward Spicer (1962, 324) observed several decades ago, it would be the people on the margins of New Spain who would be most profoundly impacted by the Spanish incursion. The Spaniards employed forced imposition, persuasion, and demonstration in their efforts to produce cultural change. The more sedentary the Native population and the closer its location to Spanish outposts, the more likely it would be to experience the full brunt of the first element of that trinity. This is not to suggest that the Navajos were beyond the reach of Spanish colonialism. They were not. But given their character and their lack of proximity, most Diné clearly did not confront the daily imposition of Spanish will in the same manner as Puebloan communities, especially those situated in the Rio Grande Valley. The Navajos were far more able to pick and choose, to take advantage of non-directed cultural change, even amidst the complications, and, at times, the horrors brought by the Spanish presence.

12

Jicarilla Apache Origins and Early White Contact

Veronica E. Velarde Tiller (2000)

The Jicarilla Apaches are a vigorous people with a tremendous enthusiasm for life, despite a history of adversity. Their past has reflected this passion for life, the essence of which derives from their conception of a personified universe. This conception includes an optimistic outlook on life, a disposition for patience and understanding, imagination, and an ability to adapt to changing environments. External flexibility and core consistency have been responsible for their survival (adopted from Gunnerson 1974, 296; Opler 1936, 205) — since they emerged from their mythical underworld to follow the Sun and Moon.

According to the Jicarilla Apache origin stories, in the beginning Black Sky and Earth Woman bore anthropomorphic Supernaturals who dwelt within the body of their mother, the Earth. Only darkness prevailed in this underworld, where all living things dwelt, and where Black Hac'ct'cin, the first offspring and Supreme Supernatural, created the first ancestral man and woman, animals, and birds out of clay, based on the impression of his own form.

The sole source of light was the eagle plumes that the people used as torches, but these provided inadequate illumination. Consequently, the numerous minor Supernaturals made a miniature Sun and Moon, which were allowed to make one circuit of the heavens. The light cast by these two bodies proved unsatisfactory, so they were brought down and enlarged. The second set was tested and permitted to rise and set four times until it provided sufficient light.

Jicarilla Apache woman in tepee village, about 1915. Photograph by H. F. Robinson.

No sooner were the Sun and Moon created than some evil shamans attempted to destroy them. Angered by this, Hac'ct'cin allowed the Sun and Moon to escape to this earth. The people pondered their misfortune, consulted with each other, sang and prayed, and considered how they could restore their two sources of light. The only alternative, they concluded, was to follow the Sun and Moon. Thus the Jicarillas were united as a people; their emergence from the underworld was necessitated by their attempt to recover the light that they had lost.

The holy people, with the guidance and help of the Hac'ct'cin, the ultimate power, facilitated their own ascent. All the powers that these underworld creatures possessed were used. These powers were given to them by Hac'ct'cin before their world debut, but during the course of the upward journey more ceremonies were given to them. At the start of the journey a ritual was performed. Four mounds of earth that had been piled in a row began to grow into huge mountains, rising toward the hole through which the Sun and Moon had escaped. Then the mountains stopped growing, making it impossible for the people and animals to complete their upward journey. Again it became necessary to use imagination and to perform ceremonies. Several different types of ladders were constructed from feathers, but they proved to be too weak. Failure was not what Hac'ct'cin envisioned; thus, he constructed four ladders of sunbeams and the people and animals were able to continue their ascent. All journeyed up to the opening with the exception of an old man and woman, who were too weak to climb and chose not to leave the land of their youth. They warned that Jicarillas would return to this underworld at death. After their emergence, the people and animals discovered that the earth was covered with water, symbolizing that life on earth was not to be easy. The Wind Deity offered to roll back the waters in the four directions to form the oceans. In his zealousness, he dried up all the waters, leaving nothing for the living creatures to drink. Prayers were offered, and soon rivers, lakes, and streams appeared. The people discovered that the earth was inhabited by monsters, who were eventually slain by one of the culture heroes, Monster Slayer. Finally, with the help of other Supernaturals, all obstacles that made the earth an unsafe place were eliminated.

When the earth was dry and safe, the people and animals traveled in all four directions in clockwise fashion. As they traveled, small groups began to break off and settle down; as they settled, the Supernaturals gave them different names and languages. The Jicarillas, however, continued to circle. The Supreme Deity was getting angry and impatient with their indecisiveness and asked them where they wanted to live. They replied, "Near the center of the earth." The Creator then made four sacred rivers to delineate the boundaries of their country: the Arkansas, Canadian, Rio Grande, and Pecos. This land became the Holy Land for the Jicarillas. They believe that they are the true descendants of the original people who emerged from the underworld, and that they retain the only true language (Opler 1936, 205; for other versions Goddard 1911; Russell 1898; Mooney 1898).

After the Jicarillas came to this world, the Supernaturals gave them elaborate laws, customs, traditions, and more ceremonials that were to be observed forever. At this time all the human attributes that the animals possessed were taken from them, though they were allowed to retain the powers they had to facilitate the emergence. For this reason the Jicarillas were warned never to abuse, molest, or otherwise mistreat animals. If an animal were to be hunted for food, the proper prayers and rituals had to be performed. Plants and mineral life were also to be respected since they too retained their supernatural attributes.

The Jicarilla world became a personified universe with which the Indians identified (Opler 1936, 205). All natural and living objects, including man, were seen as personifications of Hac'ct'cin. All living creatures and natural phenomena were manifestations of his power. Through ritual, his powers could be used for human purposes. For that reason, the more important sources of his powers — Sun, Moon, Wind, Lightning — are always represented in all the ceremonies. Within this framework, a pantheon of good and evil Supernaturals are recognized. The Jicarillas were made aware that this world consists of both good and evil and that man is not a perfect creature, but one with natural and deep blemishes in his basic character.

The culture heroes and Coyote, the trickster, were responsible for the acquisition of all the cultural and behavioral traits of man, most of which were obtained through theft and cunning rather than physical aggression. All social institutions of the Jicarillas can be traced to the character of the trickster, who points out that man is not infallible and that human foibles can be tolerated with a sense of humor.

The Jicarilla Apaches were so obsessed by their personified universe, absorbed in maintaining their cosmic order through ceremony, ritual, and the observance of their religion, that little else mattered to them. Within this seemingly harmonious and systematic universe, all natural phenomena could be explained or could be attributed to the natural order as they understood it. In spite of the existence of evil in all forms in the world, their faith in their creation seemingly remained unchallenged until the arrival of the white man.

The Jicarilla version of their origin is a symbolic one, yet it shares factual elements with recorded history. The Jicarillas are one of the six southern Athapascan groups, which include the Chiricahuas, Navajos, Western Apaches, Mescaleros, Kiowa Apaches, and Lipans. The Apachean-speaking tribes migrated out of the Canadian Mackenzie Basin, as latecomers to today's American Southwest, some time between A.D. 1300 and 1500, settling eastern Arizona, New Mexico, northern Mexico, southeastern Colorado, the Oklahoma and Texas panhandles, and west, central, and south Texas.

Out of the composite groups of southern Athapascans who relocated in the Southwest, by 1700 an identifiable group known as the Jicarilla Apaches had emerged. As their homeland, they chose the region bordered by the Arkansas River in southeastern Colorado, the northeastern plains region drained by the tributaries of the Canadian River, the flatlands of the Pecos River Valley, and the area northwest to the Rio Grande in the Chama River Valley of New Mexico. This country they deemed to be "near the center of the earth."

The Jicarilla Apaches preserved much of their fundamental Athapascan culture after settling in the Southwest, but over the centuries gradually adopted some cultural traits from their non-Athapascan neighbors. Their material culture was influenced by the Plains Indians, especially by their war and raiding complexes, while their agricultural and ceremonial rituals had definite traces of influence from the Pueblo Indians of the Upper Rio Grande (Opler 1936, 202). This cultural borrowing helped the Jicarillas adapt to their environment, which has consisted of two main geographic regions, the mountains and the plains. These geographic distinctions defined the basic social orientations of the Jicarillas into two bands: the Llaneros (plains people) and the Olleros (mountain-valley people).

This dual orientation was not discovered until the late nineteenth century when ethnographic research was conducted — long after the Jicarillas had been placed on a reservation in northern New Mexico. Historical evidence, however, suggests that it had existed for centuries. A description of Jicarilla aboriginal territory provides the key to understanding the dual-band system. Northeastern New Mexico ranges from 2,000 to 14,000 feet above sea level. The highest points are the Sangre de Cristo Mountains, with their component ridges of Culebra, Cimarron, Taos, Santa Fe, Mora, Las Vegas, and Raton. This mountain range parallels the Rio Grande on the east, extending from south of Santa Fe northward in a gentle arc to the Arkansas River in south central Colorado. A considerable part of the region is covered by these mountains, flanked on either side by high plateaus, limited by the Rio Grande on the west to a width of ten to twenty miles. This piedmont is generally level; but on the east it stretches for fifty or sixty miles and drops off in sharp escarpments toward the eastern border of New Mexico.

The semiarid plains receive little rain, usually fewer than twenty inches annually and sometimes not more than ten. The winters are subject to heavy snow and low temperatures, especially in the mountains, while summer days are hot and dry with cool breezes at night. It was in the plains that the Jicarillas began hunting the buffalo and eventually adopting the ways and methods of coping with, and living in, a plains environment.

When the Spaniards arrived in the Southwest in the mid-1500s, they established their first extensive relationships with the Rio Grande Pueblos. It was from the Pueblos that they learned of the Indians east of the Rio Grande, Indians whom the Spaniards later referred to as "Apaches." With this information and high hopes, Francisco Vazquez de Coronado's 1541 expeditionary forces journeyed through the eastern plains of New Mexico in search of the fabled Seven Cities of Cibola. To their disappointment, no cities of gold were located: their chronicles acknowledged, for the written historical record, however, the existence of the eastern branch of the Southern Athapascan Apaches. The Spaniards did not call these Indians "Apaches" until the 1600s; instead they used other names, such as "Querechos" and "Vaqueros" (Hammond and Rey 1940, 261; Hammond and Rey 1966, 87).

Until 1700, the Jicarillas were undifferentiated because of the Spanish practice of using only the name "Apache" (Gunnerson 1974, 167) to refer to all Apache bands (which included the Cuartelejos, Carlanas, Sierra Blancas, Palomas, Achos, and Calchufines). Occasionally the names of chieftains, ecological practices, or physical location were used to distinguish one band from another. The Jicarilla Apaches were not identified by that specific name, however, until 1700, when Governor Pedro Rodríguez Cubero of New Mexico ordered that a condemned criminal's head be stuck on a pole in Taos to warn the "apaches of la Xicarilla" not to harbor Spanish fugitives (Gunnerson 1974, 167). This name was applied to the Apaches living in the Taos Valley-Raton Mountains area. The word "Jicarilla" (pronounced hekäre'ya) has since been generally defined as "little basket maker," referring to a small gourd or vessel or basket. The term also designates a hemispherical vessel used to hold food or liquids. By extension, it can also refer to a chocolate cup (Gunnerson 1974, 154–58).

Over time, as a result of continuing contact with the Indians, the Spaniards noted two cultural orientations among the eastern Apaches. One group comprised semisettled horticultural people living in rancherías, mainly in the Taos, Raton, and Arkansas River region. The other included people following the buffalo on the plains, such as the Vaqueros and Carlanas. This distinguished the two Jicarilla bands.

In the decades before the Pueblo Revolt of 1680, when Pueblo-Spanish relations were becoming strained, a large number of Pueblos from the upper Rio Grande

sought refuge among the Apaches. The semisettled life-style of the Apaches was reinforced by the influence of the sedentary Pueblos, and the horticultural tendencies of
the Apaches became more pronounced. This was evident in 1692 when Don Diego de
Vargas began the reconquest of New Mexico and encountered Apaches living north of
Taos in rancherías. Captain Juan de Ulibarrí also found a ranchería of Jicarillas in the
region between the Rayado and Raton mountains in the Taos Valley (which indicated
that the Jicarillas maintained control and occupation of this region from that early
time, as they continued to do up to the late nineteenth century).

PART THREE

THE NORTHERN PROVINCE

"Hispanic heritage, in many forms, is part of the patrimony of the United States. This is nowhere more evident than in the landlocked and distant state of New Mexico, a once far north settlement that to this day bears the heritage of more than two centuries as part of Spain's New World empire." Administered from Madrid and Mexico City until Mexican independence in 1821, "for 223 years New Mexico was a very distant part of Spain's most successful colony in the Americas." Documents (histories, reports, records, memorials, accounts, journals, letters, and the like) and artifacts from this northern province bespeak exploration, conquest, and settlement — "encounters of two worlds," the European and the Native American, each new to the other (Chávez).

In seventeenth-century two-world encounters in New Mexico, three men were given or made names for themselves. One was Juan de Oñate, the "first successful colonizer [in 1598] and governor,...[who] towers over the early colonial period" (Hendricks). Another was Popay (today Po'pay), from San Juan Pueblo (today Ohkay Owingeh), "a major religious leader" who planned the Pueblo Revolt of 1680 "from the kiva at Taos" and most likely led it while "in a kiva (whether at San Juan or Taos does not matter), praying, meditating, and sacrificing for the success of the efforts of the younger men in battle" (Ortiz). The third is Diego de Vargas, whose 1690s reconquest and recolonization "dominates the historical landscape of Spanish colonial

New Mexico" (Hendricks). In recent years all three have been memorialized with statues: Oñate in 1994, Po'pay in 2005, and Vargas in 2007.

Diego de Vargas's name lives in the annual Santa Fe Fiesta, first proclaimed in 1712 and celebrated, with occasional interruptions and many changes, ever since to mark Vargas and the Spaniards' reentry into Santa Fe on September 4, 1692, after twelve years in El Paso. Later in the eighteenth century, other two-world-encounter celebrations were recounted in documents from Bishop of Durango Pedro Tamarón y Romeral's official visitation in 1760. On May 26 of that year, "the resplendent bishop administered confirmation to 192 Pecos Indians." The following September, "one of the pueblo's principal men, Agustín Guichí, a carpenter and likely head of a Pecos clown society," and two others conducted a three-day burlesque of the May ceremony, with tragic consequences for the Pecos "prelate" (Kessell). Today, "at fiestas or special gatherings of the pueblo leaders," five silver-crowned canes of office, "symbols of justice and leadership" and local sovereignty, are evident. The pueblo's lieutenant governor keeps the one bestowed during the Mexican period, while the pueblo's governor is entrusted with four — one from the Spanish colonial government, one from President Abraham Lincoln in 1863, one from New Mexico Governor Bruce King in 1980, and the fourth from King Juan Carlos of Spain in September 1987 (Sando).

13

Spain in the New World

Thomas E. Chávez

Spain's New World empire stretched across North and South America. The legacy of Spanish customs, language, religion, and mentality is indelibly etched in the Americas from the United States to southern South America. Hispanic heritage, in many forms, is part of the patrimony of the United States. This is nowhere more evident than in the landlocked and distant state of New Mexico, a once far north settlement that to this day bears the heritage of more than two centuries as part of Spain's New World empire.

Spain did not exist as a country for most of its history. The Iberian Peninsula, the southwestern appendage to Europe, would eventually become the countries of Spain and Portugal, influenced by people of various cultures who moved into the peninsula over time. Among them were people called Iberos, Basques, whose origin is unknown, Phoenicians from northern Africa (1000 B.C.), Greeks (650 B.C.), Celts in the north (600 B.C.), Romans (218 B.C.), Visigoths (476 A.D.), and Muslims, for the most part out of Africa (711 A.D.). So many subgroups under these major headings arrived that, for example, virtually every European culture is represented.

The almost seven hundred years of Roman occupation of the peninsula had a profound influence on the people of Spain. Roman language, law, and architecture are but a few of the obvious evidences of that influence.

The second most defining moment was the eight-century occupation by the Moors, from 711 A.D. until 1492. Pushed into the northern mountains by Muslim expansion,

Family tree of the Juan Martínez de Montoya family, late eighteenth century. Photograph by Blair Clark.

the Iberians, who were mostly Christians, began a crusade, as the pope proclaimed it, to retake their peninsula. St. James the Apostle became the patron of the Christian forces under the name Santiago Matamoros, St. James the Moor Killer. The Reconquest took seven hundred years and defined the Spanish character as much as the Moorish occupation influenced Spanish culture. Fully one-third of the words in the Spanish language have Moorish origins, and Moorish influence is reflected in Spanish food and art. The religious fervor of the crusade to retake the peninsula from non-Christians continued into the history of Spain, perhaps most obviously with the establishment of the Holy Office of the Inquisition and the royal proclamation declaring Catholicism the state religion. Such fervor was also channeled into the discovery, conquest, and settlement of the Americas.

The act of nation building in itself creates a national fervor. Spain became a nation as a result of centuries-long religious wars and, finally, the marriage of Isabel of Castile and Ferdinán of Aragón. The unification of their respective kingdoms created the modern country of Spain. Los Reyes Católicos, the Catholic king and queen, as they were called, succeeded solidifying their power by defeating their competitors and the last Moorish bastion at Granada. Isabel granted Columbus's petition to take his historical voyage west in an attempt to outmaneuver Portugal in the race to get to Asia. The unexpected result, as we know, was the Europeans' discovery of a continent they did not know existed. The discovery gave the new country of Spain an undreamed of opportunity to vent its patriotic and religious enthusiasm.

At roughly the same time, the Reformation, the birth of Protestantism, took place with Martin Luther's (1483–1546) attempts to get the Catholic Church to reform. Outside of the papacy, Spain would become the most obvious opponent of the Reformation. The marriage of Ferdinán and Isabel's daughter, Juana, to Phillip the Handsome, a Hapsburg, formed an alliance that gave rise to the Spanish empire that peaked during the reigns of Carlos I (1516–56) and his son Felipe II (1556–98). The empire stretched from Europe, including the lowlands, some of the Germanys, and parts of Italy, across the Atlantic, through the Americas, and across the Pacific Ocean to the Philippines. The last were named for Felipe II. The empire included people from all over the world, from African slaves and Chinese merchants to American Indians.

The Early Encounters of Two Worlds

The Americas were a new world for the Europeans, and they in turn represented a new world for Native Americans. These inhabitants, mistakenly identified as Indians, and their lands became natural and new attractions for the veterans of European wars. Indeed, the Catholic Church mandated that Spain convert all non-Catholic people whom it contacted in exchange for the exclusive opportunity to explore the land (Kamen 2003, 331–38). Add a new sense of curiosity to a sense of adventure, along with wonder and a religious mandate that created an incentive of both personal and celestial reward, and Spain with its people was positioned to move throughout the Americas.

Columbus was granted permission to sail west in quest of a short trade route to the Orient. Fortunately for him, during his first voyage of 1492–93 he spotted land about where he expected China to be. He eventually made landfall on the mainland at what is today Venezuela and Honduras during his fourth voyage of 1502–4. Realizing that Columbus had not sailed to the Orient but had encountered a new world with heretofore unknown civilizations, Spain sponsored an era of unprecedented exploration, conquest, and eventually settlement.

Within decades Spanish explorers, followed by settlers, spread throughout the Americas, which from the Spanish-speaking world's perspective were one continent, not what the English-speaking world considers two. Hernán Cortés and Francisco Pizarro, both from the poor, landlocked region called Extremadura, respectively led conquests of the Aztecs in Mexico by 1522 and the Incas in Peru by 1534. Francisco de Orellana, also from Extremadura, floated the length of the Amazon River in 1541. Fernão de Magalhães, or Ferdinand Magellan as his name became Anglicized, was a Portuguese sailing for Spain who led a crew that was the first to circumnavigate the world during a three-year journey beginning in 1519. From 1535 into the 1540s, Pizarro's original partner in the Peru venture, Diego de Almagro, and Pedro de Valdivia explored and settled southern South America.

Beyond the dates and names, Spain in the Americas is a story of varied peoples from Europe and America. The Europeans were as different and new to the Indians as the latter were to the Europeans. This encounter between Europeans and Native Americans also accelerated encounters of the latter between each other.

Intentional and not, the results were good and bad. European diseases, although unintentional, had a devastating effect on the Indians. The ideal of religious conversion could be, and many times was, overbearing and disrupting. The church's position of converting and protecting its "neophytes" was not as enlightened as it appeared. Languages, foodstuffs, farming techniques, clothing, tools, weapons, and even customs changed. All those involved became something different from what they were before the encounter. They had entered a new epoch, a new world, and would become Americans.

The viceroyalty of New Spain would become Spain's most successful "colony." From New Spain's inception, a schism developed between those who wanted to exploit the Indians and those who saw them as human beings with souls to be saved. If the argument that Indians had souls took precedence, then the Indians were subjects of the Crown and had to be treated as such. Over the years, many individual examples pointed to the appearance that those who considered Indians as chattel and property had the advantage.

Yet the larger picture offers a different conclusion. Ferdinán and Isabel proclaimed that the people in the Americas should not be brought to Europe, nor should they be abused, because they were subjects. In his letters to his king, Carlos I, Cortés expressed the dream of creating a new society through the combination of European and Native American cultures and creating a Catholic Church that would be the envy of the European world. Without the intervention of the corrupt who exist in Europe, he wrote, "there will, in a very short time, arise in these parts a new Church, where God, Our Lord, may be better served and worshipped than in all the rest of the world" (Pagden 1986, 442–43). The conquistador actually tried to create this utopia on his hacienda. He gleaned this medieval messianic ideal from the Franciscans who arrived, upon his request, soon after his conquest (Pagden 1986, 333–34, 433–55, 525 n114; also Thomas 1995, 576–79, 586).

The Franciscans, like other early priests to New Spain, expressed the belief that the New World gave them an opportunity to renew Christianity — meaning in their minds Catholicism — and create an ideal state. Realizing this ideal would set an example for the church in Europe, which had become decadent and, as a result, was undergoing its own crisis, the Reformation. The priests' ideal was not unlike the "beacon on the hill" concept expressed by Protestant English settlers almost a century later in North America.

King Carlos I, who was named Holy Roman Emperor as Carlos V, and his son, who would become Felipe II as king of Spain, heard these arguments with open minds. They initiated a series of investigations and debates over whether or not the American Indians had souls, meaning that they were human beings. Further, if the conclusion was that they were human beings, then what was the Crown's moral obligation to them? Spain was the only European country to raise this question.

The Dominican priest Fray Bartolomé de Las Casas received the assignment of presenting the argument in favor of the Indians' having souls and deserving royal protection as a matter of the Crown's obligation to God. The humanist Juan Ginés de Sepúlveda received the assignment of giving the counterargument. After more than thirty years of meetings, debates, written briefs, and hearings, Las Casas's arguments were accepted. In 1542 the Crown, under Felipe II, issued "Laws for the Government of the Indies and Good of Treatment of the Indians" that evolved into a series of royal proclamations in 1573 called the *Recopilación de las leyes de los reinos de las Indias* (Recompilation of the laws of the kingdoms of the Indies). These laws reviewed all precedents, beginning with those of Ferdinán and Isabel, and concluded that the Indians were human beings, subjects of the Crown of Spain, and merited protection by the government, measures for which the laws spelled out. These "New Laws," as they came to be called, would have a profound effect on the eventual settlement of New Mexico.

While Spain grappled with legalities, the reality in New Spain moved naturally toward acceptance of Native Americans as human beings. Simply on the basis of population numbers, *mestizaje,* or intermarriage, dictated that a new society would develop. By the eighteenth century, Jesuit writers were expressing the way they saw themselves. Clearly, they were no longer Europeans, but something better. Using history, they argued that they were products of a European heritage that included the ancient Greeks and Romans, but they had also become descendants of the "ancient" peoples of the Americas, such as the Mayas, Olmecs, Toltecs, Aztecs, and Incas. Europeans did not share this second heritage and therefore were less culturally rich. Repeating Cortés's New World dream, the intellectuals of Mexico wrote that a new culture had evolved that took the best from Europe and America and, with the New World experience, had become something different and indeed superior. This New World evolution in Mexico created an identity that came to be called "neo-Aztecism," the very expression of syncretism and recognition of Indianism.

The best expression of this concept is the story of the Virgin of Guadalupe, originally a *morena* (dark complexioned) Virgin from the Monastery of Guadalupe in Extremadura, Spain. The influence of that region and therefore its patroness on the New World cannot be overstated. Even Columbus paid homage to her when he took the first Indians transported to Europe to be baptized in her monastery. As the story goes, Guadalupe appeared to an Indian named Diego outside Mexico City, at the site of the ancient Native goddess Tonantzin, in December 1531, thus creating an expression from God that appealed directly to the Native population. The apparition and the image associated with it grew into a national icon. The Virgin's image, for example, was used on banners during the Mexican independence movement, which culminated in 1821 (Lafaye 1976).

From their arrival in the Americas, the Spaniards were in some ways living out their imaginations. They encountered new peoples living in amazing cities, some of which were as large as any in Europe. They found, garnered, and sometimes squandered wealth beyond belief. They learned of exotic new animals, plants, foods, and customs. It is no wonder that the appearance of four Spanish survivors of a disastrous expedition who, after eight years, wandered out of northern New Spain with tales of people living in rich cities would grab everyone's attention. Although not personally witness to the fact, the four repeated what had been told them by the Indians they met.

A heretofore unknown sedentary civilization in the north appealed to officialdom in Mexico City. After all, had they not found such a civilization right where they were and again to the south in Peru? The only place left for another such discovery was the unexplored north.

The viceroy quickly organized a scouting expedition, sending the Franciscan friar Marcos de Niza along with one of the four survivors from the north, a slave from North Africa called Estevan. The two men, with Indian servants, traveled north through what is today Sonora and Arizona to arrive at the Zuni pueblos in western New Mexico. There, Estevan was killed. Fray Marcos returned to report to the viceroy.

The viceroy did not hesitate to share a tale of golden cities and to personally invest some of his own funds to help form a true expedition to this faraway and newly visited land. He assigned Francisco Vázquez de Coronado to lead the expedition. Vázquez, a minor noble who had attended the University of Salamanca, would lead a group of some twelve hundred people along with the necessary livestock and other goods to feed them.

In 1540 the Vázquez de Coronado expedition traveled north out of the town of Compostela in Nueva Galicia into what is now Arizona and then New Mexico. From New Mexico he or his captains visited every pueblo and became the first Europeans to see the Grand Canyon. The expedition traveled out onto the Great Plains into Texas, and then north through Oklahoma to a place on the Arkansas River in Kansas that they called Quivira. From their camp there, scouting expeditions traveled as far as, and perhaps into, Nebraska to the north and Missouri to the east.

While all this sounds grand, glorious, and even astonishing for the distances covered, the excursion was wrought with problems and hardships. The biggest and most immediate disappointment was that the expeditionaries found no new Mexico City — there were no rich cities at all. Too, they met resistance among the Pueblo people. With the exception of the Franciscan priests and their helpers, the Coronado expedition ultimately left New Mexico, empty-handed. Despite the terrain covered and knowledge gained, the Coronado expedition, as it came to be called, was considered a failure in its day, and enthusiasm for the land of the Pueblos, which Vázquez de Coronado called Cibola, from the Zuni word for buffalo, was quickly supplanted by more pressing matters in New Spain.

Silver had been discovered at a place called Zacatecas in north-central Mexico. The rush to the new silver lodes touched off a war with the Chichimeca Indians, who proved to be fierce defenders of their homeland. Another attempt to explore New Mexico would not be made for forty years, the length of time before the war ended.

The Spanish Empire, which had expanded throughout Europe as well as the Americas, was interested in New World exploration not only for wealth but also for the knowledge it offered. This motivation can be seen in Giovanni Battista Ramusio's *Navigationi et viaggi*, a three-volume set of books printed and published in Venice in 1556. Written in Italian, the international language of the empire, the volumes describe all New World explorations as of that time, with drawings of new plants, animals, and topography and firsthand narrations of the journeys. The exploits of Fray Marcos de Niza and Vázquez de Coronado are aptly represented in the third volume, a copy of which is in the Fray Angélico Chávez Library at the Palace of the Governors in Santa Fe. The first worldwide empire, upon which the sun never set, held a fascination for the Western world.

During the forty-year hiatus after the Vázquez de Coronado expedition, the New Laws were enacted. Henceforth, all expeditions of discovery and settlement would be for religious purposes. New Mexico, or La Nueva Mexico, as the Franciscans called the far north at least as early as 1571, would be "rediscovered" from 1581 until it was finally settled in 1598 because the Franciscans sought to find out what had happened to their brethren who had stayed behind when Vázquez de Coronado left. The sedentary Pueblo Indians became prime candidates for conversion. In 1598 New Mexico was settled as a missionary field under the leadership of a prominent Zacatecas frontiersman and miner named Juan de Oñate.

A Colony of New Spain

From the establishment of that first colony until 1821, when Mexican independence was achieved, and then until 1846, when the United States Army occupied New Mexico, the area was administered from Madrid and Mexico City. For 223 years New Mexico was a very distant part of Spain's most successful colony in the Americas. To date, New Mexico has been part of the United States for a little more than a century and a half (1848–2007), or more than a half-century less than it was part of the Spanish Empire.

The Spanish-Mexican New World experience is indelibly etched on New Mexico. Neo-Aztecism, although it changed over the years, continuously influenced the people. Spanish language, religion, clothing, foodstuffs, tools, and weapons permeated lifestyles. The Spanish worldview, including concepts regarding the family, priorities, property rights, women, and Native Americans, is evident even today in New Mexico. It is not by accident that more Native Americans in New Mexico today live on the land their ancestors occupied when the Europeans arrived than Native Americans in the whole eastern half of the United States. Nor is it surprising that Mexico today is primarily an Indian nation.

The first Spanish settlement took place among a string of villages near San Juan (Ohkay Owingeh) Pueblo that Oñate named San Juan de los Caballeros, in part after his namesake. Within a few years the settlement had been renamed or moved and was called San Gabriel. The settlers who chose to remain in the distant colony soon moved out of this first capital. One person moved to Santa Clara Pueblo, where he raised sheep. Others chose unoccupied land such as the floodplain of the Santa Fe River around the present site of Santa Fe. Spanish settlers moved into that area early in the seventeenth century.

Documents now housed in the Fray Angélico Chávez Library establish that Captain Juan Martínez de Montoya established the *plaza,* or village, of Santa Fe sometime in 1607. Another of Oñate's captains, Gaspar Pérez de Villagrá, the governor's legal advisor, abandoned the colony, went to Spain, and wrote an epic poem favorably depicting the early history of the new colony. That poem, *La historia de la Nueva México*, was published as a book in Spain in 1610. One of the few original editions of the book is also in the collections of the Palace of the Governors.

Villagrá's book would be one of the earliest of many publications about New Mexico written by people who were there. Unlike Villagrá, who wrote for publication, the others wrote official reports, memorials, or accounts of what they had seen or done. The account of Fray Antonio de Espejo and Fray Antonio de Beltrán's 1583 expedition into New Mexico was translated and published in London in 1586. Fray Jerónimo de Zárate Salmerón compiled a fairly extensive account of New Mexico's missions for his superiors in 1626 and 1627, which later became well known and used. Fray Alonso de Benavides, head Franciscan in New Mexico from 1625 to 1630, returned to Spain, where he wrote and published his famous 1630 *Memorial* about New Mexico for the king. In 1634 he revised it for presentation to the pope.

New Mexico was never forgotten in the empire at large. Writers who had never been to the north wrote of or mentioned New Mexico. Fray Pedro Oroz (1972, 61–64, 312–17, 336–40) mentioned the far northern missionary field in his late sixteenth-century manuscript book, or codex. Fray Agustín de Vetancurt wrote a famous history of Mexico in which he mentioned New Mexico in connection with the Pueblo Revolt of 1680. Carlos Sigüenza y Góngora, an eighteenth-century Mexican genius, wrote a short piece titled "Mercurio volante" about Diego de Vargas, who led the reconquest of New Mexico. Later, an eighteenth-century merchant, Alonso O'Crouley, traveled to Mexico and wrote an account in which he described New Mexico, even noting that the Santa Fe River had delicious trout (O'Crouley 1972, 55).

When the French Bourbons inherited the Spanish throne from the Hapsburgs at the beginning of the eighteenth century, New Mexico had recently been resettled after the Pueblo Indian rebellion of 1680, when the Spanish colonists were exiled for thirteen years. Still the distant colony offered hardship to those who settled there. The Bourbon kings initiated a series of inspections that resulted in the Bourbon Reforms of the last half of the century. The reforms not only rearranged Spain's governance of the Americas but also represented a change in attitude that permeated New Spain, including New Mexico.

After a series of government-mandated inspections, the northern frontier of New Spain was organized and called Las Provincias Internas, the Internal Provinces. Partially as a result of a 1720 military defeat of New Mexico presidio soldiers by Indian allies of the French in distant Nebraska, the viceroy took a renewed interest in his realm's northern frontier and ordered an initial inspection of the whole north. That inspection arrived in New Mexico in 1727 and would not be the last.

All this was part of a larger picture in which Spain's northern New World experience underwent a motivational change. First came the curiosity of exploration, followed by the ideal of conversion, the goal of expansion, and finally the strategy of "reduction," or moving people into consolidated settlements, under the guise of building a northern defense against foreign intrusion. This defense was built on two primary institutions: the mission and the presidio. Physical as well as social evidence of both exists in New Mexico today. Certainly the state's many missions, both active and in ruins, speak to social influence. Santa Fe's Palace of the Governors is a vestige of the original royal buildings forming the capital's plaza, or central square, and later reestablished as a royal presidio under the Bourbon Reforms.

Life in Colonial New Mexico

Life was perilous in New Mexico during the seventeenth and eighteenth centuries. People had to survive in a land distant from the "civilized" urban centers of Mexico, and only a very few New Mexicans ever traveled there. Some journeyed into Arizona and north into the Rockies or onto the Great Plains. One New Mexican may have reached the Río Espíritu Santo, the Mississippi River, in 1634 (Chávez 1992, 20).

The old goal of the empire to find a waterway through the continent changed into New Mexico's becoming a launchpad for inland exploration of North America, a constant theme throughout its colonial history. The leaders of the expeditions mostly came up from Mexico, and New Mexicans filled the ranks. (The concept of outside leadership was not unusual for the area; of the sixty-seven colonial governors, none was born in New Mexico, and all were appointed from beyond.) As the colonial period drew to a close, one New Mexican, Juan Lucero, had made as many as thirteen trips onto the plains between 1788 and 1819. By the beginning of the nineteenth century there was not a place on the plains that New Mexicans had not explored. Their stories of hardship, bravery, determination, suffering, and success are as exciting as any.

Whether "just plain folk" of New Mexico knew it or not, the world beyond influenced them. Even items such as chinaware and Mexican copies of chinaware from the Manila galleons, which carried the empire's oriental trade, came to New Mexico. In turn, the Spanish preference for fluted soup plates and cups with handles influenced Pueblo pottery. The Spanish-Moorish designs that became so popular on Saltillo serapes were adapted not only in New Mexico's Hispanic weaving designs but also in the designs of Navajo rugs and blankets. The rugs' very material, wool, came from sheep brought to New Mexico by Spanish settlers.

Along with sheep, other foodstuffs such as chicken, pork, beef, and many fruits were brought into New Mexico at this time. The Spaniards transported chile (as it is locally spelled) from Mexico to New Mexico. All this was adapted to Native foods such as corn and beans to create common *comidas* (dishes) such as *posole*, a hominy and chile based soup. New Mexico's *sopaipilla*, a deep-fried dough fritter, originated as a Moorish food in the southern Spanish region of Andalusia, from which it was introduced into New Mexico via Mexico. Although the fritter itself is not unique to New Mexico, its local name is unusual, and it became the basis for today's Navajo fry bread.

The succession of officials who came to New Mexico, from inspectors to governors, as well as priests, brought a bit of home with them. Although no formal education existed in New Mexico, the ability to read was not unusual. Books, even in sufficient quantities to qualify as libraries, came to New Mexico and were handed down from generation to generation. Fancy clothes were worn in New Mexico for special occasions, especially among the better off. Many wills and last testaments bear witness to the material items that ended up in New Mexico. Nevertheless, distance and hardship limited the quantity of such imports. The books, chinaware, and fancy clothing arrived in an environment of adobe, or mud brick, houses with leaky flat roofs, hard dirt floors, mica or leather-covered windows, and locally made, primitive furniture. Even the official residence of the governors in Santa Fe reflected New Mexico's distance from Mexico. Although a cobblestone floor was recently discovered in the old Governors' Palace, dirt or, in a fancy attempt to emulate Spain, adobes aligned in a parquet pattern served as the floor.

New Mexicans did not construct a cobblestone or paved road anywhere during the entirety of the colonial and Mexican periods. By the end of the colonial period most of the foothills around each village, including the capital, had been denuded of trees, which had been harvested for wood to burn for cooking and heating. This in turn accelerated runoff as well as periodic flooding. During the spring and summer rainstorms, the towns could get very muddy. Along with the extremes of dank and dry, the prevailing smells of livestock, burning wood, and to some extent sewage were constant. On occasion, the pleasant aroma of a mutton stew or roasting chile overwhelmed the usual smells.

No matter where a person lived in New Mexico, life was lived seasonally and agriculturally. The seasons for planting, nourishing, and harvesting dictated the work that needed to be done. The very land on which people lived had to be parceled out according to natural river patterns and the manmade patterns of irrigation ditches, called *acequias.* The ditches were cleaned before spring runoff, the water from which was allocated among the members of the ditch system. Whole communities were organized to do the necessary work. The patron saint of farming, San Isidro, became one of the most popular religious icons for a people who, as agriculturalists in a vast landscape, had close personal relationships with their saints.

The village-dwelling people of New Mexico not only had to maintain their subsistence through work but also had to be ready to defend themselves against the nomadic raiders who surrounded New Mexico. Everyone was expected to help with defense. Every adult male, beginning as a teenager, was expected to take up his meager weapons to serve in the militia. This expectation included voluntary duty on punitive expeditions in pursuit of raiding parties. Such expeditions became exceedingly dangerous and difficult after 1700, when the nomadic Indians became horsemen. Also after 1700, every expedition included Pueblo Indian allies.

Raids were a serious and common problem. More than one Pueblo village was nearly eliminated by such raids, and whole Hispanic families were wiped out. A tradition carried over from before the arrival of the Spaniards mitigated the problem somewhat. Annual trade fairs held at peripheral locations such as Pecos Pueblo, Abiquiú, and Taos brought the adversaries together for trade. One of the more important items traded was human beings, many of whom had been captured in recent raids in New Mexico. Other captives had been taken from distant tribes such as the Shoshones and Pawnees.

Native Americans who were traded into New Mexico, along with some Pueblo Indians who ended up in Hispanic society, eventually lost their original cultural identities and acquired the culture in which they lived. These people came to be called *genízaros,* and they formed a large segment of New Mexico's population. Intermarriage, if not miscegenation, between Native Americans, especially Pueblos, and Hispanos was common. Like those who originated in Spain, virtually no family avoided racial mixture. Even New Mexico's first governor, Juan de Oñate, was married to a woman whose mixed ancestry came from Moctezuma and Cortés.

Toward the end of the Spanish colonial period, Governor Juan Baptista de Anza, appointed to New Mexico as a result of the Bourbon Reforms, secured a peace with the Comanche Indians. This lasting peace gave rise to New Mexicans' trading on the plains with these powerful former enemies. New Mexican *ciboleros,* or buffalo hunters, and *comancheros,* Indian traders, lived, hunted, and did business with the Comanches. For the most part these people were *genízaros,* detribalized Indians, who had the skills to participate in both Native and Hispanic society. Their activities cemented the peace and to some extent made allies of the Comanches.

The Bourbon Reforms also resulted in an increased interest in New Mexico on the part of the faraway government. This interest took the form of troops, their salaries, and even a remake of Santa Fe's royal fort. The reforms also encouraged trade between the different regions, so for the first time New Mexican merchants took sheep, salt, and hides south to Mexico. Mexican merchants brought utilitarian goods as well as hard specie to New Mexico. No complete makeover took place in the means of exchange, but New Mexico now had coins circulating as part of its economy.

On the eve of Mexican independence and the beginning of international trade, the old Spanish colony had finally benefited from administrative attention from the south as part of an overall administrative reorganization. After more than two centuries as part of the Spanish Empire, New Mexico's people had laid the cultural foundations that would forever influence the future.

14

Juan de Oñate,
Colonizer, Governor

Rick Hendricks

As the first successful colonizer and governor of New Mexico, Juan de Oñate towers over its early colonial period. For some he is a figure worthy of magnificent equestrian statues; for others he is a cause for revulsion. Despite the controversy that now surrounds Oñate, there is no denying that the colonists he led to New Mexico initiated the Hispanic presence in the American Southwest. Most of the elements of Spanish culture arrived with Oñate and his people. One of these was the Spanish notion of town building, although a unique expression of town, characterized by widely spaced clusters of homes, came to dominate in New Mexico. The Franciscans who came with the colonists brought Roman Catholicism to the region and established missions to proselytize among the Indians.

Background and Career

Although it is frequently said that Oñate came to New Mexico from Spain, he was actually a native of the New World. Juan and his twin brother, Cristóbal, were born to Cristóbal de Oñate and Catalina de Salazar, probably around 1552, either in the city of Zacatecas or at the family's residence in Pánuco, some five miles to the north.

Juan's father had grown up in humble circumstances in the Basque province of Álava in northern Spain, but by the time Juan was born, Cristóbal de Oñate had become a wealthy and powerful man. His business partners and many of Juan's cousins, other relatives, and neighbors were all Basques. Basques tend to think of themselves as long-suffering and

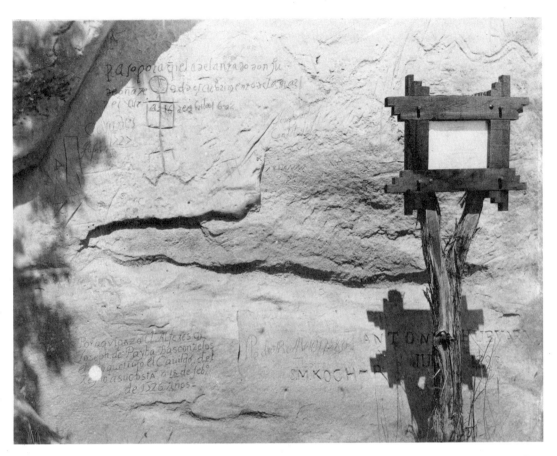

Inscription at El Morro National Monument, west-central New Mexico: "Passed by here the adelantado *Juan de Oñate from the discovery of the sea of the south on 16 April the year 1606." Photographed about 1940.*

resolute, whereas Spaniards view them as insufferably stubborn and arrogant. Juan's mother, Catalina de Salazar, was a native of Granada in southern Spain. The Oñates were men of business, principally mining, but they were also warriors. From the time Juan entered his teens he joined his father in battle against the Chichimecas, nomadic tribes of Indians who fiercely resisted the incursion of Spaniards into their territory. By his early twenties he commanded military expeditions, demonstrating his natural leadership abilities.

In 1583 the king of Spain, Phillip II, decreed that the viceroy of New Spain was to identify a man capable of leading an expedition to settle New Mexico. Several wealthy and influential men competed with Oñate for the contract. By the late summer of 1595, Oñate had prevailed and signed an agreement with the viceroy to command the expedition. He was directed to facilitate the Franciscans' conversion of the Indians. Controlling New Mexico would also protect Spain's interests in western North America against the empire's European rivals. Oñate was to locate the west coast of the American continent and search out natural harbors. He was to recruit two hundred men as colonists. All heads of household who settled in New Mexico for five years would be granted *hidalgo* status, making them members of the Spanish nobility, although at the bottom rank. Five hundred men signed on within a few weeks, and the number may have reached a thousand. Delays put a damper on the initial enthusiasm, and many gave up and left Santa Bárbara, a place four hundred miles north of Zacatecas that Oñate had chosen as the jumping-off point for the expedition.

When Oñate finally departed from Santa Bárbara, there may have been with him as many as five hundred to eight hundred men, women, and children. Several hundred individuals have been identified with some certainty (Snow 1998). After a trip of five months, the expedition of settlers and soldiers arrived at the south bank of the Rio Grande in April 1598. Once he had found a suitable place to ford, a place that came to be called El Paso (the Pass), Oñate initiated the process of staking a claim to New Mexico for the Spanish Crown. Spanish law and tradition called for elaborate ceremonies, so the travelers erected an arbor to serve as a chapel, and the Franciscans celebrated mass and delivered a sermon. Oñate read the official act of possession and affixed his signature to the document in the presence of a royal notary. Following the ceremony, there was a celebration of thanksgiving and the performance of a play one of the expedition members had written. After a few days' respite, the expedition crossed the Rio Grande and entered New Mexico.

Juan de Oñate served as governor of New Mexico for a dozen years. His tenure was tumultuous, often violent, and he became a controversial figure. He had recruited colonists largely with the promise that he would be granting Pueblo Indians to them in *encomienda,* so that the Indians would be subject to paying tribute, and through the prospect of discovering rich silver mines. It was soon apparent, however, that New Mexico held no such mineral wealth. This realization caused great disappointment among the colonists.

Some Pueblo Indians openly challenged Oñate and Spanish rule. Acoma Pueblo revolted at the end of 1599, slaying a number of Spaniards. Fear of a widespread rebellion capable of driving the Spaniards out of New Mexico led Oñate to respond by sending a force that subdued the rebels. He justified his action in the following terms (Hammond and Rey 1953, 456):

> The greatest force we possess at present to defend our friends and ourselves is the prestige of the Spanish nation, by fear of which the Indians have been kept in check. Should they lose this fear it would inevitably follow also that the teaching of the holy gospel would be hindered, which I am under obligation to prevent, as this is the main purpose for which I came. For the gospel is the complete remedy and guide for their abominable sins, some of them nefarious and against nature.

Oñate tried the Acoma prisoners and handed down harsh sentences on them. The most terrible punishment ordered was the mutilation of males over the age of twenty-five. These men were to have one foot cut off and be condemned to twenty years of servitude.

Oñate had also been instructed to explore outside of New Mexico, so in 1601 he traveled to the plains of Kansas in search of Quivira, a place visited by Vázquez de Coronado. In his absence, as many as four hundred colonists abandoned New Mexico, leaving perhaps two hundred there. In 1603 Taos Pueblo rebelled, and Oñate led a force to put down the uprising. The following year he went to what is now known as the Gulf of California in the hope of discovering the South Sea — the Pacific Ocean. These journeys meant that he was absent from the colony for long periods of time. For the settlers who remained, life was difficult. They struggled to survive shortages of food and bitter winter cold, and they came to rely on the Pueblo Indians to supply their needs. Opposition to Oñate grew, and he and his followers brutally repressed it. Finally, authorities in Mexico City began to examine the complaints against Oñate and recalled him in 1606. He returned to Zacatecas to handle his mining and financial affairs. In 1614 a new viceroy brought Oñate to trial for his actions in New Mexico. When authorities in Mexico City considered the events surrounding the rebellion of Acoma and its aftermath, Oñate was banned from New Mexico for life.

Following the death of his wife in 1619 or 1620, Oñate traveled to Spain to attempt to have himself exonerated. In 1624 he was named mining inspector for Spain. Although the position was prestigious, it carried no salary. Around June 3, 1626, Oñate entered a flooded mine at Guadalcanal to carry out an inspection. While underground in the mine, Juan de Oñate dropped dead.

After Oñate and Before the Pueblo Revolt

After Oñate left, New Mexico was marked by conflict between the Franciscans and the Spanish royal governors. Colonists chose sides, and the province moved toward civil war. Rather than abandon the enterprise entirely, the Spanish government decided to provide direct financial support and take administrative control, making New Mexico a royal colony. In the absence of mineral wealth, the Spanish Crown elected to support the Franciscans' efforts to convert the Pueblo Indians to Christianity. The Franciscans and the governors, who claimed to be acting in the economic best interests of the Spanish colonists, clashed over access to and control of Pueblo Indian labor.

Seventeenth-century New Mexico offered only limited wealth in the form of land to a handful of prominent persons who owned large tracts of irrigated farmland and pasture along the Rio Grande and its tributaries. Many of these men were *encomenderos,* persons granted the right to collect tribute from a pueblo in exchange for military protection and religious instruction. Grants of *encomienda* did not confer rights to Indian land or labor, but *encomenderos* needed Indians to work the land. Some governors and missions operated *obrajes,* or textile-making operations, which also relied on Indian labor. The Franciscans relied on Indians to tend their burgeoning livestock herds, work in mission industries, and labor in their fields.

Squabbling among the Spaniards became a sign of weakness when seen through Pueblo Indian eyes and probably inspired some Indians to rebel. Jemez Pueblo revolted in 1645, along with some Apaches. Five years later Jemez, Keres, Tiwas, and Apaches plotted an uprising that was brutally suppressed: nine leaders were hanged and many more Indians were sold into slavery for ten years.

Drought and famine marked the decade from 1665 to 1675 in New Mexico. The pace of Apache raiding on Pueblos and Spaniards quickened, and the Piro pueblos of the Salinas Basin were abandoned. The Spaniards reacted harshly to spreading rumors of rebellion, and the Franciscans became more intolerant of Pueblo religion. Suspected rebels were hanged, and the priests accused the plotters of being in league with the devil. In 1675 the governor rounded up Indians suspected of practicing witchcraft. Several of those found guilty were hanged. Among those who were punished but not executed was an Indian from San Juan Pueblo (Ohkay Owingeh) named Po'pay.

The Pueblo Revolt of 1680

A number of factors came together in August 1680 to bring about the Pueblo Revolt. The Indians resented the Spaniards for trying to stamp out their religion. Famine, disease, and increased labor demands also fueled Pueblo anger and frustration. These factors led to the Pueblos' decision to drive the Spaniards out of New Mexico. At Taos Pueblo, the charismatic Po'pay of San Juan, Luis Tupatú of Picuris, and Jaca of Taos planned a revolt in which most of the Pueblos, as well as Apaches, Navajos, and Utes, agreed to participate. The plotters chose August 13, 1680, as the day, but the Spaniards found out about the date of the coming revolt, and Po'pay advanced the schedule, leading the attack on missions and farms on August 10. Other pueblos followed within a few days as they learned of the revolt. Within a week and a half, Governor Antonio de Otermín and around a thousand colonists who had sought refuge in Santa Fe fled south as the Pueblos watched, apparently happy to let them go. Another group of survivors gathered in Isleta and then went down the Rio Grande, thinking everyone upriver was dead. By the end of September the refugees were established in El Paso.

Back up north Po'pay set about removing the remnants of Spanish civilization. Crosses and church furnishings were burned, and the names Jesús and María were banned. Indian men who had married in the church were to leave their wives and take others; those who had been baptized were to ritually cleanse themselves. Indians were to abandon the names given them at Christian baptism. Po'pay had kivas reopened and cleaned. Speaking Spanish was prohibited, as was the cultivation of Spanish-introduced crops. Po'pay's rule became oppressive; those who defied him were executed. The remarkable union of Pueblo peoples fell apart, and old animosities resurfaced. The Apaches, traditional enemies of the Pueblos, again made war on their erstwhile allies.

Otermín led an unsuccessful attempt to reconquer New Mexico in late 1681. Governors who followed made similar attempts, all of which failed. These assaults proved to the Spaniards that the Pueblos did not want them to return and showed the Pueblos how determined the Spaniards were to reconquer them. In the meantime, the New Mexico colony-in-exile barely hung on in El Paso.

Juan de Oñate: Contemporary Controversy

As he was in life, Juan de Oñate remains a controversial figure centuries after his death. In January 1998, as New Mexico began to commemorate the four-hundredth anniversary of Oñate's arrival in New Mexico in 1598, someone lopped one foot off the equestrian statue of Oñate by sculptor Reynaldo "Sonny" Rivera at the Oñate Monument Resource and Visitors Center in Alcalde, New Mexico. Situated eleven miles north of Española on Highway 68, the Oñate Center is operated by Rio Arriba County and promotes research along the Camino Real, the old royal road. Since the inauguration of the Oñate statue in 1994, it has been the focal point of demonstrations both for and against its installation. Supporters view Oñate's arrival and establishment of the colony of New Mexico as a major accomplishment in the spread of civilization across North America. Opponents consider the statue an insult to the memory of Native Americans who suffered under Spanish rule (Nieto-Phillips 2004, 210–11). The act of protest in severing one of the statue's booted feet recalled Oñate's sentence of mutilation for Acoma Indians in 1599.

Another Oñate statue, this one by El Paso, Texas, artist John Sherrill Houser, was also the subject of controversy for most of the nine years required to make it (Leyva 2007). This statue is the second in a planned series of public sculptures for El Paso known as the XII Travelers Memorial of the Southwest. In 1992 the El Paso City Council commissioned Houser to create the first two pieces and selected the historical figures to be depicted. The first statue, depicting Fray García de San Francisco, the founder of El Paso del Norte in 1659, was installed in downtown El Paso in 1996. The second statue, a forty-two-foot bronze purported to be the largest equestrian statue in the world, was originally to depict Juan de Oñate. In 2003, at the height of the local controversy in El Paso, the city council reached the decision to rename the piece *The Equestrian*. It was installed on October 31, 2006, and officially unveiled at the El Paso International Airport on April 21, 2007.

15

Popay's Leadership: A Pueblo Perspective on the 1680 Revolt

Alfonso Ortiz (1980)

In December of 1681 a small Spanish military reconnaissance ventured up the Rio Grande to a point just north of Cochití Pueblo. They were acting on the orders of Governor Otermín, who wanted to assess the Spaniards' chances for taking back New Mexico from the Pueblo people, who had rebelled successfully the year before. At this place near Cochití the Spanish soldiers encountered approximately 150 Pueblo warriors, who were obviously ready to fight. When the lieutenant in charge of the Spanish party shouted to the Pueblo warriors his concern for their souls, it is recorded that the Pueblo warriors shouted back: "You are a lot of hypocrites!"

This encounter just about sums up why the Pueblo people revolted in August of 1680. Throughout the seventeenth century prior to 1680, the Spaniards had treated the Pueblo people with consummate arrogance and complete intolerance. On the one hand the Spanish friars preached to the Pueblos about equality, brotherhood, and Christian love, while on the other Spanish soldiers brutally attempted to stamp out Pueblo religious practices. Indeed, nothing that the Pueblo people believed or practiced of an indigenous nature was called anything but devil-worship by the Spaniards. Moreover, no ordinary Pueblo Indian in seventeenth-century New Mexico could own a horse or a gun. This prohibition helps to explain how 2,500 Spaniards could control more than 16,000 Pueblo Indians. Quite reasonably, the Pueblo people saw nothing brotherly or equal about this state of affairs, and so they revolted. Hence, the Pueblo warriors who shouted back defiantly to the Spanish

*Santa Clara shield (left) and Spanish shield (*adarga)*, buffalo hide, New Mexico, late eighteenth century. Photograph by Blair Clark.*

soldiers near Cochití in 1681 were likely echoing the sentiments of all the Pueblo people of New Mexico and Arizona at that time.

One can usefully approach the events of the Revolt and its aftermath from any one of several perspectives, but since there is very little disagreement in enlightened modern scholarly circles about what happened, how it happened, and even why it happened, I shall not repeat the well-known details. Rather, I shall concentrate here on Pueblo motivations and meanings by focusing on the activities and traditional role of the much misunderstood Popay of San Juan, the prime instigator of the Revolt.

What of Popay, the man considered by his contemporaries and later historical commentators alike as the individual most responsible for focusing general Pueblo attention on a revolution, and then planning it through to its occurrence? What sort of man was he? What was his actual role in the Revolt likely to have been? Can anything be added three hundred years after the Revolt to our understanding of it? Let me take these questions in order.

First, Popay's image has improved a good deal since Francisco Xavier, secretary of government and of war for the province of New Mexico, branded him a sorcerer and persecuted him and other native religious leaders for the alleged practice of sorcery. Later historians have, with greater concern for historical objectivity and truth, but with no greater insight into the inner workings of Tewa culture, elevated Popay from sorceror to medicine man. But this is still not adequate when Popay is viewed from a Tewa perspective, given the time in which he lived. There are a few clues as to his actual place in Tewa society, in history, and in the meaning he had for his contemporaries. One clue has to do with the leader's name, considered in two aspects.

In the first aspect, that he has no Christian name, but was simply known as Popé or El Popé, suggests by itself that he was an ardent nativist. In fact, he was the only leader of the Revolt from the Christianized Pueblos who was known only by his native name, and this has to mean something. Whether he once had a Christian name as well and discarded it in defiance of the Church or of the Spaniards generally is not knowable from the published documents of the period. But the fact of Popay's later open advocacy of a general Pueblo return to native ways does indicate that he himself had rejected his baptismal name, the Church, and Spanish culture generally by the time his name first began to appear in the documents.

A careful consideration of Popay's name in a purely Tewa sense is also essential to ferreting out another understanding of possibly great significance. The name, which was always rendered by the Spaniards as Popé or Popeh, was very likely the Tewa generic term "ripe cultigens," rather than "squash mountain" or "red moon," the other possibilities suggested by modern commentators. Squash mountain, though a perfectly appropriate Tewa name — one carried by a man in San Ildefonso into the last quarter of the twentieth century — would have to be rendered *po ping* by at least some Spaniards, because the Tewa term for mountain concludes with that *-ing* sound. Yet, nowhere in the documents is Popay's name so rendered. The other possibility, *po pi*, "red moon," while closer in spelling to the Spanish renderings, is actually illogical since the Tewa people do not ordinarily think of the moon as red. But even without extending twentieth century logic back into the 1600s one has to expect that at least some Spaniards would have rendered *popé* as *po pi*, since the *-i* sound is so clear when the words "moon red," (the correct form) are uttered in Tewa.

The reason I go into this exercise in Tewa linguistics is to make the following case: If we accept my version of the meaning of Popay's name ("ripe cultigens") some other inferences become possible. One is that because the name is generic and, therefore, potent, it could not be conferred on an infant. Given the Tewa scheme of things about naming, so potent a name had to be earned, and the only appropriate channel through which one could earn such a name is through religious service after adulthood. Another consideration is that, because the term "ripe cultigens" refers to things preeminently of the summer, Popay was very likely a member of the summer moiety, and of the summer priesthood, perhaps even the chief priest.

In traditional Tewa thought, concepts and terms which refer to important aspects or phenomena of the major seasons, winter and summer, are used as names and in other symbolic ways by the winter and summer moieties, as they seem appropriate. This has been especially true of the paradigmatic things of each major season — and nothing can be more paradigmatic of the summer than the image of ripe cultigens gathered together, as in a cornucopia.

Projecting the preceding back out into history — and still assuming for the sake of argument that I am right thus far — some heretofore puzzling points from the period of the Revolt assume new meaning. One has to do with the sordid incident in 1675, in which then Governor Treviño ordered forty-seven Pueblo religious leaders rounded up and publicly flogged in Santa Fe, one of them being Popay. When they were incarcerated as well, a large delegation of "Christian Indians" marched into Santa Fe from the Tewa Pueblos, and demanded the religious leaders be released. Since they were Tewa, rather than from some other Pueblo group, one may assume that their primary concern was for the safety of Popay and the other Tewa religious leaders in the group. If Popay was a priest of the summer moiety he would have been *that important* to his people, and one can then better understand their action and their resolve in confronting the Spanish governor. Treviño was obviously impressed by their determination, for he released the religious leaders — the only time prior to the Revolt itself that a Spanish governor had caved in to native demands on a major issue.

This action by the Tewa people should have signaled something to the Spaniards about Popay's stature with his people, and it might have if they had not been so sure of the absolute rightness of their way of life and of their control. But the incident does give us a glimpse, five years before the Revolt itself, of how it could be that Popay would come to play such a prominent role in planning and organizing the events of 1680. And if what is presented here about Popay's likely identity as a revered Tewa is true, it makes it more understandable to us why he was such a credible instigator, why he was eventually believed and deferred to across two dozen communities speaking six different languages and sprawled out over a distance of nearly 400 miles, from Taos at one end to the Hopi villages at the other.

While planning the Revolt from a kiva in Taos, Popay was said (by some Indian declarants before the Spaniards) to be drawing guidance from three spirits (usually rendered "demons" by the intolerant Spaniards) who appeared to him in the kiva with instructions as to what he must do. These spirits, who allegedly came from the "Lake of Copala," were called *Tilini*, *Tleume*, and *Caudi*. I cannot find a remembered or modern version of the last two, but *Tilini* is clearly the Tewa culture hero *Tinini Povi*, or "Olivella Flower Shell Youth," one of the most revered figures in Tewa tradition. Hence, rather than invoking demons which "emitted fire from their extremities," as Spanish versions of the Indians' declarations indicate, Popay was actually doing a very wise and very traditional Pueblo thing: invoking sacred culture heroes as his ultimate rationale and guides for the rebellion he was planning.

I would even suspect that the other two spirits, who have no modern Tewa linguistic analogues, were not even Tewa at all, but perhaps Tiwa and Keresan, or at least spirits of Pueblo traditions other than the Tewa. This will have to be investigated further. If true, this makes Popay an even wiser leader and planner than even the most generous of commentators of his leadership have conceded. It also marks him almost indisputably as a religious leader, and a major one, for one among the Tewa who would invoke the most potent spiritual guides for an undertaking must first learn and earn the right to do so. And, if the evidence from the past century of research on Tewa culture is any guide, no war chief or young firebrand would be recognized to have that right. Indeed, just the very fact that Popay was making plans and directing things from a kiva points to the likelihood of his being a religious leader.

There is yet further evidence of the religious nature of the Revolt and of its inspiration. Popay and other leaders of the Revolt were also invoking a deity universal to the Pueblos, albeit one known by a name of differing spelling depending on the particular Pueblo language in which it is given. Hence, when Governor Otermín questioned three particular Pueblo captives, each speaking a different language, about the causes of the rebellion and of its leaders, he received the following replies. A *Tewa* captive asserted that the leader of the Revolt was "*Po-he-yemu*," and that he lived in the northern mountains. A *Keresan* captive said the leader was "*Payastimo*," and when asked where this "Payastimo" lived, he pointed to the mountains. A *Towa* man also said the leader was "*Paya tiabo*," and that he lived in the mountains. The point here is that all three were referring to the same deity, and not to a real man who lived in the mountains and who led the Revolt. "Po-he-yemu," by whatever name, was and is a spiritual guide who was and is invoked by Pueblo religious leaders on behalf of their people in times of need. The Revolt was such a time of need, and so "Po-he-yemu" was invoked to justify and to guide the actions of the Pueblo leaders. The correct Tewa name for this deity is *P'ose yemu*, and it translates literally as "mist-scattering," or more freely as "he who scatters mist before him."

Two other historical puzzles regarding Popay's actions before and during the Revolt will have to be thought over again carefully if the foregoing interpretation of his position in San Juan is substantially correct. First, Popay has been said to have killed his son-in-law, Nicolas Bua, or at least to have had him killed because Bua was a Spanish sympathizer who might divulge his anti-Spanish activities to the Spaniards. If Popay was a chief religious leader, as I contend, he could not have taken life — any kind of life — or knowingly participated in its taking. Chief religious leaders throughout the Pueblos have, as far back as the ethnographic and historical record goes on them, foresworn the taking of any kind of life as a condition of their ascension to religious leadership. Such men could not fulfill their charge of working for peace, harmony, continuity of tradition, and the efflorescence of life if they were also capable of taking life. This is why, unto modern times, the people of each Pueblo hunt for the religious leaders, and why young men in particular sow and harvest for the chief priests.

The other puzzle is multi-faceted and more complex. It has to do with the fact that no one has ever been able to say definitively what Popay was *doing* during the Revolt itself, nor how he lived afterwards until his death *circa* 1688. Despite the fact that at least one writer has rather fancifully imagined Popay surveying his troops from the top of some hill overlooking Santa Fe during the siege like an Indian Napoleon, those who know even a little bit about Indian military leadership in aboriginal America are aware that by the very nature of Pueblo military leadership any leader who would stand on a hill while his men fought would soon be dodging shots from his own men. Pueblo military leaders *led*. They did not plot abstract military strategy from hilltops while battles raged below them.

But even this observation just begs the point, which is that if Popay were a major religious leader he would have been doing what such people do while battles rage. He would have been in a kiva (whether at San Juan or Taos does not matter), praying, meditating, and sacrificing for the success of the efforts of the younger men in battle. Popay planned the Revolt from the kiva at Taos, and, given his position, he could execute it no other way — reports of his joining the siege of Santa Fe with the northern army notwithstanding. Pueblo religious leaders lead by prayerful retreat and sacrifice, not by anger or confrontation, and if this has been true during the past century, it was likely even more true in 1680.

Popay's life after the Revolt until his death sometime before the Spanish reconquest is beclouded because there exist no eyewitness reports by people close to him after the Spanish expulsion. If he participated in the burning of Spanish churches and church articles, as some stated, it would not undermine my understanding of him as a religious leader. Even a two hour perusal of the primary documents of the Revolt era would help any objective person understand just why it was that the Pueblos wanted so desperately to have the land cleansed of the Spaniards and their priests, and of everything which reminded of the Spanish religion. Indeed, the frequency of claims by Pueblo people during the Revolt and its aftermath that the devil was helping them in their efforts to expel the god of the Spaniards underscores the extent to which they felt oppressed by the Church. It was not likely simple mockery in which they were indulging, for anything which was defined as opposing the wishes of the Christian god would no doubt have been preferable to them.

But if Popay did try to set himself up as the leader of all of the Pueblos after the Revolt in a non-religious sense, as others have claimed, such an act on Popay's part would indicate that he had left his priestly leadership role at San Juan behind him, not necessarily that he never had such a role. After all, he did move to Taos to plan the Revolt, and it is within the realm of responsible conjecture that he would see himself being needed in a wider leadership role to ensure the long-term success of the Revolt. In any case, we really cannot say for sure what Popay's life was like after 1680 from the published documents, and he was dead before the Spanish resettlement in 1693.

If Popay himself was not likely a war leader, it was very likely, even necessary, that many of those who came to see him at Taos were. Pueblo religious leaders may interpret the signs about the earth for the people, and thereby inspire. They may even help plan something they can define as cleansing and purifying the earth, but they cannot execute the plans if they involve military action. This is where the war chiefs come in, for they are the ones who actually lead and direct the fighting. Judging by the many well-coordinated movements of Pueblo warriors (both from particular Pueblos and as parts of larger liberating armies during the Revolt), the Pueblos were well led.

The humbling lesson the Spaniards learned from the Pueblo Revolt, although they might not have realized it immediately, was that they could not remain absolutely "Spanish" if they were to learn to live in peace in the great valley of the Rio Grande and in the province of New Mexico. That is to say, they had to give up their arrogance toward nature and toward indigenous life forms and cultures, and they had to give up their absolute intolerance toward religious beliefs and practices other than their variant of Roman Catholicism. Other invaders have discovered, at the end, that they too had to learn of the spirit of place and of how to belong from those who already had roots and a sense of being at one with the land.

During the eighteenth century and beyond in New Mexico the Spaniards of Europe learned to *belong*, to the extent that they were able to overcome their attitude of fear and contempt toward indigenous institutions and beliefs.

Indeed, the unique cultural mosaic that has existed in New Mexico since the mid-nineteenth century owes its existence to the fact that, during the eighteenth century, the increasingly native Hispanics and the undeniably hispanicized Pueblo peoples learned to live and let live. They learned to respect one another as brothers and sisters, and even to become friends and religious kinsmen, *compadres* and *comadres*. This is only one aspect, albeit the most general, of the legacy of the Pueblo Revolt of 1680.

For the Pueblo people specifically, the greatest legacy of the Revolt of their ancestors has been that they have been able to endure with their cultural integrity intact, free to speak their native languages and to perform their ancient dances. Because of a desperate, despair-born gamble on the part of the Pueblo people of 1680, their descendants have lived to find that their well-being and continued cultural integrity is regarded as essential to the well-being of all of New Mexico and of the Southwest. A successful revolution, it seems to me, can leave no greater legacy than this.

Oil-on-canvas portrait of don Diego José de Vargas Zapata y Luján Ponce de León (1640–1710), painted by Manuel Cabrera Kabana after an original in Spain dating to the 1660s. Photograph by Blair Clark.

16

Diego de Vargas,
Reconqueror, Governor

Rick Hendricks

No other figure dominates the historical landscape of Spanish colonial New Mexico in the way its reconqueror and recolonizer does. The Pueblo Indians hate him for his role in the battles against their ancestors in the 1690s, yet an annual festival in Santa Fe joyously commemorates his reconquest of New Mexico. Namesake of schools and shopping malls throughout the state, Diego de Vargas, ironically, never wanted to come to New Mexico and was always eager to leave.

Background and Career

Baptized on November 8, 1643, in the church of San Luis in Madrid, Vargas received from his mother, María Margarita Contreras y Arraíz, the name Diego José de Vargas Zapata Luján Ponce de León y Contreras. He was a member of the middling nobility, content with his life in Spain. In 1664 he married Beatriz Pimentel de Prado Vélez de Olazábal in the two families' summer home of Torrelaguna, thirty miles north of the Spanish capital. There is every indication that he might never have come to the New World in 1672 had he not needed to settle the estate of his father, Alonso de Vargas, who had died in the royal service in Guatemala. Vargas served in a number of minor posts in New Spain before purchasing the governorship of New Mexico in 1688 for a five-year term.

Diego de Vargas was a man of the past. He came to New Mexico in search of mineral wealth — a veritable mountain of silver. He wanted to cloak himself in glory by regaining territory lost to the Spanish Crown for more than a decade. He also hoped to make a place for himself in heaven by delivering thousands of Pueblo converts to Catholicism.

In early 1691 he took up the post in El Paso, but he was unable to turn his attention northward for more than a year while he campaigned in neighboring provinces to the south and prepared for the reconquest of New Mexico. Writing to his son-in-law, Ignacio López de Zárate, on April 9, 1692, Vargas revealed his love for his family and another motive for his decision to become a provincial governor: the need to settle the matter of his daughter's dowry.

> How pleasant to write again of the constant affection I owe you. I contemplate the comfort of having my heart's treasures, my beloved children, protected. Not only is Your Lordship their brother-in-law, but also their true father. They live very securely under your wing. You can be certain that you will always find in me attention and ready affection for all that is dear to me. I wish I had the good fortune of showing you their depth. Out of such consideration, I could have done no more than to have exiled myself to this kingdom, at the ends of the earth and remote beyond compare. From its distance, I seek the means to fulfill my wish of paying Your Lordship the dowry once and for all. (Kessell 1989, 167–68)

Vargas also revealed his true feelings about New Mexico, a place he considered at the end of the Earth. He told López de Zárate of his plan to launch the reconquest of New Mexico on St. Lawrence's Day, August 10, 1692. He had chosen that day because it was the twelfth anniversary of the Pueblo Revolt, an event that the former New Mexicans living in El Paso vengefully recalled every year. A week later, Governor Vargas and his troops crossed the Rio Grande and began the initial phase of the reconquest, a ritual repossession and armed reconnaissance of the pueblos. The colonists fleeing the Pueblo Revolt in 1680 had carried Oñate's original royal standard out of New Mexico; Vargas returned the banner to Santa Fe. By mid-December 1692, Vargas and his men were back in El Paso. From there he launched a recolonizing expedition in October of the following year. Vargas parlayed his fame as reconqueror into a title of Spanish nobility, that of Marqués de la Nava de Barcinas.

In contrast to the ceremonial tour of the pueblos of 1692, the recolonizing expedition of 1693 was marked by bitter warfare between the advancing Spaniards and the Pueblo Indians. By bringing colonists, the Spaniards were obviously coming to stay, and the Pueblos resisted their advance.

The Pueblo Revolt of 1680 had destroyed much of the Spanish New Mexico that Juan de Oñate and his colonists had constructed in the late sixteenth and early seventeenth centuries, but remnants of the colony held on for a dozen years in El Paso. The most enduring aspect of the colony was the families who returned to New Mexico with Vargas in 1693. Two other groups of colonists joined them in New Mexico, one from Mexico City and Puebla and another from the Zacatecas area. Vargas tried to recruit colonists who would build a stable colony. Those who enrolled in Mexico City came largely from the artisan class, and the settlers drawn from the mining areas around Zacatecas were primarily laborers and farmers. These people initiated cottage industries based on their crafts and became small farmers. After these two large movements of people, New Mexico never experienced another large influx of settlers from the south. People who later found their way to the colony came in very small groups.

Vargas spent most of his first term as governor of the province of New Mexico, from 1691 to 1697, fighting a protracted war against the Pueblo Indians. During 1693 and 1694 his army fought a series of pitched battles against various pueblos, and the colony's survival hung in the balance. A second Pueblo revolt erupted in 1696, which threatened the Spanish presence in New Mexico. After another series of sieges and battles, often against fortified defensive positions atop mesas, the Spaniards put down the rebellion.

In 1697 Pedro Rodríguez Cubero replaced Vargas as governor of New Mexico. In anticipation of a reappointment, Vargas remained in Santa Fe and became involved in a bitter contest with the *cabildo,* the municipal council, of Santa Fe and with his successor, Rodríguez Cubero. The reality of life in New Mexico had fallen short of the expectations of many colonists. Hundreds deeply resented the arrogant Spaniard, Governor Vargas, and testified in the *cabildo*'s suit against him, alleging malfeasance and bad government. The legal wrangling by the parties' agents before authorities in Mexico City lasted for years. Viceregal authorities eventually exonerated Vargas of all charges. He gained the hoped-for reappointment to the governorship of New Mexico and began his second term in 1703. He died in March 1704 while campaigning against Apaches, probably of dysentery.

After Vargas

The Vargas era was the beginning of the ongoing presence of Hispanos in New Mexico. Never again after Vargas would the colony be threatened as it had been during the period before his arrival and during his years of service. Many families who came with Vargas or who were recruited by his lieutenants have descendants still living in New Mexico, an amazing continuity of people and place. In addition, the people who came in the Vargas era account for the origins of much of the Hispanic population of Colorado and for families in many other parts of the United States and northern Mexico. The culture and traditions that the founding families carried with them to New Mexico are as alive as they were more than four centuries ago. The names of their descendants fill the telephone directories of New Mexico, where Pueblos and Spaniards remained at relative peace after the conclusion of the second Pueblo revolt in 1696.

Vargas and Santa Fe Fiesta

Diego de Vargas is inextricably linked to a public celebration held every September in Santa Fe. Fiesta celebrates Vargas's entry into Santa Fe on September 4, 1692. The first Fiesta was proclaimed in 1712 by the governor of New Mexico at the time, José Chacón Medina Salazar y Villaseñor, the Marqués de la Peñuela, at the behest of one of Vargas's most trusted lieutenants, Juan Páez Hurtado. Early Fiestas were largely religious, consisting of church services and a procession of the image of the Virgin Mary in the advocation of Our Lady of the Rosary (and Our Lady of the Assumption), known in New Mexico as La Conquistadora. La Conquistadora was brought to New Mexico in 1625, carried out in 1680 at the time of the Pueblo Revolt, and returned by Vargas in 1693. Although the historical record is incomplete, it seems certain that the processions were halted at some point later in the eighteenth century and resumed by 1770. From that time on, processions of La Conquistadora have continued uninterrupted (Wilson 1997, 181–84).

In the late nineteenth century, Fiesta was associated with occasional trade fairs held to attract settlement and tourism to New Mexico (Horton 2001). The 1911 Vargas pageant, which was put on by the Alianza Hispano-Americano, was fueled by a nationwide craze for historical pageants (Wilson 1997, 195–96). According to Chris Wilson (1997, 207–8):

> By the late 1920s, Vargas's "peaceful" reconquest of 1692 had emerged as the sole focus of the annual Fiesta pageant. The selection of this episode rather than the bloody reconquest of 1693 (which had been reenacted in 1883, 1912, 1922, and 1924) complemented the emerging public rhetoric of tricultural harmony. Starting in 1920, the Fiesta opened with a reading of the 1712 fiesta proclamation of "Vespers, Mass, sermon, and procession through the Main Plaza" to commemorate de Vargas's 1692 conquest. The most direct descendant of this proclamation — the Conquistadora processions — had occurred in June since the 1700s. The proclamation, nevertheless, gave the modern Fiesta a stamp of historical continuity that few other communities could match. The proclamation also accounts for the preeminence of Vargas rather than [Governor Pedro de] Peralta, who founded Santa Fe in 1610. By focusing solely on the Spanish reconquest, the pageant became more an expression of ethnic than community-wide identity.

La Conquistadora provoked controversy in 1990 and 1991. As the five-hundredth anniversary of Christopher Columbus's voyages to the Americas neared, new protests erupted. Native Americans opposed the use of title of the image, which celebrated their military subjugation by the Spaniards. Hispanos countered that her title referred to "Our Lady of Conquering Love" and to Mary's winning of souls for Christianity. In July 1992 Archbishop Robert F. Sánchez tried to appease all parties by announcing that the image would henceforth be known as La Conquistadora, "Our Lady of Peace" (Wilson 1997, 230).

As for Vargas, he finally got his statue. Sculptor Donna Quastoff's life-size bronze statue commemorating his deeds was dedicated on June 3, 2007, in Cathedral Park in Santa Fe. Presiding at the unveiling ceremony was Gilbert Romero, president of the Caballeros de Vargas, a religious and civic organization dedicated to preserving the memory of Diego de Vargas, which led the fund-raising campaign for the statue.

Mission ruin at Pecos Pueblo National Monument, north-central New Mexico, about 1925–45. Photograph by T. Harmon Parkhurst.

17

The Memorable Visitation of Bishop Pedro Tamarón, 1760

John L. Kessell

Was there no other way? The raft looked flimsy. The Río del Norte — today's Rio Grande — swollen by the late spring run-off, was at full flow, an expanse of roiling, reddish-brown water between the bishop and the desert vegetation visible on the far side. Well aware of quicksand, old hands in El Paso warned that the river was always dangerous "because of its sandy and turbulent bottom."

A tourist at heart, Dr. Pedro Tamarón y Romeral, sixty-some years old and the last bishop of Durango to conduct a visitation of colonial New Mexico, prayed for a safe crossing. Tamarón recalled in his journal for May 6, 1760: "The loads, mules, horses, muleteers, one hundred live sheep for food in the uninhabited areas, and other supplies were taken across." His attendants escorted the prelate to the water's edge early next morning. "It was very high and overflowing....When I boarded the raft, the river was covered by Indian swimmers, some pulling lines, others making them fast. I made a happy crossing to the other side" (Adams 1954, 36, 40).

Eighty years earlier, vigorous Fray Francisco de Ayeta, trying to get provisions to refugees streaming south away from the Pueblo Revolt, had driven a six-span mule team and heavily loaded freight wagon into the rushing water just above El Paso, got stuck, and had to be rescued by swimmers who carried him to shore (Hackett and Shelby 1940, 1: cv). Whether or not Tamarón knew about Ayeta's close call, the bishop gave thanks and waited on the far bank while two dismantled vehicles were brought across and reassembled. Called *quitrines* in Spain, *volantes* in the Americas, these were light, open carriages with two tall wheels, a non-folding top, and long shafts on either side of a single horse or mule.

Four days north of El Paso, at the "dread site of Robledo," Tamarón prayed that smoke seen in the nearby sierra did not signal an Apache attack. This time, thank God, it was a forest fire. At the *paraje,* or campsite, of San Diego, he watched water barrels being filled from the river for a ninety-mile dry stretch known as the Jornada del Muerto — the Journey of Death. Once safely through it, the bishop noted "the livestock were so thirsty that they ran" to reach the river again.

Tamarón's party numbered sixty-four men in all, most of them armed. Dressed for the road in black cassock, the bishop sat side-by-side in one of the *volantes* with Franciscan superior Jacobo de Castro, who wore the distinctive blue habit of the Mexican province. The two men conversed amiably but with a certain restraint. For more than a century, New Mexico's Franciscans had resisted efforts by bishops of Durango to impose episcopal jurisdiction over the remote colony.

As the column drew even with the deserted pueblo of Socorro on the opposite bank, the two churchmen shared an unplanned intimacy. The going was rough. Ravines had sheared off the Camino Real, the royal roadway. All of a sudden, in the bishop's words, "the volante in which I and the Father Custos were riding suffered a severe upset. The Father Custos fell from the side and received a blow which hurt him. I escaped injury, because I fell on him. Therefore I took a horse and continued my journey on it" (Adams 1954, 41, 42).

Just south of Santo Domingo Pueblo the episcopal cavalcade met a welcoming committee from Santa Fe led by Governor Francisco Marín del Valle, who had descended the long downhill stretch called La Bajada from the capital in his two-seated coach. After dinner the governor rode a horse back to Santa Fe, leaving Tamarón his carriage.

In the coming weeks the bishop and his escort, defying the heat of mid-June, traveled to most of the New Mexico pueblos, likely on horseback. San Felipe, however, lay on the river's west bank. At a narrows just north of the pueblo, the bishop found himself being helped into "a good canoe" for the crossing (Adams 1954, 65–66).

A month later, he was back in El Paso. Another full year on the road to Durango lay ahead of him, for his diocese was immense. Preparing himself physically and spiritually for the Camino Real southward, naturally the bishop prayed.

Unknown to him, at the easternmost pueblo, Pecos, Bishop Tamarón had made a lasting impression. Solidly built, square-jawed and solemn, yet curiously dwarfed by his own vestments, he had processed with great dignity, planting the butt end of his pastoral staff with every other step and moving so smoothly that the high-peaked miter he wore did not bob up and down but seemed instead to float on an even plane.

On Monday, May 26, 1760, a date his secretary recorded in the mission register, the resplendent bishop administered confirmation to 192 Pecos Indians, signing a cross with holy oil on the forehead of each and intoning in Latin: "I confirm thee with the chrism of salvation, in the name of the Father, and of the Son, and of the Holy Spirit." The repetition was monotonous. Unnoticed in the shadows of the cavernous, dimly lit church, one of the pueblo's principal men, Agustín Guichí, a carpenter and likely the head of a Pecos clown society, studied the prelate's every move, his clothing, his attendants, his gestures (Kessell 1979, 336, 339–41).

The following September, once the harvest was in, Guichí called on his memory. Long a feature of Pueblo tradition, ritual clowns — through their antics of gluttony, obscenity, sex-role reversal, and extreme individuality, along with burlesques of outsiders — reinforced the boundaries of Pueblo culture (Hieb 1972). Now the resourceful Pecos leader saw to every detail. He designed and cut out episcopal vestments, fashioning the miter of parchment stained white. A bent reed became his staff. Mateo Cru, another Pecos, dressed up as the Franciscan superior while a third man painted himself black to play the bishop's valet. Then, "to the accompaniment of a muffled drum and loud huzzas," a colorful, exuberant chorus led the three actors, each astride a burro, into the pueblo's main plaza, where the sham bishop, with scrupulous sobriety, passed between two rows of kneeling women, bestowing his blessings upon them.

The burlesque lasted three days. Bishop Guichí reconfirmed his people, lining them up, marking a cross with water on the forehead of each, then cuffing them to symbolize the laying on of hands. Next day at a comic mass he distributed bits of tortillas as altar bread.

Finally, well pleased by the festivities, Agustín Guichí withdrew to his plot of corn and sat down under a juniper tree. His program had gone well. Late in the afternoon, as it began to get dark, he was still sitting there when a bear attacked him, clawing his scalp where the miter had rested and tearing his right hand to pieces. Then, strangely, the bear turned away and ambled back toward the mountains. Before he died, Agustín Guichí repented, exhorting his brother and sons never to repeat his grave sin.

When the real bishop heard the story, he had it published. To Bishop Tamarón, the message was clear. This was no coincidence. God's swift punishment of Agustín Guichí served as a warning to all the Pueblo Indians to honor "His Holy Church and her ministers" (Adams 1954, 50–53).

Guichí's ill-fated parody broadcast to succeeding generations another, more enduring message. Neither oppressive Spaniards, nor marauding nomads, nor smallpox, nor vicious strife among them — not even the repeated decimation of their race — had broken the spirit of the Pueblo peoples.

Jim Hena, governor of Tesuque Pueblo, explaining canes of office to his family, about 1966. Photograph by Bill Jack Rogers.

18

The Silver-Crowned Canes of Pueblo Office

Joe S. Sando (1992)

Following the institution of the Spanish form of government among the Pueblos, each governor received a silver-crowned cane of office. Like the American symbol of justice represented by the blindfolded lady holding a balancing scale, the canes given to the pueblo governors are symbols of justice and leadership. A Christian cross is engraved on the head of the cane, indicating that the cane had the blessing of the Catholic church, and its owner had the support of the Spanish Crown. The Franciscan priests apparently originated the giving of canes, taking as their watchword, "The cane and staff to be their comfort and strength, and their token against all enemies," from Exodus 4 and Numbers 17. But several versions exist of the origin of the Spanish canes.

Some historians write that Governor Juan de Oñate issued the canes when he met with the Pueblo leaders at the time of his arrival, accompanied by the original colonists. Another version, according to Chester A. Faris, a former Bureau of Indian Affairs employee, is that the king of Spain, in the 1620s, issued a royal decree for each pueblo, at the close of the calendar year, to choose by popular vote their civil officials. Each elected official was presented with a cane to indicate his authority. When each pueblo had selected its succeeding governor, the cane was handed over to the new governor in appropriate ceremonies.

When Mexico won independence from Spain, sovereignty was established by the new government, and new canes, silver-crowned, were presented to the pueblos. They were again authorized to function in line with previous custom. Today, these Mexican canes (or staffs) are held by the pueblo lieutenant governors.

Another cane is held in the possession of each pueblo governor. It is the Abraham Lincoln cane, which was presented to each pueblo governor in recognition of his authority under the United States Government.

The story of the Lincoln canes is this: In November 1863, Dr. Michael Steck of Pennsylvania, superintendent of the Territorial Indian Service, was called to Washington. While he was there, President Lincoln decided on belated recognition of the Pueblo Indians. Seventeen years had passed since General Kearny had taken control of the Territory of New Mexico for the United States.

Lincoln ordered silver-crowned canes, one for each pueblo. Inscribed on each cane was the name of the pueblo, the year 1863, and the signature of the president, "A. Lincoln." These canes were symbols of the new sovereignty, extending continued authority for the Pueblo form of government.

Dr. Steck returned to the Territory, bringing with him several of the pueblo land patents, and a Lincoln cane for each of the pueblo governors, to be used by them according to their custom and to be passed on to their successors.

A third cane was presented to the governors by New Mexico State Governor Bruce King during his second term in 1980. This cane was presented in order to reaffirm the sovereignty of the pueblo governments. And in September 1987, King Juan Carlos of Spain, while visiting New Mexico, gave a second Spanish cane to the governors. Now each governor has four canes. Thus for more than three centuries there has been continued recognition of Native American government — the most enduring local government in America.

Today, the pueblo governor with his canes is always in evidence at fiestas or special gatherings of the pueblo leaders. In the home of a governor, one can see all the canes prominently displayed. And it is still the tradition to have all the canes of the higher civil officials blessed on January 6, the feast day of the Three Kings.

The pueblo canes are symbols to the people that all power and authority exist in their own form of government; that their government is responsible to the people; and that they owe allegiance to the United States of America. On the other hand, the canes are also symbols of the United States Government's responsibilities for and trusteeship of the pueblos.

PART FOUR

LINKING NATIONS

During the quarter-century in which New Mexico "remained an integral, if remote and often beleaguered part of the vast region of New Spain that gained its independence" and became the Mexican Republic in 1821, New Mexicans observed celebrations on September 16 for Mexico's "official Independence Day, much the way the Fourth of July is celebrated in the United States." The first news of Mexican independence after the Treaty of Cordova was signed on August 24, 1821, reached Governor Facundo Melgares in Santa Fe by September 17, 1821 (Tórrez). As had been the case since the sixteenth century, word came via the Camino Real de Tierra Adentro (royal road of the interior land), the 310-mile route between Santa Fe and El Paso and thence through Chihuahua and Durango into Mexico City, for a total of 1,450 miles, which "served as the primary route of trade, supply, transportation, and communication between New Mexico...and the northern provinces of New Spain and Mexico City" (Jones).

Just two months later in Santa Fe, on November 17, Governor Melgares welcomed Missouri businessman William Becknell, leader of the *seis Americanos* (six Americans) whom don Pedro Ignacio Gallego had accidentally met "shortly after three o'clock on a Tuesday afternoon, November 13, 1821,...at Puertocito de la Piedra Lumbre, a small gap in the foothills of the Sangre de Cristo Mountains known today as Kearny Gap." This chance encounter, "one of the major events in New Mexico history,...led to the opening of the Santa Fe Trail and the invasion of New Mexico by the United States Army in

1846." Some eight hundred to a thousand miles long — depending on whether one traveled via the shorter Cimarron Cutoff or the longer Mountain Branch — the Santa Fe Trail, "from Becknell's trip in 1821 until it was overtaken by the completion of the Atchison, Topeka and Santa Fe Railroad into New Mexico in 1880, was always a commercial route, a trail traveled by businessmen seeking profits" (Olsen). The booming nineteenth-century commerce and communication between Missouri and Mexico City is epitomized in trail travelers' storying at Pecos Pueblo, then said to be the birthplace and special trust of the Aztec ruler Montezuma (Kessell).

19

Mexican Patriotism in New Mexico, 1821–1846

Robert J. Tórrez

During the struggles for Mexican independence, New Mexico was spared the turmoil and fighting that characterized the decade between the *grito de Dolores* — the "shout" issued by a priest named Hidalgo — in 1810 and the Treaty of Cordova in 1821. New Mexico remained steadfastly loyal to the royalist cause during this time, its leaders occasionally issuing stinging condemnations of the "disorders" sweeping Mexico. Once independence was achieved, however, New Mexicans witnessed an orderly transition from being subjects of the Spanish king to being citizens of the new Mexican nation. This seamless transfer of sovereignty is characterized by the fact that Facundo Melgares, the last Spanish-era governor and a staunch royalist, continued in the same office under the new constitutional regime. For the next twenty-five years New Mexico remained an integral, if remote and often beleaguered part of the vast region of New Spain that gained its independence from Spain and became the Mexican Republic (technically a constitutional monarchy in its early stages) in 1821.

Although New Mexico is often portrayed as isolated and cut off from the centers of government, local officials were well informed about what was going on in Spain and Mexico during the decade preceding independence. New Mexico's Spanish- and Mexican-era archives make it clear that despite the thousands of miles separating New Mexico from the centers of government, local officials received regular news of developments in Spain and Mexico. New Mexicans were kept informed of events following the invasion of Spain by Napoleon

Mexican national coat-of-arms formed with words of the national anthem, about 1911.

Bonaparte in 1808 and the subsequent abdication of Charles VI; they were updated about the Regency Council's efforts to rule in the king's name and about the establishment of the Cortes, or Spanish congress. When the Cortes issued a decree inviting its American colonies to send delegates to Spain, New Mexico was quick to respond.

It is unknown when this invitation arrived in New Mexico, but soon afterward Governor José Manrrique convened a meeting of the province's leading men. From among those present, they selected don Pedro Bautista Pino, a wealthy merchant, livestock owner, and prominent public official, to represent New Mexico in faraway Spain. Don Pedro undertook this arduous journey in late October 1811, traveling south on the Camino Real to the port of Vera Cruz, where he boarded a ship for

Spain. His principal contribution to the Cortes was a book that has become known as the *Exposition on the Province of New Mexico, 1812*. The book served as a report to the Cortes on conditions in New Mexico and is one of the most widely cited sources of information about New Mexico for that period. The efforts of the Cortes to initiate a constitutional monarchy and provide Spain's colonies with a modicum of independence, however, came to nothing. In 1814 Ferdinand VII, Charles's son, returned to the throne and repudiated the Spanish constitution of 1812. As subsequent events demonstrated, the Crown was unable to contain the growing nationalism that swept the Americas. Padre Hidalgo's *grito de Dolores* had been heard throughout Mexico, and like it or not, New Mexico was swept along with the tide.

The Mexican Struggle for Independence

Mexico celebrates the birth of its independence movement on the sixteenth of September. This pivotal moment in Mexican history is usually attributed to Miguel Hidalgo y Costilla, a priest in the parish of Dolores, a small town in what is now the state of Querétaro, northeast of Guanajuato. On the night of September 15–16, 1810, Padre Hidalgo called together his small congregation and issued what is called the *grito de Dolores* (shout of Dolores). The text of the speech Padre Hidalgo made to the small gathering of Indian and mestizo parishioners that night has apparently been lost to history, but his words sparked a powerful movement that culminated in Mexican independence in 1821.

Every September 15, an overflow crowd gathers in the evening at the Zócolo, the great plaza of Mexico City that fronts the Palacio de Gobierno, for the opening ceremonies of the following day's celebration. At eleven o'clock, the president of the republic and other government officials emerge from the Palacio onto a balcony that overlooks the plaza to ring the same bell that Padre Hidalgo used to gather his parishioners that fateful night in 1810. The president and his retinue then shout "¡Viva Hidalgo, viva Morelos, vivan los heroes de la independencia, viva México!" The ceremony is repeated in cities throughout Mexico, commemorating *el 16 de Septiembre* as the nation's official Independence Day, much the way the Fourth of July is celebrated in the United States.

Despite the honor given Padre Hidalgo, the revolt he called for in his *grito* was short-lived. In March 1811, Hidalgo's rebel force was defeated by troops loyal to the Spanish Crown. The father of Mexican independence and other leaders of the independence movement were captured, found guilty of treason, and executed. For the next several years, the Mexican War for Independence consisted mainly of isolated guerrilla movements. Then Agustín Iturbide, commanding the Spanish army in Mexico, decided in 1821 to negotiate with Vicente Guerrero, one of the principal guerrilla leaders. These negotiations resulted in the February 24, 1821, Plan of Iguala, the Mexican declaration of independence, which was recognized by Spain on August 24 of that year.

News of Mexican Independence Reaches New Mexico

The earliest news of Mexican independence arrived in New Mexico during the week of September 17, 1821. That day Governor Facundo Melgares acknowledged that he had received instructions dated August 27, 1821, ordering all local government officials to swear allegiance to *la Independencia*. Melgares noted that he and Santa Fe's *ayuntamiento,* the local town council, had taken the oaths "with all the solemnity possible" in the presence of the military chaplain, local clerics, and a gathering of the population. He also acknowledged that the order was being circulated to all the *alcaldías,* or local political jurisdictions, in the province. Some weeks later, local officials received a copy of a manifesto from Durango, Mexico, dated September 9, 1821, that announced the *grito de libertad* issued at Iguala. Indications are that this document arrived in New Mexico in late October that year along with the actual *Acta de Independencia del Imperio* of September 28, 1821. This "Acta" and other documents related to the declaration of Mexican independence and organization of the new government were being distributed locally by late November and early December 1821 (Weber 1973).

While news regarding independence was being distributed throughout the province, another extremely important event was unfolding in the plains of eastern New Mexico. Early on the morning of November 2, 1821, militia captain Pedro Ignacio Gallego and a company of 148 men left Abiquiú, a frontier town in northern New Mexico, with orders to proceed to San Miguel del Vado to investigate reports of Indian raids on the villages in that vicinity. On November 13, 1821, the day after his expedition left San Miguel, Gallego reported dryly: "About 3:30 p.m. encountered six Americans at the Puertocito de la Piedra Lumbre. They parlayed with me.... Not understanding their words nor any of the signs they made, I decided to return to El Vado" (Olsen and Myers 1992, 10).

With these unremarkable words Captain Gallego described one of the most important encounters in New Mexico history. Somewhere a few miles southwest of present-day Las Vegas, New Mexico, he had met the trading expedition of William Becknell. This chance meeting was the first contact between men of the new Mexican nation and the United States, an event that set in motion decades of commerce and cultural contact over a wagon route that was to become known as the Santa Fe Trail.

Santa Fe Celebrates Mexican Independence

The first documented public celebration related to Mexican independence in New Mexico took place on January 6, 1822. On that day, a mass, a procession, dances by Indians from the pueblo of Tesuque, and a *loa*, the reading of a dramatic poem prepared in honor of the occasion, culminated three days of patriotic activities. At the front of the procession walked a young child holding a sword, symbolizing the Plan of Iguala. The boy was followed by three girls bound together by a tricolor ribbon, symbolizing the three guarantees of the plan — independence, religion, and union.

After Indian dances on the plaza, the crowd dispersed to a variety of games and entertainments. That evening the *loa* was performed by the *alférez* (lieutenant), Santiago Abreu, vicar Juan Tomás Terrazas, and presidio chaplain Fray Francisco de Hozio. Following the *loa,* a dance at the Palace of the Governors that lasted until four-thirty in the morning was attended by the city's "persons of distinction." All the ladies in attendance wore green sashes with "Viva la Independencia del Imperio Mexicano [Long live the independence of the Mexican Empire]" imprinted on them.

In the spring of 1822, the recently installed provincial *diputación,* or legislative council, drafted a resolution of support for the imperial government. The resolution assured the council's superiors in Mexico that New Mexico's citizens considered themselves an integral and loyal part of the new nation and were prepared to shed their blood in defense of the established government. It also contained a succinct acknowledgment that they considered themselves citizens of a greater America — the terms *America septentrional,* or North America, and *estos leales Americanos,* "these loyal Americans," used in reference to themselves.

Subsequent public celebrations related to Mexican independence in New Mexico took place on December 10–12, 1822. Three days of ceremonies celebrated the installation of Agustín de Iturbide as emperor of Mexico, during which local government officials took a public oath of allegiance to their new leader. The ceremonies opened on the evening of December 10 with bonfires, the ringing of bells, artillery salutes, music, the planting of a "very tall" flagpole at the center of the plaza in Santa Fe, and the raising of a white flag inscribed with unspecified symbols of Mexican independence.

Other activities included daily parades through the streets and around the plaza featuring floats decorated in patriotic themes, local officials and dignitaries mounted on horses, files of marching soldiers, musicians, and two troupes of *matachines* dancers. The report of these events makes it clear that the public enjoyed not only the formal aspects of the celebration but also several theatrical presentations written for the occasion. Dances by members of several of the pueblos, table games, and a series of grand dances culminated the festivities every evening. The report of the celebration proudly concluded that "there was not the slightest disorder in any of the entertainments, as everyone was extremely happy with their exaltation of the Emperor to the throne."

A few months later, when news of the deposition of Iturbide as emperor arrived in New Mexico, local government transitioned seamlessly to functioning as a republic. During subsequent months, officials in Santa Fe noted compliance with congressional actions that ordered the substitution of the term *Nacional* wherever the name *Imperial* had appeared, as well as subsequent publication of the federal national constitution of 1824. A vivid report of the solemnization of the new constitution by the *ayuntamiento* of Santa Cruz de la Cañada on December 17, 1824, describes the ceremonies in which the *alférez,* Venedicto García, "proclamó por tres veces la constitución con estas voces, 'Viva la constitución federal de los Estados Unidos Mexicanos'; a la que el publico respondió lo mismo [proclaimed the constitution three times with these words, 'Long live the federal constitution of the United Mexican States'; to which the public responded with the same]." Similar ceremonies were apparently held at every *alcaldía*, although only a few reports, including those of the solemnizations at Santa Fe and the pueblo of Jemez, have survived.

On December 4, 1824, the Mexican government published a decree establishing official national religious and civil holidays, or *dias festivos*. These included the *fiestas religiosas*, or religious festivals, of Holy Thursday, Good Friday, Corpus Christi, and Nuestra Señora de Guadalupe and the civil celebrations of *16 de Septiembre*, in honor of the "primer grito de Independencia [first shout of Independence]," and October 4, in honor of the "sanción de la constitución [of 1824]."

This decree was acknowledged in Santa Fe on February 18, 1825, so it is possible that a celebration of the sixteenth of September was held as early as that year. One document from the Mexican Archives of New Mexico, dated August 11, 1827, describes the "Prevenciones y Formalidades" planned at Chihuahua to celebrate "the glorious shout of Independence" on the sixteenth and seventeenth of that month. It is possible that New Mexico officials used this document as a model for activities in Santa Fe.

New Mexican Celebrations of September 16

There is, however, no hard evidence of an actual sixteenth of September celebration in New Mexico until 1829. Documents dated between June and August 1829 show that the *diputación,* or territorial legislative council in Santa Fe, considered a proposal submitted by Ramón Abreu, Melquides Antonio Ortega, and Guadalupe Miranda asking for formal establishment of New Mexico's first *sociedad patriotica,* or patriotic society. On June 12, 1829, a committee assigned to study the proposal reported its enthusiastic support. Two months later, *gefe [jefe] político* (political boss) José Antonio Chaves issued orders for the first documented celebration of *16 de Septiembre* in New Mexico and appointed a committee to organize and direct the festivities. No report of civic participation in these 1829 festivities has survived, but the military orders Chaves issued for September 15 and 16 suggest that plans were made for an elaborate and extended celebration in which the presidio troops participated fully.

Indications are that September 16 was observed regularly, if not annually, for the next several years. On July 14, 1832, Ramón Abreu introduced a resolution to the Santa Fe *ayuntamiento* asking the governor to call a public meeting to plan for the upcoming occasion. Little more than a month later, the territorial *diputación* responded to Abreu's proposal with a resolution of its own, organizing a committee to plan the celebration of the "glorious shout of Dolores." Juan Estevan Pino and Agustín Durán were appointed to draft an invitation to the citizens of Santa Fe to decorate their homes and prepare for the occasion. Plans for this 1832 celebration include the earliest evidence of participation by the pueblos. That year, *gefe político* Santiago Abreu invited the Indians of San Gerónimo de Taos to dance at the planned September 16 celebration. José María Martínez responded to the invitation by noting that although the festivities were inconveniently scheduled during the wheat harvest in the Taos Valley, the people of Taos nonetheless accepted the invitation "with great joy."

The earliest report elaborating specific plans for *16 de Septiembre* in New Mexico is the August 25, 1835, "Plan" published by a committee composed of Santa Fe's most distinguished citizens. The administration of newly appointed Governor Albino Pérez tasked this committee with organizing the events by which Santa Fe would celebrate "the glorious anniversary" of Mexican independence that year. Its fourteen-part plan opened the celebration at midnight on the fifteenth with a protracted twenty-one-gun salute timed to conclude with the playing of the *Diana* (the Mexican equivalent of reveille and taps) at dawn. The initial canon shot would also signal a general ringing of church bells in the city, scheduled to last a full hour. At the same time, officers of the *ayuntamiento* and all government officials and troops were to congregate in front of the *palacio* and, accompanied by musicians, make a formal procession around the plaza. The procession was to halt at each corner of the square while patriotic speeches were made.

The plan included instructions for the liberal adornment of the city streets and the plaza with colorful hangings and decorations. Streets and buildings were to be illuminated with torches and bonfires throughout the evening and nighttime activities. Religious ceremonies, speeches, parades, Indian dances, games, and a grand ball were also planned. Concluding the activities on the afternoon of the seventeenth was a *corrida de toros* (bull fight) to be held on the plaza.

A lull in celebrations of September 16 in New Mexico followed the "Revolt of 1837" and the assassination of Governor Albino Pérez that year. Pérez had been appointed governor in 1835 and assigned the difficult task of implementing the "Departmental Plan" of the new Mexican constitution of 1836. This constitution converted New Mexico into a department of the Mexican Republic and replaced the *diputación,* or territorial assembly, with a Departmental Junta. The new laws also eliminated the *ayuntamientos,* or town councils, in all except the capital city, Santa Fe.

Opposition to Governor Pérez's administration and the Departmental Plan developed into a full-fledged revolt in northern New Mexico. Pérez was resented locally as an outsider who did not understand or care about local needs. This resentment was intensified by the fact that he was the first non-native governor, sent from Mexico to install a centrist constitution that reduced the autonomy and authority of local governments and imposed direct taxes on a population historically exempted from them.

The origins of the Revolt of 1837 are shrouded in mystery and speculation, but early the first week of August 1837, Governor Pérez began planning to march north with a small detachment of militia and presidio troops to deal with reports of "disorders" instigated by a "Revolutionary Proclamation" issued at Santa Cruz de la Cañada, about twenty-five miles north of Santa Fe. On August 8, 1837, the rebels routed Pérez and his troops at La Mesilla, near the pueblo of San Ildefonso. With most of his men killed or captured, Pérez managed to escape briefly to Santa Fe before attempting to flee south to Mexico. The following day, August 9, Pérez and several others were captured near Agua Fria, south of Santa Fe, and summarily executed. Accounts of his death indicate that Pérez was beheaded by his assassins and his head "kicked about with their spurred heals" (Lecompte 1985).

By August 11 the rebels had gained control of the capital and named José Gonzales governor of their "*junta popular.*" The rebel government, however, was short-lived. Within a month, the rich merchant class of the *río abajo* — the lower Rio Grande Valley — met at Tomé and proclaimed its opposition to Gonzales and his government. The framers of this "Plan of Tomé" chose former governor Manuel Armijo to lead them until the government in Mexico could provide a course of action. After several months of political maneuvering, Armijo, his forces augmented by federal troops from Mexico, crushed the revolt in late January 1838. Shortly afterward, Armijo was formally appointed governor, and New Mexico proceeded toward a slow recovery from the disastrous events of the Revolt of 1837.

There is no indication of *16 de Septiembre* celebrations for several years following the revolt, but festivities had resumed with renewed vigor by 1844. A thick folio of documents in the Mexican Archives of New Mexico describes an elaborate program organized that year by a commission consisting of twenty-nine of Santa Fe's most distinguished residents. The commission met on July 28, 1844, to begin planning for "the celebration of the anniversary of our glorious Independence." As commissions are apt to do, they first established four subcommittees that were assigned specific responsibilities. Subcommittee one was to plan for refreshments; two, to arrange for public entertainment; three, to arrange with the governor and military authorities for the firearms and other accoutrements needed for military salutes; and four, to meet with church officials to arrange for the religious ceremonies. Although no specific committee seems to have been assigned to raise funds for the celebration, several dozen persons donated or pledged altogether 434 pesos, 2 reales, to pay for the festivities.

The refreshment committee prepared a detailed report that contains a fascinating list of what its members considered "indispensable for the various refreshments for the dance planned for the 16th." Included in the long list of pastries are *marquesotes* (a caramel-like hard candy made from burnt sugar), *puches* (a pudding-like dessert), *coronas* (a fancy pastry sprinkled with gold dust or flakes), *soletas* (a ladyfinger-like pastry with icing), *encaladillas* (plain cookies sprinkled with sugar), *dulces* (divinity), and *biscochos de regalo* (a plain, biscuit-like cookie often used as a trade item). Also called for are *mirtelas* and *aguas frescas* (punch and soft drinks). In what might be the only document in New Mexico's extensive archives that may be called a recipe, the report lists the individual ingredients for each of these refreshments and the estimated cost for each. The committee suggested a budget of slightly more than 165 pesos to pay for the planned refreshments. The largest expense was the seventy-four pesos budgeted for forty-three flasks of wine and twenty-five of *aguardiente* to spice up the punch.

The entertainment committee also prepared detailed recommendations and a schedule of religious, civic, and military activities that were to begin the night of September 15. These included a general ringing of bells throughout the city, salvos of artillery, fireworks, and of course the mandatory speeches, parades, public entertainments, and religious celebrations. The events were to conclude on the seventeenth with a solemn memorial mass to honor all the Mexican patriots who had died for their country. These activities were to serve "as a joyous remembrance of the moment at which the immortal Hidalgo proclaimed our National Independence at the Pueblo of Dolores."

The 1844 celebration was tempered by the arrival in Santa Fe of six Ute chiefs and nearly two hundred warriors on September 5. The Utes had come to see Governor Mariano Martínez to press their demands for compensation for ten of their men who had been killed in an earlier campaign against the Navajos. The Utes were displeased with the gifts offered them as compensation, and the following day they angrily confronted Martínez at the Palace of the Governors. The situation quickly deteriorated into a pitched battle that left eight Utes dead in the streets of the city.

A running battle spilled over into the countryside as the Utes retreated through the villages of northern New Mexico with a detachment of presidio troops hot on their heels. It is uncertain whether or how this incident interfered with the celebrations scheduled to take place less than two weeks later. The one documented change in plans is a September 9 order to Juan Andrés Archuleta, prefect of New Mexico's northern district, informing him to cancel plans for Pueblo Indians to dance at the festivities in Santa Fe. The government felt that in light of recent incidents, their participation would make the pueblos vulnerable to Ute attacks. Despite this slight modification, indications are that many, if not all, the planned festivities went on as scheduled (Tórrez 1997).

The final celebration of *16 de Septiembre* in New Mexico took place in 1845. On September 1 that year, Governor Manuel Armijo wrote to the "*junta patriotica de esta capital*," the commission appointed to plan for that year's celebration, asking its members to use the 1844 plan as a model so that everyone could participate with the patriotic fervor characteristic of all good Mexicans. Whatever plans this commission developed have not survived, but the military orders issued for that day suggest that elaborate ceremonies were held to commemorate Mexico's "glorious emancipation."

The parades and military salutes scheduled for 1845 were the last public vestiges of Mexican pride expressed in New Mexico for many years to come. In July and August 1846, a time when committees would have been appointed to organize the following month's festivities, New Mexicans had more important issues on their minds. War had been declared between Mexico and the United States, and the American Army of the West, under the command of General Stephen Watts Kearny, was marching on New Mexico. The next national holiday celebrated at Santa Fe would be the Fourth of July.

We do not know how the first Fourth of July in New Mexico was observed in 1847. According to the November 27, 1847, issue of the *Santa Fe Republican,* however, activities organized on August 18, 1847, to celebrate the first anniversary of Kearny's occupation of New Mexico were limited to a simple military exercise and a few toasts. Otherwise, noted the paper, "no one took sufficient interest to get up a public demonstration on the occasion." One wonders whether the little interest described by the paper was a reflection that New Mexicans had no idea what the Fourth of July stood for, or whether their failure to get excited about this hallowed American holiday had something to do with their not yet feeling very American.

Expressions of Mexican Patriotism in New Mexico

The documentation reviewed here does not in and of itself prove that typical New Mexicans at one time considered themselves loyal and patriotic Mexicans. Public celebrations are not exactly proof positive of patriotism. Although New Mexicans did not participate in the armed insurrections against Spain that resulted in Mexican independence or experience the constant revolts and conflicts endured by other Mexican provinces, there is ample evidence of their support for the central Mexican government and admiration for the principals of liberty and independence. These vestiges of Mexican patriotism can be found in a number of documents unassociated with celebrations.

Expressions of Mexican patriotism are found in a March 9, 1831, proposal written by Juan Estevan Pino, Juan Felipe Ortiz, and Francisco Baca. Directed to Governor José Antonio Chaves, the proposal suggested that New Mexico desired to achieve the status of "a free and sovereign state" in the Mexican Republic and asked Chaves to solicit all the *ayuntamientos* in the territory to set aside a day during which they could present this sentiment to the territorial *diputación.* By the end of that month, a proposal and petition to the federal congress asking for admission of New Mexico as a state in the Mexican Republic known as the "Estado de Hidalgo" had been drafted by the *diputación* and signed by representatives of the *ayuntamientos* of Santa Fe, Sandia, Belén, Tomé, Sabinal, San Miguel de Socorro, La Laguna, Jemez, San Gerónimo de Taos, and the Villa de Alburquerque. Although the proposal was apparently never submitted to Mexico, because of personal opposition from the governor and other unspecified "general dissent," the document makes it clear that New Mexicans felt strongly about being an integral part of the larger Mexican federation.

Later in 1831, *gefe político* José Antonio Chaves wrote to the *secretaria de estado* concerning local response to news of recent rebellions in Mexico. He assured the central government that New Mexico was peaceful and its residents respectful of the law and authority of the central government. Chaves added confidently that sedition and other intrigues had no support locally and that if anyone dared introduce such ideas into New Mexico, the full weight of the law would be immediately brought on his head. That winter, the *secretaria* thanked then *gefe político* Santiago Abreu for a letter that had been submitted by a number of New Mexicans in agreement with the "pronunciamiento de la guarnición de Vera Cruz," a decree by the garrison of Vera Cruz in support of the duly elected government. The letter conveyed the president's thanks and appreciation for the patriotic sentiments expressed in the New Mexicans' letter and asked Abreu to personally thank each of the signatories. No copy of the letter originally submitted by these New Mexico residents has survived in the Mexican Archives of New Mexico, but the list of names to whom a copy of the *secretaria*'s letter was sent consists of a "who's who" of New Mexico politics and commerce. Abreu's successor, Francisco Sarracino, expressed strong patriotic sentiments in late 1833 in response to various circulars concerning revolutions in Mexico. "In this remote corner of New Mexico," he wrote, "no voice is heard other than that which conserves without stain the very system of popular representative federal government to which we worthily pertain."

An enthusiastic endorsement of representative democracy and support of liberty is also expressed in an 1834 letter from Manuel Sánchez, a private citizen from San Miguel de la Bajada, a small settlement a few miles south of Santa Fe near the pueblo of Cochiti. Responding to a call for his participation in an upcoming campaign against the Navajos, Sánchez noted that he was ready to sacrifice his life and property for the benefit of his beloved country, and he acknowledged the government's authority to impose on its citizens in matters of such "benefit to liberty." Although one might wonder whether the deferential tone of Sánchez's letter was more sarcasm than enthusiasm, no reason has been found to suggest that he was not proud of being a Mexican or to accept his expressions of loyalty and patriotism at face value.

As political and economic conditions deteriorated in Mexico in the 1840s and the prospect of war with the United States of America loomed, New Mexico remained steadfast in its support for the established government in Mexico. New Mexicans had no opportunity to test their oft-expressed patriotism on the field of battle, because Governor Manuel Armijo decided not to oppose General Kearny and the United States Army of the West. Yet one of the most poignant expressions of Mexican patriotism in New Mexico may be Juan Bautista Vigil y Alarid's response to Kearny's address to the people of Santa Fe on August 19, 1846. On that day, Vigil y Alarid acknowledged Governor Armijo's defection, his failure to defend New Mexico, and the de facto occupation of New Mexico by Kearny's forces. "Do not be surprised," he warned Kearny, "that we have not manifested joy and enthusiasm in seeing our city occupied by your military forces. To us the political entity of the Republic of Mexico has died. She, regardless of her circumstances, was our Mother. What son would not shed copious tears at the tomb of his parents?"

By September 22, 1846, Kearny had established a new civil government for New Mexico known as the Kearny Code and appointed Charles Bent as governor. The lack of military opposition to the American occupation of Santa Fe, however, did not mean this new government was universally welcomed by all New Mexicans. By mid-December, growing discontent with the Americans led to the arrest of several "conspirators" who were planning armed resistance to the American occupation. Despite these arrests, planning for an uprising against the *Americanos* continued.

On January 19, 1847, a large group of men attacked Governor Bent at his home at Don Fernando de Taos. By the end of the day, Bent and six officials of the recently organized American government lay dead. Within two days, the uprising had spread through much of northern New Mexico, and a force of rebels was advancing toward Santa Fe. The New Mexican insurrection known as the "Revolt of 1847" had begun.

Colonel Sterling Price, who had been left in command of the U.S. forces when Kearny departed for California the previous month, hastily organized his men and moved north to meet the oncoming rebel force. On January 24, 1847, Price's troops engaged and dispersed the New Mexicans at Santa Cruz de la Cañada. Over the next several days, the rebel force was pushed north to the pueblo of San Gerónimo de Taos, where Sterling commenced a siege on the fortified pueblo on the evening of February 3. By the end of the following day, the outgunned defenders had been routed and the insurrection crushed. Various sources estimate that between 150 and 200 rebels died at the pueblo, bringing the total estimated number of New Mexicans killed on the battlefields of northern New Mexico to nearly three hundred, although the actual number will likely never be known.

The day after Price and his men crushed the Revolt of 1847, a series of "drumhead" military courts and civil trials convicted numerous New Mexicans of charges ranging from murder and treason to fomenting "rebellious conduct" against the United States. The treason charges were later found to be improper because U.S. courts could not try Mexican citizens for treason against the United States; in January 1847 the United States and Mexico were still at war, and New Mexico was still part of the Republic of Mexico. Despite the belated recognition of this legal nuance, by the end of the summer of 1847 at least twenty-one New Mexicans had been hanged for resisting the U.S. occupation. It was a harsh introduction to American jurisprudence.

Might it not be said that this January 1847 insurrection against the United States government by the *Mexicanos* of northern New Mexico was the ultimate expression of Mexican patriotism in New Mexico (Tórrez 2005)? The idea that New Mexicans were at one time loyal and patriotic Mexican citizens is a concept that may be understood and accepted only when there is a full realization that New Mexico was at one time an integral part of the Mexican Republic. In the meantime, New Mexicans should not feel ambivalent or guilty about enjoying a *16 de Septiembre* celebration, or, for that matter, Cinco de Mayo, a holiday commemorating a Mexican victory over French forces in 1862. After all, *mas antes*, long ago, their ancestors carefully planned for these public celebrations of Mexican independence and participated in them with the enthusiasm of any Mexican citizen and patriot.

20

Perspectives on the Camino Real
in New Mexico

Oakah L. Jones (1999)

Traversing the Camino Real de Tierra Adentro [Royal Road of the Interior Land] between Santa Fe and El Paso today, the traveler may well be impressed with the historical importance of the route and the diversity of geographical features, as well as the people from at least three cultures who dwell there. The route extends for a distance of some 310 miles (496 kilometers) roughly paralleling Interstate Highway 25, with altitudes ranging from 6,954 feet (2,120 meters) at Santa Fe to 3,762 feet (1,148 meters) at El Paso. Along the way one encounters or sees, to the east, mountains of various ranges, including the Sangre de Cristos, Sandías, Manzanos, Caballos, and Franklins. However, the most prominent and continuous geographical feature is the Río Grande del Norte (also called the Río del Norte or the Río Bravo). Along or near its banks are La Bajada between Santa Fe and Bernalillo, Tomé Hill, La Jornada del Muerto, and the Mesilla Valley. Flora along the Camino Real de Tierra Adentro varies from the juniper and piñon in the north to the semi-desert yucca, chamisa, and sagebrush and finally to the lush green fields of the Mesilla Valley, where chile, cotton, vegetables, and fruits are grown in abundance.

This trail through New Mexico and its counterpart from Ciudad Juárez (the original El Paso del Norte) to the cities of Chihuahua, Hidalgo del Parral (formerly San José del Parral), Valle de Allende (formerly Valle de San Bartolomé), Santa Bárbara, Durango, Zacatecas, Querétaro, and Mexico City, a total distance of 1,450 miles (2,320 kilometers), have

Aerial view, looking south, of the Camino Real (irregular line, far left), county road, and Interstate 25 near Radium Springs, south-central New Mexico.

served as a principal route of transportation, communication, exploration, colonization, settlement, and trade for thousands of years.

Communities that have been founded by various cultures across the centuries have endured to the present day. Native American villages abound: Santo Domingo, Cochití, San Felipe, Sandía, Isleta, and three pueblos southeast of El Paso — Ysleta, Socorro, and Senecú del Sur. Spanish and Mexican towns exist in profusion: Santa Fe, Bernalillo, Algodones, Corrales, Alameda, Albuquerque, Atrisco, Peralta, Valencia, Los Lunas, Belén, Tomé, San Antonio, Sabinal, Socorro, Las Cruces, Mesilla, Doña Ana, and El Paso itself. Added to these communities are those with Anglo-American names, such as Garfield, Truth or Consequences (formerly Hot Springs), Hatch, and Anthony, along with the region of Elephant Butte and dam.

Known, used, and settled by Amerindians for hundreds of years (perhaps thousands) before the arrival of the Spaniards (Riley 1995, 113; see also Brugge 1999), the route along the Río Grande became the principal one between New Mexico and Nueva Vizcaya from the mid-sixteenth to the early nineteenth centuries. It was used by Spaniards — explorers, conquistadors, colonizers, merchants, Franciscan missionaries, travelers, soldiers, visiting officials, and those carrying mail back and forth between the northern provinces of New Spain and Mexico City. After Mexico's independence from Spain in 1821, the Camino Real continued to be used by Mexicans as the primary route for commerce between Mexico and New Mexico. In the Mexican period (1821-1846) it also served as an extension of the international trade from the United States along the Santa Fe Trail (begun in 1822) when North American goods were transported from Santa Fe to El Paso and Mexico along what became known as the

Chihuahua Trail. After the Treaty of Guadalupe Hidalgo (1848) ceded New Mexico to the United States, the Camino Real continued to be used by merchants and settlers, who brought goods and customs to New Mexico as well as products from the United States for eventual sale and trade with Mexico.

Over the course of almost three centuries, in addition to the thousands of people who settled in New Mexico, many prominent persons either traveled along the trail or participated in significant historical events nearby. Spanish explorers, such as Francisco Vázquez de Coronado, Captain Francisco Sánchez Chamuscado, fray Agustín Rodríguez, Antonio de Espejo, and Gaspar Castaño de Sosa, visited or camped along the Río Grande between 1540 and 1590, although none of them entered New Mexico via what would become the Camino Real. The expedition of Juan de Morlete, who had been sent from Saltillo to arrest Castaño de Sosa for illegal entry into New Mexico, returned by a route described as two hundred leagues shorter than the way they came; it was probably along the Río Grande to what later became known as El Paso del Norte, roughly following the trail of the Camino Real de Tierra Adentro (Hammond and Rey 1966, 46-47; Schroeder and Matson 1965, 175-76). Seven years later, in April 1598, Juan de Oñate entered New Mexico at El Paso del Norte and claimed it for the King of Spain. His colonizing expedition of men, women, children, and animals then followed the trail which he named the "Camino Real de Tierra Adentro," from El Paso del Norte to San Juan Pueblo where he established the first Spanish community near today's Española north of Santa Fe (Riley 1995, 247-48; Simmons 1991, 49, 100, 111, 195, and map, 94-95; Hammond and Rey 1953, 16-17).

Thereafter, the trail became the principal route tying New Mexico with cities in northern New Spain. Colonists, Franciscan supply caravans, and visitors to New Mexico (such as fray Alonso de Benavides) used the Camino Real. The Pueblo Revolt of August 1680 occurred under the leadership of Popé and other Pueblo leaders in the Tewa villages north of Santa Fe and the Tano pueblos south of the capital. Expelled from the Santa Fe, Río Arriba, and Río Abajo regions, Governor Antonio de Otermín, Alonso de García, and the surviving Spaniards, along with more than three hundred Amerindians from Isleta and the Piro pueblos, retreated down the road to El Paso del Norte. Twelve years later, Governor Diego de Vargas led a reconnaissance expedition northward, and in 1693, accompanied by settlers, soldiers, missionaries, and a Pueblo interpreter, Vargas followed the Camino Real de Tierra Adentro northward for the reconquest and resettlement of New Mexico. During the eighteenth century, in addition to the hundreds of people who settled the province, soldiers, ecclesiastics, merchants, and other prominent persons utilized the Camino Real. They included such notables as Juan Bautista de Anza, Pedro de Rivera, the Marqués de Rubí, and Nicolás de Lafora.

During the nineteenth century Anglos also began to use the Camino Real. For example, in the 1830s James Magoffin became a prominent merchant in the city of Chihuahua, where he was heavily involved in the Santa Fe-Chihuahua trade, and in 1841 he led a caravan with forty wagons of merchandise to St. Louis via Santa Fe, following the trail from Chihuahua to El Paso and then through New Mexico before connecting with the Santa Fe Trail (Moorhead 1958, 83-84, n. 18; Timmons 1990, 83-84). During the Mexican-American War, Cols. Stephen Watts Kearny and Alexander Doniphan led invading armies from the United States and followed a portion or all of the trail southward, accompanied by North American merchants. Samuel Magoffin, brother of James and one of these merchants, and his bride, Susan Shelby Magoffin, traveled along the Camino Real de Tierra Adentro. Susan Magoffin's diary (Drumm 1926) provides an eyewitness account of travel conditions along the trail from Santa Fe to El Paso (Moorhead 1958, 156). During the early years of the Civil War in the United States, Confederate invasion forces led by Major Henry S. Sibley and Lt. Col. John R. Baylor followed the Camino Real from El Paso to Albuquerque and Santa Fe before they were turned back on March 27 and 28, 1862, after defeats at Glorieta Pass and Apache Canyon east of Santa Fe. Forces led by Cols. John P. Slough, William R. Scurry, and Major John M. Chivington of the Colorado Volunteers thus preserved New Mexico and Colorado for the Union. Sibley's army retreated along the Camino Real de Tierra Adentro, and at Peralta, south of Albuquerque, they were defeated again by Col. Edward R. S. Canby and Union forces in the last battle of the Civil War in New Mexico (Keleher 1952, 179-80, 186). From 1878 to 1881, General Lew Wallace, the author of *Ben Hur*, resided in Santa Fe as territorial governor of New Mexico. In his journeys to southern New Mexico, he became one more famous person to follow a portion or most of the Camino Real de Tierra Adentro (Jones 1985, 138, 146)....

Perspectives

To evaluate the significance of the Camino Real de Tierra Adentro it is necessary to place the road in temporal and historical perspective. The Spanish term *camino real* literally means a royal road, but these roads were neither authorized by the king nor laid out by government officials. Instead, *caminos reales* were more accurately trails defined and developed over time for the use of colonists, merchants, ecclesiastics, government officials, and visitors. They served as primary routes for transportation, communication, and colonization. Furthermore, the Camino Real de Tierra Adentro was only one such trail during the Spanish colonial period, and its New Mexican portion was only a part of the overall trail between Mexico City, Zacatecas, Querétaro, Durango, Parral, and Chihuahua on the one hand and Santa Fe and other settlements in New Mexico on the other (Swann 1982, 61, 64-65). *Caminos reales*, often following ancient Amerindian trails used for centuries preceding Spanish contact, were established throughout New Spain, Central America, and South America during the Spanish colonial period (1519-1824). Two of them (outside New Mexico) were established in the American Southwest and northern Mexico. One ran from Monclova and San Juan Bautista in Coahuila to the province of Texas, specifically San Antonio and San Fernando de Béxar. This road, used earlier by explorers, soldiers, and missionaries, was developed for commerce and colonization during the eighteenth century. It reached San Antonio, then turned southeast to the Guadalupe River, and resumed its northeasterly direction to Los Adaes and Nacogdoches in eastern Texas (Foster 1995, 130, 148, 150, 151, 173, 185, 200, 223, 306n3, 312n19, and map, 2). After the Spanish occupation of "Antigua California" (Baja California) and the establishment of the first Jesuit missions there in 1697, a *camino real* developed to connect northern missions on the peninsula with those of Loreto, La Paz, and San José del Cabo (Crosby 1994, 196, 223, and map, 236). With the permanent occupation of Alta California (today's state of California) at San Diego and Monterey in 1796-1770 and the subsequent establishment of twenty-one missions, four presidios, and three civil communities (San José, Los Angeles, and Branciforte), a *camino real* connected San Diego with Monterey and San Francisco. It was used for essentially the same purposes as the Camino Real de Tierra Adentro (Caughey 1953, 12; Jones 1979, 230-31; Krell 1979, 4, 245, 251; Weber 1992, 344).

Yet these *caminos reales* do not detract from the significance of the Camino Real de Tierra Adentro, either its New Mexican portion or the road in its totality from Mexico City through northern New Spain to El Paso del Norte and Santa Fe. This road was important for three overarching reasons. First, it was the primary route for exploration, conquest, and colonization of New Mexico. Colonists traveled both north and south over the Camino Real de Tierra Adentro. They settled communities along the trail between El Paso del Norte and Santa Fe (earlier at San Juan de los Caballeros and San Gabriel de los Españoles). Franciscans established missions among the Pueblos and secular churches at such locations as Santa Fe, Albuquerque, and El Paso del Norte, thereby introducing and spreading Christianity. Military persons also used the Camino Real de Tierra Adentro for presidios or military garrisons at Santa Fe, El Paso del Norte, and San Elizario; for conducting inspections of New Mexico (e.g., Pedro del Rivera and the Marqués de Rubí); for campaigns against Amerindians (e.g., Diego de Vargas and Juan de Oñate); for expeditions during the Mexican-American War (e.g., Stephen Watts Kearny, Alexander Doniphan, and Sterling Price); for campaigns during the American Civil War by both Confederate and Union forces (e.g., Henry S. Sibley, John M. Chivington, and Edward R. S. Canby); and for escorting merchant caravans and mail deliveries.

Second, the Camino Real de Tierra Adentro was significant as the primary route of trade, supply, transportation, and communication between New Mexico on the one hand and the northern provinces of New Spain and Mexico City on the other. Products from Spain and other provinces of New Spain (later Mexico) were exchanged with those of New Mexico and later from the United States. Missionary supply caravans and later those of merchants brought supplies, people, livestock, and domestic and religious items to New Mexico. On their return journeys they carried New Mexican products — both Amerindian and Spanish — including hides, piñon nuts, and textiles southward for sale in northern New Spain and Mexico City.

Third, the social and cultural importance of the Camino Real de Tierra Adentro was profound. As people moved northward into New Mexico they brought with them ideas, practices, customs, traditions, and skills that became permanently implanted there. Music, sculpture, architecture, building construction (the use of straw as a binder for adobe bricks and *hornos* or beehive-shaped ovens, for example), furnishings for homes, textiles, ceramics, and the construction of *acequias* (irrigation ditches), dams, and bridges were all introduced into New Mexico. Likewise, the establishment of artisans (santeros and others) and customs (ceremonies such as Las Posadas, Los Pastores, Los Reyes Magos, La Conquistadora, Nuestra Señora de Guadalupe, and All Saints' Day) reached New Mexico, along with literature and traditional sayings. Finally, the Camino Real de Tierra Adentro played a role in establishing the diverse populace of Amerindians, Spaniards, Mexicans, Anglo-Americans, and others that created New Mexico's multicultural society.

From Amerindian trails and pueblos to Spanish explorers, conquistadores, and settlers, along with merchants, ecclesiastics, soldiers, government officials, and artisans, the Camino Real de Tierra Adentro had a significant role in the historical development of New Mexico for nearly three centuries. Even today, Interstate Highway 25 roughly parallels most of the route from El Paso to Santa Fe, serving as a principal connection between the United States and Mexico. Along with the Appalachian Trail, the Oregon Trail, the Santa Fe Trail, and other national historical trails, the Camino Real de Tierra Adentro served as a primary route of historical, international, and lasting significance in the expansion and development of the United States.

21

The Santa Fe Trail and Nineteenth-Century New Mexico: "We Encountered Six Americans"

Michael L. Olsen

One of the major events in New Mexico history took place shortly after three o'clock on a Tuesday afternoon, November 13, 1821, when don Pedro Ignacio Gallego accidentally met William Becknell at Puertocito de la Piedra Lumbre, a small gap in the foothills of the Sangre de Cristo Mountains known today as Kearny Gap. Their meeting, which led to the opening of the Santa Fe Trail and the invasion of New Mexico by the United States Army in 1846, is commemorated with a state historical marker about one mile south of Las Vegas, New Mexico.

Don Pedro Gallego was the alcalde of Abiquiú, a settlement on the northern frontier of New Mexico. He also was the captain of the local militia, known as the *militia urbana*. On November 2, 1821, he and 148 men under his leadership had left Abiquiú under orders from New Mexico's governor, Facundo Melgares. They were to follow the trail of a band of Navajos who had harried Spanish communities. Two days later another command arrived from the governor, requesting that Gallego change his plans and search for some Comanches who had raided in the vicinity of San Miguel del Vado, on the Pecos River east of Santa Fe. On his way to San Miguel, several hundred armed men from various Indian pueblos joined his forces, as did an additional 125 Spanish troops. From San Miguel this considerable army marched northeast, headed for the high plains of New Mexico.

William Becknell was a businessman who had failed at various enterprises on the Missouri frontier. Indeed, a warrant was out for his arrest on charges of nonpayment of his

March of the Caravan, Santa Fe Trail, 1849. Lithograph illustration from Commerce of the Prairies, *by Josiah Gregg.*

debts. Nevertheless, he was able to borrow several hundred dollars, which he invested in trade goods to sell in New Mexico. Up to this time, New Mexico had been closed to American trade by the laws of the Spanish Empire, but Mexico had revolted against Spanish rule. Rumors abounded on the Missouri frontier that if the revolt was successful, then Mexico would throw open its borders to outside trade. Becknell was gambling that this would happen before he got to Santa Fe. If not, he risked being arrested and imprisoned in Mexico.

Five other traders, whose names are unknown, accompanied Becknell. The party carried its trade goods on pack horses. These men had only a vague idea of how to get to Santa Fe. They reasoned that if they went far enough west across the plains of Kansas and Colorado and then turned south, they would stumble into Spanish settlements or be found by Spanish soldiers. It must have been a shock, though, when they faced Gallego's large force at the *puertocito*.

In a report to Governor Melgares, Gallego fully documented his meeting with the Becknell party. He wrote that "at 3:30 in the afternoon, I encountered *seis Americanos*.... They parleyed with me and at about 4 p.m. we halted at the stream at Piedra Lumbre." No one with Gallego spoke English. None of the Americans spoke Spanish. Each party, it seems, tried using various Indian sign languages, but to no avail. Then they made camp for the night. Although he gives no details, Gallego evidently sent back to San Miguel del Vado for someone — and here one can only speculate — who spoke French, the universal language of the North American fur trade. The interpreter arrived about one-thirty the next morning, and Gallego's hunch paid off. Becknell himself, it turned out, knew some French. The two parties now understood each other (Olsen and Myers 1992).

The next day Gallego sent Becknell and his men to Santa Fe with some of his troops. He and the rest of his force continued on the trail of the Comanches. The last portion of his report is lost, but he did get as far as the area between today's Springer and Clayton, New Mexico.

Back in Santa Fe, Governor Melgares cordially received Becknell, the first American to benefit from Mexico's emerging policy of open borders and trade. Becknell traded his goods for a significant profit, returned to Missouri, and came back to Santa Fe the next year with more merchandise. The *Missouri Intelligencer* newspaper for April 22, 1823, published his account of these two trips. The era of the Santa Fe Trail in the history of New Mexico had begun (Hulbert 1933, 56–68).

The Santa Fe Trail, 1821–1880

The Santa Fe Trail, from Becknell's trip in 1821 until it was overtaken by the completion of the Atchison, Topeka and Santa Fe Railroad into New Mexico in 1880, was always a commercial route, a trail traveled by businessmen seeking profits. Relative to the Oregon Trail, few pioneer families used it, although some American army officers and their wives and children who followed the trail after 1846 did settle in New Mexico Territory. At first, American merchants dominated the trail trade, but by the mid-1830s many Hispanic New Mexicans had invested in the wagons, mules, oxen, and trade items necessary for a profitable venture. Both groups had contacts with business houses in St. Louis, New Orleans, New York, and even London and Amsterdam that supplied trade goods.

The nature of the trail changed in 1846, when General Stephen Watts Kearny and his troops, following the trail, invaded New Mexico and annexed it to the United States. Freighting supplies down the trail for the many army posts subsequently established in the Southwest became increasingly important. During the American Civil War, Confederate troops followed the trail east from Santa Fe, intending to capture Fort Union, near Watrous, and then head north to the gold mines of Colorado. They were defeated at Glorieta Pass by U.S. Army soldiers from Fort Union and a contingent of Colorado volunteers. As the Atchison, Topeka and Santa Fe Railroad built west from Kansas, it, too, followed the trail, over Raton Pass and into New Mexico. With the completion of a spur line from Lamy to Santa Fe in 1880, the days of the Santa Fe Trail as a commercial highway and route to the Southwest were over.

When William Becknell and his companions left Missouri in 1821, they departed from the town of Franklin, on the Missouri River. A few years later a flood wiped out the town. From Franklin the eastern end of the trail moved west from one river port to the next. Eventually, most Santa Fe Trail wagons departed from Westport, Missouri, which is now engulfed by Kansas City. Leaving Westport, the trail tended west-southwest through Kansas, with some of the more notable campgrounds for caravans being at Lone Elm, Council Grove, and Diamond Spring. Once they reach the site of the present town of Great Bend, Kansas, the wagons followed the course of the Arkansas River to the vicinity of Dodge City. Near there the trail split, with one branch — the Cimarron Cutoff — crossing the river headed directly for Santa Fe via southwest Kansas, the Oklahoma Panhandle, and northeastern New Mexico. The other route, known as the Mountain Branch, followed the Arkansas into Colorado. It crossed from Colorado into New Mexico by way of Raton Pass and then made its way to Santa Fe. Until 1846 the Arkansas formed part of the international boundary between the Republic of Mexico and the United States of America in southwestern Kansas and southeastern Colorado.

Traders had to decide which of these two routes to take. Their choice was dictated by money, time, water, and the Native American peoples occupying the area. The Cimarron Cutoff, because it crossed no mountains until Glorieta Pass just above Santa Fe, was quicker than the Mountain Branch through Colorado. If a trader got his goods through early in the trading season, he could demand higher prices, because stocks of the previous year's trade items were low or sold out in Santa Fe. But the Cimarron Cutoff was more dangerous. The few streams on the high plains might dry up early in the summer or never run at all in drought years. It was especially easy to miss the Cimarron River in the Oklahoma Panhandle, because its bed was usually dry. The lack of water from that point on could doom a caravan as its mules and oxen died one by one. This was also the territory of the Comanches, the most feared and aggressive of the southern Plains Indians. Nevertheless, the lure of profits made the Cimarron Cutoff the preferred route until the early 1860s, when the withdrawal of U.S. Army troops from the west so that they could fight in the Civil War made it just too dangerous.

The Mountain Branch took longer but was safer. Water was readily available along the Arkansas and the numerous streams that flowed east from the mountains of southeastern Colorado and northern New Mexico. No Native peoples permanently occupied the foothills of the Sangre de Cristo Mountains. The Utes usually stayed west of the mountains, and the Comanches, Kiowas, and others congregated on the plains. Raton Pass was particularly difficult and time-consuming to cross until Dick Wooton cleared a toll road there in 1864, but for many, including the U.S. Army in 1846, the advantages of this route outweighed the disadvantages. Also, from the early 1830s until the late 1840s, Bent's Fort, near present La Junta, Colorado, was an important stop on the Mountain Branch. There merchants could rest, relax, refit their wagons, and perhaps do a bit of trading.

These two branches of the trail rejoined at the confluence of the Mora and Sapello Rivers at Watrous in Mora County. By the mid-1830s, the caravans might be met there by farmers from around Las Vegas in the Gallinas River valley twenty miles south. They sold the first fresh vegetables, eggs, and fruit travelers had seen since eastern Kansas. From Watrous the trail crossed the Gallinas River at Las Vegas and the Pecos River at San Miguel del Vado, went up the valley of the Pecos past Pecos

Pueblo, then over Glorieta Pass, from which it dropped down to the plaza in Santa Fe (Gregg 1954; Simmons and Jackson 2001).

A trip either way along the trail, from Missouri to New Mexico or from Santa Fe east, took six weeks or more. Hundreds of wagons made the journey every year. Traffic was heaviest in the summer, when merchants carried their goods out to New Mexico, but winter travel was not unheard of, especially if a merchant wound up his trading season late and was eager to get back to Missouri. Whenever taken, the journey was rigorous. Travelers in the summer could count on heat, dust, flies, gnats, and mosquitoes. At any time a broken axle, runaway mules, dead oxen, drought, flaring tempers, and a shortage of fresh-killed buffalo were possible. Unexpected perils might include violent summer storms with lightning and high winds or flash floods on normally tame creeks. Traders learned from experience never to camp on the near side of a creek they intended to cross, no matter how mild the weather. In late spring or early fall, ominous banks of clouds to the north might signal the arrival of a blizzard.

Josiah Gregg, in his 1844 memoir of the Santa Fe trade, *Commerce of the Prairies*, described a summer storm on the eastern plains of New Mexico:

> We were encamped at noon, when a murky cloud issued from behind the mountains, and, after hovering over us for a few minutes, gave vent to one of those tremendous peals of thunder which seem peculiar to those regions, making the elements tremble, and leaving us so stunned and confounded that some seconds elapsed before each man was able to convince himself that he had not been struck by lightning. A sulphureous stench filled the atmosphere.... It was not a little singular to find an ox lying lifeless from the stroke, while his mate stood uninjured by his side, and under the same yoke. (Gregg 1954, 76)

Another traveler, Albert Pike, caught in a blizzard at Point of Rocks, New Mexico, remembered: "Two or three hours before daylight the storm commenced with terrific violence, and I never saw a wilder or more terrible sight than was presented to us when day came. The wind swept fiercely out of the cañon, driving the snow horizontally against the wagons, and sweeping onward into the wide prairie, in which a sea of snow seemed raging. Objects were not visible at a distance of twenty feet" (Pike 1967, 16).

There could be compensations even in the midst of uncertainty and trouble. Many a person fell in love with the trail, particularly its vistas and the feeling of freedom it brought. Matt Field, a correspondent for the New Orleans newspaper the *Picayune*, took to the trail in 1839 and observed:

> Nothing in nature can be compared to the prairie but the ocean, and the similitude is most striking. The horizon bending to the land

resembles the meeting of sky and water; the rolling undulations of
the prairie are most like the heaving of old ocean; and the flutterings
of the silken grass imitate most exquisitely the ripples of the sea. Add
to this the slow rising of an object in the distance, particularly the
white top of a trader's wagon — ideas of the ocean are irresistibly
forced upon you — the distant wagon becomes a sail; the green grass
the green sea, and the wild roving herds [of buffalo], monsters of the
deep. (Sunder 1960, 281)

Oxen and mules were by far the preferred draft animals. Horses tired easily
and lacked stamina, but mules grimly persevered, and oxen, with their big feet, effi-
ciently crossed the sands encountered on the Cimarron Cutoff. Oxen, though, might
annoyingly drop dead in their traces without a sign of distress and when least expected.
Most people walked the entire distance of the trail. Exceptions might include military
officers mounted on horses or the occasional woman traveler whose husband, father,
or brother provided her with a carriage. Wagons did not carry passengers, who would
have taken up room that could be devoted to profit-earning cargo.

The style of wagons changed during the years of the Santa Fe Trail. William
Becknell took the first wagons to Santa Fe on his second trip there, in 1822. For the
rest of that decade and into the 1830s, almost anything with four wheels was used
along the trail. But by the late 1830s the trade was dominated by the famous Conestoga wagons, which merchants might have built to order in and around Pittsburg,
Pennsylvania. Later, Missouri wagon makers copied the Conestoga's essential features.
What became known as a "Santa Fe Wagon" appeared by the 1860s. It could carry
more than three tons of freight (Gardner 2000).

Santa Fe Trail Traders and Travelers

The thousands of people who experienced the Santa Fe Trail represented a cross section
of the populations of New Mexico and the United States. They included rich hacienda
owners and their wives and children, poor herders and farmers, single women, merchants, army officers and perhaps their families, artists, Native Americans, fur traders of French Canadian heritage, southern slave owners and their slaves, free African
Americans, and assorted frontier riffraff. Even Grand Duke Alexis of Russia made the
trek, coming to hunt buffalo in 1871.

Of those who traded on the trail, Miguel Antonio Otero was perhaps one of
the most important. He was born in 1829 at the Otero hacienda in Valencia County.
His family was distinguished, respected, and wealthy. As a teenager, Miguel was sent
to the United States for schooling. One of the earliest public records of him is from
a May 31, 1847, St. Louis newspaper noting his arrival in that city with several other
New Mexico youths on board the steamer *Tamerlane*. He was then eighteen and had

already been to school in St. Louis but had been called home at the outbreak of war between the United States and Mexico.

By 1851 don Miguel was studying law in New York City, and then in St. Louis, where he was admitted to the Missouri bar. At the same time he participated in his family's business activities along the Santa Fe Trail. Newspapers again noted his arrival in St. Louis, by the steamer *Kansas,* on May 24, 1851, with the intention of purchasing goods to haul down the trail. Early in July that year the driver of the stagecoach carrying the U.S. mail from Santa Fe to Independence, Missouri, reported that he had met Otero's caravan of thirty-five wagons out on the prairies, headed for Santa Fe. In 1857 Miguel Otero married Mary Josephine Blackwood, a South Carolinian whose family had business interests in St. Louis (Berry 1972, 685, 1002, 1026; Otero 1987).

Don Miguel was also active in New Mexico territorial politics in the 1850s and 1860s. He served as territorial delegate from New Mexico in the United States Congress for three terms, from 1855 to 1861. He proved to be an able politician. In the years before the Civil War he was mildly pro-slavery, demonstrating southern sympathies in Congress and supporting the passage of a Slave Code in New Mexico. His wife's family owned slaves. But he also ranked high in Abraham Lincoln's estimation, although he was a Democrat. Lincoln offered him the ambassadorship to Spain in 1861 and, when he turned that down, appointed him secretary of New Mexico Territory, somewhat the equivalent of a lieutenant governor today.

As was often the case in his day, Miguel Otero invested in many different businesses, making fortunes in some and losing money in others. His primary occupation was as a partner in Otero, Seller and Company, one of the most important freighting companies hauling goods up and down the Santa Fe Trail. But it was his role in bringing the Atchison, Topeka and Santa Fe Railroad to New Mexico for which he is perhaps most noted. This railroad had been laying track in Kansas since 1868. Otero, Seller and Company built warehouses and stores in the towns that sprang up at the ends of the tracks. As the railroad forged west, the company moved with it, building new stores. Its wagon trains would carry freight to New Mexico from the newest railroad town down what was left of the trail to Santa Fe. Don Miguel became well known to the officers of the Atchison, Topeka and Santa Fe.

By the late 1870s, the Denver and Rio Grande Railroad, laying tracks south in Colorado from Denver, was racing to beat the AT&SF over Raton Pass into New Mexico to tap into trade with the entire Southwest. As the race heated up, the AT&SF turned to Don Miguel for help. To get around certain difficulties in the laws of New Mexico, the AT&SF needed to set up a subsidiary company in the territory. It established the New Mexico and Southern Pacific Railroad, of which Otero became a vice-president. He knew whom to approach and work with in the territorial legislature. In gratitude for his services, one of the first towns the railroad established in New

Mexico, about five miles south of Raton, was named Otero. Today all traces of it have disappeared. Otero County, Colorado, formed in 1889, was also named for him.

In subsequent years Otero was a principal investor in other railroad ventures. He and a nephew owned Jemez Hot Springs and planned to open a hotel and spa there, served by a railroad from Bernalillo. At the time of his death he was active in the Las Vegas and Gulf Railroad, to be built from the Texas coast through Las Vegas, New Mexico, and on to Vancouver, British Columbia. It would have passed through some of the American West's most important mining and timber regions, but it was never constructed (Greever 1957, 159–60; Hall 1895, 242–47; Walker 1933, 87–88).

Don Miguel Antonio Otero died in 1882 at his home in Las Vegas, New Mexico. He was buried in the family plot in Riverside Cemetery, Denver, Colorado. The AT&SF provided his family and friends with a special train for the funeral, and hundreds of New Mexicans went. Colorado Governor Frederick W. Pitkin also attended. Newspapers throughout the Southwest noted his passing, with the *Daily Optic* of Las Vegas lamenting that "such men as he are seldom appreciated until after the dread summons have been served upon them" (Otero 1987, 280).

Like Otero, another great New Mexico businessman and politician, Ceran St. Vrain, got his start and made his fortune along the Santa Fe Trail. He was born on the Missouri frontier in 1802, the second of ten children. His father died in 1818, deeply in debt, and young St. Vrain suddenly had to make his own way in the world. He became a fur trapper and trader, signing on with an important St. Louis fur house, Pratte, Cabanne and Company. In 1824 he met up with William Becknell, back from two profitable trips to Santa Fe. St. Vrain convinced Bernard Pratte, his boss, to stake him to a wagon load of trade goods for the Santa Fe market. The trail became his road to success.

St. Vrain reached Santa Fe, sold out his stock, and began trapping beaver in the southern Rockies, sending the pelts back to Pratte. He met Charles Bent, another fur trapper, and in 1830 the two went into partnership, forming the enterprise that became Bent, St. Vrain and Company, the most successful and influential fur company in the Southwest. St. Vrain handled the firm's western affairs, both from its headquarters at Bent's Fort on the Arkansas River in Colorado and from his home in Taos. He became a Mexican citizen to further the company's interests. In 1832, the year Bent and St. Vrain constructed Bent's Fort, the company's fall caravan to Missouri transported $190,000 in silver, mules, and furs.

This was only the beginning for St. Vrain. In 1843 he and Cornelio Vigil, a prominent citizen of Taos, received a four-million-acre land grant from New Mexico Governor Manuel Armijo. This land lay between the Arkansas and Purgatoire Rivers in southeastern Colorado, covering the territory within a triangle drawn on a map today from Pueblo to Trinidad to La Junta, Colorado. When Vigil later died, St. Vrain became sole owner, although the U.S. Congress eventually confirmed his title to only 96,000 acres.

In 1849, Bent, St. Vrain and Company dissolved, Charles Bent having been killed in Taos in 1847. St. Vrain now adjusted himself to changing economic times. With the invasion of the Southwest by the United States and the stationing of large numbers of troops at various outposts, a lucrative market for agricultural produce arose, as did additional freighting opportunities. The army and its livestock needed to eat. St. Vrain won contracts to haul goods for the U.S. Army along the Santa Fe Trail and built a flour mill in Mora to supply the garrison at Fort Union, the largest post in the territory. He also established a brewery and a sawmill, selling the lumber at Fort Union. To oversee his new interests, he moved to Mora, which remained his principal residence for the rest of his life. St. Vrain also owned the *Santa Fe Gazette* newspaper and was the public printer for the territory, always a profitable contract to obtain. When gold was discovered in Colorado in 1859, he was on the spot, not to pan but to trade. He opened a store in Denver and quickly made another fortune.

In addition to these economic activities, St. Vrain skillfully weathered the political storms of his time. He represented American interests as United States consul in Santa Fe from 1834 to 1838. He strongly supported the acquisition of New Mexico by the United States and fought with U.S. troops when some New Mexicans resisted American occupation. When the Civil War broke out, he formed a unit of New Mexico volunteers but turned the command over to Kit Carson. St. Vrain died in Mora in 1870 and was buried, with full military honors provided by a contingent of soldiers from Fort Union, on a hillside above the town (Broadhead 1982; Mumey 1958).

Jewish merchants, many of them emigrants from Germany, also made fortunes via the Santa Fe Trail and contributed significantly to the economic and cultural life of New Mexico. In most instances, single Jewish men made their way west, recognized the potential of the trail trade, set up businesses — often crossing the plains annually with wagons and goods — and then brought brothers, cousins, nephews, wives, and in-laws to the Southwest.

Solomon Spiegelberg, Abraham Staab, and Charles Ilfeld exemplify such enterprise. Spiegelberg came to the United States as a teenager in 1842. Employed at first as a clerk in a St. Louis store, he came down the trail in 1846 in the wake of the invading United States Army. He engaged in retail trade in Santa Fe and also freighted supplies for the army and secured contracts at Indian agencies in New Mexico and Arizona. Abraham Staab was fifteen in 1854 when he landed in the United States. Two years later he was in Santa Fe working for Spiegelberg, and by 1858 he was in business with his brother Zadoc. By the 1860s their company had become the region's largest wholesale trading firm. Like Solomon Spiegelberg, the Staabs supplied army forts and Indian posts. The mansion Staab built for his wife and eight children still stands in Santa Fe.

Unlike Spiegelberg and Staab, Charles Ilfeld established his empire in Las Vegas, New Mexico, and then in Albuquerque. He came to the territory in 1865 at the age of eighteen. He settled first in Santa Fe, then in Taos, and finally in Las Vegas in 1867. Although he engaged in the trail trade, his principal success came with the shipment and sale of New Mexican commodities, notably wool and piñon nuts, to the eastern United States. The *piñones* found a ready market in "Little Italy" in New York City. A large sign on Ilfeld's store in Las Vegas carried the motto, "Wholesalers of Everything" (Tobias 1990; Twitchell 1925, 479–80).

Although businessmen dominated trade and travel, some women and children also experienced the Santa Fe Trail. Women, in fact, wrote many of the famous memoirs and diaries of trail life. Susan Shelby Magoffin's journal, published as *Down the Santa Fe Trail and into Mexico*, is the best known. Marian Russell, in her book *Land of Enchantment*, recalled the many trips she, her brother, and her mother, who was a cook for wagon caravans, took between Missouri and New Mexico. But the trail also had an effect on the lives of women from other ethnic groups and economic circumstances.

Perhaps the best-known Native American woman of trail days was Owl Woman, whose Cheyenne name was rendered in the English alphabet as Mis-stan-stur. Her father was White Thunder, who, as keeper of the sacred medicine arrows, was the Cheyennes' most important religious figure. Her husband was William Bent, brother of Charles Bent and partner with him and Ceran St. Vrain in Bent, St. Vrain and Company. William's marriage to Owl Woman was in some ways a trade alliance, because the Cheyenne were among the company's best customers. Owl Woman bore four children with William. She died in childbirth, or by some accounts in a cholera epidemic, in 1847. As with most Native American women, little more is known of her, although she did save William's life when he fell ill with diphtheria in 1845. She forced a hollow quill from a bird's feather down his clogged throat and blew a nourishing meat broth through it from her own mouth to feed him (Lavender 1972, 186–89, 255; Thompson 1974).

Gertrudes Barceló, otherwise known as Doña Tules, is the most famous Hispanic woman in Santa Fe Trail history, though she may never have ventured even one mile along the trail itself. She lived in Santa Fe, where she gained notoriety as the owner of a gambling hall. She became wealthy through her skill at the card game *monte*, the most popular game of chance in New Mexico. As in the case of Owl Woman, little is known of her private life, though as an unmarried businesswoman she had a dubious reputation. Dubious or not, few people refused an invitation to her parties and dances. She allegedly aided the American occupation of New Mexico in 1846, both by warning American authorities that there might be a revolt against them and by loaning the U.S. Army money when it ran short of funds to procure supplies. She died in 1851, and her funeral was one of the most lavish Santa Fe had ever seen (Gregg 1954, 168–69).

Charlotte Green was one of the very few African American women on the trail about whom much information exists, although some journals and diaries mention the slaves of travelers on the trail, such as "Jane," who accompanied Susan Shelby Magoffin. Charlotte was a slave of William Bent's, who also owned her husband, Dick Green. She was the chief cook at Bent's Fort, and visitors there praised her meals, so reminiscent to them of "state do'ins," or meals "back home," after weeks of trail fare. Sometimes after one of her suppers, tables would be pushed back and dancing would commence, with Charlotte much in demand as one of the few women available. William Bent granted Charlotte and her husband their freedom in 1847 in recompense for Dick's bravery while fighting with the U.S. Army in the occupation of New Mexico (Garrard 1987, 73–74; Thompson 1974, 15).

Susan Magoffin was only eighteen when she accompanied her husband, trader Samuel Magoffin, to Santa Fe and then on to old Mexico in 1846. She came from one of Kentucky's most prominent families and had an education befitting a woman of her time and status. Samuel, a friend of her father's, was twenty-seven years her senior. She traveled in a carriage and had a specially made tent in which to rest and sleep. Her comments on the food, drink, clothes, and housing she observed are especially valuable, because these aspects often went unnoticed in men's letters and journals. For instance, Mexican women shocked her sensibilities because they smoked cigarettes and wore dresses that revealed their shoulders and ankles. Susan suffered a miscarriage at Bent's Fort on her way to New Mexico. Her next child, born in Mexico, died in infancy. She gave birth to two daughters, in 1851 and 1855, after returning to the United States, but she herself died soon after the second was born. She was just twenty-seven years old (Drumm 1984, ix–xxxv).

The experiences of children on the trail are more difficult to discover than those of trail women. Marion Russell gives a glimpse of children playing tag among the wagons, just outside the circle of firelight, when the caravans had halted for the night on the prairie. Kit Carson was fifteen when he took to the trail to make his own way. When Kit's mother, Lucy, died, Kit's father remarried. Then his father died, and his stepmother remarried. Kit did not get on well with his stepfather and was apprenticed to a saddle maker in Franklin, Missouri. It was against the law for apprentices to run away, but Kit did. José Librado Gurulé was another youngster who worked on the trail. His family's *patrón*, the man whose land they farmed and to whom they probably owed money, chose José to accompany a Santa Fe Trail wagon train he was sending to Missouri. José spent eleven months on the journey and received eight dollars for his work. He was sixteen years old (Quaife 1996, 4; Russell 1993; Simmons 1986).

Miguel Otero, the son of don Miguel Antonio Otero, also saw the trail as a child. His childhood was one of privilege, comfort, and leisure. It was also full of adventure. Born in 1859, as a child he witnessed the last years of the Santa Fe Trail and the coming of the railroad. Miguel and his brother Page wanted nothing more than to grow up on the frontier. Their parents wanted them to go to school. Between 1866, when he was seven years old, and 1878, when he was nineteen, Miguel was sent to and ran away from, quit, or talked his way out of a boarding school in Topeka, Kansas, a private school in Leavenworth, Kansas, St. Louis University, the United States Military Academy at West Point, and the University of Notre Dame. Don Miguel would no more than get him sent off on the train east when Miguel Junior would hop on a train west.

As a child, Miguel came to know many of the famous frontier figures of the day. He met Wild Bill Hickock in Hays City, Kansas, in 1868, when he was nine years old. He remembered that Wild Bill

> dropped into the office of Otero & Sellar very frequently to talk to my father, who was a member of the Vigilance Committee. I took a great fancy to him and greatly enjoyed his company. At that time both my brother Page and myself had a stable with several fine saddle horses. No better horses could be found on the frontier, for they were trained buffalo hunters and seemed to enjoy the sport as much as the rider. You could fire off a gun between their ears without bothering them in the least. Wild Bill was very fond of good horses, and he was always welcome to any we had. Thus we became very good friends. He often took my brother and myself on buffalo hunts. (Otero 1987, 14)

Miguel eventually convinced his father (or wore him down) that school in the East was not for him. He clerked in his father's store in Otero and then in 1879 in Las Vegas. Twenty years later he became territorial governor of New Mexico.

The Commerce of the Trail

When William Becknell left Franklin, Missouri, on September 1, 1821, one of the principal trade goods he carried was commercially woven cotton cloth. After that, Santa Fe Trail wagons increasingly transported a bewildering array of merchandise, from luxury items such as French wines and barrels of oysters to cloth, other "dry goods," and "notions." In 1844, for example, the firm of Webb and Doan freighted articles worth a total of $6,267.22 to Santa Fe (Webb 1995, 128–29). These goods included, in part,

> Fancy, black, white, pink, and mourning prints
> Brown, and bleached sheeting
> Striped, and checked muslins
> Blue, and linen drillings
> Scarlet, and zebra cloth
> Blue, black and green alpaca
> Red, and white flannel
> Black cambric
> Striped, plaid, and black cashmere
> Bleached domestics
> French lawns
> Irish linens
> White, and fancy edgings
> Cotton flags
> Bandana, black silk, cotton, and red pongee handkerchiefs

German shawls
White cotton hose
Hickory shirts
Blue denims
Buck gloves
Black silk ties
Suspenders
Green shoe thread
Fine ivory combs
Beads
Necklaces
Gold rings
Fancy, and gilt hair pins
Pearl shirt buttons
Gilded vest buttons
Needles
Scissors
Razors
Strops
Coffee mills
Sadirons
Log chains
Shovels
Spades
Hoes
Axes
Percussion caps
Cork inkstands
Shaving soap
Candlewick

By the 1830s many of these items would have passed through Santa Fe and been shipped south for sale in Mexico, which increasingly became as profitable a market as New Mexico. Sometimes Santa Fe Trail traders themselves took freight south, but in other instances Hispanic New Mexicans bought the goods and exported them.

In return for these goods, New Mexicans largely paid cash, although furs, some wool, and thousands of mules also went east. These mules became the ancestors of the famous Missouri mule, used on farms throughout the Midwest and South in the nineteenth and into the twentieth centuries. But it was mainly silver that Americans wanted. Wealthy New Mexicans had earned silver pesos by selling hundreds of thousands of sheep on the hoof as meat and pelts in the mining districts of Mexico for more than a hundred years. This silver helped finance the development and expansion of the American frontier from the 1820s through the 1850s (Boyle 1997; Elder and Weber 1996; Gardner 1993).

The sheer quantity of trade goods available, from cloth and clothing to iron tools, changed the way people lived and worked. These goods found their way to Indian pueblos, haciendas, and towns from Mesilla to Taos. In the homes of the wealthy, window glass and iron-hinged wooden doors replaced mica panes and hanging hides, for example. Even the poor could afford a few yards of cloth, which might be used for indoor decoration and improvement. As early as 1846, Captain Philip St. George Cook, commander of a unit of the invading United States Army, noticed that householders purchased lengths of calico and attached them to their whitewashed walls above the doubled up woolen mattresses that served them as "settees" during the day, because the whitewash flaked so easily. Even the traditional religious icons in homes, the *santos*, began disappearing as cheap colored prints of Catholic saints and other religious subjects, published by Catholic presses in the United States and brought down the trail, began to flood the market and adorn homes of both the wealthy and the poor (Cooke 1964, 20; Weber 1982, 207–41).

The trail also brought a cash economy to the region. New Mexicans had never been wholly self-sufficient, of course, even on their farms and ranches. Nor did New Mexico ever have a strictly barter economy, especially with silver pesos flowing north from Mexico over the centuries. But there never had been an incentive to raise more squash or wheat than a family needed. This situation changed dramatically and suddenly with the influx of traders and their families and then especially with the troops and livestock of the U.S. Army after 1846. Now a market existed for excess production. By the 1850s, Ceran St. Vrain began contracting with farmers in the Mora Valley to plant more wheat. He guaranteed purchase of the crop, which he ground into flour at his mill on the Mora River and sold, again under contract, to the U.S. Army at Fort Union. By the 1890s the Mora Valley was the breadbasket of New Mexico, with more acreage in wheat than at any time since.

Another means of earning cash money for New Mexicans was by freighting goods for the U.S. Army, either along the Santa Fe Trail or to outlying posts such as Fort Bascom, near Tucumcari, and Fort Wingate, near Gallup. The army's distribution center was Fort Union. The army let bids on contracts for shipping goods from this central depot. Vincente Romero, from La Cueva, near Mora, was one businessman who took advantage of this opportunity. In 1866 the army hired six of Romero's teams and wagons, in this case to bring army men and their baggage all the way from Fort Leavenworth in eastern Kansas, at the rate of $8.00 per wagon per day. With the cash they earned, contractors could pay their teamsters, herders, and other employees, who, with their families, could then purchase items for sale in local stores and trading houses (McDougal 2003; Miller 1990; Sperry 1990).

The advent of this cash economy ultimately changed social relationships, political power, and even family ties. Money could now bring social prestige to those who had never had any social position. Money also bought political influence or political office. Extended families that had lived together in rural communities or at the Indian pueblos now began to split up as members took jobs for wages in the new commercial centers, traveled outside the region for their employers, or followed their own business interests.

Manuel Salustiano Delgado and his family exemplify the influence of the trail. The Delgados had long been politically and economically prominent in Santa Fe. Manuel and some of his five sons traded along the trail and down into Mexico beginning in the 1840s. They also added to their fortune by managing the business interests of other Hispano merchants. Through their trail activities and acting "as intermediaries for wealthy New Mexicans," the family and its descendants remained influential in the region into the twentieth century (Boyle 1977, 96–99).

The Santa Fe Trail Today

Although the era of the Santa Fe Trail ended in 1880, its legacy and heritage have lived on. Tales of the trail have enriched American cultural life. More than a hundred novels with a trail background have been written by novelists such as Zane Grey, whose *Fighting Caravans* (1929) and *The Lost Wagon Train* (1932) are each set on the trail. There are dozens of fictional and nonfiction children's books about the trail. Hollywood has borrowed themes from trail life for the movies, the best known of which was called simply *The Santa Fe Trail*. Produced in 1940, it starred Ronald Reagan and Errol Flynn. In the late 1930s and early 1940s, Americans danced to a popular romantic ballad, "Along the Santa Fe Trail," that Bing Crosby, the Glenn Miller Orchestra, and others recorded. Over the years, numerous tourist items have also featured the trail, such as neckties, drinking glasses, restaurant placemats, and coffee mugs.

Today the trail is firmly fixed in America's historical consciousness and in the American landscape. More than a century ago, in 1902, the Daughters of the American Revolution, fearing that knowledge of the trail was being lost as those who remembered it died, began to mark the old trail by placing inscribed stone monuments along its route. These markers are still treasured and maintained. In 1987 President Ronald Reagan approved legislation creating the Santa Fe National Historic Trail as a part of the National Historic Trails System, administered by the National Park Service.

Four National Park Service units lie on the trail: Fort Larned in Kansas, Bent's Fort in Colorado, and Fort Union and Pecos National Historic Park in New Mexico. The Park Service works with states, localities, and private landowners along the trail to protect and promote it and has marked the route of the trail along major highways in Missouri, Kansas, Colorado, Oklahoma, and New Mexico. In 1986, historians and trail buffs formed the Santa Fe Trail Association, which now has regional chapters along the entire length of the trail and is dedicated to preserving the trail and raising public consciousness about its history and importance.

Ruins of Pecos, *1846–47, from an 1848 report by Lt. James W. Abert.*

22

Pecos Pueblo:
Tourists and Tall Tales

John L. Kessell (1979)

For years the faithful remnant of the Pecos nation had suffered reason enough to abandon their ancestral pueblo. What finally impelled them to do it is not known, although some wondrous myths have been invented to account for it. The year, tradition has it, was 1838, one year after a rabid New Mexico mob beheaded Gov. Albino Pérez.

The move was calculated. They packed up their ceremonial gear, and, again according to tradition, arranged with the local Hispanos to take care of the church and celebrate the feast of Nuestra Señora de los Ángeles, la Porciúncula, every August 2, which they do to this day. The refugees may have broken their trip at Sandía. Their final destination, eighty miles west of Pecos by trail, was Jémez, the only other pueblo that spoke the Towa language....

Commenting on the Pecos migration eleven years after it happened, a talkative Jémez told Lieutenant Simpson (1852, 22–23) that,

> during one of the revolutions of the country, when he was quite a youth, this tribe, being very much harassed by the Spaniards, (Mexicans,) asked permission of the people of Jémez to come and live among them. They not only granted them permission to do this, but sent out persons to help them get in their crops,

and bring them and their property to their new abode. When they arrived, they gave them houses and fields.

There were seventeen or twenty of them, led by Juan Antonio Toya....

One year later, in September of 1839 — a year that saw a quarter of a million dollars in goods rumble past on the Santa Fe Trail — an irrepressible Matthew C. Field, actor, journalist, and rover, spent the night with Dr. David Waldo in the Pecos church. His article about the "dilapidated town called *Pécus*," which he guessed rightly "in its flourishing days must have been inhabited by not less than two thousand souls," soon appeared in the New Orleans *Picayune*. "The houses now are all unroofed," he wrote,

> and the walls crumbling. The church alone yet stands nearly entire, and in it now resides a man bent nearly double with age, and his long silken hair, white with the snow of ninety winters, renders him an object of deep interest to the contemplative traveller. The writer with a single American companion once passed a night in this old church, entertained by the old man with a supper of hot porridge made of pounded corn and goat's milk, which we drank with a shell spoon from a bowl of wood, sitting upon the ground at the foot of the ruined altar by the light of a few dimly burning sticks of pine. In this situation we learned from the old man the following imperfect story, which is all the history that is now known of the city of the Sacred Fire.

Whereupon, in purple prose, Field launched into the tale of how Montezuma had chosen the Pecos as his people and had commanded them to keep a sacred fire burning in a cave until his coming again. Josiah Gregg claimed to have seen it smouldering in a kiva. For centuries the Pecos remained faithful to the trust. "Man, woman, and child shared the honor of watching the holy fire, and the side of the mountain grew bare as year after year the trees were torn away to feed the consuming torch of Montezuma." Then "a pestilential disorder came in the summer time and swept away the people." Only three were left: a venerable chief, his daughter, and her betrothed. The old man expired. The lovers grew weak. Just before death overcame them, the young man had an idea.

Taking a brand from the fire, he grasped his beloved by the hand and led her out of the cave. "A light then rose in the sky which was not the light of morning, but the heavens were red with the flames that roared and crackled up the mountain side. And the lovers lay in each other's arms, kissing death from each other's lips, and smiling to see the fire of Montezuma mounting up to heaven."

Still, Matt Field did not reckon he had done justice to the old man's story.

He told it in glowing words and with a rapt intensity which the writer has endeavored to imitate, but he feels that the attempt is a failure. The scene itself — the ruined church — the feeble old man bending over the ashes, and the strange tones of his thin voice in the dreary midnight — all are necessary to awaken such interest as was felt by the listeners. Such is the story, however, and there is no doubt but that the legend has a strong foundation, in truth; for there stands the ruined town, well known to the Santa Fé traders, and there lives the old man, tending his goats on the hill side during the day, and driving them into the church at night.... It was imperative upon us to leave the place before day light that we might reach our destination (San Miguel) early the next morning, so that we could not gratify our curiosity by descending the cavern ourselves, but we gave the old man a few bits of silver, and telling him that the story with which he had entertained us should be told again in the great United States, we each pocketed a cinder of the sacred fire and departed (Sunder 1960, 50–51, 247–51; Gregg 1954, 188–90; Bandelier 1881, 82).

Montezuma, the perpetual fire, and a great serpent god "so huge that he left a track like a small arroyo" were off and running (summary in Simmons 1974, 127–34; also Bandelier 1881, 125–26; Curtis 1926, 19–21; Roberts 1932, 359–60).

The era of Pecos as monument had begun. The living pueblo was dead...

Epilogue

Actually, neither people nor place really died. They simply parted company.

At Jémez pueblo, the Pecos refugees settled into homes and planted fields provided by their hosts, but they did not forget who they were....

The Jémez people had welcomed the remnant of powerful Pecos. These immigrants, headed by Juan Antonio Toya, brought with them religious objects and practices to add to those of Jémez. They brought with them the Pecos bull, and fetiches, and the Pecos Eagle Catchers' society. And they brought an image of Nuestra Señora de los Ángeles, La Porciúncula, whose feast, August 2, the pueblo of Jémez began to celebrate along with that of its own patron San Diego....

They did not forget. From time to time they made pilgrimages back to their ancestral home, where they continued to maintain shrines....

While the last of the Pecos "kept the faith" at Jémez, a motley procession of traders, soldiers, and tourists was tracking through the ruins of their former homes, scratching graffiti, pocketing souvenirs, and recounting the fantastic tales of "a lost civilization."

If Thomas James (1962) heard the tales in 1821, he did not repeat them. Ten years later, Albert Pike (1967) heard them all right — Montezuma, the eternal fire in a cave, and worship of a giant snake — but he did not fix them precisely on Pecos. That came soon enough. An article by "El Doctor Masure" in the *Santa Fe Republican* of September 24, 1847, told of a visit in 1835 to the "furnace of Montezuma" at Pecos. Josiah Gregg (1954), too, said that he had descended into a Pecos kiva and "beheld this consecrated fire, silently smouldering under a covering of ashes, in the basin of a small altar."

Ever since the sixteenth century, Spanish chroniclers had associated ruins north of Mexico with the origin of the Aztecs and with Montezuma. The legendary pre-conquest feathered serpent had slithered northward even earlier. When, in the romantic atmosphere of the nineteenth century, Pecos became a bona fide and easily accessible ruin, it is no wonder that such specters took up residence here. "Ere the May-flower drifted to Plymouth's snow rock, this vestal flame was burning…and yet till Montezuma shall return — so ran the charge — that fire must burn."

Artist John Mix Stanley, with the invading Army of the West in 1846, sketched both mission church and pueblo ruins, and in House Executive Document No. 41 of the Thirtieth Congress, First Session, the former was labeled "Catholic Church" and the latter "Astek Church." Army engineers W. H. Emory and J. W. Abert related the Montezuma legend at Pecos, where "the fires from the '*estuffa*' burned and sent their incense through the same altars from which was preached the doctrine of Christ" and where "they were said to keep an immense serpent, to which they sacrificed human victims."

Yet no one topped young Pvt. Josiah M. Rice (1970), who passed by in 1851 with Col. Edwin V. Sumner's command. "There are," claimed Rice, "many traditions connected with this old church, one of which is that it was built by a race of giants, fifty feet in height. But these, dying off, they were succeeded by dwarfs, with red heads who, being in their turn exterminated, were followed by the Aztecs."

Pondering Montezuma's alleged birth at Pecos and his vow to return, the astute Adolph F. Bandelier (1881) in 1880 ascribed the tale to "an evident mixture of a name with the Christian faith in a personal redeemer, and dim recollections of Coronado's presence and promise to return." Of course it may also have become a convenient ruse employed by the Pueblos to mislead inquisitive whites. Lt. John G. Bourke (1933–1938), contemporary of Bandelier and ethnologist in his own right, found the Montezuma story "among the Pueblos who have had most to do with Americans and Mexicans and among no others." No matter, thought historian Ralph Emerson Twitchell in 1910. "This story is the veriest rot."

PART FIVE

BECOMING THE SOUTHWEST

Between the adoption of the first seal of the territory in 1851 (Office of the Secretary of State) and the dedication of Coronado State Monument at Bernalillo in 1940 (Weigle), New Mexico came to renown in the U.S. Southwest. The treaty of peace between the United States and Mexico ending the April 1846–February 1848 Mexican-American War was executed at the city of Guadalupe Hidalgo on February 2, with ratification exchanged in Querétaro on May 30 and proclamation made on July 4, 1848. The American triumph inspired the 1860s territorial seal that became the basis for the present Great Seal of the State: "It featured the American Bald Eagle, its outstretched wings shielding a smaller Mexican Eagle, symbolizing the change of sovereignty from Mexico to the United States" (Office of the Secretary of State).

From 1848 until "the conclusion of the southwestern Indian wars in 1886, no United States institution was more visible than the regular army in New Mexico Territory and the Greater Southwest," with its primary focus on "fighting and managing the region's Indians, particularly the nomadic and semi-nomadic tribes." The commands of four officers — Edwin Vose Sumner, Dixon S. Miles, James H. Carleton, and Ranald S. Mackenzie — "illustrate the army's efforts to adapt its operations to the southwestern region" (Ball). After the Civil War, "black cavalry and infantry troops were sent to New Mexico and elsewhere in the West to take part in the Indian wars and the protection of settlers." The Indians named them buffalo soldiers "because of their short curly hair and their courage and fortitude, much admired qualities of the buffalo" (Wroth).

The "Organic Act Establishing the Territory of New Mexico" was approved on September 9, 1850. Pueblo Indians had voted in the 1850 election but were disfranchised by Congress in 1854. Not until August 1948 did a three-judge tribunal hearing Isleta Pueblo war veteran Miguel H. Trujillo's case for voter registration render "a landmark decision" that "brought New Mexico into line constitutionally and granted the Indians of the state a right that should have been theirs since New Mexico became a territory." Enfranchisement was embedded in a complex of territorial and statehood issues about defining Indian homelands and assimilating Indians into American culture or acknowledging their cultural sovereignty in matters such as "religious freedom, educational choice, and Native versus Western medicine." This was the situation between the 1880s and 1920s, "long before the changes introduced in Indian Country in the 1960s and 1970s, often described as the era of 'self-determination'" (Connell-Szasz).

United States Surveyor General William Pelham arrived in Santa Fe in late January 1854 and set up an office near the Palace of the Governors. He was "to ascertain the origin, nature, character, and extent of all claims to land under the Treaty of Guadalupe Hidalgo under the laws of Spain and Mexico, a monumental task for which he was ill prepared...[because] he was unversed in the law and history of Spain and Mexico and could not read Spanish. He was, as his title implied, a land surveyor." By the late 1870s the "understaffed and underfunded" Office of the Surveyor General of New Mexico was a failing system. Land speculators, notably the Santa Fe Ring of lawyers, "judges, politicians, and businessmen," including, "besides the surveyors general, nearly every governor of New Mexico from the late 1860s to 1885," worked against rightful indigenous and Hispanic land grant holders. The "stories of land loss resulting from the United States' invasion of the Southwest" continued well into the twentieth century and still "need to be told repeatedly, whether or not the federal or state government ever provides redress or even admits responsibility for the injustice of land grant adjudication" (Ebright).

Territorial governor Lew Wallace, author of *Ben Hur: A Tale of the Christ*, a popular novel first published by Harper and Brothers on November 12, 1880, occupied the Palace of the Governors from 1878 to 1881, "at the height of the Lincoln County War." That conflict between powerful mercantile, ranching, agricultural, and political interests in the area, some backed by the Santa Fe Ring, generated "bitter memories" that persisted well into the twentieth century. The Lincoln County War "is today ranked as one of the most lawless episodes in the history of the American West." In large part this continuing notoriety comes from the saga of New Mexico's most famous outlaw hero, "a young man [born 1859?], handy with a gun, who identified himself as William H. Bonney [and who] in the less than four years of life remaining to him...would shoot his way into the history books under the name Billy the Kid" (Simmons).

Francis Boyer walked from Georgia to the Roswell area in 1896, inspired by his father's stories of New Mexico while serving with Colonel Alexander Doniphan's Army of Missouri Volunteers during the Mexican-American War. He and fellow foot traveler Dan Keyes "played a central role" in establishing the now long abandoned Blackdom, "a community of scattered homesteads, and a distinct town founded in 1920," all "built by and for blacks, people fleeing the oppression of post–Civil War life in Mississippi, Arkansas, Texas, and other southern states" (Gibson).

The Atchison, Topeka and Santa Fe Railroad broke ground in downtown Topeka, Kansas, on October 30, 1868. The first Santa Fe train entered New Mexico over Raton Pass in December 1878. Santa Fe track reached the Arizona border by July 1881, and Albuquerque businessmen organized a Territorial Fair for October 3–8 of that year. In their program and publicity they called on the Bureau of Immigration, which had been operating in an "Office in Adobe Palace [of the Governors], Santa Fe," since April 15, 1880, as a center from which "to prepare and disseminate accurate information as to the soil, climate, minerals, resources, productions and business of New Mexico, with special reference to its opportunities for development; and the inducements and advantages which it presents to desirable immigration and for the investment of capital" (Weigle).

The Santa Fe Railroad emerged from receivership in December 1895 as the Atchison, Topeka and Santa Fe Railway. By the early twentieth century, corporate advertising campaigns for it and the closely associated Fred Harvey Company of restaurants, hotels, dining car food service, museums, and tourist sales venues at the Grand Canyon, at Lamy, on the Albuquerque station platform with its grand Harvey Alvarado Hotel (opened on May 11, 1902) and next-door Indian Building, and elsewhere touted the "Great Southwest along the Santa Fe." Those campaigns extended to Santa Fe itself in 1926, when the railway purchased and leased La Fonda, a failed hotel on the Santa Fe plaza, to the Harvey Company. It became headquarters for the guided automobile Santa Fe Harvey Indian Detours, announced in 1925 and launched in April 1926 between Las Vegas, Santa Fe, and Albuquerque. The excursions enabled "rail tourists from Chicago and California to see points of historic and scenic interest in this state… [during] a pleasant break in the cross continent rail trip the year 'round" (Weigle).

Called "Land of Sunshine" since the late nineteenth century, New Mexico entered the union as the Sunshine State. Governor Clyde Tingley reorganized the State Highway Department after he took office on January 1, 1935, establishing the New Mexico State Tourist Bureau in May 1935. Florida had dubbed itself the Sunshine State by 1934, so Albuquerque advertising executive Ward Hicks and Tourist Bureau director Joseph A. Bursey adopted "Land of Enchantment," from the title of a 1906 Southwest travel book by Lilian Whiting, for the bureau's campaigns. "Land of Enchantment" first appeared on license plates in 1941, but despite efforts in 1947 and 1999, it was not designated the state's official nickname until Governor Bill Richardson signed enabling legislation on April 6, 2003.

On display in Albuquerque at the first Territorial Fair in October 1881 were "relics of antiquity exhibited by the Historical Society," an organization founded in Santa Fe on December 15, 1859. What grew into the Historical Society of New Mexico's "substantial collection encompassing documents, photographs, and 'objects of curiosity'" was initially housed in a building near the Santa Fe parish church (now the Cathedral Basilica of St. Francis), likely "the first history museum with curated exhibits west of the Mississippi" (Stevenson). In 1882 the society began meeting in the Palace of the Governors and from 1885 into the 1930s maintained a separate museum there. Its extensive collections officially became part of the Museum of New Mexico on June 29, 1977.

23

The Seal of New Mexico

Office of the Secretary of State (2003)

New Mexico's first seal was designed shortly after the Territorial Government was organized in 1851. The original seal has long since disappeared, possibly as part of the artifacts placed into the cornerstone of the Soldiers Monument in the Santa Fe Plaza. Imprints of the original seal show it consisted of the American Eagle, clutching an olive branch in one talon, and three arrows in the other. Along the outside rim was the inscription "Great Seal of the Territory NM."

In the early 1860's an unknown official adopted a new seal utilizing a design similar to today's Great Seal. It featured the American Bald Eagle, its outstretched wings shielding a smaller Mexican Eagle, symbolizing the change of sovereignty from Mexico to the United States in 1846. The smaller Mexican Brown, or Harpy Eagle grasped a snake in its beak and cactus in its talons, portraying an ancient Aztec myth. The outside rim of the seal contained the words "Territory of New Mexico," with the date 1850 along the bottom in Roman numerals (MDCCCL).

It is not clear when the Latin phrase "Crescit Eundo" was added to the seal, but in 1882, Territorial Secretary W. G. Ritch embellished the earlier design with the phrase, which translates as "it grows as it goes." This version of the seal was officially adopted as New Mexico's "official seal and coat of arms" by the Territorial Legislature in 1887.

When New Mexico became a state in 1912, the Legislature named a Commission for the purpose of designing a State Seal. In the meantime, the Legislature authorized interim

New Mexico state seal, made with assorted pieces of hardware, 1912.

use of the Territorial Seal with the words "Great Seal of the State of New Mexico" substituted. In June 1913, the Commission, which consisted of Governor William C. McDonald, Attorney General Frank W. Clancy, Chief Justice Clarence J. Roberts, and Secretary of State Antonio Lucero, filed its report adopting the general design of the Territorial Seal, substituting only the date 1912 for the Roman numerals. That seal is still in use today as the Official Seal of New Mexico.

24

The U.S. Army in New Mexico, 1848–1886

Durwood Ball

On July 6, 1849, Major Enoch Steen left Santa Fe, New Mexico, with Company H of the Second United States Dragoons. His object was to investigate the several "murders recently committed near Placero," a tiny mining community that lay on the Rio Grande a little south of Albuquerque. Company H and its commander, First Lieutenant F. L. Thomas, followed Steen south to the hamlet, where his investigations led him to conclude that "a small number of the Apacha [*sic*] tribe" — not Comanches as originally reported — were the "probable perpetrators" of the killings. Joined at Placero by Company G of the First Dragoons under Lieutenant Taylor and a company of New Mexico volunteers under Captain Chapman, Steen's party passed east through Cañon de Carnue (today's Tijeras Canyon) to San Antonito for a rendezvous with supply wagons escorted by a "sergeant + eight privates" of Company I of the First Dragoons.

From near the canyon's head, Steen's remarkable scout began. On July 9, his command — Thomas's Company H, Taylor's Company G, Chapman's volunteers, the dragoon detail, and Surgeon Rogers — coursed twenty miles southward from San Antonito to Ojo del Cuerbo along the eastern slope of the Manzano Mountains. The next day's march brought the unit to a spring near Manzano, a Hispanic community at the southern end of the range. There Steen hired a "Mexican" guide, Juan, who had been a "captive among the Apacha" for many years and "was perfectly well acquainted with their country." Juan led the column south to "Cuara" (probably Quarai),

Brigadier General James H. Carleton, about 1866.

the site of a seventeenth-century Spanish mission ruin, where Steen ordered a halt to graze the animals and, as Juan advised, assemble a small pack train.

On July 11, leaving the wagons and remaining provisions under the care of a sergeant's detail, Steen marched his column generally southeast toward the "Sierra Jumanes" until eleven o'clock that night. By the end of the following day, the soldiers had covered fifty-five miles, finally finding water in a mountain gorge. Another waterless, fifty-mile march brought Steen's troops around the Jumanes, into the Rio Pecos valley, and to Ojo de los Patos (Duck Spring). Along this trail the column discovered "tracks of horses + cattle" likely "stolen" by the Apaches at the time of the murders.

The following day, while pursuing this track, the soldiers met "a little Mexican boy" whom the Apaches had captured near Las Salinas but who had escaped them five days earlier. The hungry, exhausted child claimed that his captors had bragged about killing "three persons near Placer." Taking the boy along, Steen's column crossed the Rio Ruidoso (Noisy River), which falls from the Sierra Blanca (White Mountain). The pursuit during the sixteenth led the unit through abandoned Apache camping grounds with "remains of Twig Lodges, Camp Fires, Barked Trees" and other debris.

After spending the night at Arroyo Tularosa, Steen divided his column. He took Thomas's company into a canyon of the Sacramento Mountains while Chapman's and Taylor's men marched around their base. After a fruitless search in both directions, the two squadrons reunited at a place Steen called Laborcito de los Apaches, twenty miles to the south. That evening Juan and a few other men set out under darkness to locate the Apaches but found no villages. A day-long ride south along the Sacramento Mountains terminated at "Canion del Perri." Steen's store of provisions was nearly empty, the men and horses were exhausted, and all hope of discovering the Indians seemed to vanish in the Sacramentos. Major Steen, a frontier dragoon of sixteen years' service, pondered what to do next.

He decided to make one final thrust at the Apaches. After sending the Company I detachment back to Manzano, he launched a column under Lieutenant Thomas into the mountains. The men finally located some Apaches and engaged them inconclusively. When the supremely satisfied Thomas returned, Steen took the column about seventy miles due west to the army post at Doña Ana, near the southern end of the Jornada del Muerto (Journey of Death), arriving there on June 21, 1849.

Although Steen lost no men to wounds or death, many of the troopers were weak or ill from "fatigue and privation," and the column left on the trail "many horses completely given out." Steen reported that, in the mountains, rain fell on his men "everyday and somes twice or thrice," soaking their clothing, equipment, provisions, and animals. Between showers, oppressive sun and heat pounded everyone.

The major's arduous scout, taking his men some three hundred miles from Santa Fe to Doña Ana, was a large expenditure of men, horses, equipment, and time. The one measurable gain from the operation was Steen's detailed report, which described the deserts, grasslands, and rivers, little known to the army, below Manzano.

However, his scout demonstrated the awesome effort that any military operation, large or small, would require in New Mexico and the greater Southwest.

The addition of Texas, New Mexico, California, and Oregon to the United States between 1845 and 1848 placed enormous stress on the men and materiel of the tiny regular army — only ten thousand officers and men following the Mexican-American War. That number would ultimately settle at about twenty-five thousand officers and men following the Civil War, but the federal government expected this small professional force to defend well over two million square miles of plains, deserts, and mountains in the trans-Mississippi West. The thousands of Indians native to the region promised to challenge, canyon by canyon and valley by valley, the army's efforts to subdue them. Given the manpower shortages, supply deficiencies, and geographical challenges found in the West, the army's task was Herculean — almost impossible to achieve.

Between the end of the Mexican-American War in 1848 and the conclusion of the southwestern Indian wars in 1886, no United States institution was more visible than the regular army in New Mexico Territory and the greater Southwest. Revenue from army supply contracts helped float the regional economy, and officers and enlisted men spent their pay on products and services sold by local entrepreneurs. But the primary focus of the army in territorial New Mexico was fighting and managing the region's Indians, particularly the nomadic and semi-nomadic tribes.

At the end of the war with Mexico, federal authorities estimated that twenty thousand to forty thousand "wild" Indians inhabited the plains and mountains that lapped against the Hispanic and Pueblo Indian towns and villages in the watersheds of the Rios Grande and Pecos. The combined population of Hispanos and Pueblos approximated fifty-five thousand souls, but the nomadic Indians appeared to hold the upper hand in military affairs in 1848. New Mexicans, the U.S. Congress, and the president expected the troops of the United States Army to turn the tide against the Indians.

Between 1848 and 1886, the army vigorously operated against the region's Indian peoples. The commands of four army officers, Edwin Vose Sumner, Dixon S. Miles, James H. Carleton, and Ranald S. Mackenzie, illustrate the army's efforts to adapt its operations to the southwestern region. Given that Indian warriors generally waged guerrilla war, these commanders learned, with mixed successes, to apply methods of destruction against the societies that supported them. They purposely targeted the villages and property of Native peoples to impoverish them and bring them to the treaty table or to the reservation. In the process, federal troops inflicted casualties on noncombatants — women, children, and elders.

Lieutenant Colonel Edwin V. Sumner

Between 1846 and 1851, military government, or the army, ran New Mexico. The commanding officer of the Ninth Military Department governed the occupied territory by proclamation. Aiding his administration was a collection of judicial, law enforcement, and executive offices created by the Organic Act (or Kearny Code) in 1846 and a remnant of Mexican offices left behind by the last Mexican governor, Manuel Armijo. After crushing the Taos and Mora rebellions in early 1847, Colonel Sterling Price combined the offices of civil governor and commander-in-chief of occupied New Mexico. His successors, Majors John M. Washington and John Munroe, experienced little unrest among New Mexicans between 1848 and 1851.

In the summer of 1849 Major Washington led an armed expedition into Navajo country to the mouth of Canyon de Chelly, a sacred site. In the process, his troops killed a principal leader, Narbona, and wounded several other Navajos. The Washington expedition, manned by too few troops and encumbered by baggage and supply trains, ultimately did little to impress United States power on the Navajos, leaving behind only resentment and rage.

Washington's armed foray brought the Navajos, New Mexicans, and Americans no closer to peace. Other tribes, such as the Utes, Apaches, and Comanches, proved no less intractable. In 1850, after inspecting the Ninth Military Department, Colonel George A. McCall concluded, "The whole of the Indians of the country are ignorant of the power of the United States." If the federal government failed to impress its power on these "wild tribes," it would have to increase the troop aggregate to bring them under control. Commanding New Mexico after Washington, a frustrated Major John Munroe informed the War Department that the Navajos had resumed their raids on New Mexican communities and ranches. Only the hard hand of war, he advised, would bring the Navajos, the region's largest and most powerful tribe, to heel.

During his administration, from 1850 until 1852, President Millard Fillmore sought solutions to the military problems posed by the land and people of New Mexico Territory. In the spring of 1851 Fillmore's secretary of war, George W. Crawford, assigned Lieutenant Colonel Edwin V. Sumner, a distinguished dragoon officer, to command the unruly Ninth Military Department. A veteran of thirty-two years in the regular army, Sumner had served on American frontiers from upstate New York to coastal Texas.

During the U.S. invasion of central Mexico in 1847 Sumner led battalions of Second Dragoons and Mounted Riflemen from coastal Vera Cruz over the mountains, into the central valley, and through the gates of Mexico City. Praised for his discipline and bravery, he emerged from the conflict as the army's preeminent cavalry officer and won the admiration and trust of Commanding General Winfield Scott. The war also bestowed on him the humorous epithet "Bull" or "Bull of the Woods" when his head deflected a spent escopette ball at the Battle of Cerro Gordo. A tour of the central plains in the summer of 1850 acquainted him with the region's complex Indian affairs and a few Native leaders in the central and southern plains region. An aggressive, knowledgeable officer, Sumner seemed the logical choice for command of the Ninth Military Department, which embraced New Mexico.

On July 19, 1851, Sumner arrived in Santa Fe with a reform mission and seven hundred reinforcements. Five years previously, in August 1846, he had marched into the New Mexico capital at the head of the dragoon battalion attached to Kearny's Army of the West, but he had left for the East that fall. Now empowered to shake up the department, he was ordered to punish all Navajos, Apaches, and Utes at war with New Mexicans, reorganize the "whole system of defense," reduce the department's massive quartermaster and subsistence expenditures, and remove all army personnel from the territory's political affairs.

Wasting no time, Sumner immediately began transferring troops to the region's frontiers. The officers and men stationed in towns such as Santa Fe, Albuquerque, Socorro, Doña Ana, and El Paso, he believed, fell too easily under the spell of Mexican vice and degradation. At combat stations located toward Indian country, they would behave like regular soldiers and fight native warriors. By 1854, a year after he left the territory, the army's defensive line in New Mexico was composed of Fort Massachusetts in present-day southern Colorado, Cantonment Burgwin near Taos, Fort Union northeast of Las Vegas, Fort Marcy in Santa Fe, the depot at Albuquerque, Fort Craig south of Socorro, Fort Thorn at the southern edge of the Jornada del Muerto, Fort Fillmore in the Mesilla Valley, and Fort Bliss at Magoffinsville near El Paso, Texas. Despite the initial furor that Sumner's reorganization triggered in the vacated towns, his defensive line remained largely intact until the end of the southwestern Indian wars in 1886.

The fiery Sumner planted an additional post in western New Mexico. Navajo raids had so vexed federal authorities by late 1850 that Sumner's initial instructions included an order to campaign against them at the earliest opportunity. On August 17, 1851, impatient to whip some Indians, he led "four companies of horse[,] one of Artillery, and two of Infantry" from Santo Domingo Pueblo west toward Navajo country. Confident — overconfident — of success, the old dragoon intended to teach the Navajos a lesson in Anglo civilization and military might. Skirmishing with the Navajos on its approach, his battalion boldly penetrated some eleven miles into Canyon de Chelly, an intimidating Navajo refuge. Outraged warriors shot arrows and threw stones from the canyon rims, but the regulars were unable to reach them by either hand, horse, or gun. With the chasm's length unknown to his scouts, Sumner withdrew his column, offering his officers a lesson, however painful to him, in command prudence. Although his regulars had struck no devastating blow against Navajo hosts on the field of battle, he left a menacing U.S. calling card, Fort Defiance in Canyon Bonito, on the doorstep to the Navajo homeland. For the next thirteen years, Defiance's regulars and volunteers would claw and tear at the Navajo people until they were relocated to Bosque Redondo Reservation near Fort Sumner in 1864.

Civilians in New Mexico quickly came to hate Bull Sumner, and he returned their animosity, spite for spite. First, upon his arrival, he purged from the army payroll many dozens of civilian teamsters, artisans, and laborers. Stranded in New Mexico, these unemployed hellions added to the civil disorder that already plagued the territory and further stressed its weak law-enforcement institutions. Second, almost from the day he entered Santa Fe, he quarreled with federal officials in other departments, particularly James S. Calhoun, governor and ex-officio superintendent of Indian affairs in New Mexico. Despite Calhoun's integrity, honesty, and devotion, Sumner bore the army officer's general scorn of political appointees, who all too often disgraced frontier federal offices. Like most professional soldiers, he hated the civilian militias that slaughtered Indians from greed, from vengeance, and for sport.

On behalf of the army, Sumner also carried an institutional grudge. The transfer of the federal Indian Service from the War Department to the Department of the Interior, created in 1849, had outraged him, as it generally had galled his peers in the officer corps. By no means should the federal government, they inveighed, entrust the management of the nation's Indian affairs to the civilian Department of the Interior, whose Indian agents, all political-party hacks in the eyes of army officers, would likely abuse the Indians and exploit their federal positions for personal gain. Old Bull made Calhoun pay the toll in New Mexico. Constantly invoking departmental economy, the colonel refused to protect Calhoun's Indian agents and initially to arm civilian militias, or "marauders," as he labeled them. After only a few months in the territory, Sumner scoffed that the Indians and New Mexicans "steal women and children, and Cattle from each other, and in fact carry on the war, in all respects, like two indian [sic] nations."

Beginning in the spring of 1852, Sumner served four months as ex-officio governor, when Calhoun, his health failing, left the territory. The experience only intensified the soldier's scorn. After a year in the Southwest, he concluded that New Mexico was worthless for Anglo agriculture and industry, that New Mexicans were ignorant, indolent, and slothful, and that federal territorialism would fail miserably in the Southwest. Later reprinted in the press, his recommendation was that the U.S. government withdraw federal officials and troops, arm the New Mexicans, and let them and the Indians carry on their war in their traditional ways. Those childlike peoples would be happier, and the American people and their government would be a little wealthier. Bullied enough by Sumner's bellicosity, New Mexicans labeled him "THE BIG BUG OF ALBUQUERQUE" and complained about his callous snubs and bitter rancor.

Despite his tumultuous tenure, Sumner returned a little law and order to the towns and settlements during his military and civil administrations, and he emphatically underlined serious obstacles to regional peace: New Mexicans' slave raiding against the Indians and their often unlicensed trade with the Indians, even those with whom the United States was at war. Sumner understood that the incorporation of New Mexico and the assimilation of its peoples, Indian and Hispanic, into the United States would require the concerted reconstruction of their social, cultural, and economic institutions. He doubted that the effort was worth the cost in federal dollars and American blood. Relieved on July 1, 1853, Sumner happily vacated New Mexico Territory, a military jurisdiction requiring political talents that he had no patience to cultivate.

Dixon S. Miles

Sumner's successor, Colonel John Garland, sharply criticized his fanatical economizing and political ham-fistedness. Sumner's financial stringencies had left the army's infrastructure, its posts especially, shoddy and dilapidated, while his jealous hording of army resources had alienated New Mexicans, Hispanic and Anglo alike. In no sector of the territory were settlers any more secure, Garland claimed, than they were prior to Sumner's assumption of command in the summer of 1851. Indeed, while repairing civil-military relations, Garland tackled a war with the Jicarilla Apaches and the Utes, even employing New Mexico volunteers in those campaigns. The regulars and volunteers defeated the Jicarillas in 1854 and the Utes the following year.

In the meantime, U.S. relations with the Navajos began to unravel. As Sumner had argued in 1851 and 1852, Indian raids on the Rio Grande settlements were only half of the disorder infecting New Mexico. The federal government also had to put an end to New Mexican attacks in Indian homelands, particularly Navajo country, if it ever hoped to bring the wars to a close. With alarming frequency by 1857, New Mexicans and Navajos were plundering each other's communities for captives, sheep, cattle, and horses. Because the army would not attack U.S. citizens involved in those assaults, it targeted the Navajos in western New Mexico.

The killing of a black slave by a Navajo warrior inside the perimeter of Fort Defiance was the immediate trigger of the war in 1858. The victim, Jim, was the chattel of Major William T. Brooks, Defiance's commanding officer, who demanded that Navajo leader Sarcillos Largos hand over the killer or his people would suffer a destructive war. Largos and "other chiefs" refused.

The department's response was to dispatch Lieutenant Colonel Dixon S. Miles to Fort Defiance with instructions first to talk Navajo leaders into capturing and surrendering the murderer. But an unauthorized attack on a village at Bear Spring by regular-army captain George McLane outraged the Navajos and hardened their resolve. Miles now believed his troops would have to hunt the Navajos one canyon at a time. As Sumner and other southwestern campaigners had learned, expeditions and scouts through the deserts, mountains, and canyons broke down men, horses, and mules and wrecked weapons, saddles, and shoes at an alarming rate. The martial prospect promised little action — not even a minor skirmish — in return for the expenditure of so much sweat and treasure.

Having graduated from West Point in 1824, the fifty-four-year-old Miles had fought in wars from Florida to Mexico during his thirty-four years of service. In army circles he was considered an effective Indian fighter: he was resourceful, decisive, destructive, and lucky. His feverish conversation, his mule, and his two straw hats, one stacked on the other, always stirred comment. His orders were to prosecute a "vigorous war" against the Navajos unless they agreed to stop raiding the Rio Grande Valley settlements, returned livestock recently stolen from the Albuquerque area, and turned over Jim's murderer. The Navajos' attempt to pass off a Mexican captive as the killer confirmed to the colonel their depravity, and he bristled at their contempt for American arms: "They openly boasted we were afraid of them and dared me to meet them at Canon de Chelly." Accepting their challenge, he led 309 officers and men and a pack train north and west toward the forbidding chasm on September 9, 1858.

The second day out, New Mexican scouts captured a Navajo warrior, "well dressed, fully armed, and well mounted," in Miles's words. The man's apparent importance convinced the colonel to detain him and then to order him "shot as a spy." Miles handed the honor to his Zuni guide, José. Like Sumner, Miles believed that the wars between southwestern peoples were so ancient that the United States, the newcomer, seemed hardly relevant to them. Indeed, Miles repeatedly recommended that the departmental commander "let loose" the Zunis, Hopis, Utes, Apaches, and Hispanos to destroy their mutual enemy, the Navajos. When told his fate, the Navajo captive begged for his life, but Miles stood aside, and José shot the warrior in the head, killing him instantly.

On the third day, approaching from the south, the Navajo Expedition struck Canyon de Chelly, sacred ground to the Navajos but a "hole" to the colonel. Forty miles long, the canyon ran generally from east to west. At this point, seventeen miles above the eastern entrance, the walls towered about a thousand feet over the canyon floor, which was planted with corn and fruit trees and watered by a shallow stream. José guided the column of regulars down a debris-strewn side canyon into a cornfield at the bottom. Unlike Sumner's troops, who had been armed with short-range, inaccurate, smoothbore musketoons, Miles's infantry carried new Springfield rifles, and his Mounted Riflemen fired the long-range .58 caliber Mississippi rifle. As the column descended, the rear guard killed one Navajo warrior and wounded several others who were sniping from the rim and nearby ledges.

At the bottom, while Navajo warriors shot arrows and fired muskets from above, Miles pointed his column westward through cornfields and orchards. In a short time, he personally captured an old man hiding in a stand of corn but spared his life. The farther west the regulars marched, the lower the canyon walls dropped. That evening, when the Navajos saw the regulars bivouacked on the floor, they "commenced firing" arrows and balls into camp. Infuriated by the unmanly tactic, Miles ordered forward his Navajo captive. Through José he explained to the old man, "If they shot an arrow or fired a gun into the camp that night, I would surely hang him in the morning." The captive shouted out the colonel's ultimatum, instantly silencing the warriors' weapons. Later, Miles smugly reported, "We slept unmolested."

When the column resumed its march the next morning, it immediately received Navajo fire, but the refreshed and buoyant Miles hanged no one. Deployed onto the south rim, infantry skirmishers drove away hovering Navajo fighters. In five or six miles, the Navajo Expedition debouched from Canyon de Chelly into "an extensive cornfield," where the regulars set up camp. At dusk the Navajos began peppering the American position with projectiles, but Miles ignored the nuisance. Early in the morning of September 14, Navajo warriors infiltrated the picket line, killed one regular, and wounded three others before escaping, but their attack violated no soldierly code, and Miles remained silent. After marching through the day, the regulars again made camp, but the colonel ordered his officers to conceal their pickets after dark, giving explicit orders that the guards should discharge their weapons only if they could wound or kill their target. At dusk the Navajos resumed their harassment until a section of hidden pickets suddenly opened fire. At dawn they proudly pointed to spots and pools of blood to confirm their hits.

The Navajo Expedition pulled into Fort Defiance on September 15. Miles's column was the first U.S. Army unit to operate through most of Canyon de Chelly. His losses were two dead and three wounded. The catalogue of trophies — six Indians killed, many more wounded, four or five horses taken, and "between five and six thousand sheep" confiscated — seemed slight for all the marching and shooting, but with Sumner's expedition in 1851 included, the regulars now had seen all but a few miles of Canyon de Chelly. No longer did the place seem so forbidding or formidable to the army.

Nor did Miles stop. Scouts of infantry and cavalry poured through Navajo country — destroying as they went — well into December, when the Navajos finally sued for peace. Sumner's and Miles's operations were among the destructive campaigns demonstrating to policy makers in Washington, D.C., and to officers in the field that grappling *mano a mano,* hand to hand, was unnecessary to punish Indians in the West. Burning crops, food stores, dwellings, and other property inflicted serious material losses on the Navajos, and constant harassment subjected them to nearly unbearable deprivations. Sumner's and Miles's tactics made a deep impression on officers subsequently deployed to New Mexico and the Southwest.

On Christmas Day in 1858, Colonel Benjamin L. E. Bonneville and Superintendent James L. Collins signed terms with Navajo leaders at Fort Defiance. Tranquillity generally held throughout 1859, but New Mexican slave raids never stopped, and Navajo warriors began attacking army supply trains and grazing details in early 1860. Two hours before dawn on April 30, a thousand warriors stormed Fort Defiance, the symbol of the hated American occupation. Their tactic was highly unusual in the annals of frontier warfare, for Native warriors attacked heavily defended fixed positions only in the rarest instances. The Defiance garrison sealed the perimeter and fought off the attack through successive volleys of rifle fire, inflicting heavy casualties. The war with the Navajos was shaping up to be fight to the finish.

James H. Carleton

Departmental commander Colonel Thomas T. Fauntleroy deployed Major Edward R. S. Canby to Fort Defiance in the summer of 1860. An able frontier officer, Canby cared less about killing Navajos than about needling them, destroying their villages and crops, and ultimately driving them to the treaty table. To that end, he kept in the field at all times three mobile columns that gave the Navajos no rest and torched their fields and property at will. His hope was that the Navajo peace faction would crack down on the *ladrones*, the Navajos who prosecuted the raids on farms, ranches, and towns, and thus bring the conflict to an end. Applied throughout the fall and early winter, Canby's tactical plan had successfully divided the Navajos and compelled peace leaders to visit the placid but aggressive major in Fort Defiance and discuss implementing an armistice and undermining the *ladrones*. Peace now seemed within Canby's reach.

In April 1861, however, the outbreak of the Civil War upended Canby's Navajo campaign and brought him to Santa Fe. Taking over command of the Department of New Mexico, he now raised New Mexico volunteers for the federal service and planned territorial defenses against potential invasion from Confederate Texas. By late 1861 he had approximately four thousand volunteers and regulars on hand to block an armed incursion by three thousand Texas volunteers under Brigadier General Henry H. Sibley, who had commanded one of Canby's mobile columns in Navajo country in 1860–61.

On February 21, 1862, Sibley's Texans defeated his old commander's Union troops at the Battle of Valverde but suffered irreplaceable casualties. Marching northward, the invaders briefly occupied Socorro, Albuquerque, and Santa Fe while a Union column followed close behind. From March 26 to 28, 1862, the Texans fought a pitched battle at Glorieta Pass northeast of Santa Fe. Although they got the upper hand on the field of battle, they lost their entire quartermaster train to a raid by Colorado volunteers under Major John M. Chivington. Now operating in hostile country without supplies, Sibley's Confederates withdrew down the Rio Grande Valley to El Paso, Texas. Never again did rebellious Texans threaten Union security in the far Southwest.

In the wake of the Texas retreat, New Mexico received an army commander like no other it had experienced since Bull Sumner. As Colonel James H. Carleton marched his two thousand California volunteers from Los Angeles to the Rio Grande Valley, he drove from Tucson, in Arizona Territory, the remaining Confederate forces in the far Southwest. When the War Department called Canby east to Washington, D.C., in August 1862, he left the command of the Department of New Mexico to Carleton, a tyrannical, sober, pious, and brilliant old regular dragoon. A decade of service in New Mexico, Utah, and southern California during the 1850s had given Carleton exceptional knowledge of the arid environment, Native peoples, and desert warfare.

Promoted to brigadier general of volunteers in September 1862, Carleton turned his attention to territorial Indian affairs. In his opinion, only the absolute subjugation of the belligerent tribes, particularly the Apaches and Navajos, would guarantee the territory's security against Confederate invasion from Texas. His plan was to defeat the Indians in the field, to relocate them to reservations, and to initiate the long-term process of their assimilation into American society. No less significant to Carleton was opening the Southwest's "arable lands" and "deposits of precious metals" to exploitation by Americans, a process in which he had personal interests. With between four thousand and five thousand troops in his department, Carleton believed that he had the manpower to defeat the southwestern Indians once and for all.

Planning a war without quarter, General Carleton aimed his army first at the Mescalero Apaches in southeastern New Mexico. In October 1862 he dispatched Colonel Christopher "Kit" Carson and five companies of New Mexico volunteers to reoccupy Fort Stanton on the Rio Bonito in southeastern New Mexico. Under his instructions, mobile columns of volunteers from Forts Stanton, Mesilla, and Franklin (Texas) converged on Mescalero sanctuaries in Dog Canyon and on the Rio Peñasco. Carleton's instructions to Colonels Carson and Joseph R. West were emphatic: "All Indian men of that tribe are to be killed whenever and wherever you can find them." Under no circumstances should they cease hostilities until Mescalero chiefs personally begged for peace in Santa Fe. Some three hundred Mescalero men, women, and children died in two separate fights with New Mexico and California volunteers. An army patrol shot down Mescalero leaders Manuelito and José Largo, who were en route to treat with Carleton in Santa Fe. Although opposed to the general's war on the Mescaleros, Carson rounded up about four hundred survivors and relocated them to Bosque Redondo, Carleton's reservation experiment, near Fort Sumner on the Pecos River. About two hundred other Mescaleros escaped southward to the Guadalupe Mountains in west Texas, where they would remain until the end of the Civil War.

While he loosed his California volunteers on western Apaches, particularly the Gila bands in the mining region of Pinos Altos, Carleton next threw his New Mexico volunteers at the Navajos. Transferring the New Mexicans to Fort Canby (formerly Fort Defiance) and Fort Wingate near Mount Taylor in June 1863, the general gave the Navajos an ultimatum: surrender to military authorities and relocate to Bosque Redondo or perish in war. Any Navajos who remained in their homeland after July 20 marked themselves for assault and death.

From August to December, some five hundred New Mexico volunteers scouted for Navajos west beyond Hopi and south and southwest to the Datil Mountains and the headwaters of the Little Colorado. Old enemies of the Navajos' — Zuni Pueblos, Jemez Pueblos, and Utes — operated independently of and officially with Carson's men. Another terror was New Mexican slave raiders, whom Carleton, unlike Fauntleroy and Canby, made no effort to stop. By December the Navajos had reportedly lost "78 killed, 40 wounded, and 196 captured." The many parties of raiders also carried off about five thousand head of livestock. Despite the deaths, destruction, and captures, the Navajos still retaliated against settlements in the Rio Grande Valley.

In Carleton's mind, the summer and fall expeditions had merely softened up the Navajos; now he intended to complete their demise in the frigid cold and drifting snows of winter. Under his instructions, Carson led a strike force toward the western end of Canyon de Chelly while Captain Albert H. Pfeiffer, who had recently lost his wife and children to an Apache attack near Fort McRae, commanded two companies ordered to the eastern mouth. On January 13, 1864, Carson's men began scouring the canyon rims for passages to the floor. At the same time, Pfeiffer's men scouted the entire length of the canyon — as Navajos futilely hurled arrows, rocks, and boulders at them — rendezvousing with Carson's unit on January 15. Two volunteer companies returned through the canyon to destroy hogans (Navajo houses) and fruit orchards while Carson led the balance of his men back to Fort Canby. His operation had taken twenty-three Navajo lives, but his sustained penetration of Canyon de Chelly shattered the will of the people — already starving to death — to fight or resist. During the fall, a few hundred had come into Forts Wingate and Canby for transfer to Bosque Redondo. In only three weeks after Carson's foray, several thousand were encamped around the two posts.

Carleton had won his initial battles with the Navajos. Enduring the Long Walk — more than three hundred miles — from Forts Canby and Wingate, eight thousand Navajos, two-thirds of the nation, had transported their property, herds, and lives to Bosque Redondo in the arid Pecos River valley. Despite Carson's efforts to protect them, the Navajos suffered plundering and kidnapping by hovering, opportunistic New Mexicans along the route. Another four thousand Navajos moved westward into the Colorado Plateau, far beyond the reach of New Mexicans and the army. With Carleton's unqualified nomination, Carson, his efficient albeit reluctant field commander, received a brevet promotion to brigadier general a year later.

The Navajos won the war, however. Although Carleton was willing to hunt, harass, and kill Indians to coerce their submission, his long-term vision was to create Navajo and Mescalero pueblos on the Pecos River, transform his captive Natives into yeoman farmers and stock ranchers, and facilitate their assimilation as orderly and obedient Christians into United States society. If left on their own in the wilderness, Carleton believed, they would return to their traditional habits of plunder and murder and ultimately suffer extermination at the hands of racially motivated Anglo and Hispanic frontiersmen. Moving them onto protected federal reservations, however painful in the short run, represented the Indians' best interest in the long term.

Carleton's dreams for the Indians were noble in his time, but an avalanche of mishaps and problems scuttled his utopian Indian experiment at Bosque Redondo. Crops farmed in the river bottoms in that first summer of 1864 perished from insects, drought, and floods, forcing Carleton to provision his Indian wards at a cost of hundreds of thousands of federal dollars per month. His commissary and quartermaster departments failed to secure and ship adequate food rations, blankets, clothing, and other supplies to Fort Sumner, and the Navajos began succumbing to exposure, famine, and disease during the winter of 1864–65.

In the political and policy arena, Carleton argued bitterly with his federal Indian Service counterpart, Superintendent Michael Steck. From the beginning Steck had opposed the Navajo incarceration at Bosque Redondo as foolhardy. In no way, Steck declared, could the Pecos Valley feed and support thousands of uprooted Navajos. Ignoring Carleton's pleas and protests, the superintendent refused either to apply any portion of his departmental funds toward Bosque Redondo or to request an appropriation from his supervisor, the commissioner of Indian affairs, in the Department of the Interior. As Carson had forewarned his general, the Navajos and Mescaleros, traditional enemies, quarreled and brawled. Fed up with their captivity and the Navajos, the Mescaleros fled back to their homeland in southeast New Mexico and west Texas in December 1865.

The policy wreckage and human disaster at Bosque Redondo doomed Carleton's command of the Department of New Mexico. Cost overruns and unofficial and official reports began to catch the eye of Congress by late 1864. Also outraged over the unspeakable massacre of peaceful Southern Cheyennes at Sand Creek in southern Colorado during the winter of 1864, Congress formed the Special Joint Committee to investigate the condition of the Indians generally in the West. A subcommittee led by James R. Doolittle of Wisconsin was charged with examining Indian affairs in New Mexico. Arriving in the late summer of 1865, the committee paid special attention to conditions at Bosque Redondo. Carleton argued that isolating the Navajos and Mescaleros from their native homelands and restricting them to a controlled environment were the only probable means of driving them down the path to civilization and assimilation. Returning them to their traditional territories, even to legal reservations, would allow them to resume their "savage" or "uncivilized" ways of life.

The appalling conditions at Bosque Redondo profoundly impressed the Doolittle commission. Predicting complete failure for Carleton's experiment, it recommended that the commissioner of Indian affairs send his own special investigator to witness and record the human disaster. Another round of failed crops in 1866 sealed the fate of Bosque Redondo. On May 28, 1868, Navajo leaders treated with a new commission headed by N. G. Taylor and Major General William T. Sherman, a Union Civil War hero. On June 18, 1868, the Navajos retraced their Long March to their homeland. They returned with "1,550 horses, 20 mules, 950 sheep and 1,025 goats" — a shocking level of destitution for this once-wealthy tribe.

In the meantime, Carleton's command of New Mexico had come to an end. The expiration of his volunteers' enlistments in the summer and fall of 1864 had already reduced his Indian-fighting army to a shell of its former glory. The army reorganization and redeployment in 1866 left him only fifteen hundred troops, and his cavalry, short of serviceable horses, lacked the mobility critical to successful operations. His relations with New Mexico's political elites had also soured.

On January 21, 1866, both houses of the New Mexico Territorial Legislature adopted a resolution condemning Carleton's military policies and his failure to protect New Mexicans from Indian attacks and asking President Andrew Johnson to replace him. In April 1866 he was mustered out of the volunteer service and returned to the regular army at the rank of lieutenant colonel, one grade above his pre–Civil War majority. Five months later the War Department relieved him of departmental command in New Mexico and ordered him to join his new regiment, the Fourth

Cavalry, in Texas. Despite the failure of Bosque Redondo, the federal government would adopt Carleton's model, although changing the personnel, for its post–Civil War Indian policy.

Ranald S. Mackenzie

By late 1865, constant raids on Navajo herds and army supply trains by Comanches and Kiowas posed a serious challenge to military authorities in New Mexico. The Kiowa and Comanche homeland lay across the Llano Estacado (Staked Plains), a high, grassy tableland that unrolled eastward from the Pecos River in New Mexico to the headwaters of the Brazos and Red Rivers in the panhandle of Texas. The Indians hunted buffalo on the Llano and fled into it after raids against their enemies in New Mexico and along the Santa Fe Trail. Army units had explored the edges of the Llano, but none had tried following the Indian and trading trails that crossed it. Between 1871 and 1876, Colonel Ranald S. Mackenzie almost single-handedly collapsed the Llano as a sanctuary for the Kiowas and Comanches and destroyed a trade network, generations old, between New Mexican communities ranged along the eastern slopes of the mountains and up and down the Pecos River and the Indians who lived on the Llano.

Like Sumner and Carleton, Colonel Mackenzie was a force of nature. Graduating first in the United States Military Academy class of 1862, he served in every battle, minus Antietam, fought by units of the Army of the Potomac from Second Bull Run to Appomattox and by the Army of the Shenandoah in the fall and winter of 1864–65. He was wounded seven times. Years later, in his memoirs, Ulysses S. Grant praised Mackenzie as "the most promising young officer" in the U.S. Army at the conflict. After commanding black infantry regiments from 1867 to 1870, Mackenzie was appointed colonel of the Fourth United States Cavalry, Sumner's old First Cavalry, on December 15, 1870. At only thirty years old, he was the youngest line colonel in the army.

President Grant and Commanding General Sherman expected Mackenzie to hunt the Comanches and Kiowas in their southern plains sanctuaries and to check their raids against the Texas settlements to the south. Their object was not to annihilate the Indians but to drive them onto federal reservations, particularly Fort Sill, north of the Red River in southern Indian Territory. Death and destruction were the tools, although regretted, put at the disposal of Mackenzie and other western field commanders. Inconclusive campaigns in the summer of 1871 taught Mackenzie and his regiment the "dos and don'ts" of campaigning in the choking dust, brutal heat, sudden cold, and rugged terrain of the southern plains. Unlike many other units, his Fourth Cavalry always stripped to trail essentials — weapons, rations, and blankets — to maximize unit mobility and efficiency.

In the late summer of 1871 Mackenzie received permission to operate into the Llano Estacado. After scouting the headwaters of the Brazos, his troopers encountered defiant Comanche warriors on the Freshwater Fork of the Brazos and pursued the entire Kwahadi Comanche village westward, far into the Llano, until a sudden, violent norther — wind, rain, and sleet — forced the colonel reluctantly to order a halt. After additional forays along the Pease River, a wounded Mackenzie, who took an arrow in a thigh during a skirmish with Comanches, called off the expedition in early November. After a winter respite, the Kiowas and Comanches, driven by both domestic need and warrior culture, intensified their raids against the Texans, in one instance killing seventeen freighters at Howard's Wells. To screen the settlements, Mackenzie deployed patrols across north-central Texas. In March 1872 one of those units captured an eighteen-year-old *comanchero* (trader), Polonio Ortiz, from La Cuesta, New Mexico Territory.

Stumbling on Ortiz was an auspicious break for Mackenzie. The young man's story, that he had journeyed east in the company of other *nuevomexicanos* to steal horses and cattle or to trade for them with the Kiowas and Comanches, confirmed what Mackenzie already suspected. Indeed, since about 1800, New Mexicans had seasonally crossed the Llano to barter with Indians, especially Comanches, and to hunt buffalo. Texas cattle and horses, driven across the Llano and sold to the army and Indian reservations, were a recent addition to their traditional enterprise. Immediately employed by Mackenzie, Ortiz led units of the Fourth Cavalry to Indian sites, such as Muchaque northwest of Fort Concho, unknown to the Americans. Lethal raids and child abductions by the Indians drove the Interior Department to sanction the Kiowas and Comanches for "attack and capture" by the army. From Fort Richardson, the Fourth's headquarters, Colonel Mackenzie promised to whip the Indians and break up the *comanchero* trade that sustained them.

In early July, after scouring the headwaters of the Brazos and Freshwater Fork and tributaries of the Red, Mackenzie headed five companies of the Fourth west onto the Llano, with Ortiz as their guide. The troopers followed a wide *comanchero* trail, well watered along its entire course, and pulled into Las Canaditas, New Mexico, on August 7, 1872. Mackenzie's raid on Puerta de Luna produced no arrests of merchants suspected of supplying *comancheros;* they had already fled. After Mackenzie refitted his men at Fort Bascom to the north, his reconnaissance in force marched eastward along the southern tributaries of the Red River, a northern route of the *comanchero* trade, and reached his supply camp at Freshwater Fork on September 2. Three weeks and a day later, Mackenzie and his fourth knifed into a Kotsoteka Comanche village on McClellan's Creek, a small tributary of the North Fork of the Red River, killing 26 Natives and capturing 125 women, children, and elders. Afterward, the regulars burned all tepees and belongings. After returning to Camp Supply, the colonel broke up his expedition with his prisoners on October 11.

Two months of constant scouting had convinced Mackenzie that the eastern edge of the Llano Estacado was no barren waste but a region offering water, wood, and game enough to support a large population of Indians at any time of year. The northern *comanchero* route, reported Mackenzie, "has permanent and excellent water across the Plains and no distance of more than thirty miles between water." With Ortiz's critical knowledge and services, Mackenzie had opened the Llano to the regular army and cracked the last refuge of the Kiowas and Comanches on the southern plains.

In the summer of 1873 Mackenzie and the Fourth audaciously raided Kickapoo and Lipan villages in Remolina, Mexico, to put an end to their cross-border raids, but the following summer they returned to the Llano as a strike force in Major General Phil Sheridan's Red River campaign. As four other columns converged on Indian sanctuaries in the drainage of the Red, Mackenzie's Fourth found a large village of Comanches, Kiowas, and Cheyennes encamped along the Prairie Dog Fork, which ran through Palo Duro Canyon. Following a game trail down the precipitous incline, his troopers surprised and struck the villages, drove out the warriors, burned tepees, blankets, and other property, and captured and then slaughtered hundreds of horses. In the aftermath, Mackenzie led the Fourth on scouts to the south and west, smashing into small pockets of Comanches desperate to dodge his troopers.

The success of Mackenzie's and other columns largely drove the Comanche, Kiowa, and Southern Cheyenne holdouts onto the Fort Sill and other reservations during the winter of 1874–75, bringing the southern plains wars and the *comanchero* trade generally to an end and opening the Llano Estacado to ranchers in Texas and New Mexico. Mackenzie's plains campaigns went a long way toward fulfilling the reconstruction of the New Mexico economy urged by the exasperated Sumner in 1852.

The Red River War did not end all Indian wars in the greater Southwest. Federal troops in southern New Mexico and Arizona continued fighting the Apaches until 1886, when Geronimo and his Chiricahua Apache band finally surrendered to Colonel Nelson Miles and U.S. troops at Skeleton Canyon. By that point in the Indian wars, federal troops, with the aid of Indian auxiliaries, had elaborated the tactics of waging destructive wars on Native peoples throughout the region. A combination of harassment, fire, modern weapons, and mobility drove Native Americans to starvation and desperation. Federal troops had penetrated the farthest recesses of their homelands, leaving them no place to flee from the onslaught of United States power. Backing those successes were decades of vigorous field operations, a long history of physically brutal campaigns, destructive strikes, and vacuous failures. Across the American West, army officers drew on the mixed experiences of frontier campaigners such as Edwin V. Sumner, Dixon S. Miles, James H. Carleton, and Ranald S. Mackenzie. Some of these lessons would be carried into the United States' colonial wars in the late nineteenth and twentieth centuries.

A group of buffalo soldiers, NCO Troop L, Ninth Cavalry, Fort Wingate, New Mexico, 1899. Imperial Photo Gallery.

25

Buffalo Soldiers in New Mexico

William Wroth (2006)

At the end of the Civil War, Black cavalry and infantry troops known as buffalo soldiers were sent to New Mexico and elsewhere in the West to take part in the Indian wars and the protection of settlers. The term "buffalo soldier" is said to have been applied to the Black troops by the Indians because of their short curly hair and their courage and fortitude, much admired qualities of the buffalo. The term was first applied to Black soldiers of the 10th Cavalry Regiment in 1866 by the Kiowa Indians in western Kansas after encounters with them. It was taken as a compliment by the troops and the 10th Cavalry adopted a picture of the buffalo as the regiment's crest.

The origin of the buffalo soldiers goes back to the Civil War. Initially there was great opposition to the use of Black troops in the War; in the racist atmosphere of the day it was believed that African-Americans would not make good soldiers. However, in June 1862 the First Kansas Colored Volunteer Infantry was organized by Kansas Senator James H. Lane. In October 1862 a detachment of 225 Black troops from the First Kansas under the leadership of white officers encountered superior Confederate forces at Island Mound, Missouri and successfully held their ground against them. This first battle involving Black troops helped to defuse the prejudice against them. In May 1863 the U.S. Colored Volunteers was organized by the Army. It first consisted of a cavalry regiment, a heavy artillery regiment, five regiments of engineers, and 22 infantry regiments. By the end of the Civil War Black troops had increased substantially. There were 29 volunteer Black regiments, over 130 conscripted infantry regiments, thirteen regiments of heavy artillery, ten of light artillery, and six cavalry regiments. Nearly 200,000 Black troops served in the War, approximately ten percent of the Union forces. Black soldiers fought in 449 engagements during the War, 39 of them considered major battles.

In the reorganization of the army at the end of the Civil War, again there was opposition to Blacks serving in the army, but there also was a great need for troops, especially on the Western frontier. In 1866 Congress authorized the formation of two new regiments of Black cavalry with the designations 9th and 10th U.S. Cavalry, and four regiments of Black infantry, designated the 38th, 39th, 40th and 41st Infantry Regiments (Colored). The 38th and 41st were later reorganized as the 25th Infantry Regiment, with headquarters in Jackson Barracks, Louisiana, in November 1869. The 39th and 40th were reorganized as the 24th Infantry Regiment, headquartered at Fort Clark, Texas, in April 1869. In addition, the existing 57th and 125th Infantry Regiments included Black troops. All of these Black troops were under the command of White commissioned officers, but lower-ranked noncommissioned officers were in many cases Black.

In August 1866 eight Black companies of the 125th Infantry marched to New Mexico and soon were serving at seven Army forts throughout the territory, most of them in southern New Mexico. In September 1867 they were replaced by six companies of Black troops from the newly organized 38th Infantry who had seen action earlier in the year against the Cheyenne Indians in Kansas. As soon as the 125th arrived, they began to see action against raiding parties of Apache Indians. For both Black and White troops, the pursuit of the Apaches proved difficult due to lack of knowledge of terrain and the slowness of troop movement compared with that of the Indians. At best the buffalo soldiers could help to reduce the raiding and protect local citizens and their livestock. They also served to protect against White cattle rustlers and other outlaws in largely lawless southern New Mexico. One of the important duties of Black troops was to serve as escorts for both government and civilian parties crossing New Mexico. These included military personnel, U.S. mail carriers, supply trains of all kinds, private citizens traversing the Butterfield Overland Trail, the southern route to California, and even herds of cattle moving from one location to another.

These first buffalo soldiers to be stationed in frontier New Mexico also had many more menial responsibilities. They (as well as White soldiers) were responsible, in some cases for major construction and renovations at the forts where they were stationed and served as carpenters, plasterers, painters, and bricklayers. At Fort McCrae, for instance, Black soldiers built several new buildings, put a new roof on the hospital, and made 25,000 adobe bricks for a new officers' quarters, which they also built. They along with other workers constructed the mostly adobe Fort Selden, no doubt under the guidance of Hispanic adobe masons. The Black soldiers were also responsible for other menial work, such as fuel gathering, always a difficult task in the sparse desert environment of southern New Mexico. The men would have to go as far as fifteen miles from the fort to find adequate wood supplies and often had to laboriously dig up mesquite roots for fuel. By the early 1870s, due to complaints by officers in New Mexico, the Army began to contract for many laboring jobs and for supplies such as fuel, hay, and building supplies, thus freeing the Black soldiers from many of these onerous tasks.

After two years in the territory the 38th Infantry left New Mexico in October 1869. A period of relative peace with the Apaches followed for a few years, but by 1875 more Black troops were needed. In December 1875 the 9th Cavalry led by Colonel Edward Hatch marched from Texas to New Mexico and were stationed at nine different forts. They continued the effort to curtail the raiding of the Apaches in southern New Mexico and soon earned a good reputation for their behavior. A newspaper editor in Mesilla described them as "quiet, sober, polite, and unobtrusive" and maintaining "perfect discipline." However, their efforts against the Apaches yielded few substantial results due to the Indians' superior knowledge of the terrain and abilities in desert raiding.

The Black soldiers of the 9th Cavalry also played an important role in the effort to maintain law and order in frontier New Mexico. They participated in both the Colfax County War in 1876 and the Lincoln County War in 1878. In an effort to quell the disturbances in Colfax County, Governor Samuel Axtell called Black soldiers from Fort Union into Cimarron to arrest rancher Clay Allison who was one of the leaders of a group opposed to the Maxwell Land Grant Company. Axtell, who was allied with the interests of the company, thought that Allison, an unrepentant Southerner, would resist arrest by Black soldiers. He did not resist but was quickly released by the military authorities. It was said that Axtell planned to have several leaders of the opposition to the company killed by the troops, but this claim was never proven, and an incriminating letter said to be written by Axtell was denounced as a forgery by him. The presence of Black troops in the tense situation existing in Cimarron led to a confrontation between several of them and two Texas cowboys. In March 1876 three Black soldiers were shot to death in the bar of the St. James Hotel. After the killings more soldiers were stationed in Cimarron where they stayed until the middle of April. A few months later the Texas cowboys were caught and one of them killed by a sheriff's posse.

In the Lincoln County War Black soldiers stationed at Fort Stanton were again used by the local authorities in an effort to vanquish their enemies. Several times in the early months of 1878 Black soldiers came into Lincoln to aid law enforcement officers on both sides of the dispute between Alexander McSween's forces and those associated with James Dolan. In July 1878 the "five-day battle" began in Lincoln, and McSween and his men were held under siege in his home. Sheriff George Peppin, a Dolan supporter, asked for help from Colonel Nathan Dudley at nearby Fort Stanton. Dudley soon arrived with a small squad of troops and officers including eleven Black cavalrymen. Dudley and his men were supposed to be neutral in the conflict, but in actuality they lent support to Dolan's forces. When the latter set McSween's house on fire, Dudley refused to do anything to help. In the desperate attempt to escape from the burning house, McSween and several of his men were shot and killed by Dolan forces. Dudley was later brought before a military court for his actions. Among the witnesses called were two Black ex-soldiers who had become employees of McSween. Although they and others testified against him, Dudley was acquitted of all the charges.

In the years 1879 and 1880 Black cavalrymen of the 9th Cavalry played a major role in the pursuit of the Apache leader Victorio. They engaged in numerous fights against the Apaches and at least twelve men were killed in action. Eight Black soldiers received the Congressional Medal of Honor for bravery during this campaign. The Victorio campaign finally came to an end in October 1880 when Mexican soldiers, backed up by U. S. Army troops who had crossed the border, killed Victorio in the mountains of Chihuahua. The death of Victorio did not end the Apache wars. He was replaced by Nana who was equally committed to fighting the army. Several more bloody encounters involving buffalo soldiers took place in the first half of 1881. In spite of repeated encounters with Nana and his warriors, the Army forces never won a decisive victory against him, but they did force him to retreat into the mountains of Chihuahua in the fall of 1881. With the Apache threat thus effectively ended, the 9th Cavalry left New Mexico in the final months of 1881.

Buffalo soldiers did not return to New Mexico until 1887 when the 10th Cavalry was moved from Arizona to new headquarters in Santa Fe. Four units of the 10th Cavalry along with eight companies of the 24th Infantry were stationed at Fort Bayard near Silver City where they served until 1896. The 24th Infantry was led by Colonel Zenas R. Bliss, who had served with distinction in the Civil War. Unlike some other White officers, Bliss was not prejudiced against his Black troops. He often praised their work in his reports and tried to protect their interests. With the Apaches no longer raiding, the buffalo soldiers under Bliss played a role in maintaining the peace during this period, going on frequent scouts to investigate minor incidents. Among their final duties in New Mexico was the closing and dismantling of Fort Selden in 1891 and Fort Stanton in 1896, an indication of the peaceable conditions now reigning in the territory. Here ended the role of the buffalo soldiers in New Mexico in the Indian Wars of the nineteenth century.

26

Cultural Encounters:
Native People, New Mexico, and the
United States, 1848–1948

Margaret Connell-Szasz

Americans knew the year as 1848. For citizens who had supported the war with Mexico, the Treaty of Guadalupe Hidalgo, which increased the size of the United States by one-third, heralded the culmination of the nation's expansion. Conversely, the treaty severed Mexico City's connection with its northern frontier. Residents of the newly created Territory of New Mexico, whose vast desert and mountain lands stretched west to California, faced a new imperial capital along the Potomac River. For New Mexico Indians the year 1848 bore less import — they chronicled their lives by the seasons rather than the Western calendar. But the arrival of the Americans, who had assumed control in Santa Fe two years earlier, could not be so easily dismissed.

Long before Europeans arrived, each of the Native peoples had formed an integral relationship with its homeland. Whether the Diné Bikéyah of the Navajos, the Sacramento and Sierra Blanca Mountains of the Mescalero Apaches, or the defensive mesa home of the pueblo of Acoma, the land and the people remained connected through the people's belief in a supernatural power that pervaded the universe. Rooted in origin stories and reinforced in ritual and ceremony, this spiritual link with the land set them apart from the Europeans and lent them a sense of conviction in their unique destiny. After Spanish settlement, beginning in the late 1500s, adaptation had moderated that sense of uniqueness, but in 1848 Natives retained a separate identity. Still, they had long known the

Chiricahua Apaches four months after arriving at Carlisle Indian School, Pennsylvania. Back row, left to right: Samson Noran, Fred'k. Eskelsejah, Clement Seanilzay, Hugh Chee. Middle row, left to right: Ernest Hogee, Margaret Y. Nadasthilah. Front row, left to right: Humphrey Escharzy, Beatrice Kiahtel, Janette Pahgostatun, Bishop Eatennah, Basil Ekarden. February, 1887. Photograph by J. N. Choate.

Spaniards and Mexicans; they did not yet know the Americans, who would pose further challenges to the tenacity of their beliefs.

Resolving Homelands and Defining Status, 1848–1913

Like the Apaches, their Athabaskan-speaking cousins, the Navajos, or Diné, lived on the perimeter of the central corridor of Spanish settlement. From their arrival, Spaniards had focused their energy on the sedentary Natives who lived along the Rio Grande and its tributaries, whom the Spaniards had dubbed Pueblo, or village, Indians. Although they fought the Spaniards and later the Mexicans, the Navajos did not experience the daily contact with the settlers that the Pueblos endured.

Well after their arrival in the Southwest in the 1300s or earlier, the Navajos had moved from the Dinétah (northwestern New Mexico), expanding westward during the eighteenth century into Diné Bikéyah, a vast land centered on the Colorado Plateau and bounded by the Navajos' four sacred mountains (Brugge 1983, 494–95; Iverson 2002, 19–20). By the end of the eighteenth century, Canyon de Chelly (Tséyí) had emerged as the "heart of Diné Bikéyah" (Iverson 2002, 28). Although they continued hunting and gathering as well as trading, the Navajos thrived increasingly as farmers and herders, raising sheep, goats, and horses first acquired through extensive contact with Pueblo peoples, especially during the Pueblo-Spanish wars of the late 1600s, and cultivating maize and squash (Jorgensen 1983, 695, 701). Unlike the Pueblos, they remained mobile, moving their sheep seasonally from winter to summer pastures.

Before 1848, Navajos had participated in the pervasive trade in livestock and slaves encouraged by the Spaniards and Mexicans, which pitted several groups — Spaniards, Mexicans, Navajos, Utes, Pueblos, and other Natives — against each other in a relentless cycle of raid and counterraid (Brooks 2002, 235–57; Brugge 1983, 495–96). Upon the arrival of the Americans, the Navajos learned that the U.S. stance against raiding was firmer than the positions of previous imperial powers. In 1846, when Stephen Watts Kearny and the Army of the West reached Santa Fe, Kearny pronounced the Pueblo Indians a peaceable people, and the Navajos, hostile. The die was cast.

This inauspicious beginning to Navajo-American relations exploded during the American Civil War, when the Diné encountered General James H. Carleton, governor and commander of New Mexico Territory. Carleton had one goal in mind for relations with Native people: U.S. control over the "enemy Indians" — Navajos and Apaches — by removing them to a forty-square-mile reservation at Fort Sumner, on the east bank of the Rio Pecos, where they could be taught to farm and adopt "civilized ways." Not incidentally, the plan ensured that Americans would gain the Navajos' land, a region "much larger in extent than the state of Ohio" (Iverson 2002, 50). Carleton ordered Colonel Christopher (Kit) Carson to round up all Navajos, even in the remote depths of Canyon de Chelly, where his men would destroy cornfields and peach trees and force-march thousands of Diné to their new home, several hundred miles across New Mexico from Diné Bikéyah. The Americans knew this location as Fort Sumner and Bosque Redondo. The Navajos would dub it Hwéeldi, the prison camp. They would call the entire disaster the Long Walk.

The Long Walk remains the dividing point in Navajo memory. All events happened either before or after the Long Walk. From 1863 to 1868 the United States incarcerated more than nine thousand Diné at Fort Sumner, until the Treaty of 1868 freed them to return to Diné Bikéyah. A fourth of the Navajos died before their return. Before they went to Hwéeldi they had known hunger, but along the Pecos many of them starved. Before they went to Bosque Redondo they had lived in bands without any central leader. Afterward, they eventually came together as a nation. And today the Diné keep the memory alive. A Navajo woman recalled her grandmother's story: "When I tell my grandchildren about the Long Walk, they don't believe me. I tell them that they wouldn't be as they are today if their ancestors hadn't gone through the confinement and even died of hunger" (Roessel 1973, 116).

Like the Navajos, the Mescalero Apaches had long retained their mobility on the perimeter of the Spanish and Mexican settlements. Unlike the Navajos, the

Mescaleros remained hunters and gatherers; in addition to wild game, they relied heavily on women's harvesting of agave (mescal), along with berries, piñon and other nuts, seeds and wild greens. Moving widely across the land between the Rio Grande and the Rio Pecos, often east of the Pecos, in a region that now lies in New Mexico, Texas, Chihuahua, and Coahuilla, they reflected the diverse cultures they met in the Southwest borderlands and the buffalo-hunting patterns of the southern Great Plains (Opler 1983c, 431, 433, 437). Throughout the Spanish and Mexican periods they had the smallest population of any Native group on the southern plains, yet in the mid-eighteenth-century the Franciscan missionary at San Antonio described the Mescaleros as "more proud and domineering than the rest of them [Apache bands]" and as a people who "held more influence" than others (Anderson 1999, 112).

During the 1860s the Mescaleros tasted the bitterness of General Carleton's master plan for "enemy Indians" when he forced them into imprisonment at Bosque Redondo. Badly outnumbered by Navajos — only five hundred Mescaleros amid nine thousand Navajos — the Mescaleros came into conflict with the Diné, and the combination of this disagreement, annual crop failures, a lack of wood for fuel, and generally deplorable conditions led them to flee. In November 1864, "all but nine of the Mescalero slipped away from the Bosque," traveling south to their homeland in the mountains (Opler 1983c, 422). But their troubles with the Americans were just beginning.

Although the Navajos acquired the core of their reservation in the Treaty of 1868, the Mescaleros' sudden departure forced them into a different trajectory for securing a federally sanctioned reservation. In 1871 the U.S. Congress arbitrarily ended its long-established policy of negotiating treaties with Indian nations. By 1873, when the Mescaleros gained their reservation, federal policy dictated that only the president had the power to create an Indian reservation, by issuing an executive order. For decades afterward the federal government refused to offer the tribe any assurance that its land would remain inviolable. Well into the twentieth century, successive threats to the Mescalero reservation, including legislation introduced by New Mexico Senator (later Secretary of the Interior) Albert B. Fall to close the entire reservation by creating a national park on Mescalero land, almost tore the Mescaleros' homeland from their possession.

Congress did not confirm Mescalero title to the reservation until 1922, almost fifty years after the initial executive order that created it (Opler 1983b, 423–24). Although the Mescaleros complained to the United States that the territory set aside for them was too small for their needs, their complaints went unheard. Rather than increase the size of the reservation, the federal government responded by moving other Apaches onto Mescalero land.

Initially, the Lipan and Jicarilla Apaches may have shared a homeland in northern New Mexico, but sometime between the 1300s and the 1600s they appear to have taken their own paths. The Jicarillas remained in the northeastern borders of Apachean territory in the Southwest, and the Lipans moved southeast along the southern plains to the land lying between the Rio Pecos and the Rio Colorado (Opler 1983a, 385; Tiller 1983, 440; Tiller 2000, 4). By the mid-1700s, when the Lipans emerged as the easternmost of the plains Apaches, they included a number of smaller bands drawn from other groups (Anderson 1999, 112). Caught in the crossfire of Indian policy that Texans crafted after annexation, which called for removal or extermination of all Native people in the state, the Lipans had been driven into Mexico. In the early twentieth century, a small group of those refugees, numbering thirty-seven people, arrived on the Mescalero reservation.

A decade later, another group of Native refugees returned to the Southwest after being held by the United States for twenty-seven years as prisoners of war. In 1886, after the surrender of the prominent Chiricahua Apache Geronimo, the United States government had shipped virtually all the Chiricahua Apaches, some 498 people — warriors, Apache scouts for the U.S. Army, and families alike — to Florida for what proved to be one of the longest prisoner-of-war terms in the history of warfare between the United States and foreign nations. In 1912, four years after Geronimo's death, the remaining 261 Chiricahuas, who had been held at Fort Sill, Oklahoma, since 1894, learned that they would be set free and given the choice of joining the Mescaleros or remaining at Fort Sill. Of this number, 187 chose New Mexico, and 84 remained in Oklahoma (Debo 1989; Opler 1969, 1983b, 1996; Stockel 2004). The United States did not offer a third choice, their own reservation.

Only a decade after the United States set aside the Mescalero reservation, it sent another group of Apaches there. Vacillating for decades over its decision concerning a Jicarilla reservation, the Office of Indian Affairs (OIA, predecessor to the Bureau of Indian Affairs, or BIA) proved receptive to the blatant aggressiveness of recently arrived New Mexicans, who were eager to consolidate all Indians on a few reservations. As early as 1864 the United States asked the Jicarillas to remove to the Bosque Redondo reservation, but the negative assessment of a Jicarilla leader who visited the site enabled them to escape that disaster. In 1868 the Indian Office considered and rejected the notion of removing them to the newly created Southern Ute reservation, just north of the border with Colorado. By 1880 the United States had reluctantly set aside an executive-order reservation in northwestern New Mexico, but as soon as it was created, pressure by Congress on behalf of local constituents forced the United States to renege on its promise, and in 1883 it ordered the Jicarilla Apaches to join the Mescaleros. The Jicarillas responded half-heartedly to removal, and no sooner did they arrive than some of their leaders began pushing for their return. By the end of 1886 several hundred Jicarillas had fled, and by 1887, with the aid of powerful supporters, they finally procured the reservation set aside for them in 1880 (Tiller 1983, 452; Tiller 2000, 77–98).

When President Grover Cleveland signed the executive order in February 1887, the Jicarillas moved quickly to claim their land, which lay near the headwaters of the Rio Chama. Due largely to federal ineptness, the Jicarillas had already lost their original homeland, which included separate regions, each claimed by one of their two distinct groupings. The Ollero band (the potters) had lived in the Abiquiú–Tierra Amarilla area, north of Santa Fe. Their counterparts, the Llanero band (the plains dwellers), had lived in the vicinity of the Rio Cimarron, later the site of the Maxwell land grant. Both bands had survived through hunting and gathering, but when they moved to their reservation in 1887, writes historian Veronica E. Velarde Tiller, "they witnessed some of the worst suffering they had ever known." It was an era of tragedy that could be attributed largely to the bungling of the federal government (Tiller 2000, 98).

The Pueblo Indians, who represent a number of different languages, including Tewa, Tiwa, Towa (Tanoan), Keres, and Zuni, have deep roots in the land. From their initial encounters with Spaniards in the seventeenth century through the Pueblo-Spanish wars of the late 1600s and later the Mexican-American War, the Pueblo survivors of warfare and disease had remained in the central corridor of Spanish-Mexican settlement. By 1848 they had lived in proximity to Spaniards and Mexicans for some three hundred years, and successive generations had learned to adapt while applying pressure on colonial authorities. Yet like other Indians of New Mexico, they would face disruptive U.S. and New Mexico policies in the coming century that would guarantee confusion over their status — whether Indian or citizen — and massive loss of their land base, even though General Kearny and his officers had described them in 1846 as the "once peaceable and inoffensive masters of the country" (Simmons 1979b, 208).

The Pueblo legacy of these generations of colonialism spoke to the difference between Spanish- and Mexican-Indian relations and U.S.-Indian relations. The Pueblo role in the Spanish and Mexican periods had led to an acknowledgment of certain rights that proved to be a stumbling block for U.S. Indian policy. These rights included the famous Spanish land grants, in which the Pueblos were openly recognized "as hereditary possessors of the land they tilled and used," and, by 1820, the final year of Spanish rule, the liberal extension to the Pueblos of "full citizenship and legal equality." Following precedent, the Treaty of Cordova of 1821, which recognized Mexican independence from Spain, granted to all Indians "Mexican citizenship and protection of lands held under the Spanish regime" (Simmons 1979a, 182, 192; Simmons 1979b, 206). But as historian Marc Simmons has pointed out, the Mexican government failed to protect Indian land and water rights. In New Mexico this official neglect had enabled Spanish-speaking settlers to encroach heavily on Pueblo land (Simmons 1979b, 207).

When the United States entered the scene, the federal government stumbled upon an existing government-to-government relationship between individual pueblos and Mexican officials that it simply could not comprehend — especially because its evolving Indian policy would soon adopt the erroneous notion that Indians were "wards" of the federal government rather than sovereign nations. Still, during the early years after the Treaty of Guadalupe Hidalgo, the status of Pueblo citizenship had yet to be resolved, and under this murky state of affairs New Mexicans in 1850 voted favorably on a state constitution (Congress chose, instead, to create New Mexico Territory). The Pueblo Indians voted in this election because, shortly before, the territory's military governor had issued a proclamation declaring that Pueblos had the right to vote. Given the colonialist stance of U.S. Indian policy at this time, as well as the narrow boundaries of the franchise in America, members of the U.S. Congress could scarcely acknowledge Indian voting rights. In 1854 the House expressed these sentiments by declaring that Pueblo Indians were not citizens and therefore did not possess the franchise. The congressional ruling notwithstanding, during the 1850 vote on New Mexico's constitution and for four years thereafter, the Pueblos established a legal precedent, even though New Mexico would ignore it for almost a hundred years.

Between 1854 and 1913, the citizenship status of the Pueblos shifted full circle. Numerous legal wrangles complicated the issue, but in its two most dramatic decisions, the U.S. Supreme Court established diametrically opposite positions. The core issues focused on the legal status of Pueblos as U.S. citizens or Indians, and how this would affect their landownership. If they were citizens, then they had full title to their land. If they were Indians, then their land was entitled to federal protection. In *United States v. Joseph* (1876), the court declared that Pueblo land was not entitled to protection because the Pueblos had complete title to their land. In *United States v. Sandoval* (1913), the court reversed its earlier opinion, declaring that Pueblos were entitled to the same protection offered to other Indians in the United States. In short, the federal government would treat them as wards.

The vacillation of the Supreme Court would have a tremendous effect on the Pueblo land base. By the 1920s, New Mexico Senator Holm O. Bursum would seek to resolve the issue of Pueblo landownership and water rights by introducing the infamous Bursum bill (1922), which would have placed the burden of proving landownership on the Pueblo Indians themselves, requiring a search for records from the Spanish and Mexican eras. The bias reflected in this measure, which blatantly supported claims by Hispanos and others who had moved onto Pueblo land, prompted an intensive movement for the reform of federal Indian policy, led by John Collier, later commissioner of Indian affairs. The bill also spawned the revival of the All Pueblo Council (later the All Indian Pueblo Council), which represented the nineteen Indian pueblos of New Mexico. The Pueblos took their case to Washington, D.C., helping to defeat the Bursum bill. Shortly thereafter Congress passed the more balanced Pueblo Lands Act of 1924 (Iverson 1998, 60–61; Kelly 1983, 213–54, 295–300; Philp 1977; Sando 1976, 95; Simmons 1979b, 214–16).

Cultural Sovereignty versus Cultural Colonialism, 1880s–1940s

By the final decades of the nineteenth century, most of the tribes of New Mexico lived on land that had been acknowledged during the Spanish-Mexican era (the Pueblo land grants) or that the federal government had set aside for them since 1848. Like other Natives across Indian country, New Mexico Indians had ceased to fight in military

battles against the United States. Most Americans interpreted the surrender of Geronimo as the last act of Indian defiance, excluding the tragic killings at Wounded Knee,
South Dakota, which dealt a staggering blow to the spiritual revitalization movement
known as the Ghost Dance. Because most Indians had been confined to reservations, U.S. policy makers seized the opportunity to alter their cultures by introducing
the mainstream ideas of civilization that characterized American culture during the
immigration era of the 1880s to the 1920s. They reasoned that this might prove a good
diet for both immigrants and Native Americans. In short, policy makers believed that
Indians should become Christians and landowning farmers who had been schooled
in the "three Rs." Those who delivered these policies represented the epitome of late-
nineteenth-century European-American imperialism.

New Mexico Natives struggled with these policies at many levels. Key issues
that fomented dissension within and among the Pueblo, Apache, and Navajo nations
included religious freedom, educational choice, and Native versus Western medicine.
This era came long before the changes introduced in Indian country in the 1960s
and 1970s, often described as the era of "self-determination." Yet even though self-
determination for Native people was not in vogue between the 1880s and the 1920s,
Indians of New Mexico fought to retain their rights against great odds.

During the 1880s, at the height of the push for Indian assimilation, the Office
of Indian Affairs, with the support of Congress and the Supreme Court, created
measures to impose social, legal, and cultural control over reservation Indians.
Supreme Court rulings and congressional measures took away much of the tribes'
legal rights among their own people, including jurisdiction over major crimes. The
OIA mandated new Codes of Indian Offenses that relied on Courts of Indian Offenses
and the cooperation of the Indian police for enforcement. Crimes included any customs contrary to the mainstream, such as polygamy. Any Indian could be brought to
a reservation Court of Indian Offenses over these matters and punished accordingly
(Tiller 2000, 128–29).

In New Mexico, before the *United States v. Sandoval* ruling in 1913, only the
Apaches and Navajos could be subjected to this discipline. After 1913, when the United
States redefined the Pueblo people as Indians, federal policy makers began to scruti-
nize Pueblo religious practices, especially Pueblo dances. Indians of the Great Plains
had long endured OIA interference with the Sun Dance, which they had taken underground, into the remote regions of their reservations. But the vast spaces of the plains
could not be duplicated by those who danced on their village plazas along the Rio
Grande and west to the Hopi Mesas. In the late 1910s and the 1920s, the Indian Office
stumbled into a religious hornet's nest when Indian Commissioner Charles Burke
issued a directive — Circular 1665 — encouraging OIA superintendents to repress
Indian dances, which "under the most primitive and pagan conditions" were "apt to
be harmful." Burke's directive, supplemented in 1923 with a "Message to All Indians"
urging them to restrict their dances to monthly, mid-week, daylight events that would

be cancelled entirely during the summer months, struck home among both Plains and Pueblo Indians. It also spurred a widespread, acrimonious debate because it emerged during the emotional controversy over the Bursum bill (Kelly 1983, 295–348).

In the 1920s, religious conservatives in the United States were battling people who supported the trend toward an urban, secular society — epitomized in the famous 1925 Tennessee trial of high-school teacher John Scopes for violating state law by teaching the theory of evolution. The issues in Indian country, especially among the Pueblo Indians, including the Hopis in Arizona, echoed the nationwide dispute. The contestants in this microcosmic battle in the Southwest pitted "Progressive Christian" Pueblo Indians, who opposed traditional ceremony and leadership, against Pueblos who supported traditional ceremony and beliefs. It also set liberal reformers led by John Collier and his organization, the American Indian Defense Association, against conservative reform leaders of the old-line Indian Rights Association. Finally, it placed Charles Burke and the OIA superintendents in the middle, where they were pummeled by all sides (Kelly 1983, 300).

The crux of the struggle emerged early in 1924, when Superintendent for the Northern Pueblos C. J. Crandall notified Commissioner Burke that Taos Pueblo leaders had requested withdrawal of two of their boys from the federal school. The boys were scheduled for eighteen months of religious instruction, which required considerable time in the kiva, the Pueblos' underground ceremonial structure. Burke and Crandall suggested a compromise, but Taos rejected their offer, whereupon Burke visited Taos in April of that year in an attempt to resolve the issue. Of the various reports on this meeting, John Collier chose to believe the one declaring that Burke had intended to "deliver an ultimatum that two boys withdrawn from the school for religious purposes would have to be returned." Collier responded by suggesting that "'the damfool Burke,' by insisting upon the 'sacredness of his authority,'" had "played into their hands" (Kelly 1983, 308). The participants in this cause célèbre pressured the commissioner from all sides, and by summer Burke had grown weary of the acrimony and began to retreat from his conflict with the Pueblos. He pulled back from his insistence that the Taos boys attend school, although Crandall extracted a promise from Taos that all its children would attend school through sixth grade (Kelly 1983, 320–21).

The question of religious freedom dovetailed with the question of education. By the 1920s, the commissioner believed that mandatory schooling had to include all Indian youths. Federal Indian boarding schools, such as Carlisle Indian School (1879–1918) and Haskell Institute (1884–), earned controversial reputations in the late nineteenth and early twentieth centuries. Most of these schools taught Indian youths well beyond the chronological scope of this essay; still, they could not provide sufficient space for all Indian children, many of whom attended no school until the 1950s. The majority of public schools, unlike certain federal Indian boarding schools during the 1930s, ignored Native methods of teaching and the substance of Native knowledge. Those who taught Western education to Indians, from the Spanish colonial period forward, believed that Native youths should absorb the social, cultural, and economic systems of the colonial powers. Rarely did these outside teachers stop to acknowledge the merits of the education Natives gave their children. This cross-cultural dichotomy formed the core of the debate between Commissioner Burke and the leaders of Taos Pueblo.

The Office of Indian Affairs had introduced educational colonialism into New Mexico in the late nineteenth century. Although schools opened sporadically among the Navajos and Apaches, the Pueblo Indians proved more accessible (Opler 1983c, 423–24; Tiller 1983, 454–55). By the early twentieth century the OIA had opened day schools among more than half a dozen of the nineteen pueblos. At the pueblos of San Juan (Tewa), Jemez (Towa) and Laguna (Keresan), the OIA introduced local federal schools as early as the 1870s. For the children of the pueblo of Santa Ana (Keresan), day schools did not begin instruction until the early 1900s.

By contrast, in 1870 the pueblo of Santa Clara chose an independent route toward education by hiring an instructor to teach Santa Clara youths to read and write in Spanish (Hyer 2001, 276). Mission schools, especially Roman Catholic ones, had long provided some European education among the Pueblos, in one instance as early as the 1620s. Pueblo historian Joe Sando (Jemez) quotes a late-nineteenth-century U.S. Indian agent at the pueblo of Jemez, who observed in 1871 that "this village contains 344 inhabitants, of which only four persons can read and write; . . . These Indians desire a school and I have employed Jose Ma. Garcia, at $40 a month to teach the children." The statistics at Jemez bear a marked resemblance to territorial literacy rates of the post–Civil War decades. In 1880, 60 percent of New Mexicans, many of whom had once lived under the government of Mexico, could not read, and 65 percent could not write (Sando 1982, 169; Edelman and Ortiz 1979, 333). Determined to change this state of affairs, the Presbyterians also jumped aboard the bandwagon in the 1870s by establishing missionary schools at the pueblos of Laguna, Jemez, and Zuni.

Day schools met the stringency of federal budgets far more easily than the federal boarding schools. Still, the late nineteenth century marked the heyday of boarding schools, and the Southwest proved a prime target for bureaucrats responding to towns eager for the federal largesse that these institutions guaranteed. During these decades the OIA added two off-reservation boarding schools in New Mexico, the Santa Fe and Albuquerque Indian Schools. Set in the heart of Indian country but still removed from the reservations themselves, these two manual labor elementary schools targeted Pueblo children for their primary source of enrollment. A smaller number of Navajo and Apache children attended the schools, but most Navajo and Apache youths continued to be educated through traditional learning patterns (Hyer 1990).

New Mexico Indian families also parted with their children when they boarded the trains that would carry them to eastern Indian boarding schools. A small number of Pueblo children left their homes at the pueblos of Cochiti, Jemez, Laguna, and likely other villages to attend Carlisle Indian School in Pennsylvania. Carlisle also enrolled Chiricahua Apache children living as prisoners of war in the East, and some Navajo youths as well. The students at this famous institution came from across the continent, including the Southwest and Alaska, to gain a Western education. Given the vast distances and the school's pejorative attitude toward Native cultures, most of these young people remained in Pennsylvania for several years. Some did not return home for a full decade, and a large number, who are buried in the cemetery there, never returned at all. Among the Southwest Natives who attended Carlisle, those who eventually returned to Cochiti and Jemez Pueblos reportedly led the Progressive factions in their respective villages (Lange 1959, 30–33).

Children enrolled in federal schools, whether on or off the reservation, often carried home the diseases they caught in overcrowded school dormitories. Tuberculosis and glaucoma, a disease of the eye that can lead to blindness, frequently traveled with returning children. Some children sent home by school superintendents died shortly after they arrived in their pueblo, hogan, or log dwelling. Others lingered, spreading their illness to further members of their family. In 1912 a medical doctor serving the Navajos decried the removal of Navajo children to nonreservation schools: "It was a terrible mistake, for they began returning them dying of TB. I was frantic. I had no place to keep them" (Davies 2001, 88; Trennert 1998).

The Indian Health Service did not awaken to the dangers inherent in these institutions until the mid-twentieth century. In the meantime, Native people suffered from these diseases, and their numbers dwindled. Veronica Tiller charts the decline among the Jicarilla Apaches, whose population of 824 people in 1891 had shrunk to 594 in 1921 (Tiller 2000, 131–40).

New Mexico Indians during the Great Depression and World War II

The Crash of 1929 and the Great Depression that followed forced many Americans to alter the lifestyles they had enjoyed during the 1920s. For many New Mexicans, especially the Indians, the depression intensified the economic conditions that already circumscribed their lives (Engstrom, Korte, and McDonough 2004, 461). The Jicarilla Apaches proved an exception. By the 1920s, the federal government was finally jolted into the realization that the Jicarillas needed to be participants in the livestock industry, and it issued sheep from the tribal herd to each family. This change, together with the government's assistance in the fight against tuberculosis and its persuasive efforts to encourage the Jicarillas to adopt the Indian Reorganization Act (IRA) of 1934, "inaugurated a new era for the Jicarilla Apache" (Tiller 2000, 159–80).

Unlike the Jicarillas, most of the tribes in New Mexico voted against the IRA, the reform measure urged by Commissioner of Indian Affairs John Collier in 1934. Although scholars later criticized the IRA, most of them would agree that it generally offered Indians a brief reprieve from three-quarters of a century of assimilation restrictions. The IRA ended the allotment of Indian land, a measure that had taken from Indian people two-thirds of their remaining land base. Any tribe that voted to accept the full legislation gained the right to enter the economic world as an incorporated business with a revised form of government and a constitution based on a U.S. model. Both the Jicarilla and the Mescalero nations accepted these measures. The Navajo nation rejected the IRA, and the majority of the Pueblos also voted against it.

The story of the Navajos' rejection of the centerpiece of Collier's administration (1933–45) is far too complex to relate here, but a quick synthesis places the major cause for that rejection in Collier's demand for livestock reduction among the Navajo. He blamed the herds for the increasing land erosion on the Colorado Plateau. Since their adoption of sheep, sometime after the arrival of the Spaniards, most Diné had relied on their herds of sheep and goats for their sustenance. Although they also depended on horses, sheep were central to their lives. They provided wool for weaving and food for daily existence, ceremonies, and family gatherings. Sheep served as the educational medium for Navajo children, who learned the lessons of life — responsibility and caring attentiveness — as they herded their family's flocks. During the livestock reduction program, the Navajos lost more than half their entire stock population, leading some to dub this the "Second Long Walk." One Navajo woman recalled these years as the time when "the sheep were taken away" (Chamberlain 2000, 83; Roessel and Johnson 1974, 148). The Navajo "backlash against Collier," historian Peter Iverson notes, "left a bitter legacy" (Iverson 2002, 145).

Most of the Pueblo Indians followed suit by rejecting the Indian Reorganization Act. Half a dozen of the nineteen pueblos have an IRA-type government today, including Laguna, which was the earliest of the pueblos to adopt a Western-style elective form of government. The majority govern themselves through more traditional forms that remain intricately connected with the spiritual leadership in each pueblo. The Spaniards' treatment of Native religion, which served as a major cause of the Pueblo Revolt of 1680, continues to justify secrecy for Pueblo religion into the twenty-first century.

Still, Collier's legacy of the "Indian New Deal" also brought some gains to Native people of New Mexico. The Southwest became one of the strongholds of the Indian Civilian Conservation Corps (ICCC), under the auspices of which the federal government employed tribal members to build roads, plant trees, and construct small dams on Native land. Other Native New Mexicans found employment with the Works Progress Administration (WPA). Pablita Velarde, a renowned Santa Clara artist, found a position with the WPA after studying art with teacher Dorothy Dunn at the Santa Fe Indian School. During the 1930s, as Indian education programs under the guidance of W. Carson Ryan and W. W. Beatty urged acknowledgment of Native cultures, the Santa Fe Indian School led the way with its innovative art program, in which students found the freedom to paint from their own cultural experiences. Pablita Velarde relied on this training when she painted a group of murals for Bandelier National Monument, which remained a historic portrayal of Santa Clara Pueblo long after she won an international reputation for her earth paintings.

World War II had a major effect on all the Indians of New Mexico. Whether tribal members left their reservations to work in war factories, raised crops for the war effort, purchased savings bonds, or served in the armed forces — the army, navy, air force, or marines, including the Navajo Code Talkers — all these Native citizens contributed heavily to the victory of the United States and its allies and changed their own lives as well.

Native Americans of New Mexico: Citizens or Not?

By the years immediately after the war, New Mexicans had probably forgotten that Pueblo Indians had once voted in a territorial election. When New Mexicans wrote a new state constitution and entered the union in 1912, they denied the franchise to all "Indians not taxed." Veteran Miguel H. Trujillo, a member of the pueblo of Isleta, fought to overcome this legal injustice. A graduate of Albuquerque Indian School and Haskell Institute, Trujillo had taught in federal Indian schools until he enrolled at the University of New Mexico, where he received a degree in education in the spring of 1942. Shortly thereafter he enlisted in the U.S. Marine Corps, where he served until the fall of 1945. On his return, he received his master's degree in education, eventually becoming a principal at a federal school at Laguna Pueblo.

In 1948, like other Native veterans, Trujillo attempted to register to vote. When the state denied the franchise to the veterans, Trujillo decided to take the case to court. He chose lawyers well experienced in Indian affairs, including Felix Cohen, who later completed the classic *Handbook of Indian Law*. In early August 1948, the special three-judge tribunal assigned to hear Trujillo's case rendered its decision, declaring that, according to the U.S. Constitution, New Mexico's constitution was unconstitutional. Indians had the right to vote in New Mexico. A landmark decision, this ruling brought New Mexico into line constitutionally and granted the Indians of the state a right that should have been theirs since New Mexico became a territory. Like other Native people of New Mexico, whether Pueblo, Navajo, or Apache, Miguel Trujillo had reconfirmed the persistence of the Natives of the state.

General and Mexican governor of New Mexico Manuel Armijo (1793–1853), pastel drawing, about 1846.

27

Hispanic Land Grants and
Indian Land in New Mexico

Malcolm Ebright

When Surveyor General William Pelham arrived in Santa Fe in late January 1854 to set up shop in a building near the Palace of the Governors, he was overwhelmed by the responsibilities of sorting out the ownership of the territory the United States had acquired from Mexico under the 1848 Treaty of Guadalupe Hidalgo. Pueblo Indians owned some of the land, recipients of Spanish and Mexican land grants owned some, and the United States government owned the rest. It was Pelham's job, among other responsibilities, to determine precisely who owned what. He was instructed by General Land Office commissioner John Wilson to ascertain the origin, nature, character, and extent of all claims to land granted under the laws of Spain and Mexico, a monumental task for which Pelham was ill prepared. Although he was the most conscientious, hard-working, and honest of the handful of men to serve as surveyors general in the late 1800s, he was unversed in the law or history of Spain and Mexico and could not read Spanish. He was, as his title implied, a land surveyor.

Nevertheless, Pelham was supposed to learn about the Spanish and Mexican legal system in New Mexico, collect the documents relating to land grants there from the Spanish archives, and organize and protect these documents. He was sorely disappointed by the meager resources available to him to perform this important task. What he found when he asked Governor David Meriweather for the archives was almost as appalling as what he found when he was shown the office he would be inhabiting and the place where those archives would be stored.

Like most other buildings in Santa Fe at the time, Pelham's office near the Palace of the Governors was a typical native home with a dirt floor. The adobe walls had to be covered with canvas in order to protect his papers from the dirt. Pelham had to protect the documents from thieves as well. Although he slept in one room of his office, he had to hire a night watchman and keep a guard dog because of the perceived danger that thieves could scale the wall, let themselves down from the roofs of adjoining houses, or dig through the walls to gain access to the archives. Neither protection was provided for in Pelham's salary and expenses, and when he requested reimbursement for law books, expert translators, and even candles for the night watchman, his requests were denied.

When Governor Meriweather showed Pelham the archives, the surveyor general was shocked to find a mass of papers put up in bundles as large as goods boxes without any reference to what had been put in them. Eventually Pelham was able to sort through the archives and find papers for 197 land grants. Given this chaotic situation, it is amazing that there was not more corruption and incompetence in settling New Mexican land titles under the Treaty of Guadalupe Hidalgo. Even so, it would take fifty years before the land grant issues were settled, and the adjudication of land grants in the state remains controversial to this day.

Indian Land and the Pueblo League

In much of the present-day United States, little remains of the Natives who first occupied the land except ruins of their settlements. Only in the Southwest are intact Indian pueblos still in existence, housing people who still perform their ceremonies, use their land, and irrigate their fields. In New Mexico, nineteen pueblos remain of the several hundred that were there when Juan de Oñate brought the Spaniards who began the permanent settlement of New Mexico in 1598.

In New Mexico as elsewhere, Native Americans held different beliefs about landownership from those of Europeans. Each pueblo had its sphere of influence, sometimes overlapping the spheres of other pueblos and often bounded by a sacred mountain in each of the four directions. The nearer one traveled to the center — the pueblo's house blocks, ceremonial kivas, gardens, and fields — the greater the intensity of land use. Although Pueblo Indians did not consider the use of this land as ownership in the European sense, soon after the Pueblo Revolt in 1680 they began to resist encroachment on their land and to adopt the concept of ownership and make it work to their advantage.

A new land and water regime did away with the abusive pre-Revolt practice whereby Pueblo land was essentially owned by Spaniards who held pueblos such as Acoma and Taos in *encomienda,* meaning that the Spaniards received tribute from pueblo members. Moreover, although legally the *encomenderos* were prohibited from using forced Indian labor, they often ignored the law and did so anyway. After the revolt a new accommodation was negotiated whereby the Indians would own their own land. If Spaniards wanted to use Indian laborers, they had to pay them. By the mid-1700s governors such as Tomás Vélez Cachupín, who administered the courts, began making grants of land to Pueblo Indians, to mestizos, or people of mixed-blood descent, and to Spaniards. Under Governor Vélez Cachupín, Pueblo Indians in New Mexico also received some protection in the courts from trespass on their land and other interference with their rights.

In order to prevent trespass when a Spaniard requested land near a pueblo, a procedure was developed called "measuring the Pueblo league." Beginning in the 1700s, the pueblos were considered entitled to a league (five thousand *varas*) in each direction from the center of the pueblo. If the Spanish grant was within this measurement, then the Spaniard's petition was usually denied. Based on customary procedure rather than a specific law, this came to be called the Pueblo league. Eventually the surveyor general recommended confirmation of a Pueblo league of about 17,420 acres to each pueblo, although some received more land because of a specified land grant to the pueblo.

Spanish Settlement and Land Grants in New Mexico

The settlement of the Americas after the Spanish conquest of Mexico in 1521 gave rise to the Spanish land grant system that is still in evidence in the Southwest. Grants of land made to loyal Spanish soldiers became the favored method of colonization, providing the incentive needed to induce these soldier-citizens to settle the land and defend it from attack by nomadic Indians.

Land grants made to Spaniards in the Southwest were primarily either private grants, whereby the grantee owned the entire grant after he had settled on the land, or community grants, whereby a group of settlers received a grant that included both private property and community-held land. On a community grant, each member received a tract of property for a house site and garden plot while the remainder of the land was used in common for grazing, watering animals, gathering herbs, firewood, and building timber, hunting wild game, and fishing. Because the resources on the common land were available to every member of the community, it was possible to survive and even thrive on the small individual parcels. Grantees on community grants who had been in possession for at least four years owned their private tracts outright and could sell them to purchasers, who then became part of the community, with the obligation to defend the settlement from attack and the right to use the common land.

The process by which an individual or community received a land grant remained essentially the same whether the request was for a private or a community grant. Anyone seeking a land grant could address a petition to the governor describing the land sought and his qualifications for receiving a grant and stating that there were no adverse claims. The governor would then refer the petition to the local alcalde for his recommendation on whether the grant should be made, the primary considerations being whether the land was being used or was claimed by others, the sufficiency of the petitioner's qualifications, and, in the case of a community grant, the availability of resources such as pasture, water, and firewood.

If the alcalde's recommendation was favorable, the governor would make the grant, directing the alcalde to perform the final step: the ceremony of delivery of possession. On an appointed day, the grantees and neighboring landowners went to the land with the alcalde. This was the last chance for anyone to object, and sometimes the alcalde was called upon to settle a protest on the spot. If the alcalde found that the grant would not be prejudicial to anyone, he proceeded with the ceremony of delivery of possession.

If feasible, the grantees, the alcalde, and neighboring property owners walked the boundaries, placing monuments — usually a mound of stones or a cross — on the boundary lines or corners. Usually the most basic kind of survey was lacking, and boundaries were described by natural landmarks such as mesas, ridges, rivers, and neighbors' property. To complete the act of possession, the alcalde took the grantees by the hand and walked them over the land while they plucked up grass, threw stones in the air to signify their dominion over the land, and shouted, "Long live the king!" Soon after this ceremony the grantees took possession of their land, dug their irrigation ditches, built their homes and a church, and planted their fields. After four years of possession they owned the land grant.

The U.S. Invasion of New Mexico and the Treaty of Guadalupe Hidalgo

In August 1846 the Mexican Department of New Mexico, governed from faraway Mexico City, was changed forever by the approaching U.S. Army of the West, headed by General Stephen Watts Kearny. Before he entered Las Vegas, New Mexico, at eight o'clock on the morning of August 15, Kearny received notice of his promotion to brigadier-general.

In Las Vegas Kearny climbed to the roof of an apartment building fronting the plaza and, with alcalde Juan de Dios Maes at his side, addressed the assembled citizens. He promised: "Not a pepper, not an onion, shall be taken by my troops without pay.... I will protect you in your persons and property and in your religion" (Twitchell 1909, 49–50). After administering the new oath of allegiance to Maes and two others, the Americans moved on toward Santa Fe, where they arrived in the mid-afternoon of August 18, 1846.

Some eighteen months later, Kearny's promises were put into legal language in the Treaty of Guadalupe Hidalgo, which ended the Mexican-American War, one of the harshest in modern history. With the United States Army advancing on and finally occupying Mexico City, Nicolas Trist, the representative of U.S. President James K. Polk, and representatives of the Mexican government negotiated a draft treaty on February 2, 1848.

The Mexican representatives proposed an article providing that land grants valid under Spanish and Mexican law would be considered valid by the United States and would be protected. This provision became Article 10 of the proposed treaty, but in his message to the Senate, President Polk urged its deletion, so the version of the treaty ratified by the Senate had Article 10 "stricken out." In order to allay the concern of the Mexican government over the deletion of Article 10, the Mexican representatives asked the United States to sign an explanation known as the Protocol of Querétaro. The protocol stated that the United States did not intend to annul legitimate grants by deleting Article 10, defining legitimate titles as those that were valid under Mexican law before the cutoff date of May 13, 1846. With this written assurance to the government of Mexico, ratifications of the Treaty of Guadalupe Hidalgo (Ellis 1975, 10–31) were exchanged on May 30, 1848, and a proclamation was made on July 4, 1848.

Even with the deletion of Article 10, the surveyor general was instructed to apply the laws of Spain and Mexico as the standards or criteria for the legitimacy of land grants. Grants valid under those laws should be confirmed by the surveyor general. Thus, for the surveyor general to determine which land grants were valid under the Treaty of Guadalupe Hidalgo, he had to learn about the history and laws regarding the settlement of New Spain and New Mexico.

The Surveyor General of New Mexico

Being a much poorer state than California, New Mexico found that Congress tended to minimize the importance of settling its land grant titles. By the time Congress established the Office of Surveyor General of New Mexico in 1854, six years had passed since the signing of the Treaty of Guadalupe Hidalgo. The delay had created uncertainty about New Mexican land grant titles, which speculators were quick to take advantage of. Land speculators were the first to file for confirmation of huge grants they had acquired by purchase rather than by settlement, such as the Maxwell grant in northeastern New Mexico and southern Colorado.

Hispano settlers, on the other hand, did not understand or trust the American system of landownership. When called upon to bring their documents to Santa Fe and file claims, many Hispanos declined, fearing the government would lose their documents. Others felt adequately protected under the Treaty of Guadalupe Hidalgo and did not file a claim. Most Hispanos never conceived of the possibility that the common lands of their community grants were in jeopardy if they did not file for confirmation, because under their laws and customs, common land could not be sold.

The surveyor general's responsibility was to report to Congress his recommendations about whether land grant claims should be confirmed or rejected. But the boundaries of land grants were not surveyed until after they were confirmed, so neither he nor Congress had any idea how much land was being confirmed. Added to this, the procedure followed by the surveyor general lacked due process of law as required by the United States Constitution. No hearing was held at which the interested parties could present evidence and cross-examine opposing witnesses. Nor was any notice given to those whose property rights might be affected.

Thus, the surveyor general acted almost entirely on the basis of evidence submitted by the claimant who sought to have a land grant confirmed. If that evidence, including affidavit and deposition testimony of witnesses, was flawed and self-serving, as was often the case, there was no opportunity to correct errors through cross-examination or introduction of conflicting evidence. Self-serving affidavits could thus influence the recommendation of the surveyor general and then be incorporated into the decision by Congress to confirm or reject the land grant. The Tierra Amarilla grant, for example, which the Mexican government had made to Manuel Martínez as a community grant, was confirmed to Francisco Martínez, Manuel's son, as a private grant because of errors of fact and mistranslations in the papers submitted to Pelham by the father.

Because of the understaffing and underfunding of the surveyor general's office, the reluctance of many Hispanos and Native Americans to submit their documents to the United States government, and the lack of due process in the procedures followed, the surveyor general system often confirmed huge grants of millions of acres — such as the Maxwell grant — to one or two persons. By the late 1870s it was clear that the surveyor general system was not working. Bills were drafted to set up a true adjudication of land grants in New Mexico through a court system modeled partially on the procedure followed in California in 1851.

The Court of Private Land Claims

In early March 1891, Congress established the five-judge Court of Private Land Claims. Its procedures heavily favored the government, resulting in numerous unjust decisions. As in the surveyor general system, the claimant had the burden of proving the existence of the grant and the performance of all conditions. Previously the claimant had been aided by certain presumptions that eased the burden of proof, such as the presumption of the existence of a community grant from the existence of a settlement on that grant in 1846. Under the Court of Private Land Claims, all these presumptions were eliminated.

In addition, the experts most familiar with the land grant archives, who had researched Spanish and Mexican law, all worked for the government. Because claimants seldom had the means to hire experts, they were wholly dependent on the skill and honesty of the attorney they hired to represent them. Unfortunately, many land grant lawyers were more concerned with their own interests than with their duty to pursue their clients' interests with vigor. Yet the government pursued every case vigorously, appealing many on highly technical grounds. As the government won more appeals in the United States Supreme Court, new precedents were established in the government's favor. As a result, claimants' lawyers conceded many cases without a trial.

The Supreme Court and the Court of Private Land Claims used several specious grounds to reject perfectly valid grants. These included requirements that the grant be recorded in the Spanish or Mexican archives of New Mexico and that there be strict compliance with each of the procedural steps of the grant. These technical reasons had seldom, if ever, been the basis for land grant rejections by Spain or Mexico, but U.S. courts rarely looked to see how the Spanish and Mexican governments had treated land grants in Hispanic New Mexico.

Several grounds had justified the rejection of land grants by Spanish and Mexican authorities. These included forgery of documents, insufficient proof that a grant had been made, failure to notify owners of adjacent land, failure to meet a basic condition of the grant, revocation of the grant by Spanish or Mexican officials, and failure to settle the land for four years after the grant was made. These grounds would clearly have justified U.S. courts in rejecting grants, for under international law those courts should have adjudicated land grants in the same way Spain and Mexico would have. Instead, the courts often found it more expedient to rely on an inapplicable Spanish or Mexican law or a commentary on Hispanic law as the basis for a decision.

If Article 10 had not been eliminated from the Treaty of Guadalupe Hidalgo, its mandate to confirm all grants to the extent that Spain or Mexico would have confirmed them might have provided a guide for land grant adjudication. As it was, the land claims court and the Supreme Court followed no consistent principles, and both were highly erratic in their land grant decisions.

The Santa Fe Ring and Land Grant Speculation

Lawyers involved in land grant speculation, joined by some judges, politicians, and businessmen, were known as the Santa Fe Ring, a corrupt network established for mutual material gain. Besides the surveyors general, nearly every governor of New Mexico from the late 1860s to 1885 was a member of the Santa Fe Ring. Ironically, some members of the ring were Hispanos. With the Santa Fe Ring working against their interests, it was no wonder that Hispanic land grant settlers, unfamiliar with Anglo laws and language and often unaware of court proceedings involving their land grants, had little chance of protecting their property.

Unlike conquistadors such as Juan de Oñate, who conquered New Mexico for Spain in the hope of finding gold and silver, the Anglo Americans who came to New Mexico in the nineteenth century saw the land itself as the real material wealth. Speculators such as Thomas Catron, Stephen Elkins, Henry Atkinson, Charles Beaubien, and Antonio Joseph saw the land as an asset that could be sold for money. It was not a sacred domain that could never be owned but only used, as the Native Americans believed and as Hispanos believed about the common land of their community land grants. This battle between competing visions of the land still goes on in New Mexico as Indian pueblos, Hispanic community grants, and speculative land developments exist side-by-side.

Contemporary Hispanic and Native American property owners whose land has been lost because of the American invasion are still protesting and seeking redress from the United States government for losses against which the Treaty of Guadalupe Hidalgo promised to protect them. Although the United States did establish a bureaucracy to adjudicate Hispanic and Native American land rights, much of the land formerly owned and used by indigenous people found its way into the hands of lawyers, land speculators from the Santa Fe Ring, and the federal government. In addition, Indian agents as well as government officials past and present helped prepare the way for and participated in a huge shift in ownership of land grants away from indigenous ownership.

The stories of land loss resulting from the United States' invasion of the Southwest need to be told repeatedly, whether or not the federal or state government ever provides redress or even admits responsibility for the injustice of land grant adjudication. Keeping these stories alive helps keep alive the culture and history tied to that land. Attempts to cut the land away from the stories that give it life are still being made as the government continues to try to justify its land grant adjudication in the light of the promises made in the Treaty of Guadalupe Hidalgo. Cutting the land away from the stories that give it life can happen only if we forget.

28

Billy the Kid and the
Lincoln County War

Marc Simmons (2006)

"Every calculation based on experience elsewhere fails in New Mexico." So spoke Lew Wallace, once the youngest major general in the Union army, author of *Ben Hur*, and governor of New Mexico Territory at the height of the Lincoln County War.

Wallace's remark was not idly made, for during his three years governorship at Santa Fe, 1878–1881, he discovered to his dismay that the rules of politics and the rule of law, as he knew them in the East, did not apply there. Crooked lawyers, devious land speculators, claim jumpers, and cattle rustlers were as common as thorns on a cactus. And even many territorial officials and prominent business leaders engaged openly in corruption, on the theory, it would appear, that in this turbulent land, honest men were prime candidates for the poorhouse.

Governor Samuel B. Axtell, Wallace's immediate predecessor, for example, had been removed from office after his administration was linked to frauds, mismanagement, underhanded plots, and murders. He was a member of the notorious Santa Fe Ring, a group that controlled much of the Territory's economy and political life. Both Axtell and the Ring played an unsavory role behind the scenes in the Lincoln County War, leading President Rutherford B. Hayes to appoint Lew Wallace as house-cleaner and peace-maker.

Lincoln County, the focus of Wallace's attention during his term of office, had been carved out of the remote southeastern corner of the Territory in 1869. Stretching from the Texas line westward to the San Andres Mountains, it comprised more

William H. Bonney ("Billy the Kid"), New Mexico, about 1878–80. Copy of tintype generally thought to have been made by an itinerant tintypist working on the street in Fort Sumner, New Mexico.

land than several New England states combined and, in fact, was the largest county in the nation.

Its sparse population was thinly scattered around the fringes of the arid Tularosa Basin, through a half dozen mountain ranges, and along the valley of the middle Pecos River. Some of its people were Hispanic farmers, originally from older settlements on the Rio Grande. A sprinkling of Texans owned ranches, large and small, down the east side. And there was an uncounted host of drifters, many of them on the run from the law and looking for a place to hide. By the mid 1870s, Lincoln County was already famous as an outlaw haven.

But there were other men who sought out this far country because in its untapped resources they perceived opportunities for economic development and personal profit. As was true elsewhere in New Mexico, achievement of those goals required gathering and holding the reins of political power. The Lincoln County War was a naked struggle for power unlike more traditional conflicts in the West born of personal feuds or rivalries between cattlemen, sheep raisers, and homesteaders. And behind it all lay the sinister and, to this day, shadowy hand of the Santa Fe Ring.

Among the early opportunists was a trio of Irishmen: Lawrence G. Murphy, James J. Dolan, and John H. Riley, operators of the only mercantile business in the county seat of Lincoln. Their "Big Store" monopolized trade in the area, charged farmers and ranchers exorbitant prices, and held beef contracts for the supply of neighboring Fort Stanton and the Mescalero Apache Reservation.

Murphy and his partners maintained close ties with the Ring, depending upon its patronage and influence to win government contracts. They had the ear of Governor Axtell. Lincoln County Sheriff William Brady was their willing tool. For a time the tight mercantile monopoly, so carefully structured, seemed unassailable.

Allied against the proprietors of the Big Store, however, were three able men looking to enhance their own fortunes. One was John S. Chisum, who had driven a cattle herd out of Texas in 1873 and founded a ranch of king-size proportions on the Pecos near modern Roswell. Rustlers over a two year period stole 10,000 head of his stock, and he believed many of the animals had been purchased by Murphy's firm at Lincoln to fill beef contracts.

The second man, a friend of Chisum's, was Alexander McSween. A recently arrived Kansas lawyer, he had a hunger for political office and power. Basically honest, he looked with alarm upon the shoddy, often illegal, business practices of the Murphy-Dolan-Riley interests.

The third member of the group was a likable and ambitious Englishman in his early twenties, John Henry Tunstall. Funded by his father in London, he had come to Lincoln County determined to create a ranching empire. Establishing his headquarters on the Rio Feliz southeast of the county seat, he quickly discovered that the Big Store had local commerce and politics securely under its control.

McSween and Tunstall, finding that they had common aims, joined forces and opened a bank and a rival store in Lincoln. Much of their financial backing came from the pocket of John Chisum. By breaking the monopoly and undercutting prices, the new company was an overnight success.

About that time, Murphy went into semi-retirement because of ill health, leaving James Dolan to deal with the situation. Long-abused customers were abandoning the Big Store in droves and going over to the opposition. By fair means or foul, Dolan decided the competition had to be destroyed.

Into this charged atmosphere rode a young man, handy with a gun, who identified himself as William H. Bonney. In the less than four years of life remaining to him, this youthful desperado would shoot his way into the history books under the name Billy the Kid.

By all accounts, he scarcely looked the part of a killer. Under five feet, eight inches tall, Billy was slender and sinewy with noticeably small feet and hands. Even after he had turned twenty, folks who knew him declared that he could pass for a sixteen-year-old.

The beardless Kid had a pointed chin and a short upper lip which exposed protruding front teeth and gave him a chronic grin. Women, if credence can be given to numerous reports, found him attractive.

Less unanimous are contemporary statements regarding his disposition. His legion of enemies delighted in picturing him as reckless and cruel with an inborn instinct for murder. From that view of Billy's character sprang the often-repeated claims that he shot his first victim at age twelve — a rogue who insulted his mother — and that by the time he died at twenty-one, he had slain a man for every year of his life. Both assertions were false.

Friends and partisans, on the other hand, testified that the Kid was easy-going, jocular in manner, loyal, and kindly disposed toward those giving him half a chance. But, they were quick to admit he was a remorseless and dangerous enemy. Some of the men who opposed him discovered that when they fell before his six-gun.

By the historical record, six killings, not twenty-one, can be credited definitely to the Kid. He appears to have had a hand in three others, during gunfights when lead flew in all directions. But even those, proclaimed his supporters, occurred because evil men backed him into a corner. The ongoing argument over Billy's motives and deeds forms but one of the many elements that cast a mythical glow over his personal history.

Controversy surrounds almost every aspect of his career, including even the place and date of his birth, which unsubstantiated reports place in New York City, November 23, 1859. The first valid reference to the youth does not surface until March 1, 1873. On that date records show that the widow Catherine McCarty married William H. Antrim in Santa Fe with her two young sons, Joseph and Henry McCarty, as witnesses. Henry, the future Billy the Kid, was then fourteen years old, and though high-spirited gave no other indication of the turbulent life that would be his.

The Antrims soon moved to Silver City, and the following year Catherine died of tuberculosis, leaving her sons adrift. Without her steadying hand, little Henry was soon at odds with the law. When a companion stole a bundle of clothes from two Chinamen, he was accused of the theft and lodged in the Silver City jail. Escaping by climbing up a chimney, he headed for the Arizona line — now and to the end of his days, a fugitive.

During the next two years, Henry Antrim (he had taken his stepfather's surname) worked quietly in southeastern Arizona as cowboy, farmhand, and teamster. Then, during the summer of 1877, he shot to death blacksmith Frank Cahill, who had been bullying him in a saloon near Camp Grant.

A coroner's jury ruled that the slaying "was criminal and unjustifiable, and that Henry Antrim, alias Kid, is guilty thereof." Had the young man's plea of self-defense been sustained, giving the verdict in his favor, much of what followed might have been avoided.

Jailed once more, the Kid escaped again and rode hard for New Mexico. After a brief stopover at Mesilla, on the Rio Grande forty miles above El Paso, he set a course for Lincoln County. Crossing the Guadalupe Mountains, where Apaches stole his horse, he descended to the Pecos Valley, arriving there footsore and hungry during the fall of 1877.

A hospitable ranching family gave him grub and a new mount. Moving upriver, he stayed briefly with the Chisum outfit. After several weeks he traveled east and landed at Tunstall's ranch. The foreman, Richard Brewer, offered him a job.

Using the alias William H. Bonney to cloak his identity, the Kid enjoyed several months of calm, herding cattle. Quickly he came to admire his new boss, John Henry Tunstall, who was just a few years his senior. And the liking was reciprocated. Of Billy, Tunstall remarked to an acquaintance, "That's the finest lad I ever met. I'm going to make a man out of that boy yet. He has it in him."

The Kid's sense of loyalty toward this man explains much about his conduct in the terrible sequence of events that soon unfolded.

James Dolan now was moving swiftly to counter the threat posed by the McSween-Tunstall firm in Lincoln. By illegal means, he obtained a writ of attachment on all their properties. His ally, Sheriff Brady, agreed to send a deputy with a large posse to Tunstall's ranch to serve the writ.

When word of the maneuver reached the Rio Feliz, young Tunstall decided to go to Lincoln and try to negotiate a settlement. Some evidence suggests that the Kid, fearing treachery, pleaded with his boss to take to the hills. Tunstall refused, and gathering several of his cowboys, including Brewer and Billy, he set out for the county seat.

On the way the posse came up and the hapless Englishman was shot in the back of the head. He had made no hostile move. It was a simple case of murder.

This crime proved to be the spark touching off the conflagration which became the Lincoln County War. Death of the popular rancher-merchant aroused indignation among county residents and led his employees and friends to swear vengeance. None was more determined in that regard than Billy the Kid.

Knowing that agencies of the law were firmly under the thumb of Dolan and his associates, Tunstall's men formed a body of "Regulators," commanded by Dick Brewer, to track down members of the killer posse. Two of them were captured in March and while being taken to Lincoln were "shot trying to escape," as the popular saying went.

Governor Axtell meanwhile was being subjected to severe criticism for his seeming indifference to the spreading trouble in the southern part of the Territory. Finally he did go to Lincoln and, accompanied by Dolan, who guided his every step, he conducted a perfunctory and wholly biased investigation. As a result, he issued a proclamation authorizing the commander at Fort Stanton to assist civil law officers in keeping the peace. That meant simply that Sheriff Brady, when in need, could call out the troops to defend the Dolan faction.

The bloodshed continued to escalate. On April 1, Billy and five other Regulators slipped into Lincoln intending to serve as bodyguards for the wives and children of McSween partisans. Sheriff Brady and several deputies were seen walking down the town's one street toward the courthouse. The opportunity was too good to be missed.

From behind a plank gate, Billy and his companions opened fire. Brady and George Hindman were immediately killed. The remaining deputies shot back, and the Kid received a minor flesh wound. Concealed by friends until nightfall, he stole away and rejoined the Regulators.

The slaying of Sheriff Brady proved a major blunder. It turned public opinion against Billy's crowd and discredited their cause. Blame for the killing was also heaped upon McSween, who had nothing to do with it. Recalled one resident years afterward, "Brady…probably had faults but none that justified his being shot down like a dog."

The territorial press howled that anarchy reigned in Lincoln County. And so it seemed. A few days after the sheriff's death, the Regulators cornered "Buckshot" Roberts, another member of the posse that had killed Tunstall. At Blazer's Mill southwest of Lincoln, Roberts fought gamely and before he fell, shot Dick Brewer between the eyes.

Frank MacNab succeeded Brewer as head of the Regulators, but he died in a gunfight toward the end of April and leadership passed to "Doc" Scurlock. Ranging unchecked through the countryside, the Regulators gained the upper hand. The Dolan faction became frantic. Only the timely intervention of the Santa Fe Ring prevented its defeat.

In the capital, Thomas B. Catron, a leading Ringite, prevailed upon Governor Axtell to appoint George W. Peppin as the new sheriff of Lincoln County. Peppin, a pro-Dolan man, had been one of the deputies escaping the ambush that killed Brady. He was fully prepared to smite the enemy with fire and sword.

With this appointment, the stage was set for a showdown, and it was not long in coming. Between July 15 and 19, 1878, occurred "The Five Days Battle," the culmination of the Lincoln County War. Dolan had assembled his "troops" and under the generalship of Sheriff Peppin besieged McSween and fourteen followers in his Lincoln home.

During the affray Colonel Nathan Dudley, commander at Fort Stanton, arrived with soldiers and several pieces of artillery. But instead of intervening to end hostilities, he stood calmly by while the Peppin forces concluded the siege. The colonel's behavior can be traced to his friendliness toward Dolan and the Santa Fe Ring.

On the last day, the attackers set fire to McSween's house. Flames moved slowly through the adobe building, burning the plank floor and ceiling. Mrs. McSween left the smoking structure to plead with Colonel Dudley to spare the lives of her husband and the others. He declined.

The defenders retreated from room to room. With McSween exhausted and near collapse, Billy the Kid took charge. By dark, fire had forced them into the last room. The Kid ordered that, in turn, each man should make a wild dash for freedom. He managed to flee unscathed through the hail of lead, but Alexander McSween and four others died. In a blaze of gunfire, the war was virtually ended.

That was not entirely apparent at the time, however. Sporadic violence continued, but with both McSween and Tunstall gone, the Regulators as a group disintegrated. Shocked by reports of the Five Days Battle, President Hayes removed Governor Axtell from office and on September 30 replaced him with Lew Wallace. Also spurring him to take this action had been remonstrances from the British Foreign Officer over the killing of Tunstall.

Committed to bring order out of chaos, the new governor found the issues surrounding the war almost too perplexing to unravel. Since he was confused over who were the injured parties, he proclaimed a general amnesty for all participants. But it did not cover those who might be convicted of slaying Sheriff Brady.

Murphy died while convalescing at Santa Fe. Dolan lost his store to mortgage foreclosure, while his junior partner, Riley, left the county. Colonel Dudley, condemned for his actions during the burning of the McSween house, was relieved of his post at Fort Stanton. In January 1880 Governor Wallace was pleased to report to the territorial legislature that peace had been restored in Lincoln County.

Yet one untidy piece of business remained outstanding. Billy the Kid was still at large. With a remnant of the Regulators, he had formed an outlaw gang and turned to rustling. That played straight into the hands of the Santa Fe Ring. Since things had gone awry in Lincoln County, the Ringites made the Kid their scapegoat. The Santa Fe *New Mexican*, a mouthpiece for the group, took the lead in laying blame for old troubles and every new crime in the Territory squarely upon the shoulders of William Bonney.

In late 1880 a tall, gangling man with a walrus mustache assumed duties as the sheriff of Lincoln County. Pat Garrett had been living in the Pecos Valley around Fort Sumner and Roswell but played no part in the just-concluded war. His assignment as a lawman was to track down Billy the Kid. A standing reward of $500 for the desperado, offered by Governor Wallace, provided Garrett added incentive.

On December 21 the sheriff captured Billy and three accomplices at Stinking Springs, an abandoned cow camp twenty-five miles east of Fort Sumner. After a brief period of imprisonment in Santa Fe, the outlaw was sent by rail down to Mesilla to stand trial for the murder of Sheriff Brady.

The long arm of the Ring, reaching into the courtroom, sealed the Kid's fate. Although it could not be proved that he had shot Brady, his mere presence among the assailants, declared the judge, was sufficient for a guilty verdict. The handpicked jury readily complied, and the defendant was ordered returned to Lincoln for execution.

Back once more in the little town that figured so prominently in his life, Billy the Kid sat on the second floor of the courthouse to await the gallows. From his window, he could see the blackened ruins of the McSween residence.

On April 27, 1881, Pat Garrett departed Lincoln for the town of White Oaks to purchase lumber for the scaffold. In his absence Billy obtained a gun, hidden in the privy by a friend. Killing the two deputies left to guard him, he mounted a horse and rode out of Lincoln for the last time.

His dramatic escape threw the Territory into an uproar. Garrett, much chagrined by the turn of events, formed a posse and took up the chase. Why the Kid did not turn immediately toward Mexico will always remain a mystery. Instead, he rode northward to Fort Sumner, counting on friends to take him in. There Pat Garrett surprised him in a darkened room of the Pete Maxwell house on the night of July 14. The sheriff fired two shots and Billy the Kid fell dead.

While his foes breathed a sigh of relief, there were many, counting themselves as his friends, who mourned.

Bitter memories of the Lincoln County War persisted far into the 20th century. It is today ranked as one of the most lawless episodes in the history of the American West.

29

Blackdom, Chaves County

Daniel Gibson (1986)

In 1896, two black men named Francis Boyer and Dan Keyes began a long walk from Georgia. Their destination was New Mexico, where they were to play a central role in one of the state's most unusual and little-known communities — Blackdom. Now long abandoned, for almost two decades Blackdom was a thriving community built by and for blacks, people fleeing the oppression of post-Civil War life in Mississippi, Arkansas, Texas, and other southern states.

Little physical remains can be found of Blackdom today, just some crumbling foundations poking up through the prairie grass and bits of glass and rusted cans. But, while the community can no longer be found on maps, it continues to live on in the memories of those who lived there, illuminating a forgotten chapter in New Mexico's multicultural heritage.

Located some 16 miles due south of downtown Roswell, Blackdom was the name of both a community of scattered homesteads, and a distinct town founded in 1920, even as the black settlers were beginning to drift away, their "experiment" abandoned. At its height, the community encompassed some 15,000 acres, while its population is estimated by various sources to have topped out around 25 families or 300 individuals.

Like many other things noble in design, Blackdom actually began as a dream, a dream of Francis's father, Henry Boyer. Henry was a free Negro from Pullam, Georgia, and a wagoner in Col. Alexander Doniphan's Army of Missouri Volunteers. Sent to New Mexico to take part in the Mexican War in 1846, Henry eventually returned home to tell stories of

Farmers in the town of Blackdom, near Dexter, southeast New Mexico, about 1918.

the state's vast, unclaimed space. While technically freed by the outcome of the Civil War, blacks were still virtually enslaved through the sharecropping system prevalent in the South. Boyer's words were electrifying.

According to Lillian Collins Westfield, who was born on a Blackdom homestead and now lives in Roswell, "Most of the people came because for once they would have their own land. Most had been sharecroppers, like their parents before them. When they heard of this, they got on a train or horse and came."

For Francis Boyer and Dan Keyes, those two first pioneers, both of whom had received college educations, the trip was long and trying.

Recalls Francis's son Hobart, who also lived at Blackdom but now resides in Vado, south of Las Cruces, "People along the way would do things like make them dance while they fired bullets at their feet!" Reaching the Pecos River Valley, they at last felt unyoked and decided here they would make their new lives. For several years Francis worked for white ranchers and farmers in the area and as a bellboy in a Roswell hotel. In 1901, his wife, Ella, and budding family joined him. Still, his dream of his own farm eluded him, chiefly, says Hobart, because water was hard to come by.

"The big cattlemen, four or five of 'em, had already come in and gobbled up all the good water holes, conscripted them. So, you could get land, but no water. You could dig down about 70 feet and find a little stream, but that's all the water they thought was there! My dad was working for this man who'd come out from Indiana because of TB. This man had drilled for oil back East and decided to go deeper, looking for water. He went down to 200 feet and all he found was sand. People told him, 'See, there ain't no more water between here and hell!' But he kept drilling, cause all this talk made him mad! And, at 600 feet, he hit artesian water — the first found in the area. No one even knew it was there."

The discovery of artesian water (other sources report other individuals "discovered" the region's fame artesian sources) was to temporarily transform the Roswell region into a garden and initiate a major spurt of growth.

"Everybody went crazy," says Hobart. "New York millionaires came out, bringing in their lawyers, bankers, doctors, and retired farmers — everybody buying up the land, spreading out. It was heaven on earth. Just turn your water on and turn it off. It was booming, the whole country in there. My dad was making good money, cause the land was rich — soil all the way down 15 feet."

At last, Francis could see his dream within his grasp, and leaving Roswell late in 1901 he moved his family south to the Dexter area and established a homestead. With a loan from the Pacific Mutual Company, he dug an artesian well and tapped into the abundant water, raising sizable harvests of hay and apples.

He also began to advertise heavily, says Hobart, in newspapers and magazines in the South to attract more blacks to the area. "My dad was trying to get coloreds out here, advertising everywhere. When the exodus come, we had something to share. We'd help them get a house started and crops in the ground. But, it was hard for those wanting to get out here. Many people wanted to go to Old Mexico, or back to Africa, but the government wouldn't give them passports. Even getting out of their small towns was hard. The whites wouldn't sell them train tickets to let them leave. I remember one man arriving who told he he'd had to swim the Mississippi to get away!" At any rate, by ones and twos and in family units, blacks did begin to move into the Roswell area, gravitating to the Boyer farm where they were temporarily housed.

Lillian Collins Westfield's family arrived in 1907, settling some four miles west of what would be the Blackdom townsite in years ahead. Her father served as the mailman for the community, meeting the regular mailman about halfway between Dexter and Blackdom and then carrying the mail to a small general store that had been established by a man named James Eubank.

According to Elvis Fleming, an Eastern New Mexico University professor who wrote about Blackdom in the book *Roundup on the Pecos*, this mail service ran from 1911 to 1915. Next to the store was the other "public" building of Blackdom, a combined church, school, and community center, built with supplies furnished by the Greenfield school district, apparently to keep the local white and black children separated. Here Lillian attended a year of school. She recalls it was a one-teacher affair, with grades one through eight. Older children were taught in the basement and the younger ones upstairs. Here, too, Hobart attended church. He recalls, "We had

Methodists, Baptists, Catholics, and Seventh Day Adventists all attending the same services! Sunday school was especially lively. When we'd go to discussing the Bible, everybody would start picking it apart!"

When the Boyers had a deep well early on, the $4,000 price tag for drilling an artesian well was beyond the reach of most of the settlers. Even the $180 required to dig a shallow well proved too much for most of Blackdom's people. Instead, as Lillian relates, "A lot of people had to haul their water in barrels by horse-drawn wagons from the tanks put up by ranchers for their stock." In another vein, she remembers that "one or two families had smokehouses, and people would go out and dig up mesquite roots — as big as chairs — and we'd use them for smoking meats." Finding fuel for cooking in general, she recalls, was a problem. The only forests were some 20 miles away — a full day's outing. So instead of using wood, people in the early years collected cow chips, and later coal was shipped to the community by friends in Ratón.

"I remember the winds too," says Lillian. "There weren't hardly any trees out there, nothing to break the wind. We'd have to anchor the houses down with wire, wrapping it around the corner posts and then to a big rock buried in the ground! Once some people gave me some lambs, and I noticed that whichever way the wind blew, they'd go — even over a cliff! A storm came up one day, and I was out trying to catch my sheep and my mom saw me. She ran out and laid down on top of me, to protect me. I never saw the sheep again!"

Special occasions were celebrated at Blackdom as they were anywhere with social gatherings and good food. Recalls Hobart, "At Christmas, they'd get a big tree and set it up at the school. Everybody would come. There'd be a big program, and then people would give gifts, and finally there'd be a big eat."

Often at these social events, Lillian's mother would be called upon to play her guitar. Says Lillian, "We'd have these get-togethers — like sewing circles or ice cream socials — and everybody would ask 'Sis Mamie,' as they called my mom, to come and play her 'box.' That's what they called her guitar." Lillian, too, recalls Christmases. "I remember the one when I realized there wasn't a Santa Claus. Momma would buy things in town and put them on layaway, and just before Christmas go and collect everything. This one Christmas it was real snowy. It must have been four or five feet deep. It seemed we could just see the tops of the houses, and so she couldn't get into town. That night my father said, 'Santa might now make it tonight. It's so cold.' And I said, 'No! He's coming! He lives at the North Pole! He's used to cold.' But he didn't come."

One of the favorite holidays was "Juneteenth." Celebrated on June 19, it marked the day emancipation had been declared in Texas years before. Says Hobart, "On June 19, people would come from Roswell and Carlsbad, all over, and the cattlemen would give us two or three beefs. We'd have a big eat and a baseball game."

W. E. Utterback, a life-long white resident of the area now deceased, described this event in the book *As We Remembered It*: "About five miles west of Greenfield was a place called Blackdom. A number of Negros homesteaded this land. They were a bunch of hardworking people and gave no trouble in any way. On Emancipation Day, they invited the white folks out to a big feed. After the feed, the Negros challenged the white men to a baseball game. We got up a team from Dexter and Greenfield. I caught in that game, and we played on the open prairie with no backstop.... Their big first baseman, whom they called Y.Z. (David Profitt) hit one ball which I think landed in Orchard Park. I made the sad mistake of trying to block this Y.Z. from home plate. He came in head first and skinned my shin bones about a foot. By the way, we lost the game."

This game was not the only interaction between the community and the white people of the region. *Roundup on the Pecos* quotes Lillian's recollection: "They used to have a roundup every fall and these cowboys used to come into the area if you were home. They would come in and eat, and if they wanted to, have their bedrolls and sleep. If you weren't there, the doors were never fastened anyway. They would come in and sleep, and leave a note saying, 'I've been here.'"

White doctors were also called upon if someone was seriously ill. Hobart recalls that "people were healthy in general. We used to say the high, dry winds blew all the germs away. I was 14 before I saw a dead person."

Johnnie Mosly, who was born just beyond Blackdom, moved away and later returned before she finally settled in Roswell, remembers that many babies were delivered by midwives. Her grandmother was a midwife, and perhaps delivered Lillian's brothers and sisters. These midwives, Johnnie says, used the local herbs in their work. "Us kids used to say, 'Either they'll kill us or cure us,' and since we're alive today, I guess they worked!" During illnesses, she remembers, "Everybody was neighbors and helped one another, seeing what they could do — the wash, cooking, and such. And nobody charged anybody anything. We lived in that atmosphere."

Adds Lillian, "I recall we set up a signal system, too, because the houses were all at least a quarter of a mile apart. If someone was sick, we'd put up a white flag, and that would say, 'Come over and help.' Somehow or other, someone would get over to see what could be done, and someone else would get a buggy or horse to go and get a doctor from Dexter or Greenfield. We'd take turns caring for the sick, cooking. We were very close that way."

Food never seemed to have been lacking. Everyone had vegetable gardens, and Johnnie Mosly recalls large harvests of peaches, plums, apples, pears, and cherries. Families raised chickens, ducks, geese, hogs, turkeys, and a few had Jersey cows that yielded rich milk. Concerning the turkeys, Johnnie relates that they — like the sheep — would wander, chasing grasshoppers for miles over the gently undulating plains. And, there was some hunting. Says Hobart, "There weren't much buffalo left, but there was plenty of antelope. The white hunters would bring us one occasionally, because we were too busy working to hunt much. We did go after quail, dove, and rabbit, though. On Saturdays, 15 or 20 boys would get together and bring back a gang of rabbits."

But, adversity was waiting in the wings. Dryland farming — depending on rainfall — was chancy at best. If there were good snows, a winter wheat crop might be harvested in the spring, and one of every three or four summers brought adequate rain, says Hobart. But to sustain a large population, better water sources were needed. They were never to be acquired, and most of Blackdom's men ended up working for white farmers. The Boyers lost their own farm and deep well and had to resettle on a new homestead closer to the Blackdom townsite. Francis Boyer's granddaughter, Ethel Stubbs — a Clovis teacher — explains, "He always tried to help everyone else out who arrived, and eventually became overextended on his mortgage and the banks foreclosed."

And, what little water there was began to disappear. Says Hobart, "It was wonderful once. I can remember harvests. They'd use these steam-driven thrashing machines that puffed along like a train. They'd come down the road blowing smoke and we'd all run and yell, "Here comes the thrashing machine! Get ready.' And we got along well with the whites, mostly. Towards the end, some started coming in from the South, saying cause we worked so hard we were going to end up owning everything. But we never got a chance to demonstrate that because the water gave out. There were so many artesian wells dug that the water stopped flowing. And then, on top of that, they passed a law saying you couldn't drill new wells. That crippled us. The young people began leaving out, because there wasn't any future left.

"And then, worms got in that country, around 1916. They used to say worms couldn't live in the hot sun. There was a $50 prize if you could find a worm in a New Mexico apple. But one wet year, they took over. Apple prices went from $4 a box to 50 cents." Alkali buildup also began to become a major problem, poisoning the once fertile soil. "The yield went way down. The whole valley went down." Ditches were eventually dug to help the alkali problem, Hobart says, and adds, "It's come back pretty good now." But, Blackdom was too far west and elevated from the waters of the Pecos River to ever tap into either the water for irrigating or the ditches for drainage. The curtain was falling on Blackdom.

Curiously, though, this was the very time when the actual townsite of Blackdom was dedicated. In 1920, Francis and Ella Boyer filed a plat for the townsite, consisting of 40 acres divided into 166 lots. Many of the original homesteaders purchased lots, and to this day still own them. But others were already moving on. The Boyer family left in 1921, and the Collins family had moved into Roswell in 1916. Stragglers continued to arrive, but the exodus was over. The schoolhouse and a second church continued to be used for several years, but by the end of the 1920s, Blackdom was virtually abandoned. The Baptist church was moved south to Cottonwood, near Artesia, and Methodist services continued in it through the 1960s. State Senator Budd Hebert partially restored it for storage space, probably saving it from destruction. It was recently bought by a young white couple who plan to further renovate it and convert it to their home.

It alone seems to have survived. Several fires consumed most of the personal furniture, mementos, and photographs of Blackdom. Only a handful of original inhabitants remain, they in their seventies and eighties. As Mosly says, "The older ones are gone, and the younger ones don't recall what they left behind." Warns Hobart, "I'm told we don't have any role in the past here. If we're not careful, we won't have a history." But, Blackdom does live on — in the minds of those few survivors and the sketchy written accounts. Concludes Lillian, "The whole country was new and fresh then. It was so green, and some days the sky would be so blue! That was pioneering — really and truly! It was a beautiful thing."

An advertisement for the Montezuma Hotel and Las Vegas Hot Springs, New Mexico, in the June 28, 1890, issue of Harper's Weekly.

30

Alluring New Mexico:
Engineered Enchantment, 1880–1941

Marta Weigle

New Mexico! The first white men to set eyes upon its magnificent distances were valiant Spanish adventurers plodding weary leagues up from Mexico in search of the fabled Seven Cities of Cibola and the Gran Quivira, seeking the new, the strange and the different. Since Coronado and De Vargas wrote so largely upon the first pages of American history, New Mexico has been the Land of Enchantment for the traveler. From the sixteenth century to modern today, New Mexico has lured men from afar off. The fascination is undimmed by time. You, too, will find it, share it, never forget it. Whether you must hurry through a week or two, or whether you can linger for a year or more, New Mexico will have something new for you each day.

> — New Mexico State
> Highway Department,
> *2 weeks in New Mexico*
> *"Land of Enchantment,"* 1934

On May 20, 1934, the New Mexico State Highway Commission and the Albuquerque advertising agency Ward Hicks, Inc., launched a ten-week campaign in fourteen Oklahoma and Texas newspapers urging 810,000 readers to "take a real Vacation this summer in cool New Mexico 'Land of Enchantment.'" These ads and a thirty-two-page booklet published later that year, *2 weeks in New Mexico "Land of Enchantment,"* mark the state's first use of a new designation for what since 1912 had been called the Sunshine State. From its inception in May 1935, the New Mexico State Tourist Bureau used only "Land of Enchantment" as the state's nickname, which first appeared on license plates in 1941. Yet despite efforts in 1947 and 1999, "Land of Enchantment" was not made official until Governor Bill Richardson signed enabling legislation on April 6, 2003, some 120 years after an 1882 Bureau of Immigration publication proclaimed the territory "The Tourists' Shrine."

The Santa Fe Railroad and the Bureau of Immigration

Health for the afflicted everywhere, in the pure air and water, in the
    equitable temperature and altitude and in the medicinal hot
    springs.
Comfort and pleasure at the many new and well appointed hotels.
Scenery on natures [*sic*] grandest scale in all parts of the Territory.
Fishing, hunting and camp-life, to satisfy the most ambitious, in the
    mountains and mountain parks.
Antiquarians and archaeologists can satisfy their most fastidious
    tastes over pre-historic ruins and the remains of the hundreds
    of thousands of industrial and village population of the 16th
    centuary [*sic*].

    — "Opportunities in Brief," *New Mexico The Tourists' Shrine: Health,
        Wealth, Home,* 1882

The Atchison, Topeka and Santa Fe (AT&SF) Railroad broke ground in downtown Topeka on October 30, 1868. Founder Cyrus K. Holliday promised that "those present would live...to see the line head far down into Mexico, and meet the broad Pacific on the Gulf of California...and into the Rocky Mountains, with their hidden wealth" (Marshall 1945, 21).

The first AT&SF train entered New Mexico over Raton Pass in December 1878. The rails reached Galisteo Junction (later Lamy), with a spur line opened to Santa Fe in February 1880. According to the "Chronological Annals" appended to *The Legislative Blue-Book of the Territory of New Mexico* for the 1882 session, February 15, 1880 saw the "completion of the first railroad to Santa Fe, the oldest town on the continent, celebrated by an excursion to the Missouri river in Pullman coaches; given by the railroad company...to the Territorial Officers, Members of the Legislative Assembly and business men. The excursionists visited Lawrence, Kansas City, Leavenworth, Atchison and Topeka...: going and returning in five days; where, in 1863, the trip occupied in time one way, by U.S. mail coaches, thirty days. Thus the newest and oldest civilization upon the American Continent were brought together, and the old

Santa Fe trail of a verity became the T-rail." Track was laid to Albuquerque by April 1880 and to the Arizona border by July 1881.

The railroad's progress galvanized Albuquerque businessmen to organize a Territorial Fair for October 3–8, 1881. Their "official announcement" promised exhibition "of the products of every County in the Territory." "While the premium lists embrace all the articles usually exhibited in older countries, yet special premiums are offered to cover the natural products of New Mexico, and by that means bring samples of them together, and show, not only to our own people, but also to the many visitors that will be present, what our almost unknown land is capable of producing." Also promised were "relics of antiquity exhibited by the Historical Society, and by individuals, [that] will instruct and interest visitors and arouse visions of a pre-historic race, who have left only the ruins of their cities as mementoes of their lives and works."

Fair organizers turned to the year-old Bureau of Immigration for most of the text in their sixty-eight-page program book, *Resources of New Mexico*. Authorized by the territorial legislature on February 15, 1880, the bureau was organized on April 15 of that year with officers, commissioners, and an "Office in Adobe Palace [of the Governors], Santa Fe." *Resources of New Mexico* described "the object of the Bureau" as being "to prepare and disseminate accurate information as to the soil, climate, minerals, resources, productions and business of New Mexico, with special reference to its opportunities for development; and the inducements and advantages which it presents to desirable immigration and for the investment of capital; to have prompt replies sent to all inquiries relative to the above subjects that may be addressed to it, and to publish and distribute such pamphlets and documents as in its judgment shall tend to promote the objects of the organization."

From 1880 until statehood in 1912 the Bureau of Immigration produced more than 126 county and state publications. Between 1880 and 1885, for example, it "issued six editions (27,000 copies) of [Secretary of the Territory William G. Ritch's] *Illustrated New Mexico*, a book that grew with each edition until it reached a length of nearly 250 pages." Between April 1909 and April 1910 it distributed "142,000 pieces of printed matter; during the next twelve months, 183,000." Bureau materials were also carried by railroads such as the Chicago, Rock Island and Pacific, the Denver and Rio Grande, and the Santa Fe. The last sometimes used excerpts from bureau publications in its own extensive promotional literature (Dye 2005; Lang 1976, 207).

In 1889, Colonel Max Frost became publisher and editor of the *Santa Fe New Mexican* and secretary of the Bureau of Immigration, holding the latter post until 1907. The New Mexican Printing Company printed many bureau publications, including Frost's edited *New Mexico: Its Resources, Climate, Geography and Geological Condition* in 1890 and 1894 and his and banker-historian Paul A. F. Walter's edited *The Land of Sunshine: A Handbook of the Resources, Products, Industries and Climate of New Mexico* in 1904 and 1906. Fifty thousand copies of the latter were published by the New Mexico Board of Managers of the Louisiana Purchase Exposition with an added introduction about the territory's exhibit at that St. Louis fair in 1904.

The AT&SF and the Fred Harvey Company

The section of New Mexico included in the [Fred Harvey "Indian-detour," which became Indian Detours] plan and Albuquerque as its most important city, will get the same advertising as has been given to Southern California as a section by the Santa Fe railroad, and as is given to the Grand Canyon as a special trip. When it is realized that the busses at Grand Canyon handled 50,000 passengers last year, an idea of the magnitude of the present undertaking can be had. It will not only bring tourists directly to New Mexico and Albuquerque — something which has never been done before on a grand scale, but it will have the far more important effect of introducing easterners to the resources and beauties of New Mexico which can be seen in only few instances from the railroad car windows. It will, in a sense, be an announcement of the "open door" to New Mexico. It will result in thousands of monied people seeing the possibilities of the state where only a very few see them now.

— *Albuquerque Morning Journal*, August 21, 1925

Atchison, Topeka and Santa Fe Railroad fortunes suffered during the financial panic and depression of 1893–94, and the company was placed in receivership on December 23, 1893. Two years later, on December 10, it was sold to the Atchison, Topeka and Santa Fe Railway, with only that slight change of name, which made Edward Payson Ripley president and established executive offices in Chicago. Ripley, who served until January 1, 1920, was "a man with lifelong railroad management experience and one of the leading figures in developing the Chicago World's Columbian Exposition of 1893, [and he] turned the Santa Fe around within six months." By 1900 he "was recognized as a consummate genius in his profession." He immediately identified Fred Harvey meals "as one of the very finest advertisements that his railroad possibly could have…[and] their service quickly became the road's greatest advertisement" (Weigle and Babcock 1996, 1, 2).

The AT&SF had opened a second-floor lunchroom in Topeka in 1874. In 1876, English immigrant Frederick Henry Harvey entered into a "gentleman's agreement" with the railroad to lease the lunchroom and provide all future dining and lodging needs. Harvey's first formal contract with the railroad was signed on January 1, 1878, when he opened the Clifton Hotel in Florence, Kansas. In 1883 Harvey, later known as the "Civilizer of the West," fired unruly male waiters at the Raton, New Mexico, restaurant and hired waitresses instead. Soon he replaced all his restaurant servers with reliable young women, who became famous as Harvey Girls (Poling-Kempes 1989). A second formal contract, signed on May 1, 1889, gave Harvey "the exclusive right… to manage and operate the eating houses, lunch stands, and hotel facilities" on all company lines west of the Missouri River. Consolidated after 1895, the Fred Harvey Company continued as a family-operated, closed corporation following its founder's death in 1901, at which time it had interests in twelve states that included "15 hotels, 47 restaurants, 30 dining cars, and food service on the ferries across San Francisco Bay" (Bryant 1974, 121; Henderson 1969, 16, 44, 45).

The first major AT&SF–Harvey venture in New Mexico capitalized on the burgeoning health industry of the 1880s and 1890s, particularly climatological cures for tuberculosis. Hot springs at Gallinas Canyon near Las Vegas, where the Santa Fe completed track in 1879, had long been used by Native Americans and Hispanos for ritual and curative purposes. In 1846 the invading United States Army established a hospital there. It was sold in 1862 and converted into the Adobe Hotel, where Billy the Kid and Jesse James dined together on July 27, 1879. A Boston syndicate bought the property and in December 1879 opened a new Hot Springs Hotel, later known as the Old Stone Hotel.

In 1880 the AT&SF created the Las Vegas Hot Springs Company to purchase the hotel and surrounding property. A spur line was laid from the town, and a 270-room luxury resort hotel was constructed. Operated by Fred Harvey and named the Montezuma because the Aztec ruler was supposed to have bathed there, it opened to great fanfare on April 17, 1882. An 1883 railroad brochure called the complex "Nature's Sanitarium." The first Montezuma burned in January 1884; the second, built up on the hill rather than by the hot springs, opened in 1885 and burned down four months later. The third and present Montezuma, now part of United World College, opened as the Phoenix Hotel on August 16, 1886. It closed on September 1, 1893, while the railroad company was in bankruptcy, and reopened only during the summer seasons of the next decade until closing permanently on October 31, 1903 (Bowman 2002, 12, 15–16, 19).

The first of the AT&SF–Harvey New Mexico station hotels opened at Las Vegas in January 1899. Named for Pedro de Castañeda, chronicler of Coronado's 1540 expedition, Hotel Castañeda was designed by California architect Frederick L. Roehrig. Albuquerque's grand Alvarado Hotel, named for Coronado's lieutenant Hernando de Alvarado and designed by Chicago architect Charles F. Whittlesey, opened on May 11, 1902. It was followed in 1910 by Lamy's much smaller El Ortiz Hotel, named for an old New Mexico family and designed by Kansas City architect Louis Curtiss. Harvey Company architect and interior decorator Mary Colter, who decorated the Ortiz, both designed and decorated El Navajo Hotel, opened at Gallup in May 1923. Of these, only the Castañeda still stands, El Ortiz having been torn down in 1943, El Navajo in 1957, and the Alvarado in 1970.

Albuquerque served as prototype for the AT&SF–Harvey Indian Southwest. After her father's death in 1901, Minnie Harvey Huckel proposed that a museum to display the company's ethnographic collections be set up at the Alvarado Hotel. So began the Fred Harvey Indian Department, overseen by her husband, John Frederick Huckel, until his death in 1936. The department's main buyer, German immigrant Herman Schweizer, was "the central force" in its development, and "his influence as master collector, buyer and seller of Indian art objects was well recognized in his day" (Howard and Pardue 1996, 9, 10, 12).

Mary Colter designed the interior of the Indian Building, which opened in 1902 between the depot and the Alvarado. Travelers alighted from the trains, passed between rows of Indians displaying their work, toured the museum display rooms and demonstration areas with Indians at work on their art, and then, armed with new appreciation, entered the salesrooms. Schweizer died in 1943, marking the end of four decades of AT&SF–Harvey display and marketing that "helped create a regional identity based on an aesthetic appreciation of Indian cultures…[and] not only encouraged tourists to visit the region but also provided a corporate image for the Harvey Company and the ATSF…[with] symbols of 'Indianness' spread all along the railway line" (Dilworth 1996, 82).

There is no record explaining why the last significant AT&SF–Harvey venture was called "Indian-detour" (Weigle 1996). With railway authorization, the Harvey Company's Major R. Hunter Clarkson, who had supervised motor bus transportation at the Grand Canyon, announced in Albuquerque on August 20, 1925, the launch of "an Indian detour rail and motor way which will enable rail tourists from Chicago and California to see points of historic and scenic interest in this state and at the same time to travel on a fixed schedule…[during] three days of unusual motoring through oldest America, in the New Mexico Rockies between Las Vegas and Albuquerque… [providing] a pleasant break in the cross continent rail trip the year 'round" (*Albuquerque Morning Journal*, August 21, 1925). The first Indian Detour booklet of April 1926 called it "three days and three hundred miles of sunshine and relaxation and mountain air, in a land of unique human contrasts and natural grandeur."

Like the Harvey Girls before them, young women trained as Indian Detour Courier guides were considered crucial to the service. Albuquerque writer Erna Fergusson, who from 1921 until 1926 had operated Koshare Tours, which offered guided automobile trips to see Indians and their ceremonials in New Mexico and Arizona, was the Indian Detour Couriers' first director. Archaeologists Edgar Lee Hewett, Alfred V. Kidder, and Sylvanus G. Morley, ethnologist Frederick W. Hodge, journalist Charles F. Lummis, and Paul A. F. Walter were members of the first advisory board. Lummis wrote the lead essay for *They Know New Mexico: Intimate Sketches by Western Writers*, a fifty-six-page booklet of essays and poems produced in 1928 by the Detour's publicist, freelance travel writer Roger Williams Birdseye. In "The Golden Key to Wonderland" Lummis enthused that with "Harvey efficiency," travelers could now see "many of the wildest and noblest sceneries on this continent, and the most picturesque and fascinating types of humanity…*comprehendingly*, with guides so charming and so authentic as were never available before."

The first Indian Detour — two "Harveycars," each with uniformed chauffeur and Courier guide and carrying four tourists, called dudes — left the Hotel Castañeda in Las Vegas at nine o'clock on the morning of Saturday, May 15, 1926, and stopped at the Pecos Pueblo ruins on the way to tours of Santa Fe and nearby pueblos, with two nights at La Fonda, the Harvey hotel in Santa Fe. The third day included Santo Domingo Pueblo, lunch at the Alvarado, afternoon trips to Isleta Pueblo and Albuquerque's Old Town, and the finale — an after-dinner guided tour of the Indian Building. (Eastbound travelers reversed the order.) A November 1930 booklet listed a variety of customized tours as well as eight fixed ones: Frijoles–Puyé, Taos, Raton–Taos–Santa Fe, Carlsbad Caverns, Sierra Verde, Santa Fe–Grand Canyon, Hopi, and Navajo. In March 1931 the Harvey Company sold its interest to Major R. Hunter Clarkson, who continued the AT&SF and La Fonda association but operated limousine Couriercars and Couriercoaches instead of Harveycars.

In 1926 the AT&SF had purchased and leased to the Harvey Company a failed hotel on the southeastern corner of its namesake city's plaza. Built in 1920 on the site of hostelries dating back to the Mexican period, La Fonda Hotel had been the last major commission in Santa Fe for then resident Isaac Hamilton Rapp, who incorporated elements of his design for the State Art Museum (now the New Mexico Museum of Art, part of the Museum of New Mexico), diagonally across the plaza. For the Harvey Company, Santa Fe architect John Gaw Meem designed an addition to the Rapp structure, and Mary Colter did the interior decoration. La Fonda served as headquarters for Indian Detours, and the remodel accommodated new guest rooms, a Courier Lounge with maps, photographs, books, films, and lantern slides, and an Indian Lecture Lounge where nightly illustrated talks were given on the Southwest. The inaugural July 1929 booklet, *La Fonda in Old Santa Fé: The Inn at The End of the Trail*, proclaimed: "La Fonda of today — the present hotel was completed only in the late spring of 1929 — is another Santa Fe–Fred Harvey dream come true; a dream for the fine development of that Southwestern empire carved out in the Trail days that have passed."

World's Fair Expositions

New Mexico is both a winter and summer resort. It is in addition a land of a thousand wonders, — scenic, historical, archaeological. No other state has such tourist attractions. Its mission churches are 150 years older than those of California, and many of them are shrines for worship to the present day. Cave and cliff dwellings number tens of thousands and are vestiges of a culture thousands of years old.

Indian pueblos and hogans are as quaint and mysterious as any of the
ancient habitations of the Orient. Indian dances, such as may be witnessed in New Mexico, and church ceremonials, are more interesting
and as full of poetic and symbolic meaning as any of the Greek mysteries. New Mexico has been the meeting place of successive cultures,
of many races and tribes and each has left its imprint, each has its
survivors, making the land a treasure trove for archaeologist and
ethnologist. Nowhere else in the United States can be found so great
a variety of unique sights, glimpses of Old Spain and of scenes that
hark back to prehistoric times. It is Egypt and Babylonia, Spain and
Mexico, Colorado and California, Switzerland and the Orient, combined. Stupendous mountain masses, the loftiest peaks more than
13,000 feet high, are accessible by easy trails to their very pinnacles;
shadowy canyons, flower spangled mountain meadows, picturesque
waterfalls, whispering pine forests, babbling trout streams, vast game
preserves, the all-pervading sunshine, the mystery of the desert, the
invigorating atmosphere of the higher altitudes, the unique aspects of
irrigation, the smile of orchards and alfalfa fields, the unspoiled hospitality of flat-roofed adobe homes in which the mellifluous Spanish
is spoken, are all spanned by perfect turquoise skies that rival those
of Naples and of Andalusia. Yea, verily, here is a land of delight, of
myriad charms, of the heart's desire, well worth a visit and a stay.

> — Paul A. F. Walter, "'The Land of Heart's Desire':
> For the Tourist," 1915

In the late nineteenth and early twentieth centuries, American international expositions at Philadelphia (1876), New Orleans (1885), Chicago (1893), Atlanta (1895), Nashville (1897), Omaha (1898), Buffalo (1901), St. Louis (1904), Portland (1905), Seattle
(1909), San Francisco (1915), and San Diego (1915–16) attracted almost 100 million
people. Besides fostering economic development in the host city, these world's fairs
"provided manufacturing and commercial interests with opportunities to promote the
mass consumption of their products…[and] presented new mediums of entertainment
and opportunities for vicarious travel in other lands" (Rydell 1984, 2). The Atchison,
Topeka and Santa Fe Railroad participated in the Chicago World's Columbian Exposition, where extensive Indian archaeological and ethnological exhibits included much
southwestern material and Navajo, Apache, Papago, and Pueblo participants. Nearly
every southwestern tribe was represented at the St. Louis Louisiana Purchase Exposition, "the largest and most extensive look to date at contemporary southwestern native
life." By the time it closed, "the southwestern tribes had become the darlings of the
American public," helping "spur the developing tourist industry as well as the study of
anthropology and archaeology in the Four Corners area" (Trennert 1987, 150).

At the request of Arthur Seligman, treasurer of the New Mexico Board of Managers of the Louisiana Purchase Exposition and later governor of New Mexico, the AT&SF and the Fred Harvey Company sponsored an exhibit produced by John F. Huckel and anthropologist George A. Dorsey, who was on leave from Chicago's Field Columbian Museum and resident at the Alvarado Hotel in Harvey employ in 1903–4. *Albuquerque Morning Journal* articles on May 19 and May 20, 1904, called the ethnological exhibit "the most extensive ever made at this or any other fair" and "an entirely scientific display." The *Journal* of November 5, 1904, announced that "the Fred Harvey Indian exhibits in the division of anthropology have been awarded four prizes": two gold medals and two grand prizes, one for the best ethnological exhibit and one for the Navajo blanket exhibit. The last two were "worthy of note, for in both the ethnological and blanket exhibits the Harvey collections were pitted against those of the Smithsonian Institute, heretofore believed to be the finest in existence" (Howard and Pardue 1996, 62–63). The AT&SF–Harvey exhibit was in the fair's Anthropology Building; other state exhibits were housed in the New Mexico temporary pavilion, designed in mission revival style by Isaac Hamilton Rapp (Sheppard 1988, 46, 47).

When the new state was invited in 1913 to participate in the San Diego Panama-California Exposition, scheduled for 1915, William C. McDonald, the first statehood governor, and others saw "an excellent opportunity to promote the state's resources, enhance the economic development of its citizens, and take advantage of the millions of dollars expected to be spent… — in return for a comparatively small investment by the tax paying citizens" (Miller 1985, 13). The legislature set up a Board of Exposition Managers headed by attorney-historian Ralph Emerson Twitchell.

Albuquerque's A. E. Koehler Jr., commissioner of publicity on the board's executive staff, modeled the 254-page *New Mexico: The Land of Opportunity*, "Official Souvenir of the State of New Mexico at Panama-California Exposition San Diego 1915," on "the Exposition Book of New Mexico, issued ten years ago for the St. Louis Exposition, [which] resulted directly and indirectly, in bringing 100,000 new settlers to the State [territory], who tripled the number of farms in the State, turned the eastern livestock ranges into agricultural country, founded villages and towns, created new counties, and inaugurated a new era of growth and prosperity." The 1915 book was again "to acquaint the world with the advantages, resources and progress of the great Sunshine State [for] knowledge of the New Mexico of today is certain to result in the influx of tourists, settlers, capital, for no other state in the Union presents so great a variety of attractions for these as does New Mexico."

Isaac Hamilton Rapp designed the New Mexico Building for the San Diego exposition. It later served as the model for his design of the state's Museum of Fine Arts, which opened on the Santa Fe plaza in November 1917. Koehler called the New Mexico Building "an inspiration" whose exterior was "in greater part a replica of the Franciscan mission church on the Rock of Acoma." The main auditorium housed "the most unique moving picture theater in the world…furnished in mission style and seat[ing] six hundred people.... [It showed] 30,000 feet of motion picture films and 3,000 stereopticon views, all being explained by expert lecturers." There was a publicity room, and "in the convent are the exhibit halls, with the minerals and other exhibits, the wonderful models of historic landmarks, Indian pueblos and mission churches and various displays, maps, charts, all complying with a standard of beauty and art, set from the very start for all exhibits." The building still stands in San Diego as the Balboa Park Club (Sheppard 1988, 79–88).

Eighteen years after the San Diego exposition opened, Chicago launched its Century of Progress Exposition, the first of six enormously popular, depression-era American world's fairs that became "cultural icons for the nation's hopes and future" (Rydell 1993, 1). Originally scheduled for May–November 1933, at the urging of President Franklin D. Roosevelt it opened for a second season in 1934, when New Mexico was able to secure exhibition space in the Court of States. Governor Andrew W. Hockenhull personally raised the requisite financing.

The New Mexico State Highway Department dispatched staff engineer O. T. Jorgensen to supervise construction of the state's exhibit from Santa Fe architect Gordon Street's plans. The Pueblo-style structure boasted "a carpet of the white sands from the famous national monument near Alamogordo..., which presents a striking contrast to the rich brown hue of the *adobe* buildings, [and] is an unending wonder for the thousands who visit the exhibit every day." A corral fence, a shed, carved beams, vigas, furniture, and tin light fixtures were Spanish. Both Navajo and Chimayó blankets hung from the walls, which also "displayed paintings by eighteen New Mexico artists, some from Taos and others from Santa Fe, ...valued at $80,000, [that] were hung by [artist] Will Shuster of Santa Fe, and a requirement was made by the artists' committee which selected the paintings that none should be hung for any artist who had been in New Mexico less than fifteen years" (Shuart 1934, 11, 12).

The exhibit featured daily demonstrations by two unidentified Hispanic weavers from Chimayó under one *portal* and by Navajo weaver Ah-Kena-Bah and Navajo silversmith Fred Peshlaikai under the other. Navajo medicine man Hosteen Klah made daily sandpaintings on a stand in the center space, behind which were cases of Indian and Spanish jewelry and other handicrafts. Assisted by Peshlaikai, Klah performed a house blessingway ceremony for the exhibit's opening on July 9, 1934.

Special AT&SF trains carried New Mexicans to Chicago for New Mexico Day on August 14. An Associated Press release in the *Albuquerque Journal* that day reported that Governor Hockenhull addressed the crowds in the Court of States stadium, calling his "the most colorful of the 48 states," foremost among them "in the intangible values of culture." He said: "Oldest in point of settlement and yet the newest in the sisterhood of states, New Mexico has been the land of heart's desire for many peoples for well nigh 2,000 years.... In every sense of the word it is a modern state which at the same time has preserved for future generations antiquities, ancient ways, colorful ceremonies and quaint places which have drawn to it groups of artists and writers of wide renown."

The State Highway Department and the State Tourist Bureau

It is needless for me to tell you that you are welcome on New Mexico's soil. We are making every effort humanly possible to provide highways over which you may travel in safety and comfort. If you are on a vacation trying to get away from a noisy world, you can find seclusion in New Mexico's vast mountain domain, in beautiful haunts where human foot has never trod, where clear streams flash with trout, where a variety of game is plentiful. You will be exhilarated by a pure, cool and invigorating climate. If you are on a business trip you will find New Mexico a land of opportunities, where resources in agriculture, fruit growing, cotton, timber, livestock and minerals are practically untouched and awaiting development; also, a fascinating field for artists and writers. May you have a pleasant journey through New Mexico.

> — Richard C. Dillon, "Governor's Message:
> A Word to Tourists," 1929

On the editorial page of the July 1923 inaugural issue of the State Highway Department's official publication, *New Mexico Highway Journal*, was a notice about "Tourists and Roads": "A state that keeps its roads in good order is going to get a great deal more vacation travel from now on than it ever had before. This will go far toward paying for keeping the highway in good condition."

The department launched an official map program in 1925, but the first one directed at tourists was the *1930 Road Map of New Mexico The Sunshine State*, drafted and illustrated by the department's chief draftsman, Bertram C. Broome (Carroll 2001, 25). That year it also set up a service bureau to answer routine tourist requests for information. These efforts were complemented by the June 1933 inauguration "of a full-fledged highway patrol, carefully selected and trained, [whereby] New Mexico promises motor tourists and travelers within her borders not only scenery unsurpassed, historical settings and archaeological ruins of unique interest, fishing, hunting and recreation areas second to none, but excellent highways leading to all these regions, patrolled by a fine group of courteous, uniformed young men, alert to assist the stranded in emergency, to direct strangers, and to corral law breakers of every description" (Bennett 1933, 7).

Originally an in-house organ, the *Highway Journal* published its first tourism article, Erna Fergusson's "Acoma, the City of the Sky," in its second issue, dated October 1923. In July 1931 it merged with the State Game and Fish Department's in-house organ, *New Mexico Conservationist* (1927–31), to become *New Mexico: The Sunshine State's Recreational and Highway Magazine.* The title was changed to *New Mexico: The State Magazine of National Interest* in November 1934, and in February 1938 it became simply *New Mexico Magazine.* Initially a free publication supported by advertising, it went on sale for fifteen cents a month or one dollar a year in 1933.

Neither the Highway Department's magazine nor its other publications, such as the 32-page 1929 and 68-page 1934 *Roads to Cibola: what to see in New Mexico and how to get there* and the 32-page 1934 *2 weeks in New Mexico "Land of Enchantment,"* could match the AT&SF–Harvey success. Indian Detour publicist Roger Williams Birdseye's 1926 assessment continued to hold: "Neither the State government nor any community or group of communities within the state, is today in a position to undertake a campaign of similar magnitude and diversity" (Birdseye 1926, 9). In an effort to remedy this and capitalize on tourism in his "Greater New Mexico," Governor Clyde Tingley, soon after taking office on January 1, 1935, reorganized the Highway Department and set up the New Mexico State Tourist Bureau to initiate and coordinate national advertising campaigns.

During its first years of operation the bureau had the same three-person staff: director Joseph A. Bursey, appointed by Tingley in May (serving until 1950 and again in 1955–56), and Bursey's hires, secretary Bernice Duke and photographer Wyatt Davis. Initially, promotions were contracted to Ward Hicks's Albuquerque advertising agency, where commercial artist Willard Harold Andrews, who had moved to Albuquerque from California in 1933, did most of the design work. Andrews was responsible for the first three Tourist Bureau booklets in 1935: a new edition of the Highway Department's *2 weeks in New Mexico* (32 pages, 50,000 copies), *"The first Americans": Indians of New Mexico* (36 pages, 50,000 copies), and *Mission Churches of New Mexico* (40 pages, 25,000 copies).

Ward Hicks, who opened his agency in 1927, had laid the groundwork for the Tourist Bureau by catalyzing an informal, statewide network of businesspeople, newspaper editors, and chamber of commerce managers. He and Bursey met while the latter still worked at the capitol bureau of the *Albuquerque Tribune;* both agreed that the state needed a new nickname. Tourist Bureau secretary Bernice Duke recalled that "after Joe Bursey and Ward Hicks learned that Florida was using the slogan of 'Sunshine State,' they luckily stumbled across a book written in 1906 by Lilian Whiting [*The Land of Enchantment: From Pike's Peak to the Pacific* (Boston: Little, Brown)]...[and] the first part of the title struck the men as being tailor made for New Mexico" (Dunleavy 1984, 64). Bursey lobbied hard throughout the state to get "Land of Enchantment" accepted. It first appeared on official road maps in 1937. In 1940 Bursey persuaded Governor John E. Miles to authorize its use on license plates, which state penitentiary warden John McManus Sr. approved for the 1941 prisoner-manufactured plates.

In the early days of the Tourist Bureau, Bursey and Hicks traveled the state and determined to devise a way to mark its scenic and historic attractions. The State Highway Commission approved a design for roadside markers in 1936 and made plans for their installation and maintenance. The first signs were built by Civilian Conservation Corps workers, and later ones by Sostenes Delgado of Santa Fe (Delgado 1990). Bursey's annual report for 1938 listed fifty-one markers up by year's end, with twenty more planned for 1939. By 2002 there were more than 350, overseen by the State Highway Department and the Cultural Properties Review Committee (Pike 2004).

The summer of 1940 marked the culmination of statewide planning for the Coronado Cuarto Centennial, originally the 1930 inspiration of Roswell schoolteacher Charles M. Martin, who addressed the Roswell chapter of the New Mexico Archaeological and Historical Society on February 19, 1931: "Other states have held elaborate ceremonies at their Hundredth anniversaries. We are entitled to hold an even greater celebration at our Four Hundredth Anniversary" (*Albuquerque Journal*, April 30, 1940). In 1935 Governor Tingley signed a legislative act creating the Coronado Cuarto Centennial Commission, with University of New Mexico president James F. Zimmerman as president, Erna Fergusson as vice president, Albuquerque lawyer Gilberto Espinosa as secretary, and Santa Fe businessman Henry Dendahl as treasurer.

Zimmerman issued a declaration in 1938: "New Mexico will have an unprecedented opportunity to further the cultural relations between the United States of America and those countries lying to the South, whose historic background is so linked with ours....Through the Coronado celebration, we shall unite our colorful past with the realities of the present, and in so doing lay new foundations of spiritual relationship with our sister nations in this hemisphere." By adding Arizona, Texas, Colorado, Kansas, and Oklahoma to the plans, the commissioners were able to obtain $200,000 in federal funds in 1939, when a United States Coronado Exposition Committee was established. The Coronado State Monument at Bernalillo was dedicated on May 29, 1940.

By World War II the state had secured means for enchantment. Governor Miles began his second term of office in January 1941 by cordially inviting "new readers of *New Mexico Magazine* who live outside the State...to visit New Mexico" and extending "to those who have vacationed here before...the hospitality for a return visit in 1941." His New Year "Greetings" in the magazine echoed the objectives of the Territorial Bureau of Immigration:

New Mexico has much that it can share with the rest of the world, and each year has seen a greater number of persons come to New Mexico to share these benefits — both as vacationists and as permanent residents.

The census in 1940 showed New Mexico with the second highest percentage population gain in the Nation. We believe that strong, steady growth will continue. Our climate will continue to attract those who seek the sun and the health-giving air of the highest altitudes. Our magnificent scenic areas will continue to attract the vacationist, the hunter and fisherman, and the casual tourist. Our vast resources will continue to attract the pioneers — the rugged prospector and the wealthy investor seeking new fields of endeavor. Our towns and our rural areas will continue to attract those who seek a new start in a new land.

31

The Museum and Collections of the Historical Society of New Mexico, 1859–1977

Michael Stevenson (2006)

On December 15, 1859, a group of distinguished New Mexico citizens, all men, met in Santa Fe and founded the Historical Society of New Mexico. Its first president was Colonel John B. Grayson, a U.S. Army officer, West Point graduate and Mexican War veteran stationed at Fort Marcy. Others in that first gathering included Charles P. Clever, the U.S. Marshal in Santa Fe, *ricos* Facundo Pino and Jose Guadalupe Gallegos, and Judge Kirby Benedict, Chief Justice of the New Mexico Territorial Court. The group adopted a constitution two weeks later, setting forth a rigorous process for gaining membership and establishing a five-dollar initiation fee, a good amount of money at the time.

The scope of the Society was broad, including "History, Geography, Indian Races, Geology and Mineralogy, Antiquities and Collections, and Natural History." Shortly after the first constitution was approved, they added "Agriculture, Statistics, Botany, Biography, and Meteorology and Climatology." In this inclusive view of "history" they seem to have had in mind a New Mexican version of the Smithsonian Institution, which had opened in 1846 and its museum in 1855.

Through donations the Historical Society quickly accumulated a substantial collection encompassing documents, photographs and "objects of curiosity." Their meeting place, located near what was then *La Parroquia*, the parish church, and is today the Cathedral Basilica of St. Francis, was a building rented from one of their members, Bishop Jean Baptiste Lamy.

Room 14, Palace of the Governors, about 1924.

In it they displayed their collections at what may have been the first history museum with curated exhibits west of the Mississippi.

After the Civil War

The Civil War disrupted the fledgling organization. In 1861 Colonel Grayson resigned his commission and joined the Confederate Army, as did several other members. Grayson was assigned to command the Florida Department of the Confederacy and died shortly thereafter of "a disease of the lungs." His successor as Society president was Major John Lowry Donaldson, also a West Pointer and Mexican War veteran stationed at Fort Marcy. Somehow Major Donaldson and his remaining compatriots, all presumably Union supporters, held the organization together through the trials of the Civil War in New Mexico, including the Confederate capture of Santa Fe in 1862.

More and more Society members resigned as time went on and fewer meetings were held. At its last meeting on September 28, 1863, the Society resolved that the "room of this Society be surrendered" and that on Saturday, October 3, Curator Augustine M. Hunt "make public sale of all…property and things." There being no further business, the meeting was adjourned *sine die*, that is, without setting a date for the next meeting.

On December 26, 1880, the twenty-first anniversary of the approval of the Society's constitution, a group reconvened the organization and adopted almost ver-batim the original document. Some of this group had been active members of the first society and brought with them its institutional memory. Secretary of the Territory William G. Ritch was elected president. L. Bradford Prince, Chief Justice of the Ter-ritorial Supreme Court at the time and later territorial governor from 1889 to 1893, was elected vice-president, becoming president in 1884. Prince had a broad and abiding interest in the history and culture of New Mexico and the Southwest.

The revived Society tried to recover the lost collections from the Civil War days with some success, although none of the objects are documented as being in their later collections. Acquisition began in earnest, including documents, photographs, minerals, and "ancient pottery." As part of efforts to re-establish their museum Prince in particular lobbied hard to obtain use of the Palace of the Governors with the addi-tional agenda of working to preserve the building, which "had fallen in disrepair." In 1882 the Society was given permission to begin meeting in the Palace. In 1884 Prince convinced the U.S. Secretary of the Interior to grant the Society use of its two east-ernmost rooms.

The Historical Society's Artifact Collections

Upon gaining foothold in the Palace, Prince and his Society accelerated acquisition of objects for their new museum. He likely donated or loaned many items from his personal collection, but the bulk of those on initial display were purchased. Society reports indicate that lack of space to exhibit collections was a continual complaint, probably coming directly from Prince himself.

The first major acquisition, which cost the Society "but $254.90," was a large mineral collection originally displayed as part of the Tertio-Millennial Exposition of 1883, a "forty-five-day fair…to commemorate the 333 rd (actually 343 rd) anniversary of the founding of Santa Fe (actually the exploration of New Mexico by Coronado, in 1540)…[and] designed to publicize the territory and thereby attract investors and tourists…[with] exhibitions of minerals and produce [that] were complemented by horse races and Indian dances" (Wilson 1997, 186). Other early purchases were "the pottery made at each Pueblo — the varieties being very distinct — including the more remote ones of Moqui, Zuni, Acomo [sic], etc. This collection attracts much attention, and its value arises from its absolute accuracy. We have also a considerable number of specimens of Ancient pottery, dug from the ruins of Pueblo villages long since abandoned. Large numbers of stone implements and other articles illustrating the aboriginal civilization have been secured; but many of these we are not now able to exhibit owing to lack of room and proper cases."

Purchases totaling $656.95 between May 1884 and January 1887 included "20 pieces of ancient pottery, excavated near Los Luceros $40.00/ File of *New Mexican*, 1864 to 1880, bound $30.00/ Desk and chair of Padre Vigil $8.00/ Two finely carved wooden stirrups $10.00/ Antique Mexican bellow $6.00/ Watch of [1866 Interim] Governor [W. F. M.] Arny $5.00." Some 444 "Mexican and Indian" items were purchased from Santa Fe "curio" merchant Jake Gold at a cost of $303.05. Among the latter were "stone vessels and implements, including mortars, axes, hammers, metates, polishes, discs arrow heads, etc., from thirteen Pueblos, collections of pottery from fourteen Pueblos, and from ruins in the Gallinas and Datils, from Tesuque, Gran Queivira [*sic*] and Pueblo Quemado. Dancing dresses and ornaments, shields, macanas, lances, quivers, arrows, horn cups, medicine cases, drills, scales, weights, drums, tallegas, baskets, awls, painted skins, water jugs, necklaces, etc." Many Spanish colonial objects were among the former, which included "guns, sabres, swords, pistoles and pikes; plow, yoke, shovel, spinning wheels, trunks, petaquita, trunkstand, copper kettles, cups and other utensils; wooden and metal stirrups, violin, guitar, drums; spurs, bits, anqueras, wheels and sickles; paintings on skin, canvas and wood; ornamental crosses, etc., etc." These formed the core of what later would become the "Industrial Collection," i.e., "Spanish and Mexican period items of everyday life" and still later the core of the History Collection of the Museum of New Mexico.

The Society actively continued its acquisitions for the next several decades. As determined from acquisition records, by 1912 its artifact collections consisted of at least 500 objects (including some 125 pottery pieces) in the "Prehistoric" collection, at least 600 (including some 130 pottery pieces) in the "Aboriginal" collection, and about 500 (including more than 100 Spanish colonial bultos, retablos and paintings) in the "Spanish and Mexican" collection. At the time the "American" collection was very small, with only a few items. The mineral collection still on display evidently remained little changed from the 1883 Tertio-Millennial Exposition time except for the 1904 "donation of very large and magnificent specimens of copper ore from the 'Big Copper Mine' near San Pedro." Other notable acquisitions during the late Territorial period included the 1904 donation of "a most valuable oil portrait of Gen. Stephen W. Kearny"; "a collection of silver articles manufactured by the Navajo Indians"; "a collection illustrating the basketry of the Territory"; more than fifty "large ollas of the old type of pottery" from the Pueblos; a "great iron door" from the old county jail; two iron cannon originally from Fort Marcy; and an 1866 Arthur Kellner watercolor showing a "birds-eye view of Santa Fe."

From the beginning in 1859 the Society had also been very active in acquiring an extensive collection of documents, including newspapers of the time and thousands of photographs. The 1909 report notes that "a very important collection, being the greater part of the documents officially filed in the Northern Jurisdiction (Santa Cruz) during the Mexican regime, is probably soon to become the property of the Society." Also noted in 1909 is that "the collection of photographs of officials of the Territory is receiving constant additions to keep it up with the times."

An important acquisition reported in 1912 was "the collection of historical articles connected with the adoption of the State Constitution, presented by Hon. Nathan

Jaffa. In order to have these very interesting historical objects properly displayed, the Society had a special case built in Denver for this exhibition at a cost of $77...." These items included the pens used by President William Howard Taft, the President of the Senate, and the Speaker of the House to sign the Statehood Enabling Act.

Only about a hundred objects, most of them "American," were added to the Society's collections between 1912 and 1930. With the Museum of New Mexico gradually taking over the curation of the Society's exhibits and the care of its collections in the 1930s, the Society stopped actively acquiring items by purchase. They did continue to receive donations, including some large collections, into the 1950s.

The Historical Society's Museum, 1885–1930

When it opened in 1885 the Society's museum exhibited the mineral collection in the northeast room and "articles of historic interest" in the southeast room of the Palace. The mineral collection at least stayed in the northeast room for a number of years; the 1909 report notes that some criticism of it had been received, quite possibly from those who did not think a mineral exhibit appropriate in a Historical Society museum. Shortly after 1885 the east hallway and the old Territorial Law Library were also given to the Society. It is likely that some of the Pueblo pottery and other "Aboriginal" objects were placed on exhibit in this room, as was later the case.

As the museum and collections grew and with Prince appointed Territorial governor in 1889, the need for some full-time help was apparent. Around this time the Society hired Henry Woodruff to look after its museum and collections. Initially paid the handsome sum of six dollars per week, Woodruff and his wife Sarah worked in that capacity until he died in 1930.

In 1907 there was another expansion when the "rooms just vacated by Judge Laughlin" were acquired and remodeled. The front-most was used to exhibit more of the Pueblo pottery collections, including excavated materials from western Socorro County acquired in 1896. According to the 1909 Historical Society report:

> The back room is now the library, and has been appropriately furnished with book cases and show cases, the latter for documents and maps. The small adjoining room has been fitted up for the use of students and writers who wish to consult the library. A suitable table, with all attendant conveniences, has been procured, and adds greatly to the comfort of those desiring to make notes and extracts. The walls of this room are covered with paintings, on skin and wood; and the splendid collection of photographs referred to in our last biennial report, finds its home here.

The Historical Society was by then in control of nearly all the east end of the Palace but soon afterward suffered a blow to its ambitions.

On February 19, 1909, acting governor Nathan Jaffa approved a request from Dr. Edgar Lee Hewett to locate his School of American Archaeology (later the School of American Research and now the School for Advanced Research) in the west end of the Palace of the Governors with the caveat that it "be renovated and alterations 'made so as to keep it in external appearance as nearly as possible in harmony with the Spanish architecture of the period of its construction, and preserve it as monument to the Spanish founders of the civilization of the Southwest'" (Lewis and Hagan 2007, 14). In 1909 Jaffa also signed legislation authorizing "a Museum for the Territory of New Mexico" to be operated by Hewett as a division of his School.

Hewett opening his own museum, largely consisting of displays of archaeological materials from several excavations by himself, Nusbaum and others, in the west end of the Palace sparked a rivalry between the two museums and their directors. Beatrice Chauvenet (1983, 79–80) reports an August 1954 interview with Ina Sizer Cassidy, wife of painter Gerald Cassidy, who

> told of being invited by the former Governor and Mrs. Prince to a tea given by the Historical Society in *their* part of the old Palace. The party was held on the same afternoon that Dr. Hewett was to lecture in *his* part of the Museum. When Mrs. Cassidy, on leaving the tea early, explained to her hostess that they wished to hear Dr. Hewett, Mrs. Prince attempted to dissuade them. "You are newcomers to Santa Fe and should not get mixed up in our local controversies," she told Ina earnestly. "There is no need for you to hear Dr. Hewett."

Between 1909 and 1913 Hewett and his key protégé Jesse L. Nusbaum undertook a complete renovation of the Palace, including the Historical Society rooms. This required all Society exhibits to be moved into temporary storage and completely disrupted their museum. Acquisitions stopped almost completely during this period, and they never again picked up the earlier pace, particularly for the Spanish and Indian items favored by former governor L. Bradford Prince.

Nusbaum's renovations of Prince's east end of the Palace aggravated tensions between the two museums. Ina Sizer Cassidy

> was much amused by the direct action taken by Hewett and Nusbaum to unify the building. For some years the portion occupied by the Historical Society had had no direct access to the rest of the old Palace, and the Princes steadily refused to allow doors to be cut between their bailiwick and the Museum proper. One weekend after the custodian had gone home, while former Governor and Mrs. Prince were occupied elsewhere, Nusbaum moved in a crew of workmen who chopped two doorways through the thick walls, installed

lintels, frames and wooden doors, and plastered the broken walls neatly so that one scarcely realized that the work had been done. When Monday morning came, there was nothing the indignant leaders of the Historical Society could do to seal themselves off once more. (Chauvenet 1983, 80)

In 1912 Hewett even convinced Governor William C. McDonald to recommend that the Society be moved out of the Palace entirely, but Prince in turn convinced the Legislature to allow both the Society and its museum to remain where it was.

January 4, 1913, minutes of the Historical Society record that "a valuable piece of pottery" in its museum was discovered missing one morning following a meeting in Hewett's end of the building the night before. Prince then ordered locks placed on the doors to his museum. This in turn infuriated Hewett, who insisted that as custodian of the entire building he must have access to the Society's end. Hewett then convinced the Museum of New Mexico Board of Regents to request that the keys be turned over to him. Still it took an order from the Legislature for this to happen. Prince complied reluctantly and eventually a compromise was reached.

Whether or not the tensions with Hewett affected Prince's health, he began to decline. In 1916 he and his wife moved back to the family home in New York, where Mrs. Prince had already been spending quite a bit of time and where the Governor maintained business and political connections. In 1918 the *New York Times* reported him as "critically ill at the old Prince homestead at Broadway and Lawrence Street, Flushing."

Despite his health problems Prince continued to visit Santa Fe frequently, presiding over most Society meetings and remaining as its president until his death in New York in December 1922. With Prince's death the Historical Society began taking a much more accommodating approach to working with Hewett, especially after Ralph Emerson Twitchell became president in 1924 and Paul A. F. Walter in 1925. Walter held that position for more than three decades.

Beyond Governor Prince

The decline in viability of the Historical Society's museum began in the 1920s, likely hastened by Governor Prince's return to New York and his death there. In 1922 the Society "deferred" to the Museum of New Mexico and Hewett in "Indian materials" collecting, as announced in the Biennial Report of 1923–24: "It was urged by President Ralph Twitchell that the society should not compete with the state museum in the acquisition of Indian materials, indicating a change in the collecting policy of the organization." In the 1925–26 report Twitchell is quoted: "It is not the business of a Historical Society to maintain a museum, but…fortunately we now have the wholehearted cooperation of the State Museum. The time to standardize has come; the day of the curio cabinet has gone."

That standardization had taken place by the 1932–33 Biennial Report: "Under the guidance of Dr. Edgar L. Hewett, director of the [State] Museum, his assistants, as well as the staff of the library and the Historical Society, all exhibits of the society have been rearranged and scientifically displayed in period rooms and chronological order." Despite its no longer being in control, in the report the Society was proud to take credit for and even boast of this more "scientific" exhibition put together by the Museum staff while acknowledging the Museum's help in providing space: "The exhibits are declared to be the most interesting and most attractively displayed of any American historical society. Through the generosity of the museum authorities additional space has been allotted the Society until its exhibits now occupy one-half of the palace."

The Society had by this time replaced Henry Woodruff with Hester Jones, both "a hostess to the thousands who pass through the Palace of the Governors" and "a scholarly and painstaking curator." In 1933 Jones became Recording Secretary of the Society and held the post for more than two decades.

From the 1920s on the Society acquired more than three hundred individual objects by either donation or purchase, including three Rio Grande weavings donated by Mrs. Henry Dendahl in 1954. Following World War II it received three very large collections. The Manderfield Collection donated in 1949 contained about 180 items, including 75 pieces of women's clothing. It was deemed of such importance that it was put on display in the "Manderfield Sala" in a "blockbuster" exhibit with a special opening hosted by young ladies in period dress. The Helen Schultz Ilfeld collection of more than forty items, including clothing and jewelry, was donated in 1953. The Society received a donation of about fifty items, mostly clothing, from the estate of Cleofas Martínez Jaramillo in 1957.

During the Museum of New Mexico's reorganization between 1959 and 1961 the History Bureau was formed and assigned lead responsibility for exhibits in the Palace. The Society's collections had been reorganized in the 1950s and integrated with the Museum's by the latter's curators E. Boyd, responsible for the Spanish colonial art, and Marjorie Lambert, in charge of the historical collections with Indian items. Arthur J. O. Anderson, Associate Museum Administrator for History and Publications, was responsible for the history and document collections.

The Commission of Public Records was created in 1959 and charged with establishing the State Records Center and Archives to undertake responsibility for all official state records, including those nominally in the hands of the Historical Society. Senior archivist and later state historian Myra Ellen Jenkins split the Society's documents between the State Archives and the Palace's Library. They are now housed next door to the Palace in the Fray Angélico Chávez History Library and Photo Archives.

At the beginning of its second century the Historical Society itself began to reorganize and revitalize. A new charter in 1959 no longer included museum and collection responsibilities. The final disposition of the Society's collections is documented in a

June 29, 1977, letter from Society president Lorraine Lavender to the Board of Regents of the Museum of New Mexico and George H. Ewing, Director of the Museum of New Mexico. In this letter the Historical Society "gives to the Museum of New Mexico all of its right, title and interest in those collections acquired prior to 1960 and presently housed in the Museum of New Mexico. This is done with the understanding that the Museum of New Mexico will provide a credit line giving credit to the Historical Society of New Mexico whenever all or part of those collections are used."

Today there are more than 300 Historical Society items, primarily Spanish colonial works of art, catalogued in the collections of the Museum of International Folk Art, over 500 in the collections of the Museum of Indian Arts and Culture, and more than 1200 in the Palace of the Governors/New Mexico History Museum collections. Beyond these there are tens of thousands of documents and photographs collected by the Historical society in the collections of the State Records Center and Archives and the Fray Angélico Chávez History Library and Photo Archives at the Palace of the Governors/New Mexico History Museum. Thus, the memory of the Museum of the Historical Society of New Mexico in the Palace of the Governors still lives in the collections of the Museum of New Mexico.

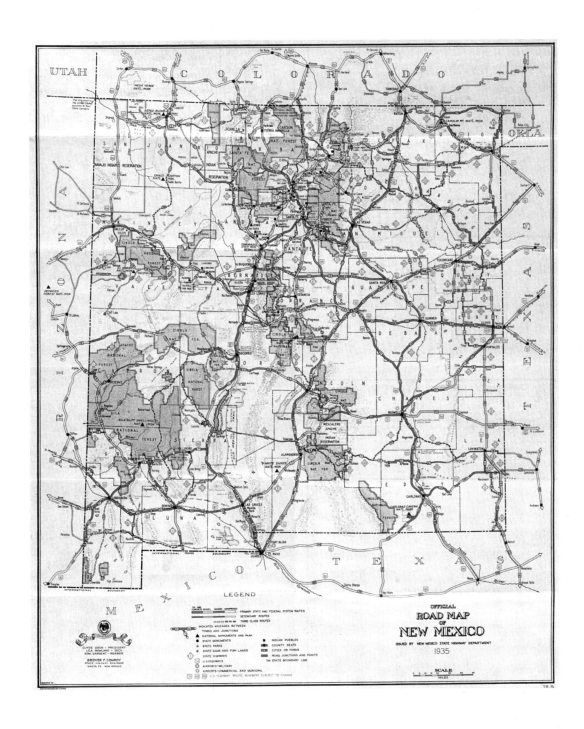

Official Road Map of New Mexico (1935). New Mexico State Highway Department. 1:3168000, 1 inch = 50 miles. Courtesy Fray Angélico Chávez History Library (NMHM/DCA).

PART SIX

THE "NEW" NEW MEXICO

Between the ratification of a state constitution for New Mexico on January 21, 1911 (Office of the Secretary of State), and the dedication of the Bosque Redondo Memorial at Fort Sumner State Monument on June 4, 2005 (Denetdale), New Mexico — proclaimed the forty-seventh state by President William Howard Taft on January 6, 1912 — came to global renown as the World War II birthplace of the nuclear age. Its first state flag, adopted in March 1915, had been designed by historian Ralph Emerson Twitchell and publicity commissioner A. E. Koehler Jr. to fly over the New Mexico Building at the San Diego Panama-California Exposition of 1915–16. Its first state song, "O, Fair New Mexico," adopted in March 1917, was written and composed in 1915 by the daughter of Lincoln County Sheriff Pat Garrett, Elizabeth Garrett, who served as a hostess-entertainer for that world's fair exhibition (Weigle).

Fifty years after San Diego, New Mexico secured a place in the National Statuary Hall Collection, which had been established in the United States Capitol in 1864. Felix W. De Weldon's bronze sculpture of United States Senator Dennis Chavez, the first of the state's two donations "to honor persons notable in their history," was received in 1966 (Architect of the Capitol and Montoya). Chavez's was not the first Statuary Hall sculpture to honor a New Mexico figure. Indiana's second donation, made in 1910, was Andrew O'Connor's marble statue of Territorial Governor Lewis (Lew) Wallace, a native of that state. On September 22, 2005, the reception of New Mexico's second donation, Cliff Fragua's marble sculpture of

Pueblo Revolt leader Po'pay, "marked the first time at which every state in the Union has been represented by two statues in the collection" (Architect of the Capitol).

During the first three decades of statehood, borderland sagas of land, livelihood, and conflict within, between, and among Mexico, Texas, Arizona, Colorado, and New Mexico continued. World War I broke out in Europe in August 1914, but the United States maintained neutrality until April 1917, some nineteen months before hostilities ended on November 11, 1918. On July 12, 1917, 1,140 striking copper miners, "about one-third of whom were Mexicans," were "deported" from Bisbee, Arizona, and "dumped unceremoniously in the desert of southern New Mexico near the town of Columbus," which Mexican Revolutionary leader Francisco ("Pancho") Villa had raided in the predawn hours of March 9, 1916. At Columbus, at the Madrid mines, at the Gallup mines, and elsewhere, interethnic tensions flared as "small farmers and workers, often the same people, struggled to hold their own as agribusiness joined the state's mining interests" (Deutsch).

In the 1930s the dirge of the Great Depression and the promise of the New Deal affected all New Mexicans, as they did all Americans (Deutsch, Szasz, Montoya). On May 6, 1935, President Franklin Delano Roosevelt signed an executive order establishing the Works Progress Administration (WPA) "to implement work relief programs and effect a monumental government intervention that integrated a vast cultural infrastructure." New Mexicans on the WPA Federal Writers' Project recorded testimony of the region's centuries-old, covert, and sorrowful legacy of slavery and peonage. By "telling of a silence, they [broke] through it, pointing to the most pressing issues of the day" (Rael-Gálvez). Writers' Project workers were also responsible for the state's contribution to the WPA American Guide Series, *New Mexico: A Guide to the Colorful State*, published in August 1940 during the Coronado Cuarto Centennial (Szasz).

World War II began on September 1, 1939, with the German invasion of Poland, but the United States remained officially neutral until after the Japanese attacked Pearl Harbor on December 7, 1941. Synchronized to coincide with Pearl Harbor, though on December 8 because on the opposite side of the International Date Line, the Japanese also attacked the Philippine Islands, where New Mexico's 200th Coast Artillery (Anti-Aircraft) had been posted since September. Its men were "credited with firing the first shots for the Allies in the Pacific theater" and were among the seventy thousand who in April 1942 were part of "the largest capitulation in the history of the American military." Only some of them survived the Bataan Death March and more than three years as prisoners of war. "A second major role for New Mexico in the war...involved the Navajo Code Talkers," whose Navajo-language "substitution system whereby military terms were encoded in familiar reservation images" stymied Japanese cryptographers (Szasz).

The war "genuinely revolutionized" New Mexico's economy and cultures. "New Mexicans who lived through the harrowing war years of 1940–45 regularly confronted two...overwhelming concerns: a haunting uncertainty regarding their soldiers serving overseas and an all-pervasive domestic secrecy" (Szasz). That which could not be told of New Mexico was foretold when the world's first atomic bomb was detonated at five-thirty on the morning of July 16, 1945, at the Trinity Site on the Alamogordo Bombing Range. It was finally proclaimed aloud in Japan on August 6 at Hiroshima and on August 9 at Nagasaki. The war in Europe ended on May 7–8, 1945, and that in the Pacific on August 14–15, with the formal Japanese surrender on September 2, 1945.

The nation's first military air base had been set up at Columbus, New Mexico, and U.S. Army Air Force biplanes assisted the army's first motorized cavalry as part of General John J. "Blackjack" Pershing's unsuccessful 1916 Punitive Expedition into Mexico in pursuit of Pancho Villa. Some thirty years later, the Roswell Army Air Force Base figured in the July 1947 Roswell Incident. In time Roswell became the epicenter for an ongoing extraterrestrial borderland saga told and untold (Gibbs).

The fifteen-month strike that began in October 1950 and shut down the Empire Zinc Corporation mine near Silver City "made national news and became part of national folklore" in the 1954 film *Salt of the Earth* (Deutsch). The following year, to commemorate the tenth anniversary of the Trinity detonation, Los Alamos Scientific Laboratory "sponsored an unprecedented event," opening "the Tech areas to newsmen, staff, and the family members of its work force," thousands of whom toured on July 17 and 18, 1955. The secrecy that had shrouded Los Alamos since 1943 finally "cracked" at noon on February 18, 1957, when "New Mexico's Governor Edwin L. Mechem became the first person to enter Los Alamos without a pass" (Hunner). Six days later, beginning in the early evening of February 24 and lasting into the early morning of February 25, Buddy Holly and his band recorded two songs, "I'm Looking for Someone to Love" and "That'll Be the Day," at the Norman Petty Studio in Clovis, one of the birthplaces of rock and roll (Silverman). Such music contributed inspiration to the protests of the 1960s, notable among them in New Mexico Reies Lopez Tijerina's storied June 5, 1967, raid on the Tierra Amarilla County Courthouse seeking "long denied justice [for] the heirs of New Mexico's land grants" (Deutsch).

In the 1960s the modern Navajo government, "which is founded upon the principles established in the Indian Reorganization Act of 1934, asserted national sovereignty...[and its] leaders fully embraced liberal ideologies as the foundation of their political system." Centennial anniversary events in 1968 commemorated a "Century of Progress" since the signing of the Treaty of 1868 that allowed Navajos to return to their homeland after the Long Walk and four years' imprisonment at Fort Sumner's Bosque Redondo. In 2003 Fort Sumner State Monument manager Gregory Scott Smith said of the planned Bosque Redondo Memorial: "It will honor the memory of thousands of Navajo and Mescalero Apache people who suffered and died as a result of the forced relocation and internment. Moreover, it will celebrate the official birth of a sovereign nation born of the tragedy of the Bosque Redondo." At its June 4, 2005, dedication, "Navajo Nation president Joe Shirley Jr. said, 'The story needs to be told, to serve as a reminder of the genocide and the holocaust that were perpetrated on a nation.' Lawrence Morgan, speaker of the Navajo Nation Council, said the memorial represented a 'slaughterhouse' and that although not all Navajos supported the memorial, it should become a tool for education and healing" (Denetdale).

The New Mexico Constitutional Convention, Santa Fe, New Mexico, 1910.
Photograph by William R. Walton.

32

New Mexico's Constitution

Office of the Secretary of State (2003)

On January 21, 1996, New Mexico's Constitution observed its eighty-fifth anniversary. The development of our State Constitution, which was overwhelmingly approved by the voters on January 21, 1911, has a long and complicated history that dates back to the time when New Mexico was first occupied by United States military forces.

In 1848, soon after the Treaty of Guadalupe Hidalgo was signed and New Mexico was formally ceded to the United States, New Mexicans petitioned Congress to establish a territorial government. Congress ignored the petition. A year later, New Mexicans adopted a new plan for a territorial government and sent a delegate to Washington. Again, Congress ignored the plan and refused to seat the delegate.

The first New Mexico Constitution was written during the summer of 1850, when local government officials drafted a plan for a state government. This first state constitution was overwhelmingly approved by voters but was quickly nullified by federal officials because New Mexico had not yet obtained Territorial status and therefore had no legal standing from which to seek statehood.

On September 9, 1850, the Organic Act formally created the Territory of New Mexico and its long struggle for statehood began. Several attempts were made to develop and implement a constitution during this period. These included proposed constitutions that were defeated at the polls in 1872 and 1889. All of these efforts, however, including the defeated joint statehood effort with Arizona in 1906, provided momentum to the statehood movement, which culminated in the 1910 constitution.

On June 20, 1910, after sixty-two years of struggle, Congress finally passed enabling legislation that authorized New Mexico to call a constitutional convention in anticipation of being admitted to the Union. On October 3, 1910, one hundred elected delegates convened at Santa Fe to draft a document, which was overwhelmingly approved by the voters on January 21, 1911. On January 6, 1912, President William H. Taft signed a proclamation declaring New Mexico the 47th state of the Union.

The past eighty-five years, however, have been a trying period for New Mexico's constitution. It currently bears little resemblance to the original document approved by the voters in 1911. While a few of its original articles have remained relatively intact — most notably those related to the Bill of Rights and Elective Franchise — most of the original twenty-two articles have undergone changes, some of them substantive.

33

The State Flags and the First State Song

Marta Weigle

New Mexico officially became the forty-seventh state of the United States of America on January 6, 1912, but it did not have a flag until the San Diego Panama-California Exposition opened on January 1, 1915. That first flag was designed by historian Ralph Emerson Twitchell, chairman of the Board of Exposition Managers, and A. E. Koehler Jr., commissioner of publicity on the board's Executive Staff, to fly over the New Mexico Building in Balboa Park. It was presented to the Second State Legislature of New Mexico and adopted as the state's first flag on March 19, 1915. According to House Bill 319, Section 1:

> A flag or banner with a turquoise blue field, emblematic of the blue skies of New Mexico; a flag of the United States of America in miniature in the upper left hand corner of the field, designating the loyalty of our people, in the upper right hand corner the figures No. 47, the forty-seventh star and state in the American Union, in the lower right hand corner the great seal of the State of New Mexico, and upon the field running from the lower left to the upper right hand corner in white the words "NEW MEXICO" be and the same hereby is adopted as the state flag or banner of New Mexico.

New Mexico state flag created by H. P. Mera, about 1925.

The designation "The Sunshine State" rings the right rim of the state seal on this so-called Twitchell flag.

The main exhibit in the New Mexico Building's central Hall of the Governors was titled *Landmarks of the Santa Fe Trail*. "Large sepia portraits of New Mexico's governors from the military occupation of 1846 to statehood" hung on the walls. Arrayed on tables in the center were Museum of New Mexico staff member John Percy Adams's models of "ancient buildings, churches, pueblos, and other edifices prominent in New Mexico's long history" (Miller 1985, 15). Among these was "a sixteen-foot-long model of the [Pecos] mesa top showing reconstructed church, South Pueblo, and main quadrangle" (Kessell 1979, 477), a major landmark of the Santa Fe Trail and by then popularly ensconced as the birthplace of the Aztec ruler Montezuma.

At Governor William C. McDonald's request, blind musician, singer, and composer Elizabeth Garrett and her "escort," friend Elizabeth (Beth) Roe, were invited to San Diego to serve as hostesses in the New Mexico Building. As the state's "First Lady of Song," Garrett was also to give a "daily program of entertainment," presenting "the songs of Old Mexico, cowboy ballads, and Indian chants." She "closed with a group of her compositions which told of mountains and valleys and apple orchards, of summer showers on mesa and desert, the *Paisano*, the roadrunner; her own songs of New Mexico." Colonel and former president Theodore Roosevelt attended a special program in his honor and afterward expressed "great pleasure to meet the daughter of my old friend, Pat Garrett,…the most noted sheriff of the Southwest, in territorial days…. In fact, I feel that he was the man who introduced law to the territory" (Hall 1983, 116).

In 1915 Elizabeth Garrett, who once said, "My father tried to bring peace and harmony to our country with his guns; I would like to do my part with my music" (Hall 1983, 9), wrote and composed "O, Fair New Mexico." The first of its three verses reads:

> Under a sky of azure, where
>   balmy breezes blow;
> Kissed by the golden sunshine,
>   is Nuevo Mejico.
> Home of the Montezuma, with
>   fiery heart aglow,
> State of the deeds historic,
>   is Nuevo Mejico.

"O, Fair New Mexico" was adopted as the official state song in March 1917, during the term of Washington E. Lindsey, the third statehood governor.

Born on a ranch at Eagle Creek in Lincoln County in 1884, three years after the death of Billy the Kid, Elizabeth Garrett died in Roswell on October 16, 1947, some three months after the Roswell Incident. She is buried in a cemetery there under a marker with the inscription "ELIZABETH GARRETT / 1947 / O FAIR NEW MEXICO."

In 1920 the New Mexico chapter of the Daughters of the American Revolution began advocating for a new flag more "representative of New Mexico's unique character," and in 1923 it sponsored an unsuccessful design competition. The members finally appealed for help to Santa Fe district public health officer Harry P. Mera, whose avocational interest in archaeology led him to choose a sun design painted on a pot from Zia Pueblo dating to the late 1800s or early 1900s. The original design showed a face inside the sun's circle, but the DAR rejected it in favor of a plain center. Mera's wife, Reba, sewed a prototype for presentation to the state legislature, which adopted House Bill 164 on March 19, 1925 (Polese 1968, 32–33):

> Said flag shall be the ancient Zia Sun Symbol of red in the center of
> a field of yellow. The colors shall be the red and yellow of old Spain.
> The proportion of the flag shall be a width of two thirds its length.
> The sun symbol shall be one-third of the length of the flag. Said

symbol shall have four groups of rays set at right angles; each group shall consist of four rays, the two inner rays of the group shall be one-fifth longer than the outer rays of the group. The diameter of the circle in the center of the symbol shall be one third of the width of the symbol.

That Mera chose a Pueblo pot design is not surprising, for "starting about 1890 and growing rapidly after 1910," what historian Richard H. Frost (1980, 5) called "the romantic inflation of Pueblo culture" transformed popular American attitudes toward the Pueblos, to whom little thought had previously been given, "apart from a pervasive belief that [they] worshiped snakes and Montezuma, and were closely related to the Aztecs." By the 1920s, however,

> in the popular mind the Pueblos were the most interesting of the American Indian tribes. Their positive qualities had grown larger than life. They were admired as ceremonialists and artists. Their pottery was sought by discriminating connoisseurs and curio-hunters. The beauty of their villages was interpreted in oil paintings displayed in prestigious eastern art galleries. Books and magazines sympathetically portrayed Pueblo life, and the style of their architecture inspired the remodeling of the capital city of New Mexico. The Pueblo Indian romance, a generation in the making, was fully ripe.

The Zia sun symbol appears at the bottom of Willard H. Andrews's centerfold map in the 1941 New Mexico State Tourist Bureau booklet *New Mexico "Land of Enchantment."* It is identified thus: "This symmetrical design, now the trademark of things New Mexican, is the symbol of the life-giving sun as conceived by the Indians of the Zia Pueblo. In red on a yellow background it forms the State flag of New Mexico."

In 1994, Representative James Roger Madalena, a Democrat from Jemez Pueblo, introduced a bill in the New Mexico Legislature to compensate Zia Pueblo $45 million for having used its sacred sun symbol on the state flag since 1925. According to an Associated Press release printed in the *Albuquerque Journal* on January 28, 1994, Madalena, whose district included Zia, "said the symbol is very sacred to the pueblo's 300 members…[and this] marks [their] first attempt to right a wrong. 'It's long overdue,' he said." The pueblo's efforts were unsuccessful, and the following year, according to an *Albuquerque Journal* editorial of January 30, 1995, "just when one might have been struck with the hypocrisy of a pueblo offering to 'sell' a sacred symbol, spokesmen said the dollar figure was merely to get the state's attention. 'We want the Legislature and the state to recognize this symbol rightfully belongs to the people of Zia,' said Peter Pino, tribal administrator, to the House Judiciary Committee." The editors noted that "the ancient symbol, long in general use in New Mexico," was not contested until 1994, so "the state can't consider paying Pueblo of Zia for past or future use of the symbol on the state flag — and, given the assertion that the money was mentioned only as an attention-getter, perhaps that point is moot anyway." They recommended: "Zia should make clear just what it would like the state to do with regard to the Zia symbol, and then the Legislature can decide on a reasonable course of action."

An Associated Press release printed in the *Albuquerque Journal* and the *Santa Fe New Mexican* on February 18, 2001, recounted how Zia tribal administrator Peter M. Pino (profile in Sando 1998, 287–91) again appeared before the state legislature and told the Appropriations and Finance Committee that "this issue has been a sore and hurt for the people of Zia for 76 years." Besides being the official state symbol, the Zia sun symbol was "widely used…by businesses and organizations, [and] Pino said the pueblo had found at least 96 private entities using the symbol." He and Zia Governor William Toribio assured lawmakers that there were no plans to sue and "no desire to stop the state from using this symbol," only a request "to approve a bill to require negotiations between the state and pueblo to determine how to compensate the pueblo for unauthorized use of the Zia symbol" and to pay "$50,000 for the Office of Indian Affairs to facilitate the proposed negotiations." Pino "contrasted the state's years of silence and inaction to a request by Texas-based Southwest Airlines for permission to use the Zia symbol on an airliner. A religious elder said a prayer at a dedication ceremony last year for the plane. The company also made a donation to the pueblo for a college scholarship fund." The amount of the Southwest Airlines donation was not disclosed, but Pino urged: "Let us start talking. Let us find a solution like we found with Southwest." His ten-year-old granddaughter Sabrina Pino "also asked lawmakers to resolve the issue and said she represented the pueblo's future generations that could benefit from any compensation from the state."

On Flag Day, June 14, 2001, the North American Vexillological Association announced the results of a three-month, online survey judging United States and Canadian flags. New Mexico's Zia sun symbol flag narrowly defeated the Lone Star flag of Texas as North America's best. According to an Associated Press release in the *Santa Fe New Mexican* on June 16, 2001: "Following New Mexico in the top 10 were Texas, Quebec, Maryland, Alaska, Arizona, Puerto Rico, the District of Columbia, the Marshall Islands and South Carolina. The bottom 10 were New Hampshire, Idaho, Wisconsin, Kentucky, Minnesota, South Dakota, Kansas, Montana, Nebraska and [last] Georgia."

Woman holding sign reading "Land or Death" at the Tierra Amarilla courthouse raid, 1967.

34

Labor, Land, and Protest
since Statehood

Sarah Deutsch

On July 12, 1917, three months after the United States entered
World War I, 1,140 striking copper miners from Bisbee, Arizona, found themselves dumped unceremoniously in the desert
of southern New Mexico near the town of Columbus. Labeled
by the press a "deportation" (for example, *Albuquerque Morning
Journal,* July 15, 1917), the incident points out both the perpetual
foreignness of New Mexico — a place to which people could
be "deported" — and at the same time the ways in which New
Mexico's labor history is inextricably bound with that of the
other forty-nine states, the region, and its neighboring nation.
The "deportation" of the strikers, about one-third of whom
were Mexicans, took place only sixteen months after Mexican
Revolutionary leader Francisco ("Pancho") Villa had raided the
same town, Columbus, New Mexico.

New Mexico's press had seen the Villa raid as an extension of the violent cross-border raids carried out under Mexico's Plan de San Diego, beginning in 1915. The radical result
of years of dispossession of the Mexican-heritage people in the
region on both sides of the U.S.-Mexican border, the plan had
enveloped south Texas in ethnic and economic violence and
raised fears in neighboring New Mexico. This volatile decade
set the stage for the unfolding of New Mexico's twentieth-
century social movements.

Labor and land were deeply linked for New Mexicans
and were interwoven with ethnic tensions resulting from the U.S.
victory in the Mexican-American War. At statehood in 1912,
the Spanish-heritage population remained the majority. As the

years passed, small farmers and workers, often the same people, struggled to hold their own as agribusiness joined the state's mining interests. Largely Spanish-speaking northern New Mexicans, with a radical heritage stretching back to the insurrection against U.S. military rule known as the Revolt of 1847, would continue to lead protests in the 1920s and 1930s aimed at ensuring autonomy. These protests linked landowner-ship and workers' rights and culminated, perhaps, in Reies López Tijerina's raid on the Tierra Amarilla County Courthouse in 1967. Sporadic, explosive, large-scale strikes in other parts of the state, such as the coal strike at Gallup in the 1930s and the famous zinc strike in the 1950s, were tied to the same mix of ethnic, economic, and social tensions and the struggle for autonomy.

Columbus and Madrid

In early March 1916, Francisco Villa and fifteen hundred of his men capped off a series of border raids by sweeping into Columbus, New Mexico. They had already attacked an English-speaking Mormon colony in Mexico and ranches on the border, and now they targeted the military encampment and town center in Columbus. Villa's revolutionaries were hungry and exhausted. They expected help from Columbus's "Mexican" residents, and they got it. Columbus Mexicans distinguished Anglo from Mexican residences and businesses. Villa's men attacked only the "gringos." The local Mexican consul took advantage of that fact to protect Anglo women in the town's hotel, claiming it held only "our people" (*Albuquerque Morning Journal* [AMJ], March 9, 1916). The women escaped. When the ruse was discovered, Villa's men shot the consul and torched the hotel. By the time U.S. soldiers sent Villa back across the border, at least sixteen Anglos lay dead, and a large part of the town had been burned. The *Albuquerque Morning Journal* called it a massacre, and Villa's men, "bandits."

The newspaper placed the raid in the context of border attacks, which had been rising in frequency and violence over the previous year in Arizona and Texas. The raids and the response to them showed the contradictory and ephemeral nature of the border. The lack of earlier U.S. federal action to end the raids infuriated many border residents. One zealous military commander who had pursued "bandits" into Mexico was undergoing court-martial. The newspaper greeted with satisfaction the news that U.S. troops were now massing on the border: "Shocked indignation occasioned by news of Villa's outrage was quickly succeeded by undisguised satisfaction in official and congressional circles over the knowledge that after three years of patient forbearance United States troops were actually on Mexican soil to avenge the death of their comrades and bring to justice the outlaws whose depredations have terrorized Americans on both sides of the border" (AMJ, March 10, 1916).

At the same time, it was clear that not all revolutionaries lived on the Mexican side of the border. On March 11 the Albuquerque paper reported on page one the suppression of a Mexican newspaper in El Paso "because of an editorial attacking the United States and defending Villa." The consolidation of Anglo business and enterprise on both sides of the border, beginning with the coming of the railroads in the 1880s, and its concomitant reduction of the economic power and land base of the older Mexican population, by the 1910s had generated sufficient rancor that Mexican revolutionaries could indeed plausibly imagine the support of U.S. citizens of Mexican descent. And whether or not they consistently received it, their imagined scenario was equally plausible to the region's newer Anglo residents. The Columbus raid, in short, was part of a larger protest about the distribution of land and economic opportunity in a region that encompassed both northern Mexico and New Mexico, with the same corporations and peoples often operating on both sides of the border (Johnson 2003; Sandos 1992).

Border violence was just one part of the massive upheaval and anxiety that permeated the region in the years immediately surrounding the United States' entry into World War I. Battles over the vote for women (New Mexico's women had school suffrage but would not win full suffrage until 1920), the "labor war" in the coal fields of Colorado, and protests by stockmen in New Mexico that "Navajos Are Getting Best of Deal" jockeyed for headline space (AMJ, March 11, 1916). On the last item, the (evidently non-Indian) stockmen complained that without the burdens of citizenship, Navajos were "permitted to take up homesteads and allotments and grazing lands, thus shutting out people who might become permanent and valuable settlers." What was clearly at stake in this complaint was who counted as "permanent and valuable settlers." As in the border upheaval, questions of borders and citizenship rammed into issues of prior occupancy and rights, markets and management. Just who was a "foreigner," anyway?

As war in Europe loomed ever closer to the United States, such questions intensified in New Mexico as in the rest of the nation. Four months after the Columbus raid, the United States celebrated "Preparedness Day," signifying its readiness to engage in the growing war. When radicals bombed the parade in San Francisco, authorities targeted two labor leaders, convicting them in a show trial with little evidence. A year later, and two months after the United States entered World War I, the incident was still making front-page headlines in New Mexico as Rena Mooney, the wife of one of the leaders, Tom Mooney, went on trial (AMJ, June 1, 1917). As labor troubles rose in 1917, workers looked increasingly, suspiciously, and even dangerously foreign. The *Albuquerque Morning Journal* differentiated between "foreigners" and other workers on strike at Jerome, Arizona, that year.

Headlines about growing labor troubles in neighboring Arizona and Colorado and concerns about access to land in New Mexico and Mexico shared space with concerns about draft registration. On the same day and in the same column, the *Journal's* front page reported "Squatters' Rights Suspended in Mexico" and "Labor May Come Into United States to Till Fields" (about the waiving of new immigration laws to allow Mexican and Canadian labor into the United States for agricultural purposes). In a story headlined "Jails Papago Chief," the paper reported that Juan Kahn-A-Rone, head of the Santa Rosa village, "was locked in the county jail today on a complaint that the chief had advised and prevented young Indians in his village from registering for the draft" (AMJ, June 9, 1917). In another column, the same issue reported that registration for the draft was lower than predicted by the Census Bureau. Three days earlier, the paper had claimed, "Registration in New Mexico Falls Below Estimate" (AMJ, June 7, 1917). Their squatting rights suspended, landless Mexicans became newly available to U.S. employers, and Native Americans, although not seen as "permanent settlers," were somehow also at fault for resisting the draft, though it was unlikely the villagers could have made up the state's deficit.

It was in this context of a constellation of fears about the country's ability to defend itself and over contested rights to land, labor, and free speech that on June 28, [1917], forty-five hundred miners employed at Bisbee, Arizona, went on strike. Over the next two weeks, as tensions rose in Bisbee, the New Mexico papers reported that southern Colorado miners, nine thousand strong, whose last large strike had culminated in the massacre of workers and their families at Ludlow, Colorado, in 1914, were prepared to go on strike again in a renewed "labor war." They also informed readers that woman suffragists picketing the White House in Washington, D.C., had been jailed, that brutal race riots had erupted in East St. Louis, leaving great numbers of African Americans dead, that hundreds of Socialists had marched in a peace demonstration in Boston with banners reading "Russia has a 6-Hour Day, why not America?", that unions in Globe, Arizona, had joined those on strike, and that federal troops might be sent to Arizona's strike zones (AMJ, June 29, July 2–5, and July 7, 1917). The Industrial Workers of the World (IWW), active in many of these strikes, denied control by "alien influence."

On July 10, 1917, the mayor of Jerome, Arizona, backed by fifty "citizens," forced sixty-seven IWW members into cattle cars and "deported" them to Needles, California (AMJ, July 11, 1917). Two days later, as mediators failed to quell labor unrest in Gallup, New Mexico, Bisbee followed suit. A "Citizen's Protective League" forced twelve hundred strikers (labeled "IWW") into freight cars and dropped them in the New Mexico desert (AMJ, July 13, 1917).

The deportation did not end the labor unrest in Arizona, New Mexico, or elsewhere. A riot at Miami, Arizona, resulted from a failed police attempt to break up an IWW meeting; quelling it required two U.S. cavalry units, rushed over from Globe (AMJ, July 15, 1917). The same day, miners threatened a strike at Madrid, New Mexico. In response, Sheriff López swore in twenty-five deputies to protect properties owned by Senator Kaseman of Albuquerque. The *Albuquerque Morning Journal* explained that because "many of the coal miners are foreigners, serious trouble is feared" (July 7, 14, 1917).

New Mexico's response to the upheaval was unique. In neighboring Texas, Anglos had responded to Mexican raids with vicious, deadly, sweeping violence against virtually any Mexicans they could find, whether U.S. citizens or not. Not so in New Mexico. Here the story comes back to Columbus, site of Villa's raid just over a year earlier, for it was in Columbus that the Bisbee deportees set up camp under the watchful eye of federal troops.

"Small City of Canvas Springs Up Between Columbus and Border," reported the *Albuquerque Morning Journal* on July 15, 1917. It was called "Camp Wobbley," after the nickname for the IWW. According to the paper, "when the unshaven and unwashed crowd marched up to the refugee camp this afternoon, they presented one of the strangest sights Columbus has seen since Villa's Mexican bandits dashed into the town on March 9, 1916." Montenegrins, Slavs, Italians, Serbs, Austrians, Welsh-men, Mexicans, and others among the 1,140 deported miners, mill men, and small merchants worked "in a blistering sun" on the hottest day of the summer setting up camp on the "plains of death." The forecast was for a high of 100 degrees. The exhausted deportees declared, "We are rearing to go back to Bisbee but not until the soldiers go along to protect us." Meanwhile, they "discussed plans for filing a blanket suit against the operators, officials and others responsible for the wholesale deportation from Arizona of those held to be members or sympathizers of the I.W.W. movement" (AMJ, July 16, 1917).

Ironically, these men, so despised by the Citizens' Protective League for their presumed disloyalty, rejected the notion of a prayer for their release through a writ of habeas corpus "on the ground that it would embarrass the federal government which is trying to find a solution of the problem involving the disposition of the men" (AMJ, July 16, 1917). That Sunday passed quietly. The men bathed and did their laundry in a horse trough, though no soap had yet been issued. "Eleven wives of deported miners came from Bisbee to visit," several of them identified as foreign — Italian and Slav — and some bringing small children. The men, who had not been charged with breaking any laws, ate "Mulligan stew" prepared from leftover scraps of their rations, and a thousand of them attended outdoor church services led by the cavalry chaplain, who "spoke on the subject of man's honest convictions. A quartet of miners sang 'Where is My Wandering Boy Tonight' and 'Throw Out the Life Line.'" A few days later, the protective troops began overseeing vaccinations and military training of the camp residents (AMJ, July 16, 17, 1917).

Meanwhile, a federal mediator prepared to meet with the miners from Madrid, New Mexico, to head off their impending strike. The *Albuquerque Morning Journal* reported that "the Spanish-American miners are not joining in the movement to union-ize the camp" (July 15, 1917). Two days later the paper reported that the Madrid miners had organized a union but for patriotic reasons would ask for neither recognition nor improved wages and hours (July 16, 1917). At the end of July and into August, the less controversial United Mine Workers at Gallup, New Mexico, with a large Mexican-heritage contingent, did go on strike. Similar "deportations," imported gunmen (boast-ing of victories at Ludlow), and an entirely Anglo local Council of Defense appeared. By the end of 1917, *El Excelsior*, a Mexican newspaper, claimed that four thousand Mexican strikers sat in the prisons of New Mexico and Arizona (Deutsch 1987, 110).

Making a distinction between unrest by "Mexicans" at the border and by patriotic "Spanish American" workers at Madrid, New Mexico Anglos did not imitate their Texas neighbors. They did not pursue wholesale violence against people of Mexican heritage in New Mexico, at the border, or elsewhere. And unlike in parts of Texas, they did not initiate a Jim Crow system that would segregate Mexican-heritage people as well as African Americans. It would have been difficult to carry off such a maneuver in a state whose majority population remained, until the 1920s, Spanish speaking. In 1919 Octaviano Larrazolo, the state's Mexican-born governor, proposed in the *New Mexico Journal of Education*, "Wouldn't it be well for every English-speaking child also to know Spanish?" and suggested that Spanish be a required language in all the grammar schools of the state (Deutsch 1987, 119).

The Postwar Years and the Great Depression

For many of the Spanish-speaking residents of New Mexico whose heritage stretched back to pre–Mexican War days, and to many of the Native American inhabitants, issues of land and labor were not easily separated. And dispossession could be an entangled process. In 1924, for example, the Pueblo Lands Act resulted in the eviction of nearly three thousand Hispanos and Anglos on behalf of Native Americans.

Particularly in the northern parts of the state, where communal landholding predominated, Hispano and many Indian villagers had watched their resources dwindle. New taxation policies and Anglo-dominated courts and court processes at a variety of levels had combined to whittle down the remaining land base. Shepherds became sheep sharecroppers. Freighters became railroad workers. Small farmers migrated seasonally to work on the tracks, in the mines, and on the commercial farms of the region. Women raised cash crops and, when they lived close enough to Anglo settlements, took in laundry or did domestic labor. Sometimes whole families migrated seasonally.

The 1920s were a difficult decade, characterized by a depressed cattle market, limited access to credit, and an average crop failure in some parts of northern New Mexico reaching 59 percent. Despite the hard times, Texans and Oklahomans seeking greener pastures and with enough capital to stake a homestead invaded the region. They built expensive irrigation projects that raised taxes at a moment, in 1926, when a new state tax law made land delinquent for three years subject to foreclosure and sale (Deutsch 1987, 128).

Ever rising numbers of Hispanic village farm families headed for larger towns such as Grants and Albuquerque or for coal-mining areas, including Gallup and Raton, in search of paying work. An even larger number left for Colorado's sugar-beet fields, seduced by labor recruiters who promised "you'd rake in the money" (Deutsch 1987, 129). Many left seasonally, finding a way to be farmers and laborers.

The Great Depression of the 1930s exploded these migration survival strategies. In the 1920s, the 14,000 Hispano families in northern New Mexico's upper Rio Grande Valley sent 7,000 to 10,000 persons north for work each year. In the early

1930s they sent only 2,000. And those sent earned only about one-third what they had before. Anxious Colorado Anglos not only helped "repatriate" about 20,000 Mexicans and their often U.S.-born children to Mexico but also complained loudly enough to Colorado's governor that he called out the National Guard in 1936 and declared martial law on the Colorado–New Mexico border.

Governor Johnson's blockade against "aliens" swept up New Mexico's migrant citizens of Mexican origin as well. Twelve Hispanos from Abiquiú and Peñasco were taken from a train, loaded in trucks, and dumped out on the prairie at the New Mexico line. While other states had closed their borders to Anglo dustbowl migrants, those in favor of and those opposed to Colorado's border closing were clear about the targets. "We are right behind you," wrote a Mr. and Mrs. Williams to the governor, "in your move to keep the Mexican race out of our state." Anglo employers, on the other hand, begged the governor to lift the blockade and allow in the "Mexicans from New Mexico" they needed for herding, lambing, harvesting, and railroad section maintenance (Deutsch 1987, 165–66).

Hispano outrage in Colorado and New Mexico helped end the blockade. Ironically, before the blockade, Hispanos had numbered among those asking the governor for protection against alien labor. They had favored deportation and vocally resented the presence of Mexican aliens on relief rolls. But when the blockade came, and despite the insistence of Governor Johnson's administration that it protected "the Colorado Spanish-American working class as well as all of Colorado labor," stories of harassment of Spanish Americans surfaced, and Hispano groups and individuals, from conservatives to the radical Liga Obrera de Habla Español (Spanish-Speaking Workers League), protested the denial of entry into Colorado of people "merely because they were of Spanish descent."

When they worked in the mines and fields and on the tracks, New Mexico's Hispanos were not simply displaced farmers and ranchers; they were workers. They listened to organizers among coal and metal miners. Sometimes they became organizers. They even brought those organizations back to their villages. Older protest traditions continued. The vigilante group Manos Negras (Black Hands) cut fences that blocked access to traditionally communal pastures and burnt barns of Rio Arriba County's Anglo and Hispano commercial farmers into the 1920s. By the early 1930s, the leftist Liga Obrera de Habla Español, which would later protest the border closing, although formed in the Colorado beet fields in 1928 with the aid of the Industrial Workers of the World, was the largest lay organization in the Hispano villages of northern New Mexico. In the early years of the depression, "La Liga secured injunctions preventing the eviction of 7,000 Spanish-speaking small landholders" (Vargas 2005, 94). The connection between their declining land base and the conditions of their labor was clear to them. They were increasingly dispossessed but not disfranchised.

In 1935 the Liga's eight thousand New Mexico members succeeded in defeating a New Mexico criminal syndicalism bill. Two years later, in a joint Anglo-Hispano action, they occupied the New Mexico governor's office. On April 9, 1937, Albuquerque's *La Bandera Americana* (whose motto was "Dedicado al Desarrollo de los Intereses del Pueblo Hispanoamericano [dedicated to the development of Spanish American interests]") reported on page one the arrest of seven people — six men and a woman — accused of an illegal meeting that resulted in a "sit-in" in Governor Clyde Tingley's office. "7 Liders de la Liga Obrera Arrestados en Santa Fe," proclaimed *El Independiente* of Albuquerque, which proclaimed itself "La Voz Hispana del Condado de Bernalillo [the Hispanic voice of Bernalillo County]." But the Liga leaders included Anglos as well as Hispanos. Four of the men had Spanish surnames, but the other two and the one woman had Anglo surnames.

Like the Liga, *El Independiente* saw farmers and industrial workers in the same frame. The masthead featured two illustrations of "Industria de N.M.," one of the plow and the other of sheep shearing. The paper reported labor news from the Colorado beet fields and strike news from across the nation and indeed the world. Only by illusion could sharp boundaries be drawn between "Mexican" and "American," "farmer" and "worker."

Gallup

At Gallup, New Mexico, the various strands came together, and the ensuing explosion in the 1930s garnered national attention. Gallup was no stranger to conflict. The 1917 strike there that had led to Bisbee- and Jerome-style deportations and citizen vigilante actions had involved Mexican-heritage strikers opposing Mexican strikebreakers imported by the company. When the United Mine Workers (UMW) tried to exploit the resulting ethnic tensions in 1922, its strike failed, and the number of Hispano citizens and Mexican nationals in Gallup grew (Rubenstein 1983; Vargas 2005, 30–113).

A decade later, the Great Depression ravaged the mining town. By late 1933, more than half of Gallup miners had little or no work. Hispanos and Mexican nationals now dominated the workforce. Most of those who had jobs worked part-time and so were ineligible for relief.

Across the state, Mexican-heritage New Mexicans faced discrimination in relief and relief work even when eligible. Leftist Unemployed Councils led protest marches demanding milk and shoes for children, allotments for families — including those of striking farmworkers — and housing security. Hispano organizations demanded equal rights for all citizens.

When the federal government enacted the National Industrial Recovery Act, with its section 7a giving workers the right to organize into unions of their choosing and bargain collectively with employers, the workers in Gallup rejected both a proposed company union and the UMW. Instead, they overwhelmingly chose the Communist-affiliated National Miners Union (NMU). That union emphasized not only militant action but cross-racial and cross-ethnic organizing. In late August 1933 the miners walked out to demand union recognition, peacefully shutting down all of Gallup's mines.

After only a day, Governor Arthur Seligman, influenced by the mine owners, local officials, and the UMW, ordered out the National Guard and put the county under martial law. The government forbade NMU meetings, and the five hundred state militiamen escorted strikebreakers around the thousand or so strikers and sympathizers, who had set up a twenty-four-hour picket line. When the militia made mass picketing impossible, the strikers turned to neighborhood squads, only to be stymied by the National Guard's "quarantining the city's working-class sectors and patrolling the roads."

The miners found the townspeople of Gallup unsympathetic. The town relied on the mining company for water and electricity. Help had to come from outside. Again, industrial and small agricultural New Mexico met when miners' families provisioned the miners from their gardens and livestock.

Some Gallup merchants broke ranks with the Chamber of Commerce and donated food and money. Members of the Farm Holiday Association, a progressive group of small farmers who demanded government intervention for small farms, in Colorado, Nebraska, and Wyoming collected food and brought it to Gallup. Strikers fanned out across the region seeking support. Despite its animus toward the leftist NMU, the New Mexico Federation of Labor, pressured by its Spanish-speaking members, "came out in support of the NMU strikers" (Vargas 2005, 99).

General Osborne E. Wood, veteran of the 1919 Boston police strike and the Great Steel Strike, among other anti-labor actions, headed the U.S. troops at Gallup. In the hope of forcing the miners to return to work, and to undermine the radical and largely Mexican-heritage and immigrant NMU in favor of the largely Anglo UMW, whose members were disproportionately still employed in the district, he arrested the entire leadership of the NMU in early October. He charged them with inciting insurrection against New Mexico. Two of the leaders were Mexican nationals, who were threatened with deportation. But the rank and file stood firm, now demanding the release of its leaders among its other strike demands. A group of about four hundred strikers and sympathizers, largely women and children, defied martial law and picketed the stockyards, where the Mexican leaders awaited deportation.

At this point New Mexico was spending about $500 a day to keep the National Guard in Gallup. Scuffles between strikers and the guard became increasingly violent. When Governor Seligman died in mid-October and Lieutenant Governor A. W. Hockenhull assumed office, Hockenhull determined to settle the strike. In late November the NMU claimed victory. All sides agreed to a negotiated settlement that included rehiring strikers, releasing jailed union leaders, and adopting the National Recovery Administration code for the bituminous coal industry.

That settlement, however, did not end Gallup's mobilization. The NMU continued to organize the community, ran candidates in state elections, and participated in a workers' dramatic group, the Club Artístico de Obreros. The NMU also organized workers on federal relief and those unemployed, a particularly crucial action because the mine operators and state government violated certain aspects of the settlement in regard to work and relief for former strikers.

Juan Ochoa led the meetings of the unemployed. An NMU organizer born in Hillsborough, New Mexico, Ochoa had arrived in Gallup in 1929 and worked for the mines until they blacklisted him after the 1933 walkout. He worked for Federal Employment Relief Administration (FERA) projects when he could and convened the Unemployed Council meetings at the Spanish-American Hall.

This level of organizing made it clear that only the most fragile of lines separated a worker from unemployment. It also led to success. After an August 1934 FERA wage cut, the NMU led relief workers on a strike that resulted in restoration of wages. They won a second, similar victory in January 1935, despite anti-Mexican and anti-Communist activity by the Elks, the VFW, and the American Legion.

Yet all was not well. Company stores profiteered. Companies violated the National Recovery Administration code and paid in scrip, which was valued only at the company store. Living conditions remained abysmal, and wage deductions forced miners into debt. Moreover, promises to rehire strikers remained, for many ex-strikers, empty. Finally, the companies had never recognized the union. In this context and in the international context of the Communists' move away from setting up Communist unions to rival existing non-Communist ones, the NMU and the UMW began a rapprochement. In February 1935 they joined in a walkout for union recognition at Diamond Coal Company. After only a day, the manager signed.

Then, in April 1935, all hell broke loose. A little over a year earlier, the Gallup American mine had sold the surface rights to the land at a place called Chihuahuaita out from under Gallup's Mexican-Hispano community, which had occupied the area since 1917. The new owner, McKinley County State Senator Clarence F. Vogel, had no intention of continuing to rent it out. He offered to sell the land to its occupants at inflated prices. About half signed, but the others, miners and unemployed mine workers, could not. Vogel began eviction proceedings toward the end of 1934.

Slowed by the courts, the first actual eviction took place on April 1, 1935. Deputy sheriffs came to the house of Victor Campos and his family, removed their belongings, and padlocked the door. In a pattern typical of eviction protests, a group of neighbors, fifty in this case, came during the night and put the belongings back in the house. Vogel watched. He recorded the names of the leaders and filed a complaint the following day, for breaking and entering, against Campos, Exiquio Navarro (the builder of the house, from whom Campos sublet), and Jeanie Lavato. All three were arrested, but only Navarro was kept — without bail until the hearing, set for April 4.

The news hit a meeting of the Unemployed Council on April 3. The council sent a committee to discuss the matter with the sheriff, who refused to allow the delegation to visit the prisoner. When the committee returned to the meeting at the

Spanish-American Hall, the fifty to one hundred members attending agreed to be at the hearing. Similarly, the Women's Auxiliary of the NMU notified its members of the hearing.

On April 4 a crowd gathered outside Justice Bickel's office, where the hearing took place. The people were denied entrance. They became increasingly aggressive, pounding on the doors, shouting, and finally cursing. The judge granted Navarro a postponement so that he could obtain an attorney, and officers took him out the back door to avoid the crowd. The crowd, however, watching at the windows, met them out back. In the press of people — about seventy-five of them in the alley — someone made a grab at Navarro, and Deputy Bogess threw a tear-gas bomb to disperse the crowd. Two gunshots followed. The first killed the sheriff, Mack R. Carmichael, instantly. His deputy lowered the sheriff to the ground and fired his own gun, killing Ignacio Velarde, and then again, hitting Solomón Esquibel with a shot that ultimately proved fatal. In the ensuing chaos, Navarro disappeared, as did the guns of Velarde, Esquibel, and the deputy who killed them.

The deputy in question, Dee Roberts, assumed the office of sheriff and swore in one hundred special deputies, drawing on the VFW and the American Legion. Together they combed the area for "radicals." They questioned hundreds, jailed two hundred, and ultimately accused fifty-five of murder. District Judge Otero dismissed charges against forty-five, holding ten to face trial. After consulting with Colorado's governor on deportations, New Mexico's governor began deporting those of the suspects he could, until more than a hundred were deported.

The officers in charge targeted members of the NMU and the Liga Obrera de Habla Español. Juan Ochoa, the successful NMU organizer, was among those held without bail, as was his fellow organizer Joe Bartol, an Austrian immigrant. The latter had arrived in the United States in 1912 and in Gallup in 1922. There he married and participated in the walkout in 1933. Like Ochoa, he had lost his job in the aftermath and turned his attention to organizing the unemployed. When he succeeded in finding work at the Southwestern mine, the mine's local elected him NMU president. The other defendants were also poor, manual laborers and migrants who had belonged to NMU-affiliated organizations.

On April 12 a contingent from the American Civil Liberties Union (ACLU), which had a new branch in Santa Fe, and the International Labor Defense League (ILD) pulled into Gallup and took the incident national. The contingent of men and women included a Washington, D.C., lawyer, a Harvard professor, and a journalist, among others. With the ILD spearheading the effort, speaking tours and demonstrations spread across the United States. Protesting letters and petitions showered the governor's office. The ILD brought in the attorney who had saved the defendants in the Tom Mooney case in California in 1917. Despite their prominence, two of the lawyers, while interviewing Bartol's wife, Julia, were kidnapped and beaten. The Gallup sheriff's office failed to investigate, Judge Otero's call for a grand jury failed to receive funding, and Congress voted down Representative Vito Marcantonio's call for a congressional investigation. The two lawyers left the state, embarking on national speaking and fund-raising tours for the defense.

When the case finally came to trial in October, the jury acquitted seven defendants and recommended clemency for the other three, including Juan Ochoa. In his sentencing, Judge McGhee railed against Communism and sentenced the three to at least forty-five and at most sixty years apiece. On appeal, the state supreme court overturned one verdict but upheld two, including Ochoa's.

By 1937 Gallup had not one dues-paying union member. In the context of renewed organizing by the UMW, however, the effort to free Ochoa and the other convicted miner continued, and in 1939 Governor John E. Miles rendered them a conditional pardon — they had to leave the state. Ochoa went to Denver, and the other miner, Manuel Avitia, went to Bisbee. Given the Colorado border closing of 1935–36 and the Bisbee deportation in 1917, their choices not only held some irony but also showed a continued deep integration, persistence, and mobility of workers and ideas in the region that belied political boundaries. Furthermore, despite these setbacks, as early as 1940 the UMW had succeeded in bringing the entire Gallup coal field under contract (Rubenstein 1983; Vargas 2005).

Grant County and Silver City

A decade later, another New Mexico strike made national news and became part of national folklore. As at Gallup, the strike drew on the state's radical heritage, its ethnic mix, and its inextricable labor and land issues. In October 1950, the members of Local 890 of the International Union of Mine, Mill, and Smelter Workers at the Empire Zinc Corporation mine in Grant County, New Mexico, walked out. They shut down the mine and stayed out for fifteen months.

It was not a large strike. The mine had only 128 employees, of whom 92 walked out. Nor were their demands, chiefly for "collar to collar" pay for time underground, easily translatable to a broader public. But as the three Hollywood artists who would bring the strike to the screen in 1954 as *Salt of the Earth* recognized, it had an elemental character (Cargill 1983). It pitted a harshly anti-union national corporation against a beleaguered group of miners, all but a dozen of them Mexican American.

They were not the lowest-paid workers in the county, but they were the ones whose company housing — unlike that of the Anglo workers — had no indoor plumbing, the ones whose wage rates were lower than in districts where Anglos worked the same jobs, and the ones who worked the more dangerous, underground jobs. The striking miners wanted equal treatment. In an era of fierce anti-communism, they ignored the persistent anti-communist attacks on their union, and like the workers at Gallup, they supported the union that fought hardest against discrimination. At the last meeting before the strike, the company's negotiator from New Jersey announced a five-cent-an-hour raise and an eight-hour-longer work week.

The striking miners established twenty-four-hour picketing. The union encouraged miners facing particular hardship to find jobs elsewhere and contribute a portion of their earnings to the strike fund. The union offered some concessions in its original demands, but the corporation determined to exert total control over the conditions of work. It was uninterested in bargaining. In June 1951 the company initiated a back-to-work campaign, and the pickets blocking the road to the mine became a major issue. Sheriff Goforth, elected with the support of the mine workers by a three-vote victory, faced enormous pressure from Empire Zinc and other business interests in the county, as well as from the district attorney, Thomas P. Foy.

With company funds, Goforth hired twenty-four special deputies to escort miners back to work. The picketers held fast. Goforth's men arrested a dozen of them, all but one of them union officers, and the other, a middle-aged woman. New picketers immediately replaced those arrested. No would-be worker made it past the line. When the company secured a restraining order from the judge against the union local, women from the union's auxiliary took over the picketing duties. The women had already written leaflets, letters, and scripts for the union's weekly radio show and worked as announcers on the show and as fund-raisers. But no one had expected them to take over the picketing. Goforth was stymied. Strikebreaking workers saw it as a golden opportunity to pass through a weaker barrier. They were wrong. Nearby, Silver City's judge issued six arrest warrants against the women for assault and battery. No one got through the women's line.

The women began to speak out in union meetings, asking the men to cover for them at home. The law officers also became more aggressive. In the early morning of June 16, Goforth came out to make good on the warrants and escort some miners to work. He had no more success than his predecessors. Enraged, he ordered everyone in his way arrested — sixty-two in all, including a six-week-old baby. As the deputies carried out his orders, new women took the places of those arrested. One frustrated deputy threw a tear gas grenade at the women, only to have a stiff wind clear the smoke away within minutes. Several cars tried to push through the line; women began to struggle with the officers. Miners watching from the hillsides threw rocks and curses. The women's line held. The cars turned back.

At the county courthouse, the sixty-two arrested women and children were crammed into a jail built for twenty-four. They sang and played cards; the miners brought them lunch. The women were outraged but excited. The arrests hardly seemed to have the desired effect of breaking the strikers' spirit. The desperate district attorney called New Mexico Governor Edwin Mechem for help. Mechem was appalled. "The state police," he told reporters, "will not go to Silver City as strike breakers." The assistant district attorney then offered to free the women if they would avoid the strike line. They refused. He caved. By midnight they were free (Cargill 1983, 208–9).

It was the women's story, rather than the men's, that swept the nation. All the major radio networks, popular national magazines such as *Time* and *Life,* and the *New*

York Times covered the story of the women's battle. The local press urged the company to negotiate. Empire Zinc refused. The struggle continued, but the union could not maintain its high-water mark of public support, particularly with a largely Mexican American labor force and a left-wing union in the fiercely anti-communist early 1950s. The governor continued to refuse to enforce anti-picketing injunctions by the local courts and offered his services as a mediator. Empire Zinc rejected his offer as well.

By the end of August, violence was rising. Early in the morning of August 23, 1951, as cars and trucks once again tried to break through the women's line, strikers vandalized the vehicles. The truck driver behind the front car suddenly revved up, pushing the car in front before the women blocking it could jump aside. The cars knocked them over, injured. A crowd of men supporting the women came toward the cars. The driver's son pulled out a pistol, aimed it in front of the approaching men, and fired. One of the bullets ricocheted. It struck a former union member, newly returned from serving in the Korean War. The strikebreakers retreated, news spread, and within hours miners had shut down the entire district. The state police arrived, and the strike "merged with a nation-wide walkout" (Cargill 1983, 231).

The national strike ended before New Mexico's Empire Zinc strike, partly because of President Truman's invocation of Taft-Hartley Act powers as an emergency war-time injunction. As anti-communism and the war in Korea accelerated nationally and locally, local citizens beat up the union's organizers, and Mechem finally ordered state police to enforce the injunction prohibiting blocking the road to the mine. Knowing the state penitentiary was considerably larger than the county jail, the strikers abided by the injunction. But the strike continued.

Finally, in January 1952, Empire Zinc agreed to negotiate. Both sides adjusted their demands. The company raised hourly wages and provided new insurance plans and some grievance and negotiating procedures. It refused to consider demands for improvements in company housing — hot water and inside baths. The issue was corporate control, something made particularly clear by Empire Zinc's statement, after the miners returned to work, that it would provide modern plumbing after all. It was made even clearer by the company's refusal to drop court proceedings against the union. The remaining strikers ratified the new contract, ending New Mexico's longest strike.

Tierra Amarilla

It was at another courthouse that protest in New Mexico again topped the nation's headlines. When Reies López Tijerina and his armed confederates marched into the Tierra Amarilla County Courthouse on June 5, 1967, to make a citizens' arrest of officials who had, in Tijerina's eyes, long denied justice to the heirs of New Mexico's land grants, issues of land and labor, housing and justice once more came to a head.

Tijerina, born in Texas in 1926 and raised there, had been an activist in New Mexico's land grant claims for almost two decades by the time of the raid. He posed the struggle as one of Indo-Hispanos against Anglos, and he saw people with Spanish surnames who served state government in these matters as having sold out to the oppressors. The raid failed in its immediate aim. A running gun battle and an arrest followed, and Tijerina was eventually tried and acquitted. But he galvanized action among the dispossessed and brought what had dwindled into a local, relatively hopeless issue to national attention, where it had not really been since the Court of Private Land Claims had claimed to resolve the issue some sixty years earlier (Tijerina 2000).

Like many other New Mexico Hispanos, such as the miners at Gallup and some at Empire Zinc, Tijerina and his followers split their time between trying to farm and migrating for wage labor. Although few other Hispanos had Tijerina's utopian fervor, many could identify with the struggle and the desire to reclaim land rightfully theirs. In the context of escalating black-white violence elsewhere in the nation over issues of poverty and economic and civil rights, and in the context of exposés about migrant farm labor that had helped end the Bracero program of immigrant "guest workers," the nation had, in the late 1960s and 1970s, a new way to read issues that Tijerina and others had been trying for decades to bring to national attention. On the federal level, pressure could be brought to resume litigation, revisit old land claim settlements, and examine educational programs that denigrated or denied New Mexico's Hispano past, language, and culture. On the state level, however, New Mexicans experienced escalating violence wrought in part by fears of dispossession by current holders of disputed land.

The courthouse raid brought enormous publicity to Tijerina and the land issue in New Mexico. Tijerina and his followers continued their protests, creating coalitions with other civil rights groups across the country and repeatedly facing arrest and incarceration until, finally, Tijerina took refuge in Mexico.

There is a certain symmetry to this twentieth-century story. New Mexico's present, like its past, remains tightly bound with that of Mexico as well as with the United States. Tijerina sought crucial information about the land grants in Mexican archives. The land grants continue to be litigated, and Mexicans continue to cross the border, legally and illegally, in search of better opportunities. Some Anglos on the border recruit them; others see them as akin to Villa's men — threats to law, order, and prosperity — and they create groups they call militias to police the border.

The border between Mexico and New Mexico remains, as it was at the beginning of the last century, an illusory demarcator of people and ideas. Who, after all, is foreign to the region? Not all Hispanos were dispossessed. There remain ranches in Hispano hands in both northern and southern New Mexico. And there remains the long history of a polyglot, racially diverse workers' struggle for rights, both civil and economic.

The New Mexico Writers' Project. Left to right: Clem Chávez, map maker and artist; Pat Chávez, assistant. Santa Fe, New Mexico, 1936. Works Progress Administration.

35

Testifying to the Silence of Servitude: Two New Mexico WPA Writers' Project Interviews

Estevan Rael-Gálvez

"Sun, silence, and adobe," mused Charles F. Lummis — "that is New Mexico in three words." These three words open *The Land of Poco Tiempo* (1893), Lummis's best-recognized book on New Mexico. Despite the many static and diminishing portrayals that follow, the Anglo American journalist and travel writer had nonetheless pointed to a profound sense of New Mexico and perhaps inadvertently to one of its most telling traditions.

A part of this tradition exists in an actual place where wisdom does *not* sit still, a place that is known and remembered as *la resolana*. This place is literally the south side of a building or a plaza, shielded from the wind and bathed in the rays of the sun. What makes this place dynamic is that for generations men have gathered there to articulate careful observations of their world, relating the memory and wisdom of those who came before them and ultimately telling New Mexico whole. Yet set against the adobe walls, the sun reflecting the stark nuances of everything it touches, some stories, even when told, hold silence still.

In the fall of 1938 and the spring of 1939, respectively, Simeon Tejada sat down and visited in *resolanas* with eighty-four-year-old José Maria Mares of Black Lake, New Mexico, and eighty-three-year-old Manuel Jesús Vasques of Peñasco, New Mexico. What these two old men told, what Simeon heard and wrote, and what was eventually translated from Spanish into English extended remarkable stories of village foundations, family origins, and, most noteworthy of all, an obscured institution in the heart of two New Mexico communities. Although

285

these foundational narratives belonged uniquely to New Mexico, by the late twentieth century these stories, like their subject, also belonged to the nation as a whole.

Laboring to Listen and Listening to Labor

When Simeon Tejada sat down in the *resolana* with the elderly Vasques and Mares, he was himself sixty years old. Even then, what Tejada could have told of his own life and reflections on his origins would have been revealing. Although he had become a citizen of the United States of America and had undoubtedly immersed himself in the New Mexico landscape, people, and their customs and history, this was something he had begun to learn only in the preceding few decades.

Born in the medieval village of Covarrubias, Spain, Simeon had decided at the age of thirty-one to leave for the United States. The reasons for his departure have long since been lost, but his was the quintessential immigrant experience in this country, starting with his arrival at Ellis Island on April 29, 1910. The Spaniard settled near Schenectedy, New York, working and waiting for more than a year until his wife, Florentina, one daughter, and three sons arrived from their own long journey across the Atlantic. Joining Florentina's brothers, by then already living in New Mexico, the Tejada family first settled in Optimo, just miles from Wagon Mound. Twelve years later the family moved west to Taos. There Tejada worked as a farmer during the next decade. By 1935, however, Tejada was about to become a part of the largest governmental intervention into cultural production in the history of United States, the project that would bring him right to the doors of Mr. Mares and Mr. Vasques.

In the face of the nation's economic depression of the 1930s, the Works Progress Administration (WPA), part of President Franklin Delano Roosevelt's New Deal, launched programs designed to implement work relief and effect a monumental government intervention that integrated a vast cultural infrastructure. As a play on the acronym and perhaps also as a social critique of this intervention, in New Mexico the WPA became known as "El Diablo a Pie," the Devil on Foot. One of several WPA programs, the Federal Writers' Project (FWP) employed writers, teachers, photographers, reporters, editors, journalists, librarians, and research workers to collect historical and cultural information. Although the program's policy was to keep its writers relatively anonymous, many of them and their so-called informants are known because the typed versions of their interviews include their names. A subsistence farmer, Simeon Tejada was one of sixty-five hundred writers drawn from the relief rolls of every state in a project that put bread on the table by hiring people to listen to and record the creativity of expression of a nation.

In New Mexico, writers under the Federal Writers' Project were instructed to interview older residents from various communities, identify cultural events that would be of interest to travelers, and catalogue the origins of place names. Remembering the creativity of the nation also involved recording the history of its people — who they were — which included defining and describing their occupations. From the interviews, written down by the interviewers from memory, emerged the stories of farmers, waitresses, teachers, miners, artists, and many others.

The occupation of Manuel Vasques must have been particularly definitive for Tejada, because following his visit he gave the interview the title "History of a Buffalo Hunter." During this interview, Vasques could not recall how he had come to live in the household of Juan Policarpio Romero, but at the age of eight he had been "herd boy" for a flock of goats belonging to Romero. Manuel went on to recount the story of a buffalo hunt that took place in 1877, when he was twenty-one. He was accompanied by several men, including a Navajo Indian named Juan Jesús Romero, whom Policarpio had "also raised." Most of the men on that hunt worked for meager wages, earning about fifty cents a day. Yet neither Manuel nor Juan Jesús earned so much as a penny.

Recognizing the disparity at the same time that he accentuated the full extent of his own labor, Manuel noted that Juan Policarpio Romero never paid him a single cent for his labor, not a cent for serving as a shepherd for his flock of goats, not a cent for the making of coffins, for which he was known and for which his *patrón* was evidently paid, not a cent for his services as a buffalo hunter or horse trader with the Indians. Stating that he had never once stepped into a schoolhouse or learned to read, Manuel noted, in a poignant revelation, that during the time his *patrón* lived, he had "never held one single penny in his hand." His *patrón* died in 1932.

It was the singular failure ever to hold the one thing we now take for granted — a penny — that for the aging Vasques seemed most to define his place and position in the world. What Tejada and Vasques knew in 1939 of the then recent debate in the halls of the U.S. Congress over the value of one's labor cannot be determined. Yet given that it was one of the framing themes of their discussion, at least as recorded by Tejada, it is interesting that less than a year had passed since Congress had passed the Fair Labor Standards Act. A major provision of the act was the establishment of the nation's first minimum wage, initially at twenty-five cents an hour, along with a maximum work week of forty-four hours. When Vasques was interviewed, he could remember his life only in terms of the seventy-five years that had marked his unremunerated labor. One thing about which he was silent was the obscurity of his origins.

Of his origins, Vasques could recall only that he was born in Chamisal, New Mexico, on January 31, 1856. According to Tejada, he "did not know how he came to live at the home of Don Juan Policarpio Romero of the village of Peñasco," which accentuates the question of his displacement all the more. The answer revolves around one of the leading issues of the day, servitude and peonage. Indeed, in the year after Vasques's birth, in an effort to counter the growing movement toward making New Mexico a slave state, New Mexico's U.S. attorney, W. W. H. Davis (1857, 303) described the advantages of the system of labor existing in New Mexico as he saw them:

> A peon can perform as much work, and can be hired for about what
> it will cost to clothe and feed a Negro, with the further advantage of

the master having no capital invested in him, which he must lose at the death of the slave. The present labor of the country is so much cheaper than any that could be introduced, that a person would hardly be justifiable in risking his capital in slaves with so little prospect of profitable return. The peons have been trained to the management of flocks and herds and are much better adapted to this pursuit than the Negro could possibly become; and there is no other employment which would yield so much profit to the master for the labor of the slave.

Beyond Davis's compelling, comparative discourse on servitude, peonage was the leading issue of the day. Litigation over the issue had in fact reached the New Mexico Supreme Court in 1857. In the ruling *Jaremillo [sic] v. Romero,* revealing the long history of peonage as custom and addressing a stark legal interpretation, Justice Kirby Benedict defined peons in the following way:

They appeared as servants, menials, or domestics, "bound" by some kind of "service" to their masters. Generally they had none or small amounts of property. The most wealthy and powerful families were flattered in their pride in displaying their retinues of these dependents. Many had been raised from childhood within the households of such families. One fact existed universally: all were indebted to their masters. This was the cord by which they seemed bound to their masters' service.

This image of master and servant bears much more consideration. This class of servitude, though significantly understudied, was foundational in the development of New Mexico, economically and culturally. Literally this lower class of laborers included thousands over the centuries, affecting the poorest of families and often creating a permanent lower class.

The Vasques family was no exception. Manuel Jesús's journey toward living in Romero's Peñasco household actually began less than five miles away in Chamisal. Church records reveal that Manuel Jesús's father may have been recorded as unknown at the time of his baptism, so that the child was identified solely as the son of Maria Dolores de Jesús Vasques. When the federal census enumerator arrived in Chamisal in 1860, the five-year-old Manuel was identified in the household with his mother, Dolores, four sisters, two brothers, and Mauricio Argüello, a stepfather. The family was listed with absolutely no real estate, and Mauricio was identified as a shoemaker with only $150 to his name. Ten years later Manuel was enumerated in the 1870 federal census in Juan Policarpio Romero's home, identified as a fourteen-year-old "domestic." This was the household Vasques would become a part of, living and serving in it.

Vasques was not the only one serving in the household. In recounting his own story, he also shared that of the Navajo Juan Jesús, who had been baptized in 1865 and incorporated into the Romero household. Although the story of Juan Jesús is sparse, if Tejada had indeed immersed himself in the history and culture of New Mexico, then the presence of former American Indian slaves would not have appeared unusual to him. Many former slaves were then still living. The story of one of these persons had recently been shared with Tejada.

Out of the Shadows of Slavery

One of the best-recognized products of the Federal Writers' Project embodied a concerted effort to document the legacy of slavery. Interviewers were charged explicitly with writing down the recollections of thousands of aged African Americans about their lives under the American South's "peculiar institution." It was a moment when many of those who had lived through slavery were still alive. Many scholars had already been working diligently to overturn Reconstruction-era stereotypes and fully recognize the importance of slavery in U.S. history. This project similarly proposed to counter decades of the institution's invisibility, revealing that at the heart of American history was the foundational story of African American slavery.

The critical importance of this effort cannot be overemphasized. Yet in regions such as the Southwest, no one was looking for these types of stories. Part of a larger context of both narratives of slavery and American Indian histories, José Maria Mares's story is still relatively unknown, and it is almost unique as a firsthand account by one of thousands of American Indians who were captured and held as servants in households throughout New Mexico during the nineteenth century. A few other early-twentieth-century writings represent people who recollected the presence of indigenous servants, but only one other firsthand account has been located. Mares's narrative offers an entry into the particular, if not peculiar, colonialism and its foothold of slavery experienced by indigenous people of the Southwest. This is why the Tejada-Mares interview in Mares's *resolana* in 1938 is so remarkable.

Only forty inhabitants resided in Black Lake when Simeon Tejada arrived at the home of eighty-four-year-old José Maria Mares. Following that interview Tejada wrote that Black Lake's "first inhabitants were Don José Maria Mares and his second wife, Doña Jenara Trujillo, in the year 1886." (Mares had married Adelaida Argüello in 1875, become a widower in 1881, and married Trujillo in 1882.) The couple "moved to Black Lake with their three year old son named Amadeo." According to the Mares-Tejada account, to get to Black Lake, the family traveled by wagon. "Don José Maria went through a lot of hardship. He went to the Lake because the Government gave him a ranch, where he built himself a log cabin, [and] to be able to feed himself and family he would hunt deer and bears take the hides to Taos, a distance of 30 miles which he walked, sell them there, buy his food, carry it on his back the same way he did the hides, and walk back to the Lake." Although Mares had lived at Black Lake for fifty-two years, his journey there was deeply storied.

Tejada reported that "Don José Maria Mares is uncertain as to the date of his birth." But unlike Vasques, who could not remember how he had come to live in Romero's home, Mares at least could recall how he was displaced: he was captured in 1857, "when he was about nine years old."

> The parents of Don José Maria Mares were Navajo Indians. When he was about nine years old, a party that was hunting Indians captured him, his brother and three Indian girls, that was in 1857. They were taken to Taos and sold to Don Juan Mares, the said José Maria and the three Indian girls, who adopted them as his own children. In 1861 they were baptized, he was given the name of José Maria, one of the girls Guadalupe, the other Candelaria and the other Prudencia, this last one went back to the Navajo Reservation near Gallup when the United States Government liberated slavery. Don José Maria Mares and the three Indian girls were baptized in Taos by Father Gabriel… in 1861.

In describing his captivity and particularly the emancipation of Prudencia, Mares reveals a full understanding of his place in the history of U.S. slavery. Like Vasques's childhood displacement, which coincided with slavery's becoming a defining issue at the end of the 1850s, Mares's peculiar displacement coincided with the expansion of the issue of servitude in policy discussions to include American Indian slavery by the 1860s.

Chief Justice Kirby Benedict, who had already taken up the question of "free labor" as it had come before the Territorial Supreme Court in 1857, had by 1865 also spoken on the issue of Indian slavery. He testified that "the Indian persons obtained… are treated by those who claim to own them as their servants and slaves." By 1868 the move against abolishing the system locally had reached beyond military intervention and into the courts.

Exactly seventy years before Tejada's visit to the Mares household, W. W. Griffin, a U.S. commissioner, arrived in New Mexico with the charge of emancipating, through the courts, American Indians still held in households throughout the territory. Griffin ultimately brought 435 cases before a grand jury, charging each person with holding either Indian slaves or peons. Accordingly, Vicente F. Mares was charged with holding five Indian slaves. Although Tejada's 1938 account recognizes that José Maria's original owner was Juan Mares, ecclesiastical, census, and probate records reveal that Juan Mares died in 1865, bequeathing all his holdings to his wife and children. Three years later, when Griffin arrived, he did not account for the fact that Juan's widow, Juana Gonzales, remained the head of household, and he charged her son with the crime instead. The 1870 federal census lists Gonzales as head of the household, which still held at least four Indian slaves, including José Maria. What should not be lost in translation is that these slaves were passed down across generations.

Acknowledging the long history of the slave trade, the grand jury nevertheless failed to indict any of the accused, on the basis of a lack of evidence that they had intentionally or maliciously violated the law. Although Griffin would claim that in spite of the paralyzing blow dealt him by the grand jury, he had more than shaken the practice of Indian slavery in New Mexico. He claimed that because of his efforts, many slaves and peons were released, although careful research into family, state, and federal records reveals otherwise. Nevertheless, in the end, the documents Griffin produced tell a great deal about the people involved in the practice of holding Indian slaves.

One part of this telling is that those charged with the crimes were intricately connected to one another through kinship and community. For instance, among the many others charged with holding Indian slaves in their households were Vicente Mares's brother, Felipe Mares, his future wife, Benina Lee, and his mother-in-law, Luz Tafoya. The priest in the Tejada-Mares narrative, Father Gabriel Ussell, was also charged with the crime of holding an Indian slave. Even Manuel Jesús Vasques's master, Juan Policarpio Romero, was charged, not with holding a peon (Vasques) but with holding one slave, the Navajo Juan Jesús Romero. Collectively, the Mares brothers, Lee, her mother, Father Ussell, and Romero held seventeen Indian slaves. Each of those captives had a story. Most of these remain untold.

Toward a Conclusion

As they might have appeared in 1938 and 1939, even now these two stories of captivity and servitude are seemingly out of place as slave narratives in the United States of America, which continues to echo not only of another place but of another people. What remains most striking about the stories of Manuel Jesús Vasques and José Maria Mares is the wonder that they were collected at all. Considering that more than two thousand slave narratives were collected from the American South, the existence of so few firsthand accounts of American Indian slaves in the Southwest is astonishing. Vasques's and Mares's stories are two rare first-person narratives of captivity and slavery, not far removed from the experiences of ex-slaves interviewed by Federal Writers' Project workers in the South.

Although foundational to New Mexico and to the United States, these rare stories have been obscured over time, part of the erasure of the real violence associated with captivity and servitude. This obscurity even bears upon the way writers and historians have retold the two men's stories. Geographer Robert Julyan (1998, 40), for example, glossed Mares's captivity as, "Years earlier, in 1857, Mares had been captured by Indians while he and his brother were hunting." Casting Mares as having been captured by Indians differs dramatically from the Mares-Tejada interview: "When he was about nine years old, a party that was hunting Indians captured him, his brother and three Indian girls." Interpretation is critical, for history is a contest of stories.

The original interviews with Mares and Vasques are not the unfiltered perspectives they may at first appear to be. One can only imagine what the actual chats in the *resolanas* revealed. Following the interview, Tejada sat down to recollect the conversation and inscribed it in Spanish. This telling was then sent to translators — Josie Sanchez for the Mares account and Lorin W. Brown for the Vasques account — who converted the story from Spanish to English. Later it was edited by other Writers' Project workers. Just as memory is often subject to scrutiny, this process and the documents it produced should be subjected to the question, What is lost in translation? The answer is part of the story of silence.

If Charles F. Lummis's three words — sun, silence, and adobe — are indeed New Mexico, they lack only the stark contrasts and details that the Vasques and Mares narratives both reveal and conceal. The present tense of testimony is incredibly powerful, and these two narratives of the 1930s WPA project are particularly illustrative of this strength. Telling of a silence, they break through it, pointing to the most pressing issues of the day. In these two accounts, the tellers' origin stories emerge as violent and obscured displacements that, along with the story of free labor, marked each man's consciousness in memories that remained palpable in old age. This legacy has been quieted over the years, by whispers as much as by silence, hushed aside even by those who have inherited the story, people who carry, in their faces and hands, if not the story's geography then certainly its memory in aching consciousness. In the end, it is imperative to recognize that these were not simply imagined stories. They were experienced, they were lived, and they remain telling of who we are as New Mexicans.

36

New Mexico during the
Second World War

Ferenc M. Szasz

The Second World War began on September 1, 1939, when the German Wehrmacht invaded Poland. But as the United States remained officially neutral, the fighting in Europe seemed light years away from regional concerns. Newspaper headlines covered the fall of France and the Battle of Britain, of course, but local issues commanded the brunt of New Mexico's attention.

Throughout 1940, for example, the state devoted an enormous amount of energy to commemorating the four-hundredth anniversary (1540–1940) of the European arrival in the Southwest. Begun in 1935, the Coronado Cuarto Centennial Commission, as it was termed, helped arrange about 175 folk festivals across New Mexico, Arizona, west Texas, Kansas, and Oklahoma, including fiestas, rodeos, cowboy reunions, local city celebrations, and Native American dances. The most extravagant ceremonies involved seventeen massive "Entrada" pageants, in which some five hundred to a thousand people, all dressed in period costumes, reenacted the Coronado story in eighteen dramatic episodes. The federal government issued a commemorative Coronado stamp, first released from the main Albuquerque post office on September 7, 1940, and the Cuarto Centennial Commission inaugurated a scholarly book publishing project that lasted for several years afterward.

Perhaps the key publication sponsored by the commission, together with the University of New Mexico, was *New Mexico: A Guide to the Colorful State*, a volume in the famed WPA American Guide Series, published by the New York firm Hastings House in August 1940. Written largely by New

A Japanese picture, captured in the Philippines by the U.S. Army, showing the infamous death march of 1942 from Bataan approaching Camp O'Donnell. Associated Press photograph from the United States Army.

Mexicans from around the state and initially edited by Ina Sizer Cassidy of Santa Fe, the *Guide* provided the first significant national introduction to what had become the "Land of Enchantment" since the establishment of the New Mexico State Tourist Bureau in 1935. Part encyclopedia and part tourist brochure, the book benefited from writers who found something intriguing to say about every area of the state.

The 571-page *Guide* provides a fascinating glimpse into this era. In 1940, New Mexico's population was slightly over half a million, but it averaged only six people per square mile. As the *Guide* frankly admitted, the state was still "in many respects a frontier" (*New Mexico* 1940, vii, xx, 8). The largest city, Albuquerque, claimed only 35,000 people, while Santa Fe at 20,000 and Las Vegas at 12,000 ranked second and third, respectively.

Moreover, the vast expanse of land in New Mexico — fourth largest of the then forty-eight states — harbored a variety of distinct subcultures. Straddling the middle and northern Rio Grande Valley and stretching west to Zuni, Pueblo Indians tilled the land as their ancestors had done for centuries. In the northwest, Navajo herdsmen pastured their sheep and goats throughout their sprawling reservation in New Mexico, Arizona, and Utah. Scores of compact Hispanic farm villages dotted the central Rio Grande Valley as well as the northern counties, where people spoke a Spanish dialect that Coronado's soldiers would easily have recognized. In the far northwest, Latter-day Saints had created a thriving agricultural community along the San Juan River, whereas Anglo American cattle and sheep ranchers, usually hailing from states of the former Confederacy, dominated the southern plains and the fertile Mesilla Valley. Outside the major towns and cities, the *Guide* advised visitors to carry their own water, carefully noting that it recommended tours only to "the most accessible places."

Harsh though the New Mexico environment might have appeared, the *Guide* also emphasized the haunting beauty of the landscape, especially the seemingly endless space. "The needs of the Nation have not pressed the resources of the State to development," it solemnly noted, "but the time will come" (*New Mexico* 1940, 8). With the Japanese attack on Pearl Harbor on December 7, 1941, the time had indeed arrived.

Although the demands of almost four years of war affected every state in the union, they genuinely revolutionized New Mexico. Young men from provincial backgrounds found themselves fighting in every corner of the globe, and when they returned they refused to accept the social status quo. Faced with potential food shortages, the state's commercial farmers, sheepmen, and cattle ranchers devised ingenious means to produce better and more abundant agricultural products. And a drastically increased federal presence — especially as seen in the top-secret city of Los Alamos — introduced a scientific and technical expertise to the state that would totally transform its economy in the postwar years.

All this is clear in retrospect. But the New Mexicans who lived through the harrowing war years of 1941–45 regularly confronted two other overwhelming concerns: a haunting uncertainty regarding their soldiers serving overseas and an all-pervasive domestic secrecy. I look at the uncertainty first.

Bataan

All families with relatives in uniform kept their fingers crossed for the duration, but the hand of fate rested with terrible force on those who joined the New Mexico National Guard. During the 1930s, Great Depression poverty had combined with patriotism to encourage several hundred New Mexicans to sign up with the guard. Originally a cavalry unit, the guard had special appeal to skilled riders; indeed, General Douglas MacArthur once affectionately termed its men "my New Mexico horsethieves." But in the late 1930s the guard shed the cavalry designation to become the 200th Coast Artillery (Anti-Aircraft).

On January 6, 1941, the unit was federalized and sent to Fort Bliss, Texas, for additional training. Because of the men's excellent training record and the fact that many of them spoke Spanish, the army posted the 200th to the Philippine Islands in September 1941. Its primary assignment revolved around the protection of Clark Air Field, northwest of Manila. (A splinter group, the 515th, was later created from the 200th, but the latter remained the primary unit.) Equipped with antiquated World War I equipment and ammunition, the 200th confronted the full force of a Japanese invasion on December 8, 1941. (The Japanese attack was precisely coordinated with the attack on Pearl Harbor, but because the Philippines lie on the opposite side of the International Date Line, it was officially the next day.) Thus, New Mexico's 200th Coast Artillery has been credited with firing the first shots for the Allies in the Pacific theater.

Then its troubles began. Overwhelmed by thousands of battle-hardened Japanese veterans, fresh from the conquest of parts of China, the 200th helped cover the retreat of American and Philippine troops south into the Bataan Peninsula. Both official and unofficial radio broadcasts urged the troops to hold on, because relief would soon arrive. But the relief never came (Dyess 1944). Much of the U.S. Pacific Fleet lay at the bottom of the bay at Pearl Harbor, and U.S. military officers had long decided that the Nazi conquests in Europe demanded first attention. As one top cabinet member sadly noted, there are times in war when men must die (Cave 1996; Griffin and Matson 1989; Sides 2004).

Armed with antiquated weapons, ill with malaria, and virtually starving, the Bataan soldiers faced insuperable odds. When President Franklin D. Roosevelt ordered General MacArthur to depart for Australia, his seconds in command, Generals Edward King and Jonathan Wainwright, found themselves forced to surrender approximately seventy thousand U.S. and Filipino troops, including the roughly eighteen hundred men of the New Mexico 200th, in April 1942—the largest capitulation in the history of the American military. From the various surrender points, the men were force-marched on a sixty-five-mile journey, without food or water, to Japanese prisoner-of-war camps. Those who fell or could not continue were bayoneted or shot, in what later became known as the Bataan Death March. The survivors then faced more than three years as POWs in the most brutal of circumstances as the Japanese government refused to abide by the rules of the 1929 Geneva Convention.

Back home, the suffering of families and friends of the 200th proved almost as agonizing, for they received virtually no information about the men — only the official U.S. government notice that they were now Japanese POWs. By happenstance, only ten days after Bataan fell, famed BBC reporter Alistair Cooke visited Deming, New Mexico, home base of the 200th and a community that had lost 150 men out of a population of 2,000. Discovering the entire town in mourning, with businesses closed and shades drawn, he quietly noted that no British village could match Deming "on the count of personal sacrifice" (Cooke 2006, 111).

For almost two years, news regarding the Bataan POWs filtered back with agonizing slowness. As late as January 1944, New Mexicans knew the fates of only two hundred of the eighteen hundred men. Dr. V. H. Spensley of Albuquerque created the Bataan Relief Organization, which devoted countless hours to gathering any scraps of information it could. In March 1943, Douglas MacArthur promised Spensley that although he could tell him little that he did not already know, "if I live, I shall return to save them" (*New York Times*, March 6, 1943).

This agonizing uncertainty became painfully accented in late January 1944, when the U.S. military finally released the account compiled by escaped POW Lieutenant Colonel William Dyess. The Dyess Report, which provided the nation with the first authenticated version of the Bataan Death March and the atrocious conditions of the Japanese POW camps, made headline news across the state. A spokesman from Carlsbad, which had lost more than a hundred men at Bataan, said that Japan must "pay for [its] inhumanity." From Santa Fe a general declared that such inhumane treatment "must not go unanswered."

The rage that swept the state reminded people of sentiments following the attack on Pearl Harbor (*Albuquerque Journal*, January 28, 1944). For most Americans, the national rallying cry was "Remember Pearl Harbor," but for New Mexicans, the phrase that appeared on many newspaper mastheads read, "Remember Pearl Harbor and Bataan." Of the approximately eighteen hundred members of the 200th, only about nine hundred returned alive. New Mexico thus had the dubious distinction of having lost more servicemen in proportion to its population than any other state in the union.

The intense suffering and maddening uncertainty surrounding the fate of the 200th account for the prominence of the name "Bataan" throughout the state today. Santa Fe boasts a Bataan Memorial government building, Taos and Albuquerque both have Bataan Memorial parks, and Deming has erected an impressive monument. The list could be extended. Truly a small-town tragedy, the Bataan story is woven into the very fabric of New Mexico history.

Code Talkers

A second major role for New Mexico in the war — also surrounded by secrecy and uncertainty, this time until 1968 — involved the Navajo Code Talkers. Although the army had drawn on Native American languages for codes during the First World War, the idea of using the Navajo language for this purpose originated with engineer Philip Johnson, who had spent his youth on the reservation as the son of a Presbyterian missionary.

Marine Corps officers initially expressed skepticism, but they changed their minds after a successful demonstration of the versatility of the Navajo language. Shortly afterward the Marines recruited twenty-nine Navajo young men, ranging in age from sixteen to thirty-four. In July 1942 the *New York Times* reported that twenty-nine "Navajo Indian warriors" had finished their Marine Corps training and were now ready for assignment (*New York Times*, July 5, 1942). What the *Times* did not report was that the men trained as marines during the day and then spent endless hours at night devising what turned out to be an unbreakable military code.

Because the Navajo language remained unwritten in 1942, and only about nineteen non-Navajos spoke it — none of them Japanese — the young marines might simply have used the Navajo language itself. Instead, they forged a substitution system whereby military terms were encoded in familiar reservation images. The term "fighter plane" became the Navajo words for "iron rain," dive bomber, "chicken hawk," submarine, "iron fish," and so forth. The United States was simply "our mother." As Code Talker Carl Gorman later recalled, "I went in to fight for Indian lands. The Navajos have always thought this is our land, and we have all the rights to fight for it" (*Albuquerque Journal Magazine*, June 9, 1981).

Japanese cryptographers eventually concluded that the American code was transmitted in the Navajo language, but they could go no further. They even tortured Navajo POW Joseph Kieyoomia of the 200th, but he knew nothing of the secret Code Talker program.

One might assume that the Code Talkers were heaped with honor after 1945, but the military decided that it might need the code in the future and so instructed the approximately four hundred Code Talker veterans to say nothing. The onset of computer-based cryptography allowed the military to change its mind, and in 1968 the Marine Corps released the Code Talker story to the nation. The Code Talkers held their first public reunion in 1971.

Although many from the original group had passed on, the survivors finally began to receive the honors they had long deserved. In 1982 President Ronald Reagan awarded Congressional Gold Medals to the remaining members of the original twenty-nine, and Silver Medals to the others. A decade later the Code Talkers marched in President Bill Clinton's inaugural parade. Veteran Sam Billison lived long enough to provide the voice — in Navajo — for the G.I. Joe Code Talker doll. Tribal spokesmen proudly noted that the power of the Navajo language had become a weapon that helped win the most destructive war in history (McClain 2001; Paul 1973).

New Mexicans in Other Combat Areas

In addition to defending Bataan and serving in the Code Talkers, New Mexicans served on every battlefront of the war. About one hundred New Mexicans were stationed at Pearl Harbor, and at least five perished in the attack. Three others participated in the 1942 Jimmie Doolittle raid over Japan, and one, Sergeant Paul Leonard of Artesia, earned a Distinguished Flying Cross for his role as a gunner in the attack. Several WACs worked as drivers for Los Alamos scientists. The monthly series "New Mexicans in the War" by *New Mexico Magazine*, usually accompanied by photographs, revealed how extensive their assignments were.

Las Cruces native James Buchanan Williams enlisted in the famed Tuskegee Airmen, an African American team of pilots who flew support for bombing runs in the European theater. "We were fighting a war to free others," Williams later observed, "and we were still considered subhuman...it was unusual for us to be in combat" (*Aggie Panorama*, March 1974, 15; Thomas, Billington, and Walter 1994). In March 2007 President George W. Bush awarded all surviving Tuskegee airmen, including three New Mexicans, the Congressional Gold Medal. From all regions, all ethnic groups, and all walks of life, New Mexicans between 1941 and 1945 found themselves scattered around the globe.

Ranching and Agriculture

As the 1940 *Guide* observed, the state's economy revolved largely around ranching and agriculture. The war proved revolutionary there as well. In 1940 the state claimed more than thirty-four thousand farms and ranches, but many farms hardly ranked above the subsistence level, and numerous ranches on the Great Plains lay more than a hundred miles from the railheads necessary to market their cattle.

From the onset of United States participation in the war, area farmers and ranchers recognized that increased food production would be crucial on many fronts. In early 1942 the federal government inaugurated a "Food for Victory" campaign, which publicized an elaborate "food pyramid" to remind citizens to eat properly, because "America Needs You Strong" (Gold 1950; Wilcox 1947). In addition, the state's agricultural producers recognized that the United States would probably eventually be feeding the starving populations of Europe. Indeed, in 1948 the *New York Times* ranked food shortages as "the world's number one economic problem."

Although state agricultural interests ranged from apple orchards in the northern Rio Grande Valley to commercial vegetable production near Grants and cotton growing in the Mesilla Valley, the sheep and cattle industries were the most prominent and best organized. Both knew how important their products would be to any victory. In a world before synthetic fibers, wool proved essential not only for domestic clothing but also for military blankets, uniforms, and flight jackets, especially for flying crews, because many Allied aircraft remained unheated. State wool producers chalked up the Russian defeat of the German invaders largely to the fact that the German army had not been sufficiently supplied with adequate winter woolen coats.

So, too, with the cattle industry. The government's food pyramid recommended meat at least once a day, and state ranchers understood that they would have to drastically increase production to help feed the armed forces. Unlike the Detroit auto industry, which could shift from automobiles to tanks within a few months, ranchers knew they would need years to increase their output. They remained fully aware, as their motto put it, that "wool and beef will win this war."

Generally conservative in lifestyle and politics, the state's ranchers kept one eye firmly on the future. Many recalled the boom-and-bust period after the First World War, and nearly everyone remembered the terrible drought and dustbowl years of the 1930s (Weigle 1985). They also recognized that New Mexico was a fragile land. It could never absorb a dramatic expansion of pasture for cattle or sheep. Thus, industry spokesmen viewed their wartime assignment as less a call to produce "more" — the land simply could not take it — than to produce a better product. Sheepmen were urged to cull weak ewes and to breed ewes only with the strongest rams. Similarly, ranchers were urged to market 15 percent more cattle, but only through systematic culling and better breeding practices (Keleher 1942).

Agents from the New Mexico Agricultural and Mechanical College (later New Mexico State University) assisted in both endeavors. In 1944 the Bell Ranch in northeastern New Mexico introduced to the state the very latest scientific research on range cattle improvement. This included keeping careful records on every breeding animal, ignoring "looks," and breeding only for increased fecundity (Remley 1993).

Fortunately, Mother Nature generally smiled on New Mexico for most of the war years. During this time, Great Plains cattlemen sowed the seeds for their unprecedented postwar prosperity. Although cattle and sheep did not increase markedly in numbers from 1940 to 1945, their value per head almost doubled. Hog and dairy cow production showed similar increases (Cockerill 1958).

The new federal-state program of standardization and better breeding affected commercial vegetable growers as well. Much of the state's prewar vegetable harvest had been decidedly helter-skelter. From 1942 forward, authorities placed an emphasis on sorting crops by size and grading all fruit and vegetables. Growers quickly realized that standardized grades of peanuts, carrots, onions, potatoes, tomatoes, cabbages, and beans brought higher prices. The erection of new canneries also made it easier to market produce, and from 1941 to 1943 the state's agricultural production tripled. As one writer observed, "the New Mexican farmer is building a highly significant war industry by producing more and better vegetables for state and nation" (Hood 1943).

So many New Mexico farm and ranch boys had been drafted, however, that fall harvest seasons always produced moments of crisis. The shortage of farmworkers remained so acute that local draft boards tracked down state residents who had moved to California to work in the well-paying aircraft and shipbuilding industries and gave them the choice of either returning to agricultural work or being drafted.

In the absence of men, New Mexico women found themselves called upon to assume a new set of duties. Those who lived in towns were soon driving taxis and running filling stations, among other occupations. Women not only supervised the raising of children but also sewed garments for the Red Cross and headed local war bond drives — in which New Mexico invariably led the nation in per capita giving. With new materials at a premium, ranch women learned to improvise, repair, and conserve. Often they roped, cut, and branded cattle alongside the men. As Grant County ranch wife Lorene Threepersons (1943) observed, "cowboys in this part of the world are as scarce as coffee and sugar."

Although gasoline rationing in New Mexico proved twice as generous as in the East, new agricultural machinery was hard to come by. From 1942 onward, horses and mules began to make a comeback on regional farms. This move was cheered by Lieutenant Colonel F. H. Hamilton of the U.S. Army Re-Mount Service in Silver City, who had long argued that increasing horse herds would prove essential to both the military and civilian fronts. He urged farmers to rely on work horses for short hauls rather than waste precious gasoline. The return of the horse, he maintained, would greatly aid the war effort: "Let's go horsemen! Here's a chance to bring the horse back into his own" ("Mustang" 1942).

The horse did make a brief comeback, and the dude ranch industry replaced automobiles with pack trains whenever possible. Writing from Santa Fe in 1943, Ruth Laughlin remarked that riding had become not only a form of exercise but also a sure means of transportation. "Horses have come into their own again," she noted, "and are available at every ranch and resort" (*New York Times*, June 13, 1943). Renewed reliance on horses had special appeal on the sprawling Navajo reservation. Reservation horse races resumed their former popularity, and most Navajos attended the wartime annual Gallup Inter-tribal Indian Ceremonial in horse-drawn wagons.

As the war dragged on, the demand for fall agricultural labor became even more acute. In 1945, American farmers estimated that they needed a million extra workers to bring in the crops. New Mexico farmers actively recruited Navajo women and children along these lines, and from 1942 forward the federal government began importing foreign workers at harvest time. By 1944 almost seventy thousand Mexican workers — participants in the famed Bracero program — helped bring in the harvests.

In 1944–45 the government drew on the efforts of more than a hundred thousand prisoners-of-war as well. Because New Mexico housed two large POW camps, at Roswell and Lordsburg, such labor lay readily at hand. Many German and Italian POWs originally hailed from peasant families and knew well the demands of the harvest season. Although local farmers grumbled that POW labor never proved as efficient as free-market labor, in general the prisoners performed satisfactorily. The exception lay in cotton picking. There the POWs had no previous experience, and few could master the demanding labor of filling the long cotton sacks in the Mesilla Valley (Schmid 2005).

Quite literally, the Second World War transformed New Mexico agriculture. By 1954 the number of state farms had dropped by thirteen thousand while the average acreage of those remaining had more than doubled. With increased size came increased production, efficiency, and profits. Aided by the wartime creation of improved food processing plants, oil mills for peanuts and cottonseed, and better fruit and vegetable grading, packing, and cooling facilities, New Mexico agriculture began to gain a national reputation. In the postwar decade the Clovis cattle auction ranked twenty-fourth in the nation, and the Roswell sheep auction came in at sixteenth. In 1954 an agricultural writer observed that during the mid-1920s, New Mexico had been scorned by the East for producing poor cotton, low-grade wool, and inferior cattle. No longer. By mid-century the state's agricultural production ranked favorably with that of any other state in the nation (Cockerill 1958, 5–7).

The Economy

The demands of the war turned New Mexico's economy upside down. Severe gasoline rationing cut the number one industry — tourism — to a trickle. But a much-increased federal presence via scattered government installations more than made up the difference.

The federal presence could be felt in almost every area of the state. Clovis, Albuquerque, Carlsbad, Alamogordo, Fort Sumner, and Roswell all housed Army Air Corps bases, each with a different emphasis. Roswell and Carlsbad trained bombardiers; Fort Sumner instructed glider pilots. The Albuquerque airfield (today's Kirtland Air Force Base) became the key installation for the region. Even Grant County, which had no military installation, benefited as the wilderness area north of Silver City became a popular recreation point for soldiers and civilians.

Increased governmental demands for precious metals reinvigorated the state's slumping mining interests. Marginal mines switched from placer gold to producing zinc, lead, and iron. The upsurge of demand for pumice and fluorspar in the Grants region even overshadowed the extensive Bluewater Irrigation District production of carrots and other vegetables (Kutnewsky 1943).

The two largest state universities felt the effects as well. With so many students and faculty serving in the military, class sizes plummeted, but the Naval Reserve Officer Training Corps program at the University of New Mexico, as well as similar military projects at New Mexico Agricultural and Mechanical College, helped take up the slack. In 1943 UNM introduced an engineering program primarily for women. Assorted anti-Hitler rallies on the campuses helped raise funds for the various war bond drives.

The Japanese Internment Camp in Santa Fe

By consensus, the federal government's most grievous wartime error came with President Roosevelt's February 19, 1942, executive order to displace all persons of Japanese ancestry living in the West Coast region and send them to scattered internment camps for the duration. New Mexico did not lie within the designated coastal war zone, so the state's approximately four hundred Japanese-American families did not suffer the same degree of humiliation as their West Coast relations. Indeed, shortly after war was declared, the Italian American mayor of Gallup sought out the leading Japanese farmer of the region to assure him that nothing would happen to either one of them. Similarly, a proposal to evacuate the Japanese growers from the Grants region was overwhelmingly voted down. Roy Nakayama, who grew up in the Mesilla Valley, fought in the Battle of the Bulge and served time in a German POW camp. When he returned to New Mexico State University after the war, he proved vital in creating the state's chile industry (Tod 1994).

Although Japanese residents of the state did not suffer relocation, in March 1942 Santa Fe became home to a major Japanese internment camp. Of much lower profile than the camps at Manzanar, California, and Poston, Arizona, the Santa Fe center held a total of 4,555 internees — largely Japanese — during its four years of existence. This camp was unique because it was run by the U.S. Immigration Service and housed enemy aliens as well as people the government considered "militant" (Melzer 1994).

For reasons that remain unclear, the Santa Fe Internment Camp has received relatively little publicity. Only scattered photos survive, and few Santa Feans mourned its closing in the spring of 1946 (*Santa Fe New Mexican*, March 20, 1946).

The original camp eventually evolved into the Casa Solano subdivision, with the only remnant of the war years reflected in the large shade trees planted by the internees. But the emotions of the war smoldered for more than half a century, and when Santa Feans proposed in the late 1990s to erect a monument to the camp, the City Different became embroiled in bitter controversy. The monument proposal drew angry responses from local Bataan veterans, who vehemently opposed the idea. The City Council meeting that eventually passed the proposal almost erupted into a fist-fight. In March 2002 the monument was dedicated, and with this, the secrecy that had surrounded the camp forever disappeared.

Los Alamos

If uncertainty and secrecy cloaked the stories of the Bataan prisoners, the Navajo Code Talkers, and the Santa Fe Internment Camp, they absolutely dominated the saga of Los Alamos. From its inception in 1942 to the president's announcement on August 6, 1945, the scientific laboratory on the Hill remained the most closely guarded secret of the war.

Alerted by British research that a nuclear weapon in German hands was a real possibility, the army created a new oversight agency, the Manhattan Engineer District, and in the summer of 1942 placed General Leslie R. Groves in charge. The mission of the Manhattan Project proved both simple and complex: to produce an atomic weapon in the shortest possible time. Under Groves's blunt but forceful direction, the Manhattan Project confiscated enormous tracts of land in eastern Tennessee and south-eastern Washington State to erect two gigantic factories, Oak Ridge and Hanford, to produce the fissionable materials uranium 235 and plutonium. Shortly afterward, in the spring of 1943, the government took over the campus of the New Mexico Ranch School in Los Alamos as well as several nearby Hispanic ranches on the Pajarito Plateau.

There, amid perhaps the most scenic fifty square miles in the nation, they erected a secret scientific laboratory with one goal: to beat the Germans to the atomic bomb. The isolation, vast spaces, and sparse population made New Mexico ideal for such a project. Rail and air connections proved adequate, military police might easily guard the laboratory, and G2 (Army Intelligence) could quickly spot inquiring strangers. Moreover, the director of Los Alamos, J. Robert Oppenheimer, harbored a deep affection for the region, for in the early 1920s it had helped restore him to health. Locating the laboratory on the mesa, he once observed, allowed him to unite his two great loves: physics and New Mexico (Szasz 1984, 2006).

From 1943 to 1945, Los Alamos grew from a handful of buildings into a bustling community of about seven thousand people, all of them engaged in the most intense industrial-scientific effort the world had ever seen. Oppenheimer convinced most of the top physicists of the day to join the team, including refugees Edward Teller and Hans Bethe. In late 1943 and early 1944 an equally talented group of British scientists, including Soviet spy Klaus Fuchs, arrived as well.

Oppenheimer presided over this brilliant, multi-talented conglomeration with consummate skill. "He was one of the smartest men the world has ever seen," recalled former colleague Robert Duffield, "and there is no doubt he was the director, the boss." Working fifteen-hour days, six days a week, the scientists produced two types of nuclear weapons: the uranium bomb, Little Boy, which destroyed Hiroshima, and the plutonium weapon, Fat Man, which destroyed Nagasaki. Although the uranium weapon was never field tested, the plutonium bomb proved so complex that the scientists asked for an actual test before any combat use.

After considerable searching, the army chose a location in the northwest section of the Alamogordo Bombing Range for the test. Oppenheimer gave it the name "Trinity Site." In a frenzy of activity during the spring of 1945, army workers erected the largest outdoor laboratory in the world about thirty miles east of Socorro. At the epicenter — under armed guard on a hundred-foot steel tower — rested "the Gadget." There, at five-thirty on the morning of July 16, 1945, the Los Alamos scientists detonated the world's first atomic weapon. The light proved as intense as that of the sun, and the sound waves broke windowpanes as far away as Gallup. The blast could have been seen from the moon.

Any explosion of this magnitude would naturally have commanded front-page headlines, but army security pressured local newspapers to print only a "planted" story that an ammunition dump had accidentally detonated and that it might be necessary to temporarily evacuate certain parts of the state.

Thanks to army security, no East Coast paper carried the tale of the explosion. Only the *El Paso Herald-Post* challenged security by headlining the event. But the official explanation fooled few locals. "I know a bomb when I see one," said a regional ranch woman (Szasz 1984, 87). Consequently, many New Mexicans became privy to a secret that the world would not comprehend until August 6, the day President Harry S. Truman officially revealed the Allied bombing of Hiroshima.

With Truman's announcement, the veil of secrecy that had surrounded Los Alamos collapsed. "Los Alamos Secret Disclosed by Truman," headlined the *Santa Fe New Mexican*. "Deadliest Weapon in World's History Made in Santa Fe." The atomic age had its origins in New Mexico.

Celebration of the End of the War

Although historians have argued that there was no single day when the Second World War ended, there is general agreement that the peace arrived in two distinct installments. On May 7, 1945, the Germans officially surrendered, and President Truman declared May 8 as Victory in Europe (VE) day. In New Mexico, however, where the focus lay largely on the Pacific theater, prevailing sentiment agreed that the task was only "half done." Governor John J. Dempsey requested that VE Day be commemorated as a day of patriotic and religious observance "rather than a day of merry making." As the editor of the *Santa Fe New Mexican* (May 8, 1945) put it, "we can be grateful, but we cannot be ecstatic."

About three months later, after the Allies had dropped atomic weapons on Hiroshima and Nagasaki, after the Soviet army had joined the Pacific conflict, and after a bitter internal struggle in the Japanese cabinet, Japan officially surrendered, on August 14, 1945. The most destructive war in the history of humankind had finally come to an end. In gratitude, Truman requested that the nation observe the following Sunday, August 19, as a National Day of Prayer and Remembrance, dedicated to the memory of those who had lost their lives and giving thanks to God for the victory (*Public Papers* 1961, 223).

New Mexicans greeted Truman's initial announcement of the surrender with wild abandon. From Farmington to Las Cruces, cars began impromptu parades — all with horns blaring — followed by endless parties. Unlike the restraint of VE Day, on August 14 the state dissolved in a paroxysm of joy. Farmington staged an impromptu street dance, and "pandemonium" reigned in Lordsburg. The victory celebration continued all week.

The arrival of the Sunday Day of Prayer and Remembrance, however, found the state in a very different mood. Like the rest of the nation, New Mexicans filed into churches and synagogues with mixed emotions, complicated further by the painful memories of Bataan and the recent disclosure of Los Alamos. By chance, the famed Gallup Inter-tribal Indian Ceremonial had been scheduled for the same weekend, and many Indian nations, including the Hopis, Navajos, Zunis, Lagunas, Cheyenne, Arapahoe, and Kiowas performed impromptu Victory Dances, which received enthusiastic applause and calls for encores (*Gallup Independent*, August 20, 1945). The 1945 Gallup festival would have been the perfect occasion on which to honor the Navajo Code Talkers, but they had to wait another twenty-three years.

Thus, sporadically during the week and officially on Sunday, August 19, Native Americans, Protestants, Catholics, and Jews gathered either separately or together to praise God for the Allied victory and mourn the painful losses. As an Associated Press reporter observed, the national sentiment could be summarized in a single phrase: "Thank God, thank God — it's over at last" (*Clovis News Journal*, August 15, 1945).

Legacy

In New Mexico, the Second World War changed everything it touched, and it touched virtually everything. Afterward, the state would never again be the same. Many soldiers and civilians — including some German POWs — were so charmed by the region that they returned to live there permanently. The city of Albuquerque grew from thirty-five thousand people to more than a hundred thousand in ten years. Returning Native American veterans dominated postwar tribal councils, and after a campaign by Laguna veteran Miguel Trujillo, the state extended the franchise to Indians in 1948. Simultaneously, Native American, Hispanic, and Anglo state veterans drew on the G.I. Bill to further their education.

The war years also helped shape the state's emerging literary scene. During the conflict, Albuquerque resident Ernie Pyle and Alamogordo-born Bill Mauldin emerged as the foremost war correspondent and cartoonist of the day, respectively. Pyle died from a sniper's bullet at Ie Shima in 1945, but Mauldin returned to Santa Fe to pursue a distinguished career as a professional cartoonist (Melzer 1996).

War issues slowly made their way into regional postwar fiction. Laguna native Leslie Marmon Silko drew on this theme for her classic *Ceremony* (1967), as did N. Scott Momaday (Kiowa and Jemez Springs resident) for his prizewinning *House Made of Dawn* (1968). Hispanic veterans Bill Gurulé, Paul Trujillo, and Sabine Ulíbarri all penned memoirs of their service years (Rivas-Rodriguez 2005). Peggy Pond Church wrote her classic *House at Otowi Bridge: The Story of Edith Warner and Los Alamos* in 1960.

Oklahoma native Tony Hillerman drew on the G.I. Bill to major in journalism and later moved to Santa Fe to edit the *New Mexican* for several years. His witnessing of a Navajo healing ceremony spurred his interest in Native America and propelled him into his current position as the premier novelist and popularizer of the American Southwest.

The scientific and technological legacy of Los Alamos also continued to reshape the state. During the immediate postwar years, no one could say for certain that the nation's nuclear research would remain on the Hill. The attributes that had made Los Alamos so attractive in 1943 — its isolation and sparse population — now seemed to be detriments. Several people suggested moving the laboratory closer to the nation's prestigious East Coast universities. General Groves and the new director of the lab, Norris Bradbury, protested, and by 1948 the Atomic Energy Commission had decided not only to keep the Los Alamos lab where it was but also to dramatically upgrade its facilities. By 1950, new construction had turned Los Alamos into the finest scientific laboratory in the world.

In late 1945 the former Z division of Los Alamos moved to Albuquerque to become Sandia Laboratories, the chief supplier of atomic weapons for the military during the entire postwar era (Szasz 2006). The earnest efforts of Senator Clinton P. Anderson (Democrat), who served on the Joint Congressional Committee on Atomic

Energy from 1951 to 1972, and later similar efforts by Senator Pete Domenici (Republican) ensured that New Mexico received more than its share of federal research dollars. Anderson once credited atomic energy as the key to the research and development structure of New Mexico. In 2004 the state received about $2.7 billion in science-related federal funds. The opening of the controversial Waste Isolation Pilot Plant Project in 1999 near Carlsbad — the first permanent low- and medium-level nuclear waste repository — was deemed appropriate. Because New Mexico had inaugurated the nuclear age, it seemed fitting that it should also permanently hold its nuclear waste products.

Ever since 1945, the world has linked "atomic" with New Mexico, a connection unlikely to disappear in the twenty-first century. And perhaps therein lies the ultimate legacy of the Second World War on the Land of Enchantment.

Leased Wire
Associated Press

Roswell Daily Record

RECORD PHONES
Business Office 2288
News Department
2287

ROSWELL, NEW MEXICO, TUESDAY, JULY 8, 1947.

Movies as Usual

Levees broke and flood waters rolled into the town of Grand Tower, Ill., but while the manager of the movie theater sweeps out the water that has entered the lobby, these youngsters are standing in line for tickets for the night's performance. (AP Wirephoto)

Claims Army Is Slacking Courts Martial

Indiana Senator Lays Protest Before Patterson

RAAF Captures Flying Saucer On Ranch in Roswell Region

House Passes Tax Slash by Large Margin

Defeat Amendment By Demos to Remove Many from Rolls

Security Council Paves Way to Talks On Arms Reductions

No Details of Flying Disk Are Revealed

Roswell Hardware Man and Wife Report Disk Seen

Ex-King Carol Weds Mme. Lupescu

Former King Carol of Rumania and Mme. Elena Lupescu relax aboard the S. S. America bound for Cuba and Mexico on May, 1941. A member of Carol's household in Rio de Janeiro said the ex-king and his companion for 23 years in reign and exile were recently married at their hotel Copacabana Palace suite. (AP Wirephoto)

Some of Soviet Satellites May Attend Paris Meeting

Roswellians Have Differing Opinions On Flying Saucers

American League Wins All-Star Game

Miners and Operators Sign Highest Wage Pact in History

Woodburn Compares Farm Progress in Past Twenty Years

Cotton Acreage Is Above 1947 Figure

Dairymen of Area Hear Lecture Serie

Bulletins

Controls Off on Most All Building

Air Force General Says Army Not Doing Experiments

Two Oil and Gas Leases Are Filed

QUICKIES by Ken Reynolds

Held For Threatening Father in Law's Life

Welcome to Roswell

"The intelligence office of the 509th Bombardment group at Roswell Army Field announced at noon today, that the field has come into possession of a flying saucer." Roswell Daily Record, July 8, 1947.

37

The Roswell Incident:
An Unsolved Mystery or
an "Unsolvable" One?

William E. Gibbs (1993)

More than forty years after young army public-relations officer Walter Haut issued his 1947 news release that the Army Air Corps at Roswell, New Mexico, had in its possession a flying saucer, the whole affair burst again upon the national media scene. Popular writer Whitley Strieber followed his account of interplanetary contact, *Communion* (1988), with *Majestic* (1990), a similar work devoted to the "Roswell Incident." More than fifty million people viewed a presentation of what "might have taken place northwest of Roswell, New Mexico, on a stormy night in July, 1947." A simulation of this incident was shown twice as part of the "Unsolved Mysteries" series, and other presentations soon followed. NBC's Faith Daniels featured the affair at Roswell in a segment of her "A Closer Look" program. Shortly thereafter, in July 1991 Larry King on CNN's "Larry King Live" queried two experts with highly divergent opinions regarding the contention that extraterrestrials had crashed in the Roswell vicinity on that rainy summer evening.

Simultaneously with the King show, one of his guests, Kevin D. Randle (with coauthor Donald R. Schmitt), released the long-awaited and extensively researched book, *UFO Crash at Roswell* (1991). Months later, the publication of a similar research endeavor by Stanton T. Friedman and Don Berliner continued to focus even more national interest on this attention-starved community, nestled along the Pecos River on the high plains of southeastern New Mexico. City officials scurried to capitalize on this newfound publicity, and the Chamber of Commerce, along with the local newspaper, the *Roswell Daily Record*, actively supported a public symposium conducted by Randle and Schmitt on "the affair of '47." T-shirts soon appeared featuring a cartoon labeled "Roswell Incident," with cows observing extraterrestrials emerging from a crashed saucer and wondering what would happen to property values. In the fall of 1992, a UFO museum opened in the heart of town. What had been a mysterious incident of the 1940s turned into a media phenomenon of the early 1990s.

The claim that alien spacecrafts had crashed near Roswell and that materials as well as extraterrestrial bodies had been removed (and/or covered up) by the Army Air Corps (later the Air Force) has brought international attention to the community. These claims raise many philosophical questions, considering such epistemological issues as skepticism, the origins of knowledge and the distinction between belief and knowledge. This forces those trying to make an objective appraisal to confront the question of whether such a contention (as the presence of extraterrestrials) can be proven and, if so, on what basis. This essay takes up all these questions.

In order to look critically at these claims of extraterrestrial contact, it is first important to consider why the incident near Roswell has received such national attention. Over the years, there have been thousands of reported UFO sightings around the world. Why, then, has the public been especially receptive to claims pertaining to the Roswell Incident? Is it because this case affords those already convinced the best chance to prove their case? More specifically, does this affair offer the best opportunity to demonstrate that those experiences upon which their beliefs are based do, in fact, constitute proof? This question can best be answered by putting the incident in historical context.

Public responses to sightings of not readily identifiable or unidentifiable foreign objects (UFOs) have ebbed and flowed since the first wave of such experiences occurred in 1896–97 (Jacobs 1975). Peak periods of receptivity usually coincided with conditions that heightened consciousness of what might be called "peculiar" phenomena. At the turn of the century, writers Jules Verne and H. G. Wells popularized the idea of airship travel, but most people tended to pursue more commonplace explanations. Few Victorians attributed the objects to extraterrestrial origins. Fears associated with World War II and the tense cold war atmosphere that followed generated an especially receptive audience. The year of the Roswell Incident (1947) was a particularly bountiful one for such sightings. As people were conditioned during this period of atomic anxiety to report anything unusual, there were more than 850 such sightings that year alone. Thought by many to be the manifestation of considerably more than a "mild case of meteorological jitters" (Jacobs 1975, 8), Americans far and wide pleaded for some explanation. Was the government testing something? Were the Russians developing some sort of mysterious weapon? Were extraterrestrials finally making contact?

These inquiries, some serious, some frantic, put the Air Force on the defensive. Charged with responsibility for matters pertaining to air space, the Air Force responded as best it could. Because of the anecdotal and ephemeral nature of the evidence, however, and because it lacked any material proof (or so it maintained), the Air Force acted with circumspection. Air Force spokesmen regularly argued that the sightings were simply misidentifications. They were the product of jittery witnesses suffering from a form of mass hysteria or mass hallucination. Some interested parties, however, maintained that the Air Force had to act in that fashion, not because it had no evidence but because it was sensitive to what might be called the "War of the Worlds" hysteria, a mass panic precipitated by Orson Welles's "Mercury Theater" radio production just a decade earlier. For whatever reason, in the late 1940s the Air Force made a concerted effort to be tight-lipped, not only about facts but also about its interest (or lack of interest) in such information.

A number of allies came to the aid of the Air Force during the early 1950s. Representatives of the print media reinforced military contentions. David Lawrence's *U.S. News and World Report* identified the alleged saucers as the Navy's "ol' Flying Flapjacks." Bob Considine in *Cosmopolitan* magazine stepped up the assault on the witnesses, characterizing them as "screwballs" and as members of the "lunatic fringe" suffering from "cold war jitters" and "mass hypnotism." Harvard astronomer Donald H. Menzel, writing in both *Look* and *Time* magazines, added considerable scholarly weight to the Air Force position. Characterizing himself in this case as "the man who shot Santa Claus," Menzel insisted that movies such as *The Day the Earth Stood Still* activated the national imagination. Witnesses had merely observed mirages or reflections created by ice crystals floating in clouds, by refraction or by temperature inversions (Jacobs 1975, 21, 188).

In 1953 the CIA quietly convened a panel of distinguished scientists to conduct an impartial study of UFO data. After looking rather superficially at some evidence for about twelve hours, the so-called Robertson Panel reached a highly political cold war conclusion: "The continued emphasis on the reporting of the phenomena (UFOs) does in these parlous times, result in the threat to the orderly functioning of the protective organs of the body politic" (Jacobs 1975, 94). Apparently the panel feared that numerous reports of sightings would make the populace susceptible to mass hysteria and thus vulnerable to enemy psychological warfare. This might lead to the erosion of respect for civil authority. As historian David Jacobs pointed out, the CIA had identified a new threat to national security: the UFO reports, not the UFOs themselves. At this juncture claims of sightings were characterized as little more than a collection of "kooky" beliefs that pointed to the "unstable" nature of some of the American citizenry.

Largely in response to the Robertson Panel report, the Air Force's Operation Blue Book, which had been created to investigate reported sightings, was largely diverted to performing public-relations work. While it did carefully compile accounts of sightings from 1953 until its demise in 1969, Operation Blue Book used classification strategies to convince the public of the identifiable origin of all reported UFO phenomena. Typically the Air Force pursued a policy of denying credibility of the claims and, especially, debunking those who had reported them. In effect Operation Blue Book shifted the focus of public attention from the claim to the claimant.

But a formidable adversary appeared during the 1950s in the person of retired Marine Maj. Donald Keyhoe. For the next twenty years Keyhoe would lead the offensive on behalf of the extraterrestrial origin of UFOs. He constructed arguments that are still integral to the contemporary furor over the credibility of the claims relative to the Roswell Incident, publishing his third book on flying saucers in 1955. Avoiding the fantastic, sensationalist claims of the contactees or abductees (those who maintained they had been in personal contact with the extraterrestrials), Keyhoe argued that the controversay revolved around the question of proof. He insisted in his books, the last published in 1973, that the real obstacle to generating the hard physical or empirical evidence to verify the existence of flying saucers was the Air Force and other government institutions, such as the CIA. Keyhoe shifted the argument from "Do UFOs exist?" to "Is the government conducting a cover-up designed to prevent any resolution of this problem?" In numerous studies, he contended there *was* such a conspiracy to deceive. For many people the mere probability of deception tended to confirm the existence of all corroborating evidence. Keyhoe had turned the Air Force's policy of "plausible deniability" on its head.

Picking up allies here and there, the most well known being the noted astronomer W. Allen Hynek, Keyhoe sought to organize the forces of the convinced to pressure the federal government to conduct investigations of the Air Force's handling of the affair. The National Investigations Committee on Aerial Phenomena (NICAP), with Keyhoe functioning as executive director and Vice Adm. R. H. Hillenkoetter, the first director of the CIA, on the board of directors, lobbied Congress during the late 1950s and early 1960s. The Air Force strenuously resisted, fearing that such hearings would lend credibility to Keyhoe's and NICAP's allegations of a cover-up. The Air Force used briefing techniques for congressional bodies to stymie NICAP and accused such civilian groups of being motivated either by religious reasons, the desire for financial gain, the need for an emotional release or just plain ignorance.

In the three years following the Lonnie Zamora incident in Socorro, New Mexico, in 1964, a wave of sightings brought the matter to a head in the American Southwest. The *Ft. Worth Star Telegram* (Jacobs 1975, 194–95) challenged the Air Force to stop kidding about the "fiction" of flying saucers: "It's going to take more than a statistical report on how many reported saucers turned out to be jets and weather balloons to convince us otherwise." Journalist John Fuller accelerated the process with television appearances and excerpts from his book on a sighting in Exeter, New Hampshire, published both in *Saturday Review* and *Look*. Fuller appeared to accept Keyhoe's theory of an Air Force cover-up. Continued pressure, some of it emanating from a highly publicized sighting at Hillsdale College in Michigan, added to the uproar for congressional hearings. In April 1966, the House Armed Services Committee called a meeting. An Ad Hoc Committee to Review Project Blue Book, as well as the House Science and Astronautics Committee, heard testimony and called for an independent university investigation. This led to the study conducted at the University of Colorado by noted scientist Edward U. Condon.

The Condon Committee convened in October 1966 and after considerable controversy, finally made its report public in 1968. It concluded that a systematic scientific study of UFOs contributed little to the body of knowledge and added that extraterrestrial contact was the least likely explanation for these numerous anomalous sightings. Even though science had ostensibly been brought to the rescue of those seeking a rational explanation, critics immediately questioned whether the study had been either systematic or scientific. Denying that any of these investigations established extraterrestrial origins of these sightings and, thus, any security threats to the nation, the Air Force promptly canceled Operation Blue Book in 1969; with it went all allegations of any cover-up.

But interest did not disappear in the ensuing decade. Buoyed by man's landing on the moon and a revived tendency to look to the heavens for answers to such problems as nuclear holocaust and dwindling natural resources, various UFO organizations kept the issue alive. W. Allen Hynek established his Chicago Center for UFO Studies, which worked with Mutual UFO Network (MUFON) to systematically record and research sightings. NICAP also continued its program, and Arizona senator Barry Goldwater, among others, soon joined the board of directors.

Probably of greater interest was the fact that, contrary to the impression that all government inquiries ceased with the Air Force's announcement of the termination of Operation Blue Book, the federal government continued to pursue, free from any obligation to divulge its findings publicly, the question of UFO presence. Several significant books have carefully chronicled these largely covert government operations. These include Lawrence Fawcett and Barry Greenwood's *Clear Intent: The Government Cover-Up of the UFO Experience* (1984), Timothy Good's *Above Top Secret* (1988), Howard Blum's *Out There: The Government's Quest for Extraterrestrials* (1990) and Tim Weiner's *Blank Check: The Pentagon's Black Budget* (1990), to name just a few.

With the 1980s, a decade that experienced both a resurgence of religious fundamentalism and a growing interest in New Age metaphysics, new life was breathed into the 1947 Roswell Incident. Almost nothing had been written about it during the previous three decades, but the sparse information that had surfaced tended to confirm Keyhoe's cover-up theory. It is ironic, however, that there was no mention of the Roswell Incident in any of Keyhoe's books published between 1950 and 1973. Yet rumors of the crash continued to circulate locally, and those interested could look at the July 8, 1947, headlines of the *Roswell Daily Record*, which announced to the community that Army Air Corps base personnel had recovered some materials alien in nature. But the subsequent explanation released by the Eighth Army Corps in Fort Worth apparently convinced the press that the materials found were from a high-altitude weather balloon. This account of a UFO crash on the high plains of New

Mexico some seventy-five miles northwest of Roswell, and the subsequent cover-up, likely would have remained buried for some time without the efforts of Stanton T. Friedman and William Moore.

Friedman, a nuclear physicist long active in UFO research, and Moore, a former English teacher who had already enjoyed some publishing success in the field, met over pizza on a cold night in January 1978 in Morris, Minnesota, to share notes. Although Friedman and Moore had limited familiarity with the Roswell sighting, a valuable lead revived the Roswell Incident for them. After speaking at Louisiana State University in Baton Rouge, Friedman followed up on a suggestion that sent him to Houma, Louisiana, home of retired Air Force Lt. Col. Jesse Marcel. This was the critical contact that gave credence to those recollections of old-timers that had long circulated around Roswell and among a few ufologists (those who study UFOs). This appeared to be an especially promising lead in the pursuit of factual verification — the process of transforming a belief into an established fact.

As the intelligence officer of the 509th Bomb Group at Roswell Air Field in 1947, Marcel had driven to the crash site and picked up some of the material. He returned to Roswell and flew the material to Fort Worth, Texas, where he witnessed the alleged cover-up. Marcel would have to be characterized as a primary witness for he reported his own experiences, not hearsay. Although recounting the story some thirty years after the event, Marcel recalled being notified through the base officer, Col. William "Butch" Blanchard, that the local sheriff, George A. Wilcox, had called the base. Wilcox indicated that a rancher, W. W. "Mac" Brazel, had arrived at his office with some strange materials he had found at a crash out at the Foster ranch, where Brazel worked. Blanchard then dispatched Marcel and a counterintelligence officer to inspect the situation and pick up additional items at this ranch, located some seventy-five miles to the northwest not far from Corona, New Mexico. Upon his return more than a day later, Marcel took the peculiar debris to his home to show his family, including his twelve-year-old son Jesse, Jr. He then carried it on to the base. After a staff meeting early Tuesday morning, July 8, 1947, Blanchard ordered 1st Lt. Walter Haut, the base public-relations officer, to issue a press release to the effect that a flying disc had been recovered. Haut recalled that Blanchard, whom he considered a very level-headed fellow, paraphrased what he wanted Haut to write. The Roswell *Morning News* had already gone to press before Haut took the release there, but the *Roswell Daily Record* (July 8, 1947) plastered the story across its front page, claiming, "RAAF Captures Flying Saucer on Ranch in Roswell Region" in its afternoon headlines. Specifically, the article stated that no details of the flying disc had been revealed. Indicating that the intelligence officer of the 509th released the account about noon, it explained that the information had come from a local rancher, and that the sheriff's office had notified Maj. Jesse Marcel, who had loaned it to higher headquarters (*Roswell Daily Record*, July 9, 1947). While news was going out over the wires and telephone calls were flooding the Roswell circuits, Marcel was ordered to fly the wreckage to the Eighth Air Force Headquarters at Carswell Air Force Base in Fort Worth, where Big. Gen. Roger Ramey inspected the materials carefully. After some delay, during which Marcel was out of the room, Ramey held a press conference. He announced that the materials had been identified as a Rawin Sonde weather balloon. On Wednesday, July 9, the *Roswell Daily Record* declared, "General Ramey Empties Roswell Saucer," explaining that the find was in fact a weather balloon. With this, virtual silence descended over the matter for the next thirty years. Mac Brazel also submitted to a number of interviews on that Wednesday during which he, too, admitted that the debris came from a weather balloon.

After Friedman and Moore had interviewed a number of witnesses, essentially to corroborate as well as elaborate upon Marcel's account, Moore (along with writer Charles Berlitz of *Bermuda Triangle* fame) published the findings, plus a good deal more, in book form as *The Roswell Incident* (1980). Berlitz and Moore (1980, 3) argued that absolute proof of UFO presence required a corpus delicti, or more accurately, physical (empirical) evidence. They explained, however, that the material evidence that would constitute the empirical proof of alien presence included bodies, which had actually been whisked away by the military to Wright Field near Dayton, Ohio, where they had been, and likely would continue to be, concealed. This book revived the Keyhoe argument of earlier decades. Unfortunately the work strayed far from facts compiled by Friedman and Moore and frequently became little more than a hodgepodge of conjecture and speculation. While it did little to lend credibility to UFO research, the book did point to the Roswell Incident as one in which government complicity might well be established. Moreover it broached the epistemological question of what constitutes "knowledge" and "proof" of extraterrestrial contact.

In what Stanton T. Friedman called "a race with the undertaker," he and Moore pursued additional leads during the 1980s, publishing a number of monographs that corrected and supplemented the Berlitz/Moore publication. With public recognition the critics, most specifically author Phil Klass, who had built a reputation on his skepticism and debunking skills, also took to the field. While the convinced piled up more evidence, mostly of a secondary variety, to support the Marcel account, the critics challenged the hearsay nature of that evidence. They especially questioned the nonexistence of any physical proof. Klass responded to observations that the UFO community was acquiring a greater interest in what was identified as the "Crashed Disc Syndrome." He explained that this would be more aptly termed the "Credulous Dementia Syndrome." Klass rejected the cover-up theory. He asked whether there had not been additional UFO crashes in this country, where evidence might not have been so effectively suppressed, or at least crashes in other countries where governments would be readily willing to make the findings public. This "king of the skeptics" argued that crash claims, such as that at Roswell, violated a basic tenet of ufology — that the technology of extraterrestrials is so advanced that it never fails and that the pilots never make errors. Previously used to explain the absence of any physical evidence by the defenders of a UFO presence, Klass (1983, 282, 284) gleefully pointed out the contradiction.

Amidst the flurry of interest in the Roswell Incident coming from both the convinced and the skeptics, two young researchers launched the most comprehensive study to date. Kevin Randle, a free-lance writer and UFO investigator, and Don Schmitt, associated with the Hynek Center for UFO Research, interviewed hundreds of witnesses and perused thousands of documents in their quest for the corpus delicti or the next best thing: evidence of the cover-up.

Mark Rodeghier, science director of the Center for UFO Studies, established in his foreword to Randle and Schmitt's *UFO Crash in Roswell* (1991, 7–9) that this book at the very least called into question continued government censorship, which strongly suggested a cover-up. In their work the authors built upon the rather extensive research by Moore and Friedman, generally filling out with secondary evidence the Mac Brazel saga. They consulted with Mac's son, Bill, along with other Corona, New Mexico, neighbors, to substantiate his account. But Randle and Schmitt's queries did not confirm a number of Moore and Friedman's claims. The most significant of these involved the matter of the "alien bodies." According to Randle and Schmitt, on the afternoon of July 8, Colonel Blanchard had Brazel flown out to the ranch, where they located a second crash site and directed men to it. Randle and Schmitt maintain that bodies were found at this crash site in the vicinity of the ranch. Relying on the diary of Grady L. "Barney" Barnett of Socorro, New Mexico, they contend that Barnett's claims to having found bodies on the San Augustin Plains west of Socorro were designed to mislead, whereas in fact, Barnett had literally run upon the extraterrestrials far east of the city near the original crash site. They then established to their satisfaction that four bodies were found there, transferred to Roswell Army Air Force Base and later sent to Wright Field (Randle and Schmitt 1991, 80–107).

Randle and Schmitt's research provided more corroboration for the allegations of an Army Air Corp cover-up, suggesting that there was something to hide: the material evidence. Additional testimony from various media people, both in Roswell and around the state, established that Brazel's story did change over the day of July 8 when he was in military custody, that an effort to suppress the Haut news release might have taken place and that, contrary to Gen. Roger Ramey's public statement, a CIA top secret memo confirmed that the material flown to Fort Worth by Marcel was, in fact, forwarded on to Wright Field. They also established continued government sensitivity to "goings-on" in the environs of the crash, even four decades after the incident. Still short of actually having the physical evidence, Randle and Schmitt again turned to Maj. Don Keyhoe's question of decades earlier: what does the government have to hide?

What can a reader conclude about the rise and fall of interest in the Roswell Incident? Does the belief held by many that extraterrestrials crashed in the general proximity of Roswell, New Mexico, on or about July 3, 1947, constitute knowledge of that fact? Is it true? Does the belief that bodies were actually found and transported to Wright Field, as some maintain, have any basis in fact? Is it true? Whether among the convinced or the skeptical, one has to admit that these are remarkable beliefs, and they form the basis of a number of extraordinary claims. In fact their justification through factual verification would force a revolutionary change in worldview equivalent to that effected by Galileo in his relegation of humans to a more peripheral position in the solar system. Humankind would have to reassess its place in the scheme of things and question its assumed physical and intellectual superiority. A severe strain would be placed on religious doctrines and dogmas that tie ultimate reality almost exclusively to earthly functions. The question of right and wrong would have to be extended to humanoid behavior (Christian 1986, 492–93, 499–500). Darwin's publication of *Origin of Species* (1859) would pale in comparison to this disclosure, *if* it could be proven.

Famed science author Carl Sagan once observed that "extraordinary claims require extraordinary evidence" (Gray 1991, 75). Therefore, any such claims have to be substantiated beyond a shadow of a doubt. As a result, a simple belief, no matter how widely and sincerely held, will simply not sustain the claim that extraterrestrials crashed in Roswell, New Mexico, in 1947, and that the federal government has for years covered up this fact. In other words, a mere belief to that effect, no matter how widely held, does not constitute knowledge of the alleged fact. If mere belief did equate to fact, then the Earth would have to be considered, in fact, flat during the Middle Ages because a number of people *believed* this to be true. Such a belief, or a body of such beliefs, must be justified through some type of physical verification and/ or sound, logical reasoning. Short of concrete evidence to verify the claims associated with the Roswell Incident, any conclusions must rest on the strength of the arguments put forward to logically sustain the contention that such evidence might actually exist, but is inaccessible because of the government conspiracy to conceal. It should be kept in mind, however, that simply proving the *existence* of a cover-up does not establish that the government had concealed UFO materials. Unfortunately the government conceals many things from its citizens. Furthermore, it must be acknowledged that even convincing indications of a UFO cover-up to not irrefutably establish the existence of concrete evidence; they merely strengthen the logical inference, or probability, that such material evidence does in fact exist.

Consequently, any critical appraisal of the claims associated with the Roswell Incident moves from the question of empirical, scientific verification to that of determining the strength of those inductive arguments put forth in support of the cover-up conspiracy. In evaluating any such arguments, two criteria need to be considered: the conclusion must follow with a great deal of probability from the premises, and the premises submitted in support of the conclusion must be true. Thus, if every statement submitted in support of the crash on the high New Mexico desert is true, then it is reasonable to assume, with considerable confidence, that there was some type of government complicity. As a result, the conclusion that something anomalous did take place might be considered a reasonably probable one. Note that this conclusion would only be a reasonably probable inference upon which one could base a strong conviction or belief; it would not be an absolute, indisputable fact.

But this matter of the truth of the various contentions put forth as evidence has to be seriously considered. Are the various propositions in support of an extraterrestrial presence near Roswell, New Mexico, verifiably true? Certainly the apparent discrepancy among different scholars relative to certain key points, most specifically the location and/or existence of the bodies, calls into question the veracity of that claim. Randle and Schmitt identify the location of a second crash site, about which surprisingly little appears to be known, about two and a half miles from the first crash site. Friedman, however, locates it on the San Augustin Plains west of Socorro, New Mexico, over a hundred and fifty miles removed. Moore (1985, 174–76), in another essay, has expressed serious doubts whether the evidence strongly supports the contention that bodies were found on the San Augustin Plains. Even more controversial, the MJ-12 Documents, which are purported to consist of briefing papers prepared for President Dwight Eisenhower and confirmation of a government cover-up in the Roswell matter, are endorsed as factual by Moore, at least partially accepted by Friedman and rejected for lack of any support by Randle and Schmitt (1991, 231, 299; also Greenwood 1989). The serious division among UFO scholars on basic questions of fact, plus the fractious nature of their exchanges relative to such matters, not only prevents consensus but also undermines the credibility of their claims.

Another matter that might generate reservations about the credibility of the claims is the abundance of secondary and/or hearsay evidence in support of them. In an interesting study of evidence, one historian has argued that observation, imagination and memory can, unconsciously, so distort evidence that false stories can obtain a currency that makes them a part of accepted public knowledge ("Case of the Eyewitness" 1969). Virtually every observation derived from primary sources is three decades or more removed from the July 1947 incident. These include the evidence gleaned from interviews with Jesse Marcel, Dr. Jesse Marcel, Jr., and retired M. Sgt. Lewis S. Rickett, the counterintelligence agent who assisted in the retrieval of the debris from the Brazel site. Numerous supportive comments, particularly on the recovery of the bodies and their transportation to Dayton, are secondhand or circumstantial. The accounts by key participants in this saga derive largely from this type of source, including Mac Brazel, Walter Haut, George A. Wilcox, Barney Barnett, Glenn Dennis and Oliver S. "Pappy" Henderson. Brazel had been dead long before Friedman, Moore and colleagues revived the incident late in the 1970s. Thus Brazel's actions were reconstructed from Marcel, and Brazel's sister, son, neighbors and friends. Walter Haut admitted to never having actually seen any of the materials and, in fact, denied he had received any "blistering rebuke," asserted to have been issued for having written the initial press release. George A. Wilcox, the Chaves County sheriff, had passed away long before the renewed interest surfaced, and the information relative to his activities and attitudes came from his family, primarily his daughter, Phyllis McGuire. Both Barney Barnett and his wife, Ruth, had died as well, and the Barnett experiences were recalled by his friend L. W. "Vern" and Jean Maltais. Glenn Dennis, formerly a local mortician who had friends at the air base in 1947, admits to being unable to prove any of what he recalled others had told him about what happened with the alien bodies at the base. Capt. Pappy Henderson's testimony relative to flying the bodies to Wright Field is fundamental to the case, yet does not come from Henderson himself but largely from his wife, Sappho. Few would question that these are honest, good-faith recollections, such as Walter Haut's memory of Jesse Marcel referring to the materials found as "not of this world." But as studies of evidence establish, witnesses can be influenced by emotion, along with predisposition, and their testimony might be subject as well to contamination from familiarity with accounts from other sources. In fact, Sappho Henderson recalled that her husband's confession to her was precipitated by his reading an article on the incident (Randle and Schmitt 1991, 82). Certainly after all the publicity the entire Roswell affair has generated over the past few years, it would be difficult to imagine how future witnesses could be free from the influence of previously circulated accounts. On the basis of these observations relative to the abundance of evidence that has surfaced lately, one would still have to conclude that the arguments put forth do not even convincingly establish the existence of a UFO cover-up, let alone confirm an extraterrestrial presence. Therefore the Roswell Incident essentially remains an unsolved mystery.

This conclusion leads to one final question: is such a mystery solvable? It is necessary to recognize that the failure to construct strong and virtually incontestable arguments in support of a cover-up does not irrevocably undermine claims of UFO presence in the Roswell Incident. In other words, just because the convinced cannot prove their claims beyond a shadow of a doubt doesn't mean that their contentions are necessarily false. Moreover, the evidence of continued government complicity, extensively demonstrated by the publications of Fawcett, Greenwood, Good, Blum and Weiner, only activates what philosopher William James (1956) once called "The Will to Believe." Of course the government could "fess up" and bring forth the evidence, documentary or otherwise. This is unlikely, however, either because it simply doesn't have any such material or, possibly, for any number of other reasons, including its fear of generating a "War of the Worlds" hysteria. In an era when New Age literature, featuring such notables as Jean Dixon and Nostradamus, has virtually run Plato and Aristotle off many bookstore shelves, this fear may not be too farfetched. Consequently the government is not likely to do anything. The memory of Donald Keyhoe will remain alive as cries of "cover-up" continue to circulate far and wide. Furthermore, new evidence, more and more removed in time from that rainy July night in New Mexico, will surface to sustain the old arguments, keeping alive the Roswell Incident indefinitely. On this basis the people of Roswell might be well advised to publicize their recently opened UFO museum, for interest in this "unsolved" and probably "unsolvable" mystery is likely to persist for some time to come.

Los Alamos protective force members scrutinizing vehicles leaving Los Alamos through the main (east) gate guard station. View is toward the Sangre de Cristo Mountains, about 1947–50.

38

Toward Normalizing Los Alamos: Cracking the Gates

Jon Hunner (2004)

"The destiny of all nations during the twentieth century will turn in large measure upon the nature and the pace of atomic energy development here and abroad."

President Dwight Eisenhower in a press release from the White House, February 17, 1954

The public furor at Los Alamos over the revocation of Oppenheimer's security clearance subsided in the fall of 1954. Although Hill personnel still revered Oppenheimer, the laboratory continued its research into the various applications of atomic energy, the community advanced its modernization drive, and families pursued the postwar American dream. All this occurred in an atmosphere of suspicion and apprehension about the Soviet Union's intentions in the Cold War. Los Alamos's mission remained vital to the nation's security, and so this unique town continued to invent itself as a modern suburb in order to adequately recruit and retain personnel.

The process of normalizing Los Alamos could be applied to the secrecy at the site. Cracks in the secrecy that surrounded the residential section and even the Tech Area began to appear. In commemoration of the tenth anniversay of Trinity, LASL sponsored an unprecedented event. It opened the Tech areas to newsmen, staff, and the family members of its work force. On July 17 and 18, 1955, thousands of people toured the technical areas that now spread over the plateau tops and among the canyons and viewed top-secret experiments. At Omega West in the bottom of Los Alamos Canyon, visitors saw nuclear reactors. As one reporter observed: "The three machines, christened in the curious, grimly humorous jargon of atomic scientists are called Topsy, Godiva, and Jezebel" (*Sunday Denver Post*, July 31, 1956). The Godiva model fissioned at a rate of a billion atoms a second. A Manhattan Project veteran, associate director Ralph Carlisle Smith briefed reporters and explained Godiva's name by saying it was a bare reactor like the Englishwoman horse rider. When the critical assembly attained a chain reaction, a warning sign flashed "Route 2," telling the visitors the safest path away from the building if something went wrong. Smith told the journalists: "Always run into the wind." But he insisted: "Only a human consciously trying to make a series of mistakes could get this reaction out of control" (*Albuquerque Journal*, July 18, 1955; July 16, 1955). Like all careful scientists, laboratory officials plotted escape routes in case the worst happened.

One journalist, after visiting the previously closed labs, reported that two things impressed those around him: "the hugeness of the entire installation and the safety precautions taken." Detection equipment for monitoring radioactivity was seen "all about the area," and laboratory officials emphasized that all radioactive material was handled by remote control. Indeed, some visitors tried the remote control arms, but none could compete with the resident operator who maneuvered the mechanical hands to unscrew an eyedropper from a bottle and squeeze three precise drops out of it (*Albuquerque Journal*, July 17, 1955).

In addition to the influx of journalists and visiting scientists, spouses and children toured the workplaces of their partners and parents for the first time, some after more than ten years of living on the Hill. With open access to the Tech Areas, families thronged through the various sites on the Pajarito Plateau to see what went on behind the closed doors. Interspersed among the mute assemblies of technical equipment were exhibits that entertained. In one area, Elizabeth Graves, wife of Alvin Graves (who survived the Slotin accident and went on to direct the Nevada Test Site), demonstrated an electrical current passing through her body and discharging out through her fingertips and her hair. In another building, an exhibit called "cooking your dimes" allowed visitors to put dimes into a counter that measured radioactivity. The units of measurement were "rare, medium, or well-done, according to how much radioactivity they had picked up" (*Albuquerque Journal*, July 17, 1955; July 18, 1955). How the dimes picked up their radioactivity was not disclosed. Other exhibits included playing peek-a-boo through the holes in the water-boiler reactor and observing a monkey in the medical research laboratory.

Families wandered through the Tech Areas with different expectations. Some children, although intrigued with the interactive exhibits, were more impressed by entering parts of the plateau that had been off-limits to them. Visitors came from the entire range of workers on the Hill. Mrs. Marvin Anna, whose husband had electrically wired many of the laboratory buildings for the Zia Company, stated that she and her two children enjoyed "seeing the places where [*sic*] he had so often spoken about" (*Albuquerque Journal*, July 18, 1955). Suzanne Ray, whose father was a guard, felt strange going through the labs. She said: "Growing up there, I never really thought that was where they had the bomb made." A journalist concluded: "Although foot weary from the tour, most families decided it had been well worth their while 'seeing where Daddy works'" (*Albuquerque Journal*, July 18, 1955). Visiting where a spouse or parent worked brought new realizations to some and a feeling of normalcy to others.

The laboratory's Open House, which allowed families and journalists into the technical areas for the first time, exhibited no nuclear weapons. Thus, the real work at LASL remained hidden from these guests. Instead, the Open House offered a sophisticated science fair with nuclear reactors, remote-controlled arms, particle accelerators, and "cooked" dimes. The safety in the Tech Areas impressed many of the visitors who saw the numerous radiation monitors positioned throughout the workshops. With the Open House such a success, especially with the families on the Hill, it became an annual event at LASL....

In 1954, a bill was introduced into the U.S. Congress by Senator Clinton P. Anderson (D-N.Mex.) and Representative Carl T. Durham (D-N.C.) that proposed to allow private ownership of land and residences at the AEC towns of Hanford, Oak Ridge, and Los Alamos. That year, the Joint Committee on Atomic Energy halted the bill, but it was reintroduced in 1955. The bill rattled many people at Los Alamos, who strongly resisted the opening up of their community to the outside world and even the opportunity to purchase their own homes. Consequently, the AEC issued this opinion: "After giving full consideration to the security, economic, and community relations aspect of a plan to alter community access controls at Los Alamos, the Atomic Energy Commission concluded that present procedures should not be changed at this time" (*New York Times*, May 1, 1955). However, plans to permit the residents of Oak Ridge and Hanford to purchase property proceeded....

After years of reversing its policies to accommodate the residents' desires, the AEC shocked the people of Los Alamos. On Friday, February 15, 1957, the AEC announced that on the following Monday, February 18, the residential areas of Los Alamos would lose their access control. After that Monday, the gates would open and people would not need passes to enter the town. Indeed, the security guards would leave the gates they had monitored twenty-four hours a day since January 1943 and be reassigned to the Tech Area. There was little advance warning of this decision, and many Hill residents expressed dismay. Ed Grilly, a chemist at LASL, was chagrined: "It will make my wife lock the door and we will have to be more careful about the house belongings and the children, but I suppose we have been rather careless up here." Ruth Haley, who had lived at Los Alamos for thirteen years, said: "It really doesn't make too much difference but I would rather have seen them shut." However, others in the community were delighted. Mrs. Herman Hoerlin told a reporter that she was "100 percent in favor of it" and "very, very happy about the whole thing." The police chief, Ralph Kopansky, commented: "There undoubtedly will be many friendly taxpayers who will wish to visit Los Alamos to see how their tax dollars have been and are being spent." Whatever their feelings about access control, residents could do nothing to prevent the loss of their guards, gates, and fences (*Santa Fe New Mexican*, February 17, 1957).

The AEC gave several reasons for reversing their previous policy of keeping the residential areas of Los Alamos behind fences. The announcement listed four advantages to removing the gates: "1. The recruitment of scientific personnel will benefit. 2. Private financing of home sites on Barranca Mesa will be facilitated. Action has been taken to opening these home sites for privately owned homes. 3. Private interest in leasing Government owned land and buildings for commercial purposes will be enhanced. 4. Removal of the gate controls will save approximately $100,000 a year in direct costs" (*Santa Fe New Mexican*, February 17, 1957). After the transfer of the main technical areas to South Mesa, there were few security reasons to justify access control to the town, except to accede to the wishes of residents. Since World War II, the AEC often had followed the policy begun by General Groves of deferring to the wishes of the people of Los Alamos to keep up morale. Now, however, the AEC's overriding concern about cutting costs and its wish to create a more "normal" community at Los Alamos forced final removal of the access controls.

At noon on February 18, 1957, under an overcast sky and lightly falling snow, the guards at the main gate were relieved of their duties, and New Mexico's Governor Edwin L. Mechem became the first person to enter Los Alamos without a pass. Paul Wilson, manager of Los Alamos for the AEC, escorted Mechem into the town and addressed the assembled crowd with these remarks: "To me, this little ceremony is symbolic of several things. First, it indicates the continued desire and effort to make Los Alamos part of New Mexico and to make it a more normal community. Second, it is symbolic of [the] continuing effort on the part of the AEC to make available for public use information pertaining to the peaceful uses of atomic energy. Third, it is symbolic of the freedom of the American people and their desire to live without unnecessary restrictions" (*Santa Fe New Mexican*, February 18, 1957; February 19, 1957; *Albuquerque Journal*, February 19, 1957)....

So the opening of the gates ended an era. Los Alamos was the last of the nation's atomic communities to take down the security fences that surrounded the residential areas. The people of Los Alamos weathered this change to their town as they had the previous ones. From 1943 to 1957, change had transformed the Pajarito Plateau several times. Los Alamos residents, driven by the urgency of the arms race, had invented and reinvented their community in the glare of the national media and, in doing so, had focused attention on what a model Cold War community should be. Even though the town of Los Alamos struggled to create a recognizably normal community through

Open Houses, church building, and conversions like the Gate Drive-in, it could not escape its unique status. Federal officers used it as an experimental community to test civil defense strategies. Curriculum reform emphasizing math and science swept the Hill's educational system to better prepare students for a nuclear and technological world. The fences did come down, and Los Alamos became more like an ordinary place than ever before, but the community remained a company town, dependent on the federal government for funding, personnel, and guidance.

Norman Petty Recording Studios sign, Clovis, New Mexico, March 27, 1992.

39

Not Fade Away: Buddy Holly's Surprising Clovis Studio

Jason Silverman (2006)

These are the birthplaces of rock and roll: Memphis, Chicago, New Orleans, the Mississippi Delta, and Clovis. That's right — the tiny town of Clovis, New Mexico, was one of the centers of the 1950s rock explosion. It was there, in a converted grocery at 1313 Seventh Street, that Charles Hardin Holley, aka Buddy Holly, recorded all of his greatest songs.

He didn't do it solo, however. Holly combined forces with Clovis native Norman Petty, a musician and self-taught producer, and together, they created a remarkable string of hits, including "Peggy Sue," "O Boy," "Rave On," "Everyday," "Words of Love," "Maybe Baby," "Not Fade Away," and "That'll Be the Day." Without Petty and his Clovis studio, it's likely that music history would have taken a different path. For the streamlined, crystal-clear style that Holly and Petty perfected, a style that could be called the Clovis Sound, was a central influence on John Lennon, Paul McCartney and Keith Richards.

Few of Norman Petty's neighbors in Clovis would have expected, or may have even known, that this quiet man would change rock-and-roll history. But a closer look at his life's work demonstrates how motivated Petty was. As a third grader at Clovis's La Casita Elementary School, he directed the school band. He started his first group, the Torchy Swingsters, while in junior high. As a professional musician in the early 1950s, he notched several hits, including a cover of Duke Ellington's "Mood Indigo."

Though successful, Petty was frustrated by the clock-watching, profit-driven industry practices of the major studios.

Meaning to record the songs of the Norman Petty Trio, he purchased his uncle's vacant store, located next door to his parents' filling station, and built a state-of-the-art studio of his own. It was a visionary move. In 1954, independent music producers were a rarity, even in big cities. And Petty was just twenty-seven.

Around the same time, about ninety miles south, in Lubbock, Texas, Buddy Holly's career was blossoming, in a small-town kind of way. Musically gifted as a child, he was performing professionally by his teens, playing his own weekly radio show by sixteen and gigging throughout Texas. In 1956, with the help of country great Marty Robbins, Holly scored his first record deal. Decca Records intended to turn the nineteen-year-old Holly into a country music star.

But all three of Holly's Nashville sessions were disasters. A Decca executive called Holly "the biggest no-talent I ever worked with," and Holly was uncomfortable with the arrangements of the songs and the demands of the cutthroat music business. He returned home after the first session, watching the charts for his single and doing occasional construction jobs.

That summer, Holly made his first trip to the Norman Petty Studio in Clovis to rehearse for his second Decca session. Bringing back tales of Norm Petty's expertise, he convinced Lubbock singer-songwriter Buddy Knox to make the drive north, too. Soon, Knox's Clovis-made "Party Doll" was climbing the charts, eventually reaching number one. In the meantime, Holly grew increasingly impatient. Decca wasn't turning him into a star. Why not follow Knox's lead and do it himself?

And so he did. Immediately after Decca dropped him in January 1957, Holly contacted Petty, and in the early evening of February 24, 1957 (the studio operated only at night, due to the noise of the filling station next door), Holly and his band began making music. By 3:00 a.m., they had recorded two songs: "I'm Looking for Someone to Love" and, in just two takes, "That'll Be the Day."

Over the next fifteen months, Holly and his band, which solidified into the Crickets, recorded sixteen more classics in Clovis. The Petty-Holly relationship, at least in the studio, proved to be remarkably productive. Holly's experience with Decca in Nashville had revealed the narrow-mindedness of major label operations. With Petty in Clovis, the increasingly confident singer was encouraged to experiment and let loose his musical genius.

According to Robert Linville, it's impossible to single out either Holly or Petty as the primary force in the creation of the Clovis Sound — the two worked as a team. A Texan who made Clovis his home, Linville sang with the Roses, Petty's backup vocal group. The Roses can be heard on "It's So Easy," among other classics.

"Buddy and Norman had so much respect for each other as individuals, and had so much in common," Linville told me. "They were both years ahead of their time. Buddy was self-made, with no formal training, and Norm couldn't even read music. And they had the same sensibilities. Norm and Buddy were both perfectionists, and so we all had to be, too. That's why you are still hearing those songs today."

The Holly-Petty sessions burned with creativity, and featured many innovations: Crickets' drummer Jerry Allison playing his knees (on"Everyday") or an empty box (on "Not Fade Away"), Petty coaxing delicate, soulful sounds out of the celesta, a kind of miniature xylophone (on "Everyday"). The Clovis Sound was a product of the collective energy as much as of any single person.

The result, a crisp, timeless, and wholly distinctive music, served as inspiration and encouragement to a generation of musicians. Among the disciples were the Beatles, who saw Buddy Holly and the Crickets on their 1958 British tour. John Lennon, Paul McCartney, and company paid homage with their arthropodal choice of name, their guitar licks, and their fashion choices (Lennon once said the Beatles' first forty songs consciously mimicked Holly, and in 1975, Paul McCartney purchased the publishing rights to all of Holly's Clovis songs). The Rolling Stones scored their first hit with a cover of "Rave On," and the songs of countless other musicians, including those of Bob Dylan and Elton John, bear the imprint in one way or another of the Clovis Sound.

Though the musical explosion that Holly and Petty created was miraculous, their relationship was not without problems. Some say that Holly regretted relinquishing a portion of the writing credit for his songs to Petty. And the increasingly popular Crickets, having allowed Petty to manage their income, grew suspicious after tasting less of the fruit than they expected. Niki Sullivan, the Crickets' original rhythm guitarist, compared Petty to Jesse James, who knocked over banks in broad daylight. HiPockets Duncan, Holly's first manager, told an interviewer that Petty took about 90 percent of the profits, rather than the customary 10 percent.

Hard feelings notwithstanding, many of the accusations about Petty seem ludicrous. Some claim that Petty broke up the Crickets by turning the band against Holly. In the Holly biography *Rave On*, Philip Norman goes as far as to implicate Petty in Holly's tragic death, claiming that Holly wouldn't have taken the fateful 1958 flight that claimed his life had Petty not withheld earnings from Holly. Holly's death, in a plane crash in an Iowa cornfield less than two years after his first Clovis recording, remains one of the tragic moments in rock-and-roll history, and was memorialized in Don McLean's 1971 hit "American Pie."

Those who knew Petty best wholly dispute the allegations. According to Linville, Petty was fair, consistent, and honest. In any case, he deserves his place in music history. Other producers, including Sam Phillips (whose Sun Records helped launch Elvis Presley), have been inducted into the Rock and Roll Hall of Fame. Petty, who died in 1984, has been largely forgotten. The Oscar-nominated 1978 film *The Buddy Holly Story* didn't even mention Petty or Clovis, instead showing Holly recording his songs in his own garage.

Keeping Petty out of the equation is simply unfair, according to Kenneth Broad, the co-administrator of the Petty estate. Petty, after all, used tiny Clovis as a launching pad not only for Holly but also for Roy Orbison and Waylon Jennings (both Holly protégés), along with the Raton-based group the Fireballs, whose "Sugar

Shack" was the biggest hit of 1963. And the Clovis-based Roses were recently inducted into the Rockabilly Hall of Fame in Nashville. The list of important musicians Petty discovered is impressive even by Nashville or New York City standards.

"[As a producer] Mr. Petty's philosophy was that creativity didn't come by the clock," Broad said. "He wouldn't rent the studio by the hour. You paid by the song, and he'd spend all the time necessary to get it right. And though there have been nasty things written about him, I've never heard anything negative about him from anyone who knew him well. He was a gracious, generous individual and a genuine good friend."

Broad and others helped restore the Norman Petty Studio to a pristine state. "It's just like the day we buried Buddy," said Linville, a pallbearer at Holly's funeral, who sometimes takes his morning coffee there and reflects on the timeless music he helped create.

Pilgrims from around the globe who come to visit see the old Baldwin piano and Hammond organ that Petty's wife, Vi (who Holly considered an honorary member of the Crickets), used to play, along with the mixing equipment, some of which Petty built himself. "People wonder why we don't use the studio today," Broad said. "It just wouldn't be the same without Mr. Petty there to turn the knobs."

40

The National Statuary Hall Collection: Dennis Chavez

The Architect of the Capitol (2006)

The National Statuary Hall Collection in the United States Capitol is comprised of statues donated by individual states to honor persons notable in their history. The entire collection now consists of 100 statues contributed by 50 states. All fifty states have contributed two statues each.

New Mexico: Dennis Chavez

Dennis Chavez was born in Los Chaves, Valencia County, New Mexico, on April 8, 1888. He left school at the age of 13 to work as a grocery clerk and later worked in the city's department of engineering. As a result of acting as a Spanish interpreter for Senator Andrieus A. Johns, Chavez came to Washington, serving as a clerk in the Office of the Secretary of the United States Senate from 1917 to 1920. He graduated from Georgetown University Law School, was admitted to the bar in 1920, and returned to Albuquerque to practice law.

He began his political career in the New Mexico House of Representatives in 1923. He was a member of the Democratic National Committee from 1933 to 1936, a member of the U.S. House of Representatives from 1931 to 1935, and an unsuccessful candidate for the United States Senate in 1934. In 1935, Chavez was appointed to the Senate to fill the vacancy left by the death of Bronson M. Cutting. Elected to that seat in 1936, he served until his death.

Chavez supported the New Deal and championed the rights of American Indians and Puerto Ricans. He worked for reciprocal trade agreements, especially with Latin America.

Statue of United States Senator Dennis Chavez. Plaque at base reads, "A friend to all. He championed the poor." Cast in bronze by sculptor Felix de Weldon (1907–2003) and placed in the National Statuary Hall of the United States Capitol, March 31, 1966.

He was known for his legislation establishing the federal Fair Employment Practices Commission along with various child care programs. He died in Washington, D.C., on November 18, 1962, and was interred in Albuquerque.

United States Senator Dennis Chavez, campaign portrait in race against Patrick Hurley, 1952.
Photograph by John LeRouge Martinez.

41

Dennis Chavez and the Making of Modern New Mexico

María E. Montoya (2002)

On May 20, 1935, Dennis Chavez entered the U. S. Senate chamber to take his oath as senator of the United States. New Mexico governor Clyde Tingley had recently appointed Chavez to take the place of Senator Bronson Cutting after the latter's untimely death. As Vice President John Vance Garner called Chavez to the front of the chamber to administer the oath, Senator Charles L. McNary of Oregon suggested the absence of a quorum. McNary's question must have confused Chavez, since the Senate chamber looked full to him. Nevertheless, the vice president asked the clerk to call the roll. As the clerk called each senator's name, he stood and answered. However, as six of the senators answered, they stood and turned their backs as Chavez walked down the aisle toward the front of the chamber. Then they left the chamber in protest.

Why did the senators do this? Did they resent Chavez because he had been appointed to take the place of their beloved colleague Bronson Cutting? Chavez had run against Cutting for the Senate and lost in a close election. Chavez then launched a complaint against Cutting for voter fraud. Unfortunately, Cutting died in a plane crash as he returned to New Mexico to answer those charges. Although Cutting was a Republican, he had been a progressive who strongly supported Roosevelt's New Deal. Many senators, including those who had walked out of the chamber, felt that Roosevelt and the Senate had not sufficiently supported Cutting and had let the proceedings drag on. Now Chavez had unjustly profited from the tragedy. Or did the senators who turned their backs to Chavez resent having a Mexican American, someone who many of them thought below their station, in their elite midst?

Curiously, whether this snubbing of Senator Chavez on the first day of what was to become his illustrious Senate career occurred remains unclear. There is no discussion of the incident in the official records of the Senate and only a brief mention in Chavez's personal papers. Nevertheless, historical myth and legend have perpetuated the story about the painful induction of Dennis Chavez into the most prestigious club in the United States. Veracity aside, this story remains a telling moment about how New Mexicans have perceived themselves in relation to the rest of the United States. Statehood and all its privileges aside, Chavez's induction has been seen as emblematic of how poorly New Mexicans, particularly Mexican American and Native American citizens, had been treated by the federal government and eastern lawmakers. New Mexico's low status in Washington, however, would end as Chavez came to wield immense power within the Senate during his career.

The Senate's snubbing of Chavez in the midst of the New Deal can be read in two ways. First, in the eyes of many lawmakers, Chavez epitomized the political corruption that plagued several western states. For many eastern critics, Chavez's questioning of the election results, and implicitly the democratic process, illustrated that New Mexicans were incapable of non-partisan self-government. This negative, and somewhat racist, view of New Mexicans had pervaded American political rhetoric since 1848 and the Mexican-American War, when senators such as John Calhoun wondered how New Mexicans with their "mongrel" heritage and "debased" political system could thrive in the American republic. Anti-New Mexican rhetoric ebbed and flowed throughout the territorial period (1850–1912) as New Mexican legislators tried to gain statehood and the rights of citizenship for their people. The U.S. Senate probably did not view Dennis Chavez, a young Mexican American from a poor family, as an appropriate replacement for the older, dashing, and patrician Bronson Cutting. Chavez represented a kind of populism and ethnic politics that the Senate liked to believe it was above.

Second, the senate's treatment of Chavez can be read as illustrative of the overt hostility and racism of the nation toward Mexican Americans in the 1930s. Chavez came to the Senate just as state and local governments in the American Southwest were engaged in some of their most discriminatory behavior against Mexican nationals and Mexican American citizens in U.S. history. City and state governments all across the Southwest, with the help of the federal government, deported Mexican nationals and Mexican American citizens. How many people were "repatriated" is unknown, but probably more than a half million people were torn from their jobs, homes, and families and shipped across the border to an alien place. Newspapers and public officials from Los Angeles to Denver to Albuquerque denounced the "hordes" of Mexicans who crossed the border and pushed American citizens out of work just at the moment that the nation faced its most devastating economic crisis — the Great Depression.

Ironically, until the early 1930s American businesses such as the mining and logging industries, agricultural interests, and the railroads had welcomed Mexican laborers because these men provided a readily available and relatively cheap labor force. The female immigrants, moreover, gave wealthy American families across the Southwest a reliable supply of domestic workers — cooks, nannies, home nurses, maids, and laundresses. After the stock crash and the onset of the Great Depression, however, Mexicans and Mexican Americans were no longer welcomed. Government officials and vocal citizens feared that people of Mexican heritage would overcrowd relief agencies and prohibit "deserving" — read white — Americans from receiving government aid.

Within this historical context of discriminatory political rhetoric and repatriation, Dennis Chavez constantly reshaped his ethnic identity, but not his political agenda, as he struggled for power within the Senate. He was consciously aware of the political and public role he played, not only for himself within the world of the Washington beltway and New Mexico's *patrón* politics, but also for his constituents, most of whom still suffered as second-class U.S. citizens in terms of employment, voting, and education. Acknowledging the low status of most Mexican Americans in the middle of the twentieth century, Chavez was quoted as saying, "If they [Mexican-Americans] go to war, they're Americans; if they run for office, they're Spanish Americans; but if they're looking for a job, they're damned Mexicans." Chavez astutely observed that the racialization of Mexican Americans depended on the political climate as well as the class status of Mexican Americans within American society. Chavez knew that money and higher class status allowed more opportunity for racial minorities, and he worked hard to equal the playing field for all New Mexicans, regardless of social or economic status. During his illustrious career, Chavez attended the most elegant of state dinners in Washington, D.C., yet despite his prestigious social position, he always remembered what it was like to grow up poor and hungry for success. It was for the people who came from similarly disadvantaged backgrounds that Chavez worked the hardest during his career, which spanned from the New Deal to the cold war.

Senator Dennis Chavez was born Dionisio Chavez on April 8, 1888, in a small community just outside of Albuquerque, New Mexico, in Valencia County. He was the eldest son of a farming couple, David Chavez and Paz Sanchez Chavez, who eventually raised eight children. Seven years after Dennis was born, the Chavez family moved to Albuquerque to find better employment opportunities for the family and to allow the children to attend school. Because the family was in such dire economic circumstances, however, Dennis had to drop out of school after the eighth grade and worked as a grocery delivery boy. He worked long days that began at 6 A.M. Thirteen-year-old Chavez earned $2.75 a week, which he added to his family's income.

Dennis Chavez, however, never gave up on the idea of educating himself. He had an intense interest in biography and history, and many of his neighbors commented on the long hours he spent in the public library, reading voraciously. His interest in history perhaps encouraged him to think about politics long before he could vote. More-over, his father was a stalwart in Hispano Republican politics, and although Dennis Chavez disagreed politically with his father and eventually joined the Democratic Party, he admired and mimicked his father's political activism. There was also a much more practical side to Chavez's desire to attain an education. When not working or reading history, Chavez attended night school and studied land surveying. His extra studying paid off; in 1905 Chavez went to work for the Albuquerque city engineering department. In his new position, he earned five times more than he had as a grocery deliverer.

After changing jobs and earning financial stability, Chavez found his place in the city. First he married Imelda Espinosa in 1911. Then he began to take an active role in New Mexico politics, particularly in the struggle to secure statehood in 1912. Four years later he entered his first political campaign but lost his bid for county clerk. In that same election year, however, he also acted as the Spanish interpreter for Andreius A. Jones, a successful Democratic candidate for the U.S. Senate. Jones rewarded Chavez by giving him a job as a clerk in his Washington, D.C., office. While clerking, Chavez was accepted into Georgetown University law studies by special examination because he did not have a high school diploma. After three years of night law school, he earned his Bachelor of Law (LL.B.) Degree in 1920 at the age of thirty-two.

Chavez and Imelda returned to Albuquerque, where he established a law prac-tice and restarted his political career. He quickly won a seat in the state House of Rep-resentatives and constantly campaigned for Democratic candidates across the state. In 1930 he easily won a seat in the U.S. House of Representatives as part of the New Deal landslide that swept the nation. After that success, he was consistently associated with Franklin D. Roosevelt and his policies. In 1934 Chavez felt confident enough to take on the popular Bronson Cutting for his U.S. Senate seat. Chavez lost that race, but the Democratic governor, Clyde Tingley, then Chavez's strong supporter, intervened and appointed Chavez to the empty seat left after Cutting's unfortunate death.

Although Dennis Chavez had already established a successful political career prior to his appointment as senator, he cut his political teeth on President Franklin D. Roosevelt's New Deal. Moreover, he was largely responsible for New Mexico's political shift in the 1930s, when the state became a stronghold for the Democrats. During the New Deal and World War II, New Mexico moved away from the Republican Party, with which it had been closely aligned during the first part of the twentieth century, and sought the largesse of the federal government through the Democrats. The major reason for this shift was that for the first time in the state's history the federal govern-ment, because of New Deal programs, began to pay close attention to local problems and met the needs of the state's people. New Mexicans' benefits from these New Deal programs resulted from Chavez's power in the Senate and his ability to bring federal government patronage to his constituents.....

The New Deal spawned a myriad of national programs. Among the most popular and well known, the Agricultural Adjustment Act and the Taylor Grazing

Act benefitted the state tremendously. There were, however, two other sets of programs that more clearly addressed the most troubling problems facing the majority of New Mexicans at the height of the depression: inadequate job training, unemployment, and hunger. First, the federal government, through programs such as the Work Projects Administration (WPA), attempted to revive the culture and arts of New Mexico's Hispano and Pueblo Indian populations. Second, through programs such as the Civilian Conservation Corps (CCC) and the National Youth Administration (NYA), the New Deal trained New Mexico's youth to participate more fully in the industrial and market economy slowly emerging in New Mexico. Although Senator Chavez supported all programs that brought money and aid to the state, he was particularly interested in measures that retrained New Mexicans to move away from their agriculturally based lifestyles to become better educated workers.

One of the most enduring legacies of the New Deal for New Mexicans was the impact of the WPA and the Public Works Administration (PWA) in the state. Many of New Mexico's public buildings, from the capitol in Santa Fe to the University of New Mexico to the Colfax County Courthouse, benefitted from the fine craftsmanship and artwork of professional artists and burgeoning artisans. Moreover, potters and weavers from the Rio Grande Pueblos, as well as Hispano *santeros* and weavers, were paid to rediscover and work in their historic arts and crafts. Artists such as Pablita Velarde recalled the important role that the WPA played in helping them to practice their art during the lean years of the depression. Since New Mexico already had a national reputation in the art world, because of patrons such as Mabel Dodge Luhan, the state was an ideal place for the WPA to experiment with aiding artists and reviving traditional arts and crafts. Reformers such as Mary Austin, who had gained notoriety because of her book *The Land of Little Rain*, saw Hispanos and Pueblo Indians as people who stood outside the modern world. She and others who urged this revival of traditional arts and crafts thought that Hispanos and Indians could provide a model for the rest of American society of how to live a simpler life more in harmony with nature. Perhaps Austin and others saw what capitalism had wrought in the form of the depression and the dust bowl, and they wanted Americans to return to their preindustrial origins. Because this view was an oversimplified and romantic vision of the state's residents, relief agents saw the Pueblos and Hispano villages as vestiges of a premodern, preindustrial utopia that needed to be preserved.....

Even though Senator Chavez supported these programs and worked to secure their funding, he did not see this first set of programs as directly addressing New Mexico's most pressing economic needs. Instead he used his influence to bring a second set of programs to the state, best exemplified by the CCC and the NYA, both of which took different views of how New Mexicans should face the hardships brought on by the depression. These programs trained young men in the industrial and vocational arts so that they could find wage work outside the agricultural sector. The NYA, created under the WPA, was a particularly favorite project of Senator Chavez, and he worked to keep it well funded. The program took a two-pronged approach to dealing with New Mexico's youth. The student aid program provided a small stipend of $6 to high school and college students to encourage them to stay in school and not join the workforce, which provided few opportunities. In return, the students performed clerical work, library duties, and, in some cases, research for school staff, teachers, and professors. The second program addressed the problem of unemployment among those young people who simply could not afford to stay enrolled in school. The NYA paid them $17 a month, and they worked primarily in the area of public works, providing upkeep of public facilities, beautification of parks, and construction of playgrounds, swimming pools, and other recreational facilities. These young people also served as recreational leaders and worked in hospitals, schools, and libraries.

In New Mexico, the NYA pumped more than $1 million into the economy during the program's first three years of existence. About one-fourth of the funding went to students enrolled in school, the rest to students seeking employment. By the time the program ended, more than three thousand New Mexican students had been helped by the program. Chavez, through his constituents, realized the benefits of this program. Whenever the program was threatened, he worked to maintain the funding levels that had made it such a success. For example, in 1937, when Congress discussed decreasing the program's budget, E. H. Wells, president of the New Mexico School of Mines, complained directly to Chavez, who immediately went to work to ensure that funding was not cut to the NYA. Even after World War II began and there was talk of phasing out the program, Chavez worked to preserve the program by changing the NYA's mission. After 1941 it trained young people to work in the defense industry to meet the labor shortage resulting from the military buildup and the simultaneous departure of young men to the war.

The CCC was similarly situated to provide job training and an introduction to industrial life for the nation's young men. Unlike the NYA, however, this program targeted men over the age of eighteen: young men who were beyond high school age but not college bound. The CCC addressed two of the major problems facing the nation at the height of the depression. First, the program tried to diminish the problem of massive unemployment and the consequent mobility of jobless young men who roamed the country, riding on railcars and looking for work. These down-on-their-luck men came to be exemplified by the hobo: the dirty young man, the bindle stiff with his worldly possessions tied to a pole. The CCC also tried to alleviate the environmental destruction that faced the nation as a result of the dust bowl. Nation-wide, thousands of young men went to work planting trees, creating trails and roads, fighting fires, and improving the nation's national parks. In New Mexico, the CCC carried out a number of ambitious projects, including the creation of all the buildings and roads at Bandelier National Monument. The program also ran a separate set of programs within the pueblos, which were administered by the CCC in conjunction with the Bureau of Indian Affairs (BIA), employing only Native men. In exchange for the labor they provided on these projects, the men and their families were paid $25 a month (quite a large sum during the depression). Five dollars went to the recruit, and the other $20 went directly home to his family. This cash infusion into the New Mexican economy provided an essential component for the recovery of the state.

The CCC, aside from simply putting cash into the economy, also left a long-term legacy to the state's inhabitants when preparing its young men to face the rigors of a wartime economy. The Department of War oversaw the supplying and assembling of the CCC camps, and so a military model was stylized to establish the hundreds of camps across the nation. Men applied and were inducted into the camps, where the young recruits spent the first couple of weeks in a "boot camp" environment that helped them adjust to the rigors of camp life. The men rose at 6 A.M., showered and shaved, made their bunks, and cleaned up before reporting for reveille at 7 A.M. After breakfast, men were sent to the agency they worked for — the National Park Service, the National Forest Service, or the Bureau of Reclamation, just to name a few — to complete their work for the day. In the evening, after they had eaten, the men had free time, although they were encouraged to improve themselves through working on their high school diplomas, acquiring a trade, learning to read English, or undertaking other kinds of personal improvement. The time that these men spent in the CCC prepared them to enter the rapidly changing world that resulted from World War II. Many graduates from the CCC went directly into military service or used their new skills as carpenters, mechanics, welders, and heavy machine operators to work in the military-industrial complex developing in New Mexico, Colorado, California, and in other parts of the American West....

Ironically, Senator Chavez had been reluctant about the U.S. entry into World War II. He consistently counseled President Roosevelt to remain neutral. Chavez even voted against the first Lend-Lease Bill in March 1941, which provided aid to the Allies fighting Hitler. By October 1941, however, he had changed his position and solidly backed Roosevelt's support of the Allied forces in Europe. Moreover, after the bombing of Pearl Harbor, Chavez became a supporter of U.S. entry into the fighting, and through his work on the Defense Appropriations Committee, he worked to prepare Americans to win the war. In foreign policy, Senator Chavez was integral to the success of the Good Neighbor Policy, which sought to create closer ties between the United States and nations to the south, especially Mexico. Roosevelt and other advocates of the policy hoped that by creating better relationships, Mexico would become a strong ally against the Axis powers. Americans still remembered the Zimmerman Telegraph incident from World War I, when Germany had supposedly proposed an alliance with Mexico, which if successful would return the territory lost during the Mexican-American War to Mexico. Chavez, with his command of Spanish and his interest in the Caribbean and Latin America, became an important player in Roosevelt's foreign policy initiative. His position as an American statesman and a diplomat was a role that he would play throughout the rest of his political career in expanding this idea of good neighborliness. Chavez worked to improve relations with Mexico and pushed for the creation of the Pan American Highway, which sought to link the Americas through a modern highway system.

Today Los Alamos National Laboratory is just the most famous imprint that the federal government left on the New Mexican landscape as a result of World War II and its aftermath. During World War II and the ensuing cold war, Senator Dennis Chavez came to wield immense power within the U.S. Senate. Through his influence he brought many federal facilities — White Sands Missile Range, Sandia National Laboratories, and Kirtland Air Force Base — and consequently opportunities and jobs to New Mexico. In 1960, when Senator Chavez served as chair of the Senate Defense Appropriations Committee, President Dwight D. Eisenhower recommended one of the largest ever peacetime budgets for military preparedness. Chavez, however, recommended a budget that added $1 billion more to the Eisenhower budget, saying, "There can be no price tag on freedom," revealing his commitment to fighting the cold war. His desire to fund the cold war at such an intense level, however, also revealed Chavez's political pragmatism since he sought to funnel much of that spending to his own state's constituents. New Mexico's residents were one of the great beneficiaries of this increased federal spending during the cold war years, when thousands of New Mexicans went to work for the federal government in a myriad of jobs brought to the state by Chavez's deft political skill in the Senate.

This increased federal spending had two profound influences on New Mexico's economy and political position nationwide. First, the cold war and New Mexico's ability to attract federal contracts made it extremely dependent on the U.S. federal government. For every dollar that New Mexicans pay in federal income taxes, they receive almost $4 in direct federal benefits in federal paychecks and appropriations to the state's facilities. Although New Mexicans have entered the modern world of high-tech enterprise, they have continued to depend on the federal government to provide those jobs and contracts. During the nineteenth century, New Mexico maintained a colonial relationship with the rest of the United States because of its dependence on eastern and foreign investment. Still, New Mexico in many ways remained in that same colonial stance throughout the late twentieth century. Since the New Deal and World War II, the state has continued to depend on the largesse of the federal government and expenditures associated with the cold war buildup of the military-industrial complex.

Second, the cold war era brought increased opportunity for many New Mexicans, particularly for Mexican Americans and Native Americans. Because of the increased federal presence in contracts, as well as in civil rights protection and fair employment practices, many New Mexicans began to reap the benefits of industrialism and wage work. The prevalence of the federal government allowed for thousands of New Mexicans to work their way into America's middle class. These federal jobs provided wages and benefits that allowed New Mexicans to complete high school, go to college or vocational school, own homes, and begin to take their share of the American dream. Senator Dennis Chavez seemed to understand that civil rights and fair-employment-practices legislation had to go hand in hand with federal appropriations for the military-industrial complex if New Mexicans were to benefit. Throughout the latter part of his career, Chavez pushed for civil rights protection for African, Native, and Mexican Americans. He also drafted the Fair Employment Practice legislation that sought to protect American workers from job discrimination, which, regrettably, did not pass when he first introduced it into the Senate. Unfortunately, Senator Chavez would not live to see the sweeping civil rights legislation and fair employment legislation the Lyndon Johnson administration passed as part of its Great Society programs. Nevertheless, it is important to remember that Chavez pioneered the push for fair employment and civil rights in the 1940s, long before his colleagues in the Senate came around to accepting the legislation.

Senator Chavez died in 1962 after a long struggle against cancer. At his death he was the fourth-highest-ranking senator in the U.S. Senate. He had come a long way in his career since his first date in the Senate chamber in 1935, when many questioned his ability and right to be a U.S. senator. Chavez had lived to prove them all wrong and alleviate any doubt about his capabilities as a legislator and political leader. Throughout his career, Chavez transformed New Mexican politics and the state's economy. Through his influence, New Mexico left the fold of the Republican Party and became a Democratic stronghold that lasted well into the 1960s. Just as Chavez had supported Roosevelt's New Deal, he also chaired the Viva Kennedy campaign in New Mexico and voiced his support for President Kennedy's and Johnson's visions of America. But Chavez's most enduring legacy in New Mexico was that he helped usher its economy and people into the modern world of the twentieth century. Whether through New Deal programs such as the WPA or the NYA or through later military buildup, Chavez always made sure that New Mexico received a generous share of federal appropriations. Chavez worked consistently to ensure that New Mexicans were well trained, fairly employed, and had access to the best jobs and opportunities available to Americans during the middle part of the twentieth century.

Navajo Indian captives under guard at Fort Sumner, east-central New Mexico, during the Bosque Redondo incarceration, about 1864–68. Photograph by United States Army Signal Corps.

42

The Navajo-Diné Century of Progress, 1868–1968, and the Bosque Redondo Memorial

Jennifer Nez Denetdale (2007)

On 4 June 2005, hundreds of Diné and their allies gathered at Fort Sumner, New Mexico, to officially open the Bosque Redondo Memorial. Sitting under an arbor, visitors listened to dignitaries interpret the meaning of the Long Walk, explain the four years of imprisonment at the Bosque Redondo, and discuss the Navajos' return to their homeland in 1868. Earlier that morning, a small gathering of Diné offered their prayers to the Holy People.

In the past twenty years, historic sites have become popular tourist attractions, partially as a result of partnerships between state historic preservation departments and the National Park Service. With the twin goals of educating the public about the American past and promoting their respective states as attractive travel destinations, park officials and public historians have also included Native American sites. Mindful that Native people must be involved in all levels of planning and establishing historic sites, they have invited Natives to participate. This endeavor purports to incorporate Native perspectives into the design and content of historic sites projects.

As is true of other memorials that were established to remind the public of significant American events involving its Native peoples, the Bosque Redondo Memorial was created to recognize Navajo experiences. By acknowledging these struggles, the memorial also brings Navajos into the American historical narrative, thereby signifying that, as a modern nation, the United States has embraced multiculturalism. The memorial perhaps will also illuminate the unjust treatment Navajos received from the United States and possibly inspire reconciliation. The memorial, which has drawn Navajos' embrace and skepticism, serves as a point from which to reflect upon the ways that their experiences under American colonialism have been understood by both Navajos and non-Indians.…

A Century of Progress, 1868–1968

In 1968 Navajo leaders announced a series of cultural events to commemorate the signing of the Treaty of 1868. Like non-Navajo scholars, they declared that the treaty between the Diné and United States and the People's return heralded the birth of the Navajo Nation. From the 1960s to the 1970s, American historians characterized the survival of the Navajos under American conquest as mirroring that of Anglo frontiers-men and women in conflicts with Mexicans and Indians. For example Iverson (1981, 10) explained the significance of the Navajo experience at Bosque Redondo and their return to their homeland:

> Previously, the Navajos had had things in common culturally, but politically there had been little centralization. They had lived in widely scattered locations, and authority was vested solely in local head-men. Their allegiances and frames of references were based on a far more limited area. But now things would be altered. They had gone through the common crucible of the Long Walk experience. Now, through the treaty of 1868, they would be returned to a portion of their old home country, but they would return to a reservation with strictly defined borders. Their political boundaries had been estab-lished: the Navajo Nation had begun.

The image of a crucible — of people withstanding incredible odds — is common in American history (e.g. Weber 1988; Dippie 1976). According to this type of history, after surviving U.S. genocidal policies, Navajos agreed to become both American and Navajo citizens, their choice affirming America's story as a liberal nation that embraces multiculturalism.

One of the purposes of the 1968 anniversary events was to provide Navajo citizens with opportunities to reflect upon the meaning of the past one hundred years since their return from captivity. American nationalist notions of progress empha-sized society development toward a more civilized and democratic state (modeled on white civilized society) and a universal history inclusive of all people and cultures (see Smith 1999). The modern Navajo government, which is founded upon the principles established in the Indian Reorganization Act of 1934, asserted national sovereignty in the 1960s, a decade during which Navajo leaders fully embraced liberal ideologies as the foundation of their political system (Wilkins 2002; Wilkins 1999). The events of the mid-nineteenth century were a portent for the formation of a Navajo nation.

Navajo leaders and their non-Indian allies identified 1868 as a watershed that marked the beginning of the modern Navajo Nation and the accompanying discourse about the wonders of development for the Navajo people. At the same time, some Navajos formed grassroots organizations to empower their communities and condemn their leaders' support of policies that impoverished Navajos and kept them dependent on the federal government and internal white control.

The creation and perpetuation of a modern Navajo nation hinged on fostering a collective consciousness through cultural events and ceremonies. Navajo leaders collaborated with non-Indian and Navajo intellectuals and educators to implement cultural awareness of their national past (Anderson 1991, 6; McClintock 1993). Beginning in January 1968, cultural events took place throughout the year. These occasions included a round-up in June, Centennial Days celebration in July, and tribal fairs in August and September, culminating in a re-enactment of the return from Hwéeldi [the prison camp] along one of the routes that the Navajo captives had taken to and from Fort Sumner. The tribally owned *Navajo Times* and the *Gallup Independent* — a border-town paper — announced the centennial events and published images of Navajo progress. These images included photographs of the development of natural resources and exhibits of Navajos utilizing Western technologies for agriculture. Listing many accomplishments, the dominant Navajo narrative heralded the establishment of the modern Navajo government after returning from Bosque Redondo and the successful Navajo entrance into modern American society.

Navajo chairman Raymond Nakai delivered a speech at the opening of the centennial year that recapped the meaning of the one hundred years following the Navajos' return from their nightmare:

> The Century of Progress which we commemorate has not been an easy one hundred years. It was initiated by the tragic and heartbreaking "long march" from Ft. Sumner. It marked a struggle of a proud people, accustomed to roam unfettered over the vast expanses of this great western United States. It reflects the slow, but steady progress of our people to this very moment. However difficult has been our struggle, never was the faith of the Navajo people the least bit diminished in their ultimate place in society. Never did the Navajo despair. Always, he sought and fought for a better way of life. All in all, this past one hundred years does reflect great progress on the part of our people. (Link 1968, 108)

Nakai's speech was published in two centennial publications: *Navajoland, U.S.A.: First Hundred Years, 1868–1968* (1968) and *Navajo: A Century of Progress, 1868–1968* (1968). These two books explain that the political history of the Navajos prior to 1863 was essentially nonexistent and that the Navajo Nation emerged after the United

States politically organized it in the 1930s and 1940s (Allen 1968; Link 1968). Both publications avoid discussing the violence that Navajos experienced as the Americans brought them "democracy" and "peace."

Many images from this period, which were disseminated in a number of fairs beginning in the early 1950s, celebrated the development of Navajo natural resources such as coal, natural gas, and uranium, which ostensibly meant that Navajos would have access to electricity, running water, and other modern conveniences. Monies from development projects would allow Navajo children to receive Western education. Benefits from modernity for Navajo women would include suburban-style homes and appliances that eased their domestic life. Certainly, for women, the messages about Navajo entrance into the modern nation also meant that they had accepted Western concepts of appropriate gender roles. At the same time that Navajo leaders heralded the benefits of modernity, they also expressed ambivalence, for modern life seemed to contradict Navajo cultural values. The images of prosperity were balanced with messages about the necessity of retaining cultural continuity with the past. As Povinelli (2002) has observed, such declarations have been interpreted as the successful integration of Native people into the modern nation; thereby rendering invisible the intolerance and hatred of indigenous cultures that espouse distinctively different beliefs and values from those of the settler nation. Further, the discourse of the multicultural nation ensures that the United States does not have to acknowledge that it used coercion and repression to achieve its goal of assimilating its indigenous inhabitants into its polity.

By the 1980s, however, fractures in the images of prosperity began to appear as critics noted that the Department of the Interior, which oversaw Indian affairs and was supposed to aid the Indian tribes, worked hand-in-hand with corporations to bilk the Navajo tribe out of much-needed monies. The development of natural resources such as coal, gas, and uranium, meant to ensure Navajos' arrival into mainstream America, did not improve their lives. In fact the growth was directly connected to the forced relocation of thousands of Navajos in northern Arizona over the span of several decades. The coal and uranium mining also caused environmental degradation (Grinde and Johansen 2001). The uranium boom left Navajo miners and their families struggling with death, cancer, and other consequences related to radiation exposure (Eichstaedt 1994; Navajo Uranium Miner Project 1997).

Navajo leaders negotiated, and are continuing to negotiate, water rights agreements that benefit developers in the Southwest and American citizens, but have done little to alleviate the poverty of their own people (Wilkinson 2004). The opening of the Navajo sawmill, which had been lauded as profitable, was closed after Navajos who formed Diné Citizens Against Ruining Our Environment (CARE), a grassroots organization dedicated to preserving Navajo lands and resources, raised questions about forestry practices that were destroying the natural environment. This questioning, combined with federal resource-management requirements, eventually led to the closing of the sawmill in Navajo, New Mexico (Gabriel 1994; Sherry 2002). Moreover, as postcolonial critics have pointed out, ideologies of nations, based on Western concepts, reinscribe relationships of hierarchy, domination, and asymmetry, including gender roles, which have included women's limited participation in the political arena.

Native scholars such as Vine Deloria Jr., David E. Wilkins, Taiaiake Alfred, Andrea Smith, and Joanne Barker have problematized the roots of Native governments and articulated the ways in which those governments have become dominated by a foreign sovereign settler state. Alfred (1999; 2005), a Mohawk political theorist, calls for indigenous critiques that will demythologize Euroamerican conquest of Native peoples and enable a movement toward reorientation and recover of indigenous politics and political traditions in their present-day societies. The articulation of the Navajo past and the meaning of the Long Walk and the Bosque Redondo experience by Navajo leaders in the 1950s, 1960s, and 1970s reflects the ways in which tribal governments have been co-opted by the United States. In addition continuous challenges by Navajo activists are forcing their leaders to question the doctrine of state sovereignty and white society's dominion over the Navajo Nation and its lands.

The Treaty of 1868 and the Bosque Redondo Memorial

The seeds to establish the Bosque Redondo Memorial were planted in the 1968 centennial commemoration. Over several decades, Navajos and their allies kept attention focused on the creation of a memorial. In 1968 the town of Fort Sumner bought a section of the Bosque Redondo and deeded it to the state of New Mexico for that purpose. Early on Navajo visitors to Fort Sumner noted that little evidence remained of the army fort and prison camp, where their ancestors had eked out a living. As a reminder of their ancestors' experiences, representatives of the Navajo Nation established a rock cairn to commemorate the spot on 14 February 1971 (McNitt 1970; Stewart 1970a; Stewart 1970b).

Gregory Scott Smith (2003), manager of the state monument in 2003, acknowledged the bitter history of the relationships between Navajos and white Americans and declared the memorial's significance: "It will honor the memory of thousands of Navajo and Mescalero Apache people who suffered and died as a result of the forced relocation and internment. Moreover, it will celebrate the official birth of a sovereign nation born of the tragedy of the Bosque Redondo." Like other memorials, such as the one to preserve the memory of the Sand Creek massacre in Colorado, the Bosque Redondo monument acknowledges the United States' record of injustices against its indigenous peoples. Perhaps the memorials will force Americans to begin questioning the facade of American superiority and exceptionalism.

In their remembrances of the Long Walk and the Bosque Redondo, Navajos have pointed to the Treaty of 1868 as an indication that the United States recognized Navajo sovereignty. A year after the 1968 centennial, the tribal council passed a resolution to name their tribe the "Navajo Nation." This official act affirmed and declared Navajo sovereignty (Iverson 2002, 245). On 1 June 1999, Treaty Day, Navajo educators and leaders brought the original treaty document from the National Archives in Washington, D.C., to Cline Library at Northern Arizona University in Flagstaff, Arizona, for a yearlong celebration of Navajo nationhood. Thousands of Navajos journeyed to view the document. On Treaty Day, Navajos gathered at the university campus to commemorate the Treaty of 1868. Sight of the treaty unleashed a flood of stories passed down through Diné memory. While the People remembered the nightmare of the 1860s, when Americans subjugated their ancestors, they also told stories of how their ancestors sacrificed to enable the People's return to their beloved homeland, where they could begin the process of rebuilding their lives (Iverson 2002, 36).

In 1992 the New Mexico State Legislature passed a House measure directing the Office of Cultural Affairs to establish the Bosque Redondo as a memorial to the Navajo people. With federal and state monies, a structure was created to house a museum and a visitor center. Although additional funding is required to complete the memorial site, the memorial officially opened on 4 June 2005 (Cisneros and Smith 2003). Planners included Navajos in establishing the memorial and organizing the official dedication. However, they also expressed concern that all participants remain "civil" as Navajos and non-Navajos presented their interpretations of the Navajo past.

In November 2005, the National Park Service held a conference in Window Rock, Arizona, to invite Navajo responses to the proposal for creating a national memorial to the Long Walk and the Bosque Redondo experiences. A day of listening to testimony about the Long Walk and Hwéeldi made clear that the 141 intervening years had not dimmed the impact on Navajo bitterness. Waiting patiently all day and listening to speakers explain the importance of establishing the memorial, local Navajo community members finally got a chance to share their stories. Just as their grandparents had heard and conveyed the stories to the next generation, the participants shared their own, which were filled with images of violence, hunger, sickness, and loneliness. There were moments when emotions threatened to overcome the presenters and the audience alike. At the same time that the People mourned, they also celebrated the courage and resilience of their grandmothers and grandfathers. Our ancestors who survived Bosque Redondo and returned to Dinétah had persevered by remembering the teachings of the Holy People. Our memories were a testament to the People's vision, courage, and resilience.

To what extent do American narratives of the past merge with Navajo memories? Do Navajo and non-Indian perspectives about the American past contrast dramatically? The official commemoration of the Bosque Redondo offers some clues. During the course of planning the events for 4 June, I served as a consultant at the request of the organizers. One coordinator from a state office in Santa Fe requested my vita — to see if I might be qualified to speak — and solicited recommendations for speakers. The person cautioned me that "they" were interested in speakers who would not be controversial and who would not call the Bosque Redondo "a concentration camp." Although the planners and organizers hoped for a "civil" program throughout the dedication, Navajo leaders were forthcoming in naming their ancestors' humiliating and atrocious experiences at the Bosque Redondo prison camp. Navajo Nation president Joe Shirley Jr. said, "The story needs to be told, to serve as a reminder of the genocide and the holocaust that were perpetrated on a nation." Lawrence Morgan, Speaker of the Navajo Nation Council, said the memorial represented a "slaughterhouse" and that while not all Navajos supported the memorial it should become a tool for education and healing (Moffett 2005; *Indian Country Today*, June 13, 2005). Other speakers such as Lt. Gov. Diane Denish hoped that America had learned something from this horrific time in history and that it would not be repeated. These speakers noted that the Navajo Nation, having survived this trauma, had grown stronger. It was, however, obvious on that same day that many Americans still had not made the connection between America's imperial past and the present imperial war in Iraq.

As Sen. Pete Domenici delivered his remarks, Nicole Walker, a Diné woman, entered the area where dignitaries sat, interrupted him, and began addressing the crowd. In memory of her ancestors who had survived the forced march to Hwéeldi, Walker and her family members had begun walking down U.S. Highway 83 to Fort Sumner at three o'clock in the morning. Her granddaughter carried the Navajo Nation flag for the contingent. Walker's grief, expressed in her wailing, moved the audience into a silence that could be heard. In the midst of Walker's interruption, reporters and photographers rushed to the front to capture for a larger audience this moment of fracture in the "official" program (*Albuquerque Sunday Journal*, June 5, 2005). Certainly Walker's dramatic performance indicates that Navajos still resist non-Indians' interpretations of their past, especially regarding the Long Walk and the Bosque Redondo. Navajo citizen Chester C. Clah wrote about the dedication in a letter to the *Navajo Times* (June 23, 2005):

June 4, 2005, will always be remembered as a day of healing and it certainly gave me a spiritual boost. Our ancestors were at last recognized for their sacrifice and hardships they encountered. Tears were shed openly when Nicole Walker made her entrance wailing like our grandmothers did back then. I want to thank her for her undying effort to put across to the dignitaries what exactly the U.S. government put our people through.… Our ancestors were like Christ. They made the ultimate sacrifice to retain our homeland.

Clah went on to urge his fellow Navajos to visit the memorial and pay tribute to our grandmothers and grandfathers. On January 27, 2006, the Navajo Nation council decided not to support the state of New Mexico and the National Park Service's call to establish the Long Walk trail system (*Gallup Independent*, January 28, 2006; *Navajo Times*, February 2, 2006). That vote indicates the ambivalence that many Navajos still feel toward speaking about their past.

Map of the Territory of New Mexico (1873). 1": 760 320". Courtesy Fray Angélico Chávez History Library (NMHM/DCA).

PART SEVEN

MY NEW MEXICO

"New Mexico History is worth remembering," state historian Estevan Rael-Gálvez writes in his "Welcome to the New Mexico Digital History Project" (newmexicohistory.org): "To remember is to call something to mind, pass it back through your heart, make it whole and finally it is, as the Spanish word 'recordar' implies, to awaken. Here, remembering the past is like opening a gift. Remembering invites us to listen to what we hear and to look at what we see; it also invites us to pull back the layers that make it contested — people, places, moments in time and the stories that reveal the fullness of the human condition. Yet, like any gift worth holding onto, it also carries a responsibility. We must be able to learn from those who have gone before us and we must be able to teach our children to appreciate the value of this historical understanding. It will invite them, in turn, to make History that is also worth remembering." Telling and heeding the (hi)stories of "My New Mexico" is eminently worthy of such remembering, responsibility, and awakening. The nuclear world emerged here (Allen, Okawa, Hunner), and New Mexico remains a long-storied place of heroic migrations and the mingling of many peoples (Hughes, Torres and Rudnick, Nieto-Phillips, López, Hunner, Agoyo).

Navajo uranium miners gathered at the Mexican Water chapter house to discuss inadequacies of the Radiation Exposure Compensation Act, May 1993. Photograph by Peter Eichstaedt.

43

Radiant Beings, Laguna Pueblo

Paula Gunn Allen (1998)

In 1939, the year I was born, some uranium was dug up from Laguna Pueblo land. As Gossips have it, that uranium went into the making of the Bomb, the ones exploded in New Mexico and over Hiroshima and Nagasaki. A few days before I began to write this piece, my father, E. Lee Francis, former Lieutenant Governor of New Mexico and a man who delights in personal reminiscences, mentioned that he saw the bomb blast — though whether it was Fat Man or Little Boy, I don't know. He was receiving livestock out around Zuni, and even at that distance he saw the cloud. "What did it look like?" I asked. "Like smoke," he said. "It looked like smoke."

I guess he didn't know exactly what he'd seen for some time; maybe he realized what he'd seen when Americans learned that the United States had dropped the Bombs on Japan. It must have frightened them, my father, my mother, and her family, for Bobby, my mother's then eighteen-year-old brother, was somewhere over there. On the Pacific, anyway, or at least not in Europe. His few brief letters said little about where he was. Under wartime security, citizens and soldiers alike were mushrooms. Surely local folk were unaware that the earth the strangers (they had to be Anglos, Eastern Anglos, at that) dug up and took away would be milled somewhere and transformed into radiant death.

In the 1950s we schoolchildren were subjected to frequent Bomb Alerts — one of the many acts of terrorism, euphemistically called Civil Defense — visited upon our cowed heads. In the wake of one of these, my best friend, Teresa Baca, and I talked about the Bomb. She told me that her mother, Concepción, told her the people of Cubero saw a ring around the moon a few days before the first bomb test, and they knew that something awful (awe-full) was about to occur. (A person probably gets more accurate information relying on her sense and particular tradition than from textbooks or media!) I think Concepción saw the smoke the same day my dad did. They were both very far away from Stallion Gate, where it was detonated, one up around Zuni, one in Cubero. But in New Mexico in the 1940s you could see forever. The people of Nagasaki and Hiroshima saw forever — became forever — when the sky exploded above their unsuspecting heads, a couple of months after my dad and my friend's mom saw the omen of global transformation. I think that during that awe-full summer the Earth gave forth her new self, and all that is was transformed.

Following the local Gossips' hints, my mother and I visited the area where we thought the original uranium had been dug up forty years before. We walked over the rough land, trying to locate the site of the first uranium dig. It lay somewhere near the old road that had led from Laguna to its daughter-village, Paguate, but even its traces had been obliterated when the new paved road was built to expedite hauling huge supplies of uranium ore from the mine. We both knew that the petrified body of the old giant-ess that my great-grandmother used to tell about marked one side of that vanished road, and her equally petrified head, flung far from the torso, marked the other; we knew that the road had opened off old Highway 66 directly across from the door to Laguna Trading Post. The lost road had begun almost at the door of the old Gunn house, where we went on Feast Day at Laguna.

Mother and I figured that the giantess's remains lay close to the site we were seeking. But even knowing, we failed to find it. It was ever so much easier to find the huge tract of land overturned by Anaconda Company's vigorous mining at Jackpile mine, near Paguate. The huge rectangular heaps of flat-topped earth eerily resemble the sandstone mesas that dot the surrounding terrain, but they are not sandstone. Piled close upon one another, they are clearly human-made, and in their arrangement, they echo the image of eastern cities: towering artificial structures huddled together in fear and pain.

This year on Memorial Day, my friend Pat Smith, her friend Margaret Wimsatt, and I drove out there. I wanted to see Marquez, fabled community of my youth — my father's youth, really. I had heard his stories about it, but I had never been there. Marquez is located only a few miles from Laguna Village, just up from Paguate. It lies within the Seboyeta Land Grant, a large Mexican-American tract held by its heirs since it was granted to them by the King of Spain in the sixteenth century. When I returned to New Mexico in January of 1990, Pat and I agreed to go out to Marquez because there was mining activity out there and eerie goings-on persisted; tales of strange sightings had filtered through from there for decades.

I recall one legend in which I participated: it involved UFOs, several members of my family, a telescope, and a balmy midsummer's night in Cubero. I ran across my nephew's hastily scribbled notes, dated 6/8/75, among some papers last month. The time was between 9:15 and 11:10 P.M., the place was my parents' home on the bluff above Cubero. The notes record, "Bright object appearing very prominently in the southwest sky, conditions slightly cloudy, 63 degrees F. observed by.... Also appeared to expel bright projectiles; colors emitted were green, red, and blue alternating flashing (unreadable) of at 1–2 second intervals. Observed a bright..." Here the note ends because the next page is missing. At the time we were pretty sure that the lights were circling the peak of Mt. Taylor, lying to the north of Cubero, and they seemed to head toward the other flank where uranium mining operations were underway. That side of the mountain was near Seboyeta and the fabled Marquez.

So our little band of adventurers piled — somewhat creakily — into my BMW and headed west from Albuquerque. In the heat of the early summer day we traveled on I-40. Expanding beneath the forever sky, our thoughts leaped outward to catch the echoes of *katsina*, or *yei*, the profound thrumming of mountain spirits of this land. The sky magnified our souls, and our spirits rejoiced in the huge beautiful around us; it was *hozho*, beauty. In minds dilated to fullest extent as when birth is imminent, we flew, aloft on the spread wings of the forever sky, gaze and hearts held safe by the brown, blue, and lavender reaches of the land. Turning off the freeway, we drove the old highway from Mesita (the easternmost Laguna village), past Laguna village to the turnoff my mother and I had taken so many years before.

This day, our band's mission was to visit the shrine at Portales, north of Seboyeta (my father's birth home), and pay our respects to the Virgin who had saved his life when he was an infant. His older sister, a three-year-old, had given her infant brother a screw to play with, and he had swallowed it. Turning blue, he all but suffocated. His frantic grandmother and mother grabbed the choking baby and set off for Portales on their knees, praying to the Virgin the whole way. They crawled a couple of miles and offered him to the Madonna, dedicating him to her. Somehow, the screw passed through his entire digestive tract and was expelled into his diaper.

The following day his parents took him to Albuquerque — at the time a very long trip on a narrow highway that wound through quite a bit of Valencia County before coming into Albuquerque by way of Bernalillo to the north. The doctor pronounced the infant well, remarking that it was a miracle that the screw had not ripped his tiny intestines on its journey. In thanks, we had a family gathering at Portales every year, praying beneath the shelter of the massive white sandstone overhang that shaded the holy spring. The last picnic was the summer after my *jide* (grandfather in Arabic) died. That would have been about twenty years ago.

I grew up in the midst of oral legends that came from Laguna, Lebanon, Germany under Hitler, and family, as well as legends of the literary kind from around the world. My mother was possessed with eclectic albeit refined aesthetic tastes, and my father was (and is) an inveterate storyteller. Mother didn't see a great deal of literary difference in Laguna traditions, stories from the Bible (only the King James version satisfied her literary judgment), Greek and Roman mythology, and a variety of materials from England. When I was very small, my sister took me on a journey to Grandma's rock garden to hunt for fairies and little people — both kinds of beings as familiar to Laguna (or so Grandma Gunn's stories indicated) as to the British Isles.

Given my background, it is natural for me to perceive otherworldly correlations between the Bomb, the mines, and the stories — correlations that reveal the transformational nature of the powers nuclear fission unleashed. The raw ore from which uranium is milled is called yellowcake, and a supernatural female featured in much of the ritual Keres tradition is named Yellow Woman (which signifies Yellow Corn Woman). I don't think it's an accident that yellowcake is found in great abundance in the lands of Yellow Woman, where yellow corn grows in abundant sweetness. It is interesting that the Mayan word for *corn* is the same as for *dawn*, though exactly what that correspondence signifies for the Keres is unclear. It is also strangely coincidental that some naturalists see yellow corn as an antidote to poisoning by strontium 90, as many narratives in the oral tradition assert that no natural poison exists that is not closely accompanied by its antidote. And, too, the color of the feminine in the Laguna system is not pink, the color of the Sandias east of Albuquerque at sunset, but yellow, the color of sweetcorn, pollen, corn tassels, and sunrise.

There is an old story about Yellow Woman in which she is abducted by Whirlwind Man. (In other versions she is abducted by Evil Kachina, or by Sun Man.) According to the story, Yellow Woman went to the river to get water for her sisters and herself. There she was accosted by Whirlwind Man, who compelled her to go with him. She left her water jar by the river, a clue to her plight. Whirlwind Man carried her off to the other world where he remanded her to his mother's custody. There she performed the tasks that every intended wife must perform for her future in-laws. Meanwhile, her concerned sisters, Red Corn, White Corn, and Blue Corn set about trying to find Yellow Woman, and eventually succeeded. Appropriate to Keres custom, Whirlwind Man sent Yellow Woman home laden with lavish gifts from his mother for herself and her sisters.

When Pat, Margaret, and I stopped along the road at Jackpile mine to view the strange grass growing where the company had filled one of its pits, we saw Whirlwind Man and what might have been his mother, brother, or wife, whirling in the far distance. We didn't tarry long. But the grass is brilliantly green there; it looks like the grass that grows in England and Scotland; it doesn't look like the tough grass natural to this part of New Mexico, the grass that blankets the earth all around the site except for where the mining had occurred. Fortunately, we viewed the green, green grass from the relative safety of the car. Luckily, it was hot and we were disinclined to get out and poke around on the ground, where we might have found something extremely dangerous that day.

Another story bears on the issue of nuclear fission and its effects. This one is far more central to Laguna thought than even the Yellow Woman ritual narratives, for it is at the heart of Laguna cosmogony. Naotsete, Sun Woman, was one of the original goddesses who, with her sister Icsity and Spider Woman, created the heavens, the earth, the gods, the animals, plants, the arts, the laws, and all institutions, abilities, and phenomena needed for planetary life. Eventually, she and her sister quarreled over who was the elder, and Naotsete decided to go away. She, like her sister, had a "medicine bag" (I like to picture it as a beautifully cross-stitched woven purse) that contained a number of yet-to-be-born qualities or phenomena, and they discussed who would keep the various items. Naotsete took writing, or so some of the stories say, along with metal, mining, and metallurgy because her sister didn't want them. Accompanied by one of her sons (the other stayed with her sister), Naotsete went away to the east. But it was said that someday she would return; some say that she came back when the Spaniards found their way into Pueblo country, but tribal Gossips say that the Bomb's detonation marked her return.

No versions that I have heard or read suggest that the end of the world follows closely upon Naotsete's return; indeed, given the facts of the past five hundred years, I'd say that the Bomb is as likely to result in the liberation of the Native people as in their (continued) demise. Gossips hint that her return signals the end of Western colonial domination and the destruction of the patriarchy. The legend suggests that it heralds something even we can't conceptualize — something only Grandmother Spider, Thought Woman, can dream, something transformational. It is clear that the fission of the atom signals loud and bright that something sacred is going on in the universe. And it is equally clear that respect for that Great Mysteriousness — the kind of respect that Whirlwind Man and his mother show for Yellow Woman and her people — is demanded in such a sacred time. Perhaps it is because of our collective disrespect of Her awesomeness, rather than radioactive substances per se, that we sicken and die.

This is not to suggest that nuclear fission is an unmitigated blessing, but rather to reiterate a point that all ritualists know: the approach of the sacred is fraught with great danger; the liminal state, which one enters at the moment of transformation, is as likely to yield disaster as its obverse. True ritualists go through long periods of cleansing and isolation before being so bold as to approach the sacred amidst the most stringent secretiveness, all of which point to the danger of approaching sacred occasions. Modern people, of course, do not recognize the peril; raised on Walt Disney's notions of supernatural events coupled with intellectually toxic empirical (the word comes from the same source as "imperial") thought, they play with the sacred as though it were a toy, then, shocked at its devastating response, look angrily around for someone to blame for their folly. Yet what went on at Los Alamos during the making of the Bomb eerily echoes the ancient ritual practices.

*Reverend Watanabe (second row, far right) at the Santa Fe Internment Camp,
New Mexico, about 1943–45.*

44

Finding American World War II Internment in Santa Fe: Voices through Time

Gail Y. Okawa

I was born during a World War II blackout, I've been told. My mother was carried to Queen's Hospital in an ambulance, probably one of the only vehicles allowed on the road under those conditions in Honolulu even a year after Pearl Harbor was attacked. As a child, I was shielded completely from the war with the exception of duck-and-cover exercises in preschool and the wailing sirens of ambulances that terrified me for years.

I didn't know that my maternal grandfather, Tamasaku Watanabe, was absent for my first three years and don't remember exactly when he appeared in my life, a tall, quiet, almost austere man, a Presbyterian minister who was a physical presence once or twice a year when he came to visit us in Honolulu from the island of Maui. My warmest memory of him comes from sometime in my preadolescence. When he was on one of his visits, I had to stay home from school one day with a cold and made egg salad and Spam sandwiches for our lunch. A man of few words, he expressed his enjoyment and approval of the simple meal by smiling impishly and remarking that I should open a sandwich shop — a compliment I've never forgotten.

When I was in high school in Honolulu, I first learned from a neighbor that this grandfather had been imprisoned in an American internment camp on the mainland during World War II. My family had never talked about it, and neither did he. I was shaken and ran home to question my parents; I remember them confirming the fact of his internment and saying only that "he came back a changed man." It seemed to be a closed subject at that point and I don't remember pursuing it. He died of cancer in 1968 while I was away from home, teaching college in Virginia.

Many years later, in the 1990s, my mother shared some letters that her father had written to her from addresses in Lordsburg and Santa Fe, New Mexico. Most were on light blue government aerograms printed with English, German, Italian, and Japanese imperatives — "DO NOT WRITE HERE! NICHT HIER SCHREIBEN! NON SCRIVETE QUI! KAKU NAKARE" — and stamped with "Detained Alien Enemy Mail EXAMINED by (censor's initials) U.S.I. & N.S. [United States Immigration and Naturalization Service]." In some cases, "Prisoner of War Mail" had been crossed out and "Internee Mail" written in its place, to me an interesting confusion and conflation of terms and people. In all, there were eight letters from the Lordsburg Internment Camp and twenty-seven from the Santa Fe Detention Station, later called the Santa Fe Alien Internment Camp, according to return addresses.

The first time I read these letters, I realized that my grandfather wasn't at all absent from my childhood. He approved of my Japanese middle name, Yukie, commenting in his halting English that "the sound is very nice as for a girl's name" (February 1, 1943). After receiving no mail from Sumi, my mother, for several weeks, he wrote: "I am worried about your health and baby Yukie and all your family members. Please write to me how you are getting along." I also learned how involved he was in my earliest years through his comments on my baby pictures: "I do not hear Yukie's voice, but I get used to see her picture [on] my desk. Her innocent face attracts me from the bottom of my heart. Now in my old age I feel I could understand more why Jesus loved a small child" (May 26, 1943).

A few months later he began referring to me by my English name: "Gail is very happy to grow nicely day by day. I have now received eleven of her pictures. They show a good process of her growth" (October 2, 1943). When I was about eighteen months old he wrote: "Your writing of Gail is very interesting because I can see how lovely she is growing day by day. I hope she will grow without any mishap" (June 27, 1944). And a year later he commented in Japanese on two more snapshots: "Gail has really grown, hasn't she? Just like the photo of Sumi taken in Stockton, Gail looks exactly like Sumi when you were little. I'm happy to know that she will be going to kindergarten in September" (June 6, 1945). As caring as he became to me through these letters, I wondered why he would have been arrested. What was he charged with? Where was he imprisoned? By whom? What kind of life did he lead in those facilities? Who were his friends and associates? What kinds of dilemmas did he face, and how did he face them?

I came to know that Reverend Watanabe was one of nearly nine hundred Japanese immigrants, or Issei, in Hawaii who experienced a fate still relatively unknown to the general American public. On August 10, 1936, more than five years before Pearl Harbor, President Franklin D. Roosevelt wrote a memo to his chief of operations stating that "every Japanese citizen or non-citizen on the Island of Oahu who meets these Japanese ships or has any connection with their officers or men should be secretly but definitely identified and his or her name placed on a special list of those who would be the first to be placed in a concentration camp in the event of trouble." In his 1980 master's thesis, Paul Clark noted that the first camp was being constructed in New Mexico at Fort Stanton as early as January 1941. On December 7, 1941, the U.S. Department of Justice (DOJ) — using such previously prepared lists — seized and separately imprisoned nearly eight thousand Japanese resident aliens from the continent and the then territories of Hawaii and Alaska. Tetsuden Kashima (2003) gives a total of 17,477 persons of Japanese ancestry eventually imprisoned by the Justice Department. In February 1942 came the better-known mass removal of 120,000 American-born Japanese and their immigrant parents from the West Coast, ordered by FDR's Executive Order 9066 on February 19. The ten resulting prison camps, such as those at Manzanar and Tule Lake in California, Minidoka in Idaho, and Amache-Granada in Colorado, were established and overseen by the War Relocation Authority (WRA) created under that order. The WRA and DOJ incarcerations differed in their histories, administrations, prisoners, and treatment of prisoners (see Kashima 2003).

Like my grandfather, those imprisoned from Hawaii were predominantly male immigrants, heads of households, and community leaders who in most cases were detained for reasons no more substantial than that they were Japanese. Although many were long-time residents of the United States, as Japanese immigrants they were designated "aliens ineligible for citizenship," on the basis of their race, by discriminatory naturalization laws in the 1920s and then, on the basis of the Alien Enemies Act of 1798, labeled "alien enemies" when hostilities broke out between the United States and their country of origin. Plans for their imprisonment were premeditated and covert, founded upon long and complex surveillance operations. All were exiled from Hawaii to the U.S. mainland. In all, the Justice Department oversaw thirteen camps, and 4,555 of the Japanese internees passed through or were imprisoned in Santa Fe, New Mexico, over the course of the war.

My Road to Santa Fe

I had set foot in Santa Fe first in the 1980s when I attended a conference of the Association for Asian Studies, presented a paper on Japanese traditional toys, and met Yvonne Lange of the Museum of International Folk Art, who encouraged my folk toy research. I continued to be drawn to the area after that — to the Pueblo cultures, the adobe buildings, the folk art and Native culture museums, the stark surrounding landscape of juniper trees and tumbleweeds, the Sangre de Cristo Mountains. Only on my trips in 1999 and 2000 did I have a vague awareness of my grandfather's presence there decades before. At those times, no one I talked to could tell me where the internment camp had been located; it was as if it had never existed.

In the fall of 2001 I learned that a group called the Committee for the World War II Santa Fe Internment Camp Historical Marker was attempting to raise funds to establish a memorial marker at the Santa Fe Internment Camp site. Excitedly, I contacted Colonel Joe Ando, U.S. Air Force (Retired), the son of an internee and co-chair of the committee. Finding this effort in progress, having the reality of the internment camp finally confirmed, and learning that there were others who sought to preserve this nearly forgotten part of history inspired me to develop a research project focusing on my grandfather and other Japanese immigrants from Hawaii in U.S. Justice Department internment camps during World War II.

After the terrorist attacks on the World Trade Center and the Pentagon on September 11, 2001, the Civil Liberties Act of 1988 took on new meaning for me. Signed by President Ronald Reagan forty-three years after the end of World War II, the act offered an apology by the U.S. government on behalf of the nation to surviving American-born Japanese and their immigrant parents who had been unjustly imprisoned. The reasons cited were "racial prejudice, wartime hysteria, and a failure of political leadership," and I feared that these forces might be rekindled against other groups. Suddenly my research took on considerable urgency, and I planned a trip to Santa Fe in March 2002, devoted to collecting whatever I could on the internment camp and the experience of the Japanese immigrants held there. Having contacted Joe Ando, I received helpful information and encouragement from him and also made plans to meet with him during that time. This fifth trip to Santa Fe became pivotal to my project and launched my study.

Staying with Carolyn ("Carrie") Vogel, a friend who taught at Northern New Mexico Community College and supported my project, I fought the urge to enjoy the sunny blue skies in Santa Fe and worked for days in the New Mexico State Library's Southwest Collection, getting oriented, then searching through vertical files and microfilms. I also spent time in the New Mexico State Archives next door, wearing ill-fitting white gloves and poring through files of correspondence from the governors who served during the war years. A chilling letter to Governor John E. Miles surfaced from "Lloyd," who wrote that "all Japs are skunks. And no matter where a skunk is born, or under what star or flag, he is still a skunk — same stripe, same odor, same characteristics.… Planting Jap colonies over this country would be worse than filling our water with typhus germs." A very different sentiment appeared as a brief note from F. A. Brookshier on a petition addressing "the question of locating a colony of Japanese farmers on the Maxwell tract": "During my twelve years of teaching school, including nine years here as superintendent, I have taught racial tolerance and the rights and duties of American citizens. This [relocation of Japanese farmers] is a part of the democratic process."

A tip from Joe Ando also led me to seek out Thomas Chávez, former director of the Museum of New Mexico's Palace of the Governors, whose 1999 newspaper article drew attention to the existence of the Santa Fe camp, and then to search the files of the Fray Angélico Chávez Library next to the Palace of the Governors. From an address found in a file, I contacted Koichiro Okada, who had written a master's thesis titled "Forced Acculturation" and who kindly gave me a copy of this unpublished work, which gave rare attention to the Issei in the Santa Fe Internment Camp (SFIC) during World War II.

Finally, with Joe's directions and the help of strangers, Carrie and I were able to find the site of the internment camp, now the thriving housing development of Casa Solana. As we drove through it, passing home after neat, middle-class home, I kept hoping to see some remnant of the camp, some indication that my grandfather had been there for two and a half years of his life, something he might have seen. But of course it seemed that there was nothing left. As we drove up the hill to a ridge that might have overlooked the camp, I noticed a high barbed-wire fence silhouetted against the sunset and imagined that he might have looked out through similar fences at similar sunsets.

The cumulative work, especially reading archival documents, book chapters, and journal and newspaper articles, proved invaluable in establishing a foundation on which I could begin to construct scenarios of the Santa Fe internment experience. It also helped me to gain a sense of past anti-Japanese attitudes in New Mexico, fueled by the large contingent of New Mexicans involved in the Bataan Death March, as well as an evolving sense of Santa Fe's community history. This was a history apparently plagued by divisions and conflicts brought to the fore by the SFIC marker project and eventually healed by the courage of a few civic leaders. The only reference to Reverend Watanabe, however, was his name on a roster of SFIC internees that I found on microfilm.

As a result of my commitment to this research and my being a family member of an internee, Ando and Chávez invited me to attend the dedication of the SFIC historic marker just three weeks later. I felt it was a monumental privilege for a researcher in the early stages of a project to be included in an event of such significance. Not only was it to be memorable historically as something long overdue, but I knew it was also of great social and political importance to Santa Feans, having learned of the community strife that surrounded the establishment of the marker. I decided to make the trip back to Santa Fe from Washington, D.C.

And it was indeed a special day. On April 20, 2002, many participants, on a hill overlooking Santa Fe, saw the coming together of people of different ethnicities, communities, and generations and their efforts toward common goals: establishing a stone marker at Frank S. Ortiz Park to recognize the historical fact that during World War II a U.S. Justice Department internment camp existed on the site of the present Casa Solana neighborhood; memorializing the experience of thousands of Japanese immigrants and American-born citizens of Japanese ancestry unjustly incarcerated there between 1942 and 1946; and healing old wounds.

Under an intensely blue and sunny sky, the event was also a baptism of wind and dust for some 250 participants and onlookers — and for the marker itself, a six-ton granite boulder with a bronze plaque engraved with the following:

At this site, due east and below the hill, 4555 men of Japanese ancestry were incarcerated in a Department of Justice Internment Camp from March 1942 to April 1946. Most were excluded by law from becoming United States citizens and were removed primarily from the West Coast and Hawaii. During World War II, their loyalty to the United States was questioned. Many of the men held here without due process were long time resident religious leaders, businessmen, teachers, fishermen, farmers, and others. No person of Japanese ancestry in the U.S. was ever charged or convicted of espionage throughout the course of the war. Many of the internees had relatives who served with distinction in the American Armed Forces in Europe and in the Pacific. This marker is placed here as a reminder that history is a valuable teacher only if we do not forget our past.

With loyalty and patriotism having been so critically in question sixty years before — and with echoes of those questions so prevalent in post-9/11 America — the Pledge of Allegiance conveyed layers of unspoken meaning. To the crowd of local residents, visitors from places as distant as Alaska, Hawaii, and Washington, D.C., and honored guests from the state and city, Chávez said, "We are here not to celebrate an event about which none of us is proud; we are here to commemorate an event that happened; it is our history."

The biting wind and dust we felt may not have been so different from the conditions experienced by the men in the Santa Fe Internment Camp more than half a century earlier. Representing the internee families, Joe Ando commented on the self-censorship among these men: "In many Japanese American families across this country, our fathers never spoke to their children about their experiences in the camps. It was a shameful, it was a painful experience." And because of the secrecy surrounding the Department of Justice facilities, camps such as the SFIC were more misunderstood.

In the late 1990s, because of such historical misunderstandings, some New Mexico World War II veterans, who confused Japanese immigrants with the Japanese enemy, vehemently protested the proposed marker and caused a significant controversy in the Santa Fe community. In the end, Santa Fe's Mayor Larry Delgado broke the tie vote of the City Council in favor of erecting the marker. A cooperative effort of citizens of different ethnic and racial backgrounds, the establishment of the SFIC marker represented a collective rather than a single ethnic triumph.

I was moved by the attendance of internee families from all over the country and the social, political, and spiritual gravity of the event. At the luncheon reception following the dedication, Joe Ando asked me to speak to the crowd, and I surprised myself by overcoming my shyness and addressing the large audience as an intimate one, bound by the common inheritance of internment and, among non-Japanese

Americans, the desire not to forget. The attentiveness of the audience brought the gravity of my project home to me. I began to realize my place and the place of my research in relation to the Japanese American community, the New Mexico community, and the American public at large.

Letters and Other Writing

After nearly a year of research, mainly in the National Archives in Washington, D.C., and Maryland, I began to gather some of the notes and documents I had collected on my grandfather's life and internment and composed a brief biography of Reverend Watanabe. I wrote this in the form of a letter to him in order to actualize my discoveries and feelings about his life in some way — to objectify him less, perhaps, by writing his biographical narrative *to* him.

> Dear Grandpa:
>
> You've been gone now for 35 years and I am myself growing older — in fact virtually the same age as you were when you were arrested on December 7, 1941, wrenched from your parsonage in Ola'a on the Island of Hawai'i, never to return to it. While you lived, I knew nothing of these years of your life. Now I read through the papers you left to us — to me — so carefully bundled and labeled in boxes for someone later to discover, and I feel oddly that I am knowing you for the first time.
>
> How confused you must have been on that day in 1941 when the soldiers arrested you! You had immigrated to the United States in 1905 as a young man of 22, arriving in Seattle, then moving to San Francisco a year before the Great San Francisco Earthquake struck the city. So profoundly were you influenced by that destruction that in September 1912 you entered the San Francisco Theological Seminary to study the Christian faith.

Ordained by the Presbyterian Church of the U.S.A., Reverend Watanabe began his ministry in Stockton and Sacramento, California, in both places serving at a Japanese Church of Christ. He and my grandmother, Yuki, had four children, a son, a daughter, and then two younger sons.

> My mother remembers that the youngest, given the English name Ernest, was struck by a Standard Oil truck and killed at the age of two.... Yet when the Hawaiian Board of Missions called you to the Hawai'ian Islands, you packed up your family — Grandma and the three remaining children, ages 9, 6, and 4 — and made your way across the vast Pacific Ocean.

After arriving in Honolulu, Hawaii, in late November 1922, my grandfather moved his family to the island of Maui in December and began a long ministry there. In early 1935 the Board of Missions transferred him to Ola'a, on the island of Hawaii, and he began his fourth ministry at the Ola'a Japanese Christian Church. There he served Japanese laborers who worked on the nearby sugar plantations. The Japanese consulate appointed him to serve as its representative in this remote location, doing humanitarian work by keeping routine records, helping immigrants with affairs related to their Japanese citizenship, and facilitating the expatriation of American-born children of immigrants. (Because the Japanese government considered the American-born children of Japanese parents to be Japanese citizens, legal expatriation documents had to be filed for dual citizens to claim exclusively U.S. citizenship.)

> As tensions between the U.S. and Japan intensified and assets of citizens of Japan were being frozen, you were asked by the General Secretary of the Board of the Hawaiian Evangelical Association to provide an affidavit attesting to "the ownership, purposes, activities, finances, and operations of the Ola'a Japanese Christian Church" (Watanabe, Affidavit, 1941). You complied with the request on August 9, 1941, as the minister and head of your church. So dedicated were you to teaching your parishioners "the Christian Gospel and the fundamentals of Christianity; to train[ing] them in the fundamentals of the Christian moral and ethical code" and "the highest ideals of Americanism" (Watanabe, Affidavit, 1941), that you must have been shocked and confused to be treated otherwise — as disloyal, as subversive, as sinister.

At least five years earlier, by order of President Roosevelt, the U.S. military and government had begun conducting surveillances and keeping lists of American residents of Japanese origin. By November 21, 1941, a document titled "Memorandum: Seizure and Detention Plan (Japanese)" and stamped "SECRET" on each page had been drawn up by Lieutenant Colonel George W. Bicknell and his staff, including extensive lists of Japanese immigrants (who were barred from U.S. citizenship) and U.S.-born Japanese (who were citizens) in Hawaii, who would be apprehended in case of war. This became known as the "ABC List," and it included Japanese consular agents and aliens or American citizens who were religious leaders, language school teachers, merchants, and other civilians.

> Though you were simply working for "the benefit of the people of Ola'a" (Watanabe, Affidavit, 1941), I know now that you were on Bicknell's "A-list" of Japanese consular agents. Thus, you were apprehended on December 7 , even before war was declared with Japan by Congress on December 8 — a fact that compounds the injustice and

unlawfulness of your arrest, for you were not yet, by definition, an "alien enemy": "a citizen of a country with which the United States is at war" (National Japanese American Historical Society et. al). As you describe it later in your petition for release, "I was apprehended on the 7th of December 1941 at my parsonage in Olaa, Hawaii, T.H., and taken into Kilauea Military Camp, Hawaii, and detained there until the time of removal to Sand Island, Honolulu, T.H., on the 23rd February 1942" (Watanabe, Petition, 1945).

Reading your hearing in the National Archives made me feel both intensely angry and intensely sad. You had four members on your hearing board. Rather than relying on a translator, you chose to speak for yourself and rely on your own abilities to speak and understand English, even under duress, reflecting your confidence and faith in the language and the American justice system. Many of the questions were routine, though one of the members seemed to want you to take sides on who should win. You did not give the simplistic question a simplistic answer, but said, "In my work as Christian minister I say, I am very sorry…I don't like the war…only I want [peace] to come quickly" (Watanabe, Hearing, 1942). The vote went in your favor: three for release; one, McLaughlin, for internment for the duration of the war. Unfortunately for you, however, Hawai'i was under martial law then, and the Military Intelligence Board supported the minority vote. You were to be interned. Your May 1945 notes for a petition tell us the arduous route of your journey from Kilauea Military Camp to Santa Fe Internment Camp over four long years:

Kilauea Military Camp	1941-12-7 to 1942-2-23
Honolulu Immigration	1942-2-24 to 1942-3-4
Sand Island [O'ahu, Hawai'i]	1942-3-4 to 1942-5-23
Angel Island [California]	1942-6-1 to 1942-6-4
Fort Sam Houston Internee Camp [Texas]	1942-6-7 to 1942-6-17
Lordsburg Internment Camp [NM]	1942-6-18 to 1943-6-22
Santa Fe Alien Internment Camp [NM]	1943-6-23

According to this document, you arrived in New Mexico in 1942 and were held at Lordsburg Internment Camp for a year until you were moved to Santa Fe, where you stayed for the duration of the war.

In theory, the Geneva Convention of 1929 was the operative document in the Department of Justice internment camps, because people like you were designated "alien enemies." But since the document was originally intended for prisoners of war, its application was still a matter of interpretation and depended on the camp commander. Its tenets gave you, as civilian internees (CIs), the right to self-government, involving the election of your own leaders, who would then communicate with the camp officials. At the Santa Fe Internment Camp, which was composed exclusively of men and which was the largest of the Japanese camps, you were at one time elected chief of your barracks.

My grandfather's papers reveal that he wrote copiously in Japanese at both Lordsburg and Santa Fe — an official roster of names and records of barracks activities when he was barracks chief, and sermons and short articles in church newsletters as part of his ministry. He wrote many letters to family and associates on the outside. In one of his letters to my mother, he mentions using a play about the prodigal son for Christmas services the previous year and asks, "If you found out a good play for old folks, please send it as soon as possible" (October 2, 1943). The following month he wrote in some exasperation: "Sumi, really it is very hard a request to get Christmas play [from] old men. So we decided to play the same play which last year we had." At some point he may have composed a play titled *An Evening in Bethlehem,* also presumably for Christmas services.

Finding librettos of Noh plays dated from his time at the Lordsburg Internment Camp and learning that groups of internees gathered to chant these pieces, I was reminded of my brief study of Noh theater during my first visits to Japan in the 1970s. It was an amazing discovery — finding that I had a common interest with my grandfather. I wished I could have shared experiences with him and discussed our favorite Noh plays, the pitches and tones of the chants.

Some internees were brave by opposing the injustice; some were brave by enduring it while maintaining their personal integrity. Though I don't know how you really felt while you were interned, I can surmise that your continued ministry to others in the camps sustained you to a large extent. Among your many papers, I found a handwritten message in English and Japanese: In English, the title is "I am really on the path," and I suspect that you copied it down because it struck a chord. At any rate, it must have had great meaning for you to take pains in translating it into Japanese, perhaps for your parishioners:

I am really on the path…

1. If I always look for the best in each person, situation, and thing.

2. If I forgive everybody without exception, no matter what he may have done; and if I then forgive myself whole-heartedly.

3. If I regard my job as sacred and do my day's work to the very best of my ability (whether I like it or not).

4. If I take every means to demonstrate a healthy body and harmonious surroundings for myself.

5. If I take every opportunity wisely to spread the knowledge of truth to others.

6. If I devote at least one hour a day to prayer, meditation and Bible reading.

7. If I practice the Golden Rule of Jews instead of merely admiring it. He said "whatsoever you would that men should do to you, do ye even so to them." The important point about the Golden Rule is that I am to practise [*sic*] it whether the other fellow does so or not.

This reveals that you may have seen your internment experience as the greatest test of your faith and dignity as a human being.

Among the many letters that you wrote home to your family — and I have been fortunate enough to read those saved by my mother and uncle — you assure them of your well-being in an effort not to worry them. But there must have been times when the isolation and loneliness and cold of Santa Fe winters became difficult. In February 1944, along with around two hundred other men, you signed a petition written to the Military Governor of the Territory of Hawaii, "asking for an immediate transfer of all of us from Santa Fe Detention Camp to some similar internment camp or camps located and maintained under your command in Hawaii" (Shigenaga et al., Petition, 1944). After more than two years of imprisonment on the mainland, you wanted to go home. The signatures themselves, primarily written in English, many with the beautiful penmanship of the Palmer Method, are moving, for they represent the assertions of each man, preserved collectively in this way for us.

In May 1945 you finally wrote your own petition to the Office of the Provost Marshal General, requesting release from internment and return to Hawai'i: "Although I am foreign born and not eligible to be naturalized citizen of this country, [I] am an American citizen by spirit since I have lived nearly two third[s] of my life in this country.... I did not apply for the repatriation, because it was my intention to go back to Hawaii no matter how long that will take to become reality" (Watanabe, Petition, 1945). Your reference to being an American citizen in spirit highlights your loyalty in the face of racist exclusion, and though this is a very public and official document, I have come to understand something of the events of your life and your perspectives on life through it.

In August 1945, as the world knows, an atomic bomb was dropped on Hiroshima, the prefecture of your birth. Though the war with Japan "ended" soon after that, you and many others were not returned to Hawai'i until three months later, in November 1945. The legacy of your experience and that of others like you who endured internment must be in what we who follow can learn from your political misfortune and your personal fortitude. We must be vigilant to the acts and words today echoing those that surrounded your unjust and unwarranted imprisonment. And we must understand that though you were silent, like so many others, about this difficult time in your life, you were no less affected by the degradation, no less courageous for bearing it. I wish I had attempted to know you then; I feel that I am beginning to know you now. Maybe it's not too late.

> *Your granddaughter,*
> *Gail*

Pilgrimages

On February 14, 2007, I made my way through blizzard conditions from northeastern Ohio to the Pittsburgh International Airport to fly to New Mexico once again — a five-year pilgrimage of sorts, to lay some flowers at the historical marker in Santa Fe. My friend Carrie and I picked our way through the snow-soaked earth, hopping from grass clump to grass clump to avoid the mud. We left red asters. It was a gesture, incense only in my mind.

On this visit I also gave an illustrated talk at the College of Santa Fe. Organized by the Office of the State Historian, it was titled "Through My Grandfather's Eyes: American World War II Internment from Sand Island, Hawai'i, to Santa Fe, New Mexico." This was a different kind of pilgrimage — a chance for me to thank those who had worked so hard to establish the memorial and inspired me to start my research five years earlier. It was also a time to publicly acknowledge the passing of the Reverend Paul Seto (1921–2006), a Presbyterian minister like my grandfather and a marker committee member, and the Reverend Shingetsu Akahoshi (1907–2007), a Buddhist minister and internee survivor who had crossed paths with my grandfather in the Santa Fe Internment Camp as a young man and who gave me a story from the camp, a precious gift of his memory of and regard for my grandfather — the only one I have.

Two days before, in Albuquerque, I had met a young woman named Lisa Pacheco by chance at a conference. Her grandmother, Lucia Ortiz Trujillo, had been a child in Santa Fe during the war, she said. She would ask her if she remembered anything. And she did, indeed. Lisa told me:

My Grandma Lucy was eight years old when [Japan] bombed Pearl Harbor. During the next summer, 1942, she was nine years old and remembers playing with a group of kids her age near the train station by her older sister Melinda's neighborhood on Manhattan Avenue. (The group probably consisted of her younger sister Bernadette and a cousin or two.) She recalled that Japanese men were being transported by train to the internment camp. On more than one occasion the train pulled into the station and the Japanese men would throw candy bars to my grandma and the other kids. At that time, candy bars were very hard to come by because of wartime rationing, and she and the other kids really looked forward to the Japanese men's generous gifts. They would get really excited when they heard the train coming and run toward it in hopes of getting some candy. She remembers walking around with the same kids all the time, and when they were in the area that is now called Casa Solana, they'd walk near the camp and see all the guards and fences and people inside. She said if it wasn't for the candy, she might not even remember any of it.

Could one of those men on the train or one of the people the children saw inside the fences have been my grandfather? Even now voices and stories still come from unexpected people and places, tying us all together through space and time.

Four months later, thousands of miles away on the island of Hawaii, I met Masa, an elderly son of Shinjiro Yoshimasu, who had been a barracks mate of my grandfather's in Santa Fe more than six decades before. He told me of his 1997 journey to Santa Fe in search of the internment camp and, although no marker existed then, his luck at finding someone at the Palace of the Governors who knew its location. The tall trees in the Casa Solana development, this man said, were planted by the Japanese internees decades earlier. For us as descendants of those men, the trees stand as a proud testament to the internees' attention to the natural beauty around them and to their will to survive.

The Road Hog, El Rito 4th of July Parade, northern New Mexico, 1968. Photograph by Lisa Law.

45

Taos: Hippies, Hopper, and Hispanic Anger

Larry Torres, as Told to
Lois Palken Rudnick (1996)

By the time film actor Dennis Hopper arrived in Taos, the counterculture had worn out its welcome. From the 1920s on, local people had tolerated a parade of brilliant eccentrics — D. H. Lawrence, Georgia O'Keeffe, Aldous Huxley, among others — at the home of Mabel Dodge Luhan. But the hippie invasion was perceived as a threat to an isolated community that still spoke the Spanish of Cervantes and traced its mores to medieval Spain. It responded with anger and violence.

> —*Taos High School language teacher Larry Torres, a 16th-generation Taoseño, describes how the confrontation changed his life in this interview adapted from* Utopian Vistas: The Mabel Dodge Luhan House and the American Counterculture, by Lois Palken Rudnick *(University of New Mexico Press, 1996).*

Nineteen sixty-six. I was 14, I suppose, or something like that. And we were told that the hippies were coming, 50,000 of them. We had these visions of 50,000 longhaired English speakers moving in on us. Now you have to remember that the school system was only consolidated in 1963 here in Taos County. Before that time, we all belonged to the little schoolhouses all over the valley. [Now] we were made to speak English formally in the classroom. So we went from a superconservative Hispanic society to an avant-garde society overnight....

[Before the hippies] there had been crackpots. Let's call them [that] because we called them *los locos*, these Anglos like Mabel. Also, we were mistrustful. Something had occurred in Los Alamos, and we were not told what it was.... There was a man here in Taos who used to walk around through the Taos fiestas every year. He had long hair, always wore glasses and always wore a long white dress, a tunic. A lot of the older people distrusted him and would make the sign of the evil eye against him. Other people were seen kissing his hands and feet and treating him like a holy man.

It was not until years later that we found out that this was a government spy who was looking for Communists among the literati of Taos. So there was a great mistrust for all Anglo-speaking people in this immediate area.... Suddenly, we were told that 50,000 hippies were coming out of Haight-Ashbury. We didn't know what Haight-Ashbury was, anyway. But what happened was, they trickled in here.... Without us realizing that they had come.

Now, suddenly, Mabel's house was revived [by Hopper], and we were high school students, and [we understood that] there were great pot parties going on at this house.... The drug scene became very, very, very big. Drugs had been virtually unknown to me as a child. The strongest thing I can remember doing is going to the corral and rolling dried horseshit cigarettes. [These are] the same ingredients that give a hallucinogen to the mushroom that is growing in the manure. So for centuries we have been smoking horseshit cigarettes here in Taos, and we were pretty much drugged out. But we didn't know it. And we certainly didn't recognize it as a drug.

Suddenly, they came and offered us new and different things, and we were eager for new and different things, because now our English was good enough. Enter Peter Fonda and Dennis Hopper. They came and did *Easy Rider*. They were the first Anglos to give recognition to the Spanish people. They incorporated them into the film.... When the film was shown here in Taos, everybody went wild. It was the first time they had seen Anglos and Spanish and Indian people together, saying, "Look! There's so and so. Look!"

A memory of hippie days: I was waiting tables at Casa Cordova, trying to be French. [Dennis and David Hopper and Peter Fonda were] sitting at table four. Gordon Douglas ran in and said, "They killed Sharon, they killed Sharon." And, as I was eavesdropping, suddenly the tale of the murder of Sharon Tate came into focus.... I was pretending that I'm waiting on them, but I was listening with all my soul. I remember Dennis Hopper poking Peter Fonda and saying, "We have an eavesdropper." And Peter said, "He's a friend," and he winked at me and wrote me off, which is exactly what I needed to hear the rest of it. Sharon, who had been in *The Valley of the Dolls*, was a friend of all these people, and they were all known. They were the rebels of Hollywood.

It was said that when they were looking for Charles Manson, he had fled to the communes of Taos, New Mexico. So I remember there was great fear and trepidation all over the valley for weeks, people locking their doors securely. Already the hippies had made quite an impact. Now a madman [was coming] who just confirmed everything we thought of hippies in the first place: murderers, pot smokers.

Dennis Hopper thought he had made a great many friends in the valley because he had made Taos famous, although this was not true. He was going up El Salto Road, which is where I lived in Arroyo Seco. Suddenly, the Seco boys decided they didn't want the goddam hippie on the road, and they got off the truck, and they were going to beat the hell out of Hopper. Now the reason they were going up the road, I suspect, was probably to visit El Salto, the seventh of the seven waterfalls that come down the holy mountain. It was [rumored to have been] used in prehistory for human sacrifice. Now Dennis and his friends were going up there, probably to drink and smoke and just to commune with the spirit of the old generation. Because Dennis Hopper was very much in tune with what had happened there with Mabel and with [D. H.] Lawrence and with [Dorothy] Brett, and Willa [Cather], and all those others. Suddenly, our local boys decided these honkies had no right going up there and getting minted and getting under our falls. So they cornered them against the Indian fence [that borders Taos Pueblo].

Dennis Hopper pulled out a gun. And, suddenly, they were up in arms, the whole valley. *These longhairs pulled a gun on our children!* See, the boys never told their fathers that they had plotted to beat the hell out of Hopper. So, suddenly, I remember there was a meeting at the schoolhouse in Arroyo Seco to see what we were going to do about the hippie problem, and it was decided we'd do something covert. The sheriff, the police department, was called in, and they said, "Do what you want. We won't be around when you do it." The ringleaders at the time were great businessmen in town, and they didn't like the longhairs. It was a communal effort to drive them out.

I remember cornering hippies at the [Manby] spring and although we knew nothing about religion, we'd go up to them and say, "So you guys believe in partying naked, do you?" You know, we'd be drinking beers and just trying to goad them into something. And one of them tried to say to us, "Well, you guys think you're temples of the holy spirit, but you're acting this way." We didn't know what temples of the holy spirit was, so they were beat up anyway.

We had a lot of people who worked at Human Services. Suddenly, the bill for food stamps went sky-high because these guys were coming in. Do you know what kind of resentment there is from people who are just trying to eke out a living, who are not given food stamps? Suddenly, they see a longhair at the counter buying things that they can't afford with food stamps.

So all of these things created such a resentment of [the Luhan] house. When we knew that Hopper was in it [people kept their distance from him]. Dennis himself, when I waited on him, was a lousy tipper for starters, never more than a quarter or 50 cents, which used to irk me. Secondly, he never took off his goddamn hat. It was always dusty, and he had two eagle feathers sticking out of it.

Two years after the hippies, 1970, the Chicanos arrived in town. The Brown Berets marched in from California with Ché Guevara on their T-shirts, and they told us who have considered ourselves to be Hispanic all these years, "You're Chicanos." The most anybody had ever told us was that we were Mexicans, and we knew damn well we weren't Mexicans because Mexicans were wetbacks to us. Any Mexican who made it this far up was a poor man looking for a job. We were centuries-old families over here. *Suddenly, these guys arrive and tell us we're "Chicanos," and they can't even tell us what a Chicano is.*

So, there was a big identity crisis. Now suddenly, not only did we have to deal with Anglos, we had also to deal with our own cultural identity. I went down to New Mexico State in Las Cruces in 1971, and when I arrived in the first Spanish class, they said, "Oh, you're Spanish," in that tone of voice. Already they realized that the people of Taos considered themselves totally different from people elsewhere.

So when I look at the cultural roots of where I am, why I became a Russian teacher, number one I think the hippie movement had a greater impact on me than I realized. I became a Russian to become un-American in the early '70s. I didn't like what I saw of American culture. I did not want to become an English American because I hated those longhairs.

I left in 1972 to study in the Soviet Union. I was sent off by the government. They gave me a full stipend, scholarship, and I went off and [got] a degree from the University of Leningrad. It wasn't until I was on the other side of the world that I discovered that all these people that I had known early in life were really interesting, fascinating people. I was amazed once traveling through the Gobi Desert that somebody asked me about Mabel…D. H. Lawrence…it just floored me.

I had such a terrible, terrible image as a Hispanic that I became French instead. It wasn't until years later, [when] I was living in deep Siberia, or traveling and teaching in France, that I suddenly realized those same things that they were telling me in those little villages over there was what I had. And then I started cultivating my Hispanicity again, and my American patriotism again. It wasn't until I started teaching in Memphis, Tennessee [in 1985] and I made my first trip to Washington, D.C., that I finally felt some patriotism and belonging. But the hurts, the hurts are still there for a lot, a lot, of our people.

46

Albuquerquean Joe Powdrell

Debra Hughes (2006)

Joe Powdrell moved to Albuquerque from Texas when he was young and has lived in Albuquerque for over forty years. He and his father own and manage Powdrell's Barbecue. He went through junior high and high school in Albuquerque and graduated from the University of New Mexico on a track-and-field scholarship. Powdrell earned his master's degree from the University of California, Fresno, in public administration. He served in Vietnam and is president of the Albuquerque chapter of the National Association for the Advancement of Colored People.

We had family here as early as the late 1930s. My dad had an uncle and two cousins. Our family migrated westward from Louisiana to East Texas to West Texas — that's where I was born — to New Mexico, and there are those who have gone on to the far West Coast. We came in pursuit of opportunity — everything this democracy offers, social justice. When I was about twelve [in 1958] we moved here. When you ask what was most pronounced or what stands out to me, it's clear to me now...but it wasn't clear to me then. Regard for your humanity was different. We here in Albuquerque had to grow, to learn how to regard others in an integrated society. We're almost there, but we still grapple with it some, and that's the end of that story!

Joe Powdrell

I went to school in what Albuquerque would call the South Broadway and South Valley area: "South San Jose." It was mainly made up of blacks and Hispanics. There was a family there that had come from Mississippi, and their place was where people started — we were in their small house. There were eleven kids in my family, and it was a confined space.

Back in Odessa, Texas, Mom and Dad lived in a partitioned tent in '44, where one side was living quarters and the other a restaurant...so they've always had barbecue places. My dad's grandfather had given him a recipe for sauce and barbecue, and he used that. Here, they opened a place on South Broadway in 1962. It lasted five months. Dad was working on the other side of the mountains for Valley Gold Dairy. He was hauling hay provided by Bruce King. They got to be good friends and still are. He did construction for Bob Stamm, and they became good friends. They still get together and laugh.

In 1969 we started a restaurant again. I attribute our success to the cultural and societal wave in this country. It was the Age of Aquarius — do you know what I mean? We went from making barbecue sauce out of a pot to using fifty-gallon vats. All along we would tell ourselves, "Be honest, put out a good product consistently and joyfully. Be content! After all, look at where you've come from."

The restaurant business has been a challenge — some family members have gone to find different forms of work. Oh, but the things we've been a part of here — you can't put a value on it — all the way from funerals to births and everything in between. The political things, the cultural things, the weddings, the divorces; people graduating from college in their seventies. We've been on the ground floor of the Balloon Fiesta and catered that from its beginnings. We've been at the fair. We fed ten thousand people at a political party, where the winner wanted to say thank you to the people. We've met some prominent people in the process — Billy Graham, Bill Cosby, Martin Luther King's daughter, Malcolm X's daughter, Spike Lee, Danny Glover, Muhammad Ali. All this depends on how you regard your experience…for me, I'm rich in experience.

Warren (Joe) Nieto, the author's uncle, as Coronado in a reenactment of the entrada *during the Fiesta de San Lorenzo, Bernalillo, New Mexico, 1976.*

47

Making Spanish-American Identity: My Language of Blood

John M. Nieto-Phillips (2004)

nos'tal'gia
1: the state of being homesick
2: a wistful or excessively sentimental yearn-
ing for return to or of some past period or
irrecoverable condition

Preface

I was seven years old when my father was laid off at the machine shop in El Monte. It was 1972. Southern California's economy had slid into a recession, and the nation was at war. Today it amazes me that my parents managed to feed and clothe seven children on a part-time nurse's salary. But they could not shield us from their mounting worries. As spring became summer, my father was still jobless and grew visibly anxious and tense. Evening meals, once boisterous, chaotic events, became solemn rituals to be avoided. But as they inevitably do, things changed.

One day, my father drove up behind the wheel of a giant GMC delivery truck that read, in large white letters on navy blue canvas, "Los Angeles Times." He parked it in our front yard. Within days he had stripped the truck down to its chassis and welded onto it the metal carcass of a whale, or so it seemed. Over the next three months he worked day and night, stitching it with electrical wiring, then wrapping it in plywood and metal siding. He cut out windows like gaping eyes, transforming the thirty-five-foot mass into our gleaming new home on wheels. When he was finished, neighbors gathered round and gawked at the largest camper they had ever seen. Who knows how he managed to pay for it. What everyone wondered was where he would park it, if not right where he built it, on the dirt patch that was once a carpet of grass. It was a monstrosity.

The next year, early August, my parents piled everyone inside and set off for New Mexico. My mother had made a *promesa* to return to Bernalillo for the three-day fiesta that honors San Lorenzo, her hometown's patron saint. She was intent on dancing again among the Matachines. At least one dance, she said, to remember our ancestors and to thank God for our health. When she told me this I knew what was coming next. The story.

I knew the story by heart. I had learned it on my mother's knee. Among our families the story was so often recited, it took on the lyrical qualities of a prayer. It flowed from my *bisabuelo*'s lips in Spanish, from my grandfather's in Spanglish, from my mother's in English. The story was as familiar as Christmas posole and Grandpa Tomás's thick, handmade tortillas. It bored me.

> In 1540 the brave conquistador *Francisco Vásquez de Coronado came looking for the Seven Cities of Gold. He camped near Bernalillo and claimed New Mexico for the king of Spain. But he found no gold. Disappointed, Coronado retreated to Mexico. Next came Don Juan de Oñate. In 1598 he and hundreds of settlers conquered the land and tried to Christianize the Indians. When the Indians resisted, he punished two dozen of them by cutting off their right feet. There was a long drought and starvation until, in 1680, Popé led his fellow Indians in a revolt that sent the Spaniards running for their lives. Thirteen years later, Diego de Vargas returned accompanied by Spanish settlers and soldiers. He made peace with the Pueblos. To celebrate the* reconquista *of the region, De Vargas and his followers danced the Matachines in Bernalillo on* el dia de San Lorenzo, *August 10, 1693. And it has been danced there each year ever since.*

I rolled my eyes each time I heard it. I recall once asking my mother who cared about all these events, since it was so long ago and all those people are dead now. In a flash she grew indignant, then almost sullen. She answered that *she* cared and that I had better care if I wanted to know my roots. This is *your* history, she said. Whatever, I thought.

Though for years to come I wanted to erase such stories from my memory, their imprint on my young mind was deep and lasting. They also caused me a great deal of anguish and posed dilemmas that would plague me through my childhood and into my adult years. Why does my mother's family keep on insisting we are Spanish? Most of our neighbors were from Mexico, and I couldn't possibly go around our neighborhood proclaiming *we* are Spanish and not Mexican — as if we were somehow better than them. We were all working-class families with lots of kids. The better-off kids lived across the Pomona freeway. Maybe *they* were more "Spanish" than us, I thought. Plus, if I ran around boasting we were Spanish, Big Mary (María L.) across the street, a bilingual teacher proud of her Mexican roots, might get offended. And that would be the end of tamales and cookies at her place.

To complicate matters, I had often heard it said that we were also part Indian, that Nano (Luciano Nieto, my great-grandfather) was orphaned and raised at Sandia Pueblo. The lore was that somewhere in our family tree there was a forgotten Indian branch and that's what explained why our skin got dark brown every summer. This information presented me with yet more quandries. How could we be Spanish and Indian at the same time, but not Mexican? How could Spaniards have made it to New Mexico without first mixing with the Indians? And what did all this matter anyhow? Our regular pilgrimages to Bernalillo never rendered any answers.

As a child, I felt trapped by our supposed "Spanish" heritage. I was cursed with it. Double-bound by the pride I was supposed to possess and by the impossibility of speaking about "our history" among my friends, I grew ashamed of my family and our history. The source of that shame was the unspoken truth: that the grandeur of the past bore little relation to our humble, working-class status. One symbol of that status was the "mud house" my mother grew up in, which we visited almost every year, as if it were a shrine to our ancestors. Situated in the ancient section of Bernalillo called Las Concinitas, the house was but a few sections of adobe walls, cracked and melting into earthen mounds. Because of the shame, I pushed down all questions of my identity, pushed them into a sort of abyss of painful dilemmas. I submerged these questions for years and tried to ignore them, tried to forget them. I learned French, became a high school All-American athlete (sports were my ticket to college), and generally tried to blend into the ethnic patchwork of Los Angeles.

But there came a day in my late teens that I stared into the abyss and, as Nietzsche once wrote, the abyss stared back. When my Grandpa Tomás died, I was suddenly afflicted with a serious case of nostalgia. For reasons that have become only somewhat clearer to me with age, I yearned to revisit the dilemmas of my childhood, to recover that which I had repressed or forgotten — as well as that which never really existed. I became a collector of memorabilia of all sorts, saved museum tickets and brochures, scanned newspapers and magazines for articles on history and lore, and suffered to know every name and date that defined my family's past. I sat for hours with great uncles and great aunts and listened to tales of their lives — usually the long versions. After my visits, I would write everything down, every story or anecdote. Many times in my excitement, I would forget important details or jumble them and have to reconstruct bits and pieces in subsequent visits. Or I would invert the sequence of events. When I did not misremember names, I made them up entirely. Such is the nature of memory, especially when one is afflicted with nostalgia....

Epilogue

Wonderful article and a lesson to all of us about wanting to be something we're not or in forgetting that part of us that isn't fashionable.

> – *Jerry Pusey, Oceanside*

Thank you for an enlightening article. I am a Valdivia who argues with others here in New Mexico about the lineage issue. I tell them their ancestors would have had to fly here on a 747 more than 400 years ago to escape mixing bloodlines with so-called Mexicans. Your article is the education we all need.

> – *Steven Valdivia, Albuquerque*

The above two letters to the editor appeared in the *Los Angeles Times*, 21 February 2000, in response to an article by José Cárdenas ("Roots and Reality," 25 January 2000) detailing the efforts of some Latinos who had formed a genealogical society in an effort to retrace their Spanish roots.

Nostalgia Isn't What It Used to Be

Somewhere there is a black-and-white photograph of two young girls on an outdoor stage gleefully dancing the *jarabe tapatío*. One has braided black hair and is festooned in a white blouse and vivid Mexican skirt; the other is dressed as a young man, in dark pants trimmed with metal buttons and a bright satin shirt, and she sports the wide-brimmed sombrero of a *charro*. The two are facing each other and beaming with delight as relatives and neighbors look on. All are smiling or clapping. Someone has strewn a pocketful of coins across the stage, and they glisten in the afternoon sunshine. "I don't know what happened to the money," my mother says. "It never occurred to me to take the money."

The year was 1940, and the occasion was the celebration of the Coronado Cuarto Centennial, a series of statewide events that commemorated four centuries since Europeans first set foot in the region. Organized in part by a local chapter of LULAC (the League of United Latin American Citizens [*Albuquerque Journal*, December 24, 1939]), the Bernalillo festivities were particularly memorable to long-time residents. Nuevomexicanos who had grown up in the vicinity were well aware that Coronado and his entourage had encamped just across the Rio Grande, at what were now mere remains of the Tiwa pueblo Kuaua. This fact of history was long a source of local pride. When the Cuarto Centennial officials came to town on 29 May 1940, to dedicate the Coronado State Monument at that site, citizens gathered excitedly to welcome Spain's ambassador to the United States, Juan Francisco de Cardenas. After several addresses had been made, Pueblo Indians performed traditional music and dances, and the fiestas began.

Ostensibly, the mission of the Cuarto Centennial was to educate the local and national public about the legacy of "the first white man" to visit the region; to that end, it generally succeeded. However, the official promotional literature suggests that the underlying objective was to showcase New Mexico's history for tourists and thereby to garner revenue (Pan 1995). Much to the dismay of state officials, the two hundred events that comprised the yearlong festivities failed to draw throngs of vacationers bearing cameras and money. True, some events lured sightseers with flamboyant reenactments of Coronado's *entrada* — for example, more than five hundred participants reenacted the historic event in an Albuquerque football stadium, to a crowd of thousands — but few of the commemorative events achieved the status of a full-fledged tourist spectacle. Festivities remained, by and large, modest affairs staged and attended by townsfolk. They drew only a fraction of the tourist traffic that planners had predicted.

A few outsiders finally ventured into the far-flung communities where many events were staged — in towns such as Raton, Farmington, Tularosa, Estancia, Mesilla, and so forth. Those who did must have felt, at least in some measure, like interlopers. Such was the feeling Sarah Gertrude Knott had during the three months she toured the state as an aide to Albuquerque businessman Clinton P. Anderson, president of the organizing Coronado Cuarto Centennial Commission. Having immersed herself among nativos and Native Americans, Knott (1940) commented on how strange and yet enlightening the experience was:

> In Albuquerque I felt like the foreigner I was. "Natives," as the Spanish-Americans are called, and Indians milled through the streets. The Anglos, the term for all those neither Spanish-American nor Indian, were lost in the crowd. However, I did not feel foreign in spirit to the gracious, hospitable people. We had a common bond of love in the folk traditions. At the end of three months, more than two hundred festivals were set in Indian, Spanish-American, and Anglo communities throughout the state. I soon saw there was a vast difference between the traditional expressions of New Mexico and any other group I had known. There are three distinct racial groups, three different philosophies of life, three sets of folk traditions — confusing, yet challenging.

Knott's brief experience as a "foreigner" in Albuquerque is poignant testimony to the class and cultural divide that set Anglos apart from "native" communities. Generally speaking, tourists and middle-class Anglos appreciated New Mexico's "traditional expressions" within the safe and sterile confines of Santa Fe or Albuquerque, and, as Knott's statement attests, even those tourist settings attained an exotic air when "Indians" and "Spanish-Americans" outnumbered Anglos. Leaving the well-worn tourist path for more intimate environs of satellite communities along the Rio Grande was something few Anglos dared to do.

Having failed to rake in projected tourist dollars, the Coronado Cuarto Centennial's enduring impact was mostly intrinsic and not material, local and not national. It afforded Anglos and Nuevomexicanos an occasion both for historical reflection and half-serious recreation. Communities staged pageants, fiestas, and reenactments of Coronado's entrada; schoolchildren studied and dramatized various aspects of the Spanish conquest; politicians exhorted audiences to embrace equally the Indian, Spanish, and American contributions to the state; and boosters marketed New Mexico as a veritable "kaleidoscope of living history sung and danced in fiesta, religious drama, and ancient ceremonial" (Knott 1940).

In 1940, New Mexico's history was indeed "living," at least in the hearts and imaginations of Cuarto Centennial participants and spectators. It was elaborated and played out in pageants, recited in classrooms, discussed in newspapers, and reconstituted in a series of official textbooks and teaching tools. The combination of festivity and instruction made the year memorable to everyone involved. To that extent, then, the Cuarto Centennial had fulfilled at least one of its objectives: to arouse historical appreciation. But more important, it reaffirmed a now pervasive claim by Nuevomexicanos to the Spanish past and symbolically revitalized their Catholic identity, attachment to the soil, and pride in their language....

The Photo

In researching this book, I once asked my mother if she sees any irony in her performance of the jarabe tapatío, the "Mexican hat dance" that grew popular following the Revolution, to celebrate the Spanish conquest. She begins to explain that, culturally, we are all "mexicanos"; we have the same values, the same religion, the same language. Then she hesitates. "I was a little girl back then, and it was just something I was asked to do. I was very happy to do it."...

Spanish American identity in New Mexico was conceived in myth and is sustained by memory. And memories, of course, are subject to change, manipulation, distortion. Those that are incongruent with our expectations and immediate needs are often cast off into oblivion — el olvido or l'oubli. On the other hand, those that affirm our sense of self and community, and that empower us in the present or help explain our marginality, are...larger than life. As Latinos comprise an ever-larger proportion of the U.S. population, historians will invariably have to address the perplexities of memory in framing "Latina/o History." Until recent years, the historiography has emphasized nation-specific diasporas and narratives, broadly conceived as Mexican-American/ Chicana/o, Puerto Rican, Dominican, Cuban, and so forth. But the predominant framework of Latina/o historical scholarship is yet uncertain. Which landmark events will historians consecrate in text? Which myths and memories will predominate? More important, which memories will be cast off?

I have never actually seen that photograph of my mother dressed as a charro, dancing the jarabe tapatío, and I am beginning to doubt whether one actually exists. But she insists it must. My mother distinctly recalls seeing someone in the crowd snapping photos with a Brownie camera that was popular back then. As a historian, I feel compelled to confirm or dispel her recollection with tangible evidence. But that obligation will go unfulfilled. Instead, that moment will remain preserved in her memory — and here, in these pages.

Surveillance aircraft patrolling the border along the Rio Grande, about 1950.

48

Tricky Mirror: Mexican Immigrants in New Mexico

María Cristina López

I grew up in the 1950s on the south side of the Río Bravo–Río Grande in Ciudad Juárez, Chihuahua. This was a period of stability and relative prosperity in Mexico. After the Mexican Revolution of 1910 a national identity had been forged in the arts, the literature, and the consciousness of Mexicans. We were proud of our mestizo heritage, "la Raza Cósmica," as the Mexican educator José Vasconcelos called it. We abhorred the acts of the Spanish conquistadores and were suspicious but admiring of the United States. Our heroes were Cuauhtémoc, the last Aztec emperor, Benito Juárez, the reforming nineteenth-century president of Mexico, and the revolutionary president Francisco Madero. Pancho Villa was too close to home to loom large in our minds.

In grade school we spent one whole year studying the history of the Native peoples of Mexico and skipped three hundred years of colonization. We celebrated the War of Independence and cried when we read about "La Invasión Norteamericana," the Mexican-American War of 1846–48. What we learned about these events could be summarized in two facts: the courage of "Los Niños Héroes," the military cadets who jumped to their death wrapped in the Mexican flag rather than surrender to the U.S. forces of General Winfield Scott, and the blatant theft of more than half of Mexican territory by the United States with the aid of General Santana, the traitor.

I remember a continuing argument with my cousin Carmen from Mesilla Park, New Mexico, whom we would hold accountable for the loss of that land. To my sister and me, she represented the United States, and we wanted her to answer for these actions. Carmen always stood her ground and blamed Santana's ambition for the sad consequences. But no one ever mentioned the other loss — the people, our ancestors. There were 100,000 Mexicans living in the Southwest before it became part of the United States.

Years later Carmen learned the history of her New Mexico family. Longino Mestas, her grandfather's grandfather, had lost his land in the 1860s because of some legal technicality. Carmen believes Longino Mestas was one of the three thousand New Mexicans who opted to move to Mexico after the Treaty of Guadalupe Hidalgo was signed, only to find out five years later that the borderline had been redrawn after the Gadsden Purchase and they were back in U.S. territory. At the beginning of the twentieth century Carmen's grandfather began sharecropping on what used to be his family's land, and finally, after forty years of hard work, he was able to buy back the property. On it still stood the small adobe building where his grandfather had been born and the chapel where he was baptized. Few people were that fortunate. Was Longino Mestas an immigrant from the United States to Mexico or an immigrant from Mexico to the United States?

The imposed border between Mexico and the United States represented an attempt to turn the people who remained on the other side into strangers. As the years passed, it seemed as if the total erasure of historical information on both sides of the border had created a psychological *frontera* more divisive and harder to cross than the political one. Yet taking into consideration the anti-immigrant campaigns waged at the national and regional levels during times of economic recession, New Mexicans have managed to maintain a connection with Mexico that dates back to before the arrival of Europeans on this continent. Today, in the first decade of the second millennium, New Mexico, a border state, leads the country having passed some of the most progressive legislation dealing with the human rights of immigrants.

Mexican Immigrants Arrive in New Mexico

Until the early 1920s, people from Mexico walked across the river to New Mexico, or to El Paso and then to New Mexico, as they had been doing for generations to visit family and friends, for trade reasons, and to find work. Although many were driven by economic insecurity, others were motivated by political unrest.

One of the most notable turn-of-the-twentieth-century immigrants was Octaviano Larrazolo, the fourth governor of New Mexico and the first Hispanic U.S. senator. Larrazolo was born in 1859 in Valle de Allende, Chihuahua, where most of my father's aunts and uncles come from. After the French occupation of Mexico in 1864–67, the Larrazolo family found itself in an unstable economic and political situation and decided to send Octaviano, then ten years old, to study in the United States. He would receive the tutelage of Bishop Salpointe, who had recently been appointed to look after the spiritual needs of Arizona, Mesilla, New Mexico, and San Elizario, Texas.

Larrazolo attended parochial school in Las Cruces and then traveled to Santa Fe to continue his studies at St. Michaels College. His first job was as a schoolteacher in San Elizario, where he had a second job as a farmer in order to save money to bring his parents and three siblings to live with him. He became an American citizen in 1884 and continued his law studies, being accepted to the Texas bar four years later.

In 1895 Larrazolo moved to Las Vegas, New Mexico, desiring to be more involved in New Mexico politics. Throughout the Southwest he became known as the "silver-tongued orator." During his remarkable career, Governor Larrazolo defended the rights of both native New Mexicans and Mexican immigrants to high-quality education and the preservation of the Spanish language. He was the first politician to envision the value of bilingual education both for the cultural integrity of the Hispano community and as a means to a multifaceted collaboration with Latin America (Larrazolo 1986).

Mexican Immigrants Work in the Mines and on the Railroad

At the turn of the twentieth century the extension of the railroad and the development of coal, copper, iron, and silver mines in the western part of the state created a need for cheap labor. Workers from Mexico could easily satisfy this need because of their geographical proximity and the difficult political and economic situation in their country (García-Acevedo 2000). The transnational movement of people from Mexico to New Mexico and the contributions these families made after settling in the state have remained invisible. The stories that follow describe the experiences of Mexican immigrants in different parts of New Mexico as told by their descendants, with the intention of starting to fill in the gaps in the history of our state.

Rosemary Burrola Chavez's great-grandfather, Catarino Martínez, came to New Mexico Territory from El Valle de Buenaventura, Chihuahua, in 1880. He homesteaded a piece of land outside Silver City and for many years made his living as a farmer; later he sold firewood. His daughter Guillerma married Valentin Burrola, who at that time worked in the Kelly and Tokay mines. Burrola exemplifies the enterprising spirit of many immigrant men of the times. He went on to work for the Southwest Coal and Mutual Coal Companies. Before World War II he had a claim on a manganese ore mine in the foothills across from San Marcial, New Mexico. These were the Buena Vista Mines.

Like many other young men all over the United States, Valentin and Guillerma's sons enlisted in the armed forces to serve their country. Both Rosemary's father, William Burrola, and her uncle Joe were veterans of World War II, survivors of the Bataan Death March and prisoners of war for three and a half years. Two other brothers joined later:

> My Grandmother Guillerma had great faith and passed that faith on
> to her family. She asked the Lord to return her boys, all four, safely

home, and promised to go on her knees to the Catholic Church on their return. They returned and on her knees she went about six blocks to the church in thanksgiving. She also walked to Zuni, N.M., to the "Santo Niño" in thanksgiving, about 30 miles from Gallup; my dad accompanied her. So when my kidneys were failing at age 1½, my father prayed to the Santo Niño in Zuni for a miracle of healing for me. When the doctor in Pueblo, Colorado, successfully treated me and I came home to recuperate, he walked also to Zuni, N.M., in thanksgiving.

Rosemary's paternal grandparents bought a home in the area of Gallup called Chihuahuaita, where all the families of Mexican descent lived. This community had originated in 1917 when the Gallup American Coal Company had brought in Mexican workers as strikebreakers and then leased to them home lots next to the west side of Gallup. In 1934 the coal company sold the property to McKinley County State Senator Clarence F. Vogel, who had no intention of continuing to lease the land. He gave the residents the choice of buying their lots for an inflated price or moving out. It was the Great Depression, and many miners were unemployed and could not afford the payments. Vogel decided to evict those who had failed to pay. The first eviction took place on April 1, 1935, when sheriff's deputies carried out the personal belongings of one of the families and put a padlock on the door. But that night members of the community came together and decided to place the family's possessions back inside the house.

There followed a series of events that culminated in the death of Sheriff Mack R. Carmichael. A manhunt began to find all the possible suspects, and at one point fifty-five people were charged with attempted homicide. One way to get rid of some of the so-called troublemakers without taking them to trial was to have them deported by the Immigration and Naturalization Service. More than a hundred Mexican miners from the Gallup area had to leave the country in 1935 (Rubenstein 1983). They joined the other victims of a national trend during the Great Depression toward repatriating Mexican workers, who were seen as a burden to the economy. Eventually more than a million people, some of them American citizens, were forced to relocate (Balderrama and Rodríguez 2006). In New Mexico, six thousand Mexican workers returned to Mexico between 1930 and 1932 (García-Acevedo 2000). After the war, Rosemary Burrola Chavez's 's father built the family's home in Chihuahuaita.

Today, many of the grandsons and great-grandsons of Catarino Martínez still work at the Dodge Phelps mine in Silver City. Catarino's granddaughter says that through the years, Mexican families have suffered discrimination, having to live in segregated neighborhoods and bury their dead in the Mexican cemetery. She remembers being punished for speaking Spanish as a child, and that the playgrounds and bathrooms were segregated.

Juan and Florita López, Rosemary's maternal grandparents, came to New Mexico during the Mexican Revolution to work for the railroad. It was the practice at the time for American businesses involved in ranching, mining, and the railroad to import laborers from Mexico, and the couple was transported north by train. The Lópezes arrived in Arizona and later were moved to South Guam, near present-day Coolidge, about three miles east of Gallup. Rosemary's mother, Sally, remembers the section houses made of cinder block and the concrete floors: "They were so cold. The families had two rooms each, and all the rooms were attached in a row. The laborers were of different nationalities, not only Mexicans. They weren't far from the tracks, but luckily, no one was ever killed. They had a small, one-room schoolhouse across from Highway 66. They were poor but managed." Her dad was a laborer, building and maintaining the rails. After he retired, Mr. López and his wife were given free passes to go by train anywhere in the United States, but they couldn't afford to travel. Rosemary's grandmother once went to Fresno, to see her son Catarino before he left for England during the war. "She also went to Albuquerque with my mother to see her daughter Teresa, who was hospitalized at St. Joseph's Hospital."

The family was eventually relocated to Gallup, to live again in section houses. "My grandfather, with the help of his first two sons-in-law, built a home in town. I understand the neighbors were not happy about the fact that they were Mexicans." Rosemary's mother remembered the children being called "stupid Mexicans" and shunning her and others because they were poorly dressed. They were told to speak English and spoke Spanish only at home. When her sisters and brothers had families, they spoke to their children mostly in English. They didn't feel the urgency to teach them Spanish. Rosemary's generation spoke only Spanish to their parents, picked up bits and pieces at their grandparents' homes, and later studied the language at school. "I believe, due to their feeling of isolation, the families were closely knit, spending holidays and celebrations together. Made to feel they weren't as good as others, they didn't all reach out for more in their life. Now, three and four generations later, we their children know different. Many of us own businesses, have received college degrees, and contribute to our communities with our talents."

Rosemary married Richard S. Chavez from Santa Fe, and in 2007 the two lived in Gallup, where they had raised their five children. They owned Glenn's Bakery, which was managed by their oldest son. The second son owned the Coal Street Pub, and his wife, Angel's Café con Leche coffee house. The third son was a mechanical engineer. The elder daughter worked at home raising her two children, and the younger one was a kindergarten teacher staying at home with her first child.

Mexican Immigrants Work in Agriculture and Ranching

Starting in the 1920s, agriculture and ranching in southern and eastern New Mexico experienced steady growth and created many opportunities for farmworkers from Mexico. Elma Samora's family on her mother's side, the Cortezes, came to Artesia in the twenties from Presidio, Texas, across the border from Ojinaga, Chihuahua. They settled in a farming community called Seven Rivers, between Artesia and Carlsbad. Elma's grandfather, Mauro Cortez, worked for his cousin Hilario Brito in exchange for a place to live. The other members of the family worked on other farms, picking cotton in "exchange for vegetables or whatever was being planted." Elma says they never considered themselves poor, "because they eventually owned a cow and some chickens." But her mother talks about those years in Seven Rivers as hard times. She remembers the invasion of grasshoppers and how her "grandfather would send all the kids to the field with a big stick to hit the cotton." They did this in the evening to drive the grasshoppers to the trees before they ate the cotton plants. A chicken coop was also placed nearby so the chickens would eat the insects.

Elma's father's family came to Seven Rivers from Zacatecas, Mexico. Manuel García married Mercedes Cortez, and they began to raise a family. In the early years money was scarce, so the family had to live in a tent. After working hard, they were able to save enough money to buy a lot in Artesia for "the lump sum of $40."

In the 1930s, Mexican people lived on the north side of Artesia in a section of town called La Loma. Most of them attended St. Anthony's, the only Catholic church in town. Elma's mother recalled how the Mexican families were continually humiliated by other parishioners. She tells of a Dr. J. J. Clark, who used to rap their legs with a cane every time she and her sisters walked by where he was sitting in the church. According to Elma:

> Mr. José Alvarado decided it was time to build their own church in their own neighborhood. All the residents of La Loma participated in this project, making the adobes by hand and carrying water and sand from the river. There were fundraising projects like a play organized by Mercedes Cortez García and Elodia Alaniz Samora. Our Lady of Grace Church was dedicated almost a year later, in May 1942. According to an article in the *Artesia Advocate*, the local newspaper, there was a "Dedication Luncheon Honoring Anglos Who Made Church Erection Possible. Hosted By Dr. J. J. Clark." None of the people who actually built the church were honored or acknowledged.

Elma continues telling the story of segregation:

> As the Mexican population grew, the need for a cemetery came up, and after discovering they could not select a plot in the Anglo one, a site for the Mexican cemetery was chosen and it was named San Marcos. I believe prior to this people just buried their dear ones out in the country. As a child I did not understand why we had these two different places, one across from the other. The grave sites at San

Marcos were nothing but dirt, and on the other side of the fence was this beautiful resting place with grass, trees, and flowers. In later years the two were joined.

Because of the booming cotton industry, the demand for agricultural workers increased, and Mexican workers came with the Bracero program, a guest-worker program initiated during World War II. Lupe, Elma's sister, was director of the HELP program, which advocated for migrant workers' rights to fair treatment and worked to improve substandard housing. Lupe was responsible for organizing the Concilio, an advisory board of members of the farming community. One of its first projects was to buy a tract of land to provide housing for the farm laborers. The houses are still there. The other task of the Concilio was to work with the migrant women to develop marketable skills that would get them out of the fields. Sewing, making piñatas, and caring for children were some of the training they received.

All of Elma's brothers and sisters attended college in the 1960s. In the 1980s a group of people gathered at Our Lady of Grace Church to organize and elect Hispanos to government positions at the local and county and eventually at the state level. José Luis Aguilar was thus elected councilman for Artesia. The group campaigned door to door, one district at a time, held enchilada dinners to raise funds, and were successful at electing Hispanic candidates to the school board and county commission positions.

In addition to politicians, Artesia had three doctors, a postmaster, and many educators and successful businesspeople of Hispanic ancestry. Elma says, "We are specially proud of the doctors who decided to come back to their communities and contribute." Today, one of these doctors makes house calls to the elderly, visiting many *tíos* and *tías* whose roots go back to the first immigrant families who came to Artesia.

Life is not without contradictions. One of Elma's former students, an immigrant himself, is now cafeteria manager, in charge of preparing meals for all the district's schools. "Because we now have a border patrol training center in Artesia," he said to Elma, "pues cómo la ve, maestra, que estoy preparando comida para los que andan detrás de mi gente [what do you think, teacher, I am preparing food for those who are after my people]."

Mexican Immigration during and after the Mexican Revolution

The Mexican Revolution of 1910–21 was the first social revolution of the twentieth century, brought about by the extreme economic inequality most small farmers and urban workers experienced during the thirty years of dictatorship of Porfirio Díaz. A small Mexican oligarchy became very wealthy along with foreign investors who profited from the development of the oil and railroad industries, not to mention mining and textile production. Yet the vast majority of the Mexican people could hardly make a living. These were some of the factors that contributed to the beginning of a popular uprising against the federal government led by such different individuals as Francisco I. Madero, Pancho Villa, and Emiliano Zapata. It is estimated that between 1899 and 1928, at least half a million Mexican immigrants entered the United States legally, most of them coming before or after the war of revolution (Griswold del Castillo 1990).

The family of José de Jesús Ríos came across the border during the Mexican Revolution to avoid having to join the federal army to fight against the soldiers of Pancho Villa. The family was from San José de la Boca, Durango. Jesús's mother, Josefa Ríos Rivera, left everything behind and had to be escorted by General Arrieta so that her young sons would be allowed to leave Mexico. José de Jesús was seven at the time, the youngest of twelve children, seven boys and five girls. They went to Texas first, where the oldest sister, Sirina, lived, and then they followed two of Jesús's brothers-in-law, who worked for the railroad in Raton, New Mexico. Seven years later José de Jesús found work in a mine in Dawson, New Mexico. Eventually he would become supervisor of a group of miners much older than he, all of them immigrants from Slavic countries, Italy, and Greece.

In 1919, after basic training in Deming, Jesús Ríos was on his way to Fort Bliss in El Paso when the war ended in Europe. He returned to Santa Fe, where his family had relocated after the coal mine closed in Raton. A few years later he met Teresita Gabaldón and fell in love. The two were married for sixty-three years.

They raised their five daughters and three sons to be proud of their cultural heritage as Mexicanos and Nuevomexicanos and to speak Spanish. He taught them to say their prayers, the Our Father and Hail Mary, in Spanish. Pancha, one of the daughters, remembers being reprimanded for speaking Spanish with one of her little friends in the schoolyard and coming home to tell her father. After Jesús Ríos spoke to the principal, the children were never again chastised for using their language.

Ríos's first business, and one that his sons and daughters continue to this day, was the sale of firewood and hauling of freight. He began selling from his mother-in-law's home on Abeyta Street and later bought property on Canyon Road and Camino del Monte Sol. Today the wood yard is surrounded by high-end restaurants, galleries, boutiques, and fancy homes. Developers have had their eyes on this prime piece of real estate, but in 2007 the Ríos family was not ready to sell. There have been times when one of the Canyon Road residents has tried to have the business removed, but to no avail.

The story goes that in 1947 a neighbor took Jesús Ríos to court, complaining about the noise his saws made. As Ríos walked into the courtroom, the attorney for the other side said, "Here comes Pancho Villa." Ríos replied, "If I were Pancho Villa, none of you clowns would be standing there."

His son León, who took over Ríos Excavating and Demolition, says that his father was ahead of his time in many ways. He recycled everything he could, taking apart hundreds of buildings piece by piece. He did not believe in smashing old buildings into bits. Jesús Ríos supplied materials all over town, including the red cedar slabs that he laid on the ceiling of Cristo Rey Church.

León tells of the amazing partnership between his parents. Teresita kept the books and sold wood while his father was out doing other work. At the same time she supervised fifty to sixty workers and made sure there was always food on the table for their nine children. There are countless stories of the Ríoses' generosity toward their neighbors and their laborers.

For longer than anyone can remember, Sunday afternoons have been open house at the Ríoses' home. Friends and family gather around the large kitchen table to share a meal and enjoy good conversation. When Jesús Ríos was alive he had many stories to tell, punctuated by the wisdom of his *dichos* (sayings) and a great sense of humor. "La fuerza del soldado me hace entrar a la guerra [life's obligations have to be met]" was one of his favorite sayings, according to Socorro Rios, his daughter. In the Museo Cultural de Santa Fe there is a room dedicated to José de Jesús Ríos, replete with photographs and newspaper and magazine articles recounting the life of this hardworking, larger-than-life patriarch.

The New Transnational Workers

The second devaluation of the peso in the middle 1980s prompted unprecedented growth in Mexican migration to northern New Mexico. Immigrants found work in the hospitality industry, landscaping, construction, and private homes. Small businesses owned by immigrants began to appear on the south side of Santa Fe: restaurants, bakeries, *tortillerías,* and food markets.

In the past, immigrants from Mexico for the most part had been young men, working to send money home. In time some of them brought their wives and children to live in the United States. Since the late 1980s a new trend in transnational labor migration has been observed — the migration of women on their own to make a living in the north, mostly in the domestic service sector. In urban locations on the U.S. side of the border, these women continue to fulfill the familial obligations of parenting and caretaking of parents long established in agrarian settings in Mexico.

Olivia (not her real name) grew up in Santa Clara Namiquipa, a rural area in the state of Chihuahua. Her family lived from the sale of beans and corn they harvested. They had some fruit trees and farm animals, and as Olivia put it, "they lived from year to year, working hard but never being able to get ahead or save money." There were eight children in her family, five boys and three girls, and she is the next to the youngest. After finishing high school, Olivia worked as a secretary in a government office, and when that job ended she thought seriously about coming to the United States to work. She wanted to help her parents financially, because she saw them getting old and having no savings for their later years. She dreamed of having them come to visit their children in the United States, to see what their lives were like there.

She chose to come to New Mexico because it was near Chihuahua and she had other family members already living in Santa Fe. She had heard there were jobs available in the tourist industry:

I remember the exact date I arrived in Santa Fe, November 13, 1994. For two years I worked literally day and night to save money to find my own apartment and to buy a car. I worked cleaning houses from Monday through Saturday, from eight in the morning to six at night. I came home, had dinner, and then I went to my next job at a spa, where I worked from seven-thirty at night till one o'clock in the morning. Monday was my day off. After those two years I had saved enough money to go back to Chihuahua and help my parents get visas to be able to come and spend time with me two or three times a year.

Olivia's father had worked in New Mexico during the 1950s with the Bracero program. He had been a ranch hand on cattle ranches in Magdalena, Socorro, and surrounding areas. Even before that, as a child he would go to Ciudad Juárez, on the border, and sneak back and forth across the river to find work. Those were the days when, if a Mexican was caught crossing, the Immigration and Naturalization Service — La Migra — would just take him or her back to the other side. Not anymore. Today, if someone is deported and crosses back without papers, it is considered a felony, and the person can spend up to five years in jail. People are increasingly being forced to stay in the United States. Workers who return to Mexico to see their families or who are coming to the United States for the first time have to travel different and more difficult routes to get to the U.S. side.

Olivia came to the United States the way many immigrants do, with a visitor's visa, and remained in this country after her permit expired. She is one of 12 million immigrants working in the shadows under the threat of deportation. This is, in the eyes of many people, a low-grade form of terrorism that increases during periods of intense anti-immigrant rhetoric in the media.

Olivia is not hopeful about a legalization program for her in the near future, although she believes that people who have worked hard and contributed to the U.S. economy should have a chance to stay there legally. She remembers that in 1986 the Immigration Reform and Control Act gave many undocumented immigrants an opportunity to become legal residents of the United States. She planned to continue working to ensure a life full of opportunities for the baby boy she was expecting. He will not have to worry about documents.

Olivia's husband, Jorge, was unsure he wanted his son to grow up in this country. He thinks children in the United States become selfish, forget about their family, and lose respect for their elders. "People have been very good to me here," Olivia counters. Her employers have been fair and supportive. Still, it has not been easy. Sometimes the isolation has seemed overwhelming. A wave of longing for familiar celebrations, places, and faces washes over her at times. On the other hand, as a woman raised in a rural Mexican community with very traditional ways, she appreciates being independent and having the freedom to make decisions about her life. Both Jorge and Olivia want to raise their child with the best of both cultures — they want him to be bilingual and to respect all human beings.

The Education of a Mexican Immigrant

I arrived in Albuquerque, New Mexico, in 1963 and soon found out that Nuevomexicanos cringed when I said the word "Mexican." Politely they told me to say I was Spanish. "I'm 150 percent Mexican," was my reply. I was a visitor, a foreign student always able to return to the safety of my homeland. Why were enchiladas, burros, and *corridos* Spanish? I remember feeling a twinge of sadness, a sense of rejection I did not understand. But when I spoke to my friends' parents or *abuelitos* (grandparents) in Spanish, we were Mexicanos — we shared a culture and an intimacy that felt like home.

Six or seven years later I was no longer a visitor. I was married, had a baby, and was a participant in a social movement working to forge a new world in which peace, justice, and equality would reign. New Mexico was my home. When I visited family in Mexico, strangers would ask me where I was from. My Chihuahuan accent was fading, and sometimes I stumbled for a word in Spanish or used English words and phrases. I no longer tolerated gender double standards, and I challenged classist statements. "Tenga mucho cuidado, mijita, no ande diciendo todo lo que piensa, es peligroso [Be careful, my girl, don't go saying everything you think; it's dangerous]." I was not acting like a nice Mexican girl. I was beginning to feel off center on both sides of the Río Grande–Río Bravo. *Dislocada culturalmente.*

Gradually, the historical pieces started to fall into place. The Chicano movement drew the faces and documented the struggles of the people who lived in the territory from California to Texas. I learned about César Chávez and the farmworkers' fight for better conditions in the fields, about Corky González and the Crusade for Justice in Colorado, about La Raza Unida in Texas. The first time I heard about the Treaty of Guadalupe Hidalgo and its relationship to the people and their land was when I heard Reies López Tijerina speak.

It was clear to me that the Mexicanos who lived north of the border had a long history of oppression due solely to their ethnicity, *su mexicanidad.* The benefits of a stable and wealthy economy were a myth for a colonized people. I had not shared that part of their history, but now I was here and I was part of that *mexicanidad* whether my New Mexican friends accepted me or not. The dominant society put us all in the same pot. There were moments of cultural intimacy when that internal wall temporarily disappeared. When we played guitar and sang *rancheras,* we were home — not in a geographical or political space but in a cultural and emotional one.

It was only when I started studying the history of the Spanish language in New Mexico that most of the pieces fell into place. The Treaty of Guadalupe Hidalgo, instead of protecting the culture, land, and civil rights of the people, marked the beginning of a campaign to divest Nuevomexicanos of their language and ethnic identity.

Before and during the Mexican-American War, newspaper articles from the East Coast characterized Mexicanos as people incapable of governing themselves, as drunks, as untrustworthy and quick to use guns to resolve arguments. Demonizing a people in order to gain support for an unjust war is a tactic used by many governments. I learned that most people had chosen to stay on the U.S. side after the war because their land and their roots were there — almost three hundred years of history. Nuevomexicanos resisted the attack on their culture then, and the resistance continues today.

The term "Spanish American" became popular at the turn of the last century when New Mexico politicians and large landowners in favor of statehood began using it to appeal to Washington. The label came from the top down. The people in the northern villages of New Mexico wore the name as a mask when they spoke English. When they spoke Spanish they called themselves Mexicanos; they ate *comida mexicana,* sang *canciones mexicanas,* and even spoke *mexicano.*

Spanish has survived against all odds in northern New Mexico, and this is what keeps the culture alive. After World War II and up until the 1960s, Nuevomexicanos were consistently punished for speaking their language in school and were ridiculed for their Spanish accents in English. No wonder the next generation attempted to protect their children from the same humiliation by not teaching them Spanish.

As I learned this historical information, my internal barrier disintegrated; I was no longer offended or defensive. I am able to have *diálogos abiertos,* open dialogues, with my friends and students who say they grew up believing the word "Mexican" was contaminated and the border was there to protect them from the Mexicans. Through self-reflection, education, and introspection about the we-they dichotomy between Mexicanos and Nuevomexicanos created by lies, myths, and historical voids, the barriers have gradually disappeared.

In 1994, Proposition 187 passed in California, marking the beginning of an anti-immigrant campaign that spread like wildfire across the country. Economic hardship has historically spurred xenophobic sentiments seeking an easy target to blame. Proposition 187 denied education, social services, and health care to undocumented immigrants. Other states followed suit, but not New Mexico. At the 1995 legislative session in Santa Fe, legislators from both northern and southern New Mexico spoke eloquently about New Mexico's historical ties to Mexican immigrants and underlined the state's commitment to providing educational and human services to immigrant children. Nuevomexicanos against Proposition 187 organized rallies and marches in Albuquerque and Santa Fe to express New Mexicans' opposition to such types of legislation.

New groups were born in the 1990s to work to protect the human rights of immigrants in New Mexico. One in particular, Somos un Pueblo Unido, based in Santa Fe, has led local and statewide campaigns to create and change policies to benefit immigrants. In the state of New Mexico, undocumented immigrants can obtain driver's licenses with appropriate identification, and undocumented students have access to higher education and are eligible for the State Lottery Scholarship. The cities of Albuquerque and Santa Fe have passed resolutions that in essence say that no city resources will be used to persecute immigrants regardless of their immigration status. In 2006 New Mexico cities saw the largest demonstrations in the history of the state, which joined millions of people in Los Angeles, Chicago, Dallas, and many other cities across the country in marching for comprehensive immigration reform, equality, and justice. This political activism is supported and sometimes led by local Nuevomexicanos who know the history and make the connections between the two Mexicos.

Go to almost any town in New Mexico and you will find families of Mexican ancestry, those who came after 1848, with stories of hardship and success. Newcomers are always looked upon with suspicion, seen as competition for jobs, yet after a generation and intermarriage they become part of the local community. Transnational workers are defying geographical borders. By creating networks of family members and friends, they are able to live on both sides of the line.

Lime plastering workshop in Mesilla, southwest New Mexico.

49

Driven by History:
Pursuing the Past in
Twenty-First-Century New Mexico

Jon Hunner

I drove into a career in history. In the 1980s I operated an art transport business out of Santa Fe. Sitting behind a steering wheel for endless hours bored me, and on one of my trips to Denver, I thought I saw Santa Fe Trail ruts along Interstate 25 just north of Watrous. In fact what caught my attention were some ditches dug for a gas line, and the subtler trail ruts curved around the hills on the opposite side of the highway. But this experience rekindled an interest first planted in me as a Boy Scout, when in 1967 my Albuquerque troop hiked from Cimarron to Fort Union along the historic trail. After the trail ruts along the interstate grabbed my interest, I began devouring histories of the Santa Fe Trail.

The trail had me by my collar and would not let go, so when it came time to make a career change, Mary Ellen, my wife, said, "Why don't you become a historian? That's all you are reading anyway." Taking her advice, in 1990 I went to graduate school at the University of New Mexico (UNM) to become a historian of the American West. During my time there, Richard Etulain, one of my professors, remarked that there were many historians of the frontier West but, with the twentieth century almost over, few who specialized in the more recent period.

History as Autobiography

Often we choose to focus on a particular past for autobiographical reasons. I am no different. My father, Paul Hunner, administered nuclear weapons for the U.S. Air Force. In what is now called "stockpile stewardship," he helped safeguard the warheads in top-secret storage facilities. One November in the late 1950s, my father and mother, Anna, drove me and my two brothers to the parade field at Sandia Air Force Base in Albuquerque. Flanking the flagpole, where most military bases showcased their artillery pieces, rested replicas of Fat Man and Little Boy, the atomic bombs dropped on Japan. To young boys these replicas looked more like playground equipment than weapons of mass destruction. The Hunner boys jumped on Fat Man, and my father quickly plucked us off and herded us back to our station wagon. At our nightly dinner table, we did not ask Dad what he did at work that day, but he did hang photos of mushroom clouds from nuclear bomb tests on our family room walls.

To uncover my family's secret past and to take advantage of Etulain's suggestion about the twentieth-century West, I turned away from the Santa Fe Trail and the frontier West and became a historian of the atomic bomb and Los Alamos. I earned a Ph.D. in United States history in 1996 with a dissertation on the social and cultural history of the Atomic City, now published by the University of Oklahoma Press under the title *Inventing Los Alamos*. We often do history because of our own past and our own history, and sometimes history just grabs us by the neck and won't let go.

Even before I graduated from UNM, I started teaching at New Mexico State University (NMSU) in Las Cruces. Since 1995 I have directed the Public History Program (PHP) in the Department of History, in which students learn to work as historians outside the classroom. The PHP offers courses in museum studies, historic preservation, oral history, historic editing, and heritage tourism. Public historians curate exhibits and conduct educational programs in museums, save historic buildings, record the oral histories of elders of their communities, research the heritages and histories of towns and villages, give tours of historic places, edit books and journals, and preserve historic documents and photographs in archives. In brief, public historians collect, preserve, document, and present the history and heritage of a region. Public historians like those at the New Mexico History Museum are driven by history to engage the public in the pursuit of the past.

Southern New Mexico has always been on the border, whether it was a frontier between different groups of Native Americans a thousand years ago, between New Spain and its colonial outpost in Santa Fe four hundred years ago, or between the United States and Mexico as it is today. Today's international border is a distinct line drawn in the Chihuahuan desert, but the linguistic, economic, and cultural borders between the two countries are notably fuzzy. The yeasty blend of languages, beliefs, cuisines, and fashions that spreads north and south from the international boundary makes this region and indeed the whole of New Mexico a historically diverse place where various people have lived and interacted for millennia.

The southern part of New Mexico is neither solely United States nor Mexican, but a mixture of the two. In fact New Mexico is more than the "tri-cultural" mix celebrated by chambers of commerce across the state. In language, food, religion, and traditions, New Mexicans embrace a varied mixture of beliefs and activities to live their lives. Those of us who record, preserve, and interpret the history of New Mexico work at the intersection of many places and events — on the border between New Mexico, Texas, and Mexico, on the border between academic and public history, and on the border between the past and the future.

Pursuing New Mexico's past in the twenty-first century involves exploring local history and heritage. Many New Mexicans devote their time and money to collecting, preserving, interpreting, and exhibiting the rich stories of their culture and history. Driven by a desire to understand themselves, their families, and their communities, to search for meaning, to educate themselves, and to have fun, New Mexicans turn to the past in their everyday lives to prepare for the future.

We are all historians. We know about our own lives, about our family's history, even about the past of our communities and regions. Not all of us produce history for academic purposes or public consumption, such as in books or museum exhibits, but we look to the past for guidance, insight, and identity. Thousands of people in the state connect with the past, in their own ways and for their own reasons. What follows is an exploration of some of the people and their historical projects in southern New Mexico. These are just a few examples of the ways people in the borderlands pursue the past in the twenty-first century.

Human Systems Research and Cañada Alamosa

In a light industrial park in Las Cruces, in an indistinct trailer, eight volunteers shift through more than 150,000 items from an archeological excavation one hundred miles to the north. Fran Clark, one of those volunteers who is a trained archeologist, works one day a week classifying the remnants of a society that thrived in central New Mexico more than a thousand years ago. Since 1999, amateur and professional archeologists have excavated the ancient pueblo ruins at Cañada Alamosa during summer field schools conducted by Human Systems Research of Las Cruces. From there, the objects found in the excavations are driven down to Las Cruces. As one of the team of volunteers, Fran looks at pieces of broken pottery and stone flakes to evaluate how humans made and used them. She commented on her work: "What we do on a weekly basis is pretty boring, but what will come from it is pretty exciting once we're done."

The significance of this pre-Columbian site resides in its location — it was at a frontier of Native American culture from A.D. 600 to 1400. At Cañada Alamosa, the northern Pueblo (or Chacoan) culture from the northwest part of New Mexico met the Mogollon people from the southern part of the state. Over the centuries, four distinct Native American cultures lived in the canyon and interacted with other peoples both near and far away. For Fran and the other volunteer archeologists, these small pieces of pottery and stone flakes are "time and culture markers" that offer insights into the civilizations of long ago. They are some of the only evidence left of those who lived there.

When asked why she volunteers to sort through the excavated objects, Fran replied that the importance of the site attracted her. As Mike Hughes, another volunteer, said about the Cañada Alamosa site: "It's a special place. It's easy to picture what old women were doing there a thousand years ago." Fran also feels a deep commitment to Human Systems Research and to Karl Laumbach, its associate director of research and public relations. Karl and HSR are dedicated to the site and the ethical care of the ancient objects. Fran is also convinced that the report Karl is writing about the excavation will be a path-breaking account of these early people of New Mexico.

The Barela-Reynolds-Taylor State Monument

In Mesilla, New Mexico, the Mary and J. Paul Taylor family has preserved local history and heritage for decades — indeed, for generations. Mary was a historian who in 2004 published *A Place as Wild as the West Ever Was,* and Paul is a retired school administrator and former state representative. The Taylors and their seven children grew up in a hacienda on the west side of the plaza of Mesilla that they bought in 1953. In addition to raising their family in the adobe home, originally built in the 1850s, Mary and Paul have collected countless artifacts, art objects, pieces of furniture, textiles, and *santos,* or images of saints. In 2004 the Taylors donated their home and many of the objects in their collection to the state of New Mexico. In the future, New Mexico State Monuments will turn the home into a museum celebrating not only the Taylor family but also the history of the Mesilla Valley and New Mexico.

In an extensive oral history interview conducted by participants in the Public History Program at NMSU, members of the family talked about how history had driven their household. In his interview, Michael Romero Taylor observed: "You know, the intent of the folks giving this property to the state is to make it available to the public…to really provide it as a place where people can come and learn about the history of this valley, the history of this house, the history of Mesilla.… Historic preservation was always in there, and Dad and Mom were really proponents of that balance of keeping the historic integrity of Mesilla, but at the same time creating some economic vitality." Keeping a healthy balance between preservation and development is a constant challenge in Mesilla, as in many other communities around the state.

Representative J. Paul Taylor talked about his own hopes for the museum: "We would hope that at the time it passes to the museum…that people will enjoy viewing the house…that has been lived in and loved by a number of people.…We hope that when people come through the house, through the *zaguan* [vestibule], into the parlor, make their rounds through the rooms, visit the *portal* [porch], that they would have some essence of life in Mesilla by families that live here now." For the Taylors and many others in New Mexico, pursuing the past is virtually part of their hereditary makeup, passed down over the generations through their family's heritage DNA.

Preserving Historic Adobe Buildings and Their Communities

Pat Taylor, a son of Mary and Paul Taylor's, upholds his family's preservation tradition as he revitalizes historic structures in southern New Mexico and west Texas. From his start as a building contractor, Pat has taken on some challenging restorations. During the 1990s he assembled a workforce of local teenagers and young adults to save the Nuestra Señora de la Candelaria adobe church at Doña Ana. He then collaborated with Jean Fulton to bring about the same success with the Nuestra Señora de la Purísima Concepción mission church at Socorro, Texas. Pat is the regional coordinator for Cornerstones Community Partnerships, a nonprofit organization dedicated to working with communities to preserve their historic adobe and stone structures, and Jean is its preservation programs coordinator. At both churches, an active community group provided not just a dedicated workforce but also leadership and local guidance to complete the restorations. To aid the community members who were the driving forces behind these restorations, Cornerstones Community Partnerships provided expertise and assistance, but the projects would not have succeeded without the deep commitment by local people to save their historic churches.

Beginning with the restoration of Nuestra Señora de la Purísima Concepción, Doña Ana has revitalized the historic neighborhood around the old church. Chris Wilson, the J. B. Jackson Professor at UNM's School of Architecture and director of its Historic Preservation and Regionalism Program, has collaborated with State Senator Mary Jane Garcia and the citizens of Doña Ana to create a plaza just to the south of the church. The plaza invents a new tradition, because this town, which dates to the 1840s, had no plaza before this. Now the people of this historic village on the Camino Real can enjoy a central social place.

To aid in restoring historic adobe structures in the region, Pat Taylor brought *maestros* (masonry experts) from Mexico to teach historic preservationists in the borderland the lost art of lime plastering. Back in the 1930s, cement began to replace lime and mud plaster on the exteriors of adobe structures. But cement stucco locks moisture inside the mud brick walls. With water trapped in the walls, the mud bricks dissolve. Lime plaster is permeable and allows the walls to breathe, which helps preserve these historic structures. Consequently, for the long-term health of many historic adobe buildings, lime plaster should replace cement stucco on the outside walls. With this skill lost north of the border, Pat brought in experts from Mexico to reintroduce traditional lime plastering.

During the work at Nuestra Señora de la Purísima Concepción, a young community member named Albert Palacios joined in. Albert later commented: "These responsibilities have somehow stimulated my intellectual and creative juices. Working on the project has helped me step closer to what I need to be when I enter the real world. The challenge has also led me to discover an architectural wonder in my own backyard." For Albert, doing history in his backyard sparked his interest, and he has been accepted to the University of Texas at Austin to pursue a degree in architecture and historic preservation.

Oral Histories in Southeast New Mexico

One hundred and fifty miles east of the Mesilla Valley, Virginia Dodier directs the Carlsbad Museum and Art Center, the oldest municipal museum in the state. Virginia has embarked on the Eddy County Oral History Project, an ambitious endeavor to interview Hispanos and people in the farming and ranching industries in southeastern New Mexico. She is driven to do this for several reasons. First, her family is from the borderlands. Second, when she arrived in Carlsbad in 1999 to direct the museum, she found scarce archival documentation about Hispanos in southeast New Mexico. She wondered about the people of Mexican origin who built the canals and flumes for the Carlsbad Irrigation District and who worked in the region's mines, farms, and ranches. To obtain stories of the people who helped build Eddy County, who came north from Mexico at the turn of the twentieth century, Virginia tracked down their descendants.

Virginia interviewed Apolonio (Polo) Fernandez Muñoz. As a young man, Polo fought in World War II and earned a Silver Star for his courage in liberating the Philippines. Upon his return from the war he worked in the nearby potash mines and also became politically active, both locally and with the League of United Latin American Citizens (LULAC). Eventually Polo was elected to the Carlsbad City Council, the first Mexican American to serve in that body. During his interview with Virginia, he talked proudly about helping to break the "color bar" that prevented Hispanos from obtaining jobs in the mines and with the city. The oral histories of Polo and others in the Eddy County Oral History Project are starting to fill the gap in knowledge about the vital contributions that Hispanos have made in southeast New Mexico. Although funding is scarce, Virginia is driven to record the life histories of people there. These interviews are deposited at her museum and in the library at NMSU's Carlsbad branch.

Making History Come Alive in the Classroom

George Torok, who teaches history at El Paso Community College, stumbled onto using local history in his classrooms when he looked for a project that his students could tackle over the course of a semester. George has his students conduct research and interviews to create the texts for nearby historical markers and signs. For non-history majors at a community college, this is an accessible project that gets them interested in history.

Along similar lines, the Public History Program at NMSU uses nearby and local history to enliven the teaching of history as well as to prepare undergraduates and graduate students for careers in history outside the classroom. Documenting significant buildings in historic districts, interviewing elders of a community, assembling books of historic photographs, creating living history learning events at museums such as the New Mexico History Museum and the New Mexico Farm and Ranch Heritage Museum — all such projects bring history to the public.

Since 2001 the PHP has conducted "Time Travels through New Mexico's History." In the Time Travels classes, university students research a distinct time period and develop characters from that era. During the last third of the semester, local classes of schoolchildren from the fifth to the twelfth grade join us at a specially prepared site at the Farm and Ranch Museum where the university students act out their characters as if they were living in the past. Since Time Travels began, more than fifteen hundred students have experienced the Spanish colonial period in the year 1776, the wild West in 1889, and the Great Depression in 1937. Using local historic and cultural resources, students learn about history by connecting with the nearby historic environment.

Corridos *and Cultural Preservation*

To assist in pursuing the past in the twenty-first century, the New Mexico Humanities Council (NMHC) grants funding to people and organizations to conduct historical projects. Like participants in many other heritage organizations in the state, Executive Director Craig Newbill and members of the Board of Directors of NMHC drive around the state to attend meetings and see the many projects that New Mexicans are carrying out to commemorate their past. One example involves an exhibit and public programming effort concerning *corridos*, Spanish ballads that often focus on local people and themes. In 2006 the Silver City Museum rented *¿Nuevo Mexico: Hasta Quando?* a part of the exhibition *Corridos sin Fronteras: A New World Ballad Tradition,* assembled by the Smithsonian Institution. Curated for the Smithsonian by Enrique Lamadrid of the University of New Mexico, the *corridos* exhibit had four panels with eight listening stations that played the ballads. Some of these songs held local importance for Silver City because they were about the Empire Zinc Company labor strike in the early 1950s, immortalized in the 1954 film *Salt of the Earth.*

In order to make the exhibition more relevant to the public, Susan Berry, director of the Silver City Museum, worked with local people to hold musical performances in conjunction with *¿Nuevo Mexico: Hasta Quando?* The museum offered two evenings of musical public programming during the exhibition's stay in Silver City. The first evening of performances had Lamadrid and Luis Quiñones playing and singing *corridos* with local themes. The words of one ballad, which originated in the early 1950s, told of the Empire Zinc strike, but the tune came from a 1906 mining conflict in Mexico that helped launch the Mexican Civil War. Another song during the evening told of Juan Chacón, a leader of the Empire Zinc strike. This ballad was first performed at Juan's funeral in 1985. The second evening of performances hosted an Albuquerque dance troupe, Las Flores de Baille, that sang, danced, and performed a program of *corridos*. The evening also presented many songs telling the tales of women in the Mexican Civil War after the turn of the twentieth century.

Some of the *corridos* focused on local people and themes. For example, one told the tragic tale of a local Silver City man who was at the wrong place at the wrong time and was murdered by a mentally deranged person. Although this had happened years before, the widow attended the evening. Because of such connections with local history, the songs held special meaning for the audience, which sang along with the performers. At the end of both performances, many people hugged each other, and as Director Berry observed, "There were smiles all around."

After the *¿Nuevo Mexico: Hasta Quando?* exhibit played in Silver City for five months, it moved to the Branigan Cultural Center in Las Cruces. Again, songs about local people brought the past alive to the citizens of the Mesilla Valley. A *corrido* about Lorenzo Banegas, a local survivor of the Bataan Death March, told of that terrible event and the courageous New Mexicans who fought in the Philippines during the first days of World War II. Again, Enrique Lamadrid came to play and talk about *corridos*, funded by New Mexico Humanities Council.

Climate Change Threatens Cultural and Historic Resources

Cultural and historic resources are as vulnerable to natural disasters in southern New Mexico as anywhere else. The summer thunderstorms of 2006 hit the borderland particularly hard. Torrential rains hammered Alamogordo, El Paso, Ciudad Juárez, and Hatch, flooding homes and businesses. Hatch, the chile capital of the world, suffered some of the worst devastation. During a storm on August 15, walls of water swept down from the surrounding hills, flooded 402 of the town's 480 dwellings (many of them historic), and damaged 55 of the 80 businesses, causing 60 years' worth of deterioration overnight.

A collection of agencies, including the New Mexico Historic Preservation Division, the National Trust for Historic Preservation, NMSU's Engineering Technology Department, and FEMA, assisted with the recovery of this small but vital agricultural town. Cornerstones Community Partnerships again stepped in as Jean Fulton and Pat Taylor consulted with town officials and property owners on how to repair water-damaged adobe homes. Displaced families gratefully moved into trailers provided by FEMA, but Jean fears that Hatch residents will replace their adobe homes with wood frame structures or trailers, thus losing the historic character of the village. In 2006 and 2007, Cornerstones sponsored workshops in Hatch on foundation stabilization and ways of drying out adobe brick walls.

A second effort to rescue the history of Hatch involved the village's official documents. After the flood, the Hatch Town Hall lay under four feet of water. Six bound volumes containing all the minutes of the town's governmental meetings and all resolutions and ordinances passed since 1927 were stored in fireproof filing cabinets. As City Clerk Kathy McConnell said, "They were fireproof, but not waterproof."

Kathy called Shirley Clark, the city clerk of Las Cruces at the time, for help, and Shirley rushed up to Hatch that same day.

Shirley helped Kathy contact Steve Hussman, director of the Rio Grande Historical Collection (RGHC, the archive at NMSU), for advice. Steve told them that the drenched documents had to be frozen immediately and suggested that a local grocery store might allow its meat locker to be used for that purpose. A local supermarket did freeze the soggy papers, and then the volumes were driven to the RGHC conservation lab at NMSU. Each page of the mainly onionskin papers was delicately separated and dried out. Saving the meeting minutes, ordinances, and resolutions preserved those essential documents, and as Kathy noted, "these papers are a good history of Hatch." As the worldwide environment changes because of global warming, natural disasters like those that hit the borderlands in the summer of 2006 will continue to threaten our state's historic and cultural resources.

The Past versus the Present versus the Future

In a fascinating juxtaposition of old and new, the effort to identify, interpret, and preserve El Camino Real de Tierra Adentro (the royal road to the interior lands) crosses state and even national borders. The Camino Real ran for fifteen hundred miles from Mexico City to Santa Fe. For part of New Mexico's Spanish colonial era, (1598–1821), it was the longest trail in North America. Dedicated volunteers in Mexico, Texas, and New Mexico have helped preserve the existing traces of the trail.

As a bi-national historic trail, the Camino Real presents interesting challenges to heritage preservationists. The Camino Real Trail Association (CARTA) has worked closely with the National Park Service and the Bureau of Land Management to develop a management plan for the trail. In conjunction with this plan, CARTA is certifying potential historic sites along the trail and creating working relationships with local groups.

Of particular concern in preserving the remnants of the Camino Real is the location of the New Mexico Spaceport. As North America's proposed primary site for launching private rockets into space, the spaceport, east of the town of Truth or Consequences, will be situated near and possibly destroy some of the distinctive trail ruts from the royal road. CARTA is taking the lead in addressing the potential effects of the spaceport on the remains of the historic trail. Indeed, the exciting possibility of having a historic site that celebrates the preferred mode of travel in the seventeenth and eighteenth centuries — by ox cart and mule — at the same place where the frontier of commercial space travel is launched seems like a win-win situation. However, the struggle continues to convince some of the state's officials that the trail is a valuable site not just for history enthusiasts but also for space tourists.

Another opportunity in looking to the future to celebrate our past arrives in 2012 with the centennial of New Mexico's statehood. Since 2004, a core group of heritage preservationists, state officials, museum professionals, and public historians from around the state have held regular meetings to discuss and plan for the centennial. In the summer of 2006, the New Mexico Humanities Council began organizing and funding a series of community meetings in Carlsbad, Gallup, Las Cruces, Las Vegas, Roswell, and Silver City to hear how New Mexicans wanted to commemorate the anniversary. Ideas that emerged from these meetings included sponsoring student-created art murals with historic themes, identifying and restoring endangered buildings in participating communities, certifying businesses, ranches, farms, and churches that have existed since 1912, writing a "March to Statehood" pamphlet for distribution to schools and establishing after-school Centennial History Clubs, and producing a "This Day in New Mexico History" for daily broadcast on the radio. Some of the ideas are already being worked on; others await funding and collaborators to initiate an ambitious series of public programming, exhibits, and heritage projects leading up to 2012.

50

The National Statuary Hall Collection: Po'pay

The Architect of the Capitol (2006)

The National Statuary Hall Collection in the United States Capitol is comprised of statues donated by individual states to honor persons notable in their history. The entire collection now consists of 100 statues contributed by 50 states. All fifty states have contributed two statues each.

New Mexico: Po'pay

> Marble by Cliff Fragua. Given in 2005. Location: Rotunda, pending selection of a permanent location by the Joint Committee on the Library.

Po'pay was born around 1630 in the San Juan Pueblo, in what is now the state of New Mexico; his given name, Popyn, means "ripe squash" in the Tewa language. As an adult he became a religious leader and was responsible for healing as well as for his people's spiritual life. He also knew of his people's suffering under Spanish settlers, who forced them to provide labor and food to support the Spanish community. The Spaniards also pressured them to give up their religion and way of life and to adopt Christianity — those found practicing their religion were tortured and sometimes executed.

In 1675 Po'pay and 46 other Pueblo leaders were convicted of sorcery; he was among those flogged, while others were executed. In 1680 Po'pay organized the Pueblo Revolt against the Spanish. According to legend, to coordinate the timing of

Sculptor Cliff Fragua working on a granite statue of Po'pay for the National Statuary Hall in the United States Capitol, about 2004. Photograph by Marcia Keegan.

the uprising, he and his followers sent runners to each pueblo with knotted deerskin strips. One knot was to be untied each day, and the revolt would begin on the day the last one was untied. However, the Spaniards arrested two of the runners, and the pueblos were quickly notified to accelerate the revolt. The attacks began on August 10, two days before the last knot would have been untied. The Spaniards took refuge at Santa Fe; the besieging Indians cut off their water supply but soon permitted them to leave the area. The Pueblo Revolt helped to ensure the survival of the Pueblo culture and shaped the history of the American Southwest.

In 1997, the New Mexico Legislature selected Po'pay as the subject of the state's second statue for the National Statuary Hall Collection and created the New Mexico Statuary Hall Commission, whose members were appointed by Governor Gary Johnson. Four sculptors were selected to create maquettes, and Cliff Fragua was awarded the commission in December 1999. It will be the seventh statue of a Native American in the collection; the others are King Kamehameha I [Hawaii, 1969], Will Rogers (who had Cherokee ancestors) [Oklahoma, 1939], Sakakawea [North Dakota, 2003], Sequoyah [Oklahoma, 1917], Washakie [Wyoming, 2000], and Sarah Winnemucca [Nevada, 2005].

The seven-foot-high statue was carved from pink Tennessee marble (making it the only colored marble statue in the collection) and stands on a three-foot-high pedestal comprised of a steel frame clad in black granite. It is the first marble statue contributed to the collection since that of South Dakota's Joseph Ward, which was given in 1963; the other statues given since that time have been bronze. Its acceptance [September 22, 2005] marked the first time at which every state in the Union has been represented by two statues in the collection. In addition, Po'pay is historically the first person represented in the collection to be born on what would become American soil.

No image or written description of Po'pay is known to exist. Sculptor Cliff Fragua describes the statue thus:

> In my rendition, he holds in his hands items that will determine the future existence of the Pueblo people. The knotted cord in his left hand was used to determine when the Revolt would begin. As to how many knots were used is debatable, but I feel that it must have taken many days to plan and notify most of the Pueblos. The bear fetish in his right hand symbolizes the center of the Pueblo world, the Pueblo religion. The pot behind him symbolizes the Pueblo culture, and the deerskin he wears is a humble symbol of his status as a provider. The necklace that he wears is a constant reminder of where life began, and his clothing consists of a loin cloth and moccasins in Pueblo fashion. His hair is cut in Pueblo tradition and bound in a *chongo*. On his back are the scars that remain from the whipping he received for his participation and faith in the Pueblo ceremonies and religion.

Fragua, an Indian from Jemez Pueblo, studied sculpture in Italy, California, and New Mexico; he created his first stone sculpture in 1974.

Herman Agoyo and Joe Sando at the unveiling ceremony of the Po'pay statue, Ohkay Owingeh (San Juan Pueblo), May 21, 2005. Photograph by Marcia Keegan.

51

Po'pay: A Pueblo Perspective on the Leader of the First American Revolution

Herman Agoyo (2005)

We have no physical description of Po'pay ("Po pay" — Ripe Pumpkin), no photograph, no rendering in ink — not even some murky, handwritten remarks as to the man's height, weight, dimensions or the amount of space he may have occupied in a room. Yet, to anyone who has lived in the Southwest, his face is as familiar as is the face of any recognizable hero. It is the face that has lived in remarkable continuity throughout the history of my Pueblo people. To the outside world, however, Po'pay and the Pueblo Revolt remain pretty much unknown.

I was born at Ohkay Owingeh (San Juan Pueblo), the same village that gave birth to Po'pay. Ohkay Owingeh is the largest of the six Tewa-speaking villages, with over 2,000 tribal members. The village is located in the Rio Grande Valley just 30 miles north of Santa Fe, New Mexico. Known to many as the "mother home" of the Tewa people, Ohkay Owingeh has always played a central political and economic role in the Southwest.

In 1598, Ohkay Owingeh's characteristics as a political and economic center were recognized by the Spaniards, who proclaimed it the first capital of Northern New Mexico. This village was given another name, San Juan de los Caballeros (*caballeros* is Spanish for "gentlemen"), by Juan de Oñate to symbolize the generosity and hospitality provided by our tribal members. Today, as the headquarters of the Eight Northern Indian Pueblos Council and the Bureau of Indian Affairs Northern Pueblos Agency, Ohkay Owingeh remains a political center of Pueblo life in modern New Mexico.

I received my first years of education in Ohkay Owingeh. Later I attended the Santa Fe Indian School, and it was there that a priest friend of mine encouraged me to seek a four-year college degree. This was a radical idea in the mid-1950s, as so much fine government work had gone into preparing us Indians for vocational careers. I was the only one of my class to go immediately to a four-year college.

As I stand and look back years away from that time, I have come to the conclusion that it was not the lack of substantial educational opportunities that was most detrimental; rather, it was the fact that all that schooling taught me many things of the world but nothing of myself or my people and our history. I learned about the causes of the American Revolutionary War and all the wars between then and now. I learned about Plato, ancient Greece, and the rise and fall of the Roman Empire, but not one word was ever spoken of the great leader of the Pueblo Revolt of 1680, Po'pay. In fact, even the Pueblo Revolt itself has been merely a footnote in most history books, if it's mentioned at all.

In 1976 my wife, Rachele, and I took a delegation of forty from San Juan Pueblo to Washington, D.C., to help commemorate the Bicentennial. However, we traveled to the capital not so much to celebrate the Bicentennial but in dedication to our great leader, Po'pay. Here each state is allowed to place two statues of prominent figures from its history. At that time New Mexico had only placed the bronze figure of the Honorable Senator Dennis Chavez, leaving one remaining space. Beneath the watchful eyes of those giants of the past, Rachele asked, "Why not Po'pay?" I thought about it. So, why not Po'pay?

After almost thirty years, that empty spot — the last vacant space in the great Statuary Hall of the United States of America — will soon be occupied. Over these thirty years we have celebrated the Tricentennial of the Pueblo Revolt, promoted and garnered Po'pay's acceptance as our state's second and final representative, and raised funds on a local level and through the state government to finance this endeavor. Most recently, we have chosen a local sculptor, Cliff Fragua, from Jemez Pueblo, the only Native American artist to be represented in Statuary Hall, and we have transported a ten-ton block of Tennessee marble to Jemez Pueblo for his use in creating the statue. We have promoted educational programs in our schools so that our children will learn why New Mexico celebrates its status as a true multicultural state. All of this is to honor a man that most of America knows little or nothing about.

In this book you will learn about the Pueblo Revolt and Po'pay. The history of the Revolt is fairly straightforward. Where the story becomes unclear is with the contradictory legends of Po'pay himself. Was he a war captain or a medicine man? Was he involved in the battles or did he view them from a nearby hilltop — or was he locked away in prayer and supplication as some have suggested? Did he have a Spanish name that was later discarded or was he always Po'pay? To the Spaniards he became known as "El Pope." They characterized him as mad and evil — a sorcerer, a rabble-rouser, a man of no distinction and an opportunist who later abused his authority.

It is likely, however, that in reality he was a religious leader, because this would have given him access to the inner sanctuary of Taos Pueblo, from where he and other leaders planned the revolt. The Spanish historical records clearly connect him with the Revolt. On December 18, 1681, a Tesuque Pueblo Indian named Juan testified under oath, before "Señor Governor" Antonio De Otermín and "Secretary of Governmental War" Francisco Xavier, that the chief mover and organizer of the Revolt was a "native of the Pueblo of San Juan, named El Pope." On December 19 and 20, this testimony was corroborated by Joseph, a Spanish-speaking Indian; Lucas, a Piro; Pedro Naranjo; and the brothers Juan and Francisco Lorenzo of San Felipe Pueblo, who also, under oath, identified Po'pay as the leader of the Revolt.

In 1980, San Juan Pueblo elders revealed his Tewa name, family lineage, moiety (two-party system for dual organization), and the approximate location of his residence in the Pueblo. Po'pay's name was of the summer moiety. His role after the Revolt is unclear, but the event that he led in 1680 was vital to the survival of the New Mexico Indian Pueblos and historically significant as the first American revolution.

Here, then, is our offer of respect and honor for the man, Po'pay. This history and these contemplations are put forth so that there may be knowledge and acceptance of the man who surrendered himself to the immorality of war and all of its heartaches in order that his people would survive, that they would continue to live and pray in the manner of their ancestors, and that the sun would continue to shine and the rain would continue to fall.

Hispanic Family, New Mexico. Back to front, left to right: Andrés A. Gallegos (1938–64); Juanita (Jane) Trujillo (b. 1945); Juan C. Borrego (1882–1964); Apolonio Gallegos (1904–85); Delfino Borrego (1909–98); Clara Borrego (1919–2004). June 1949. Photograph by Anacleto (Tito) G. Apodaca.

EPILOGUE

Telling New Mexico into the
Twenty-First Century:
The New Mexico History Museum

Frances Levine

The 2009 opening of the New Mexico History Museum
(NMHM), adjacent to the Palace of the Governors on the Santa
Fe plaza, initiates new dialogue in telling New Mexico. As a
major cultural attraction, NMHM, the Palace, the Fray Angélico
Chávez History Library and Photo Archives, and the Palace
Press together offer New Mexicans and visitors a comprehensive
state history museum that narrates New Mexico from its prehistoric sequences to the present. For the first time, the Palace can
tell its important story as witness to four centuries of contact
between peoples of many cultures.

Nearly four hundred years old, the Palace of the
Governors is the oldest public building in the United States.
It became a Registered National Landmark in 1960 and was
designated an American Treasure in 1999. Countless people,
important and ordinary, have lived, worked, and convened
business and government affairs within its thick adobe walls.
As the most important artifact of our state's patrimony, its preservation has been one of the central missions of the Museum of
New Mexico since it began in 1909. The Palace has since doubled
as historic structure and history museum, a task too great even
for this venerable building, which is now complemented by the
New Mexico History Museum.

The NMHM collections of nearly 20,000 objects,
750,000 historic photographs, and thousands of manuscript
pages grew from the antiquarian efforts of a small group of
men who started the Historical Society of New Mexico in
1859. Their devotion to the Palace saw this national landmark

rescued from several threats — demolition at the hands of harried territorial governors who found the building's maintenance needs burdensome and residents whose attempts to modernize the ancient adobe were careless or incompatible. Their collections of objects, documents, and photographs, now housed at the Palace, the Museum of Indian Arts and Culture, the Museum of International Folk Art, and the State Records Center and Archives, laid foundations that have sustained scholarship in New Mexico anthropology and history and commemorated its public and domestic life through the centuries.

Today, the collection, curation, and exhibition of these "tellings" are a partnership between museum and community. History museums such as NMHM are no longer simply community or state attics filled with long-forgotten objects and yellowing letters. They are becoming places that honor the past while serving as ongoing partners in education, civic engagement, and social change. The best play a strong role in framing social policy and provide a long-term perspective on what makes communities and states unique. They inspire by telling of those who came before and of those who are making our history today — in large or more personal ways.

Few states have the time depth and breadth of our cultural history. NMHM presents an opportunity to change the way most Americans think about our national history. Its exhibitions situate our national identity in a broader cultural perspective, recognizing the "tellings" of Pueblo, Navajo, Apache, Spanish, and Mexican contributions to American history.

The New Mexico History Museum honors our ancestors and inspires our descendants. It is a partner in the education of our children and in every citizen's journey of life-long learning. It is a pillar of our civic life, showing New Mexicans and visitors alike how we have built on the foundations of the long archaeological record and nearly four hundred years of European history. It is a place that not only houses and tells New Mexico's past but also shares the responsibility of envisioning and shaping its future.

Acknowledgment of Sources

LIGHT, LAND, WATER, WIND

Jake Page, "Natural New Mexico: Light"
Reprinted by permission of Jake Page. Originally published as "Introduction" in *The Smithsonian Guides to Natural America: The Southwest — New Mexico and Arizona* (Washington, D.C.: Smithsonian Books, and New York: Random House, 1995), text by Jake Page, pp. 24–25. Page's quotations are from D. H. Lawrence's 1931 essay, "New Mexico," and John DeWitt McKee's 1957 essay, "The Unrelenting Land," both of which are reprinted in *The Spell of New Mexico,* edited by Tony Hillerman (Albuquerque: University of New Mexico Press, 1976).

Larry S. Crumpler, "Land of Volcanoes"
Reprinted by permission from L. S. Crumpler, "Land of Volcanoes," *New Mexico Magazine*, vol. 79, no. 1 (January 2001), pp. 60–67.

William deBuys, "The Sangre de Cristo Mountains"
Adapted from "Introduction: Place" and scattered other passages in William deBuys, *Enchantment and Exploitation: The Life and Hard Times of a New Mexico Mountain Range* (Albuquerque: University of New Mexico Press, 1985).

Sylvia Rodríguez, "Waterways: Acequias"
Reprinted by permission from Sylvia Rodríguez, *Acequia: Water Sharing, Sanctity, and Place*, pp. 2–3, 6–8. Copyright © 2006 by the School for Advanced Research, Santa Fe, New Mexico. *Acequia* is a School for Advanced Research Resident Scholar Book.

Roland F. Dickey, "Windscapes: Chronicles of Neglected Time"
Reprinted by permission of V. B. Price, editor, *Century: A Southwest Journal of Observation and Opinion*. Originally published in *Century* on March 16, 1983, pp. 9–11.

Paul M. Jones, "Minescapes: Memories of Santa Rita"
Excerpts from *Memories of Santa Rita*, written and self-published by Paul M. Jones, 1985. According to Jones, writing in the original book (p. 9): "These are my recollections of life in Santa Rita from 1923 until I joined the Navy in 1938. I kept no diary, and therefore all incidents are from memory, which might conceivably play tricks on me as I grow older. Although minor facts may differ slightly from the actual, all is as true and factual as memory will allow, and aided by some of my old friends from that era.... Many of the people in these stories are still alive and some of them are living in Grant County. Nothing in these pages is intended to bring embarrassment or hurt of any degree to anyone. If such comes to pass, it will be strictly accidental and I apologize in advance."

Rina Swentzell, "Pueblo Space: An Understated Sacredness"
Reprinted by permission of Rina Swentzell. Originally published as "An Understated Sacredness" in *MASS: A Publication of the School of Architecture and Planning* (University of New Mexico), vol. 3 (Fall 1985), pp. 24–25.

Haniel Long, "The Carlsbad Cavern"
Quoted from "The Cavern," in *Piñon Country*, by Haniel Long (Haniel Long Papers, Collection 672). Source: Department of Special Collections, Charles E. Young Research Library, UCLA. Reprinted by permission. Long's *Piñon Country* (New York: Duell, Sloan and Pearce, 1941) was part of the twenty-five-volume American Folkways Series of studies of regional American life edited by Erskine Caldwell in the 1940s and 1950s.

BEYOND HISTORY'S RECORDS

Alfonso Ortiz, "Indian People of Southwestern North America"
Reprinted by permission of the Smithsonian Institution from Alfonso Ortiz, "Introduction," in *Handbook of North American Indians*, vol. 9, *Southwest*, pp. 1–4. Copyright © 1979 by the Smithsonian Institution. The planned but yet uncompleted twenty-volume *Handbook of North American Indians*, William C. Sturtevant, general editor, includes two volumes on the Southwest (vol. 9, published in 1979, and vol. 10, in 1983), both edited by Ortiz.

Tom R. Kennedy and Dan Simplicio, "First Contact at Hawikku (Zuni): The Day the World Stopped"

This essay emerged from the authors' abiding interest in and experience with the issues pertaining to "first contact" at Zuni. Both served key roles on the planning team for the exhibit *Hawikku: Echoes from Our Past*. Kennedy oversaw the installation of that exhibit and continues to administer tours to the Hawikku site. Simplicio has considered intercultural contact from the perspectives of cultural resource management and service as a Zuni tribal councilman. It is their hope that an interpretation center can someday be developed at Hawikku to explore the issues surrounding first contact.

Peter Iverson, "Diné (Navajo) History: 'Black Clouds Will Rise'"

Reprinted by permission from Peter Iverson, *Diné: A History of the Navajos*, pp. 7–8, 11–14, 18, 19–20, 21–23. Copyright © 2002 University of New Mexico Press. This selection is from chapter 1, "'Black Clouds Will Rise': To 1846." Iverson's unpublished sources are AnCita Benally, "Hané' Béé'ééhanííh: With Stories It Is Remembered" (master's thesis, Arizona State University, 1993), and Harry Walters, "A New Perspective on Navajo Prehistory" (n.d., photocopy in Iverson's private collection). The newspaper articles are "Descendants of the Anasazi?" by Zarana Sanghani, *Gallup Independent*, April 29, 2000, and "Social Strife May Have Exiled Ancient Indians," by George Johnson, *New York Times*, August 20, 1996.

Veronica E. Velarde Tiller, "Jicarilla Apache Origins and Early White Contact"

Reprinted by permission of Veronica E. Velarde Tiller from "Prologue: Jicarilla Apache Origins and Early White Contact," in *The Jicarilla Apache Tribe: A History*, by Veronica E. Velarde Tiller (Albuquerque: BowArrow Publishing Company, rev. ed., 2000), pp. 1–6. First published by the University of Nebraska Press in 1983. A revised edition of 1992 was also published there as a Bison Book.

THE NORTHERN PROVINCE

Thomas E. Chávez, "Spain in the New World"

The author writes: "This essay derives from a lifetime's interest in New Mexico's history and twenty-five years working at the Palace of the Governors. My wife, Celia López-Chávez, also a historian, discovered Villagrá's records in the archives of the University of Salamanca. I have always been impressed with the Jesuit priests Francisco Clavijero and Francisco Alegre, who wrote impressionistic histories of Mexico in the eighteenth century that, in my mind, clearly define Mexico as a 'patria' versus a colony."

Rick Hendricks, "Juan de Oñate, Colonizer, Governor"
A more extensive treatment of Juan de Oñate and his place in the history of New Mexico was published as Rick Hendricks, "Juan de Oñate, Diego de Vargas, and Hispanic Beginnings in New Mexico," in *New Mexican Lives: Profiles and Historical Stories*, edited by Richard W. Etulain (Albuquerque: University of New Mexico Press, 2002), pp. 45–77. The most approachable work on Oñate is Marc Simmons, *The Last Conquistador: Juan de Oñate and the Settling of the Far Southwest* (Norman: University of Oklahoma Press, 1991). This popular biography by one of the foremost historians of the Spanish Southwest draws from published sources, primary and secondary. Simmons's bibliographic essay is a good place to begin a search for additional material on Oñate. The history of Oñate's New Mexico through the eyes of a participant and poet is available in *Historia de la Nueva México, 1610: Gaspar Pérez de Villagrá, a Critical and Annotated Spanish/English Edition*, translated and edited by Miguel Encinias, Alfred Rodríguez, and Joseph P. Sánchez (Albuquerque: University of New Mexico Press, 1992).

Alfonso Ortiz, "Popay's Leadership: A Pueblo Perspective on the 1680 Revolt"
Reprinted by permission from *El Palacio*, vol. 86, no. 4 (Winter 1980–81), pp. 18–22.

Rick Hendricks, "Diego de Vargas, Reconqueror, Governor"
A more extensive treatment of Diego de Vargas and his place in the history of New Mexico was published as Rick Hendricks, "Juan de Oñate, Diego de Vargas, and Hispanic Beginnings in New Mexico," in *New Mexican Lives: Profiles and Historical Stories*, edited by Richard W. Etulain (Albuquerque: University of New Mexico Press, 2002), pp. 45–77. The fundamental work on Diego de Vargas and his era in New Mexico is the multivolume documentary edition *The Journals of don Diego de Vargas* (University of New Mexico Press). These volumes of translated and heavily annotated documents are the work of John L. Kessell and his colleagues at the Vargas Project. Individual titles are *Remote Beyond Compare* (1989), *By Force of Arms* (1992), *To the Royal Crown Restored* (1995), *Blood on the Boulders* (1998), *That Disturbances Cease* (2000), and *A Settling of Accounts* (2002). The only narrative of the Vargas period remains J. Manuel Espinosa's *Crusaders of the Rio Grande: The Story of Don Diego de Vargas and the Reconquest and Refounding of New Mexico* (1942; Salisbury, N.C.: Documentary Publications, 1977). A new synthesis of the Spanish period is Carroll L. Riley's *The Kachina and the Cross: Indians and Spaniards in the Early Southwest* (Salt Lake City: University of Utah Press, 1999).

John L. Kessell, "The Memorable Visitation of Bishop Pedro Tamarón, 1760"
As Bishop Tamarón composed a description of his vast diocese, word reached

him of the Pecos Pueblo Indians' burlesque of his visitation and the fate of the perpetrator. We do not know who the eyewitness was, but Tamarón had the story published in 1763. It first appeared in English translation in Eleanor B. Adams, *Bishop Tamarón's Visitation of New Mexico, 1760* (Albuquerque: Historical Society of New Mexico, 1954).

Joe S. Sando, "The Silver-Crowned Canes of Pueblo Office"

Reprinted by permission from Joe S. Sando, "Epilogue: The Silver-Crowned Canes," in *Pueblo Nations: Eight Centuries of Pueblo Indian History* (Santa Fe, New Mexico: Clear Light Publishing, 1992), pp. 243–44. *Pueblo Nations* is a revised update of Joe S. Sando, *The Pueblo Indians* (San Francisco: Indian Historian Press, 1976).

LINKING NATIONS

Robert J. Tórrez, "Mexican Patriotism in New Mexico, 1821–1846"

This essay is based almost entirely on original documents from the *Calendar of the Microfilm Edition of the Mexican Archives of New Mexico, 1821–1846* (Santa Fe: State of New Mexico Records Center, 1970). This wonderful and underutilized archival collection contains the surviving records of the Mexican-period government in New Mexico. Another excellent source of primary documents for the Mexican period is found in the *Calendar to the Microfilm Edition of the Sender Collection, 1697–1884* (Santa Fe: Archives Division, New Mexico State Records Center and Archives, 1988). Additional book-length sources for the Mexican period include David J. Weber, *The Mexican Frontier, 1821–1846: The American Southwest under Mexico* (Albuquerque: University of New Mexico Press, 1982); Janet Lecompte, *Rebellion in Rio Arriba, 1837* (Albuquerque: University of New Mexico Press, 1985); and Jill Mocho, *Murder and Justice in Frontier New Mexico, 1821–1846* (Albuquerque: University of New Mexico Press, 1997).

Oakah L. Jones, "Perspectives on the Camino Real in New Mexico"

Reprinted from Oakah L. Jones, "Perspectives on the Camino Real in New Mexico," in *El Camino Real de Tierra Adentro*, vol. 2, compiled by Gabrielle G. Palmer and Stephen L. Fosberg (U.S. Department of the Interior, Bureau of Land Management, 1999), pp. 335–37, 343–44. Reproduced with permission of the New Mexico Bureau of Land Management, United States Department of the Interior.

Michael L. Olsen, "The Santa Fe Trail and Nineteenth-Century New Mexico: 'We Encountered Six Americans'"

The literature of the Santa Fe Trail is extensive. Many primary documents have been reprinted, as have diaries, letters, journals, and memoirs from trail days. Anyone seeking additional information should start with Jack D. Rittenhouse, *The Santa Fe Trail: A Historical Bibliography* (Albuquerque: University of New Mexico Press, 1971), and with the issues of *Wagon Tracks: Santa Fe Trail Association Quarterly*, which has been in continuous publication since November 1986. The New Mexico State Records Center and Archives holds many of the important original papers concerning New Mexico's role in the Santa Fe Trail, including the report of don Pedro Ignacio Gallego to Governor Facundo Melgares, describing his meeting with William Becknell.

John L. Kessell, "Pecos Pueblo: Tourists and Tall Tales"

Reprinted from John L. Kessell, *Kiva, Cross, and Crown: The Pecos Indians and New Mexico, 1540–1840* (Washington, D.C.: U.S. Department of the Interior, National Park Service, 1979), pp. 458–63, 465, 471–73. Public domain.

BECOMING THE SOUTHWEST

Office of the Secretary of State, "The Seal of New Mexico"

Reprinted from "State Seal," *New Mexico Blue Book, 2003–2004* (Office of the Secretary of State of New Mexico, 2003), p. 68. Public domain. On the following page, readers interested in more on the various earlier seals are referred to a December 1993 article in *New Mexico Magazine* by Robert Tórrez, "State Seal Receives Eagle Eyed Scrutiny."

Durwood Ball, "The U.S. Army in New Mexico, 1848–1886"

Primary sources for this essay include *Letters Sent by Headquarters of the 9th Military Department, the Department of New Mexico, and the District of New Mexico, 1849–1890*, M1072 (Washington, D.C.: National Archives and Records Service, 1979), microfilm; *Register of Letters Received and Letters Received by Headquarters, 9th Military Department, 1848–1853*, M1102 (Washington, D.C.: National Archives and Records Service, 1980), microfilm; *Register of Letters Received and Letters Received by the Department of New Mexico, 1854–1865*, M1120 (Washington, D.C.: National Archives and Records Service, 1980), microfilm; Annie H. Abel, ed., *The Correspondence of James S. Calhoun* (Washington, D.C.: Government Printing Office, 1915); Ernest Wallace, ed., *Ranald S. Mackenzie's Official Correspondence Relating to Texas, 1871–1879*, 2 vols. (Lubbock: West Texas Museum Association, 1967–68); Joe F. Taylor, "The Indian Campaign on the Staked Plains, 1874–1875:

Military Correspondence from the War Department Adjutant General's File, 1874–1875," *Panhandle-Plains Historical Review 34* (1961): 1–216; 35 (1962): 215–357. Published secondary works include Robert M. Utley, *Frontiersmen in Blue: The United States Army and the Indian, 1848–1865* (New York: Macmillan, 1967), and *Frontier Regulars: United States Army and the Indian, 1866–1891* (New York: Macmillan, 1977); Paul Andrew Hutton, *Phil Sheridan and His Army* (Lincoln: University of Nebraska Press, 1985); and Durwood Ball, *Army Regulars on the Western Frontier, 1848–1861* (Norman: University of Oklahoma Press, 2001).

William Wroth, "Buffalo Soldiers in New Mexico"

This essay is a slightly revised version of Wroth's contributed research essay on the website of the New Mexico Digital History Project under People: Occupations (© 2004–2007, New Mexico Office of the State Historian). "The goal of the New Mexico Digital History Project is to create a virtual engagement with New Mexico history past and present. We invite visitors to navigate through themes that explore the wisdom of places, the significance of events, the complexity of the human condition and the transformative power of storytelling. The website showcases historical documents and brings visitors face to face with New Mexico's premier archival collections, video footage, oral histories and photographs. Each of the navigations incorporates essays and interpretive research that contextualizes these archival materials" (newmexicohistory.org).

Margaret Connell-Szasz, "Cultural Encounters: Native People, New Mexico, and the United States, 1848–1948"

The author writes: "This essay draws heavily on the expertise of scholars who have explored Native New Mexico history. In this regard, I am indebted to a number of old friends and acquaintances, including David Brugge, the late Morris Opler, Henrietta Stockel, the late Sally Hyer, Veronica Tiller, Carol Venturini, Peter Iverson, the late Alfonso Ortiz, and Joe Sando. For the 1850–54 voting situation and the concluding biography of Miguel H. Trujillo, see Carol A. Venturini, 'The Fight for Indian Voting Rights in New Mexico' (master's thesis, University of New Mexico, 1993), pp. 8, 160–75."

Malcolm Ebright, "Hispanic Land Grants and Indian Land in New Mexico"

The author writes: "The literature on Spanish and Mexican land grants was very thin prior to the famous Tierra Amarilla courthouse raid of June 5, 1967. That event, which made headlines around the world, is how I learned about the land grant problem in New Mexico. Two years later I was employed by the New Mexico State Planning Office to coauthor a report on land grants and land titles in New Mexico. See White, Koch, Kelley, and McCarthy, and the New Mexico State Planning Office, *Land Title Study* (State Planning Office, 1971)."

The University of New Mexico Press, Albuquerque, has published five valuable books in its New Mexico Land Grant Series, edited by John R. Van Ness: Victor Westphall, *Mercedes Reales: Hispanic Land Grants of the Upper Rio Grande Region* (1983); G. Emlen Hall, *Four Leagues of Pecos: A Legal History of the Pecos Grant, 1800–1933* (1984); Charles L. Briggs and John R. Van Ness, eds., *Land, Water, and Culture: New Perspectives on Hispanic Land Grants* (1987); Suzanne Forrest, *The Preservation of the Village: New Mexico's Hispanics and the New Deal* (1989); and Malcolm Ebright, *Land Grants and Lawsuits in Northern New Mexico* (1994). Sunflower University Press, Manhattan, Kansas, has published two books about land grants in northern New Mexico: John R. Van Ness and Christine M. Van Ness, eds., *Spanish and Mexican Land Grants in New Mexico and Southern Colorado* (1980), and Malcolm Ebright, ed., *Land Grants and the Law* (1989). For land grants in southern New Mexico, see J. J. Bowden, *Spanish and Mexican Land Grants in the Chihuahuan Acquisition* (El Paso: Texas Western Press, 1971).

For books on specific land grants, see Malcolm Ebright, *The Tierra Amarilla Grant: A History of Chicanery* (Santa Fe: Center for Land Grant Studies, 1980); John R. Van Ness, *Hispanos in Northern New Mexico: Development of Corporate Community and Multicommunity* (New York: AMS Press, 1991); María E. Montoya, *Translating Property: The Maxwell Land Grant and the Problem of Land in the American West, 1840–1900* (Berkeley: University of California Press, 2002); and Malcolm Ebright and Rick Hendricks, *The Witches of Abiquiú: The Governor, the Priest, the Genízaro Indians, and the Devil* (Albuquerque: University of New Mexico Press, 2006). On the Pueblo league and Indian land and water, see Malcolm Ebright and Rick Hendricks, "The Pueblo League and Pueblo Indian Land in New Mexico," in *Ysleta del Sur Pueblo Archives*, vol. 4 (El Paso: Book Publishers of El Paso, 2001) and James A. Vlasich, *Pueblo Indian Agriculture* (Albuquerque: University of New Mexico Press, 2005).

Marc Simmons, "Billy the Kid and the Lincoln County War"
Reprinted by permission from Marc Simmons, *Stalking Billy the Kid: Brief Sketches of a Short Life*, pp. 17–33. © 2006 by Sunstone Press. Simmons concludes his book with a section of "Selected Readings" (pp. 188–92), beginning with "the bibliographer and western writer Jeff C. Dykes [who] in 1952 published a basic reference tool, *Billy the Kid, The Bibliography of a Legend* (University of New Mexico Press)." Simmons recommends "a handful of books that have appeared in recent years, ones that I believe are especially significant and reliable," including, on the Lincoln County War, Robert M. Utley, *High Noon in Lincoln: Violence on the Western Frontier* (Albuquerque: University of New Mexico Press, 1987); John P. Wilson, *Merchants, Guns and Money: The Story of Lincoln County and Its Wars* (Santa Fe: Museum of New Mexico Press, 1987); Frederick Nolan, *The Lincoln County War: A Documentary History* (Norman: University of Oklahoma Press,

1992); and Joel Jacobsen, *Such Men as Billy the Kid: The Lincoln County War Reconsidered* (Lincoln: University of Nebraska Press, 1994). He writes: "The best introductory biography for a general audience is Robert M. Utley, *Billy the Kid: A Short and Violent Life* (Lincoln: University of Nebraska Press, 1989).... For those eager to plow deeper into the field of 'Billy books,' I can recommend a few additional titles. Jon Tuska's *Billy the Kid: A Handbook* (reprint, Lincoln: University of Nebraska Press, 1986) is a concise bio-bibliography which also tells at length how historians, fiction writers, and film makers have used and exploited the Kid's name. Also in that vein is Stephen Tatum, *Billy the Kid: Visions of the Outlaw in America, 1881–1981* (Albuquerque: University of New Mexico Press, 1982)."

Daniel Gibson, "Blackdom, Chaves County"

Reprinted by permission of the author from Daniel Gibson, "Blackdom," *New Mexico Magazine*, vol. 64, no. 2 (February 1986), pp. 46–47, 50–51.

Marta Weigle, "Alluring New Mexico: Engineered Enchantment, 1880–1941"

This essay is derived from a book manuscript in progress on tourism: "Alluring New Mexico: Engineered Enchantment, 1821–2001."

Michael Stevenson, "The Museum and Collections of the Historical Society of New Mexico, 1859–1977"

This essay is adapted from the January 9, 2006, draft of "The Museum and Collections of the Historical Society of New Mexico," written for the Palace of the Governors docents and staff. A version was published in *La Crónica de Nuevo México*, the official publication of the Historical Society of New Mexico, no. 72, July 2007. Most of it is based on Historical Society of New Mexico records in the Fray Angélico Chávez History Library and Photo Archives, Museum of New Mexico, and the New Mexico State Records Center and Archives. Also see History Unit Staff, "Historical Society of New Mexico Donation to the Museum of New Mexico," *El Palacio*, vol. 90, no. 3 (Fall–Winter 1984), pp. 7–13.

THE "NEW" NEW MEXICO

Office of the Secretary of State, "New Mexico's Constitution"

Reprinted from "New Mexico's Constitution," *New Mexico Blue Book, 2003–2004* (Office of the Secretary of State, 2003), p. 42. Public domain.

Marta Weigle, "The State Flags and the First State Song"

This essay is derived from a book manuscript in progress on tourism: "Alluring New Mexico: Engineered Enchantment, 1821–2001." According to *New Mexico*

Blue Book, 2003–2004 (Office of the Secretary of State, 2003), pp. 71–72: "In 1928, America's most famous march composer and conductor, John Philip Sousa, presented Governor A. T. Hannett and the people of New Mexico an arrangement of the state song embracing a musical story of the Indian, the Cavalry, the Spanish, and the Mexican. 'Así Es Nuevo Méjico,' written by contemporary composer Amadeo Lucero, was sung with guitar accompaniment to the assembled members of the 1971 legislature by Lieutenant Governor Roberto Mondragon and was promptly adopted as the Spanish-language version of the State Song.... Michael Martin Murphey, a Taos resident, wrote 'The Land of Enchantment' and in March 1989, the legislature took action to declare it the state ballad.... Pablo Mares, a distinguished music educator, conductor and composer wrote 'New Mexico — Mi Lindo Nuevo Mexico' in 1983, and in March 1995 the legislature adopted it as the state bilingual song."

Sarah Deutsch, "Labor, Land, and Protest since Statehood"

This essay relies heavily on the author's own research and, for its coverage of the Gallup and Empire Zinc strikes, on two foundational essays in Robert Kern, ed., *Labor in New Mexico: Unions, Strikes, and Social History since 1881* (Albuquerque: University of New Mexico Press, 1983): Jack Cargill, "Empire and Opposition: The 'Salt of the Earth' Strike," pp. 183–267, and Harry R. Rubenstein, "Political Repression in New Mexico: The Destruction of the National Miners' Union in Gallup," pp. 91–140.

Estevan Rael-Gálvez, "Testifying to the Silence of Servitude: Two New Mexico WPA Writers' Project Interviews"

This essay is derived from a book manuscript in progress, "The Silence of Slavery: Narratives of American Indian and Mexican Servitude and Its Legacy," based on the author's 2002 doctoral dissertation, "Identifying Captivity and Capturing Identity: Narratives of American Indian Slavery." New Mexico WPA Writers' Project manuscripts of the two Simeon Tejada interviews, "History of the Black Lake" (October 26, 1938) and "History of a Buffalo Hunter" (April 17, 1939), are in the New Mexico State Records Center and Archives (NMSRCA), where biographical material on the Mares and Vasques families, including probate records, census records, and church records, may also be found. Justice Kirby Benedict's papers include the 1857 definition of peonage (in Benedict, *Jaremillo* [sic] *v. Romero*, p. 194). The 1865 testimony on Indian slavery is taken from F. Rives and J. Rives, *Congressional Globe: Containing the Debates and Proceedings of the Second Session of the Thirty-ninth Congress*, Senator Doolittle reporting, "Condition of Tribes," February 23, 1867 (Washington, D.C.: Printed at the Congressional Globe Office, 1867). The Griffin cases may be found in the Territorial Papers of the United

States Senate, 1789–1873, New Mexico, NA-RG 46, which are also on microfilm in the NMSRCA.

Ferenc M. Szasz, "New Mexico during the Second World War"

This essay is derived from the author's more than two decades of teaching a class titled "The United States during the Era of the Second World War," as well as interviews and archival research for his three books treating Los Alamos and the early history of the atomic age: *The Day the Sun Rose Twice: The Story of the Trinity Site Nuclear Explosion, July 16, 1945* (Albuquerque: University of New Mexico Press, 1984), *British Scientists and the Manhattan Project: The Los Alamos Years* (New York: St. Martin's Press, 1992), and *Larger Than Life: New Mexico in the Twentieth Century* (Albuquerque: University of New Mexico Press, 2006). The Coronado Cuarto Centennial Commission records are housed in the Center for Southwest Research, Zimmerman Library, University of New Mexico.

William E. Gibbs, "The Roswell Incident: An Unsolved Mystery or an Unsolvable One?"

Reprinted by permission from William E. Gibbs, "The Roswell Incident: An 'Unsolved' or 'Unsolvable' Mystery?" in *Great Mysteries of the West*, edited by Ferenc Morton Szasz, pp. 145–60. © 1993 by Fulcrum Books. Gibbs notes: "I am especially grateful for the valuable information provided by Cliff Stone, Ralph Heick, Stanton T. Friedman, and Steve Bell. In addition I would like to thank Professors Austin Q. Male and Wendell Affsprung as well as the members of the Introduction to Philosophy class at New Mexico Military Institute for their helpful criticism of the manuscript. None of these individuals is responsible, however, for any errors in this paper."

Gibbs cites five books by Donald E. Keyhoe: *The Flying Saucers Are Real* (New York: Fawcett Publications), *Flying Saucers from Outer Space* (New York: Holt, 1953), *The Flying Saucer Conspiracy* (New York: Holt, 1955), *Flying Saucers: Top Secret* (New York: Random House, 1968), and *Aliens from Space* (New York: Doubleday, 1973). Other volumes cited are (in order of citation): Whitley Strieber, *Communion: A True Story* (New York: Avon Books, 1988); Whitley Strieber, *Majestic* (New York: Berkley Books, 1990); Lawrence Fawcett and Barry J. Greenwood, *Clear Intent: The Government Cover-Up of the UFO Experience* (New Jersey: Prentice Hall, 1984); Timothy Good, *Above Top Secret* (New York: Morrow, 1988); Howard Blum, *Out There: The Government's Quest for Extraterrestrials* (New York: Simon and Schuster, 1990); Tim Weiner, *Blank Check: The Pentagon's Black Budget* (New York: Warner Books, 1990); and William James, *The Will to Believe and Human Immortality* (New York: Dover Publications, 1956).

Gibbs uses an unpublished MUFRON paper by Stanton T. Friedman, "Update on Crashed Saucers in New Mexico" (1991), pp. 1–2, and a letter from Friedman to Gibbs dated June 16, 1991. The "CIA top secret memo [that] confirmed that the material flown to Fort Worth…was…forwarded on to Wright Field" is from teletype, FBI, Dallas, to Director and SAC, Cincinnati, July 8, 1947: "This memo, obtained through the Freedom of Information Act and circulated among various UFO researchers, stated that the material was purported to be a flying disc but resembled a high-altitude weather balloon with a radar reflector. It added that the material was sent to the Wright Field office because of the national interest in the case."

Gibbs interviewed Walter Haut on September 11, 1991. Of "RAAF Captures Flying Saucer on Ranch in Roswell Region," *Roswell Daily Record*, July 8, 1947, p. 1, "Haut recalled…that the newspaper copy had been changed somewhat for, as he observed, 'one did not "loan" things to their immediate superiors.'"

Jon Hunner, "Toward Normalizing Los Alamos: Cracking the Gates"
Reprinted by permission from Jon Hunner, *Inventing Los Alamos: The Growth of an Atomic Community*, pp. 197–99, 216, 218–19, 221–22. © 2004 by the University of Oklahoma Press, Norman, Publishing Division of the University. All rights reserved.

Jason Silverman, "Not Fade Away: Buddy Holly's Surprising Clovis Studio"
Reprinted by permission from Jason Silverman, *Untold New Mexico: Stories from a Hidden Past*, pp. 27–31. © 2006 by Sunstone Press. Originally published in different form in the *Santa Fean*, October 2001. The essay is based on author interviews with Kenneth Broad and Robert Linville. The Decca executive's "the biggest no-talent" remark is from Ellis Amburn, *Buddy Holly: A Biography* (New York: St. Martin's Griffith, 1995), p. 49. Other works referenced are Norma Jean Berry, "Norman Petty Recordings Put Clovis on Map," *Clovis News-Journal*, December 20, 1959; *The Buddy Holly Story*, Steve Rash, director, 1978; and Philip Norman, *Rave On* (New York: Simon and Schuster, 1996).

The Architect of the Capitol, "The National Statuary Hall Collection: Dennis Chavez"
Reprinted from the website of the Architect of the Capitol (aoc.gov), June 2006.

María E. Montoya, "Dennis Chavez and the Making of Modern New Mexico"
Reprinted by permission from *New Mexican Lives: Profiles and Historical Stories*, edited by Richard W. Etulain, pp. 242–53, 258–62. © 2002 by University of New Mexico Press.

Jennifer Nez Denetdale, "The Navajo-Diné Century of Progress, 1868–1968, and the Bosque Redondo Memorial"
Reprinted by permission from Jennifer Nez Denetdale, "Discontinuities, Remem-

brances, and Cultural Survival: History, Diné/Navajo Memory, and the Bosque Redondo Memorial," *New Mexico Historical Review*, vol. 82, no. 3 (Summer 2007): 295–316. © 2007 by the University of New Mexico Board of Regents. All rights reserved. Denetdale notes: "Navajos refer to themselves as the Diné, which means the People. Throughout my paper, I use all three terms — Navajo, Diné, and the People."

The "postcolonial critics" Denetdale refers to are Partha Chatterjee, *Nationalist Thought and the Colonial World: A Derivative Discourse* (London: Zed Books, 1986); Nira Yuval-Davis, *Gender and Nation* (Thousand Oaks, Calif.: Sage Publications, 1997); Chandra Talpade Mohanty, Ann Russo, and Lourdes Torres, eds., *Third World Women and the Politics of Feminism* (Bloomington: Indiana University Press, 1991); and Jennifer Nez Denetdale, "Chairmen, Presidents, and Princesses: The Navajo Nation, Gender, and the Politics of Tradition," *Wicazo Sa Review* 21 (Spring 2006), pp. 9–28. The "Native scholars" are Vine Deloria Jr. and Clifford M. Lytle, *The Nations Within: The Past and Future of American Indian Sovereignty* (New York: Pantheon Books, 1984); David E. Wilkins, *American Indian Sovereignty and the U.S. Supreme Court: The Masking of Justice* (Austin: University of Texas Press, 1997); Andrea Smith, *Conquest: Sexual Violence and American Indian Genocide* (Cambridge, Mass.: South End Press, 2005); Taiaiake Alfred, *Peace, Power, and Righteousness: An Indigenous Manifesto* (New York: Oxford University Press, 1999); and Joanne Barker, ed., *Sovereignty Matters: Locations of Contestation and Possibility in Indigenous Struggles for Self-Determination* (Lincoln: University of Nebraska Press, 2005). In order of mention, the newspaper articles are Brenda Norrell, "In Honor and Remembrance: Bosque Redondo Memorial Dedicated to Navajo and Apache," *Indian Country Today*, June 5, 2005; Leslie Linthicum, "Dark History: Memorial to Navajos' 19th Century Captivity in Bosque Redondo Opens with Painful Remembrances and Vows of 'Never Again,'" *Albuquerque Sunday Journal*, June 5, 2005; Chester C. Clah, letter to the editor, *Navajo Times*, June 23, 2005; Kathy Helms, "Council Says No to Long Walk Trail," *Gallup (New Mexico) Independent*, January 28, 2006; and Jason Begay, "Council Mixed on Reform, Nixes Long Walk Trail," *Navajo Times*, February 2, 2006.

MY NEW MEXICO

Paula Gunn Allen, "Radiant Beings, Laguna Pueblo"
Reprinted from Paula Gunn Allen, *Off the Reservation: Reflections on Boundary-Busting, Border-Crossing Loose Cannons*, pp. 101–107. Copyright © 1998 by Paula Gunn Allen. Reprinted by permission of Beacon Press, Boston.

Gail Y. Okawa, "Finding American World War II Internment in Santa Fe: Voices through Time"

Portions of this essay were published in "Letters to Our Forbears: Reconnecting Generations through Writing," *English Journal*, July 2003, pp. 47–51, and in "Unbundling: Archival Research and Japanese American Communal Memory of U.S. Justice Department Internment, 1941–45," in *Beyond the Archives: Research as a Lived Process*, edited by Gesa Kirsch and Liz Rohan (Carbondale: Southern Illinois University Press, 2008). Most of the essay is based on archival materials: Governor John E. Miles Papers, 1939–1942, New Mexico State Records Center and Archives, Santa Fe; National Archives and Records Administration II, Record Group 389, College Park, Maryland; and Tamasaku Watanabe Papers, Gail Y. Okawa Collection, Honolulu, Hawaii. Paul F. Clark's 1980 master's thesis, "Those Other Camps: An Oral History Analysis of Japanese Alien Enemy Internment during World War II," was completed at California State University, Fullerton.

Debra Hughes, "Albuquerquean Joe Powdrell"

Reprinted by permission from Debra Hughes, *Albuquerque in Our Time: 30 Voices, 300 Years*, pp. 123–24. © 2006 by Museum of New Mexico Press.

Larry Torres as Told to Lois Palken Rudnick, "Taos: Hippies, Hopper, and Hispanic Anger"

Reprinted by permission from Lois Palken Rudnick, *Utopian Vistas: The Mabel Dodge Luhan House and the American Counterculture*, pp. 335–39. © 1996 by the University of New Mexico Press. The title "Hippies, Hopper, and Hispanic Anger" and the italicized introduction to the excerpt are as published in the *Santa Fean*, April 1996, pp. 37–39.

John M. Nieto-Phillips, "Making Spanish-American Identity: My Language of Blood"

Reprinted by permission from John M. Nieto-Phillips, *The Language of Blood: The Making of Spanish-American Identity in New Mexico*, 1880s–1930s, pp. ix–xii, 207–12. © 2004 by University of New Mexico Press.

María Cristina López, "Tricky Mirror: Mexican Immigrants in New Mexico"

The author writes: "This essay is derived from a presentation I gave on 'The Legacy of the Treaty of Guadalupe Hidalgo' at the Symposium Commemorating the 150th Anniversary of the Treaty of Guadalupe Hidalgo, Santa Fe, February 1998. While preparing that paper I found very little documentation on the lives of Mexicans once they migrated to New Mexico after 1848. For this essay I interviewed the following persons, to whom I am grateful for their patience and generosity: Elma Samora, who is planning to write the story of her family in Artesia in the southeastern part of the state; Rosemary Burrola Chavez, who is researching her family tree in the Silver City and Grants areas; Socorro, León, and Francisca Ríos of Santa Fe, who talked about their father, Jesús Ríos; and Olivia and Jorge (not their real names) of Santa Fe, who spoke of their present lives."

Jon Hunner, "Driven by History: Pursuing the Past in Twenty-First-Century New Mexico"

The author writes: "Many people have both knowingly and unknowingly contributed to my history of the state. For this essay, I interviewed Elmo Baca, Susan Berry, Virginia Dodier, Garland Court, Fran Clark, Jean Fulton, Steve Hussman, Karl Laumbach, Kathy McConnell, Dr. Jeffrey Sheppard, Rep. J. Paul Taylor, Mike Taylor, Pat Taylor, and Dr. George Torok. Organizations that preserve the history and heritage of the state also contributing to this chapter include the Branigan Cultural Center, Cornerstones Community Partnerships, the Camino Real Trail Association, the Carlsbad Museum and Art Center, Human Systems Research, the New Mexico Humanities Council, New Mexico MainStreet, the Public History Program and the Rio Grande Historical Collection at New Mexico State University, the Silver City Museum, and the School of Architectural and Regional Planning at the University of New Mexico."

The Architect of the Capitol, "The National Statuary Hall Collection: Po'pay"

Reprinted from the website of the Architect of the Capitol (aoc.gov), June 2006.

Herman Agoyo, "Po'pay: A Pueblo Perspective on the Leader of the First American Revolution"

Reprinted by permission from Herman Agoyo, "Preface," in *Po'pay: Leader of the First American Revolution*, edited by Joe S. Sando and Herman Agoyo (Santa Fe, N.M.: Clear Light Publishing, 2005), pp. xi–xiv.

References Cited

Abert, James W. *Report and Map of the Examination of New Mexico; made by Lt. J. W. Abert, of the Topographical Corps, in Answer to a Resolution of the U.S. Senate.* Washington, D.C.: 30th Congress, 1st Session, Senate Executive Document no. 23, 1848.

Adams, Eleanor B., ed. 1954. *Bishop Tamarón's Visitation of New Mexico, 1760.* Albuquerque: Historical Society of New Mexico.

Alfred, Taiaiake. 1999. *Peace, Power, and Righteousness: An Indigenous Manifesto.* New York: Oxford University Press.

———. 2005. "Sovereignty." Pp. 33–50 in *Sovereignty Matters: Locations of Contestation and Possibility in Indigenous Struggles for Self-Determination*, ed. Joanne Barker. Lincoln: University of Nebraska Press.

Allen, Perry, ed. 1968. *Navajoland, U.S.A.: First Hundred Years, 1868–1968.* Window Rock, Arizona: Navajo Tribe.

Anderson, Benedict. 1991. *Imagined Communities: Reflections on the Origin and Spread of Nationalism.* Rev. ed. New York: Verso.

Anderson, Gary Clayton. 1999. *The Indian Southwest, 1580–1830.* Norman: University of Oklahoma Press.

Balderrama, Francisco E., and Raymond Rodríguez. 2006. *Decade of Betrayal: Mexican Repatriation in the 1930s.* Rev. ed. Albuquerque: University of New Mexico Press.

Bandelier, Adolph F. 1881. "A Visit to the Aboriginal Ruins in the Valley of the Río Pecos." Pp. 35–135 in *Papers of the Archaeological Institute of America*, America Series, vol. 1. Boston: A. Williams and Co.

Bennett, R. W. 1933. "Motoring New Mexico." *New Mexico,* (June): 7–9, 53.

Berlitz, Charles, and William L. Moore. 1980. *The Roswell Incident.* New York: Berkley Books.

Berry, Louise. 1972. *The Beginning of the West: Annals of the Kansas Gateway to the American West, 1540–1854.* Topeka: Kansas State Historical Society.

Birdseye, Roger Williams. 1926. "Selling New Mexico Right." *New Mexico Highway Journal* 4, no. 9 (September): 7–9.

Bourke, John G. 1933–38. "Bourke on the Southwest." *New Mexico Historical Review* 8–13: passim.

Bowman, Jon, ed. 2002. *Montezuma: The Castle in the West.* Santa Fe: New Mexico Magazine.

Boyle, Susan. 1997. *Los Capitalistas: Hispano Merchants and the Santa Fe Trade.* Albuquerque: University of New Mexico Press.

Broadhead, Edward. 1982. *Ceran St. Vrain, 1802–1870.* Pueblo, Colorado: Pueblo County Historical Society.

Brooks, James F. 2002. *Captives and Cousins: Slavery, Kinship and Community in the Southwest Borderlands.* Chapel Hill: University of North Carolina Press.

Brugge, David M. 1983. "Navajo Prehistory and History to 1850." Pp. 489–501 in *Handbook of North American Indians,* vol. 10, *Southwest,* ed. Alfonso Ortiz. Washington, D.C.: Smithsonian Institution.

———. 1999. "Captives and Slaves on the Camino Real." Pp. 103–10 in *El Camino Real de Tierra Adentro,* vol. 2, comp. Gabrielle G. Palmer and Stephen L. Fosberg, ed. June-el Piper. Cultural Resources Series, no. 13. Santa Fe: Bureau of Land Management, New Mexico State Office.

Bryant, Keith L., Jr. 1974. *History of the Atchison, Topeka and Santa Fe Railway.* New York: Macmillan.

Cargill, Jack. 1983. "Empire and Opposition: The 'Salt of the Earth' Strike." Pp. 183–267 in *Labor in New Mexico: Unions, Strikes, and Social History since 1881,* ed. Robert Kern. Albuquerque: University of New Mexico Press.

Carr, Pat. 1979. *Mimbres Mythology*. El Paso: Texas Western Press.

Carroll, Curtis. 2001. "Enchantment or Bust: State Highway Maps Reflect the Times and Spirit of New Mexico." *New Mexico Magazine,* (January): 25–27.

Caughey, John W. 1953. *California*. 2d ed. Englewood Cliffs, New Jersey: Prentice-Hall.

Cave, Dorothy. 1996. *Beyond Courage: One Regiment against Japan, 1941–1945*. Rev. ed. Las Cruces: Yucca Tree Press.

Chamberlain, Kathleen P. 2000. *Under Sacred Ground: A History of Navajo Oil, 1922–1982*. Lincoln: University of Nebraska Press.

Chávez, Thomas E. 1992. *Quest for Quivira: Spanish Explorers on the Great Plains, 1540–1821*. Tucson, Arizona: Southwest Parks and Monuments Association.

———. 2006. *New Mexico: Past and Future*. Albuquerque: University of New Mexico Press.

Chauvenet, Beatrice. 1983. *Hewett and Friends: A Biography of Santa Fe's Vibrant Era*. Santa Fe: Museum of New Mexico Press.

Christian, James L. 1986. *Philosophy: The Art of Wondering*. 4th ed. New York: Holt, Rinehart and Winston.

Cisneros, Jose, and Gregory Scott Smith. 2003. "The Bosque Redondo Memorial: Long Deserved, Long Overdue." *El Palacio* 108, no. 4 (Winter): 14–18.

Cockerill, P. W. 1958. *A Statistical History of Crop and Livestock Production in New Mexico*. Las Cruces, New Mexico: Agricultural Marketing Service.

Cooke, Alistair. 2006. *The American Home Front, 1941–1942*. New York: Atlantic Monthly Press.

Cooke, Philip St. George. 1964. *The Conquest of New Mexico and California in 1846–1848*. Chicago: Rio Grande Press.

Crawford, Stanley G. 1988. *Mayordomo: Chronicle of an Acequia in Northern New Mexico*. Albuquerque: University of New Mexico Press.

Crosby, Harry W. 1994. *Antigua California: Mission and Colony on the Peninsular Frontier, 1697–1768*. Albuquerque: University of New Mexico Press.

Curtis, Edward S. 1926. *The North American Indian*, vol. 17. Norwood, Massachusetts: The Plimpton Press.

Davies, Wade. 2001. *Healing Ways: Navajo Health Care in the Twentieth Century*. Albuquerque: University of New Mexico Press.

Davis, W. W. H. 1857. *El Gringo; or, New Mexico and Her People*. New York: Harper and Brothers.

Debo, Angie. 1989. *Geronimo: The Man, His Time, His Place*. Norman: University of Oklahoma Press.

Delgado, Deane G. 1990. *Historical Markers in New Mexico*. Santa Fe: Ancient City Press.

Deutsch, Sarah. 1987. *No Separate Refuge: Culture, Class, and Gender in an Anglo-Hispanic Frontier in the American Southwest, 1880–1940*. New York: Oxford University Press.

Dilworth, Leah. 1996. *Imagining Indians in the Southwest: Persistent Visions of a Primitive Past*. Washington, D.C.: Smithsonian Institution Press.

Dippie, Brian W. 1976. *Custer's Last Stand: The Anatomy of an American Myth*. University of Montana Publications in History. Missoula: University of Montana.

Drumm, Stella M., ed. 1926. *Down the Santa Fe Trail and into Mexico: The Diary of Susan Shelby Magoffin, 1846–47*. New Haven, Connecticut: Yale University Press. Reprint, 1984, Lincoln: University of Nebraska Press.

Dunleavy, Julie. 1984. "New Mexico: A Pioneer in Southwestern Tourism." *New Mexico Magazine,* (November): 61–65.

Dye, Victoria E. 2005. *All Aboard for Santa Fe: Railway Promotion of the Southwest, 1890s to 1930s*. Albuquerque: University of New Mexico Press.

Dyess, Lt. Col. William E. 1944 [2002]. *Bataan Death March: A Survivor's Account.* Lincoln: University of Nebraska Press.

Edelman, Sandra A., and Alfonso Ortiz. 1979. "Tesuque Pueblo." Pp. 330–35 in *Handbook of North American Indians,* vol. 9, *Southwest*, ed. Alfonso Ortiz. Washington, D.C.: Smithsonian Institution.

Eichstaedt, Peter. 1994. *If You Poison Us: Uranium and Native Americans.* Santa Fe, New Mexico: Red Crane Books.

Elder, Jane, and David Weber. 1996. *Trading in Santa Fe: John M. Kingsbury's Correspondence with James Josiah Webb, 1853–1861.* Dallas: Southern Methodist University Press.

Ellis, Erl H. 1983. *Colorado Mapology.* Frederick, Colorado: Jende-Hagan Book Corporation.

Ellis, Richard N., ed. 1975. *New Mexico Historic Documents.* Albuquerque: University of New Mexico Press.

Engstrom, David W., Alvin O. Korte, and Katie McDonough. 2004. "Understaffed, Underfunded: The Emergence of Social Welfare in New Mexico, 1940s–1950s." *New Mexico Historical Review* 79: 459–88.

Foster, William C. 1995. *Spanish Expeditions into Texas, 1689–1768.* Austin: University of Texas Press.

Frisbie, Charlotte J. 1987. *Navajo Medicine Bundles, or Jish: Acquisition, Transmission, and Disposition in the Past and Present.* Albuquerque: University of New Mexico Press.

Frost, Richard H. 1980. "The Romantic Inflation of Pueblo Culture." *The American West,* (January–February): 5–9, 56–60.

Fugate, Francis L., and Roberta B. Fugate. 1989. *Roadside History of New Mexico.* Missoula, Montana: Mountain Press Publishing Co.

Gabriel, Trip. 1994. "A Death in Navajo Country." *Outside,* (May): 78–84, 195–99.

García-Acevedo, María Rosa. 2000. "The Forgotten Diaspora." Pp. 216–38 in *The*

Contested Homeland: A Chicano History of New Mexico, eds. Erlinda Gonzales-Berry and David R. Maciel. Albuquerque: University of New Mexico Press.

Gardner, Mark. 1993. *Brothers on the Santa Fe and Chihuahua Trails: Edward James Glasgow and William Henry Glasgow, 1846–1848*. Niwot: University Press of Colorado.

———. 2000. *Wagons for the Santa Fe Trade: Wheeled Vehicles and Their Makers, 1822–1880*. Albuquerque: University of New Mexico Press.

Garrard, Lewis. 1987. *Wah-to-yah and the Taos Trail*. Norman: University of Oklahoma Press.

Goddard, Pliny Earle. 1911. *Jicarilla Apache Texts*. Anthropological Papers of the American Museum of Natural History 8. New York.

Gold, Bela. 1950. *Wartime Economic Planning in Agriculture: A Story in the Allocation of Resources*. New York: Columbia University Press.

Gray, William D. 1991. *Thinking Critically about New Age Ideas*. Belmont, California: Wadsworth.

Greenwood, Barry, ed. 1989. "A Majestic Deception." *Just Cause* 20 (September): 1–10.

Greever, William. 1957. "Railway Development in the Southwest." *New Mexico Historical Review* 32: 151–203.

Gregg, Josiah. 1954. *Commerce of the Prairies*. Edited by Max L. Moorhead. Norman: University of Oklahoma Press.

Griffin, Marcus, and Eva Jane Matson, comps. 1989. *Heroes of Bataan, Corregidor, and Northern Luzon*. Las Cruces, New Mexico: Yucca Tree Press.

Grinde, Donald, and Bruch Johansen. 2001. "The Navajos and National Sacrifice." Pp. 204–20 in *The Multicultural Southwest: A Reader*, eds. A. Gabriel Meléndez, M. Jane Young, Patricia Moore, and Patrick Pynes. Tucson: University of Arizona Press.

Griswold del Castillo, Richard. 1990. *The Treaty of Guadalupe Hidalgo: A Legacy of Conflict*. Norman: University of Oklahoma Press.

Gunnerson, Dolores A. 1974. *The Jicarilla Apaches: A Study in Survival.* Dekalb: Northern Illinois University Press.

Hackett, Charles Wilson, and Charmion Clair Shelby, eds. 1940. *Revolt of the Pueblo Indians of New Mexico and Otermín's Attempted Reconquest, 1680–1682.* 2 vols. Albuquerque: University of New Mexico Press.

Hall, Frank. 1895. *History of the State of Colorado,* vol. 4. Chicago: Blakely Printing Co.

Hall, Ruth K. 1983. *A Place of Her Own: The Story of Elizabeth Garrett.* Santa Fe, New Mexico: Sunstone Press.

Hammond, George P., and Agapito Rey, eds. and trans. 1940. *Narratives of the Coronado Expedition, 1540–1542.* Albuquerque: University of New Mexico Press.

———, eds. 1953. *Don Juan de Oñate: Colonizer of New Mexico, 1595–1628.* Albuquerque: University of New Mexico Press.

———. 1966. *The Rediscovery of New Mexico, 1580–1594: The Explorations of Chamuscado, Espejo, Castaño de Sosa, Morlete, and Leyva de Bonilla and Humaña.* Albuquerque: University of New Mexico Press.

Henderson, James. 1969. *"Meals by Fred Harvey": A Phenomenon of the American West.* Fort Worth: Texas Christian University Press.

Henry, Jeannette, Vine Deloria Jr., N. Scott Momaday, Bea Medicine, and Alfonso Ortiz, eds. 1970. *Indian Voices: The First Convocation of American Indian Scholars.* San Francisco: Indian Historian Press.

Hieb, Louis A. 1972. "Meaning and Mismeaning: Toward an Understanding of the Ritual Clown." Pp. 163–95 in *New Perspectives on the Pueblos,* ed. Alfonso Ortiz. Albuquerque: University of New Mexico Press.

Hood, Margaret Page. 1943. "V is for Vegetables." *New Mexico,* (May): 7–9, 32.

Horton, Sarah. 2001. "Where Is the 'Mexican' in 'New Mexican'?: Enacting History, Enacting Dominance in the Santa Fe Fiesta." *Public Historian* 23, no. 4 (Fall): 41–54.

Howard, Kathleen L., and Diana F. Pardue. 1996. *Inventing the Southwest: The Fred Harvey Company and Native American Art.* Flagstaff, Arizona: Northland Press.

Hulbert, Archer. 1933. *Southwest on the Turquoise Trail: The First Diaries on the Road to Santa Fe.* Colorado Springs: Steward Commission of Colorado College and Denver Public Library.

Hyer, Sally. 1990. *One House, One Voice, One Heart: The Education of Native American Children at the Santa Fe Indian School.* Santa Fe: Museum of New Mexico Press.

———. 2001. "The Pueblo Artist as Cultural Broker." Pp. 273–93 in *Between Indian and White Worlds: The Cultural Broker,* ed. Margaret Connell-Szasz. Norman: University of Oklahoma Press.

Iverson, Peter. 1981. *The Navajo Nation.* Westport, Connecticut: Greenwood Press.

———. 1998. *"We Are Still Here": American Indians in the Twentieth Century.* Wheeling, Illinois: Harlan Davidson.

———. 2002. *Diné: A History of the Navajo.* Albuquerque: University of New Mexico Press.

Jacobs, David M. 1975. *The UFO Controversy.* Bloomington: Indiana University Press.

James, Thomas. 1962. *Three Years among the Indians and Mexicans.* Philadelphia: J. B. Lippincott.

James, William. 1956. *The Will to Believe, and Other Essays in Popular Philosophy, and Human Immortality.* New York: Dover Publications.

Johnson, Benjamin Heber. 2003. *Revolution in Texas: How a Forgotten Rebellion and Its Bloody Suppression Turned Mexicans into Americans.* New Haven, Connecticut: Yale University Press.

Jones, Oakah L. 1979. *Los Paisanos: Spanish Settlers on the Northern Frontier of New Spain.* Norman: University of Oklahoma Press.

———. 1985. "Lew Wallace: Hoosier Governor of Territorial New Mexico, 1878–81." *New Mexico Historical Review* 60: 129–58.

Jorgensen, Joseph G. 1983. "Comparative Traditional Economics and Ecological Adaptations." Pp. 684–710 in *Handbook of North American Indians,* vol. 10, *Southwest,* ed. Alfonso Ortiz. Washington, D.C.: Smithsonian Institution.

Julyan, Robert. 1998. *The Place Names of New Mexico.* Rev. ed. Albuquerque: University of New Mexico Press.

Kamen, Henry. 2003. *Empire: How Spain Became a World Power, 1492–1763.* New York: HarperCollins.

Kashima, Tetsuden. 2003. *Judgment without Trial: Japanese American Imprisonment during World War II.* Seattle: University of Washington Press.

Keleher, William A. 1942. "The New Mexico Agriculture College and the 'Food for Victory' Program." *New Mexico Stockman,* (March): 14–18.

————. 1952. *Turmoil in New Mexico, 1846–1868.* Santa Fe, New Mexico: Rydal Press.

Kelley, Klara, and Harris Francis. 1998. "Anthropological Traditions versus Navajo Traditions about Early Navajo History." Pp. 143–55 in *Diné Bikéyah: Papers in Honor of David M. Brugge,* eds. Meliha S. Duran and David T. Kirkpatrick. Albuquerque: Archaeological Society of New Mexico.

Kelly, Lawrence C. 1983. *The Assault on Assimilation: John Collier and the Origins of Indian Policy Reform.* Albuquerque: University of New Mexico Press.

Kessell, John L. 1979. *Kiva, Cross, and Crown: The Pecos Indians and New Mexico, 1540–1840.* Washington, D.C.: National Park Service, U.S. Department of the Interior.

————, ed. 1989. *Remote Beyond Compare: Letters of don Diego de Vargas to His Family from New Spain and New Mexico, 1675–1706.* Albuquerque: University of New Mexico Press.

Kirchhoff, Paul. 1954. "Gatherers and Farmers in the Greater Southwest: A Problem in Classification." *American Anthropologist* 56, no. 4: 529–50.

Klass, Philip. 1983. *UFOs: The Public Deceived.* Buffalo, New York: Prometheus Books.

Knott, Sarah Gertrude. 1940. "North of the Border." *Survey Graphic* 29, no. 6 (June): 339.

Krell, Dorothy, ed. 1979. *The California Missions: A Pictorial History.* Menlo Park, California: Lane.

Kutnewsky, Fremont. 1943. "War Mines at Grants." *New Mexico,* (February): 11–13, 30–31.

Lafaye, Jacques. 1976. *Quetzalcóatl and Guadalupe: the Formation of Mexican National Consciousness, 1531–1813.* Translated by Benjamin Keen. Chicago: University of Chicago Press.

Lang, Herbert H. 1976. "The New Mexico Bureau of Immigration, 1880–1912." *New Mexico Historical Review* 51: 193–214.

Lange, Charles H. 1959. *Cochiti: A New Mexico Pueblo, Past and Present.* Austin: University of Texas Press.

Larrazolo, Paul F. 1986. *Octaviano Larrazolo: A Moment in New Mexico History.* New York: Carlton.

Lavender, David. 1972. *Bent's Fort.* Lincoln: University of Nebraska Press.

Lecompte, Janet. 1985. *Rebellion in Rio Arriba, 1837.* Albuquerque: University of New Mexico Press.

Levy, Jerrold E. 1998. *In the Beginning: The Navajo Genesis.* Berkeley: University of California Press.

Lewis, Nancy Owen, and Kay Leigh Hagan. 2007. *A Peculiar Alchemy: A Centennial History of SAR, 1907–2007.* Santa Fe, New Mexico: School for Advanced Research Press.

Leyva, Yolanda. 2007. "Monuments of Conformity: Commemorating and Protesting Oñate on the Border." *New Mexico Historical Review* 82: 343–67.

Linford, Laurance D. 2000. *Navajo Places: History, Legend, Landscape.* Salt Lake City: University of Utah Press.

Link, Martin A., ed. 1968. *Navajo: A Century of Progress, 1868–1968*. Window Rock, Arizona: Navajo Tribe.

Lummis, Charles F. 1893. *The Land of Poco Tiempo*. New York: Scribner.

Marshall, James. 1945. *Santa Fe: The Railroad that Built an Empire*. New York: Random House.

McClain, Sally. 2001. *Navajo Weapon: The Navajo Code Talkers*. Tucson, Arizona: Rio Nuevo Publishers.

McClintock, Anne. 1993. "Family Feuds: Gender, Nationalism and the Family." *Feminist Review* 44 (Summer): 61–80.

McDougal, C. L. 2003. "The Santa Fe Trail and the Mora Land Grant: The Effects of Trade on a Traditional Economy, 1846–1880." *Wagon Tracks: Santa Fe Trail Association Quarterly* 18, no. 1: 8–14.

McNitt, Frank. 1970. "Fort Sumner: A Study in Origins." *New Mexico Historical Review* 45: 101–17.

Melzer, Richard. 1994. "Casualties of Caution and Fear: Life in Santa Fe's Japanese Internment Camp, 1942–46." Pp. 213–40 in *Essays in Twentieth-Century New Mexico History*, ed. Judith Boyce DeMark. Albuquerque: University of New Mexico Press.

———. 1996. *Ernie Pyle in the American Southwest*. Santa Fe, New Mexico: Sunstone Press.

Miller, Darlis. 1990. "Freighting for Uncle Sam." *Wagon Tracks: Santa Fe Trail Association Quarterly* 5, no. 1: 11–15.

Miller, Michael. 1985. "New Mexico's Role in the Panama-California Exposition of 1915." *El Palacio* 91, no. 2 (Fall): 12–17.

Mooney, James. 1898. "The Jicarilla Genesis." *American Anthropologist,* old series 2: 197–209.

Moore, William L. 1985. "Crashed Saucers: Evidence in Search of Proof." Pp. 174–76 in *MUFON Symposium Proceedings*. Fredericton, New Brunswick: UFO Research.

Moorhead, Max L. 1958. *New Mexico's Royal Road: Trade and Travel on the Chihuahua Trail.* Norman: University of Oklahoma Press.

Mumey, Nolie. 1958. "Ceran St. Vrain, Frontiersman, Indian Trader, Territorial and Political Leader, and Pioneer Businessman." *Denver Westerners Monthly Roundup* 14, no. 1: 4–16.

"Mustang, The." 1942. *New Mexico Stockman* (January): 32.

Navajo Uranium Miner Oral History and Photography Project. 1997. *Memories Come to Us in the Rain and the Wind: Oral Histories and Photographs of Navajo Uranium Miners and Their Families.* Boston: Navajo Uranium Miner Oral History and Photography Project.

New Mexico: A Guide to the Colorful State. 1940. New York: Hastings House.

Nieto-Phillips, John M. 2004. *The Language of Blood: The Making of Spanish-American Identity in New Mexico, 1880s–1930s.* Albuquerque: University of New Mexico Press.

O'Bryan, Aileen. 1956. *The Dîné: Origin Myths of the Navajo Indians.* Smithsonian Institution, Bureau of American Ethnology Bulletin 163. Washington, D.C.: Government Printing Office.

O'Crouley, Pedro Alonso. 1972. *A Description of the Kingdom of New Spain.* Translated and edited by Seán Galvin. San Francisco: John Howell.

Office of the Secretary of State, comp. *New Mexico Blue Book, 2003–2004.* Edited by Kathryn A. Flynn. Albuquerque, New Mexico: LithExcel.

Olsen, Michael L., and Harry C. Myers. 1992. "The Diary of Pedro Ignacio Gallego." *Wagon Tracks: Santa Fe Trail Association Quarterly* 7, no. 1: 15–20.

Opler, Morris E. 1936. "A Summary of Jicarilla Apache Culture." *American Anthropologist,* new series 38: 202–23.

———. 1969 [1942]. *Myths and Tales of the Chiricahua Apache Indians.* New York: Kraus Reprint.

———. 1983a. "The Apachean Culture Pattern and Its Origins." Pp. 368–92 in *Hand-*

book of North American Indians, vol. 10, *Southwest,* ed. Alfonso Ortiz. Washington, D.C.: Smithsonian Institution.

———. 1983b. "Chiricahua Apache." Pp. 401–18 in *Handbook of North American Indians,* vol. 10, *Southwest,* ed. Alfonso Ortiz. Washington, D.C.: Smithsonian Institution.

———. 1983c. "Mescalero Apache." Pp. 419–39 in *Handbook of North American Indians,* vol. 10, *Southwest,* ed. Alfonso Ortiz. Washington, D.C.: Smithsonian Institution.

———. 1996 [1941]. *An Apache Life-way: The Economic, Social, and Religious Institutions of the Chiricahua Indians.* Lincoln: University of Nebraska Press.

Oroz, Fray Pedro. 1972 [1584–86]. *The Oroz Codex.* Translated and edited by Angélico Chávez, O.F.M. Washington, D.C.: Academy of American Franciscan History.

Ortiz, Alfonso. 1969. *The Tewa World: Space, Time, Being, and Becoming in a Pueblo Society.* Chicago: University of Chicago Press.

Otero, Miguel Antonio. 1987. *My Life on the Frontier, 1864–1882.* Albuquerque: University of New Mexico Press.

Pagden, Anthony, trans. and ed. 1986. *Hernán Cortés: Letters from Mexico.* New Haven, Connecticut: Yale University Press.

Pan, Denise. 1995. "Commercializing the Spanish Past: The Coronado Cuarto Centennial, 1935–1940." Pp. 81–109 in *Explorations in American History,* eds. Sandra Varney MacMahon and Louis Tanner. Albuquerque: University of New Mexico Center for the American West.

Paul, Doris A. 1973. *The Navajo Codetalkers.* Pittsburgh: Dorrance Publishing.

Philp, Kenneth R. 1977. *John Collier's Crusade for Indian Reform.* Tucson: University of Arizona Press.

Pike, Albert. 1967. *Prose Sketches and Poems Written in the Western Country.* Edited by David J. Weber. Albuquerque: Calvin Horn.

Pike, David. 2004. *Roadside New Mexico: A Guide to Historic Markers.* Albuquerque: University of New Mexico Press.

Polese, Richard L. 1968. "The Zia Sun Symbol: Variations on a Theme." *El Palacio* 75, no. 2 (Summer): 30–34.

Poling-Kempes, Lesley. 1989. *The Harvey Girls: Women Who Opened the West*. New York: Paragon House.

Prince, L. Bradford. 1910. *New Mexico's Struggle for Statehood: Sixty Years of Effort to Obtain Self Government*. Santa Fe: New Mexican Printing Co.

Povinelli, Elizabeth A. 2002. *The Cunning of Recognition: Indigenous Alterities and the Making of Australian Multiculturalism*. Durham, North Carolina: Duke University Press.

Public Papers of the Presidents of the United States, Harry S. Truman... 1961. Washington, D.C.: U.S. Government Printing Office.

Quaife, Milo Milton. 1966. *Kit Carson's Autobiography*. Lincoln: University of Nebraska Press.

Randle, Kevin D., and Donald R. Schmitt. 1991. *UFO Crash at Roswell*. New York: Avon Books.

Reed, Paul F., ed. 2000. *Foundations of Anasazi Culture: The Basketmaker-Pueblo Transition*. Salt Lake City: University of Utah Press.

Remley, David. 1993. *Bell Ranch: Cattle Ranching in the Southwest, 1842–1947*. Albuquerque: University of New Mexico Press.

Rice, Josiah M. 1970. *A Cannoneer in Navajo Country: Journal of Private Josiah M. Rice, 1851*, ed. Richard H. Dillon. Denver: Old West Publishing.

Riley, Carroll L. 1995. *Río del Norte: People of the Upper Río Grande from Earliest Times to the Pueblo Revolt*. Salt Lake City: University of Utah Press.

Rivas-Rodriguez, Maggie, ed. 2005. *Mexican Americans and World War II*. Austin: University of Texas Press.

Roberts, Helen H. 1932. "The Reason for the Departure of the Pecos Indians for Jemez Pueblo." *American Anthropologist* 34: 359–60.

Roessel, Ruth, ed. 1973. *Navajo Stories of the Long Walk Period*. Tsaile, Arizona: Navajo Community College Press.

———, and Broderick H. Johnson, comps. 1974. *Navajo Livestock Reduction: A National Disgrace*. Chinle, Arizona: Navajo Community College Press.

Rubenstein, Henry R. 1983. "Political Regression in New Mexico: The Destruction of the National Miner's Union in Gallup." Pp. 91–140 in *Labor in New Mexico: Unions, Strikes, and Social History since 1881*, ed. Robert Kern. Albuquerque: University of New Mexico Press.

Russell, Frank. 1898. "Myths of the Jicarilla Apaches." *Journal of American Folklore* 11: 253–71.

Russell, Marian. 1993. *Land of Enchantment*. Albuquerque: University of New Mexico Press.

Rydell, Robert W. 1984. *All the World's a Fair: Visions of Empire at American International Expositions, 1876–1916*. Chicago: University of Chicago Press.

———. 1993. *World of Fairs: The Century-of-Progress Expositions*. Chicago: University of Chicago Press.

Sando, Joe S. 1976. *The Pueblo Indians*. San Francisco: Indian Historian Press.

———. 1982. *Nee Hemish: A History of Jemez Pueblo*. Albuquerque: University of New Mexico Press.

———. 1998. *Pueblo Profiles: Cultural Identity through Centuries of Change*. Santa Fe, New Mexico: Clear Light Publishers.

Sandos, James A. 1992. *Rebellion in the Borderlands: Anarchism and the Plan of San Diego, 1904–1923*. Norman: University of Oklahoma Press.

Schmid, Walter. 2005. *A German POW in New Mexico*. Albuquerque: University of New Mexico Press.

Schroeder, Albert H., and Dan S. Matson. 1965. *A Colony of the Move: Gaspar Castaño de Sosa's Journal, 1590–91*. Santa Fe, New Mexico: School of American Research.

Sheppard, Carl D. 1988. *Creator of the Santa Fe Style: Isaac Hamilton Rapp, Architect.* Albuquerque: University of New Mexico Press.

Sherry, John W. 2002. *Land, Wind, and Hard Words: A Story of Navajo Activism.* Albuquerque: University of New Mexico Press.

Shuart, Harry E. 1934. "New Mexico Goes to the 'World's Fair': The State's Exhibit at A Century of Progress Is One of the High Spots in the Big Show." *New Mexico,* (July): 10–12.

Sides, Hampton. 2004. *Ghost Soldiers: The Epic Account of World War II's Greatest Rescue Mission.* New York: Anchor Books.

Simmons, Marc. 1974. *Witchcraft in the Southwest: Spanish and Indian Supernaturalism on the Rio Grande.* Flagstaff, Arizona: Northland Press.

———. 1977. *New Mexico: A Bicentennial History.* New York: W. W. Norton.

———. 1979a. "History of Pueblo-Spanish Relations to 1821." Pp. 178–93 in *Handbook of North American Indians,* vol. 9, *Southwest,* ed. Alfonso Ortiz. Washington, D.C.: Smithsonian Institution.

———. 1979b. "History of Pueblo-Spanish Relations since 1821." Pp. 206–23 in *Handbook of North American Indians,* vol. 9, *Southwest,* ed. Alfonso Ortiz. Washington, D.C.: Smithsonian Institution.

———. 1986. "José Librado Gurulé's Recollections, 1867." Pp. 120–33 in *On the Santa Fe Trail,* ed. Marc Simmons. Lawrence: University Press of Kansas.

———. 1991. *The Last Conquistador: Juan de Oñate and the Settlement of the Far Southwest.* Norman: University of Oklahoma Press.

———, and Hal Jackson. 2001. *Following the Santa Fe Trail: A Guide for Modern Travelers.* Santa Fe, New Mexico: Ancient City Press.

Simpson, James H. *Journal of a Military Reconnaissance from Santa Fé, New Mexico, to the Navajo Country.* Philadelphia: Lippincott, Grambo, and Co.

Smith, Gregory Scott. 2003. "A Concern for the Future." *El Palacio* 108, no. 4 (Winter): 19.

Smith, Linda Tuhiwai. 1999. *Decolonizing Methodologies: Research and Indigenous Peoples*. New York: Zed Books.

Snow, David H. 1998. *New Mexico's First Colonists: The 1597–1600 Enlistments for New Mexico under Juan de Oñate, Adelante [sic] and Governador*. Albuquerque: Hispanic Genealogical Research Center of New Mexico.

Sperry, T. J. 1990. "A Long and Useful Life for the Santa Fe Trail." *Wagon Tracks: Santa Fe Trail Association Quarterly* 4, no. 3: 14–17.

Spicer, Edward H. 1962. *Cycles of Conquest: The Impact of Spain, Mexico, and the United States on the Indians of the Southwest, 1533–1960*. Tucson: University of Arizona Press.

Stewart, George R. 1982. *Names on the Land: A Historical Account of Placenaming in the United States*. 4th ed. San Francisco: Lexikos.

Stewart, Ronald L. 1970a. "An Indian Shrine at Fort Sumner." *El Palacio* 77, no. 2: 36.

———. 1970b. "Fort Sumner: An Adobe Post on the Pecos." *El Palacio* 77, no. 4: 12–16.

Stockel, Henrietta H. 2004. *Shame and Endurance: The Untold Story of the Chiricahua Apache Prisoners of War*. Tucson: University of Arizona Press.

Sunder, John E., ed. 1960. *Matt Field on the Santa Fe Trail*. Norman: University of Oklahoma Press.

Swann, Michael M. 1982. *Tierra Adentro: Settlement and Society in Colonial Durango*. Boulder, Colorado: Westview Press.

Szasz, Ferenc M. 1984. *The Day the Sun Rose Twice: The Story of the Trinity Site Nuclear Explosion, July 16, 1945*. Albuquerque: University of New Mexico Press.

———. 2006. *Larger than Life: New Mexico in the Twentieth Century*. Albuquerque: University of New Mexico Press.

Tapahanso, Luci. 1997. "This Is How They Were Placed Here for Us." Pp. 39–42 in *Blue Horses Rush In*. Tucson: University of Arizona Press.

Thomas, Gerald W., Monroe L. Billington, and Roger D. Walter, eds. 1994. *Victory in World War II: The New Mexico Story.* Las Cruces: New Mexico State University.

Thomas, Hugh. 1995. *Conquest: Montezuma, Cortés, and the Fall of Old Mexico.* New York: Simon and Schuster.

Thompson, Enid. 1974. "The Ladies of Bent's Fort." *Denver Westerners Roundup* 30, no. 9: 4–8.

Threepersons, Lorene. 1943. "A Ranch Wife in Wartime." *New Mexico Stockman,* (February): 26–27.

Tijerina, Reies López. 2000. *They Called Me "King Tiger": My Struggle for the Land and Our Rights.* Edited by José Angel Gutiérrez. Houston: Arté Publico Press.

Tiller, Veronica E. 1983. "Jicarilla Apache." Pp. 440–61 in *Handbook of North American Indians,* vol. 10, *Southwest,* ed. Alfonso Ortiz. Washington, D.C.: Smithsonian Institution.

———. 2000. *The Jicarilla Apache Tribe: A History.* Albuquerque: Bow Arrow Publishing Co.

Timmons, W. H. 1990. *El Paso: A Borderlands History.* El Paso: Texas Western Press.

Tobias, Henry J. 1990. *A History of the Jews in New Mexico.* Albuquerque: University of New Mexico Press.

Tod, Nancy. 1944. "The Deeds of Roy Nakayama." *Southern New Mexico Historical Review* 1 (January): 2–8.

Tórrez, Robert J. 1997. "Celebrations of Mexican Independence and a Fracas at the Palace in 1844." *Compadres,* (November), pp. 5–8.

———. 2005. "The New Mexican 'Revolt' and 'Treason Trials' of 1847." *Nuestras Raíses* 17, no. 1: 3–10.

Treaty between the United States of America and the Navajo Tribe of Indians, With a record of the discussions that led to its signing. 1968. Flagstaff, Arizona: KC Publications.

Trennert, Robert A. 1987. "Fairs, Expositions, and the Changing Image of Southwestern Indians, 1876–1904." *New Mexico Historical Review* 62: 127–50.

———. 1998. *White Man's Medicine: Government Doctors and the Navajo, 1863–1955.* Albuquerque: University of New Mexico Press.

Twitchell, Ralph Emerson. 1909. *The Military Occupation of New Mexico, 1846–1851.* Denver: Smith-Brooks Co.

———. 1910. "The Ancient Pueblo of Pecos." *Santa Fe Employees' Magazine* 4 (October): 27–32.

———. 1925. *Old Santa Fe: The Story of New Mexico's Ancient Capital.* Santa Fe: New Mexican Publishing Co.

Udall, Stewart L. 1987. *To the Inland Empire: Coronado and Our Spanish Legacy.* Garden City, New York: Doubleday.

Vaillant, George C. 1966. *Aztecs of Mexico: Origin, Rise, and Fall of the Aztec Nation.* Rev. ed. Baltimore, Maryland: Penguin Books.

Vargas, Zaragosa. 2005. *Labor Rights Are Civil Rights: Mexican American Workers in Twentieth-Century America.* Princeton: Princeton University Press.

Villagrá, Gaspar Pérez de. 1933. *History of New Mexico (Alcalá, 1610).* Translated by Gilberto Espinosa. Los Angeles: Quivira Society.

Walker, Charles. 1933. "Causes of the Confederate Invasion of New Mexico." *New Mexico Historical Review* 8: 76–97.

Waters, Frank. 1950. *Masked Gods: Navaho and Pueblo Ceremonialism.* Albuquerque: University of New Mexico Press.

Webb, James Josiah. 1995. *Adventures in the Santa Fe Trade, 1844–1847.* Lincoln: University of Nebraska Press.

Weber, David J. 1982. *The Mexican Frontier, 1821–1846: The American Southwest under Mexico.* Albuquerque: University of New Mexico Press.

———. 1988. *Myth and the History of the Hispanic Southwest: Essays by David J. Weber.* Albuquerque: University of New Mexico Press.

———. 1992. *The Spanish Frontier in North America.* New Haven, Connecticut: Yale University Press.

Weber, David J., ed. 1973. "An Unforgettable Day: Facundo Melgares on Independence." *New Mexico Historical Review* 47: 27–44.

Weigle, Marta. 1985. *New Mexicans in Cameo and Camera: New Deal Documentation of Twentieth-Century Lives.* Albuquerque: University of New Mexico Press.

————. 1996. "'Insisted on Authenticity': Harveycar Indian Detours, 1925–1931." Pp. 47–59 in *The Great Southwest of the Fred Harvey Company and the Santa Fe Railway*, eds. Marta Weigle and Barbara A. Babcock. Phoenix, Arizona: Heard Museum.

————, and Barbara A. Babcock, eds. 1996. *The Great Southwest of the Fred Harvey Company and the Santa Fe Railway.* Phoenix, Arizona: Heard Museum.

Wilcox, Walter W. 1947. *The Farmer in the Second World War.* Ames: Iowa State College Press.

Wilkins, David E. 1999. *The Navajo Political Experience.* Tsaile, Arizona: Diné College Press.

————. 2002. "Governance within the Navajo Nation: Have Democratic Traditions Taken Hold?" *Wicazo Sa Review* 17 (Spring): 91–129.

Wilkinson, Charles F. 2004. *Fire on the Plateau: Conflict and Endurance in the American Southwest.* Washington, D.C.: Island Press.

Wilson, Chris. 1997. *The Myth of Santa Fe: Creating a Modern Regional Tradition.* Albuquerque: University of New Mexico Press.

Woodbury, Richard B. 1979. "Prehistory: Introduction." Pp. 22–30 in *Handbook of North American Indians*, vol. 9, *Southwest*, ed. Alfonso Ortiz. Washington, D.C.: Smithsonian Institution.

Woods, Betty. 1950. *Fifty Trips to Thrills.* Edited by George Fitzpatrick. Santa Fe: New Mexico Magazine.

————. 1973. *101 Trips in the Land of Enchantment.* Edited by George Fitzpatrick. 4th rev. ed. Santa Fe: New Mexico Magazine.

Wroth, William. 1983. "*La Sangre de Cristo*: History and Symbolism." Pp. 283–92 in *Hispanic Arts and Ethnohistory in the Southwest: New Papers Inspired by the Work of*

E. Boyd, ed. Marta Weigle with Claudia Larcombe and Samuel Larcombe. Santa Fe, New Mexico: Ancient City Press; Albuquerque: University of New Mexico Press.

Yazzie, Albert W. 1984. *Navajo Oral Tradition*. Rough Rock, Arizona: Navajo Resource Center, Rough Rock Demonstration School.

Yazzie, Ethelou, ed. 1971. *Navajo History*. Rough Rock, Arizona: Navajo Curriculum Center, Rough Rock Demonstration School.

Zolbrod, Paul, trans. 1984. *Diné bahane': The Navajo Creation Story*. Albuquerque: University of New Mexico Press.

Contributor Notes

Each contributor of a previously unpublished essay to *Telling New Mexico* provided a contributor note. The notes for authors of reprinted pieces are taken from those in the original publications, as indicated by dates given alongside essay titles. A biographical sketch is included for each of the five deceased contributors.

Herman Agoyo, a lifetime member of the San Juan Pueblo Tribal Council, was serving the pueblo, at the time he wrote his essay in 2005, as its realty officer and Native American Graves Protection and Repatriation Act (NAGPRA) representative. He had been lieutenant governor four times and served as governor in 1992. Agoyo has also chaired the All Indian Pueblo Council and been executive director of the Eight Northern Indian Pueblo Council (ENIPC). He was co-founder of ENIPC's Arts and Crafts Show and founder of the American Indian Week of the Indian Pueblo Cultural Center in Albuquerque. He is co-chairman of the New Mexico Statuary Hall Commission and former president of the New Mexico Statuary Hall Foundation. He also finds time to be an active member of San Juan Pueblo's Senior Olympics program and to publish poetry and articles.

Paula Gunn Allen (1939–2008) was an award-winning American Indian poet, novelist, and scholar. Of both Laguna Pueblo–Métis–Scot and Lebanese descent, she grew up on the Cubero land grant and at Laguna Pueblo. Allen earned her B.A. in English and M.F.A. in creative writing from the University of Oregon and her Ph.D. in American studies from the University of New Mexico. She taught at Fort Lewis College, the College of San Mateo, San Diego State University, San Francisco State University, the University of New Mexico, the University of California, Berkeley, and the University of California, Los Angeles, from which she retired in 1999 as professor of English, creative writing, and American Indian studies. Among her scholarly books are *Studies in American Indian Literature: Critical Essays and Course Designs* and *The Sacred Hoop: Recovering the Feminine in American Indian Traditions.* Her *Pocahontas: Medicine Woman, Spy, Entrepreneur, Diplomat* was nominated for a Pulitzer Prize. Among her awards were the Hubbell Prize for Lifetime Achievement in American Literary Studies from the Modern Language Association, the Lifetime Achievement Award from the Native Writer's Circle of the Americas, and a Lannan Foundation Fellowship.

The Architect of the Capitol is responsible to the United States Congress for the maintenance, operation, development, and preservation of the United States Capitol Complex, which includes the Capitol, the congressional office buildings, the Library of Congress buildings, the Supreme Court building, the U.S. Botanic Garden, the Capitol Power Plant, and other facilities.

Durwood Ball is an associate professor of history at the University of New Mexico and editor of the *New Mexico Historical Review.* He is the author of *Army Regulars on the Western Frontier, 1848–1861.* He has also published numerous articles on frontier military history.

Thomas E. Chávez is a historian who currently works as a consultant. He was director of the Palace of the Governors for twenty-one years and, for a short period, executive director of the National Hispanic Cultural Center. Among his books are *Manuel Alvarez, 1794–1856: A Southwestern Biography*; *An Illustrated History of New Mexico*; *Spain and the Independence of the United States: An Intrinsic Gift*; *Wake for a Fat Vicar: Padre Juan Felipe Ortiz, Archbishop Lamy, and the New Mexican Catholic Church in the Middle Nineteenth Century* (with Fray Angélico Chávez); and *New Mexico: Past and Future.* He is working on a multivolume catalogue of all the documents pertinent to Benjamin Franklin extant in the archives of Spain. He has received many awards from organizations including the City of Santa Fe, the New Mexico Endowment for the Humanities, the Daughters of the American Revolution, and the University of New Mexico Alumni Association.

Margaret Connell-Szasz is a professor of history at the University of New Mexico, where she teaches courses on American Indian and Alaska Native history and Celtic history. She has also taught at the University of Exeter, England, and at the University of Aberdeen, Scotland, where she is a research fellow in the School of Divinity, History and Philosophy. She has published widely in American Indian history. Her latest book is *Scottish Highlanders and Native Americans: Indigenous Education in the Eighteenth-Century Atlantic World.*

Larry S. Crumpler, Ph.D., at the time his essay was originally published in 2001, was research curator of volcanology and space science at the New Mexico Museum of Natural History and Science. He had published numerous research papers about volcanic fields in New Mexico and Arizona as well as — on the basis of his experience with several NASA planetary missions — the volcanoes of Mars and Venus.

William deBuys teaches documentary studies at the College of Santa Fe. He is the author of six books, including *Enchantment and Exploitation: The Life and Hard Times of a New Mexico Mountain Range* and *River of Traps: A New Mexico Mountain Life*, which was a finalist for the Pulitzer Prize in 1991. His most recent book, *The Walk*, is set in the same remote valley as *River of Traps*.

Jennifer Nez Denetdale (Diné) was, in summer 2007, an associate professor of history at the University of New Mexico. She is the author of *Reclaiming Diné History: The Legacies of Navajo Chief Manuelito and Juanita* and is working on a history of Navajo women.

Sarah Deutsch is a professor of history and dean of the Faculty of Social Sciences at Duke University. Among her publications on the North American West are *No Separate Refuge: Culture, Class, and Gender on an Anglo-Hispanic Frontier in the American Southwest, 1880–1940*; "Landscape of Enclaves: Race Relations in the American West, 1865–1990," in *Under an Open Sky*; "Contemporary Peoples/Contested Places" (with George J. Sanchez and Gary Y. Okihiro), in *The Oxford History of the American West*; and "Being American in Boley, Oklahoma," in *Beyond Black and White: Race, Ethnicity, and Gender in the U.S. South and Southwest*. She is currently writing a book manuscript titled "Making the Twentieth Century West, 1898–1942."

Roland F. Dickey (1914–2000) grew up on his family's sheep and cattle ranch near Clovis, New Mexico. He received his B.A. in English from the University of New Mexico. During the late 1930s Dickey worked for the New Mexico Federal Art Project, directing its art teaching and exhibition center in Roswell, where he served as director of the Roswell Museum of Arts and Culture (1938–41). He enlisted in the U.S. Army in 1943. Dickey worked as an editor in Albuquerque, Socorro, and Milwaukee and was director of the University of New Mexico Press (1956–66), where he edited the *New Mexico Quarterly*. Author of *New Mexico Village Arts* (1949), he was president of the Historical Society of New Mexico and the Albuquerque Historical Society. "Windscapes: Chronicles of Neglected Time" was one of several columns Dickey wrote for *Century: A Southwest Journal of Observation and Opinion*, edited by V. B. Price and published in Albuquerque in 1980–83. Dickey described himself for the December 16, 1981, issue of *Century* as being "of the macaroon school of writing, set off on a Proustian track by familiar objects."

Malcolm Ebright is a historian, an attorney, and director of the Center for Land Grant Studies. His most recent book (with Rick Hendricks), *The Witches of Abiquiú: The Governor, the Priest, the Genízaro Indians, and the Devil*, won a prize (shared with David Caffey's *Frank Springer and New Mexico*) for the best history book in 2006 from the Historical Society of New Mexico. Ebright has often testified as an expert witness in litigation dealing with land grants and water rights and has written numerous books and award-winning articles on New Mexico land and water history, including *The Tierra Amarilla Grant: A History of Chicanery* and *Land Grants and Lawsuits in Northern New Mexico*. He continues to work with indigenous communities, helping them protect their land and water rights.

William E. Gibbs, as of 1993, had taught history at the New Mexico Military Institute in Roswell, New Mexico, for more than fifteen years. He was at that time the author of several articles on the influence of race and ethnicity on U.S. foreign relations, a subject of special interest to him.

Daniel Gibson writes for national magazines. In 1986, when he wrote the essay reprinted here, he worked for the New Mexico Office of Indian Affairs.

Rick Hendricks works in the Archives and Special Collections Department at New Mexico State University Library and teaches occasional courses in the Department of History. He was a co-editor on the Vargas Project, which produced six volumes on the administration of seventeenth-century governor Diego de Vargas. Among his other New Mexico books are *The Witches of Abiquiú: The Governor, the Priest, the Genízaro Indians, and the Devil* (with Malcolm Ebright); *New Mexico Prenuptial Investigations from the Archivos Históricos del Arzobispado de Durango* (with John B. Colligan); and *The Navajos in 1705: Roque Madrid's Campaign Journal* (with John P. Wilson). He recently completed the book manuscript "New Mexico in 1801: The Priests' Report."

Debra Hughes, a writer and editor, is an Albuquerque native who, in 2006, lived in Tucson, Arizona.

Jon Hunner is the director of the Public History Program at New Mexico State University, where he also teaches New Mexico and United States history. Among his books are *Inventing Los Alamos: The Growth of an Atomic Community* and two co-authored volumes in the Images of America series, *Las Cruces* and *Santa Fe: A Historical Walking Tour*. He has conducted numerous public history projects in New Mexico, including surveys of the historic districts of Columbus, Las Cruces, Las Trampas, and Mesilla; oral histories of the Rep. J. Paul and Mary Taylor family of Mesilla; and living history re-creations of the Spanish colonial and Great

Depression periods at the New Mexico Farm and Ranch Heritage Museum and the Palace of the Governors. In 2004 he received the Heritage Preservation Award from the New Mexico Historic Preservation Division for his work in public history around the state.

Peter Iverson was, in 2002, Regents' Professor of History at Arizona State University. He is a leading scholar of twentieth-century American Indian history.

Oakah L. Jones was, in 1999, a professor emeritus of history at Purdue University, residing in Albuquerque. He received his M.A. and Ph.D. from the University of Oklahoma. He taught Latin American history and the Spanish borderlands for thirty-three years at the U.S. Air Force Academy, the University of Colorado in Colorado Springs, Florida State University in the Panama Canal Zone, Purdue University, and St. Mary's University in San Antonio, Texas. His research interests are the Spanish frontier in North America, colonial Latin America, Mexico, and Guatemala. He is the author of five books, editor of three, and author of numerous articles and book reviews.

Paul M. Jones, of Silver City, "died in his home early Sunday morning," October 2, 1990, according to his obituary in the *Silver City Daily Press and Independent*. "Born May 3, 1919, in Pottesville, Texas, he had been a resident of Silver City since 1981. Mr. Jones was a retired superintendent of preparation and processing with Dole Pineapple Co. in Honolulu, Hawaii. He was owner of Jones Drilling in Grant County from 1947 to 1957. He was the author and publisher of a book, *Memories of Santa Rita* [1985], and was a World War II veteran, having served with the U.S. Navy's Pacific fleet."

Tom R. Kennedy has completed his twelfth year at Zuni Pueblo, serving first as executive director of the A:shiwi A:wan Museum and Heritage Center and currently as director of the Zuni Tourism Office. While at the tribe's museum, he led a Zuni team in planning and installing the exhibit *Hawikku: Echoes from Our Past* and coordinated the selection and return of more than two hundred Hawikku artifacts to Zuni. His current responsibilities include restoration and interpretation of key heritage sites, among them Our Lady of Guadalupe (Old Zuni) Mission and the Hawikku archaeological site. He also leads several regional initiatives in northwest New Mexico, among them heading a regional tourism marketing board, developing a cultural enterprise network, establishing an arts trail, and coordinating management of a major scenic byway.

John L. Kessell is a professor emeritus in the Department of History at the University of New Mexico. He was founding editor of the Vargas Project, which, thanks to colleagues Rick Hendricks, Meredith D. Dodge, and Larry D. Miller, resulted in the six-volume *Journals of don Diego de Vargas, 1691–1704*. He is the author of *Kiva, Cross, and Crown: The Pecos Indians and New Mexico, 1540–1840* and *Spain in the Southwest: A Narrative History of New Mexico, Arizona, Texas, and California*.

Frances Levine is the director of the New Mexico History Museum, which includes the Palace of the Governors, the oldest museum in the Museum of New Mexico system, and the Fray Angélico Chávez History Library and Photo Archives. She came to the museum from a position as assistant dean of academic affairs for Arts and Sciences at Santa Fe Community College, where she taught classes in New Mexico history and the ethnohistory of Pueblo and Hispanic communities in the Southwest. The author of *Our Prayers Are in This Place: Pecos Pueblo Identity over the Centuries*, Levine has served as an expert witness on land and water use adjudications for Pueblo and Hispanic communities.

Haniel Long (1888–1956) was an author, publisher, and literary visionary. After teaching English for twenty years at Carnegie Institute of Technology (now Carnegie Mellon), Long moved with his family to Santa Fe in 1929 to devote himself to writing. There he joined with Alice Corbin, Peggy Pond Church, and Raymond Otis to found Writers' Editions, a cooperative "to publish good books that otherwise might not see the light of day," both their own and by other writers living in the Southwest. Published by the Rydal Press of Santa Fe, Writers' Editions included two of Long's books: *Interlinear to Cabeza de Vaca: His Relation of the Journey from Florida to the Pacific, 1528–1536* (1936) and *Malinche (Doña Marina)* (1939), the last Writers' Edition book.

María Cristina López recently retired from teaching Spanish language and literature and heritage Spanish in the Languages Department at Santa Fe Community College. She presently chairs the City of Santa Fe Commission on Immigrant Affairs and is active as a co-founder and board member of Somos un Pueblo Unido, an immigrant rights organization. In 1990 she received the Gloria Steinem: Women of Vision Award for her work in the area of empowerment and leadership.

María E. Montoya was, in 2002, an associate professor at the University of Michigan in the Department of History and the Program in American Culture. She is the author of *Translating Property: The Maxwell Land Grant and the Conflict over Land in the American West, 1840–1900*.

John M. Nieto-Phillips was, in 2004, an associate professor of history and Latino studies at Indiana University, Bloomington.

The Office of the Secretary of State, according to the *New Mexico Blue Book 2003–2004*, p. 125, "is an elected state office, second in line of succession to the office of governor after the lieutenant governor.… The secretary is the keeper of the Great Seal of the State of New Mexico and affixes the seal to all commissions issued in the name of the governor.… In addition…the secretary of state is responsible for administering an agency with a number of ongoing functions. Probably the most visible of these is the role as the state's chief election officer."

Gail Okawa is a professor of English at Youngstown State University, Ohio, where she teaches courses in multicultural literature and sociolinguistics. In 2002 she was a scholar-in-residence at the Smithsonian Institution, where she worked on a project on U.S. language history artifacts. In 2003 and 2006 she was a visiting scholar at the Center for Biographical Research, University of Hawaii at Manoa, where she has been researching the experiences of Japanese internees from Hawaii exiled during World War II to U.S. Department of Justice internment camps on the mainland, including the one in Santa Fe, in part through the life of her grandfather. Her book on the subject is tentatively titled "More than a Mug Shot: Hawaiian Japanese Immigrants in World War II U.S. Department of Justice Internment Camps."

Michael L. Olsen is a professor emeritus at New Mexico Highlands University. He has published widely on the history of the Santa Fe Trail, especially its social and cultural aspects. He has served on the Board of Directors of the Santa Fe Trail Association, on the Citizen's Advisory Committee for the Santa Fe National Historic Trail, on the New Mexico State Records Center and Archives Advisory Board, and as a consultant to the National Park Service.

Alfonso Ortiz (1939–97) was a professor in the Department of Anthropology at the University of New Mexico from 1974 until his death in 1997. Of both Native American (San Juan Pueblo) and Hispanic descent, he earned his B.A. in sociology from the University of New Mexico and his M.A. and Ph.D. in anthropology from the University of Chicago. He taught at Pitzer College and Princeton University before returning to his home state. Among his books are *The Tewa World: Space, Time, Being, and Becoming in a Pueblo Society* (1969), the edited *New Perspectives on the Pueblos* (1972), and the two Southwest volumes (9 and 10) of the *Handbook of North American Indians* (1979, 1983). Ortiz received both a John Simon Guggenheim Memorial Foundation fellowship and the prestigious John D. and Catherine T. MacArthur Foundation fellowship. He lectured widely, and among his many public service commitments was a career-spanning involvement with the Association on American Indian Affairs, including fifteen years as its president (1973–88).

Jake Page claimed in 1995 to have been "seduced by the Southwest" a few years before and "transformed into a literal and literate desert rat." Others of his Smithsonian Institution books are *Lords of the Air: The Smithsonian Book of Birds* and *Smithsonian's New Zoo.*

Estevan Rael-Gálvez is state historian for New Mexico and chairman of the Cultural Properties Review Committee, New Mexico's policy-making and advisory board for historical preservation. He is working on a book, "The Silence of Slavery: Narratives of American Indian and Mexican Servitude and Its Legacy." Rael-Gálvez is the recipient of numerous fellowships for his academic studies, including a Ford Foundation Dissertation Fellowship and a residential fellowship at the School for Advanced Research in Santa Fe.

Sylvia Rodríguez was, in 2006, a professor of anthropology at the University of New Mexico and the author of *The Matachines Dance: Ritual Symbolism and Interethnic Relations in the Upper Río Grande Valley* and *Acequia: Water Sharing, Sanctity, and Place.*

Lois Palken Rudnick was, in 1996, director of the American Studies Program at the University of Massachusetts, Boston. She is the author of *Mabel Dodge Luhan: New Woman, New Worlds* and *Utopian Vistas: The Mabel Dodge Luhan House and the American Counterculture.*

Joe S. Sando, born into the Sun clan at Jemez Pueblo, is a well-known writer on Indian history. In 1992 he was director of archives for the Pueblo Indian Study and Research Center at the Indian Pueblo Cultural Center in Albuquerque. Sando has taught Pueblo history at the University of New Mexico and ethnohistory at the Institute of American Indian Arts in Santa Fe. He has also been a columnist for the *Albuquerque Tribune* and *Capitol Roundup.*

Jason Silverman is an award-winning journalist who has written for *Wired* magazine, the *Austin Chronicle*, the *Santa Fean, Time Out New York, Southwest Art,* and *Utne Reader.* His work has appeared in books including *The Critical Guide to Contemporary North American Directors* and *The World Is a Text.* His articles have been translated into eight languages. He also is an independent film curator.

Marc Simmons was, in 2006, a professional author and historian who has published more than forty books on New Mexico and the American Southwest. His popular "Trail Dust" column is syndicated in several regional newspapers. In 1993, King Juan Carlos of Spain admitted him to the knightly Order of Isabel la Católica for his contributions to Spanish colonial history.

Dan Simplicio was for many years a member of the Zuni Tribal Council. In that position he was known for his effective advocacy on behalf of the pueblo of Zuni, its culture, and its land. For nearly two decades he led an ultimately successful opposition to the mining of Zuni Salt Lake, a sacred place to Zunis and other Pueblo peoples. He has also been an advocate for his people on many other issues, including health, language continuance, and environmental and culture protection. A sought-after public speaker, Simplicio has addressed these concerns before the national media and legislative bodies and at conferences and symposia throughout the country. He currently teaches Zuni language and culture at Twin Buttes High School on the Zuni reservation.

Michael Stevenson was, in 2006, first vice-president of the Historical Society of New Mexico, a member and secretary of the Museum of New Mexico Board of Regents, and a trustee of the Museum of New Mexico Foundation. In 1993 he retired from Los Alamos National Laboratory as associate director for energy and environment. He is a longtime volunteer for and supporter of the Palace of the Governors and New Mexico History Museum.

Louise Stiver is senior curator at the New Mexico History Museum. She has held previous curatorial positions at the Museum of Indian Arts and Culture in Santa Fe, the National Park Service in Colorado and New Mexico, and the University of New Mexico's Maxwell Museum of Anthropology. She is the author of many published articles about Native American material culture and was photo editor of *New Mexico Route 66 on Tour: Legendary Architecture from Glenrio to Gallup*.

Rina Swentzell is from Santa Clara Pueblo. She received her M.A. in architecture and Ph.D. in American studies from the University of New Mexico. In 1985, when her essay was originally published, she lived in Santa Fe, where she worked as an educational and architectural consultant and taught culture and architecture in the Native American context at the School of Architecture and Planning at UNM.

Ferenc M. Szasz is University Regents Professor in the Department of History at the University of New Mexico, where he has taught for more than three decades. A specialist in the history of American ideas, he has written or edited some hundred articles and eleven books. *The Day the Sun Rose Twice: The Story of the Trinity Site Nuclear Explosion, July 16, 1945* is probably his best-known work. His latest book is a collection of essays, *Larger than Life: New Mexico in the Twentieth Century*.

Veronica E. Velarde Tiller holds a Ph.D. in history from the University of New Mexico. In 2000 she owned a consulting firm in Albuquerque.

Robert J. Tórrez served as state historian at the New Mexico State Records Center and Archives in Santa Fe from 1987 until his retirement in December 2000. He has contributed to several books and published numerous articles on New Mexico history and culture in *New Mexico Historical Review, New Mexico Magazine, True West, Tradición Revista,* and other regional and national publications. His monthly column, "Voices from the Past," appears in *Round the Roundhouse,* the state government employees' newspaper, and a compilation of these columns, *UFOs over Galisteo and Other Stories of New Mexico's History,* has been published. His most recent book is *New Mexico in 1876–1877: A Newspaperman's View.* He is finishing a book about crime and punishment in territorial New Mexico, "Myth of the Hanging Tree."

Marta Weigle is University Regents Professor in the Department of Anthropology at the University of New Mexico. Among her New Mexico books are *Brothers of Light, Brothers of Blood: The Penitentes of the Southwest; Santa Fe and Taos: The Writer's Era, 1916–1941* (with Kyle Fiore); *New Mexicans in Cameo and Camera: New Deal Documentation of Twentieth-Century Lives; The Lore of New Mexico* (with Peter White); and *Spanish New Mexico: The Spanish Colonial Arts Society Collection* (with Donna Pierce). She is finishing a book on tourism: "Alluring New Mexico: Engineered Enchantment, 1821–2001." In 2005 she received the inaugural State Historian's Award for Excellence in New Mexico Heritage Scholarship from the New Mexico Historic Preservation Division.

William Wroth is a cultural historian who specializes in Hispanic and Native American cultures of the Southwest and Mexico. Among his books are *The Chapel of Our Lady of Talpa; Images of Penance, Images of Mercy: Southwestern Santos in the Late Nineteenth Century;* and *Ute Indian Arts and Culture from Prehistory to the New Millennium.* Curator of the Taylor Museum of the Colorado Springs Fine Arts Center from 1976 to 1983, he has since served as guest curator for several institutions, including, in 2006, the Museum of Spanish Colonial Art in Santa Fe.

Acknowledgments

A publication about New Mexico's history was envisioned from the earliest stages of developing exhibitions for the New Mexico History Museum, opening in Santa Fe in 2009. But what would that text be? It could have been a book of scholarly debates on the meaning of our history. Or, it might have been simply a catalogue of the artifacts, documents, photographs, and maps that are on exhibit in the new museum. Several potential authors were invited to a series of workshops to discuss and help shape the book. During one of those working sessions, Marta Weigle offered to serve as volume editor for the publication. Through a series of brain-storming meetings between Marta Weigle, Frances Levine, and Louise Stiver, the publication was conceptualized as a tribute to our history

Weigle's expertise as editor was invaluable, and we could not have accomplished this volume without her. Kay Hagan became an accomplice, drafting caption text and clearing permissions for the many chapters involving reprinted material. The Palace of the Governors/New Mexico History Museum staff worked diligently and under tight deadlines to envision and conceptualize the New Mexico core history exhibition and provide accompanying graphics and photographs.

Another invaluable element of any undertaking of this magnitude is the underwriters for the volume. Michael and Marianne O'Shaughnessy generously provided funding for the authors and book production through the I.A. O'Shaughnessy Foundation. The Historical Society of New Mexico granted funding through its Jane Sanchez Legacy Fund. The Museum of New Mexico Foundation contributed additional funds. We are grateful to the Museum of New Mexico Press for their skillful final editing, their creative design, and their dedication to quality that makes them such a valuable museum partner..

Louise Stiver, *Senior Curator*
Frances Levine, *Director*

Photography Credits

DEDICATION

Shiprock, New Mexico, 1994. Photograph by Michael O'Shaughnessy

JAKE PAGE/LIGHT

Courtesy Photo Archives (NMHM/DCA), New Mexico Magazine Collection.

CRUMPLER/VOLCANOES

Courtesy Photo Archives (NMHM/DCA), neg. no. 050805.

DEBUYS/MOUNTAIN VILLAGE

Courtesy Photo Archives (NMHM/DCA), neg. no. 011569.

RODRIGUEZ/ACEQUIAS

Courtesy Photo Archives (NMHM/DCA), Nancy Hunter Warren Collection, HP.2003.29.

DICKEY/WINDSCAPES

Collection of the New Mexico Museum of Art. New Mexico Farm Security Administration Collection, Museum purchase with funds from the Pinewood Foundation with additional support from Barbara Erdman, 1990.

JONES/MINES

Courtesy Photo Archives (NMHM/DCA), neg. no. 065731.

SWENTZELL/PUYE

Courtesy Photo Archives (NMHM/DCA), neg. no. 077525.

LONG/CARLSBAD

Courtesy Marta Weigle.

ORTIZ/SW INDIGENOUS PEOPLES

Courtesy Photo Archives (NMHM/DCA), neg. no. 130232.

SIMPLICIO/KENNEDY/ZUNI FIRST CONTACT

Courtesy Photo Archives (NMHM/DCA), neg. no. 016387 .

IVERSON/NAVAJO

Courtesy Photo Archives (NMHM/DCA), neg. no. 008718.

TILLER/JICARILLA APACHE

Courtesy Photo Archives (NMHM/DCA), neg. no. 021552.

CHAVEZ/SPAIN IN THE NEW WORLD

Courtesy Fray Angélico Chávez History Library (NMHM/DCA), AC143.

HENDRICKS/OÑATE

Courtesy Photo Archives (NMHM/DCA), neg. no. 008763.

ORTIZ/PO'PAY (PUEBLO PERSPECTIVE ON REVOLT)

Courtesy Museum of Indian Arts and Culture, LA 23837/12, and Museum of
International Folk Art, F.A. 79.64-130 (Museum of New Mexico/DCA).

HENDRICKS/DEVARGAS

Courtesy History Collection (NMHM/DCA), neg. no. 011409, catalog no.
10048/45.

KESSELL/BISHOP TAMARON'S VISIT

Courtesy Photo Archives (NMHM/DCA), neg. no. 006506.

SANDO/PUEBLO CANES

Courtesy Photo Archives (NMHM/DCA), New Mexico Magazine Collection,
neg. no. 183354.

TORREZ/MEXICAN PATRIOTISM

Courtesy Photo Archives (NMHM/DCA), neg. no. 100538.

JONES/CAMINO REAL

Courtesy Bureau of Land Management, New Mexico.

OLSEN/SF TRAIL

Courtesy Photo Archives (NMHM/DCA), neg. no. 171104.

KESSELL/PECOS

Courtesy Photo Archives (NMHM/DCA), neg. no. 006504.

WEIGLE/STATE SEAL

Courtesy History Collection (NMHM/DCA), gift of Helen Smith, 10030/45.

BALL/MILITARY 1800S

Courtesy Photo Archives (NMHM/DCA), John G. Meem Collection, neg. no. 022938.

WROTH/BUFFALO SOLDIERS

Courtesy Photo Archives (NMHM/DCA), neg. no. 098373.

CONNELL-SZASZ/NATIVE EDUCATION (2 PHOTOS)

Courtesy Photo Archives (NMHM/DCA), neg. no. 002112.

EBRIGHT/LAND GRANTS/STATUS

Courtesy History Collection (NMHM/DCA), neg. no. 050800, catalog no. 9781/45.

SIMMONS/BILLY THE KID

Courtesy Photo Archives (NMHM/DCA), neg. no. 128785.

GIBSON/BLACKDOM

Courtesy Blackdom Memorial Foundation, Inc.

WEIGLE/TOURISM BEGINNINGS

Courtesy Photo Archives (NMHM/DCA), neg. no. 133942.

STEVENSON/NM HISTORICAL SOCIETY

Courtesy Photo Archives (NMHM/DCA), Clarkson Collection, neg. no. 053554.

NM CONSTITUTION

Courtesy Photo Archives (NMHM/DCA), neg. no. 008119.

WEIGLE/STATE FLAGS AND SONG

Courtesy History Collection (NMHM/DCA), 1709/45.

DEUTSCH/LABOR RIGHTS & STRIKES

Courtesy *Santa Fe New Mexican*.

GALVEZ/WPA

Courtesy Photo Archives (NMHM/DCA), neg. no. 101283.

SZASZ/NM IN WWII

Associated Press photograph from United States Army, Library of Congress, Prints and Photographs Division, NYWT&S Collection, LC-USZ62-128769.

GIBBS/ROSWELL

Courtesy *Roswell Daily Record*.

HUNNER/NORMALIZING LOS ALAMOS

Courtesy Los Alamos Historical Society, P1985-894-1-2473.

SILVERMAN/BUDDY HOLLY

Courtesy Photo Archives (NMHM/DCA), New Mexico Magazine Collection.

CHAVEZ STATUE

Courtesy Photo Archives (NMHM/DCA), neg. no. 183220.

MONTOYA/CHAVEZ

Courtesy Photo Archives (NMHM/DCA), neg. no. 057271.

DENETDALE/BOSQUE REDONDO

Courtesy Photo Archives (NMHM/DCA), neg. no. 028534 .

GUNN ALLEN/RADIANT BEINGS

Courtesy Photo Archives (NMHM/DCA), HP2006-19.

OKAWA/JAPANESE INTERNMENT/SF

Courtesy Gail Y. Okawa.

TORRES/HIPPIES IN EL RITO

Courtesy Photo Archives (NMHM/DCA), Lisa Law Photo Collection, which is part of the Lisa Law Archive, neg. no. HP.2006.36.

HUGHES/POWDRELL

Courtesy Museum of New Mexico Press, © 2006.

NIETO-PHILLIPS/SPANISH-AMERICAN ID

Courtesy John Nieto-Phillips.

LOPEZ/MEXICAN IMMIGRANTS

Courtesy Photo Archives (NMHM/DCA), New Mexico Magazine Collection.

HUNNER/DRIVEN BY HISTORY

Courtesy Cornerstones Community Partnerships.

PO'PAY STATUE

Courtesy Marcia Keegan, from *Po'pay: Leader of the First American Revolution* (Clear Light Publishing).

AGOYO AND SANDO/PUEBLO PERSPECTIVE OF PO'PAY

Courtesy of Marcia Keegan, from *Po'pay: Leader of the First American Revolution* (Santa Fe: Clear Light Publishing).

EPILOGUE/STORYTELLING

Courtesy Photo Archives (NMHM/DCA), Títo Apodaca "Mi Gente" Collection, neg. no. 142320.

COLCHA/EMBROIDERED WEAVING

Courtesy History Collection (NMHM/DCA), 4674/45.

Index

Project director: Mary Wachs
Design and production: David Skolkin and Bette Brodsky
Cover design: Bette Brodsky
Composition: Set in Adobe Garamond by Angela Taormina
Manufactured in the USA
10 9 8 7 6 5 4 3 2 1

Library of Congress Cataloging-in-Publication Data

Telling New Mexico : a new history / edited by Marta Weigle
with Frances Levine and Louise Stiver. -- 1st ed.
p. cm.
Includes bibliographical references and index.
ISBN 978-0-89013-552-5 (clothbound : alk. paper)--ISBN 978-0-89013-556-3 (pbk.: alk. paper)
1. New Mexico--History. I. Weigle, Marta. II. Levine, Frances. III. Stiver, Louise.
F796.T38 2009
978.9--dc22
2008044950

Museum of New Mexico Press
Post Office Box 2087
Santa Fe, New Mexico 87504
www.mnmpress.org

Front cover: Valles Caldera, by Robert Martin, courtesy Palace of the Governors Photo Archives, Robert Martin Collectionm HP.2005.22.

Frontispiece: Colcha-embroidered blanket, New Mexico, about 1850. Photograph by Blair Clark.

Page 4: Shiprock, New Mexico, 1994. Photograph by Michael O'Shaughnessy.